CW00556257

NORFOLK HEARTH TAX

EXEMPTION CERTIFICATES

1670–1674

THE BRITISH RECORD SOCIETY
HEARTH TAX SERIES VOLUME III

NORFOLK RECORD SOCIETY
VOLUME LXV

in association with
UNIVERSITY OF SURREY ROEHAMPTON

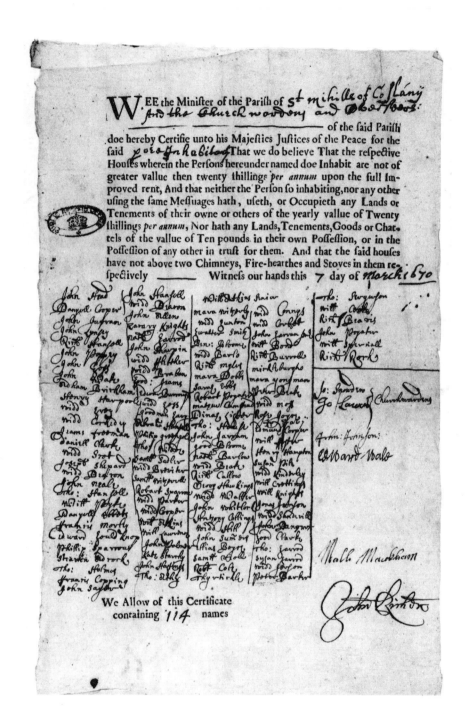

WEE the Minister of the Parish of S‍t mihills of Coslany
and the Church wardens and Overseers
——————————————— of the said Parish
doe hereby Certifie unto his Majesties Justices of the Peace for the
said poor Inhabitants That we do believe That the respective
Houses wherein the Persons hereunder named doe Inhabit are not of
greater vallue then twenty shillings *per annum* upon the full Improved rent, And that neither the Person so inhabiting, nor any other
using the same Messuages hath, useth, or Occupieth any Lands or
Tenements of their owne or others of the yearly vallue of Twenty
shillings *per annum*, Nor hath any Lands, Tenements, Goods or Chattels of the vallue of Ten pounds in their own Possession, or in the
Possession of any other in trust for them. And that the said houses
have not above two Chimneys, Fire-hearthes and Stoves in them respectively ———— Witness our hands this 7 day of March 1670

We Allow of this Certificate
containing 114 names

Public Record Office, E 179/338, f.33. Hearth tax exemption certificate
for the parish of St Michael Coslany, Norwich, 7 March 1670/1

NORFOLK HEARTH TAX EXEMPTION CERTIFICATES 1670–1674: NORWICH, GREAT YARMOUTH, KING'S LYNN and THETFORD

Edited and Introduced by
PETER SEAMAN

With Contributions by
JOHN POUND and ROBERT SMITH

Published by The British Record Society
c/o Patric Dickinson
The College of Arms
Queen Victoria Street
London EC4V 4BT
ISBN 0 901505 44 7

in association with

The Norfolk Record Society
c/o Barbara Miller, M.B.E.,
17 Christchurch Road
Norwich NR2 2AE
ISBN 0 2538298 3 9

Printed in Great Britain

CONTENTS

MAPS *by Phillip Judge*

Foreword

Once again it gives me much pleasure to introduce this, the third of the series of Hearth Tax volumes to be produced by the British Record Society in association with county record societies, in this case the Norfolk Record Society. This time, it is in a rather different form, being an edition of the surviving Norfolk Hearth Tax Exemption Certificates for the City of Norwich and the boroughs of Great Yarmouth, King's Lynn and Thetford. They contain nearly 20,000 names, many repeated from the different dates for which they survive.

The Hearth Tax returns themselves, for Norfolk, are frankly disappointing. In Houghton's figures of 1693, for the numbers of 'houses' by counties, Norfolk and Norwich was one of the most populous and probably richest of counties, with 47,180 households recorded. Peter Seaman has already published the Michaelmas return for 1664 for which only 40 out of 62 membranes survive, and that for Lady Day 1666, which only includes chargeable householders and lacks assessments for 15 hundreds. The returns are mapped in *Norfolk Genealogy*, XX, Norfolk and Norwich Genealogical Society, 1988. These lacunae, in view of the importance of the county, are lamentable. However, Mr Seaman is continuing to transcribe the assessment for the county for Michaelmas 1672, and it looks probable that we may get a more complete picture from the analysis of this.

Meanwhile, little attention had previously been paid, as it is here, to a rich collection of certificates for those exempt from the tax on the grounds of poverty. The immediate use that strikes the attention is, of course, their use to the family historian, who finds him or herself most at a loss searching for poor ancestors. However, their use is far greater than that alone. Peter Seaman has established the ratio of exempt to taxed people in Norwich (and the other boroughs), which makes these records of far more value.

We now know, too, in which wards and parishes of the city the poor and the rich congregated. He has also added to what Tom Arkell has told us of the poor, in the Hearth Taxes. In Norwich also, although those exempt were always described as 'paupers', they were by no means necessarily receiving poor relief. We seem to be thinking of a <u>strata</u> of people, including some on relief, who mainly were more prosperous than that, but not prosperous enough to pay the 2/- a year for the Hearth Tax. Lastly, after having an encapsulated social anatomy of the city and its trades laid before our eyes, we are introduced to the house-plans and descriptions of the small houses in which these people lived. We are delighted that Peter Seaman, John Pound and Robert Smith have collaborated to produce this very enlightening volume.

Margaret Spufford
Research Director

Centre for Hearth Tax Studies
University of Surrey Roehampton

Michaelmas, 2001

ACKNOWLEDGEMENTS

I wish first to thank the Councils of the British Record Society and Norfolk Record Society, and the University of Surrey Roehampton, for agreeing to publish my transcription of the hearth tax exemption certificates. In particular I wish to thank Mrs Nesta Evans, Dr Richard Wilson and Professor Margaret Spufford of those respective institutions for their expert guidance and interest. Nesta Evans has been my constant and helpful liaison with all three institutions. I wish also to thank particularly Mr Cliff Webb and Mr Roy Stephens for their technical expertise in preparing the book for publication.

Of my friends and colleagues either now or formerly at the Public Record Office, I wish to thank the following for their help at various stages of this project: Mr Hugh Byrne, Dr Trevor Chalmers, Dr David Crook, Mr Alistair Hanson, Mr Roger Kershaw, Dr Alec Mulinder and Miss Suranganee Perera.

My thanks are due also to Mr Jeremy Gibson, who informed Nesta Evans that I had transcribed the records; and to Mr Paul Rutledge and Mrs Elizabeth Rutledge.

Particular thanks are due to the two historians who have made contributions to my introduction. Dr John Pound is an acknowledged expert on Tudor and Stuart Norwich, and Mr Robert Smith is one on the buildings of Norwich and Norfolk. I thank both of them for the time and effort they have taken to enhance the quality of the introduction with their expertise. I wish also to thank Mr Phillip Judge for drawing the maps.

Peter Seaman
Public Record Office
Kew, Richmond, Surrey

Michaelmas 2001

INTRODUCTION

This volume is part of a series of hearth tax returns which are being published jointly by the British Record Society, County Record Societies and the University of Surrey Roehampton, under the direction of the Roehampton Centre for Hearth Tax Research. The aim is to publish at least one, and preferably two, hearth tax returns for every English and Welsh county. The purpose of the series is to make a major original source for late seventeenth-century economic and social history available for anyone interested in this period.[1] All the results will be tabulated and mapped. The introduction is intended to point out some of the ways in which hearth taxes can be used by historians, and to demonstrate what the exemption certificates for Norfolk tell us.

The exemption certificates published in this volume were transcribed mostly from hard copy prints from microfilm, and in some cases from photocopies of original documents. The transcripts were then checked against the original documents in the Public Record Office.

The best recent guide to the hearth tax returns is Kevin Schürer's and Tom Arkell's *Surveying the People*.[2] Arkell's clear exposition of the hearth tax legislation is essential reading for anyone wishing to come to grips with this complicated source.[3] It includes the printed instructions issued to collectors of the tax in 1664, followed by a specimen return for Old Windsor. The originals are in the Public Record Office.[4] There are also excellent introductions to several published returns; the best is that to the Nottinghamshire returns.[5]

---

[1] Original documents have been microfilmed, with a grant from the Heritage Lottery Fund, and copies have been distributed of all relevant county lists to County Record Offices.
[2] Kevin Schürer and Tom Arkell (eds), *Surveying the People*, (Oxford, 1992). Under the supervision of Mr Tom Arkell, Mrs Elizabeth Parkinson is completing a Ph.D. thesis at the University of Surrey Roehampton, on 'The Administration of the Hearth Tax, 1662-6'.
[3] *Surveying the People*, pp. 38-64.
[4] PRO E 179/265/30; Calendar of Treasury Books, VII, pp. 1362-7.
[5] *Nottinghamshire Hearth Tax 1664 . 1674*, edited by W.F. Webster with introduction by J.V. Beckett, M.W. Barley and S.C. Wallwork, Thoroton Society Record Series, XXXVII, (Nottingham, 1988). Other examples are: D.G. Edwards (ed), *Derbyshire Hearth Tax Assessments 1662-70*, Derbyshire Record Society, 7, (1982); C.A.F. Meekings, *Dorset hearth tax assessments, 1662-1664*, (Dorchester, 1951); T.L. Stoate, *Cornwall hearth and poll taxes 1661-1664*, (Bristol, 1981) and *Devon hearth tax return, Lady Day 1674*, (Bristol, 1982); P. Styles, 'Introduction to the Warwickshire hearth tax records', *Warwick County Records Hearth Tax Returns*, 1, (1957).

INTRODUCTION

Early modern taxation

In order to avoid unnecessary duplication of effort, it is intended that the description of the administration of the hearth tax should be used in the introduction to other volumes in the series. Where local circumstances vary, this description will be modified.

Regular direct taxation in the form of income tax did not exist before the late eighteenth century. In the Tudor period two medieval taxes, the fifteenth and the lay subsidy, were still in use. The former was a quota tax raised from communities, while the latter was levied on individual wealth usually assessed on land or goods, but also on wages in 1524-5.[6] Both medieval and Tudor subsidy records have been analysed by historians.[7] Until the hearth taxes of the later Stuart period, no other taxes were sufficiently comprehensive to be as useful as the Lay Subsidy of 1524-5 for the study of economic and local history. Dr Husbands wrote in 1987 that 'alone amongst the mid and late-seventeenth century taxes, the Hearth tax allows historians to draw general comparative conclusions about local economies.[8] Yet in 1992 he had to conclude that 'as yet, much of the potential of the Hearth tax to provide a general framework for the socio-economic history of the later seventeenth century still remains to be exploited at both local and national levels.'[9]

Subsidies continued to be used in the early Stuart period. Charles I introduced the much disliked Ship Money, but, as its tax threshold was high, its records are much less full than those of the subsidies. Taxation was heavy during the Civil War and Commonwealth, but its records are few. Another new tax at this time was the Excise, first introduced in 1643 and revived at the Restoration to compensate the Crown for the loss of taxes such as feudal dues and the revenue from the Court of Wards. Between 1641 and 1702 a number of poll taxes were levied. The first, in 1641, was raised to enable Charles I to pay off the Scottish army occupying parts of northern England. The next poll tax, in 1660, was similar, in that its purpose was to pay the arrears due to the army and navy as a necessary step to their disbandment.[10] Two excellent studies of seventeenth century taxation are those by C.D. Chandaman and M.J. Braddick.[11]

---

[6] Richard Hoyle, *Tudor Taxation Records*, (London, 1994), pp. 1-3.

[7] R.E. Glasscock, *The Lay Subsidy of 1334*, British Academy Records of Social and Economic History, new series, II, (1975); John Sheail, *The Regional distribution of wealth in England as indicated in the 1524/5 lay subsidy returns*, edited by R.W. Hoyle, List and Index Society, Special Series, Vol. 28, parts 1 and 2, and Vol. 29, parts 1 and 2, (Kew, 1998).

[8] C. Husbands, 'Regional change in a pre-industrial economy: wealth and population in England in the sixteenth and seventeenth centuries', *Journal of Historical Geography*, 13, (1987), pp. 348-9.

[9] *Surveying the People*, p. 77

[10] *Surveying the People*, p. 142.

[11] C.D. Chandaman, *English Public Revenue 1660-1688*, (Oxford, 1975), and M.J. Braddick, *Parliamentary Taxation in Seventeenth-Century England*, (Woodbridge, 1994).

INTRODUCTION

1. THE ADMINISTRATION OF THE HEARTH TAX; AND THE SURVIVING NORFOLK RECORDS

The Hearth Tax

The English hearth tax was a major source of government revenue levied twice yearly at Lady Day (25 March) and Michaelmas (29 September) from 1662 to 1689. Between 1666 and 1669 and from 1674 to 1684 the collection of the tax was farmed out and from 1684 to 1689 it was carried out by a Commission which managed both the Excise and the Hearth Tax. Very few returns of named taxpayers survive from these three periods, although some lists of the sums of money collected do exist.

Most of the surviving returns for 1662-66 and 1669-74 are to be found in the Public Record Office. It was only during these years that the documents had to be returned to Quarter Sessions and central Government. The hearth tax was administered county by county, and two copies of each return were made, one of which was enrolled for Quarter Sessions while the other was sent to the Exchequer. It is the latter which is now in the Public Record Office. Far fewer of the Quarter Sessions' copies have survived, and those which do are now to be found in County Record Offices and other local archive repositories.[12]

Initially the returns consisted of the assessment lists of taxpayers with the number of their hearths, and a separate return of the sums actually collected.[13] However, from Michaelmas 1664 to Lady Day 1666 and from Michaelmas 1669 to Lady Day 1674 the returns generally combined the assessment with the return of money collected. The returns were made to the Exchequer for auditing, and all those which survive in the Public Record Office are catalogued under E 179, together with the records of other taxes. Since 1995, a major relisting of all taxation records held in this class has been in progress, and many documents, which previously were not easily identifiable, have been made accessible.

Meekings and Styles[14] agreed that Sir William Petty was 'one of the progenitors'[15] of the new tax, but the former pointed out that the idea was not original, for similar taxes were already being levied in France and the United Provinces. Petty, who was one of those supporting the introduction of new kinds of taxes, set out the arguments in favour of the hearth tax in his 'Treatise of Taxes and Contributions', written in 1662.[16] Petty's 'Treatise' provides evidence of contemporary discussion of the principles and theory of taxation. The events of the years leading up to the Civil War had shown that reform of taxation was a necessity. After the Restoration, the three main sources of ordinary revenue were customs, excise and the hearth tax. Direct taxation was reserved for extraordinary expenditure such as financing war.

---

[12] The Irish hearth tax returns have survived for the 1660s for about half the counties, but the rest are lost. In 1691 the Scottish Parliament introduced a hearth tax which, like the Irish hearth taxes, continued to be levied until the late eighteenth century.

[13] *Surveying the People*, p. 41.

[14] Meekings, *Dorset* and Styles, *Warwickshire*.

[15] Meekings, *Dorset*, p. xii.

[16] C.H. Hull (ed), *Economic Writings of Sir William Petty*, 2 vols, (Cambridge, 1899).

Petty regarded the hearth tax as a form of excise, on the grounds that the number of hearths in a house could be regarded as a reflection of the owner's purchasing power. Householders, on the other hand, saw the hearth tax as a levy like the Poll Tax, but a permanent one.

Samuel Pepys wrote in his diary on 3 March 1662: 'I am told that this day the Parliament hath voted 2s per annum for every chimny in England, as a constant Revenue for ever to the Crowne.'[17] The act did not receive the royal assent until May. The hearth tax was introduced in 1662[18] as part of the financial settlement of the Restoration and continued to be levied twice a year at the rate of one shilling per hearth each six months, at Lady Day and Michaelmas, until 1689. Like the Excise, this new tax was intended to finance the conduct of normal government business by the king.

Macaulay propagated the traditional Whig view of the hearth tax as oppressive, but this is not entirely accurate. William III ordered its abolition as a political move to gain popular support, but a few years later he found it necessary to replace it with the almost equally obnoxious Window Tax. On 8 March 1689 John Evelyn wrote in his diary 'The Hearth Tax was remitted for ever: but what intended to supply it, besids greate Taxes on land: is not named'.[19] It is ironic that at the point when the hearth tax was abolished, it was at last being efficiently administered and producing the long hoped for yield.[20]

The sheriffs, 1662-1664

The 1662 Act made existing local officials responsible for the collection of the tax under the supervision of justices of the peace, the clerk of the peace and the sheriff. Householders were given six days notice to make a written and signed return of the number of their fire hearths and stoves. No instructions were given about returns from illiterate householders. These returns were collated by the petty constables before being enrolled at Quarter Sessions as the assessment for the tax. The high constables were only involved in the collection of the money raised by the hearth tax, which remained a separate process from the assessment until the revising Act of 1663.

Within four months of its introduction Pepys was writing, on 30 June 1662, about the discontent created by the new tax: 'They clamour against the Chimny-money and say they will not pay it without force.'[21] One of the chief reasons for the dislike of the new tax was the right given to constables to check the returns by entering houses, although only in the day time.

The collectors of the tax were permitted to subtract a poundage from the money they collected: twopence in the pound for petty constables, a penny for the high constables and fourpence for the sheriffs, from which a penny had to be paid to the clerk of the peace. This was an inadequate reward for the amount of work involved, and probably goes some way to explaining the

---

[17] Robert Latham (ed), *The Shorter Pepys*, (London, 1985), p. 183.
[18] 14 Charles II, c.10.
[19] Guy de la Bédoyère (ed), *The Diary of John Evelyn*, (Bangor, 1994), p. 364.
[20] Derbyshire hearth tax, xiii.
[21] *Shorter Pepys*, p. 210.

disappointing financial returns from the first collection at Michaelmas 1662. Meekings mentions a memorandum criticising the manner in which the tax was levied under the 1662 Act.[22] Although undated, it 'may be safely placed in June or July 1663.'[23] It is particularly critical of the arrangements for collecting the tax, recommending the use of 'constant receivers' in the place of local amateur officials. The lack of control over these is a major reason for the low returns in the early years of the tax. In the seventeenth century there was no means of accurately forecasting the yield of taxes, and in 1662 the House of Commons over-estimated the yield of the hearth tax.

The 1663 Act 'for the better ordering & collecting the Revenue arising by the Hearth Money'[24] concentrated on under-assessment rather than on failures in collecting the tax. The checking process was supposedly tightened, and petty constables were instructed to write their assessments in a book or roll in two columns headed 'chargeable' and 'non-chargeable', giving the names and hearths of both those liable and not liable to the tax. An extra check was introduced at hundred level, as these books or rolls had to be checked by the high constable before being signed by the justices of the peace. The clerk of the peace had to make a county copy of the enrolled new assessment as well as the Exchequer duplicate. This new assessment was generally used for the Lady Day 1664 collection. No attempt was made to reform the sheriffs' administration of the tax and this led to the failure of the 1663 Act.

The sheriffs' accounts covering the four collections of the tax from Lady Day 1662 to Lady Day 1664 in Norfolk and Norwich were declared at the Exchequer, and these declarations (as all of those for England and Wales) were recorded by C.A.F. Meekings (1914-1977), an assistant keeper of the public records, who, as Beckett says, was 'the first historian to do serious work on the Hearth Tax returns'.[25] Meekings's detailed manuscript notes on the accounts have been published.[26] These show who administered the collections of the tax for Norwich and Norfolk.

The collections for Norwich were made and accounted for separately from the rest of Norfolk. It is known that the first returns for both Norfolk and Norwich had been received in the King's Remembrancer's Office by 21 September 1662.[27] For Norwich, the account for the year ended Lady Day 1663 was submitted for John Manser and John [sic; recte George] Miris, sheriffs in 1662, by Cuthbert Brereton, gent, their deputy, and was declared on 15 December 1665. The number of registered hearths in Norwich was 7,302.[28] It should be noted, however, that an assessment for Norwich for the half year ended Michaelmas 1662 exists (see p.xxvii), giving a total of only 6,835 hearths for the city, making a shortfall of 467 hearths below the Lady Day 1663 total. The Norwich account for the year ended Lady Day 1664 was submitted for Robert Bendish and Thomas Thacker, sheriffs in 1663, again by

---

[22] It can be found in PRO E 179/159.
[23] C.A.F. Meekings (ed), *Surrey hearth tax 1664*, Surrey Record Society, vol 17, (1940), pp. xxv-xxvi.
[24] 15 Charles II, c.13, known as the first revising Act. It became law on 27 July 1663.
[25] *Nottinghamshire Hearth Tax 1664 1674*, introduction, p. xvi
[26] *Analysis of hearth tax accounts 1662-1665, 1666-1689* (List and Index Society cliii, clxiii, London, 1979, 1980).
[27] In PRO E 179/358.
[28] *Analysis of hearth tax accounts 1662-1665*, p. 179.

Cuthbert Brereton, and was declared on 16 December 1665. This time the number of registered hearths in Norwich was reduced to 6,364.[29]

For Norfolk, excluding Norwich, the account for the half year ended Michaelmas 1662 was submitted for Richard Berney, sheriff in 1662, by Roger Smyth, his deputy, and was declared on 3 June 1665. The number of registered hearths in the county was 66,609.[30] The account for the year ended Michaelmas 1663 was submitted for Thomas Meadowes [sic; recte Meadowe], sheriff in 1663, by William Randall, his deputy, and was declared on 5 December 1665. The number of registered hearths in the county was again 66,609[31]; this was because the assessment for Michaelmas 1662 was also used for Lady Day and Michaelmas 1663, as in other counties. The account for the half year ended Lady Day 1664 was submitted for Sir Jacob Astley, sheriff in 1664, by William Randall, his deputy, and was declared on 5 December 1665. This time the number of registered hearths in the county was reduced to 57,034.[32] The assessment for Lady Day 1664 was probably made in the autumn and winter of 1663-1664.

When Charles II opened the new session of Parliament on 21 March 1664, he pointed out that the revenue from the hearth tax had declined and added 'Men build at least fast enough'. The king asked Parliament to 'let Me have the Collecting and Husbanding of it by My own Officers; and then I doubt not but to improve that Receipt, and will be cozened of as little as I can'.[33] The new Act became law on 17 May 1664.[34] Clarendon was impressed by the new Act and in his autobiography called it 'a very good additional bill for the chimney money, which made that revenue much more considerable'.[35]

The first receivers, 1664-1665

One of the principal features of the new Act was the replacement of the sheriffs by specially appointed receivers. Their salary was one shilling in the pound, but this included the payments they had to make to their sub-collectors. They had to deposit bonds as security against defaults in the King's Remembrancer's office; the amount of security was based on the value of the 1662 assessment.

The receivers were appointed by the Exchequer Commission set up to administer the 1664 Act; it also instructed the Exchequer auditors to make copies of the 1662 assessments for the receivers and to send them a set of printed instructions setting out the procedures for assessment, collecting and accounting.[36] These instructions show that the Government was determined to tighten Exchequer control over the administration and collection of the hearth

---

[29] *Analysis of hearth tax accounts 1662-1665*, p. 180

[30] ibid, p. 181. Here the names of Berney (rendered as Berry) and Smyth have been transposed. They are correctly given in a document in PRO E 179/359 titled 'Norff. A briefe State of the Accompt of Roger Smyth Deputy to Richard Berney esquire late Shrieffe for ye County aforesaid & Receivor of the harth mony there for half year at Michaelmas 1662'.

[31] ibid, p. 182.

[32] ibid, p. 183.

[33] *Lords Journals*, XI, p. 583.

[34] 16 Charles II, c.3, known as the second revising Act.

[35] Meekings, *Dorset*, p. xviii.

[36] *Surveying the People*, pp. 55-64 and discussion in pp. 41-54.

tax with the aim of improving its yield. With a few exceptions, there was one receiver for each county and most county towns were joined to their county, as was the case in Norfolk. The receiver for Norfolk and Norwich was Christopher Jay, whose administration is described in more detail on pp. xxviii-xxx.

It was intended that the new officials should use the Lady Day 1664 assessment as a working document, but in fact it was the original assessment made in 1662 which was used. It was realised too late that the most recent returns would not reach the Exchequer in time for them to be copied out and sent to the receivers for the Michaelmas 1664 collection. The instructions sent with the 1662 assessment urged the receivers to 'endeavour to procure ...Copies of the Taxation for the half year ended 25th of March 1664'.[37] Most of the receivers failed to do this and were faced with using instructions which referred specifically to the Lady Day 1664 return. Not surprisingly, this led to the failure of the attempt to achieve national uniformity in the returns, and accounts for the variations found in printed returns from different counties. A further difficulty for the receivers resulted from their late appointment, which led to them being unable to make their first assessment until after the date when the Michaelmas 1664 collection was due. As a result they had to collect the money retrospectively, and their assessments became a combined assessment and return.[38]

The system of collection was stricter under the 1664 Act than it had been under the two earlier Acts. Self-assessment by occupiers was replaced by collection by the Receiver's officers, often called 'Chimney Men'. They were to collect the tax from each house, and could levy the duty by distress on the goods of anyone who refused to pay after one hour. When a distress was made the petty or parish constable had to be present, and an appeal against taking a distress could be made to one justice of the peace. Anyone who violently resisted the chimney men could be sentenced to a month's imprisonment by a single justice. No examples of resistance are to be found in the Norfolk return for Michaelmas 1664, but they do exist in some other published returns. Although the constables were no longer the collectors of the tax, they, and the chimney men, were given the right to search every house once a year to find 'what Fire Hearthes or Stoves are increased or decreased since the former Certificate'.

One of the intentions of the Hearth Tax Act of 1664 was to prevent landlords from escaping payment of the tax by dividing a house into tenements, and then letting them to poor tenants. The 1662 Act had stipulated that if a house was worth not more than 20 shillings a year, the occupant was exempt from paying the tax unless he owned land or tenements over 20 shillings a year, or land, tenements or goods of the value of at least £10. Sir William Petty saw it as essential to the success of the hearth tax that landlords should be made responsible for its payment when their tenants were excused through poverty. Petty called the tax 'an "Accumulated Excise" levied on a

---

[37] *Surveying the People*, pp. 51-3.
[38] Elizabeth Parkinson (ed), *The Glamorgan Hearth Tax Assessment of 1670*, South Wales Record Society, (Cardiff, 1994), pp xiv-xv

necessary commodity closely related to a man's general consumption and not "a particular Excise upon but one onely commodity, namely Housing".[39] Further modifications to the earlier Acts were concerned with liability to pay: everyone with more than two hearths had to pay even if otherwise entitled to exemption; if the owner had let the land away from the house, so reducing its value to under twenty shillings, or if he sublet to poor tenants exempt from the tax, it was he who paid; and anyone moving into a new house was liable for the whole six months tax due at the succeeding Lady Day or Michaelmas. Beckett mistakenly stated that all houses with *two* or more hearths were to be taxed, regardless of the standing of their occupants.[40] This led him to suggest 'a social acceptance that the less prosperous members of society were generally to be found in one-chimney houses.'[41] It is true that the majority of those exempt from paying hearth tax lived in one-hearth houses, but by no means all did so and it is probable that there are regional variations in the proportions of both taxpayers and exempt living in one and two-hearth houses.

In spite of the reforms it appears that the tax continued to produce less than was expected. On 3 September 1665 Pepys was worrying about where the money would come from to pay the fleet should the Dutch attack: 'it is said at this day our Lord Treasurer cannot tell what the profits of Chimny money is; what it comes to per annum - nor looks whether that or any other part of the Revenue be duly gathered as it ought'.[42] The Lord Treasurer was Thomas Wriothesley, second Earl of Southampton.

The receivers had expected to be permanent, but were displaced with little warning in the spring of 1666. Their assessments were therefore in many cases not sent to be enrolled by the clerks of the peace until 1667, and were not all in the Exchequer until 1669. The effects of the plague outbreak in 1665-6 and the Second Dutch War of 1665-67 may also have had some bearing on these delays.

The first farm, 1666-1669

The receivers, like the sheriffs before them, were unable to raise the level of revenue collection enough to satisfy the Government, so a third experiment was tried. It was brought on by a crisis. In January 1666 the Government found itself desperately short of money to prosecute the Second Dutch War, and decided to farm the hearth tax to a City of London consortium, for an advance of £250,000 and a rent. The receivers were therefore suddenly displaced in April 1666 by farmers who had a centralised Hearth Office in London, and who administered London directly and let other areas to subfarmers. Because outstanding loans (plus interest), raised on the credit of receipts from the hearth tax, remained to be paid to the City of London, it was laid down for the one collection of Lady Day 1666 that the subfarmers should act as receivers, and return their assessments through the Hearth Office for audit in the Exchequer. The revenue was to be paid into the City Chamber.

---

[39] Styles, 'Warwickshire hearth tax', p xv.
[40] Beckett, *Nottinghamshire Hearth Tax*, pp. ix, xi.
[41] ibid, p. xxv.
[42] *Shorter Pepys*, pp. 520-1.

The consortium's advance was spent between January and May 1666. Apart from a subsidy sent to England's ally the Bishop of Münster, it was devoted wholly to the Navy. The man appointed subfarmer for Norfolk and Norwich was Captain John Lloyd, whose administration is described in more detail on pp. xxx-xxxi.

The farm administered by the consortium of City merchants from Lady Day 1666 to Lady Day 1669 was meant to last for seven years, but 'proved to be a total failure', and was made worse by the destruction of the Hearth Office in the fire of London.[43] The farm was doomed to failure from the start because the rent had been fixed at a much higher figure than the gross current yield justified. The country was disturbed by plague and war, and in October 1666 Parliament voted to abolish the hearth tax, which encouraged widespread riots against the collectors. These three years are the period of what Braddick called 'hearth tax disorders', marked by riots against the tax in a number of counties, amongst which Norfolk was included.[44]

In King's Lynn, in November 1666, '[t]he officers of Captain Lloyd, collector of chimney money, were abused by the ruder and poorer sort of people, till the mayor sent some of them to gaol'.[45] In early December it was reported '[t]hose parts are quiet, only the common people clamour against the hearth-money collectors, and there would have been a riot but for the vigilance of the mayor and justices, in sending some of the ringleaders to prison'.[46]

In September 1668 the Privy Council heard a complaint by the farmers that two of their collectors in Norfolk, Robert Kenrick and Edward Tudor, had been 'abused in the performance of their duty by one John Soames of Aylsham...who struck the said Robert Kenrick and the constable (who was then assisting them) and used many scandalous and opprobrious words against them'. When the constable tried to place Soames in the stocks Mr William Doughty rescued him.[47]

A further impediment to the collection of the tax was the fact that justices of the peace actively obstructed the farmers. As early as September 1665, Charles II had observed that there had been, in his own words, 'such compliance in many of the Justices of the Peace with those that upon any pretence soever dispute this duty, that if he permit them to be chancellors of this payment he conceives it will soone be reduced to very little'.[48] In November 1668 the farmers invoked their option to surrender after only three years, with effect from Lady Day 1669, and responsibility for collecting the Tax passed back into the hands of the Government.

[43] *Surveying the People*, p. 43.
[44] Braddick, pp. 252-266.
[45] ibid, p. 256, quoting *Calendar of state papers, domestic series (CSPD), 1666-7*, p. 265.
[46] ibid, p. 256, quoting *CSPD, 1666-7*, p. 321.
[47] ibid, p. 261, quoting PRO, PC 2/61, f. 2.
[48] Quoted by Meekings, *Dorset hearth tax*, p. xx.

INTRODUCTION

The second receivers, 1669-1674[49]

Although the Government had been notified in November 1668 about the surrender of the farm, they took more than a year to decide what to do. They finally appointed Richard Sherwyn (a Treasury clerk) and Colonel William Webb (the late farmers' auditor) to examine and report.

In February 1670 they made their report. They recommended a return to the system of receivers of 1664-1665, but with substantial modifications, and Sherwyn and Webb themselves settled the administrative details. They reduced the administrative areas from the 48 of 1664-1665 to 35, which had been about the number under the farm. Instead of the receivers' fixed one shilling poundage of 1664-1665, they arranged a sliding scale depending on the difficulties of collection in a particular area. They provided transcripts of the subfarmers' books for 1668; prepared a manual of instructions, printed forms for exemption certificates and a model form of commission. They sifted applications for receiverships and arranged the scales of securities.

By Treasury warrant dated 21 March 1670, Sherwyn and Webb were appointed as Agents for the Hearth Money, in which capacity they supervised the receivers. (In November 1671 they were given further duties, and with exchequer official Bartholomew Fillingham they became Agents for Taxes in general.)

Warrants for the appointment of the new receivers were all ready by 11 May 1670. During the next two months the King's Remembrancer's Office was busy taking securities and swearing in the receivers, who were then given copies of the manual and transcript provided by Sherwyn and Webb, and went to their district to appoint sub-collectors, establish a local Hearth Office, prepare revised assessments and make a collection which (since a full year's duty was owing) generally covered the three instalments Michaelmas 1669 to Michaelmas 1670. The receiver for Norfolk and Norwich appointed in 1670 was Augustine Briggs, whose administration is described in more detail below.

So from Michaelmas 1669 to Lady Day 1674 the hearth tax was again administered by receivers appointed by patent, with staffs of subcollectors and help from petty constables, all under the general supervision of a small central office called the Agents for the Hearth Tax; and the administration of the tax was generally far more efficient than it had been earlier. The receivers sent in assessments to be enrolled by the clerks of the peace; these vary in form from lists of taxpayers and exempt, or lists of taxpayers only, to lists merely of variations since the last full assessment of taxpayers. The clerks of the peace continued to make the county and Exchequer duplicate assessment rolls, and the parish officials and justices of the peace the exemption certificates.

All the assessments made by the second receivers were enrolled after collection had been made, and so were combined assessment and return. Their first assessment, made in the summer and autumn of 1670, was generally for the year and a half ending Michaelmas 1670, as it was in Norfolk and Norwich. The last was generally for the year ending Lady Day 1674. The

[49] This description of the second receivers' administration owes much to C.A.F. Meekings, *The Hearth Tax, 1662-1689, Exhibition of Records*, Public Record Office, (London, 1962).

assessments made in between differed considerably from area to area. The receivers' bags of particulars of account - usually four in all - were largely filled with exemption certificates. Some clerks of the peace enrolled the names of those exempt in the parchment assessments; many did not do so.

A Treasury letter of 28 November 1670 to the clerks of the peace assumed that the new receivers would then be bringing in their first assessments for enrolment, and that these would be passed by the justices and delivered to the Exchequer by January 1671, so that the receivers' audits could begin in February. This was too optimistic, however; most of the surviving Michaelmas 1670 assessments were not passed until Sessions between April and October 1671, and most reached the Exchequer between May and November 1671. The earliest Michaelmas 1670 accounts to be declared were declared in November 1671; the bulk were declared in 1672, with stragglers between 1673 and 1677.

Augustine Briggs (1617-1684) was appointed receiver for Norfolk and Norwich on 11 May 1670.[50] He was a moderate and popular alderman of Norwich, sheriff in 1660 and mayor in 1670; and he was one of the two members of Parliament for Norwich in 1678, 1679 and 1681. His portrait has been reproduced.[51]

On 6 June his securities were taken[52]; and on 7 July 1670 Briggs was one of eight receivers who were sent a letter from the Treasury Lords, saying 'You have not taken out your commission, nor come to the Agents for managing the Hearth money for such other things as are necessary for that service. If you do not speedily collect and pay in the King's moneys, so that by the beginning of Michaelmas term next at furthest the whole year's duty due at Lady Day last be paid into the Exchequer, your commission must be made void.'[53]

Briggs's account for the year and a half ended Michaelmas 1670, that is, for the collections of Michaelmas 1669, Lady Day 1670 and Michaelmas 1670, was declared on 9 May 1673.[54] The number of registered hearths in the county of Norfolk was 81,123; and in the city of Norwich, 11,484.[55] A supporting document[56] is a book entitled 'Mr Briggs his Accompt for 3 halfe yeares ended at Michaelmas 1670'. In this account, the total number of hearths for Norwich is broken down by petty ward, but not parish, giving for each petty ward the total of hearths, and the numbers chargeable and exempt. Three other abstracts of account covering the same three half years exist;[57] they deal with money totals only.

The receipts signed by the constables of Norwich, King's Lynn and South Erpingham hundred, acknowledging receipt of payment for their assistance in collecting the tax due for the three half years ended Michaelmas 1670, still

---

[50] *Calendar of Treasury Books*, III, 1669-1672, p. 567; and a paper document in E 179/354.
[51] Basil Cozens-Hardy and Ernest A. Kent, *The Mayors of Norwich 1403-1835*, (Norwich, 1938), plate VI.
[52] *Calendar of Treasury Books*, III, 1669-1672, p. 586
[53] ibid, p. 614
[54] *Calendar of Treasury Books*, IV, 1672-1675, p. 134.
[55] *Analysis of hearth tax accounts 1666-1689*, p. 59 left hand.
[56] In PRO E 179/355.
[57] In PRO E 179/359.

exist. Those for King's Lynn and Norwich are printed in Appendix VI of this volume.[58]

Braddick notes that 'in Norfolk and Norwich the second administration of the receivers led to a substantial increase in the numbers of hearths registered, but a decrease in the numbers chargeable. This contrasts sharply with a number of counties where receivership saw increases in the number of hearths chargeable' (for example, large increases were recorded in the number of chargeable hearths in Cambridgeshire, Cheshire, Herefordshire, Lancashire, Lincolnshire, Northamptonshire, Nottinghamshire and Yorkshire). He adds 'Chandaman judges the receivers to have been a great success, particularly in contrast with the first farm, and the peculiarity of Norfolk noted here may simply reflect the efficiency of the sheriffs' administration in the early 1660s, efficiency which could not be improved upon by the receivers'.[59]

Briggs's account for the year ended Michaelmas 1671, that is, for the collections of Lady Day 1671 and Michaelmas 1671, was declared on 24 February 1674. The number of registered hearths in the county of Norfolk was 79,203; and in the city of Norwich, 11,614.[60] A supporting document of this account is the assessment for Norwich dated 24 July 1671, which is described on pp. xxxi-xxxii.

Although Briggs appears to have submitted the account for the year ending Michaelmas 1671, a paper transcribed in the present volume (Appendix VII, p. lxxxi) is headed 'Norff[olk] Norw[i]ch. The state of the Accompt of Rich[ar]d Browne Gent. Receiver Gen[e]rall of the hearthmony within the places afores[ai]d for one year End[ed] St Mich[ael] [16]71 as foll[owe]th.' Three other documents[61] connect Richard Browne with the 1671 account: one is a comparison between the 1670 and 1671 returns for Norfolk and Norwich, headed 'Richard Browne Recr. genll. of the hearth mony'; another a neat abstract of his account for Norfolk and Norwich for the year ended Michaelmas 1671; and the other a dirty and flimsy abstract of the roll for Norwich parishes and hamlets, 1671, bearing his name as Receiver General.

On 25 September 1671 there was sent a 'Treasury warrant to the King's Remembrancer to prepare a commission to Richard Browne as Receiver of Hearthmoney, co. Norfolk.'[62] And the next day, 'Treasury warrant to the King's Remembrancer to take the securities, detailed, of Richard Browne, as Receiver of Hearthmoney for co. Norfolk.'[63]

Little is at present known of Richard Browne. On 20 March 1672 the Treasury Lords sent a letter to Browne saying 'We notice the slackness of your passing your accounts or paying in your receipts of the Hearthmoney. At your peril you are to forbear to collect any of said revenue which will be due

---

[58] See also the section *Other documents published in this volume* on p. xli.

[59] Braddick, p. 251. It does not invalidate his comments, but it should be noted that for the 1669-1670 return Braddick quotes figures given by Meekings in *Analysis of hearth tax accounts 1666-1689*, p. 118 recto, ie chargeable 69,281 plus exempt 24,326 equals registered hearths 93,607. This differs from other figures given by Meekings for the same return on p. 59 left hand of the same volume, ie Norfolk 81,123 plus Norwich 11,484 equals registered hearths 92,607. The totals differ by 1,000 hearths.

[60] *Analysis of hearth tax accounts 1666-1689*, p. 59 right hand.

[61] All in PRO E 179/360.

[62] *Calendar of Treasury Books*, III, 1669-1672, p. 935.

[63] ibid, p. 936.

at Lady Day next, and none of your deputies are to intermeddle therein till further order.'[64] Browne was one of eight receivers to receive a similar letter. The next account, for the year and a half ended Lady Day 1673, that is, for the collections of Lady Day 1672, Michaelmas 1672 and Lady Day 1673, was declared on 25 November 1673. The number of registered hearths in the county of Norfolk was 79,125; and in the city of Norwich, 11,517.[65] Meekings attributes the account to Augustine Briggs, but the receiver responsible was Richard Browne. A supporting document of this account is the Michaelmas 1672 return for the county of Norfolk (see p. xxxii). Another is 'A Breife Abstract of the Hea[rth] Roll for a yeare and a half ending Lady Day 1673'[66] which for hundreds and the individual parishes within them gives totals of hearths paid, hearths certified (as exempt) and almshouses. It does the same for the city of Norwich and its parishes and the three boroughs and their wards. These figures are printed for Norwich in Appendix III (pp. lxviii-lxix) and for the boroughs in Appendix IV (pp. lxx-lxxi). There are two further supporting documents, which are abstract overall accounts of the three half years ended Lady Day 1673, bearing Richard Browne's name as Receiver General.[67]

The last account of the second receivers was submitted by Frances Browne, widow and executrix of Richard Browne. It was for the year ended Lady Day 1674, that is, for the collections of Michaelmas 1673 and Lady Day 1674, and was declared on 1 December 1674. The number of registered hearths in the county of Norfolk was 79,030; and in the city of Norwich, 11,623.[68] A supporting document of this account is 'A Briefe of the Hearth Roll for a yeare ended at Ladyday 1674'[69] which for hundreds and the individual parishes within them gives totals of hearths paid, hearths certified (as exempt) and almshouses. It does the same for the city of Norwich and its parishes, and for the three boroughs (but not for their wards).

The second and third farms, and Commission, 1674-1689

The administration of the second receivers produced reasonable results, and the gross yield of the hearth tax rose slowly from about £145,000 to £155,000 per annum. In June 1673, however, Viscount Osborne of Dunblane (who in June 1674 became Earl of Danby) arrived at the Treasury as Charles II's chief minister. He set about reducing expenditure and increasing revenue. In April 1674 the hearth tax was farmed for five years from Michaelmas 1674 up to and including Lady Day 1679, and then again from Michaelmas 1679 to Lady Day 1684.

In 1684 it appeared that the farmers were making what the Government regarded as excessive profits, so after the last collection of Lady Day 1684 the farm was not renewed. Instead, a return was made to the method of direct

---

[64] *Calendar of Treasury Books*, III, 1669-1672, p. 1209.
[65] *Analysis of hearth tax accounts 1666-1689*, p. 60 left hand.
[66] In PRO E 179/355.
[67] One in PRO E 179/359, the other in PRO E 179/360
[68] *Analysis of hearth tax accounts 1666-1689*, p. 60 right hand.
[69] In PRO E 179/335, ff 436-448.

collection of the tax. A joint Commission was set up for the Excise and the Hearthmoney.

The final period of the hearth tax, from Michaelmas 1684, was the most successful in terms of the sums raised. Hitherto the annual return from the tax had averaged £150,000 a year, but in its final years the yield rose to £216,000 per annum.[70] Its continuing unpopularity led to its abolition early in the reign of William and Mary, who were anxious to win support for their rule.

One major change in the instructions for 1684 was the requirement to list the names of inhabitants, and those responsible for any empty houses, in topographical order. This was rightly seen as the best way of preventing evasion of the tax and omissions from the lists. Had this been done when the Exchequer was in charge of administering the hearth tax, modern historians could use the returns to follow the collectors' routes. There are exceptions, for this was already possible in Warwickshire in the early 1670s, as well as for the 1678 return for the City of Worcester, which is 'virtually a gazetteer of all the households in the city in 1678.'[71]

The hearth tax lists need to be used with care, for the deceptively simple information contained within them is full of inconsistencies. Some of these arise from the changing administration of the tax, together with the differing interpretations of the rules within the separately administered counties and cities. By the fifth collection at Michaelmas 1664, the rules had been changed twice, together with a change of officials and some change of administrative areas. By the time of the Michaelmas 1670 collection, the increasing standardisation of procedures was not necessarily reflected in the county lists, which still showed an inconsistency in recording those not liable. In addition, the surviving documents represent different stages of the collection procedure - assessments of taxpayers, returns of those who had paid and fair copies of working papers compiled by many individuals, to name but a few. A discussion of the changing administration of the tax with its resultant effect on the recorded data is the subject of a forthcoming thesis.[72]

The Norfolk Hearth Tax Returns

The survival of the documents

Of the hearth tax documents of the English and Welsh counties, the survivals exist mainly in the Public Record Office, for the two periods 1662-66 and 1669-74, when they had to be returned to Quarter Sessions and to the King's Remembrancer's Office in the Exchequer.

In 1962 Meekings noted the very different survival rate of hearth tax documents in the PRO's holdings for the various counties: most of the records for Warwickshire had survived, whereas very few for Wiltshire had.[73] For

---

[70] *Surveying the People*, p. 44.
[71] ibid, p. 53 quoting Meekings and others.
[72] Under the supervision of Mr Tom Arkell, Mrs Elizabeth Parkinson is completing a Ph.D. thesis at the University of Surrey Roehampton, on 'The Administration of the Hearth Tax, 1662-6'. The Editor is grateful to Mrs Parkinson for providing this paragraph.
[73] Meekings, *The Hearth Tax, 1662-1689, Exhibition of Records*, p. 4. The surviving documents of all the counties are listed in Jeremy Gibson, *The Hearth Tax, other later Stuart Tax Lists and*

INTRODUCTION

Norfolk, partial returns exist for Michaelmas 1664 and Lady Day 1666, and a damaged return for Michaelmas 1672, as well as many membranes and fragments not yet positively dated. The surviving Norfolk hearth tax documents are listed in Appendix I, pp. lix-lxii.

The survival of historical records has always depended largely on the conditions of their storage, and in the early nineteenth century the records of the King's Remembrancer were very poorly cared for. In 1800 they were unsorted and unarranged, and kept in chests in rooms at the medieval Palace of Westminster. Those buildings were demolished in 1822 to make room for new law courts. From 1822 the records were stored in a shed made of deal boards erected inside Westminster Hall, and were carried to it loose or in sacks by labourers completely without supervision. The shed was later described as 'slight and wooden' and 'dark, damp and almost pestilential'. In 1831 the records were moved to the Royal Mews at Charing Cross, and in 1833 the record commissioners fortunately gained custody of them on the abolition of the Exchequer as an accounting office. In 1835 the records were moved to Carlton Ride, the former stables of Carlton House in Pall Mall.

During this period of frequent moves, the arrangement (such as it was) of the records was broken up and confused, the documents neglected and mistreated, and many records lost. It was reported that during one of the moves 'large quantities of parchment were purloined by the labourers employed and sold to glue manufacturers'. While the records were at the Royal Mews, 4,136 cubic feet of them were stored in two enormous bins. The records were damp, some coagulated beyond repair, and others were stuck to the walls. Seven mummified rats and a dead cat were found, and a dog searched the bins for living rats and their nests. It took three labourers three weeks to transfer the records from the bins into sacks, sustained by 'strong stimulants' to overcome the 'putrid filth, stench, dirt and decomposition'. 500 sacks of records were filled, and 24 bushels of dust and dirt were discarded.[74]

From 1837 the records were sorted and identified, and in 1858 moved into the newly-erected Public Record Office, built as a result of the 1838 Act 'for keeping safely the Public Records'.

From the surviving Norfolk documents, five dateable returns of hearth tax payers can be identified. They are as follows:

(i) Michaelmas 1662: city of Norwich only.

This was the first assessment of the hearth tax, and retrospectively covered the preceding half year. The document[75] is endorsed 'Civ Norwic 1662'. It was sealed on 8 August, and signed Richard Wenman, Mayor (1662-1663), Joseph Paine (West Wymer ward alderman) and Christopher Jay (Fyebridge ward alderman). This assessment was presumably also used for the collection of Lady Day 1663, except that the total of hearths for Michaelmas 1662 was

---

the *Association Oath Rolls* (Federation of Family History Societies and Roehampton Institute, 2nd ed., London, 1996).
[74] See David Crook, 'The records of taxation in England in the Public Record Office', in *Crises, Revolutions and Self-sustained Growth. Essays in European Fiscal History, 1130-1830*, ed W.M. Ormrod, Richard Bonney and Margaret Bonney (Stamford, 1999), pp. 427-435.
[75] PRO E 179/154/701.

6,835, and for Lady Day 1663 it was 7,302, making a difference of 467 hearths. (see p. xvii).

(ii) A published return: Michaelmas 1664: county of Norfolk only (excluding Norwich).

This return covered the previous half year, and served also for the collections of Lady Day and Michaelmas 1665. It is incomplete, and parts of it survive in six separate piece numbers. An edition of it has been published by the Norfolk and Norwich Genealogical Society.[76]

The receiver for Norfolk and Norwich, appointed on 26 July 1664, was Christopher Jay. He was a prominent Norwich alderman, and deputy lieutenant of that city, of which he was sheriff in 1653, mayor in 1657 and member of Parliament from 1661 to his death in 1677. He had influence at Court through the marriage of his cousin Jane Jay to Sir Edward Nicholas, Secretary of State to Charles II.

Jay made use of Sir Edmund Sawyer's offer to the receivers to supply copies of the Michaelmas 1662 assessment. Those for Norfolk and Norwich were transcribed on to 281 sheets of paper, and were received by Jay's agent on 3 September 1664. The Michaelmas 1664 assessment would have been made out in the autumn and winter of 1664-1665, and served also for the collections of Lady Day and Michaelmas 1665. Because the receivers were displaced with little warning in April 1666, many did not send their assessments to be enrolled by the clerks of the peace until 1666-1667, and not all of the assessments were in the Exchequer until 1669.

Jay's enrolled Exchequer duplicate was delivered before Sir Matthew Hale, Chief Baron of the Exchequer, on 3 May 1667. Getting the actual money into the Exchequer was a different matter, however. Meekings's notes suggest that on 17 June 1665 the sum of £4,650 had been paid to the City Chamber, to Sir Thomas Player, Chamberlain of London. But the total sum expected was £9,509 14s 0d (that is, £3,169 18s 0d per half year, on 63,382 hearths). On 19 January 1667 a mere £200 was paid into the Exchequer, followed by a similarly small sum of £255 1s 6d a week later.[77] The lords of the Treasury began to concentrate their attentions on Jay as well as on other receivers. The calendar of Treasury books notes, on 5 June 1667, 'Process ordered against all collectors of Chimney money (before the present farm thereof began) who have not brought in their accounts. The Auditors to report to-morrow what every collector thereof is in arrear. Mr Christopher Jay, of Norwich, ... to be arrested by the Serjeant.'[78]

On 2 July 1667: 'Mr Jaye to make oath that the moneys which he charges in the collectors' hands for the Chimney money of Norfolk are in their hands.'[79]

On 9 July 1667: 'Mr Jay called in and ordered to get in the Chimney Money remaining uncollected, and to pay the receipts for 1666, Lady Day, to Sir

---

[76] M.S. Frankel and P.J. Seaman, (eds), *Norfolk Hearth Tax Assessment, Michaelmas 1664* (Norfolk Genealogy, XV, 1983).
[77] *Analysis of hearth tax accounts 1662-1665*, p. 185, and other manuscript notes made by Meekings.
[78] *Calendar of Treasury Books*, II, 1667-1668, p 7
[79] ibid, p. 26.

Thomas Player.'[80] Jay's involvement in the Lady Day 1666 collection is discussed under (iii) below.

On 25 July 1667: 'Mr Jay called in. Ordered that before process be stayed he and his securities ... sign before Sir John Holland at Norwich the paper which is to be prepared by Lord Ashley.'[81]

On 1 August 1667: 'Process stopped against Thomas Gawdy and John Kendall, sureties of Mr Jay as late Receiver of Hearth money for Norfolk and Huntingdon.'[82]

On 2 August 1667: 'Process against Mr Jay to stop till Sept. 1 next.'[83]

On 23 May 1668: 'Write Mr Jay to attend on Tuesday fortnight to finish his Firehearth account.'[84]

On 25 June 1668: 'Mr Jay is desired to hasten his Chimney account. Process to issue against his securities. My Lords will speak with him about other matters [such] as that of his being the King's Receiver.'[85]

On 26 June 1668: 'The Treasury Lords to the King's Remembrancer to issue immediate extent against Thomas Gawdy and John Kendall, sureties for Christopher Jay, late Receiver of Hearth money for Norfolk and Huntingdon.'[86]

On 6 October 1668: 'The state of the debt of Jay, White, Price and Harlackenden to be presented to the King in Council at his return.'[87]

On 21 April 1669: 'The Treasury Lords to the King's Remembrancer for immediate process of extent against Thomas Price, late Receiver of Aids for co. Hereford, Thomas Harlackenden, late same for Kent, and Christopher Jay, late Receiver of Hearth money for Norfolk, for not having passed their accounts and for detaining considerable sums of the King's money in their hands.'[88]

Jay's arrears were calculated to be £4,335. In the calendar of Treasury books there are many other references to Jay's failure to pay these arrears. A solution was found when on 27 August 1669 a Treasury warrant was issued for a privy seal to grant Robert Foley, ironmonger to the Navy, Jay's debt of £4,335, in part-payment of a debt of £4,401 10s 2d owed to Foley by the Government.[89] It still fell to the Treasury, however, to pursue Jay's arrears.

On 20 August 1670: 'Treasury warrant to the King's Remembrancer for process to go against the sureties of Christopher Jay, late Receiver of Hearth money for co. Norfolk, on the £4,335 which he has been ordered, but has so far failed, to pay to Robert Foley, in part of a larger sum due to said Foley for iron work delivered to the Navy: process being impossible against said Jay himself by virtue of his privilege as a Member of Parliament.'[90]

---

[80] *Calendar of Treasury Books*, II, 1667-1668, p. 31.
[81] ibid, p. 46.
[82] ibid, p. 51.
[83] Ibid, p. 53.
[84] ibid, p. 333.
[85] ibid, p. 363.
[86] ibid, p 587
[87] ibid, p. 452.
[88] *Calendar of Treasury Books*, III, 1669-1672, p. 211.
[89] ibid, pp. 274 and 295.
[90] ibid, p. 654.

Some of the money appears to have been paid on 27 October 1671 by William Crow and Adrian Payne, sheriffs of Norwich, as a result of the seizure of Jay's chattels by Government order.[91]

On 12 February 1672: 'Sir Rob. Howard to write to the Attorney General that the Sergeant may take Mr Christopher Jay into custody who now uses the protection of the Temple.'[92]

On 2 July 1672: 'Entry of the reference to the Surveyor General of Crown Lands of the petition of Christopher Jay, citizen and alderman of Norwich, touching the sum of £1,000 by him agreed to be paid to Mr Foley in discharge of a debt due to His Majesty, which not being fully paid he is taken in execution at His Majesty's suit and in prison in the common gaol of Norwich; and praying liberty to go abroad [in England] and sell his land to raise money for discharge of said debt.'[93]

On 10 March 1673 Robert Foley was granted a lease, under Exchequer Seal, of a messuage in St George Tombland, Norwich, and several messuages and lands in Thompson and elsewhere in Norfolk, being parcel of the lands of Christopher Jay, extended for debt.[94]

On 23 March 1676 Treasurer Danby issued a warrant to the late Queen Mother's Trustees, to accept £200 from Christopher Jay in his capacity as Receiver of the late Queen Mother's revenue in Norfolk and Huntingdon, in settlement and discharge of a larger arrear: 'said Jay being but in a low condition, and the Trustees having been able to recover no part of said debt from him.'[95]

Christopher Jay died 'in straitened circumstances, and was buried in the church of St George's Tombland'[96] on 23 August 1677.

(iii) A published return: Lady Day 1666: Norfolk and Norwich.

This return covered the previous half year only. It is incomplete, and parts of it survive in three separate piece numbers. An edition of it has been published by the Norfolk and Norwich Genealogical Society.[97]

The man appointed subfarmer for Norfolk and Norwich was Captain John Lloyd, who, unlike Jay, does not appear to have been a local man. He had petitioned for the receivership in 1665 on the grounds of twenty years service to the monarchs at home and abroad.[98]

Because the subfarmers were not appointed until the summer of 1666, after the instalment for Lady Day became due, their paper books containing the assessment were not made out until the summer of 1666, after the collection was made. The papers therefore represent assessment and return in one. The subfarmers submitted their paper books (which might be the original papers of

[91] *Calendar of Treasury Books*, III, 1669-1672, p. 1162
[92] ibid, p. 1032.
[93] ibid, p. 1266
[94] *Calendar of Treasury Books*, IV, 1672-1675, p. 82.
[95] ibid, p. 169.
[96] Basil Cozens-Hardy and Ernest A. Kent, *The Mayors of Norwich 1403-1835*, (Norwich, 1938), p. 89.
[97] P.J. Seaman, (ed), *Norfolk and Norwich Hearth Tax Assessment, Lady Day 1666* (Norfolk Genealogy, XX, 1988).
[98] *CSPD, 1665-6*, p. 155.

the subcollectors and constables, or fair copies made from them, or a mixture of both) through the Hearth Office to the Exchequer, where they were audited from June 1667 onwards, and kept. After audit, between 1667 and 1672, the accounts were not declared but were only sworn.

Christopher Jay helped John Lloyd to collect the tax due at Lady Day 1666. His name as a receiver of collected tax appears at least three times in the surviving documents.[99] A manuscript note by Meekings, recording an abstract of the collection,[100] says 'received by Lloyd £2,573 13s 0d; by Jay £1,339 0s 0d.' The accounts were sworn on 25 June 1669 and 29 June 1670. Meekings notes the total sum of £4,751 7s 0d for 95,027 hearths, of which 83,770 were in the county of Norfolk and 11,257 in the city of Norwich. These figures represent the total of registered hearths, both chargeable and not chargeable, although in the surviving returns exemptions are not listed.

Since the publication of the Lady Day 1666 assessment in 1988, other documents belonging to that assessment have been discovered. The abstract recorded by Meekings is in a bundle labelled 'Lloyds acc[oun]t, Norfolk 1666 L[ady Day].'[101] There is also a paper book containing a neatly written return of the parishes in Loddon hundred;[102] it is similar to those[103] which have been published. Also in existence are 'John Lloyd's 3 receipts for Lady Day 1666'.[104]

In the Norfolk Record Office, among 'Papers relating to Hearth Tax etc, 1666-1696',[105] is a document listing John Lloyd's deputies 'for the viewing collecting levying and receiving of his Ma[jes]ties duty of Hearth money for the County of Norff[olk]'. 25 names are given, and the document was signed by John Lloyd on 24 January 1666 [/1667].

John Lloyd appears to have remained subfarmer for Norfolk until the last farmers' collection of Lady Day 1669.[106]

(iv) July 1671: city of Norwich only.

In the Norfolk Record Office are three of four original paper books containing the hearth tax assessment for Norwich dated 24 July 1671.[107] They are complemented by a document entitled 'A Certificate of all the Fire Harthes & Stoves in the City, July 24[th] 1671, Augustine Briggs'.[108] It reads: 'I doe hereby Certyfye that these bookes, now delivered into your hands doe Conteine an exact view of all the fire hearthes & stoves within the Citty of Norwich and County of the same Citty & accordinge to the severall view's and Lists that I have rec[eive]d from the respective Collectors of the duty of Hearth mony therein. Dated ye 24 of July 1671. Aug[ustine] Briggs'.

---

[99] Seaman, *Norfolk and Norwich Hearth Tax Assessment, Lady Day 1666*, p. vi.
[100] In PRO E 179/360.
[101] ibid.
[102] ibid.
[103] PRO E/179/253/42.
[104] In PRO E 179/355.
[105] NRO Case 7 Shelf K.
[106] *Analysis of hearth tax accounts 1662-1665*, p. 417.
[107] NRO Case 13a/48. They must be ordered as microfilm MF/RO 416/8.
[108] NRO Case 7 Shelf K.

Briggs's account for the year ending Michaelmas 1671, that is, covering the collections of Lady Day 1671 and Michaelmas 1671, was declared on 24 February 1673/4. The first batch of exemption certificates, filled in between December 1670 and April 1671, no doubt were made for the Lady Day 1671 return, which served also for Michaelmas 1671. John Pound finds that the names in that batch of exemption certificates were used when compiling the July 1671 Norwich books (see p. xlii).

Of the four original July 1671 books, number 2 is missing. It would have contained the following parishes: in North Conesford Ward: St George Tombland (part) and St Peter Parmentergate; in Fyebridge Ward: St Clement, St Edmund, St James, St Martin at Palace (part), St Paul, Pockthorpe and St Saviour (part); in East Wymer Ward: St George Tombland (part), St Helen, St Martin at Palace (part), St Peter Hungate, and St Simon and St Jude.

John Pound's informed reconstruction of Norwich in 1671 gives a total of 5,143 households and 11,591 hearths (Table 2, p.xliii). Briggs's account for Michaelmas 1671 gives totals of 79,203 hearths in Norfolk and 11,614 hearths in Norwich, giving a shortfall of a mere 23 hearths for Norwich in John Pound's estimate.

In May 2001, long after John Pound had prepared his detailed reconstruction, a piece of paper was found which proved to be a contemporary abstract, giving the totals of chargeable and exempt hearths for every parish in Norwich in 1671.[109] These newly-discovered figures are given in Appendix V, pp. lxxii-lxxiii. When the actual totals for hearths are compared with John Pound's reconstructed totals for parishes and wards in Appendix II (pp. lxiii-lxvii) and Table 2 (p. xliii), it is satisfying to note how closely they correspond.

(v) Michaelmas 1672: county of Norfolk only (excluding Norwich).

This is the Exchequer duplicate roll of the second of the three collections of the year and a half ended Lady Day 1673. The document[110] is headed 'Norff[olk]. A Duplicate of the fire Harths and Stoves within the county of Norff[olk] taken upon view for the yere endinge att the feast of St Mich[ael] the ArchAngell Anno D[omi]ni 1672 by Richard Browne Esq (his Majesties Officer appointed to collect that Duty) and his Deputyes and by him certified to Will[ia]m Burleigh Esq Clerke of ye peace for the said county and approved of by us whose hands are hereunto sett two of his Majesties justices of ye peace for the said county and enrolled in fifty & three Rolls of parchment to be certified into his Majesties Court of Exchequer according to the severall Acts of parliament made concerninge that Duty'.

Although the return purports to be for the year ending Michaelmas 1672, the lists of those 'discharged by certificate' duplicate the exemption certificates dated April 1672-March 1673 ('batch 3': see p. xxxix), and are obviously compiled from them. The roll was therefore drawn up after March 1673. On the dorse of the last membrane is written 'Norff. 1672. Jurat coram Barone Turnor' 19 September 167[3] per Edwardum Hilton generosum' (Norfolk

---

[109] In PRO E 179/360.
[110] PRO E 179/154/697.

1672. Sworn before Baron Turner[111] 19 September 167[3] by Edward Hilton gentleman). The total of the hearths for parishes and hundreds given in the roll are identical to those given in 'A Breife Abstract of the Hea[rth] Roll for a yeare and a half ending Lady Day 1673',[112] proving that the 'Michaelmas 1672' roll served also for Lady Day 1673. Indeed, the membrane numbers of the 'Michaelmas 1672' roll are written to the left of the parish names in the 'Breife Abstract', showing where the list commences in each particular membrane.

The roll is in its original order of 53 numbered membranes, with parts of all its membranes present, but each membrane has gaps in it where rodents have eaten into the roll, and the final outer membranes of the roll have lost their lower portions. The roll was repaired by the Conservation Department of the Public Record Office in 1998. The gaps in the lists of exemptions can be made good from the exemption certificates in 'batch 3' (April 1672-March 1673), and the totals for payers and exempt in each parish and hundred from the 'Breife Abstract' mentioned above. On faded or damaged membranes the sequence of parishes can also be restored by reference to the 'Breife Abstract'.

It is hoped that this roll will be transcribed and form the subject of a future publication by the British Record Society and the University of Surrey Roehampton.

Hearth Tax Exemptions

Qualifications for exemption

The 1662 Act set out three categories of exemption from the tax:

(i) persons who paid neither church nor poor rate
(that is, any 'person who by reason of his poverty or the smallnes of his Estate is exempted from the usual Taxes Payments and Contributions towards the Church and Poor').

(ii) persons inhabiting a house worth *not more than* 20s. a year and not having any other property worth 20s. a year, nor an annual income of £10
(that is, if 'the house wherein any person doth inhabit is not of greater value than twenty shillings per annum upon the full improved rent And that neither the person so inhabiting nor any other using the same Messuage hath useth or occupieth any Lands or Tenements of theire owne or others of the yearely value of Twenty shillings per annum nor hath any Lands Tenements Goods or Chattels of the value of Ten pounds in theire owne possession or in the possession of any other in trust for them'). Such persons had to be exempted by a certificate signed by the minister and at least one of the churchwardens or overseers of the poor of their parish and certified by two JPs.

---

[111] Sir Edward Turner was Chief Baron of the Exchequer from 23 May 1671 to 12 April 1676.
[112] In PRO E 179/355.

(iii) industrial hearths, private ovens, and charitable institutions such as hospitals, almshouses and free schools
(that is, 'any Blowing house and Stampe Furnace or Kiln or any private Oven within any of the houses hereby charged nor any Hearth or Stove within the scite of any Hospital or Alms house for the reliefe of Poore people whose Endowment and Revenue doth not exceed in true value the summ of One hundred pounds by the yeare').

The first hearth tax returns did not have to include exempt persons, but the first revising Act of 1663 established that future returns should record both 'chargeable' and 'not chargeable' persons.

Originally the tax was paid by the occupier of a house, not by the landlord; but the second revising Act of 1664 ensured that landlords of exempt leaseholders were liable to pay the tax. The same Act also ensured that everyone with more than two hearths was made liable even if they were otherwise entitled to exemption. It should not be forgotten that although after this Act all exempt individuals had only one or two hearths, many who paid the tax had only one or two hearths because they fulfilled the property qualification.

Arkell has pointed out the difficulties presented to contemporaries, and to subsequent commentators, by these categories and by subsequent changes in law and practice.[113] For example, the categories of exemptions overlapped, and should not be regarded as dividing the 'poor' into those automatically exempted by being unable to pay poor rates and those exempted by certificate. Also, the third category covering industrial hearths was badly worded, and did not make it clear that the Government intended smiths' forges and bakers' ovens to be liable. Furthermore, the printed manual issued by Sir Edmund Sawyer, senior Exchequer auditor, as a guide for the Michaelmas 1664 collection, was flawed and led to misinterpretation and confusion. Unfortunately a manual known to have been produced in 1670-1672 has not survived; and one produced in 1684 dates from the hearth tax's final phase, when its collection was administered by a joint Commission.

The 1684 manual, though late in date, does clarify the interpretation of some clauses of the three Hearth Tax Acts of 1662-1664. Blowing houses and stamp furnaces which were exempt, unlike smiths' forges, were defined as 'houses wherein the mineral ore is smelted down into metal'. Private ovens which were also exempted (but not public ones) were described as those 'wherein provisions for the family only and not for gain, are baked and dressed'.[114]

---

[113] *Surveying the People*, pp. 38-55 Mrs Elizabeth Parkinson also addresses these problems in her Ph.D. thesis 'The Administration of the Hearth Tax, 1662-1666', chapter 5, 'Wrestling with the not chargeable hearths'.
[114] *Surveying the People*, p. 47. One of the most evocative of all hearth tax records is a page in PRO E 179/252/32, book 4 John Webb, appointed subfarmer in August 1666, wrote a neat and detailed assessment of the parish of St Margaret New Fish Street in the City of London, recording the premises of Thomas Farrinor, the King's baker, on the east side of Pudding Lane, as having 5 hearths and 1 oven. In one of these hearths or the oven, a few days later, began the fire which destroyed most of London.

The administrators of the second farm, of 1674-1679, managed to obtain a legal judgment that empty houses should be liable to the tax; but they failed in a similar action over smiths' hearths, which remained problematic.[115]

That the Lords of the Treasury were in no doubt that smiths' forges were liable is evidenced by a rebuke sent to a Norfolk justice of the peace on 12 January 1671. 'The Treasury Lords to Francis Bacon, Esq., Justice of Peace in Norfolk. We have seen an order of yours directing William Beamont, one of the Collectors of Hearth money for Norfolk, to restore to Richard Robins, of Itteringham [in South Erpingham Hundred], blacksmith, 3s. levied on him for his smith's forge. "Wherein you take upon you to assert that it is not the meaning of the laws concerning that duty to charge smiths' forges any more than the furnaces of braziers and pewterers. What should warrant such a conclusion we cannot discern, a furnace being literally excepted, but not one word in all the [Hearth money] Acts to exempt smiths' forges, which we suppose [you] will deny to be Firehearths. Upon a question moved whether smiths' forges were liable to pay the duty or not, we (being upon advice with His Majesty's counsel learned, satisfied of His Majesty's right thereunto) did give order that where payment was denied the Receiver should take distress," and in case the party distrained brought action the Receiver should appear. We still expect these directions to be observed by His Majesty's officers, and desire you to consider well before you give any more interruption to it. We meet with very few of your opinion, and are not willing if it may be avoided to represent your proceeding to His Majesty and the Council, so we hope you will give us no further occasion.'[116]

Hearth tax exemption certificates of 1670-1674

The English and Welsh hearth tax exemption certificates are a rich but under-used source. From Lady Day 1664, hearth tax returns list both 'chargeable' and 'non-chargeable' persons. Most published hearth tax returns are transcriptions of the parchment Exchequer duplicate rolls, and so include the exempt persons listed there as well as the payers of the tax. The parchment rolls are generally robust, but may often be faded, water-damaged or eaten into by rodents. By contrast, the printed exemption certificates of 1670-1674, though of fragile paper, are usually in good condition and are clear to read.

Moreover, the exemption certificates have survived in quantity. There are 38 boxes of them for England and Wales on the repository shelves of the Public Record Office at Kew. The certificates may be flat, or folded, or rolled in bundles, or conserved and bound in guard books. The loose, folded certificates for Norfolk occupy three boxes. Norfolk also shares five guard books (in three boxes) with London. The certificates for Yorkshire occupy six boxes; those for Essex and Lincolnshire, two boxes each. Most counties have, or share, one box.

The printed forms for exemption certificates devised by Sherwyn and Webb were issued to the receivers in 1670. The first to be used in Norfolk were

---

[115] Meekings, *The hearth tax*, Case VI, exhibit 3 [p. 27].
[116] *Calendar of Treasury Books*, III, 1669-1672, p. 762.

filled in in September 1670. The forms rehearsed briefly the statutory provisions for exemption, and were worded as follows:

'We the Minister of the Parish of [place-name, & the Churchwardens and Overseers] of the said Parish, do hereby certifie unto His Majesties Justices of the Peace for the said [place] That we do believe, that the respective Houses wherein the Persons here under-named do Inhabit, are not of greater value than twenty shillings *per Annum* upon the full improved Rent; And that neither the Person so inhabiting, nor any other using the same Messuages hath, useth, or occupieth any Lands or Tenements of their own, or others, of the yearly value of twenty shillings *per Annum*; Nor hath any Lands, Tenements, Goods, or Chattels of the value of ten Pounds in their own possession, or in the possession of any other in trust for them: And that the said Houses have not above two Chimneys, Firehearths, and Stoves in them respectively
Witness our Hands this [date] day of [month and year]
[names of exempt, and signatures of minister, churchwardens and overseers]
We Allow of this Certificate containing [number] Names
[signatures of justices of the peace]'

Receivers complained frequently that persons who should have paid tax were included on these certificates. On 20 December 1671 a Privy Council Circular was issued to the justices of the peace. It remarked that 'Wee easily believe that the abuse proceeds from the too much easiness and complyance of the Ministers and from the Partiall (as is to be feared) and indirect practices of the Churchwardens and Overseers who first frame those Certificates'. The Circular suggested ways of improving matters. From 1672 the printed certificates were supposed to carry on their backs forceful reminders to the minister, churchwardens etc of their duty. At the same time an additional clause was to be inserted in the instructions on the face: 'Neither hath any of their Houses been divided, nor any Lands, Gardens, Orchards, or Out-Houses been lett apart from any of them, since the year 1663'. None of the Norfolk certificates in this volume have any such additions, however.

When supplies of printed certificates were short, or the number of exempt in a parish was very large, manuscript certificates, with a formula based on the printed form, were prepared. A departure from the usual formula was made by the minister, churchwardens and overseers of St Edmund, Norwich, in the manuscript certificate they signed on 17 September 1672: 'Wee the Minister Churchwardens & Overseers of the sayd parish doe Testefy yt ye persons within Named ar not In a Cappacety to pay ye duty of hearthmony: they (to our knowledg) not having ye worth of ten pound in ther own hand nor in ye hand of any other: & though some of them By Reason of the dearnes of Rents in this Citty may pay somwhat above twenty shillings per anum: yet have they not Above one fierhearth: & ar soe poor yt if by sicknes they be taken from ther work they must (as some of them now ar) soe the Rest must be kept By ye Charety of others.'[117] One of the justices of the peace who signed this certificate was Christopher Jay (formerly receiver of hearth tax), as alderman for Fyebridge Ward.

---

[117] PRO E 179/336, f. 28.

INTRODUCTION

The Norfolk Hearth Tax Exemption Certificates

The hearth tax exemption certificates which form the subject of this volume are for the parishes of the city of Norwich and the wards of the three boroughs of Great Yarmouth, King's Lynn and Thetford. They represent four separate returns made between the years 1670 and 1674. All of the 239 known surviving certificates for the city and boroughs have been transcribed and indexed, and only 14 are missing or as yet untraced. The 239 certificates contain 19,706 names, but this total is the result of largely the same exempt persons being listed at four different dates, and many of the names are repeated in at least one of the other three returns.

The four different dates are detailed in the descriptions of the four batches of certificates headed in italics, below.

For Norwich, a total of 12,413 exempted householders are listed: 3,009 in batch 1; 3,150 in batch 2; 3,109 in batch 3; and 3,145 in batch 4; (average 3,103).

For Great Yarmouth, a total of 3,484 exempted householders are listed: 1,072 in batch 1; the certificates in batch 2 are missing; 1,219 in batch 3; and 1,193 in batch 4; (average 1,161).

For King's Lynn, a total of 3,265 exempted householders are listed: 826 in batch 1; 822 in batch 2; 802 in batch 3; and 815 in batch 4; (average 816).

For Thetford, a total of 544 exempted householders are listed: 134 in batch 1; 140 in batch 2; 136 in batch 3; and 134 in batch 4; (average 136).

The supposed 14 missing certificates would have contained about 1,270 names; again, many of those names will appear in at least one of the other three returns. Of those 1,270 names, perhaps 1,160 would have belonged to Great Yarmouth, and the other 110 to St Margaret, Norwich in batch 3, perhaps Earlham in batches 2-4, and Hellesdon in batches 2 and 4.

These 239 certificates, although they contain many names because they are returns for the populous city and boroughs, are only 9% of the 2,599 certificates which are known to survive for the whole of Norfolk. In all, perhaps only about 140 certificates either no longer exist or are misfiled among the certificates of other counties.[118] Table 1 shows the numbers of Norfolk exemption certificates at present known to survive, by hundred, city and borough, for each of the four return periods.[119]

The four return periods are represented by four batches of certificates as follows:

---

[118] The bound 'Norfolk' certificates in E 179/335 include strays for Little Waltham, Essex (f 658), St Peter, Sudbury, Suffolk (f 740), Tintinhull, Somerset (f 814), Mansell Lacy, Herefordshire (f 844), and Kirby Knowle, Yorkshire, North Riding (f 997).

[119] The missing Norfolk certificates mainly belong to batch 2 (late 1671-early 1672) and represent Great Yarmouth borough, the whole of Henstead, Tunstead and Wayland hundreds, and parishes in South Erpingham and Freebridge-Lynn hundreds.

TABLE 1

Number of surviving Norfolk hearth tax exemption certificates

Hundred	late 1670-early 1671	late 1671-early 1672	late 1672-early 1673	late 1673-early 1674
Blofield	16	14	17	16
Brothercross	9	8	8	8
Clackclose	26	26	26	25
Clavering	20	19	19	17
Depwade	20	21	21	21
Diss	14	13	14	13
Earsham	15	15	15	15
East Flegg	6	7	6	7
Eynsford	28	30	27	27
Forehoe	28	23	25	26
Freebridge-Lynn	27	19	25	25
Freebridge-Marshland	16	16	15	15
Gallow	27	24	24	24
Grimshoe	11	11	11	11
Guiltcross	11	10	10	10
Happing	15	15	16	16
Henstead	16	-	13	13
Holt	26	26	26	26
Humbleyard	15	14	13	12
Launditch	32	31	31	31
Loddon	18	19	19	17
Mitford	18	18	18	17
North Erpingham	31	33	32	32
North Greenhoe	15	16	15	14
Shropham	20	18	19	20
Smithdon	16	12	16	15
South Erpingham	35	2	35	35
South Greenhoe	20	20	18	17
Taverham	18	18	17	17
Tunstead	26	-	26	25
Walsham	12	4	12	10
Wayland	15	-	14	14
West Flegg	11	10	10	11
	633	512	613	602
City and Boroughs				
Norwich	44	41	41	41
Great Yarmouth	8	-	8	8
King's Lynn	10	10	10	10
Thetford	2	2	2	2
Grand total: 2599	697	565	674	663

INTRODUCTION

Batch 1: late 1670-early 1671

The certificates in 'batch 1' span late 1670 to early 1671 (for the city and boroughs, December 1670 to April 1671; for the county as a whole,

September 1670 to April 1671). They were probably prepared for the Lady Day 1671 and Michaelmas 1671 returns. In Norwich, King's Lynn and Thetford, totals of hearths are *not* given against the names; in Great Yarmouth, they *are*.

In the return for the year ended Michaelmas 1671, Norwich had 11,614 hearths, of which 3,769 were exempt, representing 33 per cent of the total.[120]

Batch 2: late 1671-early 1672

The certificates in 'batch 2' span late 1671 to early 1672 (for the city and boroughs, December 1671 to May 1672; for the county as a whole, November 1671 to April 1672). They were probably prepared for the Lady Day 1672 return. In Norwich, totals of hearths are *sometimes* given against the names; in King's Lynn and Thetford, they are *not*. The Great Yarmouth certificates are missing.

Batch 3: 1672-early 1673

The certificates in 'batch 3' span 1672 to early 1673 (for the city and boroughs, July 1672 to March 1673; for the county as a whole, April 1672 to March 1673). They were certainly prepared for the Michaelmas 1672 and Lady Day 1673 returns. In Norwich, King's Lynn and Thetford, totals of hearths are *not* given against the names; in Great Yarmouth, they *sometimes* are.

In the return for the year and a half ended Lady Day 1673, Norwich had 11,517 hearths, of which 3,773 were exempt, representing 33 per cent of the total. Great Yarmouth had 5,366 hearths, of which 1,687 were exempt (31 per cent); King's Lynn had 3,509 hearths, of which 1,147 were exempt (33 per cent); and Thetford had 765 hearths, of which 181 were exempt (24 per cent).[121]

Batch 4: 1673-1674

The certificates in 'batch 4' span 1673 to 1674 (for the city and boroughs, October 1673 to September 1674; for the county as a whole, April 1673 to September 1674). They were probably prepared for the Lady Day 1674 return, the last that had to be returned to the Exchequer. In Norwich and Great Yarmouth, totals of hearths are *nearly always* given against the names; in King's Lynn and Thetford, they are *not*.

---

[120] See Appendix V (pp. lxxii-lxxiii) for this calculation.
[121] 'A Breife Abstract of the Hea[rth] Roll for a yeare and a half ending Lady Day 1673', in PRO E 179/355.

In the return for the year ended Lady Day 1674, Norwich had 11,623 hearths, of which 3,906 were exempt, representing 34 per cent of the total.[122] Great Yarmouth had 5,381 hearths, of which 1,709 were exempt (32 per cent); King's Lynn had 3,540 hearths, of which 1,218 were exempt (34 per cent); and Thetford had 740 hearths, of which 163 were exempt (22 per cent).[123]

Annotations to the certificates

Certain annotations made to the certificates, or written on papers enclosing them, can be illuminating.

Despite arguments that can be made concerning the relative poverty of the individuals listed on the hearth tax exemption certificates, the local officials who completed and submitted the certificates referred to them as paupers, even if collusion was practised to include some who should not have been included. A paper wrapper enclosing the Norwich certificates for late 1670-early 1671, and contemporary constables' receipts, was titled 'Norwich Paupers';[124] and another enclosing the certificates for Great Yarmouth, King's Lynn and Thetford for the same period, and constables' receipts for King's Lynn, was titled 'Lynn Yarmouth Thetford paupers'.[125] Even Richard Browne's 'state of the Accompt' for the year ended Michaelmas 1671 described those exempted as being 'Excused through poverty as by Severall Certificates According to the Acts of Parliament'. A certificate for the Second North Ward of Great Yarmouth in 1671, in manuscript because it lists as many as 240 names, is inscribed 'The Names of the Pore Inhabietance of the Second North warde with an Account of what fierharthes every parsonne Hath in his house'.[126] On the certificate for St Michael Coslany, Norwich, dated 7 March 1670/1, instead of certifying 'unto his Majesties Justices of the Peace for the said' parish, or city, or city and county, the officials wrote 'pore Inhabitants' (see frontispiece). This was done in other parishes also. On the back of a certificate for St Mary Coslany, Norwich, is written 'the pores bill'.[127] A person in extreme poverty might be specially mentioned, for example 'Mis Wored verey poer' in St John de Sepulchre in 1672.[128]

Occasionally the occupations of exempt persons are given on the certificates. The 1671 certificate for St Peter Mancroft, Norwich, lists the occupations of 8 of the 95 people listed.[129]

Some of the officials who signed the certificates were concerned to qualify their endorsements. In 1674 Nicholas Norgate, curate of 'St Awdries' (St Etheldreda), Norwich, wrote 'I am informed these persons are incapable of paying ye hearth mony'.[130] In 1674 Benedict Revely, minister of St George Tombland, Norwich, wrote 'I ... doe testify what I am hereby required though

---

[122] PRO E 179/335, f. 447.
[123] PRO E 179/335, f. 446.
[124] PRO E 179/338, f.68.
[125] PRO E 179/338, f.65.
[126] PRO E 179/338, f.46.
[127] PRO E 179/336, f.70.
[128] PRO E 179/337, f 8
[129] PRO E 179/338, f.36.
[130] PRO E 179/336, f.32.

not uppon personall knowledge'.[131] Robert Bendish, alderman of Middle Wymer Ward, Norwich, allowed the certificate 'unless cause be shewn to the contrary'.[132] John Richers, alderman of Coslany Ward, Norwich, was careful to say 'As I am informed this is a trew Certificate'.[133] Augustine Briggs, however, His Majesty's Receiver, seems to have been content to sign certificates on his own when necessary, without another justice of the peace. He was alderman of South Conesford Ward, which contained two of the poorest parishes in Norwich. When he certified the 104 names in St Peter Southgate parish in 1671, he wrote 'wee allow of this certificate containing 5 score & 4 names Aug Briggs Major [Mayor] & Alderman of the Ward'.[134] The certificates are important in containing examples of the signatures of the aldermen and mayors of the city and three boroughs. Some of the King's Lynn certificates bear the signature of Henry Bell (d 1686), mayor in 1670-1, and father of the architect of the same name.[135]

Some annotations may throw light on the way the supporting documents were handed in to the authorities. Five of the certificates in 'batch 3' (1672-early 1673), four of them for parishes in Clavering hundred and one in Loddon hundred (Loddon and Clavering were frequently paired administratively), have a place of delivery written on the back: 'Leave this at Mrs Heamons at the Singe [sign] of the Sunn in [Sun inn] at Gyles [St Giles, Norwich]'.[136] Another certificate, from 'batch 4' (1673-1674), has 'to Ask for Bart Carter collector by St Giles church'.[137]

Other documents published in this volume

Not only the 239 exemption certificates for the city and boroughs have been transcribed and published in this volume, but 21 other documents also. Two of them are constables' receipts for King's Lynn, with their wrapper; sixteen are constables' receipts for Norwich, with their wrapper; and one is the Receiver's state of the account for the year ended Michaelmas 1671. The receipts are published as Appendix VI (pp. lxxiv-lxxx), and the state of account as Appendix VII (p. lxxxi). They are included in this volume because the receipts and account are stored with the exemption certificates[138] and relate to the places covered in this volume.

The constables of the wards of King's Lynn and Norwich were allowed two pence in the pound for assisting the collectors in the collection of the hearth tax due for the three half years ended Michaelmas 1670, and duly signed their receipts.

---

[131] PRO E 179/336, f.38
[132] PRO E 179/336, ff.53, 72
[133] PRO E 179/336, f.62.
[134] PRO E 179/338, f.38.
[135] For example, PRO E 179/338, ff.58, 60-62.
[136] PRO E 179/336, f.573 (Hedenham). The others are ff.205 (Aldeby), 557 (Alpington), 564 (Carleton St Peter) and 577 (Kirstead).
[137] PRO E 179/336, f.558 (Alpington, in Loddon hundred).
[138] The receipts are in PRO E 179/338, ff.65-84, and the account in PRO E 179/337, f.53. A wrapper and 33 constables' receipts for South Erpingham hundred are in PRO E 179/338, ff.598-631.

2. POVERTY, WEALTH AND OCCUPATIONS IN RESTORATION NORWICH

[Editor's note: John Pound was the first historian of Norfolk to make scholarly use of the Norfolk hearth tax records, especially the three books of the Norwich July 1671 return in the Norfolk Record Office and the exemption certificates in the Public Record Office, in a paper presented to the Urban History Group at the University of East Anglia in April 1968.[139] Penelope Corfield later made use of the same sources,[140] as did John Patten.[141]]

The 1671 Hearth Tax Return for Norwich

Three books out of an original four have survived for this return. They are dated July 1671 and are held in the Norfolk Record Office, and list both payers and exempt, although there is no attempt to differentiate between the two categories. The exemption certificates in the Public Record Office, drawn up three months earlier, tally almost exactly with the names in the Norwich books and confirm that the two sources can be used in conjunction with each other with some confidence. A full analysis of the material for Norwich in 1671, broken down into parish and petty ward, is given in Appendix II, pp. lxiii-lxvii. The summary of it given in Table 2, which includes a reconstruction of the parishes which would have been contained in the missing book, is by petty ward and great ward, and provides details of an estimated 5,143 households containing 11,591 hearths, at an average of 2.25 hearths per household, just over 51 per cent of which contained a single hearth. These details closely resemble those given in a contemporary abstract return in the PRO, which records 11,614 hearths, both chargeable and exempt, for the year ended Michaelmas 1671.[142] It is important to stress the word 'household' for there is little doubt that many dwellings, especially in the Conesford area of the city, were sub-divided to house the poor.[143]

---

[139] John Pound, 'The Social Structure and Governing Classes of Norwich, 1525-1670', expanded in 'Government and Society in Tudor and Stuart Norwich, 1525-1675' (unpublished Ph.D. thesis, University of Leicester, 1976). He returned to the hearth tax material in John Pound, *Tudor and Stuart Norwich*, (Chichester, 1988), p 176, n. 7, and passim.

[140] P. Corfield, 'A Provincial Capital in the late Seventeenth Century: the case of Norwich' in P. Clark and P. Slack (eds), *Crisis and Order in English Towns, 1500-1700*, (London, 1972), pp. 263-310.

[141] It should be noted that Patten's conclusions about the Norfolk hearth tax are misleading For example, figures he gives for Diss, Great Walsingham and Wells in a table in one of his articles are found to be very inaccurate when compared with the documents. John Patten, 'The Hearth Taxes, 1662-1689', *Local Population Studies*, No. 7, (Autumn 1971), pp. 20-21.

[142] *Analysis of hearth tax accounts 1666-1689*, p. 59 right hand

[143] Large houses had been sub-divided for the use of the poor since at least the sixteenth century, as the Norwich Census of the Poor makes clear See J.F. Pound (ed), *The Norwich Census of the Poor, 1570*, Norfolk Record Society, XL, (1971), pp. 14-15.

TABLE 2

The Norwich Hearth Tax Return, 1671

Petty Wards, Great Wards and Hamlets

A=Total number of households B=Total number of hearths
C=Average number of hearths per household U=Unknown

Petty wards and GREAT WARDS	Number of households per band of hearth numbers								
	1	2	3-5	6-9	10+	U	A	B	C
South Conesford	218	39	20	3	2		282	403	1.43
North Conesford	224	106	29	8	3		370	630	1.70
Berstreet	335	129	57	14	3		538	939	1.74
CONESFORD	**777**	**274**	**106**	**25**	**8**		**1190**	**1972**	**1.66**
St Giles	78	30	25	11	3		147	341	2.32
St Peter Mancroft	105	85	99	40	22		351	1281	3.18
St Stephen	147	65	52	15	7		286	681	2.16
MANCROFT	**330**	**180**	**176**	**66**	**32**		**784**	**2303**	**2.94**
West Wymer	284	133	76	21	11		525	1090	2.08
Middle Wymer	82	80	102	56	11		331	1226	3.70
East Wymer	186	109	81	38	15	60	489	1347	2.75
WYMER	**552**	**322**	**259**	**115**	**37**	**60**	**1345**	**3663**	**2.72**
Coslany	337	137	61	13	3	61	612	1065	1.74
Colegate	145	69	52	16	4		286	621	2.17
Fyebridge	360	182	76	30	8		656	1317	2.01
ULTRA AQUAM	**842**	**388**	**189**	**59**	**15**	**61**	**1554**	**3003**	**1.93**
Hamlets	143	63	39	16	9		270	650	2.41
Grand totals	2644	1227	769	281	101	121	5143	11591	2.25
Percentage of total number of households	51.4	23.9	15.0	5.5	2.0	2.4			

The reconstruction of both households and hearths in the missing parishes has proved relatively straightforward. As pointed out above, a contemporary abstract in the PRO relating to the collections of Lady Day and Michaelmas 1671 records the number of registered hearths as 11,614, or 1,425 more than those contained in the surviving Norwich books for 1671[144] and the relevant material in the return for Michaelmas 1662.[145] These have been reconstituted, as far as possible, by making use of the printed returns for 1666,[146] combining these with the exemptions for 1671,[147] and comparing the number of hearths which emerges with both the abstract from 1671 and a contemporary abstract for 1672-1673 which lists the numbers of hearths taxed and exempted for that period.[148] This latter abstract is printed in full in Appendix III (pp. lxviii-lxix). The results from both sources show that the total of 1,402 additional hearths is not too wide of the mark.

In Table 3, showing a reconstruction of households exempted from the hearth tax in 1671, the Norwich parishes and hamlets, including the reconstructed ones, have been divided into three equal groupings: the first containing those with exemption levels from 17 to 49 per cent; the second with parishes whose exemption rate varies between 50 and 66 per cent; while the third contains the really poor parishes, ranging from 67 per cent in St John Timberhill to 91 per cent in St Peter Southgate. The divisions are arbitrary, but make for an interesting comparison. Column A refers to the number of exempted households, B to the total number of households, and C to the percentage of exempted households in the various parishes following these figures.

As the surviving material makes clear, the poor continued to predominate in Restoration Norwich just as they had in the Elizabethan city a century earlier. Some areas of the city were composed almost entirely of households in this category; rather more than 90 per cent of the parishioners of St Peter Southgate, for example, living in households containing a single hearth. Almost at the same margin were the parishes of St Michael at Thorn and St Paul, with over 80 per cent of the inhabitants exempted from the hearth tax, and those of All Saints, St John de Sepulchre and St Julian, all in the same area of the city, with 75 per cent or more of their inhabitants designated poor. In the parishes of St Martin at Oak, St Mary Coslany and the hamlet of Pockthorpe to the north-east of the city there were similarly disadvantaged proportions. In total contrast, three-quarters or more of the inhabitants of St Andrew, the Cathedral Close, St Peter Hungate and St Saviour paid the tax, as did almost two-thirds of those in the wealthy parishes of St Michael at Plea and St Peter Mancroft. These were the areas where some of the largest houses in the city were to be found, ranging in size from the huge mansions of the Duke of Norfolk and Sir John Hobart, with 60 and 50 hearths respectively, to the more modest but still large houses of the city's gentry and aldermen with between 10 and 25 hearths each. There were just over 100 houses in Norwich with 10 hearths or more. Twenty-two of these were to be found in St Peter

---

[144] NRO MF/RO 416/8.
[145] PRO E 179/154/701
[146] Seaman, *Norfolk and Norwich Hearth Tax Assessment, Lady Day 1666.*
[147] PRO E 179/336.
[148] In PRO E 179/355.

TABLE 3

Households exempted from the Hearth Tax in Norwich, 1671

A=Exempted households B=Total households C=Percentage exempted

Parish	A	B	C	Parish	A	B	C	Parish	A	B	C
St Peter Hungate	8	46	17	Hellesdon	8	16	50	St John Timberhill	84	126	67
Cathedral Close	20	100	20	St Giles	75	147	51	St Benedict	62	91	68
St Andrew	34	156	22	Trowse & Carrow	39	73	53	St Margaret	87	123	71
St Saviour	19	85	22	Heigham	51	94	54	St Martin at Palace	119	163	73
St Peter Mancroft	95	351	27	St Stephen	160	286	56	St James	62	83	75
St Michael at Plea	27	99	27	St Etheldreda	24	42	57	St Julian	95	126	75
Earlham	3	8	38	St Augustine	81	141	57	St Mary Coslany	143	188	76
St George Tombland	22	55	40	St Edmund	38	64	59	St Martin at Oak	154	202	76
St John Maddermarket	31	76	41	St Michael Coslany	137	222	62	St John de Sepulchre	120	157	76
St Simon and St Jude	27	65	42	St Lawrence	62	100	62	Pockthorpe	137	175	78
St George Colegate	63	145	43	St Peter Parmentergate	236	370	64	All Saints	66	83	80
St Gregory	61	138	44	Lakenham	32	50	64	St Michael at Thorn	146	172	85
St Helen	28	60	47	St Swithin	47	73	64	St Paul	140	164	85
St Clement	42	85	49	Eaton	19	24	66	St Peter Southgate	104	114	91
Totals	480	1469	33		1009	1707	59		1519	1967	77
				Grand Total	3008	5143	58				

xlv

Mancroft parish, some undoubtedly being inns as well as private dwellings, while St Andrew and St Stephen each had seven and St Gregory six. The remainder were distributed more or less evenly throughout the city.

Rather more than one-fifth of the houses for which we have information had between three and nine hearths, the type inhabited by all the common councillors of the city and by some of the less affluent aldermen. A similar proportion lived in households with two hearths. Some of these were exempted from paying the tax on the grounds of poverty, but most were probably above subsistence level.

We know the occupations of about one-third of those recorded in the hearth tax returns as well as their social status. Significantly, 80 per cent of building workers lived in dwellings with either one or two hearths and were thus poor or, at best, in modest circumstances, a picture which contrasts sharply with that produced by the inventories of their wealthier colleagues.[149] Over 60 per cent of the wood, leather, clothing, metal and textile workers were in similar circumstances, as were more than half of those occupied with food and drink. Worsted weavers, although some individuals were amongst the wealthiest men in the city, were especially numerous among the poorer classes, 182 having a single hearth, a further 141 only two, while butchers, tailors, cordwainers and blacksmiths were evident among the less affluent tradesmen in their own occupational categories. Only the city's merchants and professional men had small numbers in those categories, 19 and 13 per cent respectively. A large number of those following the occupations of draper, grocer, haberdasher and general merchant lived in houses containing three hearths or more, as did the apothecaries, clerks, doctors and scriveners.

Trade groupings can, of course, conceal differences between individual trades. Thus one-third of the city's carpenters and tailors and a majority of the hosiers were men of some substance. Most of the bakers and brewers were comfortably off, and both cordwainers and tailors included a number of men of middle rank. The same is true of the metal workers, where goldsmiths, ironmongers, pewterers and pinners were predominantly men of middle rank.[150]

Exemptions and the poor in Norwich

The figures for exemptions in 1671 and 1674 remained surprisingly constant, but it is, nevertheless, true that the poor were a volatile group with people moving in and out of the various parishes at surprising speed. This is most notable in certain areas of the city. Thus the exempt in St John de Sepulchre almost halved from 120 in 1671 to 67 in the following year before

---

[149] For details of wealthy building workers in seventeenth century Norwich, with assets ranging from £400 to more than £1,000, see Pound, *Tudor and Stuart Norwich*, p. 40. The median value of the inventories of five of the more affluent builders in the period 1651-1675 was £61 10s. 0d. Idem, p. 38.

[150] For the distribution of hearths among the trade groupings, see Pound, *Tudor and Stuart Norwich*, p. 45, Table 4.7, The social status of the freemen of Norwich, 1671. For a full analysis of the number of hearths per household by individual trade within trade groupings, see idem, pp. 184-186, Appendix III, Occupations and wealth in late seventeenth-century Norwich.

TABLE 4

Proportion of exempted receiving poor relief in 1673-1674

Parish	Number receiving poor relief	Number exempted	% of exempted relieved
St Etheldreda & St Julian	27	51	52.94
St Peter Hungate	4	8	50.00
St John Maddermarket	16	33	48.48
St Andrew	18	38	47.37
St Simon & St Jude	11	24	45.83
St Stephen	67	163	41.10
Heigham	25	63	39.68
St Gregory	23	60	38.33
St Martin at Palace	41	107	38.32
St Giles	27	76	35.53
St Clement	12	34	35.29
St George Tombland	8	23	34.78
St Margaret	25	76	32.89
St Peter Mancroft	34	104	32.69
St Augustine	26	80	32.50
All Saints	20	66	30.30
St George Colegate	25	84	29.76
St James	16	58	27.59
St Michael at Plea	8	29	27.59
St Saviour	10	38	26.32
St Paul	37	147	25.17
St Edmund	9	36	25.00
St Lawrence	25	103	24.27
Pockthorpe	36	152	23.68
St Martin at Oak	41	174	23.56
St Peter Southgate	25	107	23.36
St John de Sepulchre	20	87	22.99
St Peter Parmentergate	60	266	22.56
St Helen	6	29	20.69
St Benedict	13	68	19.12
St Michael at Thorn	28	148	18.92
St Mary Coslany	26	146	17.81
St Swithin	11	62	17.74
St John Timberhill	16	107	14.95
St Michael Coslany	18	140	12.86
Grand totals	814	2987	27.25

As noted in the text, those receiving poor relief include those exempted from the Hearth Tax AND those recorded solely as recipients of poor relief. The percentage of 'exempted' relieved is thus exaggerated but does emphasise the fact that exemption alone is not synonymous with absolute poverty.

rising to 81 and 87 in the two succeeding years. St John Timberhill, also in Berstreet Ward, rose from 84 in 1671 to 109 by 1673, while St Julian, in the neighbouring ward of South Conesford, fell from a high of 95 in 1671 to only 51 three years later. The most notable rise occurred in St Lawrence where the 1671 figure of 62 leapt to 102 the following year, and remained at the higher figure in the succeeding period. Those exempt in St Lawrence in 1671 were almost completely replaced by newcomers in the following year, with few of those recorded in 1671 remaining in the parish. This was exceptional, but changes of occupants were commonplace in all of the city's parishes and are reflected in the changes mentioned above. It is at least possible that many of the poorer inhabitants of the parishes were simply not recorded, for the hearth tax was essentially a fiscal measure. If individuals had nothing to contribute, and were unlikely to improve their financial status, there was less incentive to list them, particularly bearing in mind the constant changes referred to above. It seems likely that exemptions in any given year are only minimum numbers and that many of those recorded were above the level of actual destitution. This becomes clear when comparing the names of those receiving poor relief in 1673-1674 with those actually exempted from the payment of hearth tax.[151] Some people, unsurprisingly, are detailed in both lists, but the vast majority of those recorded as poor, some two-thirds of them women, appear nowhere among the names of those exempted. In the parish of St Julian, for example, no more than two of the nineteen receiving relief were listed as exempted from the hearth tax, while 45 per cent of those provided with support in All Saints and St John de Sepulchre were unrecorded. In contrast, six of the eight listed as poor in the smaller parish of St Etheldreda appeared in both lists. In every case women predominated, the proportions exceeding 90 per cent in St Benedict and St Swithin, exactly 90 per cent in St Saviour and 80 per cent or more in St Margaret and St Edmund, with a majority of the other parishes having two-thirds or more of women listed among the poor.[152] Over 300 of these, some 62 per cent, were widows. It may well be that up to 500 people in Norwich in any given year were never recorded in any hearth tax listing, and were dismissed, as suggested above, as having no financial contribution to make either then or in the foreseeable future.

By contemporary standards at least we are considering relative poverty when discussing the level of exemptions. Those exempted from the hearth tax were regarded as being far from destitute in every case, as the very full details of those receiving poor relief in 1673-1674 make perfectly clear. It is assumed that the individuals being offered support reflect households in every case, and are therefore shown as a proportion of those exempted from payment of hearth tax. At best, this can only serve as a rough-and-ready guide, for while a majority of the poor were additional to the exempt, a minority were to be found in both lists. As a result the proportions exaggerate the percentages of poor among the exempt, but to no great extent. Those parishes supporting the greatest number of 'deserving poor' are listed first in Table 4, with the rest following in descending order. There is no information available for the

---

[151] The lists of both recipients and contributors to poor relief in 1673-1674 are provided in Norfolk Record Office, Poor Law Records, Case 20, Shelf c, Book 13, passim.
[152] Only three city parishes – St John Maddermarket, St Michael at Thorn and St Stephen – and the hamlet of Heigham had fewer than half of their recorded poor listed as women.

hamlets of Eaton, Lakenham, Trowse and Carrow, nor for the Cathedral Close.

If the population remained at around 21,000 in 1673-1674 this suggests a level of poor relief rather less than 4 per cent of the whole, many of the poorer parishes continuing to rely on the largesse of their wealthier neighbours, much as they had done a century earlier when the city's poor law scheme was first reorganised. Fifteen parishes provided support for their poorer neighbours in 1673-1674, St Peter Mancroft topping the list by assisting ten other areas. St Andrew, St Martin at Oak and St Saviour provided help for four, St Clement three, and St Gregory and St Michael at Plea two. In contrast, St Paul was obliged to accept help from five other parishes, St Lawrence, St Margaret and St Martin at Palace from three, with a further nine receiving assistance from either one or two other areas.

This situation was not peculiar to the 1670s. There is evidence that it had continued to operate in much the same way since the Elizabethan period, if not earlier. The details do not survive for every parish for the preceding century, but a rate levied for the whole city in 1633-1634 produces a very similar picture,[153] while a survey by John Fransham[154] in 1720 records full details of the numbers of payers, recipients and costs of poor relief for the period 1621-1720, culled from the registers of fourteen parishes 'whose Parish-Books run back so far'.[155] If Fransham's information can be relied upon, it suggests that, broadly speaking, the amounts spent on poor relief were steadily increasing throughout the period being dealt with here, rising from a yearly charge of £286 12s. 7d. in 1671 to £384 13s. 2d. by 1675, a significant increase and one which can only reflect the extent of poverty in the parishes concerned, and may well be indicative of the situation in the city as a whole.[156]

3. SOME SMALLER BUILDINGS IN SEVENTEENTH-CENTURY NORWICH

[Editor's note: Robert Smith is an architectural historian who has spent many years studying the buildings of Norwich and Norfolk. Here he studies some of the smaller buildings to be found in Restoration Norwich, from the three per cent or so of the pre-1700 buildings that survive.]

---

[153] Walter Rye (ed), *The Norwich Rate Book from Easter 1633 to Easter 1634*, (1903), passim.
[154] Poor Law Guardian and Common Councillor for Mancroft Great Ward.
[155] J Fransham, *An Exact Account of the Charge for Supporting the Poor of the City of Norwich*, (London, 1720).
[156] The parishes detailed by Fransham were St Andrew, St Clement, St Edmund, St Etheldreda, St George Tombland, St Gregory, St Helen, St James, St John Maddermarket, St Mary Coslany, St Michael at Plea, St Peter Hungate, St Saviour and St Swithin. With the exception of St Etheldreda in Conesford Great Ward all these parishes were in Wymer Great Ward, or in the Great Ward Over-the-Water (alias Ultra Aquam) in the northern part of the city, Conesford Great Ward and Mancroft Great Ward being unavoidably excluded from his whole analysis.

INTRODUCTION

The area covered by the medieval city of Norwich was large, being comparable in size to London and covering some 217.5 hectares (537 acres). Its defence walls extend for just under three and a half kilometres (two miles) around the north, west and south sides, and on the east side the River Wensum completes the circuit. There were two closely extramural hamlets, Pockthorpe and Heigham, but apart from these, and because of the size of the city, the populace of Norwich could be contained within the medieval walls until the early nineteenth century. The seventeenth century saw the most dramatic increase in the population with conservative estimates showing that by 1700 it had reached 30,000. However, it should be emphasised that only something like 3 per cent of the pre-1700 buildings survive today, making it impossible to ascertain their comparative architectural status.

The sheer size of the medieval city could accommodate the increase in the number of dwellings needed to house the rising population, although by the late eighteenth century space was running out. This, and prevailing social attitudes, led to the inevitable creation of slums, although many references to an unhealthy environment were more politically motivated than referring to actual conditions. For instance the view that the city gates and walls were 'a nuisance, that smells rank in the nose of modern improvement',[157] and the comment that the defences inhibited the free movement of air, were a direct reaction to the feared decline in the state of eighteenth-century commerce.

The nineteenth-century slums were generally contained within, or formed, the yards and 'courts' found throughout the city. Generally speaking the yards extended back at right angles from the street frontage and often created labyrinthine complexes that extended back for some distance; in reality the 'courts' were no more than a smaller variation on the yards.

The origin of these yards is complex. Surviving examples date from the fifteenth century through to the early seventeenth century. These show a building set back from and parallel to the street. It seems likely, as a result of commercial pressures, that the street frontage would have been built up, although because of subsequent rebuilding of the more commercially viable building on the street frontage this is far from certain.

This trend in positioning the building away from the street was presumably possible due to the amount of space available, although as this was eventually absorbed to accommodate the ever-increasing population, so the space between the building and the street was encroached upon. A typical example is seen at Gurney Court off Magdalen Street. Here the late sixteenth-century house is set back from the street and is flanked on one side by an early seventeenth-century building and on the other by a slightly later block. The street frontage is formed by two seventeenth-century buildings that include a passageway through to the yard that was formed by this resulting development.

Obviously, this description of the development of the city's buildings is highly simplistic, although it does begin to point to another development in

---

[157] W. Chase, *The Norwich Directory*, (Norwich, 1783), p. v.

1

house types found in seventeenth-century Norwich, that is, the single-cell house.[159]

Writing in 1973[160] Alan Carter stated that 'An analysis of the Norwich probate inventories for the period 1580-1730 had shown that a building similar to this [a post-1507 building excavated on a site in Pottergate], i.e. one room on each of the two floors, with increasing use of the attic space throughout the period, had once been extremely common. The type as reconstructed from the documentary evidence was strongly associated with craftsmen, and the only surviving example of this type so far discovered (dated 1670) was built for a worsted weaver'.

The building is No. 63 St George's Street and it was renovated by Norwich City Architects Department in the mid 1980s. Although Carter's observation was correct the renovation work uncovered evidence that made the building more interesting and significant.

The building measures some 5.60m x 8.00m. It is constructed on the street line, and consists of a single room at ground and first floor levels plus a single room attic. There are opposing doorways in the front and back walls immediately adjacent to the side gable wall and the chimney stack is built into the opposite wall. All three floor levels were heated: see figure 1.

The walls are built with flint rubble, the door and window jambs are decorated with a simple quadrant moulding, and the chamfers on the ceiling beams are terminated with a nicked stop typical of the period. There was a contemporary stone plaque in the front wall with the initials of William and Anne Watson and the date of 1670.[161] The stone plaque surely indicates some form of social pretension but the decoration on the jambs and the ceiling beams is basic when compared with, for example, contemporary decoration found in Great Yarmouth.

The main point, however, is that the Watsons' house was in effect a single-cell unit that was added on to an adjoining building. Apart from the party wall, which was still covered with eighteenth-century panelling,[162] and part of the front wall, there is nothing left of the adjoining building. It was only when restoration work had started that a secondary doorway was discovered leading from the stairs in the Watsons' house to the adjoining property. Twenty-six other single-cell buildings have been identified within the city walls. Between them they display three variations on the basic plan form seen at No. 63 St George's Street. All date from the seventeenth century and are constructed with flint rubble walls. Thus by the later years of the seventeenth century the single-cell building was established in the repertoire of available building types.

A slight variation on the plan seen at No. 63 St George's Street occurs in the street range of No. 58 St Benedict's Street, 37-39 All Saints Green, and the

---

[159] Earlier single-cell houses have been found in excavations, although these were unheated and were presumably single storey.

[160] 'The Buildings and their Social Context' in Excavations in Norwich –1973, The Norwich Survey third Interim Report, (Norfolk Archaeology, XXXVI part 1, 1974), p. 50.

[161] This was stolen during the restoration and the existing plaque is a twentieth-century replacement

[162] By the eighteenth century flint rubble walls were superseded by walls constructed entirely with bricks. This shows that the building pre-dates the panelling.

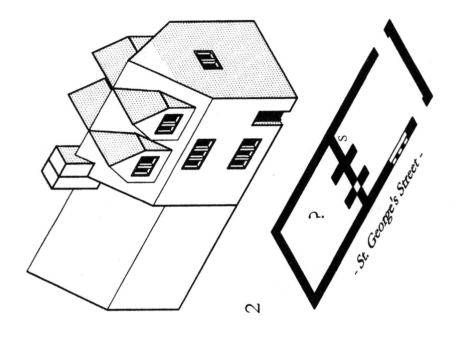

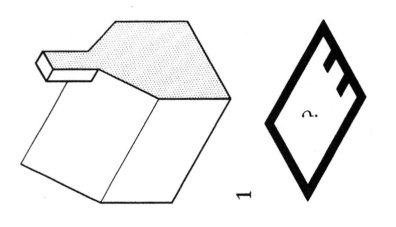

Fig. 1. T63 St George's Street

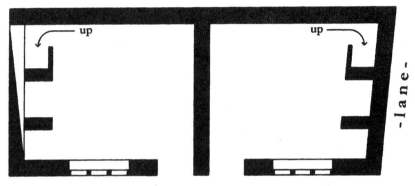

47 - 49 St. Martin's Lane

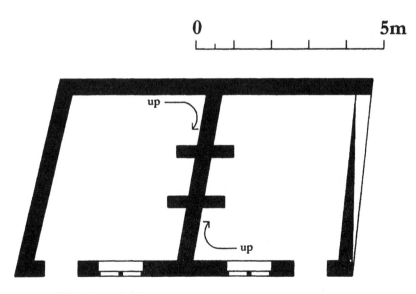

5 - 7 Timberhill

Fig. 2. 47–49 St Martin's Lane and 5–7 Timberhill

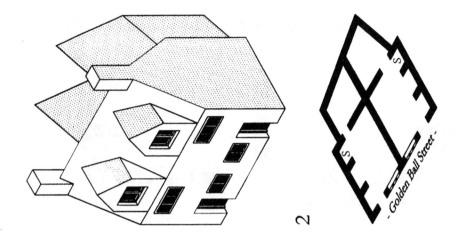

2

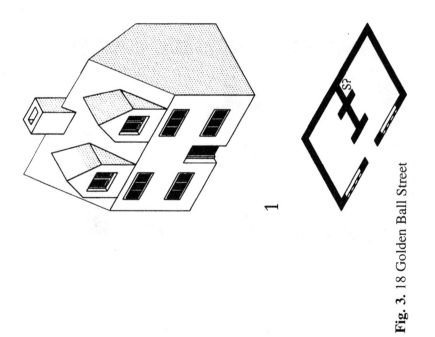

1

Fig. 3. 18 Golden Ball Street

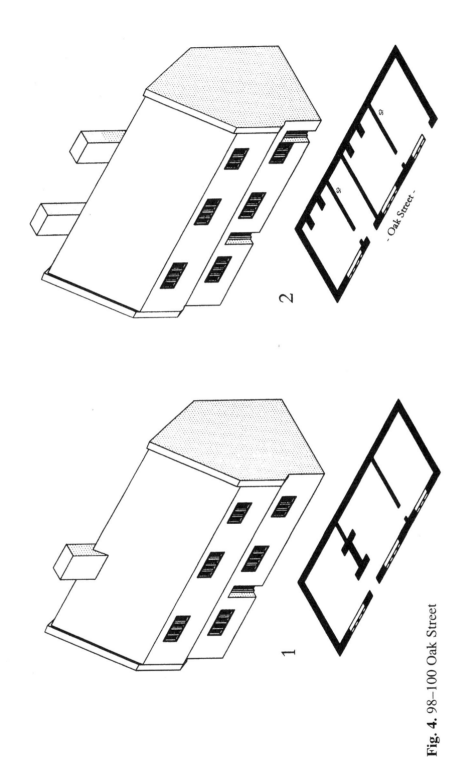

Fig. 4. 98–100 Oak Street

INTRODUCTION

building to the rear of No. 88 Upper St Giles Street. In each example the stack is on the rear wall, and in the latter example a doorway still exists that is positioned on the extreme right hand side of the front wall, although the frame was replaced in the nineteenth century.

Seven of the buildings consist of a semi-detached block that are literally a doubling-up or a mirror image of the plan form seen at No. 63 St George's Street. For instance at Nos. 5 and 7 Timberhill the building is ranged along the street frontage and the stack in the party wall serves both units. At Nos. 47 and 49 St Martin's Lane, where the block is at right angles to the road, the chimney stack is in each of the end gables and in both cases the upper floor(s) were reached via stack-side stairs: see figure 2.

At No. 28 Magdalen Street the building is in effect two single-cell units in line at right angles to the street frontage. Both the front and back rooms have a stack on the side wall although unfortunately this, apart from the roof, is the only feature, minus the fireplace, to survive commercial alterations. The roof is interesting as each of the two rooms has its own pitched roof and there is a contemporary dormer 'corridor' linking the two attic spaces. Even more interesting is the fact that a pre-war photograph[162] shows No. 28 to be part of a terrace of four identical buildings. It is possibly an early example of speculative development.

Two buildings out of the surviving examples in the city became single-cell units by alteration, presumably as a direct reaction to the increasing demand for houses. Number 18 Golden Ball Street was constructed in the early seventeenth century as a small, two storey plus attic, two-cell building with a central chimney stack. Later in the same century the stack was removed, the block divided into two throughout its full height and each new unit was given a gable-end stack plus a rear room: see figure 3.

The technology involved in constructing the rear additions was third-rate with insubstantial timber-framed upper walls with brick-on-edge infill and very basic carpentry details. Nevertheless, the decoration on the new door frames between the front and back rooms and the quadrant mouldings on the windows in the rear wall were, despite their elementary design, comparable with those found in some of the more substantial houses in the city.

A variation on this, again involving the removal of a chimney stack, occurs in Nos. 98-100 Oak Street. This building was constructed in the early seventeenth century as a two storey, three-cell building with two heated rooms and one unheated room all ranged along the street line.[163] Later in the century the stack was removed and the block was divided into two self-contained, three-storeyed units of unequal size, each with a stack on the rear wall, plus a smaller unheated room: see figure 4.

---

[162] Reproduced in George A.F Plunkett, *Rambles in Old Norwich*, (Lavenham, 1990), p. 88 (lower photograph).
[163] This type of building is relatively common in the surrounding countryside and in the market towns although it is scarce in Norwich with only two, or possibly three, examples surviving. The uncertainty over the number is due to severe alterations in one case.

This could conceivably have contained the stairs to the upper floors although later alterations make this a speculative point.

In conclusion seventeenth-century Norwich seems to have been a city of extremes that on the one hand was associated with wealth and on the other dictated by the reaction to a rapidly increasing population. For instance, the most extravagant decoration applied to a ceiling beam is found in Strangers' Hall in one of the seventeenth-century extensions to the fifteenth-century open hall. It consists of the ubiquitous nicked ending plus two bars on a straight-cut chamfer before two steps that are in front of the quadrant moulded chamfer. This decoration, however, would just about qualify to be included with the general standard of seventeenth-century decoration seen, for example, in the market town of Wymondham some ten miles south-west of Norwich.

There are very good examples of seventeenth-century stair design; one again in Strangers' Hall and another in Howard House,[164] King Street, although the former contains certain discrepancies that could suggest that it is made up with elements from another stair. Likewise, well-designed full-height fireplace surrounds exist as museum exhibits and are known through antiquarian illustrations although it must be emphasised that these are all, or were, in relatively large and exceptional buildings. From these exceptional buildings of quality there is no gradual move to the mundane in terms of architectural decoration, despite the transition through various levels of social standing.

4. CONCLUSION

This book is a record of those persons exempted from payment of the hearth tax in Norwich and the three Norfolk boroughs in the period 1670-1674. For that period, the exemption certificates for the whole of Norfolk are almost complete, whereas the records of those liable to pay the tax are sadly incomplete for the entire period of the tax. Partial returns for the county exist for Michaelmas 1664 and Lady Day 1666, and a damaged return exists for Michaelmas 1672. For the latter, however, an abstract also exists showing totals of chargeable and exempt hearths for every parish in the county. For Norwich, there are incomplete returns for Michaelmas 1662, Lady Day 1666 and July 1671. Other than those returns, there are stray membranes and fragments for parts of the county, which might be grouped together by style and binding holes, and dated from internal evidence.

The lack of a complete and undamaged return for Norfolk, and of one for Norwich, is the more regrettable because of the importance of the county in population and wealth, as demonstrated by John Houghton's estimate of the number of 'houses' in the English counties in the mid-1680s, possibly derived from the hearth tax returns of 1685. After Yorkshire, with its three ridings, totalling 106,151, comes the conglomeration of London, Middlesex and Westminster, with 100,136. Then Devon with 56,310 and Somerset with

---

[164] Most of the decorative panels associated with the stairs in Howard House were unfortunately stolen a few years back.

49,808 are followed by Norfolk with 47,180. After Norfolk come Lincolnshire, Lancashire and Kent.[165]

The survival of abstract returns of hearths does, however, allow us to build up a picture of the proportion of exempted hearths in parishes and wards, and the survival of the exemption certificates supplies us with the names of all persons exempted from payment of the tax.

In the return for the year and a half ended Lady Day 1673, Norwich had 11,517 hearths, of which 3,773 were exempt, representing 33 per cent of the total. Great Yarmouth had 5,366 hearths, of which 1,687 were exempt (31 per cent); King's Lynn had 3,509 hearths, of which 1,147 were exempt (33 per cent); and Thetford had 765 hearths, of which 181 were exempt (24 per cent).

In the return for the year ended Lady Day 1674, Norwich had 11,623 hearths, of which 3,906 were exempt, representing 34 per cent of the total. Great Yarmouth had 5,381 hearths, of which 1,709 were exempt (32 per cent); King's Lynn had 3,540 hearths, of which 1,218 were exempt (34 per cent); and Thetford had 740 hearths, of which 163 were exempt (22 per cent).

These figures show only exempted hearths as a percentage of a total number of recorded hearths. It must be remembered that the exempt had only one or two hearths; rich householders had many more. For Norwich, John Pound has gone further; using evidence including that of the incomplete 1662, 1666 and 1671 returns of Norwich hearth tax payers to extrapolate numbers of households, he has reached the conclusion that in Norwich an average of 58% of households were exempted from payment of the hearth tax in 1671. His tables and appendixes show the details for parishes and wards, illustrating what Robert Smith has rightly described as 'a city of extremes'.

The maps, apart from delineating for the first time the old ward boundaries of the boroughs, show what percentage the exempted hearths were of the total number of hearths in each parish of Norwich and each ward of Great Yarmouth, King's Lynn and Thetford in 1672-1673.

It is hoped that this book succeeds in illustrating the importance of the hearth tax exemption certificates, not only for the chief Norfolk towns, but for all places in England and Wales.

---

[165] John Houghton, *An Account of the Acres and Houses, with the Proportional Tax, &c of each county in England and Wales*, broadsheet, London, 1693; also in John Houghton, *A Collection for the Improvement of Husbandry and Trade*, xxvi, 3 February 1693. Republished and discussed in 'Note on the number of houses in England and Wales, 1690' as an appendix to D.V. Glass, 'Two papers on Gregory King', in D.V. Glass and E.C. Eversley (eds), *Population in History*, (London, 1965), pp. 216-20.

APPENDIX I

A LIST OF NORFOLK HEARTH TAX DOCUMENTS

(a) In the Public Record Office

Reference | *Description*

E 179/154/696   *8 mems.* 8 stray Norfolk paper exemption certificates.

E 179/154/697   *53 mems.* The Exchequer Duplicate Roll for the county of Norfolk (but not including Norwich), *Michaelmas 1672.*

E 179/154/700   *8 mems.* 2 membranes from *Michaelmas 1664.* 6 membranes from *undated assessments,* covering Clackclose, Clavering and Depwade hundreds. 2 mems. **printed** in M.S. Frankel and P.J. Seaman, (eds), *Norfolk Hearth Tax Assessment, Michaelmas 1664* (Norfolk Genealogy, XV, 1983).

E 179/154/701   *5 mems.* Roll for the city of Norwich, *Michaelmas 1662.*

E 179/154/703A   *2 mems.* 2 membranes from an *undated assessment,* covering Clackclose, Clavering and Depwade hundreds.

E 179/154/704   *4 mems.* 4 membranes from an *undated assessment,* covering Depwade, Diss, Earsham and Eynsford hundreds.

E 179/154/707   *5 mems. and 12 fragments.* 5 membranes from *Michaelmas 1664* and 12 fragments from *undated assessments* covering Earsham, East Flegg, Forehoe, Freebridge-Lynn, North Erpingham, North Greenhoe, South Erpingham and Shropham hundreds. 5 mems. **printed** in Frankel and Seaman, *Michaelmas 1664.*

E 179/154/709	*4 mems.* 4 membranes from *Michaelmas 1664.* **Printed** in Frankel and Seaman, *Michaelmas 1664.*
E 179/238/119	*1 mem.* 1 membrane from *Michaelmas 1664.* **Printed** in Frankel and Seaman, *Michaelmas 1664.*
E 179/253/42	*58 fos.* 3 paper books covering various Hundreds in Norfolk, *Lady Day 1666.* **Printed** in P.J. Seaman, (ed), *Norfolk and Norwich Hearth Tax Assessment, Lady Day 1666* (Norfolk Genealogy, XX, 1988).
E 179/253/43	*12 fos.* Papers covering part of Norfolk and part of Norwich, *Lady Day 1666.* **Printed** in Seaman, *Lady Day 1666.*
E 179/253/44	*11 fos.* 1 paper book covering part of Norwich, *Lady Day 1666,* and arrears for part of Norfolk and Norwich at *Michaelmas 1665.* **Printed** in Seaman, *Lady Day 1666.*
E 179/253/45	*30 mems.* 21 membranes from *Michaelmas 1664.* 9 membranes from *undated assessments,* covering Clackclose, Clavering, Depwade, Diss, Eynsford and West Flegg hundreds, and Thetford borough. 21 mems. **printed** in Frankel and Seaman, *Michaelmas 1664.*
E 179/335	*997 fos.* Bound documents, includind 505 paper exemption certificates for Norfolk, *1671-1672.* Also Norfolk arrears, *Michaelmas 1662;* and abstract of hearth roll for Norfolk and Norwich for year ended *Lady Day 1674.* Some fos. **printed** in present volume.
E 179/336	*705 fos.* A box of 705 paper exemption certificates, *1671-1674.* Some fos. **printed** in present volume.
E 179/337	*711 fos.* A box of 710 paper exemption certificates, *1672-1674;* and one folio of accounts, *1671.* Some fos. **printed** in present volume.
E 179/338	*733 fos.* A box of 671 paper exemption certificates, *1670-1671;* 3 paper wrappers and 59 folios of constables' receipts for Norwich city,

King's Lynn and Thetford boroughs and South Erpingham hundred, *1670-1671*. Some fos. **printed** in present volume.

E 179/351   In a bound volume, Part 1 folio 2 is a paper exemption certificate for Brooke in Clavering hundred, *1672*.

E 179/354   Includes: Augustine Briggs appointed Receiver from Lady Day 1669. Given *11 May 1670*.

E 179/355   Includes: John Lloyd's 3 receipts for one and a half years ending *Lady Day 1666*; Norfolk & Norwich, Mr Briggs his accompt, one and a half years ending *Michaelmas 1670*; Norfolk & Norwich, Auditor's abstract of total hearths, one and a half years ending *Lady Day 1673*.
From the abstract ending *Lady Day 1673*, figures for Norwich and the boroughs **printed** as Appendices III and IV respectively in the present volume.

E 179/356   Includes: Norff booke of Arreares Hearth mony *1671*.

E 179/358   Includes: list showing that returns for Norfolk and Norwich had been received in Remembrancer's Office by 21 Sept 1662. Also arrears for Norfolk.

E 179/359   Includes: 2 Norfolk abstracts.

E 179/360   Includes: paper book listing hearth tax payers by parish in Loddon hundred, *Lady Day 1666*. Also, in a bundle labelled 'Lloyds acc[oun]t, Norfolk *1666 L[ady Day]*': neat abstract state of account, *Lady Day 1666*; rougher abstract; neat table comparing returns 1663 and 1666; rougher table; figures per parish for certain hundreds. Also comparison between 1670 and 1671 returns, Richard Browne Recr. genll of the hearth mony. Also, in a bundle labelled 'Norfolk', neat abstract of account of Richard Browne, for year ended *Michaelmas 1671*, Norfolk & Norwich; dirty and flimsy statistics for Norwich, 1671; rough account for 3 half years ending *Lady Day 1673*, Richard Browne , Recr. generall.
Flimsy statistics for Norwich 1671 **printed** as Appendix V in present volume.

E 179/367/13	*17 mems. and 11 fragments.* 7 membranes from *Michaelmas 1664*; 10 membranes from *undated assessments* covering Clackclose, East Flegg, Freebridge-Lynn, Freebridge Marshland, Gallow, Guiltcross, Humbleyard, Launditch, Loddon and West Flegg hundreds, and Norwich and Great Yarmouth; and 11 fragments from *undated assessments* covering Blofield, Brothercross, Clavering, Depwade, Diss, Freebridge-Lynn, Freebridge Marshland, Shropham, Smithdon, South Erpingham, South Greenhoe, Taverham, Tunstead, Walsham and Wayland hundreds, and King's Lynn. 7 mems. **printed** in Frankel and Seaman, *Michaelmas 1664.*

NOTE: It is possible that previously inidentified Norfolk hearth tax records in the PRO will be discovered in the course of the current re-listing of Norfolk E 179 records, as part of the PRO's 'E 179 Project'.

(b) In the Norfolk Record Office

Reference	*Description*
Case 13a/48	3 surviving paper books, out of 4 originals, being the return for Norwich, book 3 dated 24 July 1671, so for both *Lady Day 1671* and *Michaelmas 1671.* Books 1, 3 and 4 survive. Missing book 2 would have contained North Conesford, Fyebridge and East Wymer wards. Order as microfilm MF/RO 416/8.
Case 7 shelf k	'Papers relating to Hearth Tax etc, 1666-1696'. Certificate of delivery of the books, dated 24 July 1671, signed Augustine Briggs. Also a list of John Lloyd's deputies in collecting the tax, dated 24 January 1666/7, and signed John Lloyd.
Frere MSS	In the Shropham Hundred sections of these MSS Paul Rutledge has identified hearth tax lists of payers and exempt for Hargham, Hockham and Wilby. There are others.
Aylsham Collection 203	North Erpingham Hundred: Hanworth 1662, 1664.

APPENDIX II

The Norwich Hearth Tax Return, 1671

A= Total number of Households **B**=Total number of hearths
C=Average number of hearths per household

Parishes and Petty Wards	Number of households per band of hearth numbers							
	1	2	3-5	6-9	10+	A	B	C
St Peter Southgate	102	10	2			114	129	1.13
St Etheldreda	20	12	8	1	1	42	97	2.31
St Julian	96	17	10	2	1	126	177	1.42
SOUTH CONESFORD	218	39	20	3	2	282	403	1.43
Percentages	77.30	13.83	7.09	1.06	0.71			
St Peter Parmentergate¹	224	106	29	8	3	370	630	1.70
Percentages	60.54	28.65	7.84	2.16	0.81			
St John Timberhill	64	33	23	4	2	126	264	2.09
All Saints	62	10	7	4		83	132	1.59
St Michael at Thorn	121	36	12	2	1	172	271	1.57
St John de Sepulchre	88	50	15	4		157	272	1.73
BER STREET	335	129	57	14	3	538	939	1.74
Percentages	62.27	23.98	10.59	2.60	0.56			
St Giles	78	30	25	11	3	147	341	2.32
Percentages	53.06	20.41	17.01	7.48	2.04			

The Norwich Hearth Tax Return, 1671

Parishes and Petty Wards	Number of households per band of hearth numbers							
	1	2	3-5	6-9	10+	A	B	C
St Peter Mancroft	105	85	99	40	22	351	1281	3.18
Percentages	29.91	24.22	28.20	11.40	6.27			
St Stephen	147	65	52	15	7	286	681	2.16
Percentages	51.40	22.73	18.18	5.24	2.45			
St Benedict	66	14	10	1		91	137	1.51
St Swithin	43	17	9	3	1	73	142	1.95
St Margaret	79	29	11	4		123	203	1.65
St Lawrence	49	28	18	1	4	100	219	2.19
St Gregory	47	45	28	12	6	138	389	2.29
WEST WYMER	284	133	76	21	11	525	1090	2.08
Percentages	54.09	25.33	14.48	4.00	2.09			
St John Maddermarket	11	29	21	11	4	76	338	4.45
St Andrew	32	38	48	31	7	156	587	3.76
St Michael at Plea	39	13	33	14		99	301	3.04
MIDDLE WYMER	82	80	102	56	11	331	1226	3.70
Percentages	24.77	24.17	30.82	16.92	3.32			
Cathedral Close	19	22	36	20	3	100	401	4.01
St George Tombland[2]	24	11	8	6	6	55	194	3.53
St Helen[3]	25	3	(32 unknown)			60	88	1.47
St Martin at P.[4]	90	51	17	4	1	163	302	1.91

The Norwich Hearth Tax Return, 1671

Parishes and Petty Wards	Number of households per band of hearth numbers							
	1	2	3-5	6-9	10+	A	B	C
St Peter Hungate[5]	6	5	4		3	46	153	3.33
			(28 unknown)					
St Simon & St Jude[6]	22	17	16	8	2	65	209	3.21
EAST WYMER	186	109	81	38	15	489	1347	2.75
Percentages*	40.47	26.37	20.10	9.92	3.13			

* Excluding St Helen and St Peter Hungate i.e. based on 383 households.

	1	2	3-5	6-9	10+	A	B	C
St Michael Coslany and St Mary Coslany[7]	218	84	37	9	1	410	709	1.73
St Martin at Oak	119	53	24	4	2	202	356	1.76
COSLANY	337	137	61	13	3	612	1065	1.74
Percentages	61.16	24.86	11.07	2.36	0.54			

	1	2	3-5	6-9	10+	A	B	C
St Augustine	75	44	16	6		141	259	1.84
St George Colegate	70	25	36	10	4	145	362	2.50
COLEGATE	145	69	52	16	4	286	621	2.17
Percentages	50.70	24.13	18.18	5.59	1.40			

	1	2	3-5	6-9	10+	A	B	C
St Clement[8]	19	40	15	8	3	85	249	2.93
St Edmund[9]	31	21	11	1		64	124	1.94
St James	45	29	9			83	141	1.70
St Paul	116	37	5	5	1	164	254	1.55
Pockthorpe	127	37	9	1	1	175	250	1.43
St Saviour	22	18	27	15	3	85	299	3.52

The Norwich Hearth Tax Return, 1671

FYEBRIDGE	360	182	76	30	8	656	1317	2.01
Percentages	54.88	27.74	11.58	4.57	1.22			

Hamlets	Number of households per band of hearth numbers							
	1	2	3-5	6-9	10+	A	B	C
Carrow	5	1	1	3		10	31	3.10
Earlham	3	1	2		2	8	42	5.25
Eaton	17	5	5	1	1	29	65	2.25
Heigham	50	24	12	6	2	94	210	2.23
Hellesdon	6	4	4		2	16	52	3.25
Lakenham	21	18	6	3	2	50	136	2.72
Trowse	41	10	9	3		63	114	1.81
Totals	143	63	39	16	9	270	650	2.41
Percentages	52.96	23.33	14.44	5.93	3.33			

1.   This parish comprised North Conesford Ward. Figures derived from the 1662 return.

2.   Most of St George Tombland was obtained from the 1662 listing, supplemented by additional material from the listings of exemptions in 1671/2.

3.   Nothing survives for St Helen, apart from the details of exemptions and the details of chargeable and exempted hearths in 1672/3. I have estimated the number of households by reducing the figure of population given by Gregory King in 1696 by one quarter and dividing the result by 4.25.

4.   The details for St Martin at Palace were derived from the 1662 listing. The total of 302 hearths coincides exactly with that of 1672/3.

5.   St Peter Hungate is very defective, these details being a combination of exemptions and a little additional detail from the printed 1666 return. Household numbers have been estimated as in Note 3 and the total number of hearths from the 1672/3 listing.

6.   The details for St Simon and St Jude are derived from the 1662 return.

7.   St Michael Coslany and St Mary Coslany were not clearly distinguished in the Norwich books which merely referred to 'part of St Michael'. The combined

total of 603 hearths suggests a shortfall of 106, based on the 1672/3 listing and I have followed this, estimating the missing households as 61 by dividing the 106 hearths by the average of 1.73 given by the Norwich books (i.e. 603 divided by 349). The percentages are based on the Norwich books, viz. a proportion of 551 hearths, not the 612 estimated.

8.   St Clement's details are derived from the 1662 return.

9.   The parishes of St Edmund, St James, St Paul and Pockthorpe are a combination of the exemptions for 1671 (the distinction between 1 & 2 hearths being obtained from the 1673/4 return) with those details - full for these parishes - derived from the printed 1666 listing. The total of hearths corresponds closely with that given in 1672/3, suggesting - unsurprisingly - that the composition of the larger houses had altered little, if at all, in the ensuing period. The figures for St Saviour in the Norwich books, i.e. 122 hearths, correspond exactly with one part of the parish detailed in 1672/3. The rest of the parish has been reconstituted in the way referred to above, the resulting 299 hearths being very close to the 303 referred to overall in 1672/3.

APPENDIX III

Exempted and paying hearths in Norwich, 1672-1673

Parish	Hearths paid	Hearths exempted	Total of hearths	Exempted hearths as percentage of total
All Saints	61	94	155	61
Cathedral Close	355	39	394	10
Earlham	39	-	39	-
Eaton	42	26	68	38
Heigham	130	77	207	37
Hellesdon	38	11	49	22
Lakenham	81	49	130	38
Pockthorpe	78	167	245	68
St Andrew	537	48	585	8
St Augustine	157	99	256	39
St Benedict	67	67	134	50
St Clement	167	56	223	25
St Edmund	89	45	134	34
St Etheldreda	64	28	92	30
St George Colegate	273	90	363	25
St George Tombland	184	31	215	14
St Giles	240	86	326	26
St Gregory	297	83	380	22
St Helen	57	31	88	35
St James	68	88	156	56
St John de Sepulchre	103	111	214	52
St John Maddermarket	264	39	303	13
St John Timberhill	164	141	305	46
St Julian	82	104	186	56
St Lawrence	154	103	257	40
St Margaret	98	103	201	51
St Martin at Oak	161	200	361	55
St Martin at Palace	172	130	302	43
St Mary Coslany	145	180	325	55
St Michael at Plea	251	38	289	13
St Michael at Thorn	84	188	272	69

Exempted and paying hearths in Norwich, 1672-1673

Parish	Hearths paid	Hearths exempted	Total of hearths	Exempted hearths as percentage of total
St Michael Coslany	217	167	384	44
St Paul	131	152	283	54
St Peter Hungate	141	12	153	8
St Peter Mancroft	1139	118	1257	9
St Peter Parmentergate	341	273	614	45
St Peter Southgate	27	106	133	80
St Saviour	260	43	303	14
St Simon & St Jude	145	33	178	19
St Stephen	483	188	671	28
St Swithin	81	75	156	48
Trowse	51	51	102	50
Carrow Abbey	26	3	29	10
Totals	**7744**	**3773**	**11,517**	**33**

APPENDIX IV

Exempted and paying hearths in the Norfolk boroughs, 1672-1673

Borough and Ward	Hearths paid	Hearths exempted	Total of hearths	Exempted hearths as percentage of total
GREAT YARMOUTH				
First North Ward	396	412	808	51
Second North Ward	530	336	866	39
First North Middle Ward	628	186	814	23
Second North Middle Ward	378	86	464	19
First South Middle Ward	375	108	483	22
Second South Middle Ward	466	135	601	23
First South Ward	433	228	661	35
Second South Ward	473	196	669	29
Totals	**3679**	**1687**	**5366**	**31**
KING'S LYNN				
Chequer Ward	440	151	591	26
Jew's Lane Ward	218	67	285	24
Kettlewell Ward	124	50	174	29
New Conduit Ward	219	84	303	28
North End Ward	210	159	369	43
Paradise Ward	108	148	256	58
Sedgeford Lane Ward	308	191	499	38
Stonegate Ward	267	178	445	40
Trinity Hall Ward	288	81	369	22
South Lynn Ward	180	38	218	17
Totals	**2362**	**1147**	**3509**	**33**

Exempted and paying hearths in the Norfolk boroughs, 1672-1673

Borough and Ward	Hearths paid	Hearths exempted	Total of hearths	Exempted hearths as percentage of total
THETFORD				
Bailey End Ward	301	119	420	28
Bridgegate Ward	283	62	345	18
Totals	**584**	**181**	**765**	**24**

APPENDIX V

Exempted and paying hearths in Norwich, 1671

Parish	Hearths paid	Hearths exempted	Total of hearths	Exempted hearths as percentage of total
All Saints	56	95	151	63
Cathedral Close	367	23	390	6
Earlham	39	3	42	7
Eaton	42	24	66	36
Heigham	134	85	219	39
Hellesdon	43	-	43	-
Lakenham	88	50	138	36
Pockthorpe	77	161	238	68
St Andrew	544	48	592	8
St Augustine	161	115	276	42
St Benedict	67	66	133	50
St Clement	152	49	201	24
St Edmund	92	45	137	33
St Etheldreda	64	31	95	33
St George Colegate	283	100	383	26
St George Tombland	185	30	215	14
St Giles	245	85	330	26
St Gregory	298	100	398	25
St Helen	57	27	84	32
St James	83	[96]	179	54
St John de Sepulchre	106	96	202	48
St John Maddermarket	294	40	334	12
St John Timberhill	154	134	288	47
St Julian	82	104	186	56
St Lawrence	155	108	263	41
St Margaret	101	98	199	49
St Martin at Oak	165	199	364	55
St Martin at Palace	136	122	258	47
St Mary Coslany	149	177	326	54
St Michael at Plea	254	36	290	12
St Michael at Thorn	88	204	292	70
St Michael Coslany	219	144	363	40
St Paul	133	158	291	54

Exempted and paying hearths in Norwich, 1671

Parish	Hearths paid	Hearths exempted	Total of hearths	Exempted hearths as percentage of total
St Peter Hungate	129	12	141	9
St Peter Mancroft	1141	116	1257	9
St Peter Parmentergate	341	263	604	44
St Peter Southgate	29	123	152	81
St Saviour	261	43	304	14
St Simon & St Jude	134	32	166	19
St Stephen	485	194	679	29
St Swithin	80	83	163	51
Trowse	62	50	112	45
Carrow Abbey	33	-	33	-
Precincts of the Bishop	37	-	37	-
Totals	**7845**	**3769**	**11,614**	**33**

APPENDIX VI

Constables' receipts for King's Lynn and Norwich

E 179/338, f.65

[paper wrapper]
Lynn Yarmouth Thetford paupers

E 179/338, f.66

CONSTABLES' RECEIPTS,
KING'S LYNN
(E 179/338,ff.66-67)

South Lynn Ward
18 Mar 1670/1
Received the 18th of March 1670 of Mr Ambrose Monye the sume of three shillings six pence which is for my Assisting of him in the Collection of the Duty of harth Mony in South Lynn Warde in the bounds of Lynn Regis. I say received. 3s : 6d.
Robt Clarke Constable.

New Conduit Ward
19 Mar 1670/1
Received the 19th of March 1670 of Mr Ambrose Monye the sum of five shillings which is for my Assisting of him in the Collection of the Duty of harth Mony in New Cundit Warde in the Bounds of Lynn Regis. I say received.
5s : 00d.
Tho Tue Constable.

Paradise Ward
19 Mar 1670/1
Received the 19th of March 1670 of Mr Ambrose Monye ye sum of two shillings six pence which is for my Assisting of him in the Collection of the Duty of harth mony in Parridice Warde in the Bounds of Lynn Regis. I say received. 2s : 6d.
Francis Faken Constable.

Constables' receipts for King's Lynn and Norwich

Stonegate Ward
18 Mar 1670/1
Received the 18th of March 1670 of Mr Ambrose Monye the sum of six
shillings and three pence which is for my Assisting of him in the Collection of
ye Duty of harth Mony in Stonegate Warde in the bounds of Lynn Regis. I say
received. 6s : 3d.
Wat Sly Constable.

Chequer Ward
18 Mar 1670/1
Received the 18th of March 1670 of Mr Ambrose Mony the sum of Tenn
shillings which is for my Assisting of him in the Collection of the Duty of
harth Mony in Chequer Warde in the Bounds of Lynn Regis. I say received.
10s : 00d. Will Blackborne Constable.

E 179/338, f.67

Sedgeford Lane Ward
3 Apr 1671
Aperill ye 3d 1671. Received of Henry Safford the sum of seven shillings
fower pence for my assisting him in Collecting the duty of hearth money in
Sedgford Lane ward in Lynn Regis. I say received. 7s : 4d.
by Fran Shaus Con.

E 179/338, f.68

[paper wrapper]
Norwich Paupers

CONSTABLES' RECEIPTS, NORWICH
(E 179/338, ff.69-84)

E 179/338, f.69

Eaton: St Stephen Ward
25 Feb 1670/1
February 25th 1670
Eaton Next Norwich
Received then of Henry Halls One shilling for helpeing to Collect the duty of
Hearth Money in Eaton. I say Received. js.
per me Sam Browne his x marke Constable there.

Trowse Millgate: Berstreet Ward
25 Feb 1670/1
February 25th 1670
Trowse Next Norwich
Received of Henry Halls the some of One shilling & fourepence for helpeinge
to Collect the Duty of Hearth Money in Trowse next Norwich. I say Received.
1s : 4d.
per me Tho Smoeton his x marke Constable there.

Hellesdon: Coslany Ward
25 Feb 1670/1
February 25th 1670
Helsden
Received then of Henry Halls Tenn pence for helpeinge to Collect the Duty of
Hearth [money] in Helsden. I say Received. 0s : 10d.
per me John Hudson his x marke Constable.

Heigham: West Wymer Ward
4 Mar 1670/1
March the 4th 1670
Heigham
Received of Hen Halls the some of - for Helpeing to Collect the Duty of
hearth Money in Heigham. We say Received. 03 : 04.
Jer Bell.

E 179/338, f.70

Lakenham: Berstreet Ward
21 Apr 1671
Aprill the 21 1671
Received of Henry Halls the some of twoe shillings two pence for helpeing to
Collect the Duty of Hearth Money in Lakenham. I say Received 00 : 02 : 02.
Jo Dobbs his x marke Constable.
per me Geo Pitcher his x marke Const.

E 179/338, f.71

Berstreet Ward: St John Timberhill, St Michael at Thorn, St John de Sepulchre, All Saints
25 Mar 1671
St Johns of Timber Hill, St Michaell att Thorne, St Johns of Sepulcher, All
Sts parish, in Berestrett Ward.
March 25th 1671
Received of Henry Halls the some of Eight shillings & ten pence for helpeing
to Collect the Duty of Hearth [money] in the parishes abovesaid. We say
Received. 00 : 08 : 10.
per nos Jeremyah Osborne
George Colles

E 179/338, f.72
Cathedral Close
26 Mar 1671
Received then of William Lambert Collector for the precincts of the Cathedrall of the holly and undevided [Trinity] of Christ Church for the duty belonginge to me for my aide and assistance in Collectinge the dutie for fire harths and stoves due to his majestie for one yeeres and a halfe ended at Mich[ael]mas last past the sume of Eight shillings ten pence. I say Received. 00 : 08 : 10.
by me x the marke of Michaell Virgoe Constable.

E 179/338, f.73

Coslany Ward: St Michael Coslany, St Martin at Oak, St Mary Coslany
20 Mar 1670/1
March 20th 1670. Received of John Pierson Collector for harth mony in St Mihills St Martins St Maris of Coslany ward the sume of twelve shillings & ten pence in full, for my duty according to the Act.
I say Received. 12 : 10.
by me x the mark of Steven Cocke Constable.

E 179/338, f.74

East Wymer Ward: St George Tombland, St Helen, St Martin at Palace, St Peter Hungate, St Simon and St Jude
20 Mar 1670/1
20 Marcij 1670. Received then of John Thurgar Collector of the hearth Money in East Wymer ward & the Pallace in the Citie of Norwich the sum of sixtenn shillings and six pence it beinge two pence on the pound allowed me by the Act, as Constable of the said ward for assistinge the said Collector in collectinge the sum of ninetye nine pound Due to the Kings Majestie for three halfe yeares endinge at St Michaell Last past. I say received. 16s : 06d.
Per me Edmund Mason

E 179/338, f.75

Pockthorpe: Fyebridge Ward
[31 Mar 1671]
Received then of John Thurgar Collector of the hearth money in Pockthorpe next Norwich the sum of One shillinge and nine pence it beinge two pence on the pound allowed me by the Act as Constable in the said Hamlett for assistinge the said Collector in Collectinge the sum of Tenn pounds and Tenn shillings, Due att St Michaell last past. I say received. 01s : 09d.
Daniel Cockane

E 179/338, f.76

Fyebridge Ward: St Clement, St Edmund, St James, St Paul, St Saviour
24 Mar 1670/1
24 Marcij 1670
Received then of John Thurgar Collector of the hearth Money in fie bridge
ward in the Citie of Norwich the sum of fowrtenn shillings and eleaven pence
it being two pence on the pound Allowed me by the Act as Constable of the
said ward for assistinge the said Collector in collectinge the sum of fower
score and nine pounds Eleaven shillings in the said ward, Due to the King's
Majestie for three halfe yeares ending at St Michaell last past. I say received.
14s : 11d.
by me Richard Scottow.

E 179/338, f.77

**Middle Wymer Ward: St Andrew, St John Maddermarket, St Michael at
Plea**
9 Jan 1670/1
Received of John Pierson Collector for the hath mony for my sallery for the
Kinges duty the sum of Twenty seaven shillings in full content for The ward
of Middell Wymer. I say Received.
1 : 7 : 0.
per me Fra Weston Cunstable.
January the 9th 1670.

E 179/338, f.78

North Conesford Ward: St Peter Parmentergate
6 Feb 1670/1
vj Feb 1670. Received then of John Thurgar Collector of the Hearth Money in
North Conisforth Ward in the Citie of Norwich the sum of eight shillings and
six pence beinge two pence on the pound allowed me by the Act for assistinge
the said Collector in the Collectinge of fiftie and one pounds in the said Ward
Due to the King's Majestie for three halfe yeares ended att St Michaell Last
past. I say received. 08s : 06d.
per me Edmund Girlinge

E 179/338, f.79

Colegate Ward: St Augustine, St George Colegate
20 Mar 1670/1
March 20 1670. Received of John Pierson Collector for harth mony in St
Georges of Collgate ward the sum of Thirteene shillings in full for my duty
according to the Act. I say Received. 13s : 0.
by me Petter Tomson Constable.

E 179/338, f.80

St Giles Ward: St Giles
8 Mar 1670/1
Norwich. March 8th 1670. Received of Henry Clarke Collector the sum of six shillings for my Assistance in collectinge the Kings duty of Hearth Money for thre halfe yeares due at Michaelmas last past in the ward of St Gyles. I say received. 6s.
by me Obadiah Barlow Constable.

E 179/338, f.81

St Peter Mancroft Ward: St Peter Mancroft
10 Mar 1670/1
Norwich St Peters of Mancroft
March 10th 1670
Received of Henry Clarke Collector the sum of one pound seaven shillings & two pence for my Assistance in collecting the Kings duty of Hearth Money for three halfe [years] due at Michaelmas last past. I say received.
£01 : 07s : 02d.
by me x the marke of Francis Warmell Constable.

E 179/338, f.82

St Stephen Ward: St Stephen
23 Jan 1670/1
Norwich January ye 23th 1670. Received of William Lambert the sume of Eleaven shillings and tenn pence it being for my assistance in Collecting the Kings dutie for fire harths and stoves in the Ward and parish in St Stephens. I say Received. 0 : 11s : 10d.
by me Jno Freeman Constable.

E 179/338, f.83

South Conesford Ward: St Etheldreda, St Julian, St Peter Southgate
14 Mar 1670/1
March 14th 1670. Received of Edward Edmond the sume of thre shillings and teen pen[ce] for my assistance in Colectinge his Magestis hearth mony in South Counsford ward.
3s : 10d.
by Edward Tompson.

E 179/338, f.84

West Wymer Ward: St Benedict, St Gregory, St Lawrence, St Margaret, St Swithin
20 Mar 1670/1
Received March 20 70 of Wm Lambert seaventen shillings six pence and it is in full for my paines & assistance in Collecting the duty of hearth money out of the Ward of West Wymer Norwich. I say received. 17 : 6d.
Tho Ficke his mark.

APPENDIX VII

E 179/337, f.53

Norff[olk] Norw[i]ch	The state of the Accompt of Rich[ar]d Browne Gent. Receiver Gen[e]rall of the hearthmony within the places afores[ai]d. for one year End[ed] St Mich[ael] [16]71 as foll[owe]th.

Charge   Th' Accomptant Chargeth himselfe with   li   s   d
soe much rec[eive]d of th' arreares due at
St Mich[ael]s 1670   22:16: 0

ffor
79203 hearths Norff[olk]   7920: 06: 0
ffor
11614 hearths Norw[i]ch   1161: 08: 0   9081:14: 0   9104:10: 0

Discharg[e]d   Excus[e]d through poverty as by Severall
Certificates Accord[ing] to the Acts of
Parl[ia]m[en]t for the sayd sume Amount
to in all   2472:18: 0

Salary, at 23d per li for 6491:09: 0
rec[eive]d is   622:01:01

P[ai]d into his Maj[es]t[ie]s Exch[eque]r
as by xij tallys Exam[ine]d appeare   5855:12:11

the surplusage upon the last Accompte   13:15:00   8964: 7: 0

                                           Remaynes
                                           thru   140: 3: 0

                                           totum

upon Empty houses [...] as by particulars   140: 3: 0

And soe the Accomptant is Even

xxviij [...] Ex[...] per J Jeffery

	Parish names	Percentage of exempt hearths
1	All Saints	61
2	Cathedral Close	10
3	Earlham	—
4	Eaton	38
5	Heigham	37
6	Hellesdon	22
7	Lakenham	38
8	Pockthorpe	68
9	St Andrew	8
10	St Augustine	39
11	St Benedict	50
12	St Clement	25
13	St Edmund	34
14	St Etheldreda	30
15	St George Colegate	25
16	St George Tombland	14
17	St Giles	26
18	St Gregory	22
19	St Helen	35
20	St James	56
21	St John de Sepulchre	52
22	St John Maddermarket	13
23	St John Timberhill	46
24	St Julian	56
25	St Lawrence	40
26	St Margaret	51
27	St Martin at Oak	55
28	St Martin at Palace	43
29	St Mary Coslany	55
30	St Michael at Plea	13
31	St Michael at Thorn	69
32	St Michael Coslany	44
33	St Paul	54
34	St Peter Hungate	8
35	St Peter Mancroft	9
36	St Peter Parmentergate	45
37	St Peter Southgate	80
38	St Saviour	14
39	St Simon & St Jude	19
40	St Stephen	28
41	St Swithin	48
42	Trowse	50
43	Carrow Abbey	10
44	Norwich Castle precincts	—

1. Norwich: key to parishes, showing percentage of exempt hearths per parish in 1672–1673

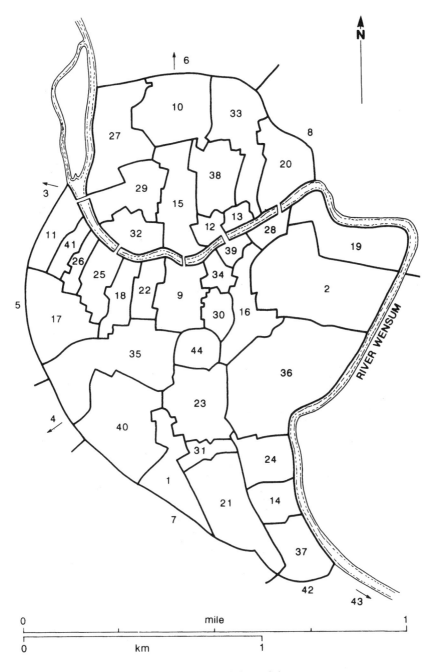

2. Map of Norwich parishes

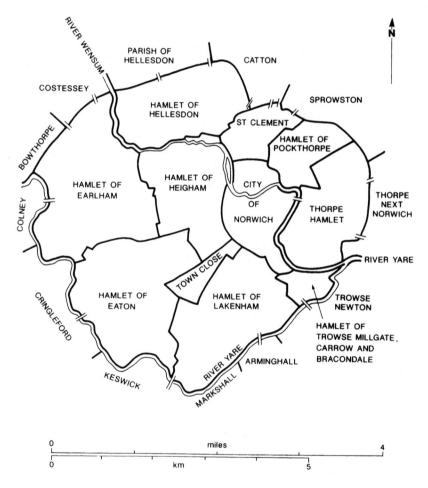

3. Map of hamlets in the County of the City of Norwich

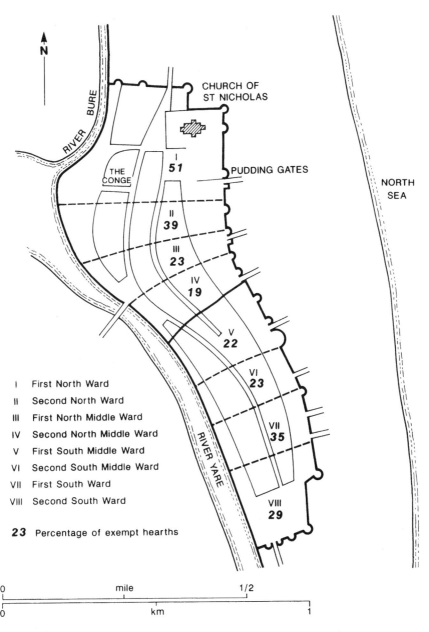

4. Map of Great Yarmouth wards, showing percentage of exempt hearths per ward in 1672–1673

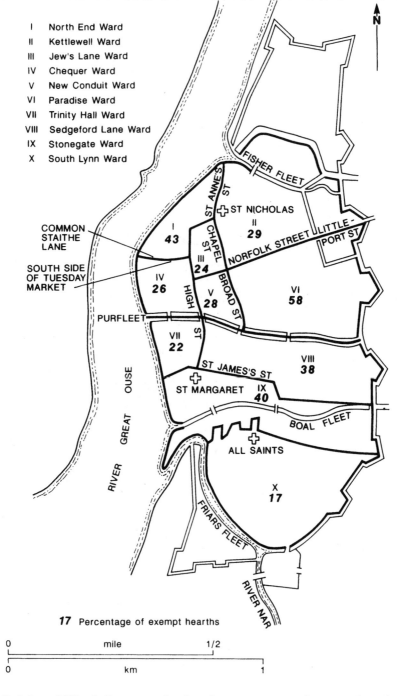

I   North End Ward
II   Kettlewell Ward
III   Jew's Lane Ward
IV   Chequer Ward
V   New Conduit Ward
VI   Paradise Ward
VII   Trinity Hall Ward
VIII   Sedgeford Lane Ward
IX   Stonegate Ward
X   South Lynn Ward

N

FISHER FLEET

ST ANNE'S ST

✠ ST NICHOLAS

COMMON
STAITHE
LANE

I
43

CHAPEL ST

II
29

LITTLE-PORT ST

NORFOLK STREET

III
24

SOUTH SIDE
OF TUESDAY
MARKET

IV
26

HIGH ST

BROAD ST

V
28

VI
58

PURFLEET

VII
22

ST JAMES'S ST

VIII
38

✠
ST MARGARET

IX
40

BOAL FLEET

RIVER GREAT OUSE

✠
ALL SAINTS

X
17

FRIARS FLEET

RIVER NAR

17 Percentage of exempt hearths

0   mile   1/2

0   km   1

5. Map of King's Lynn wards, showing percentage of exempt hearths
per ward in 1672–1673

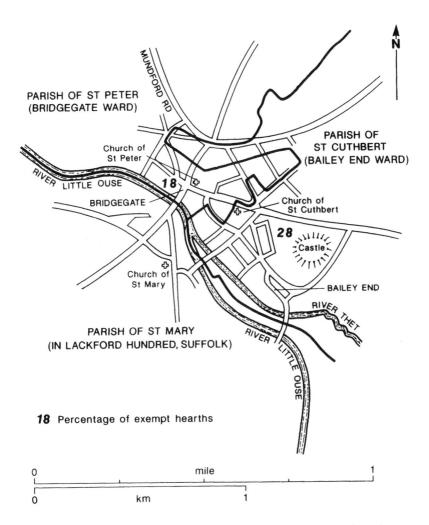

6. Map of Thetford wards, showing percentage of exempt hearths per ward in 1672–1673

7. A note on the maps

The municipal government of the city and three boroughs was altered by the Representation of the People Act of 1832[1] and the Municipal Corporations Act of 1835.[2] The maps in this book reconstruct the parishes and wards as they were in the 1670s, before the changes of the 1830s.

Norwich

"The County of the City of Norwich was separated from the county of Norfolk, by Henry IV, in 1403, and placed under the exclusive jurisdiction of the corporation. It comprises about 6,630 acres of land; being nearly fourteen miles in circumference."[3] The seven hamlets outside the city walls, but within the County of the City, enjoyed all the privileges of the city wards, and were as follows: Earlham, Eaton, Heigham, Hellesdon, Lakenham, Pockthorpe, and Trowse Millgate which included Carrow and Bracondale.

Map 3 shows the boundaries of the hamlets that lay outside the city walls. This map is based on that produced for the Municipal Corporation Boundaries Commission.[4]

Several maps showing the boundaries of Norwich parishes have been published, the earliest very detailed one being that published by the Ordnance Survey in 1884-1885 at a scale of 1:500, from a survey made in 1883. For maps showing the built-up areas in the parishes (but not the parish boundaries) the nearest contemporary ones are those of Thomas Cleer (1696) and James Corbridge (1727). The earliest map to show the built-up areas in detail is that of Anthony Hochstetter (1789).

Great Yarmouth

Map 4 is perhaps the first map ever to show the probable boundaries of the pre-1835 wards. It is based on the map produced for the Municipal Corporation Boundaries Commission.[5] That map does not show the boundaries of the old wards, but of the post-1835 proposed wards. The report

---

[1] 2 & 3 William IV, c.45, popularly known as the Reform Act.
[2] 5 & 6 William IV, c.76, popularly known as the Municipal Reform Act.
[3] William White, *History, Gazetteer, and Directory of Norfolk*, (Sheffield, 1845), p. 50.
[4] *Report of Municipal Corporation Boundaries (England and Wales) Commission*, (House of Commons Parliamentary Papers, 1837, vol. XXVII), p. 364.
[5] ibid, 1837, vol. XXVIII, p. 380.

A note on the maps

and analysis, which the map accompanies, list which old wards, or parts of them, were absorbed into the proposed wards, and that information has formed the basis of the present map.

There are two contemporary maps of Great Yarmouth in the Public Record Office, but they do not show ward boundaries. The earlier of the two is Sir Bernard de Gomme's manuscript map of 1668;[6] the other is Samuel Newton's manuscript map of 1688.[7]

A map of 1730 gives no details of building plans between the rows. Henry Swinden (d 1772) made a large-scale manuscript map in 1753; it was published by Mostyn Armstrong, County Surveyor, in 1779,[8] and was heavily relied on by William Faden for his map of 1797.[9] A map showing the towers and gates of Great Yarmouth's walls is said to exist in an edition of an earlier work,[10] and the fortifications have been included in Map 4 of the present volume.

King's Lynn

Before the present publication, perhaps only one map had ever been published showing the boundaries of the pre-1835 wards, and that is the map produced for the Municipal Corporation Boundaries Commission.[11] It forms the basis of the present map (Map 5), but the addition has been made of the Civil War fortifications, which were still very much in evidence in the 1670s. These fortifications are shown on 'The Groundplat of Kings Lyn' by Henry Bell, dated between c1680 and 1692.[12] They are also shown on William Rastrick's map of 1725.[13]

---

[6] PRO MR 1/487.
[7] PRO MR 1/488.
[8] Reproduced in A.A.C. Hedges, *Yarmouth is an antient Town*, (Norwich, 1959), pp. 38-39.
[9] Reproduced in *Faden's Map of Norfolk*, Norfolk Record Society, XLII, (1973).
[10] H. Manship, *A booke of the foundacion and antiquitye of the towne of Greate Yermouthe*, ed. C.J. Palmer (1847); the map is reproduced in A.A.C. Hedges, *Yarmouth is an antient Town*, (Norwich, 1959), p. 30.
[11] *Report of Municipal Corporation Boundaries (England and Wales) Commission*, (House of Commons Parliamentary Papers, 1837, vol.XXVII), p. 122.
[12] Reproduced in Suṣan Yaxley (ed), *The Siege of King's Lynn 1643*, (Dereham, 1993), pp. 6-7, and in Vanessa Parker, *The Making of Kings Lynn*, (1971), between pp. 2 & 3.
[13] Reproduced in Paul Richards, *King's Lynn*, (Chichester, 1990), p. 14, and in Vanessa Parker, *The Making of Kings Lynn*, (1971), between pp. 2 & 3.

A note on the maps

Thetford

Map 6 is based on that produced for the Municipal Corporation Boundaries Commission.[14] The area of St Peter's parish is too large to be shown on the present map, which is confined to the built-up area of Thetford. Other maps of Thetford were produced by Thomas Martin (1779) and George Bird Burrell (1807). The parish boundaries on the present map follow those of the Commission's map.

---

[14] *Report of Municipal Corporation Boundaries (England and Wales) Commission*, (House of Commons Parliamentary Papers, 1837, vol. XXVIII), p. 272.

EDITORIAL METHOD

Each hearth tax certificate has been given its full Public Record Office reference and folio number. The name of the parish or ward has been given its standard modernised spelling, and the date has been given as day, month and year, the year being double-dated in Old Style and New Style where the date is between 1 January and 24 March. (Under the Julian calendar then applying, the year began on 25 March, until 1752 when the Gregorian calendar was adopted, under which the year began on the preceding 1 January.)

Only the names of the exempted persons shown on each certificate have been listed. The preamble has been left out, as have the names of the minister, churchwardens, overseers and Justices of the Peace, and any notes written on the front or back of the certificate.

Of the names of exempted persons, forenames are usually abbreviated on the certificates. These have been extended and given standard modernised spelling in the transcription. Surnames are given in the exact spelling that appears in the original.

Where the number of hearths is given against a name in the original, this has been given in the transcription.

The total number of the names of the exempt is given at the end of each transcription of a certificate. The names have been carefully counted, and the total may differ from that given in the original.

NORFOLK HEARTH TAX EXEMPTION CERTIFICATES 1670-1674 NORWICH; GREAT YARMOUTH KING'S LYNN; THETFORD

Norwich

E 179/338, f.1

All Saints

[undated ?early 1671]

Stephen Danyell
widow Garwood
Amy Dix
James Stilyard
George Robertson
Edmund Dawbnye
widow Augustine
Francis Knights
Mary Sparkes
Elizabeth Mason
William Loveday
Jonathan Foster
William Holloway
Edward Pecall
Richard Tirrell
Simon Pecall
William Seaborne
Thomas Bowman
Catherine Ralph
Richard Wallis

widow Wright
Stephen Handy
Thomas Harold
Edmund Wilkins
Matthew Midleton
John Hanser
Elizabeth Hansell
William Levies
Thomas Watton, jun.
widow Mills
widow Person
Robert Strowger
Arthur Durrant
John Turner
Matthew Barnes
John Sames
Susan Downes
Philip Cooper
Henry Grime
Ann Joones

All Saints [continued]

John Money
Catherine Tuffyn
Thomas Adderton
widow Busby
Thomas Forcey
Robert Loveday
Anthony Chetleburgh
William Wodstocke
William Duffild
John Pike
Thomas Woodrow
widow Mercer
Michael Gilbert
Thomas Boole
Thomas Watton, sen.
Francis Basonwhite
Edward Varnish
William Hunte
John Diditt
William Nurse
Matthew Mote
Daniel Strowger
William Elmor
Robert Harte
Peter Nurse
John Dobson

[66 Names]

E 179/337, f.1

All Saints

25 Mar 1672

widow Mason	1
widow Tuffin	1
widow Messer	1
Ann Jones	1
widow Rolfe	1
widow Dix	1
Michael Gilbert	2
widow Mills	1
Lydia Ames	1

All Saints [continued]

John Money	2
widow Busby	2
widow Allin	1
William Tuffill	1
Andrew Custin	1
Matthew Middilton	2
Peter Nurs	2
Edmund Carr	2
William Luis	2
William Word	1
John Buddell	1
Matthew Barnes	2
John Turnner	2
Henry Gun	1
John Sames	1
Philip Cooper	1
Elizabeth Coell	1
Thomas Freese	1
Thomas Alderton	1
Robert Loufday	2
Thomas Wodderow	2
John Pick	1
William Hunt	2
Thomas Watton	2
William Woodstock	1
Francis Bassinwhit	2
Thomas Watton	2
William Mayes	2
Philip Ro...	
Robert Day	
William Nurs	1
Matthew Mott	1
Robert Strolger	2
Jeremy Scottow	2
Thomas Harrison	1
John Gillman	1
Stephen Hanba	1
Henry Wright	2
Richard Turrell	2
John Clabbon	1
Phineas Brown	2
Thomas Bowman	1
Simon Peacoll	2
Edmund Peacoll	1

2

All Saints [continued]

William Loufday	1
Jonathan Foster	2
William Sabborn	2
Richard Willis	1
Edmund Dabney	2
Sarah Asson	1
Francis Knights	1
George Robison	2
James Tilyeard	1
Abigail Garrowd	2
John Cobbinge	2
William Loveday	1
John Murunt	1
Thomas Cobb	

[67 Names]

E 179/336, f.1

All Saints

10 Feb 1672/3

George Roberson
Ann Dixe
James Stelyard
Thomas Spurgin
widow Garrod
Edward Dabny
James Sabborne
Francis Knights
William Sabborne
Jonathan Foster
William Leadey
Thomas Bowman
James Townsing
John Minns
widow Rolfe
John Clabborne
Richard Turrell
Thomas Harrod
Stephen Handes
widow Wright
The Parish House

All Saints [continued]

Jeremy Skottow
Matthew M[?ote]
William Mays
William Leavis
Gilbert Tufen
Thomas Watton, sen.
William Hunte
Robert Strolger
widow Mason
widow Messer
Ellis Brooke
Thomas Forsee
John Picke
Thomas Wodrow
Michael Gilbarte
Robert Burrell
Catherine Barns
William Doffell
Henry Barton
Francis Bassingwhite
William Bearte
Andrew Custill
Joseph Giles
Matthew Middleton
Adam Care
Cornelius Palle
Thomas Watton, jun.
William Warde
John Mancer
John Pearse
Thomas Alderton
Matthew Barnes
John Turner
John Seames
Elizabeth Hall
Philip Cuper
Ann Jones
William Hude
John Money
Catherine Tufen
Phineas Browne
widow Busby
Robert Leavdey
Peter Nurse

3

All Saints [continued]

John Budwell
Christopher Cooke
John Warde
William Wodstocke
Thomas Cobb

[69 Names]

E 179/336, f.2

All Saints

14 Nov 1673

George Robbesonn	1
widow Dix	1
James Tilliard	2
widow Garrett	2
widow Cady	
Edward Dabney	1
John Foster	1
Thomas Bouth	1
William Loveday	2
goodman Foster	1
James Sabborn	2
James Tousand	1
John Mines	1
widow Rofe	2
John Sabborn	1
John Ward	1
Thomas Cobbes	2
widow Jerfers	1
Richard Wallis	1
Richard Turrell	2
Stephen Handey	1
Robert Loveday	1
goodman Browne	1
widow Busbay	1
widow Tuffen	1
Thomas Alderson	2
John Money	2
Ann Jones	1
widow Hall	1
John Burrell	2

All Saints [continued]

goodman Copper	1
John Sames	1
goodman Barns	2
John Turnner	2
John Buddell	2
Peter Nurse	1
John Manser	1
John Parson	2
Thomas Watton	1
William Elmer	2
goodman Car	1
goodman Medelton	1
goodman Ivet	1
John Dudles	1
William True	1
John True	2
William Bart	2
William Duffell	1
goodman Strolger	1
widow Mason	2
goodman Gilbard	1
widow Barns	1
goodman Aldred	2
widow Maser	1
goodwife Brooke	2
Francis Basinwhite	1
Gilbert Tuffen	2
William Hunt	2
Thomas Watton, sen.	1
William Leves	1
goodman Hansell	2
goodman Mote	2
goodman Scotto	1
Frances Bacon	1
goodman Dedett	1
goodman Allen	2

[66 Names]

E 179/338, f.2

Cathedral Close

2 Mar 1670/1

Ellen Bradburye
goodman Shilldrake
widow Sarsnett
widow Bishopp
Thomas Shilldrake
Christopher Pallding
Elizabeth Dickinson
widow King
Anthony Siggitt
Anthony Sydell
Thomas Boswell
widow Gray
widow King
widow Robins
widow Life
goodman Holmes
widow Cooke
John Rutland
Edward Riches
Ann Jacob

[20 Names]

E 179/336, f.3

Cathedral Close

12 Feb 1671/2

Mrs Sheldrake
widow Sarsnett
Anthony Sidwell
Christopher Spalding
Elizabeth Dunnn
widow Kinge
Anthony Sigett
Thomas Boswell
widow Grey
widow Robkins

Cathedral Close [continued]

widow Life
John Paine
goodman Medcalfe
widow Cooke
John Rudland
Edward Riches
Rebecca Smith
Charles Brooke
Edmund Brent

[19 Names]

E 179/336, f.4

Cathedral Close

3 Sep 1672

widow Sheldrake
widow Sanson
Anthony Sidell
Christopher Paulden
Elizabeth Dickinson
widow King
Anthony Sedgwick
Thomas Bozwell
widow Gray
widow Robkins
widow Life
John Paine
g[ood...] Medcalfe
widow Cooke
John Rudland
Edward Riches
Rebecca Smith
Charles Brooke
Edmund Brant
Thomas Brant
Robert Taylor
Thomas Nunn
Bridget Bloy
James Welch
widow Bradbury
g[ood...] Woolly

Cathedral Close [continued]

Robert March
widow Wright
Robert More
g[ood...] Hovell

[30 Names]

E 179/336, f.5

Cathedral Close

4 Dec 1673

widow Shildrake	1
widow Tracey	2
widow Sanson	1
Anthony Sydall	2
Christopher Palland	1
widow King	2
Anthony Sedgwick	2
Thomas Boswell	2
widow Gray	1
widow Life	2
John Payne	1
Christopher Fox	1
Mrs Cook, widow	2
John Rudland	2
Edward Richards	1
widow Brant	1
Thomas Brant	2
Robert Tayler	1
Thomas Nunn	1
Bridget Bloy	1
Ellen Bradberry	1
Robert March	1
Robert More	2
Edward Hovell	1
widow Wright	1
goodwife Balderston	2
Nicholas Harman	2
goodman Bristowe	1
Charles Brooke	1

[29 Names]

E 179/338, f.3

Earlham

19 Feb 1670/1

Nicholas Wittham
William Howard
Humphrey Leeke

[3 Names]

E 179/338, f.4

Eaton

24 Feb 1670/1

John Youngs
John Fox
widow Saberton
Thomas Welloms
John Carr
Matthew Reany
John Browne
Edward Churchman
widow White
widow Chamberlin
Stephen Norton
Samuel Bancks
Henry Roberson
widow Penmman
William Syzer
Edward Fuller
Francis Smyth
Catherine Burrell
Richard Coale

[19 Names]

E 179/337, f.2

Eaton

[undated ? early 1672]

John Youngs	1
John Fox	1
widow Saberton	2
Henry Robinson	2
Thomas Budd	1
Edward Chambers	1
Samuel Banks	1
widow Chambers	1
widow Peddement	2
Edward Fuller	1
William Siser	1
Henry Fer	1
John Car	1
Francis Smith	1
Catherine Burrow	1
Matthew Reaney	1
Edward Churchman	1
John Brown	1
John Sowell	2
Emma Welham	1
Elizabeth Wellham	1

[21 Names]

E 179/336, f.6

Eaton

27 Aug 1672

John Youngs
John Fox
Henry Robeson
Thomas Budd
Edmund Chambelin
Samuel Bankes
widow Chambelin
widow Pennement
Edward Fuller

Eaton [continued]

William Syser
Henry Ferre
John Carre
Francis Smith
Catherine Borow
Matthew Reaney
Edward Churchman
John Browne
John Sowell
Emma Wellham
Frank ...
widow Sabeton
Elizabeth Wellham

[22 Names]

E 179/336, f.7

Eaton

15 Nov 1673

Francis Smith	1
Catherine Birill	1
Elizabeth Wellum	1
Elizabeth Chamberlin	1
John Car	2
Henry Fare	1
Edward Fuller	1
Samuel Bankes	2
John Pesk	1
Henry Roberso[n]	1
Thomas Bud	2
Edmund Chambers	1
John Youngs	2
Margaret Saberton	1
John Fox	2
Mary Reney	1
Edward Churchman	1
John Browne	2
Jude Penneman	1

[19 Names]

7

E 179/338, f.5

Heigham

17 Feb 1670/1

widow Beales
William B...abourt
Thomas Wats
Michael Wetherley
Edmund True
widow Elwin
widow Harison
Thomas Peachman
[?Bartholomew] Butefant
John Giberne
Robert Havors
John Skiner
widow Haridence
widow Norton
John Elwin
Thomas Burnet
widow Fuller
Nicholas Becket
John Burnet
Robert Shering
Michael Butter
John Drayton
Ralph Raynforth
William Gedney
widow Adams
Lawrence Bird
Thomas Noobs
Thomas Pecke
Samuel Gaze
Abraham Stringer
widow Avis
widow Semon
William Winter
William Waller
Philip Smyth
William Calley
John Jervis
Richard White
John Cotton
John Rackham

Heigham [continued]

widow Smyth
Nicholas Lawes
George Godward
Mary Melton
William Taller
William Firman
Nicholas Brokbanke
John Edwards
William Tompson
Eliza Millison
John Barker

[51 Names]

E 179/337, f.3

Heigham

12 Mar 1671/2

widow Beales	2
Michael Witherley	2
Edmund True	1
John Burman	1
widow Payne	1
widow Passifield	1
Richard Richardson	2
widow Melton	1
Robert Pepse	1
widow Norton	2
Grace Harridence	2
Robert Havers	2
John Elwin	1
William Taler	1
John Skinner	1
widow Caverley	1
Bartholomew Buttefant	1
John Gibberne	1
Henry Dewying	2
widow Roole	1
Thomas Burnett	2
Edmund Makings	1
widow Fuller	1
widow Adams	2

Heigham [continued]

widow Harrison	1
Nicholas Becket	2
John Burnett	2
Michael Butter	1
Ralph Rainsforth	1
Simon Rilay	1
Robert Smith	2
Robert Potter	
& his wife	2
William Gedney	2
Thomas Peck	2
Thomas Nobbs	1
Lawrence Bird	1
Samuel Gaze	1
William Sallet	1
widow Avis	1
Richard Browne	2
Abraham Stringall	2
widow Seaman	1
William Winter	2
William Waller	2
Gregory Cooke	2
John Barker	1
William Caley	1
Richard White	2
John Cotton	1
John Rackham	1
widow Smith	1
Nicholas Lawes	1
George Godward	2
Philip Smith	
William Firman	2
Nicholas Brookbank	2
William Tompson	2
John Edwards	1
widow Webster	1
Matthew Beavise	2

[60 Names]

E 179/336, f.8

Heigham

13 Sep 1672

Michael Weetherley
Edmund True
John Burman
widow Paine
widow Passifeild
Richard Richardson
widow Melton
Robert Pearse
widow Norton
Grace Haeredence
Robert Havers
John Elvin
William Taler
John Skiner
widow Caverley
Bartholomew Butefant
John Gibbrene
Henry Dowene
widow Roole
Thomas Burnet
Edmund Makings
widow Fuller
widow Adames
widow Harroson
Nicholas Becet
John Burnet
Michael Butter
Ralph Raineforth
Simon Rilay
Robert Poter's wife
William Gidney
Thomas Pecke
Thomas Nobbs
Lawrence Bird
Samuel Gaes
William Sallett
widow Avis
Richard Browen
Abraham Stringall
widow Seamon

Heigham [continued]

William Winter
William Waller
John Berker
Gregory Cocke
William Caley
Richard White
John Cotten
John Rackem
widow Smyth
Nicholas Lawes
George Godward
Philip Smyth
William Firman
Nicholas Brookbank
John Edwards
widow Webster
Matthew Beavise
Frances Boulock

[58 Names]

E 179/336, f.9

Heigham

24 Jan 1673/4

widow Jarwood	1
Daniel Disserment	1
Michael Witherley	1
Edmund True	2
John Burman	2
Elizabeth Paine	1
widow Passifeild	1
Richard Richardson	1
widow Melton	2
... Jarrum	1
Robert Clarke	1
widow Norton	1
Robert Havers	1
John Elwin	2
William Taylor	2
John Skinner	1
widow Caverley	1

Heigham [continued]

Bartholomew Buttifant	2
John Gibborne	1
Michael Downing	1
widow Roll	2
Richard Markes	1
John Hodges	1
Thomas Burnet	1
Edmund Makins	2
widow Fuller	1
widow Addams	2
widow Harrison	1
widow Beckett	1
John Burnett	1
Michael Butter	2
Ralph Ranfforth	1
Simon Royoly	1
John Elwin	1
John Davis	1
William Gedney	1
John Porter	2
Thomas Nobbs	1
Richard White	2
Samuel Gaze	1
William Sallett	1
Robert Potter	1
widow Avis	1
Richard Browne	2
Abraham Stringhall	1
widow Semons	1
William Winter	1
William Waller	1
John Barber	1
William Caley	1
Richard Bird	2
John Cotton	1
John Rackham	2
widow Smith	2
Nicholas Lawes	2
George Goddard	1
Philip Smith	1
William Firman	2
Nicholas Brookebanke	2
John Edwards	1
widow Webster	1

Heigham [continued]

Matthew Beavis	2
Francis Bullocke	1

[63 Names]

E 179/338, f.6

Hellesdon

[undated ?early 1671]

John Clarke
Richard Coopsey
Geoffrey Money
widow Goodson
John Lann
Thomas Fabbes
Thomas Doyle
Robert Oly

[8 Names]

E 179/336, f.10

Hellesdon

27 Aug 1672

John Clarke	1
Thomas Fabes	1
Geoffrey Money	1
John Lane	1
Thomas Doyle	1
Richard Copsy	1
John Godson	
Samuel Archer	
Robert Oly	

[9 Names]

E 179/338, f.7

Lakenham

7 Feb 1670/1

Henry West
John Calf
Thomas Marcoll
James Tilny
John Fitt
Robert Scott
James Dix
Benjamin Skoyles
widow Rooke
John Cotton
Roger Lemmon
Francis Cotton
widow Masterson
Edward Calfe
widow Flayle
Christopher Townsend
Thomas Gouldsmith
John Calfe
widow Wade
John Warrin
John Stanton
John Thurston
Thomas Alboro
William Summers
George Fuller
widow Skivington
Martin Brian
William Tomson
widow Stacy
Henry Ward
William Gardiner
Henry West

[32 Names]

E 179/337, f.4

Lakenham

21 Mar 1671/2

John Warrent	1
Roger Lemmon	2
Robert Scott	1
widow Skiverton	1
widow Wade	2
widow Roocke	2
Thomas Gowldsmith	1
Henry Warde	2
James Dix	1
John Fitt	1
John Cane	2
Henry Waste	1
Martin Brier	2
widow Stacy	1
widow Flayle	1
Christopher Townson	1
Edward Calfe	2
widow Masterson	2
William Sommers	2
John Stanton	1
John Thurston	1
Thomas Alborow	2
Thomas Marskoll	2
George Fuller	1
Francis Cotton	2
Robert James	2
John Cotton	1
William Rose	2
Benjamin Skylles	2
James Tillney	1
William Tompson	2
William Smeth	2
John Hunt	2

[33 Names]

E 179/336, f.11

Lakenham

27 Aug 1672

Francis Cotten
George Fuller
Robert James
Thomas Marcole
Thomas Alboro
John Thirsten
John Stanstone
William Sumers
widow Mastersin
widow Flayle
Christopher Townesend
Edward Calfe
widow Towers
Martin Brier
Benjamin Skeyles
John Calfe
Henry West
Henry Ward's house
James Dix house
John Fittes
Roger Lamon
James London
John Warrante
John Cotten
widow Wade
widow Rucke house
Thomas Goldsmith
James Tillne
Robert Scott
John Duglis
widow Stacy
William Smith house

[32 Names]

12

E 179/336, f.12

Lakenham

29 Dec 1673

John Cotton	2
Benjamin Skiles	2
James London	2
John Warrant	1
widow Calfe	1
widow Riss	2
Roger Lemand	2
John Parkin	1
widow Fytt	1
Henry West	2
John Calfe	1
widow Flayle	2
Christopher Townsend	2
Richard Summers	1
William Summers	2
John Stanton	1
John Thurston	2
Thomas Olburgh	2
Thomas Marcoll	1
Robert James	1
Francis Cotton	2
James Tillney	1
Arthur Sherman	2
widow Stacye	1
Robert Scott	2
John Daglass	2
widow Stacey	1
William Smyth	2
widow Towers	1
Henry Ward	2
widow Wade	2

[31 Names]

E 179/338, f.8

Pockthorpe

24 Mar 1670/1

John Lane
Henry Brady
widow Heard
Robert Drewry
John Waker
Adam Clarke
Peter Thurketle
John Marchell
William Wilsey
Robert Read
Francis Lessey
Edward Fuller
Henry Allin
John Weeds
widow Cortney
Robert Blackamore
Thomas Medle
widow Hodson
widow Wantlope
Edward Smyth
Robert Fox
James Nockalls
Robert Arneld
Samuel Hewit
widow Broufe
William Pecke
widow Scoale
Thomas Heard
John Sconce
Robert Baker
Thomas Manfield
Henry Baxter
widow Lodes
James Wateringe
widow Willis
William Wright
William Lane
Wolstan Haraway
widow Wantlope
Thomas Baxter

Pockthorpe [continued]

widow Cordy
widow Aible
Henry Cooke
Francis Wild
Francis Stanford
Robert Doubleday
Henry Shepheard
Michael Kempe
Edmund Bland
Clement Barnard
John Hadman
Robert Gray
George Hunt
Thomas Love
Thomas Bell
Robert Beverly
widow Skillyn
Thomas Hadden
Nicholas Greewoods
widow Wix
John Lightfoot
William Hubbard
John Smyth
John Goodwyn
widow Harper
widow Eason
George Levock
widow Larwood
Francis Wantlope
Anthony Coale
Francis Bull
John Goblett
John Clarke
George Hakney
widow Pratt
Philip Lodes
Christopher Pleasants
John Saddler
widow Smyth
Edward Harper
James Dey
widow Hansell
James Steward
Nathaniel Drinkall

Pockthorpe [continued]

John Boardly
John Hewit
Anthony Chapman
Richard Howse
Richard Nobbs
Sarah Watts
widow Barrett
widow Durdin
John Scottowe
Robert More
John Smith
Stephen Sower
Joseph Bussell
John Leane
Edward Flacknam
George Ireland
William Barber
George Wilson
Roger Godfry
Francis Kempe
Christopher Andrewes
Edmund Smyth
widow Shepheard
Francis Shepheard
Thomas Edwards
Henry Day
Francis Drewry
John Wormell
widow Saull
widow Sammon
John Love
William Palmer
Thomas Page
widow Hane
John Hill
widow Hewitt
Susan Wattson
Thomas Lodes
widow Pratt
George Cannells
John Small
Thomas Mason
widow Newarke
Humphrey Duffield

Pockthorpe [continued]

Peter Gargill
Clement Wild
Robert Field
Nathaniel Goulder
Roger Elvin
Thomas List
widow Lame
Joseph Woodworke
Edmund Shinkinge

[137 Names]

E 179/336, f.13

Pockthorpe

.. May 1672

John Lane
Henry Bradie
widow Read
Robert Dreury
John Walker
Adam Clark
Peter Thirkell
John Marshall
William Willsey
Robert Read
Francis Leasey
Edward Fuller
Henry Allen
John Weeds
widow Courtney
Robert Blackamore
Thomas Midle
widow Hodson
widow Wantlope
Edward Smith
Robert Fox
James Nockolds
Robert Arnold
Samuel Hewitt
widow Hodson
widow Bruffe

Pockthorpe [continued]

widow Peck
widow Scole
Thomas Heard
John Sconce
Robert Barbor
widow Gunner
Thomas Manfeild
Henry Baxter
widow Loads
Jane Watteringe
widow Willise
William Write
widow Lane
Wolstan Harroway
widow Wantlope
Thomas Baxter
widow Cordie
widow Able
Henry Coock
Francis Whild
Francis Stamford
Robert Dubbelday
Henry Sheppard
Michael Kempe
Edmund Irland
Clement Barnard
John Hadman
Robert Bray
George Hunnt
Thomas Love
Thomas Bell
Robert Beverley
widow Skillinge
Edmund Pullham
Thomas Haden
Isaac Grinwood
widow Wikes
John Litefoot
William Limbart
John Smith
John Goodwyn
widow Harper
widow Eason
George Leavick

Pockthorpe [continued]

widow Larwood
Francis Wantlope
Anthony Cole
Francis Bull
John Cobbett
John Clarke
George Hackney
widow Pratt
Philip Loads
Christopher Plesance
John Saddler
widow Smith
Edward Harper
George Hackney
James Dey
widow Hansell
James Steward
Nathaniel Drinckale
John Bordly
John Hewett
Anthony Chapman
Richard Howes
Richard Nobbs
Sarah Watts
widow Barrett
widow Durden
John Scottow
Robert More
John Smith
Stephen Sewell
Joseph Bussey
John Lane, jun.
Edward Flakman
George Irland
William Barbor
George Willson
Roger Godffery
Francis Kemp
Christopher Andrews
widow Sheppard
Edward Smith
Francis Sheppard
Thomas Edwards
Henry Day

Pockthorpe [continued]

Francis Druery
John Wormell
widow Salle
widow Samon
John Lowe
widow Palmer
widow Hawne
Thomas Page
John Hill
widow Hewett
Susan Wattson
Thomas Loads
widow Pratt
George Connalds
John Small
Thomas Massen
widow Newworke
Humphrey Duffeld
Peter Gargile
Clement Wild
Robert Feild
Nathaniel Golder
Roger Elven
Thomas List
widow Lamb
Joseph Woodward
Edmund Shinckin

[141 Names]

E 179/336, f.14

Pockthorpe

19 Aug 1672

Francis Bull
John Smith
John Gobbet
John Clarke
George Hackna
widow Hansell
William Allen
Jean Ags

Pockthorpe [continued]

Christopher Pleasants
John Sadler
widow Smith
John Rolph
Edward Facknam
John Harper
Roger Godfrey
widow Hodson
Francis Kemp
John Lightfoot
widow Newworke
Matthew Drinckale
John Hewett
John Boordly
James Dey
widow Rosear
widow Chapman
widow Basset
Joseph Isaacke
Humphrey Duffeill
Richard Hows
George Hunt
Peter Gargett
Thomas Banyard
Sarah Watts
William Hubbard
Lawrence Scotto
James Steward
Samuel More
William Coulsy
Thomas Betts
Joseph Bussell
Richard Barber
George Ireland
William Barber
Richard Nobs
widow Scampling
William Palmer
William Heine
George Cunnills
John Walker
widow Saul
Thomas Medler
John Warmenger

Pockthorpe [continued]

Thomas Loads
Henry Day
Nicholas Parker
Francis Sheppard
widow Sheppard
Henry Walker
Francis Tisom
Thomas Page
Thomas Paine
Robert Blackamore
widow Druery
Thomas Roberts
Robert Read
James Nockolls
Thomas Campling
Anthony Coale
widow Pratt
Robert Beverly
widow Bruff
Thomas Baxter
Clement Wild
Robert Feild
Roger Ellvin
Nathaniel Goulder
Thomas Leacy
widow Lamb
Nicholas Greenwoods
Robert Spinsbee
widow Wantlope
John Marshall
Peter Thirtill
James Knights
Robert Druery
Thomas Heard
William Johnsons
Hugh Hodson
widow Tucke
John Skons
Robert Baker
widow Hadden
Clement Barnard
John Weeds
John Hadman
Thomas Manfeild

Pockthorpe [continued]

Thomas Edwards
Edward Fuller
Henry Allen
Robert Gray
Robert Arnoll
widow Hodson
Susan Watson
Thomas Heins
widow Sammon
widow Scole
goody Clarke
Thomas Hewett
widow Watering
Francis Stamford
Henry Baxter
widow Coartney
widow Loads
widow Willows
Henry Cooke
Bartholomew Plumstead
widow Cordy
Philip Loads
Francis Wild
widow Able
Robert Dubbledy
Henry Shepard
Thomas Love
Wolstan Harrowing
Stephen Sower
widow Wantlope, jun.
William Wright
Michael Kent
John Love
Thomas Neavill
Adam Pey
widow Barrett
Robert Smith
widow Harper
Thomas Mason
Robert Bull
Robert Bell
William Wilsy
John Smith
Peter Hagon

Pockthorpe [continued]

Thomas Sparrow
Thomas Samnon
John Goodwins
widow Harper
widow Eason
Francis Wantlope
George Leavicke

[147 Names]

E 179/336, f.15

Pockthorpe

11 Apr 1674

John Brooke	1
John Flagg	1
John Marshall	1
Robert Drury	1
Robert Parke	2
Robert Robeson	1
Thomas Heard	2
John Sconse	2
John Weeds	1
Robert Baker	1
Clement Barnard	1
John Hadman	2
Thomas Manfield	1
Hugh Hodson	1
widow Tucke	1
Henry Allni	2
John Wallker	1
Susan Wattson	2
Robert Arnold, sen.	1
Robert Arnold, jun.	1
Thomas Haines	1
Robert Gray	1
Edward Fuller	1
Thomas Edwards	1
Sarah Scoles	1
Adam Clarke	2
Margaret Hewett	1
Francis Stamford	1

Pockthorpe [continued]

widow Watterens	1
widow Playford	1
Henry Baxter	2
widow Willowes	1
James Nockolls	1
Edmund Crotch	1
Ann Cordy	1
Henry Cooke	1
widow Abell	1
Robert Dubleday	1
Daniel Rust	1
Thomas Banyard	1
William Wright	1
Wolstan Harwin	1
Stephen Sower	1
Edward Presslinge	1
John Scott	1
Adam Pie	2
John Hakeney	1
John Lane	1
Michael Gant	1
William Gobbett	1
Robert Bull	2
widow Harper	1
widow Easton	1
John Carr	1
John Smith	1
William Fell	1
John Sparrow	1
Robert Noobes	2
John Goodings	1
widow Harper	1
Roger Godfry	1
Joseph Isaacs	1
John Hewett	1
Robert Clarke	2
William Gargilt	1
Francis Wantlupp	1
Thomas Bolt	1
John Smith	1
Peter Hakeney	1
William Willsey	1
widow Bull	1
William Allni	1

Pockthorpe [continued]

widow Clarke	2
Thomas Mason	1
widow Hansell	1
widow Lightfoote	1
Edward Fakenham	1
widow Smith	2
John Sadler	1
John Mallett	1
John Crompton	1
Thomas Sammon	1
William Hubbard	1
widow Hodson	1
Francis Kempe	2
widow Chapman	2
James Dye	1
widow Roseare	1
John Bordly	1
Nathaniel Drinkale	2
Joseph Bland	1
Paul Hott	1
John Lightfoote	1
widow Burr	1
widow Bassett	1
Richard Howse	2
Humphrey Duffeld	1
Peter Gargitt	1
George Hunt	1
James Knights	1
Lawrence Scottow	1
James Steward	1
widow Barrett	1
Isaac Large	2
Samuel More	1
John Rant	1
John Coppin	2
William Coulsell	1
widow Crotch	1
Joseph Bassell	1
Richard Barber	1
William Barber	1
George Ireland	1
Richard Nobbs	2
William Palmer	1
widow Hanne	1

Pockthorpe [continued]   E 179/338, f.9

George Cannolds	2	**St Andrew**
Edward Wakefield	1	
widow Shephard	1	8 Mar 1670/1
Henry Day	1	
Philip Loades	1	John Longe
Thomas Love	2	Ann Hoddy
John Warmoll	1	Elizabeth Mendham
Thomas Medler	1	Mary Smith
Francis Tissum	1	John Saffery
Thomas Baudricke	1	John W[ri]ghtt
Thomas Page	1	Peter Dringe
Thomas Paine	2	Rose Blackewell
John Hodson	1	Ann Frost
John Small	1	Jeremiah Tookle
Edward Smith	1	widow Bloy
Thomas Roberts	2	Nathaniel Barlow
Robert Read	1	widow Poole
Richard Robeson	1	widow Corye
Robert Blackmore	1	Martha Tottnell
Robert Fox	1	Martin Sharpe
Thomas Camplin	2	Edmund Pidgeon
Clement Morley	2	Henry Daynes
Thomas Locke	1	Thomas Larrood
Robert Beverly	1	William Harris
Robert Field	1	Susan London
Clement Wild	1	Thomas Skinner
Thomas Baxter	2	Judah Ramm
Robert Wakefield	1	widow Cuttinge
Roger Ellwin	1	William Pallden
Nathaniel Gollder	1	Edmund Frind
Nicholas Greenwood	1	Peter Eyers
Christopher Crotch	1	Mary Newton
Christopher Andrews	2	Augustine Woods
widow Brasse	1	Edmund Downes
widow Wantlupp	1	goodman Willison
Robert Spinsby	1	Simon Fenn
		Richard Passiver
[152 Names]		Andrew Aggs

[34 Names]

E 179/336, f.16

St Andrew

9 May [?1672]

John Long
Ann Hoddy
Elizabeth M[?en]dham
John Scarles
Mary Smith
John Wright
Peter Dringe
Rose Blackewell
Ann Frost
Jeremy Tokeley
widow Bloy
Nathaniel Barlow
widow Poole
widow Cory
Matthew Tottnett
Martin Sharpin
John Brandin
Thomas Rust
Thomas Haward
William Harris
Susan Lundon
Thomas Skinner
John Critwood
widow Ram
widow Cutting
William Pollder
Edmund Frenid
Peter Heyers
Mary Newton
Augustine Woods
Edmund Downes
Thomas Person
Simon Fenne
Nicholas Passipher
Andrew Aggs
William Woods
old Bingham
Mary Whightbread
John Tottnett

St Andrew [continued]

[39 Names]

E 179/336, f.17

St Andrew

24 July 1672

goody Mendham
widow Collens
Dorothy Haylett
Ann Frost
widow Hoddy
goodman N...s
goody Wright
goody Hemblton
goody Croker
goody Davies
John Totnell
John Hoddy
Edward Dowine
Thomas Newton
Mary Hastings
widow Younges
William Woods
John Bingham
Thomas Larrod
Ann Maunden
William Wilkinson
Judith ...a... [?Paine]
Edward Dawson
Nathaniel Rust
Ann Creasey
Augustine Woods
Edmund Freind
Elizabeth Horton
Peter Dring
Susan Lundon
Martha Sharpin
Mary Whightbread
Thomas Rost
Thomas Hawward
William Polder
widow Bloy

St Andrew [continued]

Mary Newton
widow Harrison

[38 Names]

E 179/336, f.18

St Andrew

16 Feb 1673/4

goody Mendham	1
widow Collins	1
Dorothy Haylet	2
Ann Frost	1
widow Hoddy	1
goodman Mayes	2
goodman Wright	1
goody Hamilton	1
goody Croker	1
goody Dawney	1
John Tottnell	2
George Hoddy	2
Edward Downes	1
Thomas Newton	2
Mary Hastings	1
widow Youngs	2
goody Woods	1
John Bingham	1
Thomas Larwood	1
Ann Maundy	1
William Wilkinson	1
Judith Paine	1
Edward Purson	1
Nathaniel Rust	2
Ann Creasey	1
Augustine Woods	1
Edmund Berry	2
Elizabeth Hopton	1
Peter Dring	1
Matthew Shirpin	2
Mary Whitebread	2
Titus Rust	1
Thomas Harwood	1

St Andrew [continued]

William Fowlder	1
widow Bloye	1
Mary Newton	1
widow Harrison	2
goodman Dawson	2

[38 Names]

E 179/338, f.10

St Augustine

3 Mar 1670/1

Thomas Stubbs
John Watterson
Robert Wrongey
Samuel Parker
Robert Tennant
Thomas Browne
widow Frost
John Harding
Robert Barlow
Thomas Youngs
Thomas Burch
Thomas Cotton
widow Printer
widow Honny
William Reade
widow Cott
Jacob Laquory
Augustine Newton
James Ferry
Thomas Colthorp
Lawrence Cutting
James Duckman
Thomas Tompson
Nicholas Hellsen
Samuel Leoury
John King
Abraham Drewmoy
Samuel Rudd
John Baxter
Lewis Shelow

St Augustine [continued]

John Gedge
Daniel Wanbeak
Davy Lance
Israel Veny
John Watterson
widow Bucher
Elizabeth Tillny
William Fox
William Hadman
widow Rock
widow Honey
James Claxson
widow ...llford
Thomas Dewson
Frances Whorlo
John Deday
Thomas Bateley
John Boone
widow Emms
widow Wharlow
George Emms
Martin Cobb
John Hardingham
James Honey
John Symonds
William Ames
Eli Permon
Richard Bossum
widow Harper
William Tassell
Thomas Lankaster
John Gardine
widow Garren
widow Thurtell
Matthew Neave
Sarah Hopton
John Titter
Daniel Hashow
Jacob Rickes
James Demow
Richard Gunner
widow Sheringham
James Chapman
Richard Barrett

St Augustine [continued]

Samuel Alling
widow Titter
John Bettson
Edmund Harslow
widow Wright
William Elvin
Thomas Cotten

[81 Names]

E 179/336, f.19

St Augustine

3 May 1672

Philip Burton
John Waterson
James Honey
William Ames
William Fox
George Emes
Thomas Bartlet
John Heard
John Younges
Thomas Browne
Martin Jacob
William Hadman
John Emes
Edward Hemton
John Bradley
John Willson
Thomas Stubbs
William Jarman
Peter Deday
Francis Whorle
Thomas Tomson
Thomas Cooper
Abel Shaft
widow Rickey
Thomas Beatley
Thomas Harrould
James Dishmay
Eli Vermon

St Augustine [continued]

Zachariah Mayhew
Zachariah Mullion
John Tomson
widow Bouth
Francis Perrone
Israel Peloe
Jude Lacohe
Nicholas Helsden
Richard Dasson
Davy Rickey
Richard Barrit
William Claydon
Thomas Garrowd
Thomas Dadrey
John King
Benjamin Smith
John Smith
widow Bucher
Israel Vene
Edward Gunton
John Claydon
Samuel Allen
William Farme
Thomas Caltrup
Vincent Femling
Joyce Carpenter
widow Baxster
Michael Honner
Samuel Rudd
Daniel Wambeak
James Honey, jun.
Samuel Dere
John Mendum
Henry Anderson
Edmund Loyse
Daniel Hurshor
George Rogers
Jane Pament
Philip Shambon
widow Farrum
widow Rooke
Humphrey Stride
Matthew Neave
John Greene

St Augustine [continued]

Thomas Lanckester, jun.
Richard Bossum
William Dawes
Thomas Gunell
Jacob Rickey
Thomas Armes
Augustine Nuton
widow Elvin
John Blondowe
widow Titter
John Whitebread
James Ferree
Robert Dunn
Edward Hemton

[86 Names]

E 179/336, f.20

St Augustine

31 July 1672

widow Butcher
widow Wright
John Watterson
Philip Burten
James Honey
John Semanc
William Ames
William Foxe
George Emes
Thomas Bartell
John Harde
John Younges
Thomas Bowen
Martin Jacobes
William Hadman
John Emes
Edward Hempton
John Bradley
Thomas Stubes
W[?illiam] Jarman
Peter Deday

St Augustine [continued]

John Armes
Frances Wharlo
Thomas Thomson
Thomas Cooper
Abel Shaft
widow Ricke
Thomas Batle
Thomas Harwod
James Dishmay
Eli Permon
Zachariah Mayhew
Zachariah Mullyon
John Tomson
widow Bouth
Frances Perone
Israel Peloe
Jacob Lacohe
Nicholas Helsdon
Samuel Alliny
Jude Lacohe
Richard Dawson
Davy Rickhe
Israel Venum
Edmund Gunton
Thomas Coltrup
Joyce Carpender
widow Baxter
Michael Honer
Samuel Rudd
Daniel Wambark
James Honey
Samuel Dere
John Mendume
Henry Anderson
Edmund Loyse
John Bartell
widow Jacobes
Daniel Horshshor
Philip Shambor
widow Feaver
widow Roke
Humphrey Stride
Matthew Neave
John Garden

St Augustine [continued]

Thomas Lanckester
Richard Bosume
William Dawsun
Thomas Gunell
Jacob Ricke
Thomas Ames
Augustine Newton
widow Eulviny
John Bloundewe
widow Titter
John Whitbread
James Ferny
Robert Dune
John Clayton
William Clayton
Thomas Garwod
Richard Barrit
John Kinge
John Deday

[84 Names]

E 179/336, f.21

St Augustine

3 May 1674

widow Catte	1
Margaret Wright	1
Philip Burton	2
John Willson	1
James Honey, sen.	1
James Honey, jun.	1
John Semancs	1
William Emmes	2
William Fox	1
George Emes	1
Thomas Bartle	1
John Hardye	1
young Youngs	2
Thomas Browne	1
Martin Jacob	1
Lewis Oobien	1

St Augustine [continued]

William Hadman	2
John Emes	1
Edward Hemton	1
John Bradley	2
Thomas Stubbs	1
widow Jarrum	1
Peter Denne	2
John Armes	1
Thomas Tomson	1
Thomas Cooper	1
Abel Shaft	1
widow Rickey	2
James Dismay	1
goodwife Bartle	1
Eli Vermon	1
John Tomson	1
widow Booth	1
Francis Peron	1
Davy Peron	1
widow Whorlo	1
Jacob Lacohe	1
Richard Dawson	1
Davy Rickey	2
Israel Vennie	1
Edward Gunton	1
Thomas Caltrup	1
Joyce Carpenter	1
Michael Honnerre	1
Samuel Rudd	1
Samuel Wambeake	1
Joseph Mendum	1
John Bartle	2
Thomas Mills	1
Daniel Hurshor	1
Henry Anderson	1
Philip Shambon	1
widow Feaver	1
widow Rooke	1
Humphrey Stryd	2
Matthew Neave	1
John Gardine	1
Thomas Lanckester	1
Richard Bossum	1
William Dawsen	1

St Augustine [continued]

Jacob Rickey	1
Thomas Armes	2
Augustine Nuton	1
John Blundow	1
widow Titter	1
John Whitebread	2
Robert Dunn	1
John Castelton	1
William Claydon	1
John King	1
John Deday	1
Michael Mathes	2
James Drew	1
Thomas Batle	1
William Read	1
Thomas Colton	2
William Betson	2
widow Printer	1
widow Tillny	1
Mary Bankes	1

[80 Names]

E 179/338, f.11

St Benedict

[undated ?early 1671]

widow Pamont
widow Clarke
widow Kendall
goodman Moulton
goodman Jerves
goodman Baldwin
James Powell
goodman Burgis
Isaac Pepis
Henry Palmer
Peter Blundeuwe
William Smith
goodman Hupleyawe
Nicholas Clasop
William Eagleston

St Benedict [continued]

Thomas Sanders
James Farnesby
Island Lindsey
John Watts
Richard Burgis
... Lindsey, sen.
Jonathan Parker
Matthew Dallimond
Robert Ruderam
Thomas Foulsham
Robert Robinson
Ann Palgrave
Edmund Caverly
Richard Medler
Thomas Croskett
widow Caverly
Thomas Cousten
John Warner
Nicholas Bootey
Robert Johnson
Thomas Howcrofte
John Buck
John Whood
John Beale
Richard Dixon
Benjamin Symonds
widow Russell
James ...er
John Whittam
Richard Palfryman
Jeremiah Gosse
Thomas King
Frances Barlowe
John Browne
Robert Mony
Abraham Cooper
John Whittum
Edward Lawes
John Baxster
George Wittum
James Durrant
Edward Harper
Jonathan Pickington
Go... Firman, sen.

St Benedict [continued]

William Firman
James Rutter
Francis Watts

[62 Names]

E 179/337, f.5

St Benedict

8 Apr 1672

John Wright
widow Caverly
Elias Hopkines
Robert Linchorne
William Ferman
William Godfery
William Barker
widow Randall
John Browne
John Dawis
Simon Sancroft
Nicholas Folsham
widow Durrant
John Durrant
Peter Dey
Robert Stanton
goodman Loveleige
William Bolding
Richard Burgis
William Levicke
goodman Springall
James Poull
Abraham Cooper
goodman Baud
John Witham
George Wittham
Francis Barlow
good Paufereman
goodman Cudball
John Godfery
Emanuel Brient
widow Hubbert

27

St Benedict [continued]

Thomas Howcraft
Thomas Becket
William Wattson
Edward Allen, jun.
Michael Smith
Richard Midlebrooke
widow Wollward
Richard Medly
John Robison
Elias Hobson
Robert Robison
John Sadd
Elizabeth Thurgell
Matthew Dolleman
Michael Gallant
Jonathan Parker
Nicholas Holman
Samuel Ferreby
widow Neave
Thomas Picke
William Eclestone
Thomas Sanders
William Smith
Thomas Howlings
Nicholas Crispe
Peter Blundue
Esau Hopleyaugh
Henry Palmer
widow Hubbert
John Warner
John Sparnall
Emanuel Brien

[64 Names]

E 179/336, f.22

St Benedict

18 July 1672

John Wright
Richard Burgis
William Loveit

St Benedict [continued]

Richard Medler
Richard Middellbrook
John Roberson
Elias Hopkens
Abraham Fuller
Robert Roberson
John Sad
Michael Galent
Matthew Dalimant
William Sponer
Jonathan Parker
Nicholas Hollmon
Samuel Feribey
Thomas Pecke
Thomas Sanders
William Eccellston
Nicholas Cursp
Esau Hoppellyow
Peter Blundow
Henry Palmer
Thomas Howlewes
William Smith
Thomas Coulse
Mary Hubbart
Manuel Brian
John Sparnell
John Warner
Robert Johnsons
Thomas Becket
James Powle
William Bolding
Robert Springall
Edward Lowes
Richard Pefrement
Abraham Cooper
George Wittam
John Wittam
Edward Allen
Henry Beade
Frances Barlow
Stephen Gipes
Thomas Money
John Goodferey
John Harison

St Benedict [continued]

William Goodferey
William Watson
John Lovelech
Michael Smith
John Durrant
Peter Dey
Simon Sancraft
Robert Barcer
John Daues
John Broune
Robert Linkhorn
Nicholas Foulsom
James Rutter
Sarah Robartes
Robert Stanton
William Farman
widow Randell

[64 Names]

E 179/336, f.23

St Benedict

30 Dec 1673

John Roberson
John Drayton
Richard Medler
Richard Middlebrooke
William Eccleston
Richard Burgis
Elizabeth Saphar
Richard Tunney
widow Cavele
Richard Seele
Richard Dreu
Thomas Sanders
Abraham Cooper
Edward Allyn
John Watson
Francis Pall
Benjamin Symons
John Balding

St Benedict [continued]

William Godfry
Nicholas Chrispe
Esau Hoppio
Henry Pamer
John Fane
Thomas Hovolaus
William Smyth`
Samuel Ferebe
Thomas Peck
Nicholas Holman
Jonathan Parker
Michael Gallent
Martha Dalaman
William Sponer
Abraham Fuller
Robert Roberson
Ellen Lynsey
James Powell
Robert Stanton
Elias Hopkins
Arthur Burrell
John Godfry
James Fuller
Nicholas Foulsham 2
Robert Springall
John Browne
Margaret Randall
Simon Sandcroft
William Watson
Edward Lawes
John Durrant
Peter Dey
Francis Barron 2
Thomas Money
Stephen Jeps
George Wittham
Mark Utbard
Richard Patriman
George Grundy
Daniel Disiman
Edmund Larond
Emanuel Bryant 2
John Warner
John Sparnell

St Benedict [continued]

Robert Johnson
Robert Aldrich
Michael Smyth
John Loverich
John Clark
Davy Rinibrooke

[68 Names]

E 179/338, f.12

St Clement

15 Mar 1670/1

Joseph Fenn
Abraham Tacey
Roger Cupis
widow Sweets
Edmund Barton
Matthew Durrant
John Robinson
Thomas Burton
William Gargell
Bernard Wright
Ann Beales
widow Aldredge
Thomas Wegge
Thomas Finch
Anthony Whitton
widow Allyn
Peter Norton
Margaret Brooke
Jane Whartinham
Richard Hinds
goodman Bates
Christian Riston
Edmund Tinker
Robert Coale
widow Denny
George Greene
Walter Wells
Philip Bridgman
John Gargill

St Clement [continued]

Thomas Lessingham
Charles Crogden
widow Carter
widow Derwick
Samuel Fromentall
Henry Sampson
William Cumnis
Thomas Rutter
Robert Viall
Giles Camby
Henry Harris
Abigail Everard
widow Newarke

[42 Names]

E 179/336, f.24

St Clement

25 Apr [blank ?1672]

Thomas Rutter
Robert Viall
Samuel Firmantele
good Barton
John Wickmore
John Grymley
Charles Crogden
John Lessingham
good Gargile
Philip Bridgman
Walter Wells
Robert Cole
widow Denney
Christian Resten
George Green
Joseph Fenn
Giles Candbey
Margaret Brooke
Henry Harris
Mary Clarke
Peter Norton
Thomas Finch

St Clement [continued]

widow Beales
widow Allen
widow Carter
good Mollett
Robert Hines
John Bates
good Wickmore
William Conneys
widow Sweett
Thomas Burton
Edmund Tincker
goodman Whitton
Roger Keepis
Martha Randsome
Bernard Wright
John Keepis
Abraham Taz
Abigail Evered
Richard Wright
widow Neworke
Martin Durrent

[43 Names]

E 179/336, f.25

St Clement

16 Aug 1672

Thomas Burton
Matthew Ransone
John Bats
William Coneys
John Durrent
widow Sweet
Nicholas Wickmore
Joseph Poynting
Peter Norton
Robert Cubit
George Grene
Giles Canbey
Philip Bridgman
good Gargirle

St Clement [continued]

Ann Reston
Charles Crodgen
Walter Wells
Thomas Lessingham
Robert Coole
widow Carter
widow Newarke
Robert Hynds
Abigail Everard
Abraham Taz
John Wickmore
Samuel Fromantell
widow Blunt
widow Derrick
widow Alline
Thomas Finch
John Grimley
widow Denney
Richard Wright
Bernard Wright
Roger Keepis
Thomas Mollett
Joseph Fenn
widow Beales
Thomas Rutter
Robert Viall
John Keepis, sen.

[41 Names]

E 179/336, f.26

St Clement

12 Nov 1673

John Grimley	2
Abraham Tace	2
Richard Wright	2
Richard Hynes, sen.	2
Thomas Finch	2
Giles Canbey	1
Philip Bridgman	1
Charles Crodgden	2

St Clement [continued]

Thomas Leasingim	1
widow Danny	2
Robert Cole	2
Nicholas Wickmor	2
John Gargen	2
Walter Wells	1
Thomas Helsden	2
Lancelot Allen	1
Martin Durrent	2
widow Poynten	1
John Houten	2
widow Cupis	2
Peter Norten	1
Joseph Fenn	2
widow Allenn	1
widow Eaten	2
Roger Robason	2
Thomas Burton	2
George Grene	1
Robert Vyall	2
Thomas Rutter	2
Samuel Frumety	1
Roger Cupis	2
Bernard Wright	1
Robert Brinckley	2
Edmund Tincker	1

[34 Names]

E 179/338, f.13

St Edmund

21 Feb 1670/1

Sarah Mortemy
Thomas Dey
Thomas Mortemy
Roger Skipper
Henry Church
Matthew Sancraft
Robert Mortemy
John Claxton
Robert Lacy

St Edmund [continued]

John Hidman
widow Nichols
John Pike
Robert Postle
William Burgis
John Decarle
Daniel Turner
Rachel Bradley
John Damm
John Scottowe
Richard Beachen
Francis Bloome
Lawrence Trull
Thomas Sparrow
widow Gibbins
Simon Richmond
John Crowder
John Rose
Thomas Dey
John Symonds
John Scott
widow Winckfield
widow Scott
Dorothy Wagge
Thomas Fulchers
Jeremiah Medcalfe
widow Crowder
Samuel Wagge
widow Kings

[38 Names]

E 179/336, f.27

St Edmund

2 May 1672

Robert Morteme
Thomas Dye
Simon Richmond
Lancelot Trull
widow Crowder
widow Gibbens

St Edmund [continued]

Francis Bloome
Richard Beachin
Daniel Turner
John Crowder
Thomas Dye
John Pyke
widow Nickolls
James Miller
John Claxton
William Gargin
John Scott
John Hydeman
Thomas Sparham
John Skotto
widow Scott
Thomas Fullches
Jeremiah Mettcalf
John Rose
Samuel Wegg
widow Sandcroft
Thomas Posle
Thomas Halfknits
Thomas Martem
Richard Burwell
John Decarle
widow Kinge
John Dam
widow Anger
Robert Leasey
Roger Skipper
John Symonds
Thomas Sharpin

[38 Names]

E 179/336, f.28

St Edmund

17 Sep 1672

Frances Bloome
widow Crowder
Thomas Sparham

St Edmund [continued]

Lawrence Trull
Richard Beachin
Thomas Halfknites
James Miller
Daniel Turner
John Crowder
Thomas Dye
John Pyke
widow Nickolls
John Claxton
William Gargin
widow Scott
John Scott
John Symonds
Roger Skipper
John Rose
Sarah Morteme
Thomas Fullches
Samuel Wegg
widow Sandcraft
Thomas Postle
Thomas Morteme
Richard Burrwell
John Decarle
widow Kinge
John Dam
widow Anger
Simon Richmond
Thomas Dye
Jeremiah Mettcalf
Thomas Sharpin
Robert Leasey
John Hydeman
William Symonds

[37 Names]

E 179/336, f.29

St Edmund

24 Apr 1674

Thomas Bloome

1

33

St Edmund [continued]

Thomas Sparram	1
Simon Richmond	2
William Gargin	1
Richard Boachin	2
William Connies	1
John Claxton	1
widow Crowder	1
Sarah Morteme	2
Thomas Die, weaver	1
William Simons	1
Thomas Tapper	1
Thomas Dueing	2
Jeremiah Medcalf	1
John Hideman	1
Thomas Morteme	1
Mary Skipper	1
Thomas Fulcher	2
Francis Knights	1
widow Scots	2
John Scot	1
John Simans	2
John Dam	1
Samuel Weeke	1
John Crowder	2
Daniel Turner	2
John Grave	1
widow Sandgrave	1
Thomas Die, dyer	1
widow Kinge	1
widow Nickels	1
John Pike	1
Thomas Postle	1
Robert Lesie	1
widow Trull	2
Thomas Halfeknights	1

[36 Names]

E 179/338, f.14

St Etheldreda

13 Mar 1670/1

Richard Pulley
widow Harper
widow Riser
Robert Crew
widow Campe
widow Underwod
widow Leake
Nicholas Chapman
Joseph Youngman
William Adcok
Robert Man
John Knowles
Christopher Risborow
Gabriel Wills
Edward Cokrill
John Wornes
widow Cooper
Richard Edwards
John Osler
James Sherwod
Isabel Hakene
William Griggs
Edmund Pegge
Henry King

[24 Names]

E 179/336, f.30

St Etheldreda

12 Apr 1672

Gabriel Willis
Ann Harper, widow
widow Camp
widow Lake
Nicholas Chapman
Edward Cockrell
Joseph Yongman

St Etheldreda [continued]

widow Adcock
Christopher Rsbro
John Warnes
Richard Edward
John Nowells
Robert Man
widow Underwood
widow Rising
widow Cooper
Richard Pooley
Robert Crew
Isabel Hock
James Sherwood
William Briges
Edmund Pegge
John Ossler
Henry King
widow Carffer

[25 Names]

E 179/336, f.31

St Etheldreda

10 Sep 1672

John Warnes
John Wattson
Edward Cocker
Nicholas Chapman
Joseph Youngman
William Adcok
widow Rising
widow Haper
Robert Mann
John Knowles
John Dunthorne
Peter Mathewes
widow Kempe
widow Underwood
widow Leake
Richard Edwards
James Sherwood

St Etheldreda [continued]

Henry King
Robert Crew
widow Carver
Isabel Haken
Oliver Gayford

[22 Names]

E 179/336, f.32

St Etheldreda

21 Feb 1673/4

Gabriel Miles	2
John Warnes	1
Robert Man	2
John Wattson	1
James Lanne	2
Robert Rantte	2
O...ing [? Owen] Barlowe	1
Edward Cocker	2
Nicholas Chapman	2
John Youngman	1
John Warenes	2
Thomas Wattson	2
widow Ryson	2
John Noweles	2
widow Keampe	2
widow Leacke	2
widow Undarwood	2
Oliver Saffear	2
Robert Crue	1
William Adcocke	1
widow Rising	1
Edward Pegg	1
James Sherwood	2
Isabel Hackin	2
Henry Kinge	2
Richard Eadwordes	1

[26 Names]

E 179/338, f.15

St George Colegate

[undated ?early 1671]

Samuel Lankeaster
John Adkings
Nicholas Cocke
widow Sharpe
John Barny
William Willson
Rebecca Harridence
Robert Youngs
Valentine Wetherell
Francis White
John Fayre
John Springal
Thomas Church
John Abord
Christopher Arminger
George Brice
John Edwards
John Shepperd
Peter Ames
John Harper
John France
Dorothy Feake
Elizabeth True
widow Mollinyow
widow Matthew
Nathaniel Reeder
Edmund Clarke
widow Boyton
Samuel Sayer
Ann Pasiver
widow Ames
John Shepard
Michael Beake
Henry Turner
widow Parker
John Simpson
Eli Castell
John Angell
Anthony Hernsey
widow Webster

St George Colegate [continued]

widow Thurston
O... Wattson
Moses Blundow
Nathaniel Porter
Richard Callow
Thomas Moss
William Freese
Thomas Mills
widow Dewson
John Nickolls
William James
widow Frost
widow Parker
Noah Delatree
Thomas Hansell
Thomas Davy
good Ralison
Thomas Baxter
Nicholas Skott
William Egleton
James Cushin
widow Angell
James Lanch

[63 Names]

E 179/336, f.33

St George Colegate

7 May 1672

widow Moore
John Fiddiman
Samuel Sayer
Henry Mason
John Albon
John Calfe
Philip Wilkins
Samuel Lancaster
Richard Miles
John Barney
William Willsons
widow Harridence

St George Colegate [continued]

Nicholas Scott
John Adkins
John Springall
Robert Smith
Richard Markes
William Wade
John Taggly
Edmund Bland
George Mallowes
John Cuttin
William Nickells
Thomas Biggett
widow Chapman
William James
Robert Gibb
Samuel Joy
James Edwards
John Jemson
John Harpar
John France
Henry Turner
Richard Callaway
William Aldred
John Simson
George Brice
widow Hornsey
Thomas Jewell
George England
Francis Mosse
Thomas Millis
widow Parker
Nathaniel Porter
John Edwards
Abraham Valiant
Isaac Rickey
James Lance
John Nockells
Noah Catree
Moses Blundeaw
Robert Matthew
John Feaver
Thomas Mosse
John Howlett
John Mills

St George Colegate [continued]

John Hansell
William Bryant
James Cushin
Thomas Cawthorne
widow Angell
Edward Clarke
Michael Beake
Peter Ames
widow Holt
Thomas Wilkinson
widow Waller
William Selfe

[68 Names]

E 179/336, f.34

St George Colegate

31 July 1672

Samuel Lancaster
widow Moore
John Fiddimon
widow Clarke
Samuel Sayer
Henry Mason
John Ayborn
… Farrow
widow Marcon
John Webb
Richard Myhills
William Selfe
John Barney
William Wilson
widow Harridence
John Adkins
Nicholas Scott
Robert Smith
John Tagley
William Wade
Christopher Armiger
Cock & Mills
widow Waller

37

St George Colegate [continued]

Ann Leake
Martin Aggs
Thomas Wilkerson
Michael Beake
Peter Amos
widow Sheppard
widow Howlt
John France
Edmund Bland
George Mallowe
Abraham Bubbings
[?John] Cutten
widow Frost
William Nockols
widow Chapman
James Edwards
James Marshall
... Joyce
John Fiddimon
John Harper
Thomas Cothan
James Cushin
John Money
George Brice
good Yewell
William Freese
Christopher Dowzin
Nathaniel Porter
widow Angle
widow Agston
widow Callow
good Millis
good Mosse
John Edwards
Abraham Valyent
Isaac Rickey
Noah Datree
Moses Blundeaw
John Nockolls
James Launce
John Feaver
Robert Matthews
John Howlens
Thomas Kendall

St George Colegate [continued]

James Thompson
Mary Castle
good Clarke
John Deslee

[71 Names]

E 179/336, f.35

St George Colegate

12 Nov 1673

William Wilson	1
widow Moore	1
John Fideman	1
widow Clarke	2
Samuel Sayer	1
Henry Mason	1
John Auborne	1
good Farrowe	2
widow Markall	2
Richard Miles	1
William Miles	1
John Barney	1
widow Harridunce	2
John Adkins	1
Nicholas Scott	1
Robert Smith	1
William Wade	1
Christopher Armiger	2
Cooke & Mills	2
widow Waller	2
Ann Leake	1
Martin Aggs	1
Thomas Wilkenson	1
Michael Bake	1
Peter Amos	2
widow Sheppard	1
widow Hoult	2
Thomas Marson	1
John France	1
Edmund Bland	1
George Mallows	1

St George Colegate [continued]

Abraham Bubbins	1
good Catten	1
widow Frost	1
James Edwards	1
widow Chapman	1
James Marshal	2
John Fideman	1
John Harper	1
James Cushen	1
John Money	2
good Pulley	1
William Freese	2
Christopher Dowsin	1
William Salomon	1
John Smith	1
Matthew Porter	1
widow Angle	2
widow Callowe	1
Thomas Gothen	2
John Woollsy	1
Francis Fisher	1
good Bryant	1
John Edwards	1
Abraham Valiant	1
Sarah Kirby	1
Noah Detree	1
Moses Blundewe	1
John Nockalls	2
James Launce	1
John Faver	1
Robert Mathyes	1
Henry Holt	1
Thomas Kendall	1
James Tompson	1
Mary Castle	1
widow Clarke	1
John Mahewe	1
Thomas Mosse	2
John Webb	2
Samuel Lancaster	2
good Jemson	1
Thomas Wenn	1
widow Mallowes	1
Henry Adames	1

St George Colegate [continued]

goody Davey	1
Ann Picke	1
John Eldred	1
widow Marcon	1
good Armenger	1
good Callowe	1
Francis Mosse	1
good Joyess	1
John Springall	1

[84 Names]

E 179/338, f.16

St George Tombland

7 Mar 1670/1

Robert Mann
Rebecca Diboll
widow Byce
John Lindsey
Joseph Emperor
Jasper Hedgman
widow Atterson
John Martin
Thomas Ballance
widow Price
widow Waffe
Simon Bird
William Cookoe
Edmund Foulsham
Thomas Greene
John Downes
John Denny
Thomas Bullard
Matthew Salmon
Sarah Toft
Robert Sammon
Clement Daynes

[22 Names]

E 179/336, f.36

St George Tombland

15 Feb 1671/2

Robert Man
Rebecca Dyboll
widow Byse
John Say
John Emperor
Jasper Hegman
John Marten
Thomas Ballance
widow Brice
widow Waffe
Simon Burd
William Cooke
Edmund Foulsham
Thomas Greene
Clement Daynes
John Denne
Thomas Bullard
Matthew Sallmon
Sarah Toft
Robert Sallmon
widow Neave
widow Pinchin
widow Tooly
widow Garry
widow Crooke
goodman Plummer
Robert Woorts

[27 Names]

E 179/336, f.37

St George Tombland

17 July 1672

Robert Man
widow Buise
Joseph Emprer
John Denny

St George Tombland
[continued]

John Day
Sarah Toft
Matthew Sammon
Thomas Ballance
Mary Brice, widow
Simon Bird
Edmund Foulsham
Jasper Hedgman
Robert Salmon
Rebecca Dyball
John Martyn
widow Waffe
William Cooke
Thomas Green
Clement Dayns
Thomas Bullard
widow Neave
widow Pinchyn
widow Tooley
widow Crooke
widow Gary
goodman Plumer
Philip Wilson

[27 Names]

E 179/336, f.38

St George Tombland

13 Jan 1673/4

Robert Man	2
widow Waffe	1
Joseph Emperor	1
Martin Salmon	1
Thomas Balanc	2
widow Neave	1
widow Brise	1
Simon Bird	2
Henry Huflet	1
Thomas Smith	1
Edmund Foullsam	1

St George Tombland

[continued]

Joseph Hegman	2
Robert Salmon	1
widow Pinching	1
Thomas Green	1
Clement Daynes	1
John Waffe	2
widow Toolye	2
widow Crooke	1
Rebecca Diball	1
widow Parmenter	2
widow Garie	2
William Cooke	2

[23 Names]

E 179/338, f.17

St Giles

26 Jan 1670/1

John Hoecroft
Thomas Smith
John Rust
John Harper
Edmund Harper
Richard Thurken
Edward Amis
Robert Hackney
William Croskell
goody Potter
John Browne
Edward Pettey
James Aldrush
widow Bundsnell
widow Watlinge
Henry Thurrell
Daniel Watlinge
Thomas Sympson
widow Briggs
George Smith
Elizabeth Cleare
John Berry

St Giles [continued]

old Chrithood
widow Bastey
widow Sanders
Thomas Woods
John Budwell
Nicholas Mallet
John Fenn, sen.
Hamon Peartre
Thomas Ringe
Simon Flood
Thomas Gidens
George Buddell
widow Funnell
Roger Eliot
Robert Gunton
Samuel Jefferys
John Ballence
Mercy Hoghenet
Thomas Pepes
Aquila Ferman
James Wiltsheir
Robert Reynolds
James Groome
goodman Clarke
John Browne
Thomas Crane
William Tayler
Thomas Colingder
Robert Darbey
William Wickers
Elizabeth Spacke
widow Tush
widow Bunton
Hugh Smith
John Knittes
John Gedny
Christopher Viner
Thomas Underwood
Robert Rivett
William Dexter
John Fen & old Mose
Robert Warner
... Dringlee & widow Skott

St Giles [continued]

Joseph Watlinge
Joseph Turner
Thomas Coole
John Budwell
Henry Toller
William Speding
William Crane
Thomas Lowe

[75 Names]

E 179/337, f.6

St Giles

18 Mar [blank ?1671/2]

William Croskell
John Cose & John Bery
Edward Petty
Thomas Cran
Roger Ellette
Samuel Jafres
James Elette
     [&] John Clabarn
old Crittwood
widow Bace
     & Mark Hodgne
Robert Dorby
Thomas Harper
William Wickeres
Henry Thurell
     & Robert Slad
Daniel Wattling
widow Briges
John Ruste
     & John Balenc
Thomas Stemson
goody Potter
     & William Briges
Nicholas Mallett
James Brooeck
William Edgly
Elizabeth Sparke

St Giles [continued]

Christopher Androes
widow Tushe
John Browen
James Crome
Hamon Parttre
widow Buntton
widow Wattling
old Flud
Mary Sanders
widow Bundsell
Henry Smith
John Knittes
Ellen Cler
Thomas King
John Gedney
Robert Ranells
James Willcher
Thomas Woodes
old Harper
widow Funell
William Crann
Robert Hackne
young Harper
old Smetth
Richard Thurckell
Christopher Wineyard
George Burdell
Thomas Underwood
William Tayellerd
Thomas Lowe
Robert Rivett
William Dexter
John Fen & old Mose
John Howecraftte
Robert Worner
… Dringlee & widow Skotte
Aquila Farman
Joseph Wattling
Joseph Turner
Thomas Couell
John Budwell
Henry Toller
Thomas Pa[?rker]

St Giles [continued]

William Spedeing
Thomas Geddings
Nicholas Abren
George Smith
Edward Ames

[78 Names]

E 179/336, f.39

St Giles

9 Jan 1672/3

William Crossfeild
John Cole
John Berry
Edward Peteys
Thomas Crane
Roger Ellet
Samuel Jeffery
James Ellett
John Labron
widow Base
Mark Hoges
Robert Dorby
Thomas Harper
William Vickars
Henry Thurrell
Watling Slade
widow Bridge
John Rust
John Bollence
Thomas Stimpson
widow Potter
William Briggs
Nicholas Mallet
James Brooke
William Edgley
Elizabeth Sparke
Christopher Andrewes
widow Tush
John Browne
James Crome

St Giles [continued]

Hamon Peartree
widow Button
widow Watling
old Fludd
Mary Saunders
widow Bundsnell
Henry Smith
John Knights
Helen Cleere
Thomas Kinge
John Gedney
Robert Randalls
James Wilcher
Thomas Woods
old Harper
widow Funnell
old Critswod
William Crane
Robert Harkeney
young Harper
old Smith
Richard Thurkittle
Christopher Winyard
George Burdell
Thomas Underwood
William Tayler
Thomas Lowe
Robert Vincent
William Dexiter
John Fenn
old Mosse
John Howcroft
Robert Warner
Dring Lee
widow Scott
Aquila Farmon
Joseph Watling
Joseph Turner
Thomas Cowell
John Budwell
Henry Towell
Thomas Parker
William Speeding
Thomas Goodwyns

St Giles [continued]

George Smith
Edward Amis
John Clarke
Robert Daniell

[78 Names]

E 179/336, f.40

St Giles

10 Jan 1673/4

William Crassfield	1
John Cole	1
John Berry	1
Edward Pettis	1
Thomas Crane	1
Roger Ellit	1
James Ellit	1
John Aborne	2
Mercy Hodges	1
Robert Dorby	1
Thomas Harper	1
William Vickers	1
Henry Thurrold	2
Watling Sladd	1
widow Woolbricke	1
John Rust	1
John Bullock	1
Thomas Stimson	1
William Briggs	2
Richard Mallet	1
James Brooke	1
Elizabeth Sparke	1
Christopher Andrews	2
... Fenn in the parish house	2
widow Tush	1
John Brown	1
James Croome	1
Hamon Pertree	1
widow Watlyn	1
old Flood	1
widow Bunsdell	1

St Giles [continued]

Mary Smith	1
Elizabeth Cleare	1
Thomas Kinge	2
John Gidney	1
Robert Ranolds	1
James Willcher	2
Thomas Woods	1
old Harper	1
widow Funnell	1
goody Pooly	1
Robert Hakeny	1
young Harper	1
Hugh Smith	1
Richard Thirkittle	2
William Tayler	1
... Clabborn	1
Thomas Lowe	1
William Dexter	1
Thomas Underwood	1
Henry Fenn	2
John Howcraft	1
widow Warner	1
Dring Lee	1
widow Scott	1
Aquila Ferman	1
Joseph Wattlyn	1
Joseph Turner	1
Thomas Gidding	1
George Burdell	1
William Tompson	1
Henry Toller	1
William Spedding	1
George Smith	1
Edward Amys	1
John Clerk	1
Robert Daniell	2
widow Jefferies	1
Daniel Watlyn	1
widow Francklyn	1
Edward Symonds	1
widow Pinder	1
John Ballance	1
goodman Wright	1
John Clabborn	1

St Giles [continued]

old Rivett   1

[76 Names]

E 179/338, f.18

St Gregory

3 Apr 1671

John Wrighte
Peter Head
Susan Swifte
Thomas Shacklock
John Jary
Thomas Love
Thomas Secker
widow Allen
Alice Nuttinge
Ann Chambers
Ann Smith
George Love
widow Kill
Peter Davy
John Foxe
Mary Fransome
Mary Holland
William Mony
John Tyler
widow Dale
Ann Linsey
Thomas Shacklock
John Cooke
Philip Elmer
Wi... Hoode
John Scott
Richard Gargell
Robert Burrell
Catherine Pinkny
Edmund Rixe
William Woolmer
William Brookes
Francis Eaton
John Tylor

St Gregory [continued]

Robert Parnell
Thomas Leamon
goodman Budfeild
Vincent Porter
Thomas Molbey
widow Harriss
Robert Campline
Thomas Teate
Isaac Neale
Elizabeth Beamont
John Warden
Edmund Cable
widow Huxe
widow Wright
Richard Budfeild
Richard Gorthern
widow Verdeer
Peter Verdeer
Mary Pullham
widow Mills
John Pitcher
Luke Smith
Robert Goose
Richard Russell
Richard Broughton
goodman Chubb
widow Masters
the last 5 live in
almshouses

[61 Names]

E 179/337, f.7

St Gregory

18 Mar [blank ?1671/2]

Susan Shift
widow Shacklock
Thomas Love
Thomas Secker
Alice Nutting
Ann Chambers

45

St Gregory [continued]

Ann Smith
George Love
widow Hill
Peter Davy
Mary Francim
Mary Holland
William Money
Thomas Tyler
Ann Linsey
John Coock
William Hood
John Scott
Richard Gargin
Catherine Pinckney
Edward Rich
John Tyler
Robert Sparnall
John Fox
John Wright
John Gary
William Walmer
Philip Aylmer
William Brooke
Richard Gathorne
widow Dix
… Hicks
widow Hoode
widow Cademon
Robert Goose
Thomas Leeman
Francis Eaton
widow Fromentel
Vincent Porter
Thomas Malby
widow Harrys
Robert Camplin
Thomas Teate
Isaac Neale
widow Beaumont
goodman Warden
Edmund Cabel
widow Hickes
widow Wright
Richard Budfield

St Gregory [continued]

Peter Verdier
widow Verdier
Mary Pullam
widow Milles
John Pitcher
Luke Smith
Richard Russel
Richard Broughton
John Hardy

[59 Names]

E 179/336, f.41

St Gregory

18 July 1672

widow Fromentell
Richard Rusells
widow Harris
widow Hill
Simon Hubert
widow Fox
Mary Millis
Elizabeth Beomont
Susan Linager
Peter Verdier
Nicholas Booty
John Pitchers
Edmund Cable
Deborah Verdier
Charles Cornhill
Joseph Neal
Mary Hawkes
Robert Millis
Ann Write
Henry Wood…ne
Thomas Teate
Catherine Kamplin
Vincent Porter
Christopher Maulby
Thomas Leeman
John Beomont

St Gregory [continued]

John Scot
Richard Gargen
Elizabeth Cooke
Mary Shacklock
Joseph Woolmer
Thomas Love
George Love
John Cushion
William Hood
Thomas Chambers
Mary Mott
widow Clark
Catherine Wilson
Isaac Wicks
Hannah Johnson
Dorothy Pinkney
Peter Davy
Luke Smith
Mary Holland
Francis Moore
Margaret Fransum
John Fenn
Thomas Watson
William Thompson, sen.
William Pope
William Thompson, jun.
Matthew Cooke
Thomas Martens
Henry Frend
Richard Broughton
Robert Varnell
William Bofell
John Foa...ke
John Cooke

[60 Names]

E 179/336, f.42

St Gregory

19 Jan 1673/4

Charles Dawes	2

St Gregory [continued]

Susan Wicks, widow	1
Edmund Randolf	1
widow Thornton	1
Thomas Chambers	2
John Cushing	1
George Love	1
widow Secker	1
Mary Shacklock, widow	2
Elizabeth Cook, widow	1
John Scot	1
William Hood	2
Richard Gargill	1
William Burhill	1
Joseph Nobbes	2
Catherine Masters, widow	1
Thomas Love	1
James Barton	2
widow Clark	1
widow Pinkney	1
George Skinner	2
Robert Varvell	1
Richard Broughton	1
widow Harris	1
Henry Warden	1
Vincent Porter	1
widow Fromantl	1
Thomas Teat	2
widow Camplin	1
Simon Hubbert	1
Nicholas Booty	1
Isaac Neal	2
Charles Cornhill	2
Edmund Keble	1
widow Verdier	1
widow Booty	2
widow Linagar	1
John Pitcher	2
widow Hawk	1
widow Beamont	2
widow Millis	1
widow Wright	1
widow Watts	1
Thomas Wilson	2
Joseph Woolmer	1

St Gregory [continued]

Francis Eaton	2
Matthew Crotch	1
Stephen Martin	1
Mary Hilland, widow	1
Francis More	1
Margaret Fransham	2
John Fenn, sen.	2
Robert Fox	1
Nathaniel Garrood	1
widow Allen	1
Francis Wharles	2
William Woodstock	2
widow Mott	1
Thomas Duberry	2
Peter Verdier	1

[60 Names]

E 179/338, f.19

St Helen

20 Feb 1670/1

widow Huett
widow Biggs
Matthew Thompson
widow Stewerson
widow Bassett
Thomas Back
widow Everitt
widow Shanke
Henry Cocke
Thomas Fenn
Edward Medcalfe
Andrew Howman
Christopher Buxton
Edward Mason
William Procter
Nicholas Fishooke
widow Thettford
Michael Cocke
Zachariah Burcham
Samuel Gase

St Helen [continued]

William Crome
widow Clay
John Powle
Peter Homan
John Back
Francis Jellin
Edmund Joyce
Robert Gedney

[28 Names]

E 179/336, f.43

St Helen

15 Feb 1671/2

widow Hewitt
widow Biggs
Martin Tompson
widow Stewarson
widow Somes
Thomas Backe
widow Everit
widow Shancke
Henry Cocke
Thomas Fenn
Edward Madcalfe
Andrew Homan
Christopher Buxton
Edward Mason
William Procter
Nicholas Fishacke
widow Thettford
Michael Cocke
Zachariah Burchum
Samuel Gase
William Crome
widow Claton
John Stubbs
widow Pearcavall
Arthur Wryte
Mary Aynsworth

St Helen [continued]

[26 Names]

E 179/336, f.44

St Helen

17 July 1672

widow Clayton
William Crome
Samuel Gaze
John Steward
Martin Tompson
John Backe
Francis Gillins
Robert Cocke
Peter Homan
John Stubbes
Edward Mason
William Proctor
Andrew Homan
widow Norman
Christopher Buxton
widow Everit
Thomas Fenne
Nicholas Fishooke
Edward Medcalfe
widow Bigges
Robert Gidney
James Gibson
Edmund Salmon
Zachariah Burcham
widow Joyce
Mary Ainsworth
Samuel Holmes
John Pike
Arthur Wright
John Long

[30 Names]

E 179/336, f.45

St Helen

28 Apr 1674

widow Pike	1
Arthur Write	1
Samuel Homes	1
Mary Aynsworth	1
goodman Brett	2
Thomas Stanton	1
Martin Tomson	1
John Stubbs	1
Andrew Homan	1
Edward Mason	1
Robert Cocke	1
Peter Homan	1
goodman Gase	1
goodman Buckston	2
Robert Bircham	2
Th[?omas] Fenn	1
... Medcaf	1
widow Joyse	1
Philip Rust	1
goodman Crome	1
Henry Cocke	1
Mi[?chael] Cocke	
widow Shancke	
John Steward	1
... Clayton	1
Nicholas Fishooke	1
widow Stewerson	1
widow Bigges	1
Samuel Hewet	1

[29 Names]

E 179/338, f.20

St James

14 Mar 1670/1

widow Parker
Daniel Tye

49

St James [continued]

Thomas Betts
Samuel Springhall
William Jell or Bell [sic]
John Rickey
Thomas Flower
Roger Hall
Edward Pye
Robert Coston
Robert Fletcher
Thomas Kinge
widow Youngs
Timothy Baldinyn
Peter Webster
widow Harvey
John Eaton
Samuel Hansell
John Shefield
Thomas Read
Thomas Metcalfe
John Portman
Mary Burman
John Symonds
Thomas Sammon
Edward Godfry
Henry Bray
Samuel March
John Carr
Thomas Martin
Henry Riches
John Elvin
Catherine Read
Adam Pye
John Crotch
Edward Denny
Edward Horth
John Bunn
John Leacy
Henry Knights
Nicholas Halfnett
widow Crotch
widow Saffery
widow Fletcher
Thomas Rust
Robert Wantlope

St James [continued]

Jonathan Parker
Richard Chapmann
Thomas Hardyn
John Green
Henry Hall
John Browne
William Symonds
Margaret Sowell
Peter Raspe
  or Rashbell [sic]
Bevis Nicholls
George Canham
Elizabeth Usher
Robert Hovell
John Catlynge
Mary Ulfe
Richard Burrell

[62 Names]

E 179/336, f.46

St James

29 Apr 1672

Edward Hoath
Nicholas Hobart
John Bun
William Hoath
John Simonts
Christopher Howling
Robert Scot
Nicholas Halfknits
widow Croach
Thomas Harding
Samuel Hansell
John Worker
Henry Harrison
Edward Denny
widow Safery
Richard Chapman
widow Clark
Henry Bale

St James [continued]

widow Flecher
John Greene
Thomas Mallet
Henry Gray
Henry Knights
Thomas Warters
John Croach
John Shoart
John Youngs
Samuel Homes
Peter Savage
Robert Flecher
George Cannum
John Eten
Peter Webster
Timothy Bolding, sen.
Robert Wantlope
widow Recke
Edward Pie
Timothy Bolding, jun.
Thomas Rust
Thomas Flower
Robert Costen
William Ille
Ann James
Edward Godfrey
John Browne
Daniel Tye
John Towell
John Sheffeld
Thomas Elven
Alice Read
Thomas Medcap
Thomas Kinge
John Portman
Roger Hall
Thomas Burchham
William Simons
Mary Burman
Samuel Springall
John Cattling
widow Langly
Mary Greenewod
widow Harny

St James [continued]

Samuel March
widow Read
Henry Reches
Thomas Martings
widow Barck
Elizabeth Ussher
Richard Burrell
Margaret Sowell
John Beny
Peter Raspell
Bevis Nickcolls
Robert Hovell

[74 Names]

E 179/336, f.47

St James

16 Aug 1672

Edward Hoath
Nicholas Hobart
John Bunn
William Hoath
John Simons
Christopher Howling
Robert Scot
Nicholas Halfknights
widow Croach
Thomas Harding
Samuel Hancell
John Worker
Henry Harrison
Edward Denney
widow Safery
Richard Chapman
widow Clarke
Henry Bale
widow Flecher
John Greene
Thomas Mallet
Henry Gray
Henry Knights

St James [continued]

Thomas Warters
John Croach
John Shart
John Youngs
Samuel Homes
Peter Savage
Robert Flecher
George Canam
John Eaton
Peter Webster
Timothy Bolding
Robert Wanthrog
widow Rickkey
Edward Pie
Timothy Bolding
Thomas Rust
Thomas Flower
Robert Costen
William Ille
Ann James
Edward Godfrey
John Browne
Daniel Tie
John Towell
John Sheffeld
Thomas Elven
Alice Reade
Thomas Medcap
Thomas King
John Portman
Roger Hale
Thomas Burcham
William Simons
Mary Burman
Samuel Springall
John Cattling
widow Langly
Mary Greewod
widow Harny
Samuel March
widow Reade
Henry Riches
Thomas Martings
widow Barke

St James [continued]

Elizabeth Ussher
Richard Burrell
Margaret Sowell
John Bene
Peter Raspell
Bevis Nickcols
Robert Hovell

[74 Names]

E 179/336, f.48

St James

25 Apr 1674

John Baker	2
Itchingham Lofties	1
John Towell	2
Daniel Tye	1
Henry Coppin	1
John Short	1
Peter Webster	1
Simon Ranolds	1
Arthur Moutton, sen.	2
John Tayler	1
Arthur Moutton, jun.	1
Timothy Balden	1
Thomas Flower	1
William Youngs	1
widow Spencer	1
John Emes	2
John Eaton	2
William Augar	1
Robert Wantlop	2
George Canham	1
John Shead	1
John Symonds	2
Matthew Howard	2
John Malbey	1
Robert Scot	1
Thomas Waterson	2
Samuel Springall	1
John Brown	2

St James [continued]

Henry Bale	1
Samuel Hensley	2
... Wieth	1
Thomas Harden	1
Nicholas Halfnights	2
John Miller	1
Edward Hoath	1
Joseph Jary	1
Thomas Spinks	2
John Sommon	1
John Crotch	2
William Hoath	2
John Bun	1
widow Knights	1
widow Peck	1
John Catling	1
widow Langly	1
goodwife Ranolds	2
John Read	1
Richard Collings	1
John Portman	1
John Hall	2
Thomas Medcalfe	2
Thomas Paine	1
Thomas King	2
William Symonds	1
Mary Burnman	1
John Claxton	2
widow Harny	2
John Bleiss	1

[58 Names]

E 179/338, f.21

St John de Sepulchre

28 Feb 1670/1

James Sheringam
widow Smsom
William Robinson
Mary Ford
William Mony

St John de Sepulchre
[continued]

Mary Sherod
John Sheringham
widow Skelton
Hannah Poyt
widow Allin
Thomas Barwick
Henry Feacks
John... Theoboll
Ann Arbor
John Wade
John Tungat
Thomas Osban
widow Rogers
Alexander Wade, sen.
Stephen Mute
Thomas Lesen
Mary Narbrow
John Denmes
Thomas Dausen
John Lese
Ann Pecnell
John Clexston
John Wissiter
Thomas Robinson
Anthony Person
Francis Cunnon
widow Warde
Robert Ringwood
Clement Barton
Henry Cacket, sen.
widow Lambe
Edward Allden
John Chartwrite
Thomas Holby
Richard Narburgh
widow Flower
John Tooly
widow Denme
Martha Tru
John Dunthon, sen.
John Johnson
widow Johnson
Godfrey Dum

St John de Sepulchre
[continued]

John Warrintan
Thomas Dorman, jun.
Geoffrey More
Elizabeth Johnson
Augustine Kempe
John Genies
Joseph Morly
Nicholas Picher
Deborah Osban
Esther Harttly
Stephen Rexs
Matthew Smith
widow Lankthorn
Daniel Dey
Edmund Wade
Thomas Skelton, jun.
Henry Gorbell
Gregory Noobs
Henry Searls, jun.
Henry Searls, sen.
Roger Reve
Simon Reve
Edmund Gos
Nathaniel Smith
widow Batts
Henry Watts
... Robinson
widow Dicks
William Denne
Thomas Cooke
John Heasell
Charles Machen
Thomas Tooly
Simon Baxter
Thomas Bell
Thomas Elles
Joseph Hackney
John Dunthorn
Thomas Poull
John Willmes
Alexander Wade
Michael Downeing
Thomas Hemsted

St John de Sepulchre
[continued]

William Elles
Thomas Worsley
Bartholomew Scott
John Ransom
Mary Willson
widow Pey
Henry Smith
Thomas Tooly, jun.
Thomas Tooley, sen.
Jacob Barnod
Thomas Stantom
Christopher Sprunt
Robert Ludkin
Thomas Bell
James Smith
Daniel Hemnell
Thomas Man
Thomas Ringwood
John Dunthorn, jun.
John Money
Daniel Norton
Robert Leasing
Bird Jeulm...
Smith Curton
widow Nellson
Matthew Bottwrit
John Wade

[120 Names]

E 179/337, f.8

St John de Sepulchre

3 May 1672

good Mone	1
widow Allen	1
John Waed, sen.	1
John Waed, jun.	2
John Tong...en	1
widow Rogeres	1
widow Norbor	1

St John de Sepulchre
[continued]

widow Lacy	1
old Touly	2
John Donthorn	2
John Jhonson	1
widow Jhonson	1
Thomas Dorman	1
Geoffrey More	1
Augustine Kempe	2
Edmund Waed	2
Thomas Sklton	1
Henry Soreles	1
Thomas Skener	2
Esther Rarly	1
Mrs Treu	1
old Hackny	1
Henry Cockes	1
Gregory Nobes	1
Simon Reves	1
William Deane	2
Thomas Ball	1
Thomas Baxtar	2
Thomas Eles[?]	2
Bartholomew Skott	2
widow Pye	1
Thomas Touly, jun.	1
Jacob Barney	1
Thomas Ba..., jun.	1
... Hodson & Julons	2
widow Cartor	1
good Archar	
Christopher Spront	1
widow Smeth	1
Esther Houard	1
good Smeth	1
good Worant	2
Daniel Dey	1
... Foster	1
Thomas Robarson	2
Henry Corbell	2
Thomas Parnell	2
Henry Counsalar	2
Frances Cannom	2
John Hoey	1

St John de Sepulchre
[continued]

John Garves	1
John Mancar	1
widow Porson	1
widow Betts	1
Thomas Stanton	2
John Claxon	1
Robert Reinggall	1
Mrs Wored, very poor	1
widow Caruson	1
widow Flouer	2
John Welles	2
Thomas Ringwod	2
widow Lambe	2
Edward Aldem	1
Peter ...	2
Robert Edridge	2
John Springer	2

[67 Names]

E 179/336, f.49

St John de Sepulchre

10 Feb 1672/3

Edmund Aldam
goody Mony
widow Alen
John Wade, sen.
John Wade, jun.
John Tungat
widow Rogers
widow Narbro
widow Leacy
old Toly
John Dunthorn
John Jonson
Thomas Dorman
Geoffrey More
Augustine Kempe
Edmund Wade
Thomas Skelton

St John de Sepulchre
[continued]

Henry Searls
Thomas Skinner
Mrs True
old Hakeny
Henry Coket
Gregory Nobs
Simon Reve
William Denne
Thomas Toly
Thomas Bell
Simon Baxter
Thomas Ollis
Bartholomew Skot
widow Lambe
widow Pye
John Toly
Jacob Barny
Thomas Bell
... Hatson & Julians
widow Cartar
Ann Archer
widow Sprunt
goody Smith
Esther Howard
widow Smith
goody Warrant
Daniel Dye
Roger Reve
Henry Feake
widow Burtot
Robert Foster
Thomas Robinson
Henry Corbet
Thomas Parnell
widow Counseller
Francis Cannum
Thomas Durson
John Jarvis
widow Bates
Thomas Skanton
John Claxon
Thomas Ringwood
Robert Ringwood

St John de Sepulchre
[continued]

widow Warrant
widow Curreson
widow Flower
John Willis
John Man
William Jarvis
Robert Boone
James Smith
Edmund Goss
Bridget Narbro
Mary Stimson
James Jorye, sen.
James Sheringham
Robert Leasing
Thomas Cooke the smith
Thomas Barwicke
William Abbes
Daniel Norton
Ezra Barwicke
John Carteret
John Rabards

[81 Names]

E 179/336, f.50

St John de Sepulchre

14 Jan 1673/4

John Mony	1
widow Forde	1
John Wade, sen.	2
John Gebens	1
widow Carter	1
John Roberts	1
Daniel Dey	2
widow Hackny	1
John Hueson	1
Robert Leesing	2
widow Narbrow	2
Daniel Hemblin	1
Thomas Bell	2

St John de Sepulchre
[continued]

William Gervece	2
James Smith	1
Jacob Barnord	1
Thomas Tooly	1
Henry Smith	1
Thomas Ringwood	1
Thomas Stanton	1
widow Pey	1
Ezra Barwick	1
widow Bowles	1
John Willkins	2
John Bowls	1
Thomas Parnall	2
Thomas Bell	1
Thomas Poull	1
Thomas Carter	1
John Hill	1
Thomas Elles, jun.	1
widow Parnall	1
Thomas Tooly, sen.	1
Thomas Cook	2
Thomas Elles, sen.	1
William Dean	1
Thomas Hansell	1
Robert Gemson	1
widow Bates	1
Nathaniel Smith	1
Edmund Goss	1
Simon Reeve	1
Roger Reeve	2
Gregory Nobs	1
Thomas Skelton	1
widow Carthwrite	2
Edward Allden	2
Robert Bone	1
Thomas Coket	1
widow Curisun	2
Robert Ringwood	1
Thomas Skiner	1
James Sheringham	2
Henry Scearls, jun.	2
Henry Scearls, sen.	1
Edmund Waert	1

St John de Sepulchre
[continued]

widow Smith	1
John Wade, jun.	2
widow Warrent	1
Thomas Man	2
Esther Hartly	1
Bartholomew Scot	2
Nicholas Picher	1
widow Longthorn	1
Deborah Osborn	1
William Nurs	1
Alexander Wade	1
widow Johnson	1
Henry Jorball	1
Hugh Warmtun	1
John Gervice	2
Thomas Dorman	1
Geoffrey Moore	1
Godfrey Dam	1
John Jonson	1
widow Dunthorn	1
John Tooly	1
widow Flower	1
Thomas Dawson	1
Stephen Moote	1
widow Leasey	2
John Claxton	2
Frances Cannon	2
Thomas Robinson	1
Thomas Barwick	2
Henry Feakes	2
Henry Sheringham	2

[87 Names]

E 179/338, f.22

St John Maddermarket

8 Mar 1670/1

Augustine Alldrid
John Cable
Geoffrey Parker

57

St John Maddermarket
[continued]

William Ems
Samuel Jell
Alice Tuck
George Settle
widow Vipors
Esther Holl
widow Clarke
James Horn
Edmund Cock
John Sparke
Mary Smith
Nathaniel Loyce
John King
Thomas Smith
widow Smith
John Hern
William Calf
Robert Gerling
widow Gyles
Edward Gyles
widow Norgate
John Hill
widow Maufree
widow Lambart
John Potter
Thomas Carver
George Skiner
Susanna Buttler

[31 Names]

E 179/336, f.51

St John Maddermarket

20 Apr [blank ?1672]

Robert Huchason
Samuel Gelly
George Skener
William Emes
John Howard
Simon Scott

St John Maddermarket
[continued]

John Cable
William Simonds
John Ashly
Jonas Parker
Robert Sponer
Olav Wild
William Calfe
William Alldrege
Edward Gilles
widow Norgett
John Potter
Robert Girlinge
Roger Hill
Richard Meeke
Robert Douton
James Horn
John Hurn
John Morteme
Thomas Smith
John Kinge
Nicholas Lock
John Spark
John Settlawe
John Browen
Nathaniel Locke
widow Heare
widow Smith

[33 Names]

E 179/336, f.52

St John Maddermarket

24 July 1672

Samuel Jelly
George Skiner
William Emms
John Howard
Simon Scot
John Cable
William Symonds

St John Maddermarket
[continued]

John Ashly
Jonas Parker
Robert Spooner
Olav Wilde
William Calfe
William Alldred
Edward Giles
John Potter
Robert Girling
Roger Hill
Richard Meek
Robert Huchison
James Horn
John Harn
John Mortone
Thomas Smith
John King
Nicholas Locke
John Sparke
John Setlaw
John Browne
Nathaniel Loyse
widow Hare
widow Smyth
widow Norget

[32 Names]

E 179/336, f.53

St John Maddermarket

[undated ?late 1673 or early 1674]

Samuel Jelly	1
William Eams	2
John Howard	1
Simon Scott	1
John Cable	1
William Symonds	2
John Ashly	1
Jonas Parker	1

St John Maddermarket
[continued]

Robert Spooner	1
William Calfe	1
William Aldred	2
John Potter	1
Roger Hill	2
James Horn	1
John Harn	1
Michael Croch	2
Thomas Smyth	1
John Kinge	1
Nicholas Locke	2
John Setlaw	1
widow Hare	1
widow Smyth	2
widow [?Nor]get	1
Robert Douyton	1
Robert Girlinge	2
Alice Tucke	1
Francis Allen	1
widow Maththas	1
John Sparke	1
Nathaniel Loyse	2
widow Bowman	1
Robert Huchison	1
goodman Mony	1

[33 Names]

E 179/338, f.23

St John Timberhill

2 Mar 1670/1

widow Elmor
Elizabeth Buddifant
James Butler
John Crew
John Phebe
Christopher Browne, sen.
Robert Falthorpe
widow Hunn
Peter Hurne

St John Timberhill [continued]

Robert Greenwood
widow Buckhowse
John Hunn
Mildred Salmon
Peter Hemblin
William Webster
Elizabeth Canham
widow Lancaster
John Suttell
Christopher Browne
Robert Middleton
Henry Bencelee
William Lovedy
goodman Bishopp
Thomas Ellis
widow Demay
Thomas Draper
Elizabeth Crawley
Elizabeth Cady
Thomas Spooner
Richard Gedge
widow Gilmer
Francis More
Alice Fletcher
Peter Herne
John Ransom, tailor
John Blancher
Elizabeth Trollop
Daniel Barny
widow Hanby
Philip Hicklin
widow Wettman
Peter Reason
John Hawes
   & Christopher Hatton
William Bayes
Matthew Timms
William Rutter
Oliver Smith
widow Moore
Arthur Durrant
Susan Berry
Robert Wiggett
widow Adkins

St John Timberhill [continued]

Alice Dolton
Lancelot Allen
John Scott
James Carr
Elizabeth Durrant
Matthew Flattman
William Row
John Davis
John Gilbert
John Sugar
William Allen
Winifred Brettingham
Adam Carr
John Capell
William Hye
John Stimpson
widow Ashly
widow Watts
Richard Loods
Isaac Moises
old Pye
widow Tilny
John Moore
Hugh Perriman
Henry Carver
Henry Simonts
Joseph Bullen
Ann Bell
Peter Hart
Joshua Gray
William Cofer

[84 Names]

E 179/337, f.9

St John Timberhill

[blank 1671 or ?early 1672]

widow Ellner	1
James Buttler	1
John Crew	2
John Phebe	1

St John Timberhill [continued]

Christopher Brow	2
Robert Fellthorp	2
widow Hun	1
Peter Hun	1
... Backhouse	1
John Hunn	1
William Webster	2
Peter Hambling	2
Elizabeth Cannum	1
widow Lancaster	1
John Settell	1
Robert Medleton	2
Henry Bensyn	2
William Loveday	1
good Bishopp	1
Thomas Elles	2
Michael Barker	1
widow Demey	1
widow Tillney	1
John More	1
widow Watts	1
Hugh Pedemont	1
Joseph Bullen	1
Henry Pirple	1
old Cutter	1
widow Buddefant	2
Christopher Brown	1
William Thirkittle	2
Robert Fuller	1
John Crome	1
Thomas Draper	2
John Crawley	1
Elizabeth Cady	2
Richard Gadge	1
Thomas Sponer	1
widow Gillmer	2
Francis More	1
Alice Flecher	1
Peter Herne	1
John Ransom	1
John Blancher	1
Elizabeth Trollup	1
widow Barny	1
widow Henby	1

St John Timberhill [continued]

... Hickling	1
widow Wettman	1
Peter Reson	2
John Hawes	2
Christopher Hatton	1
William Bayes	1
Matthew Times	2
William Rutter	1
Oliver Smith	1
Stephen Barns	1
widow Ca[?mpling]	2
Ann Bell	1
William Cofer	2
William Watts	1
Philip Murrell	1
George Burton	1
William Barnard	2
John Harding	2
Benjamin Rise	1
widow More	2
Arthur Durrent	1
Susan Berry	2
Robert Wiggate	1
John Heymes	1
Alice Dalton	1
Lancelot Allen	1
John Scot	1
James Car	1
Elizabeth Durrent	1
Matthew Flattman	1
William Row	1
John Davis	1
John Gillbart	1
John Suger	1
William Allen	1
Winifred Brettingam	1
Adam Car	1
Robert Smith	1
Edward Capell	1
William Heye	1
John Stimpson	1
widow Ashley	1
widow Watts	2
Richard Loads	2

St John Timberhill [continued]

Isaac Moyes	2
old Pye	2
Henry Simonds	1
Peter Hart	2
Joseph ...	2
Matthew Tims	1
Robert Royse	1
Rose Duckit	1
Thomas Smith	2

[101 Names]

E 179/336, f.54

St John Timberhill

10 Feb 1672/3

Nicholas Gosse
Matthew Times
William Bayes
Philip Hicling
James Whetman
James Gogels
Daniel Barney
Elizabeth Sudly
James Wats
Sarah Asten
William Dussten
Samuel Ogden
... Gilmer
Joseph H...
Peter Hart
Joseph Bullen
Joshua Gray
John Goslen
Roger Siser
Jane Crew
Thomas Woodrow
Susan Lancaster
John Settle
Christopher Brown
James Vickers
Peter Ha[?mbling]

St John Timberhill [continued]

John Webster
Elizabeth Cannom
Samuel Stro...er
John Hun
Ann Backhouse
Michael Barker
Mildred Samon
Robert Grenewood
Robert Midleton
Sarah More
Arthur Durrant
William Berney
John Baly
... Thirtikle
James Car
Philip Morrold
William Row
John Dawes
Thomas Scot
Edward Cossey
John Gilbird
Elizabeth Wats
John Sugar
Stephen Randall
Roger Veiens
Alice Tittelow
Henry Purple
Edward Capell
John Stimson
Margaret Lashly
James Butler
Robert Phillips
William Wats
Christopher Cuttings
Isaac Moyses
Nicholas Rouse
Richard Rodes
William High
goody Titthelow
Ann Ransum
William Bisshopp
Thomas Ellis
Henry Bensley
Robert Smith

St John Timberhill [continued] E 179/336, f.55

John ...
Robert Saberton
Thomas Scot
Elizabeth Cady
Thomas Draper
Richard Crowly
Thomas Smith
Richard Gedge
Thomas ...
Elizabeth Buddifunt
John Feby
John ...
Alice Fletcher
Francis More
Margaret ...
William ...
Christopher Browne
John Blancher
Edmund Felsted
widow Trolley
Christopher Hatten
William Plantin
Oliver Smith
Stephen Randall
John Crew
Matthew Sall
William Coster
Thomas Booth
Thomas ...
George Barlowe
Susan Sanders
William Rutter
Robert Barnard
widow Tilleny
John Crow
Henry ...
Joseph Bullen
old Cutter
... Wats

[109 Names]

St John Timberhill

21 Jan 1673/4

Nicholas Goss	2
Matthew Timms	2
William Bays	1
Stephen Randell	2
Philip Hicklinge	2
widow Cokettman	1
Sarah Austines	1
James Goggles	1
widow Thurston	1
Thomas Rounse	1
Daniel Barny	1
Samuel Ogden	1
William Dusten	1
Sarah Gilmer	2
Joseph Bullen	2
Joshua Gray	2
Roger Syser	1
Thomas Woodrow	1
Susan Lancaster	2
Christopher Browne, jun.	1
James Vicars	2
Peter Herne	2
John Gosfen	1
John Webster	1
Michael Barker	1
Elizabeth Canham	2
goodman Strowger	2
John Hunn	2
old Thirtrekle	1
Ann Backhowse	1
widow Salmon	1
Robert Greenwood	2
Robert Middleton	2
John Sugar	1
Sarah More	1
Arthur Durrant	1
William Barny	1
John Baly	2
James Carr	1
William Row	1

St John Timberhill [continued]

John Dawes	1
Philip Murrell	1
Thomas Scott	2
Edward Edfox	1
John Gilbert	1
Roger Siser	1
John Settle	2
Margaret Ashly	1
Christopher Eaton	1
Roger Vines	2
goodman Whittmer	2
Alice Titlo	1
Edward Pecall	2
old Stimpson	2
widow Trolley	1
William Plantine	1
John Crew	1
William Coster	1
Christopher Browne, sen.	2
George Burton	1
Susan Sanders	2
good Ellis	1
widow Tilny	1
widow Camplin	1
Isaac Moyses	2
James Pa...ent	1
Richard Gedge	1
John Hill	1
widow More	1
William Shinkfeild	2
widow Heigham	1
John Hawes	2
widow Fletcher	1
William Rutter	2
Thomas Booth	2
James Butler	2
William Wats	2
goodman Draper	1
widow Dixson	1
widow Cady	1
John Scott	1
John Phelinge	1
widow Hunn	1
Peter Hart	1

St John Timberhill [continued]

goodman Coster	2
Matthew Tilny	2
widow Dike	1
Philip Murrell	1
widow Camplin	1
Edward Cossy	1
goodman Dangerfe...	1
Richard Stimpson	1
James Gotto	1
Richard Loads	1
William Hye	1
old Bishopp	1
good Ranson	1
goodman Ellis	1
Thomas Scott	1
Henry Bensly	1
Richard Sabberton	1
John Blansher	2
William Allen	2
Peter Carsy	1
Matthew Saule	1
Thomas Browne	2
John Barny	1

[107 Names]

E 179/338, f.24

St Julian

16 Mar 1670/1

Samuel Rust
James Harper
widow Warterlin
widow Bassome
widow Bybrest
widow Massem
Peter Chapman
Thomas Reedder
widow Saymes
widow Cooke
Robert Pestell
widow Steward

St Julian [continued]

Nicholas Willsonne
James Hempinstall
Samuel Morteme
widow Hoth
widow Willins
widow Phillips
widow Harrisonne
widow Earlle
Richard Bowman
John Wissitter
Isaac Battes
Charles Linsey
Peter Harper
Richard Parritt
Edmund Kipping
Richard Dallesonne
John Burrell
Richard Cutter
William Milles
John Cristen, sen.
Frances Asstine
Benjamin Paggett
William Sherwood
William Norten
Simon Skarfe
William Reed
widow Davy
widow Gubs
Christopher Horne
widow Thacker
widow Houchin
Henry Brome
Walter Millem
Thomas Smith
widow Garrett
widow Harper
John Hayhem
William Blisse
James Larwood
Joel Thobald
George Yungs
Elizabeth Stimsonne
James Kipping
Robert Tyce

St Julian [continued]

John Sinderland
John Cristen, jun.
John Holland
Henry Wright
Thomas Newby
Thomas Nethersole
Thomas Ashmenall
widow Sabberton
Robert Turner
Owen Barlow
Thomas Salter
Thomas Ambrook
widow Suffild
John Burton
William Summers
Frances Clarke
James Clarke
Edmund Gosling
James Bowser
William Hamment
John Woodgard
William Astinne
James Cotham
Henry Houwling
Ann Collinton
Thomas Pilkerton
Frances Deane
Robert Collinton
John Pearce
Frances Tyssum
Thomas Mony
George Nurss
William Gybert
Thomas Cotten
William Symonds
Daniel Gray
Edmund Nockoulds
Benjamin Thurkettell
Robert Phillips

[95 Names]

E 179/336, f.56

St Julian

12 Apr 1672

Samuel Rust
James Harper
widow Waterlin
widow Cock
William Hamant
Isaac Beattes
Nicholas Wilson
widow Wiseter
Edward Nockols
widow ...
Robert Turner
Robert Phillips
James Hepenstel
William Giber
Richard Parret
Charles Lensey
Peter Harper
John Burill
Richard Cuter
Frances Asten
William Shearwood
Robert Pestell
Peter Chapman
William Norten
Simon Scarf
Daniel Gray
William Reade
Richard Dalesen
Christopher Herne
Henry Brum
widow Thacker
widow Harper
widow Brinfeter
George Nurse
Walter Miller
James Ruster
widow Hareson
Thomas Smith
John Hayam
Thomas Tayler

St Julian [continued]

William Simonds
widow Christon
Richard Boman
William Blise
James Larode
widow Masham
Joel Thobald
... Bastmen
Thomas Cotton
George Yonges
James Kiping
Benjamin Thircitell
John Senderland
widow Somes
widow Willings
John Holland
Samuel Mortema
widow Earle
Robert Tith
Thomas Ashmenal
widow Stimson
widow Davie
William Sumers
William Gubbs
John Christan, jun.
widow Sufell
Frances Clarke
James Clarke
Richard Mosse
widow Bibrest
John Woodgard
John Reeder
William Asen
Thomas Sallter
widow Fillips
Henry Wright
Thomas Newbe
John Burten
Thomas Ambruck
William Mills
Frances Denney
Mary Pagget
Robert Colenton
John Parsey

St Julian [continued]

Owen Barley
Frances Tysum
Thomas Muney
Edmund Goslen
Thomas Wethersett

[89 Names]

E 179/336, f.57

St Julian

10 Sep 1672

Edmund Larwood
Henry Carr
Richard Parrett
goodwife Jaques
Joseph Page
John Perce
Edmund Knights
Francis Deane
widow Watterin
Richard Bonne
Robert Pestell
Christopher Chace
Isaac Bates
Ann Collington
Richard Moss
James Hempinstall
Jonathan Pilkinton
Thomas Taylour
Robert Turner
Robert Phillips
William Austine
James Cotham
Ann Breviter
Joseph Teball
George Young
Owen Barley
Samuel Bootey
Thomas Ambroock
George Nurss
Robert Rant

St Julian [continued]

widow Thacker
widow Massam
Jonas Cole
Thomas Nethersole
John Broome
widow Saymes
John Sinderland
Edmund Nockolls
goodman Rush
Walter Mylom
widow Harrison
John Woodyard
widow Christian
Richard Bowman
widow Houchen
Henry Broome
Samuel Mortimer
widow Moore
widow Earle
Henry Gardiner
Robert Tyce
William Summers
widow Saberton
Thomas Cotwinn
Thomas Symonds
Nicholas Wilsonn
widow Leake
John Tills
Christopher Horn
widow Jubbs
widow Davy
Daniel Gray
widow Christian
Joseph Scarffe
William Read
John Holland
John Ostler
Catherine Willins
Ann Bybress
widow Steward
Thomas Cock
Edward Kippinn
Thomas Eddiman
Thomas Salter

St Julian [continued]

widow Phillips
Henry Wright
Thomas Newby
widow Suffield
John Burton
William Sherwood
Thomas Ashminall
Francis Austine
Benjamin Paggit
William Myles
James Barlie
Christopher Tooley
Thomas Hoath
William Hammont

[88 Names]

E 179/336, f.58

St Julian

14 Mar 1673/4

Thomas Taylour	1
Robert Turner	1
Philip Hembling	2
Robert Witherley	1
Isaac Bates	1
John Nunn	1
James Hempinstall	2
George Young	1
... Awbree	
Joel Theoball	1
Robert Williams	2
Thomas Spanton	1
Thomas Hakeney	1
John Cinderland	2
William Austine	1
widow Christian	1
Thomas Cotwinn	2
widow Saberton	1
William Hammond	1
Robert Phillips	2
widow Breviter	1

St Julian [continued]

Edmund Nockolls	2
Thomas Nethersole	1
widow Harlstone	1
Henry Broome	2
Robert Tyce	2
Samuel Mortimer	1
John Tills	2
Thomas Thurlow	1
widow Thacker	1
Thomas Davey	2
Richard Parrett	1
William Read	1
Thomas Eager	2
John Burton	2
William Sherwood, jun.	1
Thomas Newbey	2
Benjamin Padgett	1
Francis Austine	1
James Barlow	2
John Ostler	1
John Holland	2
Robert Sherwood	1
Henry Wright	2
Nicholas Wilsonn	1
Thomas Saulter	2
widow Phillips	1
William Manseur	2
Joseph Scarfe	1
Samuel Bunn	2
Thomas Hager	2

[51 Names]

E 179/338, f.25

St Lawrence

3 Apr 1671

Edmund True
Jeremiah King
Matthew Creslett
Henry Resing
Peter Paddin

St Lawrence [continued]

John Leeyes
Francis Grime
Elizabeth Frary
John Banister
Abraham Fassett
William Jackson
John Bucknam
Alice Scarfe
Nicholas Aldrige
Thomasine Carr
Thomas Ellett
Grizell Garrod
Thomas Crunn
widow Overing
Robert Copeman
Richard Adams
Margaret Morley
Richard Cock
Ann Gold
Susan Cookow
Nicholas Scott
Thomas Youngs
John Mills
John Bullingham
Mary Goldsmith
Robert Creeke
Richard Adams
John Carr
widow Powell
Thomas Kid
Peter Fideman
John Bowell
Thomas Crane
Susan Cookow
William Robinson
John Stannaway
Lawrence Vestree
Joseph Danee
William Webster
James Verdree
James Townson, sen.
James Townson, jun.
Matthew Bradford
James Wright

St Lawrence [continued]

Richard Lessingham
Isaac Loyce
James Madlee
John Hardiman
Richard Vinsent
Richard Cridge
widow Smith
Samuel Milles
Henry Hott
Thomas Shacklock
John Titelow
William Rose
Henry Ford

[62 Names]

E 179/337, f.10

St Lawrence

18 Mar [blank ?1671/2]

John Bucckenam
William Jaxon
widow Aldrige
Edward Blacke
widow Brooke
Robin Copeman
Richard Addams
John Stiles
William Rose
widow Cookeo
Thomas Youngs
Robert Goldsmith
Lawrence Say
widow Violl
John Carr
Rebecca Poul
William Saffrey
Thomas Kyt
widow Overing
Edward Dauson
John Bower
Peter Fideman

69

St Lawrence [continued]

Thomas Harridens
Thomas Mottley
Robert Crake
widow Brouster
Peter Head
Henry Hott
Nathaniel Cobbe
Peter Pattin
Samuel Miles
Thomas Spenser
John Davy
widow Lambert
widow Carr
good Ansell
widow Lungly
Richard Lesingham
Abraham Aloys, sen.
Isaac Aloys, jun.
John Davy
Abraham Aloys
John Loys
Thomas Shaklock
Robert Barton
Abraham Pelo
Thomas Crane
John Pelo
Robert Parker
Edmund Buddefant
William Gilbert
Edmund Cooke
Benjamin Danniell
Joseph Sheringham
John Smyth
John Rochister
Jeremiah Mones
Alice Barlo
John Rous
widow Farweather
William Rous
widow Clake
John Hosbone
Peter Dowell
William Benn
John Robeson

St Lawrence [continued]

William Wix
John Stannard
widow Smith
William White
Thomas Hickling
Lancelot Duckett
Thomas Earle
Richard Woods
Henry Cely
Isaac Cony
John Bannister
goodman Grime
John Colls
Henry Fords
John Rust
goodman Bowman
Joseph Davy
goodman Pully
Jeremiah Alouys
goody Gaze
Oliver Febe
John Hademan
Matthew Bradfer
James Townsan, sen.
James Towsan, jun.
Thomas Shinck
James Whright
Thomas Kinckson
Robert Dowson
goody Turner, widow
Thomas Fuller
Richard Safry
Christopher Lesingham
Charles Emperour
Thomas Child
goody Man

[102 Names]

E 179/336, f.59

St Lawrence

22 Jan 1672/3

John Buckingham
William Hagon
John Davie
widow Alldrge
widow Lambert
Edward Bloye
widow Carre
widow Brook
widow Ansell
widow Lopman
widow Langley
Richard Adhams
John Styles
William Rouse
Richard Leasingham
widow Cooke
Abraham Aloyse, sen.
Thomas Youngs
Isaac Aloye, jun.
Robert Gouldsmith
Lawrence Say
John Deytey
widow Viall
John Carre
Rebecca Poule
Abraham Aloyse
widow Savory
John Aloye
Thomas Hytt
widow Overing
Edward Dawson
John Bower
Peter Fideman
Thomas Staridens
Thomas Mottley
Robert Clarke
widow Brewster
Peter Head
Henry Hortt
Nathaniel Cob[?be]

St Lawrence [continued]

Peter Patter
Samuel Myles
Thomas Spencer
Thomas Shakloke
Robert Barton
Abraham Pelo
Robert Parker
Edmund Budefunt
William Gyllbert
Edmund Cooke
Benjamin Danell
Joseph Sheringham
John Smith
John Roschester
Jeremy Mines
Alice Barlo
John Rouse
widow Fayther
William ...ouse
widow Earle
John Ossborne
Peter Dewell
William Crane
John Robrson
William Wix
John Stannard
widow Smith
William White
Thomas Hickling
Lancelot Durkett
Thomas Earle
Richard Woods
Henry Seeley
Isaac Tonny
John Banister
Richard Grime
John Colls
Henry Fords
John Rust
John Burman
Joseph Datte
goodman Pally
goodman Gay
Oliver Febey

St Lawrence [continued]

John Hadman
Matthew Bradfer
James Thompson, sen.
James Thompson, jun.
Thomas Smith
James Wright
Thomas Kinson
Robert Dewson
widow Turner
Thomas Fuller
Richard Saviory
Christopher Sheringham
widow Emperor
Thomas Child
widow Man
John Cole

[100 Names]

E 179/336, f.60

St Lawrence

23 Mar 1673/4

John Buckingham	1
widow Hagon	1
John Davey	1
widow Lambart	1
Edward Bloy	1
widow Carre	1
widow Brooke	1
widow Hansell	1
widow Lopman	1
widow Langley	1
Richard Adams	1
Robert Copman	2
William Rowse	1
Richard Lesingham	1
widow Cookow	1
Abraham Aloyc, sen.	1
Robert Goldsmith	1
widow Ovring	2
Isaac Aloyc, jun.	1

St Lawrence [continued]

Lawrence Say	1
John Datey	1
widow Voyell	1
John Carey	1
Richard Powle	1
William Jackson	2
widow Davey	1
John Aloyc	1
Thomas Huit	1
widow Guing	1
Edward Dewsing	1
John Bowers	1
Peter Fideman	1
Thomas Haridens	1
Robert Creal	1
widow Brewster	1
Peter Head	1
Matthew Cob	2
Peter Pating	1
Henry Ford	1
Thomas Spenser	2
Thomas Shacklock	1
Robert Bartonn	1
Abraham Pelow, sen.	1
Robert Parker	1
Edmund Budifant	1
William Gilbart	1
Edmund Cookoe	1
Benjamin Danyell	1
Joseph Sheringam	1
Robert Carle	2
John Rochister	1
Jeremy Munes	1
Alice Barlow	1
John Rowse	1
widow Farwether	1
William Rowse	1
Peter Duwill	1
William Crane	1
John Robrtson	1
John Stanard	1
widow Smith	1
William Whit	1
Thomas Hickling	1

St Lawrence [continued]

E 179/338, f.26

Thomas Earle	1
Richard Wods	1
Henry Seley	1
Isaac Tuney	1
John Banister	1
Abraham Fasit	2
John Rust	1
John Coles	1
John Burman	1
John Duete	1
good Puley	1
good Jay	1
Oliver Phebey	1
John Hardeman	1
Matthew Bradford	1
old Dowsing	1
James Wright	1
Thomas Kengston	1
Robert Dowsing	1
widow Turner	1
Thomas Fuler	1
Richard Saverey	1
Christian Sheringam	2
Charles Empror	1
Thomas Child	1
widow Man	1
John Hadman	1
Ambrose Ansell	2
Arthur Powl	1
good Cotten	1
good Harper	1
widow Kid	1
good Critwod	1
Ellen Hamand	1
widow Bunn	1
Thomas Man	1
Robert Man	1
Clement Leman	1
old Chroch	1
John Wattson	2

[103 Names]

St Margaret

[undated ?early 1671]

Robert Ward
Francis Cutball
Mar... Richardson
Thomas Ebbets
Bay Blanch
Michael Depree
John Gooch
William Cutbert
William Potter
Elizabeth Bates
Edward Vines
Elizabeth Leverington
John Jarvis
widow Jay
Jeremy ...ins
Thomas Womacke
Richard Brisely
Edmund Randall
Edmund Adams
Clement Tillyard
Thomas Cuxon
widow Smith
Ann Brett
Ann Welton
William Jarvis
Henry Whall
widow Becke
Henry Caly
Mary Brand
Thomas Simonds
Philip Tylyard
Robert Rose
Anthony Purkins
Peter Cobb
Ann Tylyard
John Taylor
John Harrison
Matthew Carr
Joseph Cutlocke
William Horne

St Margaret [continued]

... Stroulger
widow Parker
Stephen Brees
William Tubby
Mary Keely
Lettice Linsey
Peregrine Ransome
Charles Levoyge
widow Urstleton
Isaac Loyce
widow Clarke
Nathaniel Stanart
Peter Head
John Burridge
Richard Tunny
widow Bates
widow Robinson
William Hargrave
William Margery
John ...
... Foster
Susan Hubbert
Daniel Parke
Oliver Phoebe
goodman Busby
goodwife Youngs
goodman Mann
widow Davy
Robert Hadman
Thomas Youngs
James Pettet
Mark Utbert
Thomas Bass
Margaret Fisher
James Hubbert
Thomas Booty
widow Juby
William Burgess
Edward Cliffton
Abraham Clarke
John Geddney
Robert Man
Henry Broughton
Ann Brett

St Margaret [continued]

Thomas Broughton
goodman Lewis
Bernard Utbert

[87 Names]

E 179/337, f.11

St Margaret

18 Mar [blank ?1671/2]

John Harrison
John Tayler
widow Tillyard
widow Ellemes
Thomas Strowger
widow Smith
widow Uftone
William Garvis
Henry Whalle
Henry Caley
widow Becke
Henry Stillyard
John Harriwine
Charles Emmirson
William Cutbarde
widow Gallfe
Edward Wines
John Garvis
John Gooche
Michael Depre
widow Levetone
Joseph Boulldine
Thomas Broutone
Henry Brouton
widow Pelle
widow Brote
William Burges
Edmund Clefine
John Godney
Mark Utburd
Bernard Utbarde
widow Stone

St Margaret [continued]

John Frosbrocke
widow Wenne
widow Cutball
widow Larwod
Thomas Ebbets
Richard Tanney
William Horne
widow Barlowe
John Tunell
Stephen Brese
William Tubbine
widow Linsey
Peregrine Ransum
Charles Lewgrave
Richard Tuney
widow Robison
Nicholas Fisher
widow ...
Daniel Clarke
goodman ...ley
William Parker
widow Leane
Richard Tuney
Isaac Heade
John Pettet
William Peavey
Robert Rose
Clement Styllyard
Richard Brisley
Edmund Addames
John Warrent
Daniel Dalle
Frances Rudrum
Abraham Rickey
widow Bates
Sarah Puckell
Thomas Bayes
John Money
Thomas Boutey
Peter Prime
Anthony Purkines
Andrew Prime
Edward Watson
John Linsey

St Margaret [continued]

Abraham Clarke
Thomas Clarke
Thomas Chapline
widow Browne
Bay Bllanch
Richard Pey
John Harris
James Parke
James Earlle
Isaac Aloyes
William Parker
Martin Baxter
Nathaniel Stanwod
Rowland Roberson
Richard Sandell

[91 Names]

E 179/336, f.61

St Margaret

18 Mar 1673/4

Thomas King	2
widow Daue	1
James Earle	2
Daniel Dale	1
Richard Cooper	1
widow Tayler	1
widow Stilyard	1
Clement Stilyard	2
Michael Pree	2
widow Gaff	1
Martin Baxter	2
widow Cutboll	1
Thomas Tunny	2
Richard Brinsley	2
John Pettet	1
widow Aylms	1
widow Leveriton	1
John Goffe	2
Thomas Strowger	1
John Tailer	1

St Margaret [continued]

Henry Cliffun	1
widow Brougton	1
widow Horne	1
John Worrant	2
Robert Wright	1
John Nobs	2
William Burgis	1
William Bouldin	1
John Lince	1
widow Barlo	1
William Parker	1
Thomas Browton	2
Henry Cale	2
Francis Dinn	2
widow Brett	2
William Loads	2
Bernard Utber	2
James Saftly	2
widow Linse	2
William Jarvis	2
Clement Stalyard	2
Thomas Bootee	2
widow Hallow	2
widow Bates	2
widow Gooch	2
Joseph Miles	2
Mark Utberd	2
Edmund Addams	2
Charles Emerson	2
widow Usselton	2
Henry Whall	2
Henry Whalleron	2
John Tuck	1
Thomas Cushin	2
widow Luce	1
Edmund Vines	1
widow Smith	1
Thomas Bates	2
Robert Roase	1
Robert Boldin	1
James Jarmey	2
Charles Lewgrave	2
Isaac Head	2
Francis Barlow	2

St Margaret [continued]

Peter Prime	1
Thomas Strowger	1
Edmund A[?dam]es	2
Francis Blanch	1
Bernard Utbert	2
Richard Tunny	1
widow Beake	1
William Briggs	2
Robert Robson	2
John Harrise	1
Abraham Clarke	1
widow Browne	1

[76 Names]

E 179/338, f.27

St Martin at Oak

8 Mar 1670/1

Robert Spenser
Anthony Kett
John Porter
Edmund Jafferis
Anthony Overton
John Huson
William Blogg
Francis Gittins
Thomas Jewson
James Munford
Elizabeth Burgar
widow Kett
widow Harper
Thomas Hyndes
widow Cadie
Richard Lawes
Nicholas Harridens
widow Downing
Elizabeth Wilkin
widow Reede
Thomas Ardnold
Robert Elvin
John Newport

St Martin at Oak [continued]

old Demow
widow Tiptoe
Daniel Dremow
widow Taylor
Francis Norman
John Arnald
John Rogers
Elizabeth Willkins
James Burton
William Wright
Abraham Browne
Richard Cocke
Thomas Watts
Thomas Dowe
Abraham Bock
Edmund Lickerell
widow Browne
John Theoderell
Samuel Warde
Thomas Stanton
Samuel March
Thomas Sparkell
Jeremiah King
Richard Cocke
widow Hewett
Thomas Waker
Thomas Wister
Paul Deme
Peter Woolfe
Nicholas Rose
John Chambers
Richard Akers
Robert Cooke
John Tompson
Anthony Wale
Robert Beecroft
Henry Wood
John Nockalls
Margaret Ameis
William Ivery
Henry Chapman
Mary Cutting
widow Woolfe
Thomas Woods

St Martin at Oak [continued]

John Bucknam
George Robbins
William Coulsell
William Fox
William Parr
Robert Wymer
Thomas Dawson
Robert Freez
Thomas Wood
Thomas Ruston
Thomas Beggett
William Nockalls
Daniel Spalding
George Thick
Thomas Church
John Andrews & Mills
widow Say
Richard Million
John Jonsons
Thomas Simson
John Deeringe
John Cumbie
Robert King
Peter Wilson
John Numon
John Tredaway
John Sutton
John Bartrum
widow Key
Hugh Brimer
Thomas Iverson
William Goultknop
Edmund Carter
John Burage
widow Mayhew
John Hutchinson
Stephen Becroft
Francis Burrage
James Russell
widow Beecroft
Robert Hall
Samuel Burne
George Warrington

St Martin at Oak [continued]   [154 Names]

widow Hopkins
widow Taylor
James Woolferton
John Overin
Ursula Browne
Joseph Howes
James Bernard
Peter Fever
Francis Wild
William Pamer
Thomas Fuller
Robert Towell
Henry Bartrum
Francis Barker
Abraham Deremon
Thomas Norford
Andrew Rudrum
George Allerd
widow Hipper
Robert Rudrum
widow Andrews
Hugh Woods
Mary Smith
Richard Swetman
Thomas Mann
widow Huitt
Robert Robinson
James Peecok
John Franke
Philip James
Robert Andrews
George Gray
Martin Fox
Henry Waker
Richard Solman
John Moore
Ursula Waters
Richard Barret
Jeremy Clapison
William Paulden
widow Woods
John Waters
Francis Scott

E 179/336, f.62

St Martin at Oak

8 May 1672

William Everits
John Ling
widow Hood
widow Low
widow Beans
William Fickling
Thomas Barny
widow Poynter
John Tredwell
William Say
widow Hone
Samuel Barny
widow Farrow
Sarah Mayhew
Robert Grieve
Daniel Spolding
Thomas Shinns
Thomas Wisseter
Robert Spenser
William Blogg
Frances Giddins
Henry Hewitt
John Jaquis
John Dawsy
widow Hewett
Thomas Tomson
goody Parish
John Waters
Edmund Pickrell
Matthew Buttle
Thomas Rouland
Thomas Norfur
Peter Patten
Richard Sammon
William Loake
George Gray
Thomas Man
John Frank

St Martin at Oak [continued]

Philip James
Charles Long
Nicholas Haridence
Richard Lawes
John More
Robert Roberson
Edmund Brett
Robert Cook
John Sutton
James Peakock
Richard Swetman
Nicholas Back
Henry Woods
Thomas Norfor
widow Hipper
Robert Rudderum
John Horshor
widow Kucow
James Barnard
Abraham Derymon
Thomas Fuller
Edmund Ward
Henry Bathrum
Robert Towell
Robert Rungry
John Wignall
Hugh Thorne
Peter Feaver
Thomas Balls
James Claxton
widow Wilkeson
Sarah Hopkins
Joseph Hone
William Palmer
Nicholas White
Frances Wild
John Crane
John Worrinton
John Blundew
Edmund Carter
James Woollbread
widow Cooke
widow Hopkins
James Russels

St Martin at Oak [continued]

Isaac Saull
Henry Hodges
John Overing
John Bonerd
John Pooly
Anthony Overton
Edmund Jeffries
widow Porter
Thomas Waters
widow Wilde
widow Downing
widow Burgor
widow Harper
John Buckinham
William Wright
Thomas Ling
Anthony Kitt
Daniel Mow
John Newport
Robert Elvin
Thomas Arnold
Frances Norman
John Rodgers
Betty Wilkeson
widow Tipto
Erasmus Goldsmith
Ralph Blogg
John Hartt
James Burton
Richard Cock
Daniel Waters
widow Dowe
Abraham Bock
widow Brown
Prudence Horne
John Theorderick
Thomas Stanton
Samuel March
Philip Greengoll
John Cottingam
John Cock
David Cocke
Daniel Wilson
Peter Woolf

St Martin at Oak [continued]

Frances Ring
Paul Demee
John Tomson
Robert Androws
John Chambers
Thomas Spitt
widow Woolf
George Robinson
Thomas Spenser
Anthony Male
widow Becraft
Frances Basye
widow Acurs
widow Walker
Michael Conlea
Henry Woods
Thomas Fox
John Sherwood
Robert Barlard
Thomas Hell
Thomas Wilkeson
Thomas Woods
Daniel Parker
Charles Pooly
William Parr
widow Dayne
William Cooper
Simon Skott
widow Barnfather
Thomas Russon
Thomas Coulsie
Thomas Church
John Johnsons
Robert Million
George Fick
John Cumbyn
Frances Dun
Thomas Iverson
John Numan
Frances Barker
Peter Willson
Richard Rivins
John Sutton
Thomas Elknott

St Martin at Oak [continued]

widow Cott
Hugh Brimer
John Brimmer
widow Key
widow Brown
Peter Mallitt
John Hammant
widow Tayler
goody Lilderston
John Dearing
goody King
widow Quailles
William Fascitt
widow Woolf
goodman Martell
goodman Gouldknop

[186 Names]

E 179/336, f.63

St Martin at Oak

13 Aug 1672

Robert Spenser
William Bloge
Francis Giddins
Henry Hewit
John Jaques
John Darcy
widow Hewit
Thomas Gempson
goody Parrish
John Waters
Edmund Pickrell
Matthew Bothell
Thomas Rowland
Thomas Norford
Peter Patten
William Loakes
Richard Samman
Thomas Maning
John Franke

St Martin at Oak [continued]

Philip James
widow Long
Nicholas Haridence
Richard Lawes
Robert Roberson
Edmund Breet
Robert Cooke
James Peacock
Richard Swetman
Nicholas Back
Hugh Woods
Thomas Norford
widow Hipper
Robert Rudderham
widow Cookow
James Barnwood
Abraham Dremon
Thomas Fuller
Edward Ward
Henry Batherham
Robert Tovell
Robert Wrongry
John Wiggnall
Hugh Thorn
Peter Feaver
Thomas Bals
James Claxton
widow Wilkerson
Sarah Hopkins
Joseph Hoaney
William Pamer
Michael White
Francis Wild
John Crane
John Warrinton
John Blondow
Edmund Carter
James Woolbread
widow Cooke
widow Hopkins
James Russells
Isaac Saule
Henry Hodges
John Overin

St Martin at Oak [continued]

John Boone
Anthony Overton
Edward Jefferies
John Luson
widow Porter
Thomas Waters
widow Wild
widow Burgar
widow Harper
John Buckenham
Thomas Hines
Anthony Kett
William Wright
Daniel Mow
John Newporte
Robert Elven
goodman Nobs
Francis Norman
John Roggers
Elizabeth Wilkerson
Ambrose Goldsmith
Ralph Blogg
John Kippit
James Burton
Richard Cocke
Daniel Waters
widow Dowe
Prudence Horn
John Theodericke
Thomas Stanton
Samuel March
Philip Greengold
John Cottingham
John Cocke
David Cocke
Daniel Willson
Peter Wolfe
Francis King
Paul Deme
John Tompson
Robert Andrewes
John Chambers
Thomas Speed
widow Wolfe

St Martin at Oak [continued]

George Robinson
Thomas Spenser
Anthony Maill
widow Beecroft
Francis Bacy
widow Acres
widow Walker
Michael Conlea
Henry Woods
Thomas Fox
John Sherwood
Robert Bulward
Thomas Hill
John Wilkerson
Thomas Woods
Daniel Parker
Charles Pooley
William Parr
widow Darcy
William Cooper
Simon Scott
widow Banfather
Thomas Russen
Thomas Coulsea
Thomas Church
John Johnsons
Robert Million
George Ficke
John Comby
Thomas Iverson
John Numan
Francis Barker
Peter Willson
Richard Revins
John Sutten
Thomas Elnott
widow Cott
Hugh Brimmer
John Brimmer
widow Key
widow Browne
John Dearing
William Fassitt
William Everate

St Martin at Oak [continued]

John Thredwell
Sarah Mayhue
Daniel Spolden
Thomas·Wisiter
John Ling
widow Hoode
William Fickler
Thomas Barney
Samuel Barney
goodman Gouldannop
Thomas Man
John Pooley
widow Dowing
Francis Dunn

[165 Names]

E 179/336, f.64

St Martin at Oak

15 Dec 1673

Thomas Jempson	1
John Jauques	1
widow Porter	2
John Dause	1
John Luson	1
Robert Turner	1
Edward Jeffris	2
Daniel Waters	1
William Fassett	1
William Blogg	1
James Bowser	2
widow Hopkins	2
widow Hewit	1
widow Wild	1
Thomas Hines	2
widow Harper	1
widow Burgor	1
Nicholas Back	1
Nicholas Harridence	1
Robert Lewes	2
Daniel Mow	1

St Martin at Oak [continued]

William Wright	2
John Newport	2
Robert Elven	1
Francis Norman	1
widow Cutting	1
widow Downing	1
Peter Woolfe	1
widow Savory	1
John Rogers	2
William Nobbs	2
Erasmus Goldsmith	2
James Burton	1
John Cubit	1
Richard Cock	1
Abraham Bock	2
John Theoderick	1
Ann Giddins	1
widow Browne	1
Anthony Kett	
Charles Greengold	2
John Hubbard	1
Samuel March	2
Davy Cock	1
John Cocke	1
Peter Woolfe	2
John Cottingham	1
Thomas Whisiter	1
Paul Deme	1
Robert Andrewes	1
Thomas Speede	1
goodman Pamer	1
Anthony Mayle	2
Francis Basea	1
widow Beecraft	1
Thomas Spenser	1
Robert Bulward	1
John Sherwood	1
Thomas Fox	1
Thomas Hill	1
Michael Condlea	1
John Wilkerson	2
John Brownson	1
Prudence Horne	1
Thomas Russon	1

St Martin at Oak [continued]

Simon Scott	1
goodman Hilderstone	2
William Cooper	1
Robert Wymer	1
Thomas Woods	2
widow Dauson	1
widow Quaile	1
William Parr	1
goodman Shinkefield	1
Daniel Spaulden	1
Robert Austea	1
Thomas Church	2
George Ficke	1
John Andrewes	1
Richard Million	1
Daniel Millson	1
John Johnsons	1
Thomas Burcham	1
John Cumbey	1
Francis Dunn	1
John Newman	1
Richard Revins	2
John Sutten	1
Thomas Elnot	1
James Waller	1
widow Cott	1
Francis Barker	1
Thomas Iverson	1
widow Browne	1
John Brimmer	1
Hugh Brimmer	1
Peter Willson	1
Michael White	1
Samuel Barney	2
widow Taylor	1
Samuel Whisiter	1
widow Beanes	1
widow Honey	1
William Say	2
goodman Theadaway	1
Thomas Woods	2
Thomas Barney	1
William Ficklen	1
John Chapman	1

St Martin at Oak [continued]

John Ling	1
widow Hood	1
William Shelling	1
John Boone	2
Francis Wild	1
goodman Roberts	2
goodman Hall	1
goodman Fox	1
goodman Goldenop	1
Isaac Sall	1
Sarah Mayhue	1
Luke Smith	1
James Woolbread	2
Edmund Carter	1
John Warrinton	1
Robert Greife	1
widow Crane	1
Joseph Honshea	1
Robert Woolbright	2
John Riches	1
John Crooke	1
Henry Gregory	1
Anthony Overton	2
William Everade	1
Bassinbon Ives	1
Thomas Rowland	1
Thomas Ewell	1
Ephraim Ellis	1
Thomas Green	1
Henry Batteram	1
Robert Towell	1
Robert Wrongrey	1
Edward Ward	1
Thomas Fuller	2
widow Cookco	1
Robert Rudderham	1
widow Mow	1
Thomas Norford	1
widow Hipper	1
James Barnwood	2
Luke Woods	1
John Scott	1
Ambrose Woolbread	2
widow Cooke	1

St Martin at Oak [continued]

Philip James	1
John Franke	1
Robert Cooke	1
Christopher Tommas	2
Henry Greif	1
Thomas Balls	1
Thomas Man	1
Richard Fresin	1
Richard Lawes	2
Robert Bemment	1
widow Willkerson	1
George Gray	1
Richard Sammon	1
Thomas Dunn	1
John Waters	2
Edmund Pickrell	1
Thomas Norford	1
Peter Feaver	1
William Loake	2
Peter Patten	1
John Pooley	2

[174 Names]

E 179/338, f.28

St Martin at Palace [in East Wymer Ward]

23 Mar 1670/1

Mary Harris
Benjamin Goss
John Pomfery
Thomas Browne
Francis Grimes
widow Mason
Thomas Thompson
John Wilde
William Myles
Thomas Tant
widow Brotherhood
Thomas Jary
Charles Dewell

St Martin at Palace [continued]

Thomas Curbey
William Maggs
Daniel Read
widow Fisher
Nicholas Viall
John Breesse
William Trull
Richard Tills
widow Garwood
widow Ward
Richard Wells
John Elvin
George Gay
Samuel Dasson
George Emperor
widow Blyth
Lawrence Whitmore
Thomas Gase
Richard Scot
Stephen Shippe
Nicholas Dix
William Browne
widow Springhall
Thomas Norman
widow Elsegood
Edward Whitmore
widow Wilson
Thomas Bona
John Golden
Ann Dey
Richard Pattinge
Henry Lemend
William Strangleman
John Vincent
widow Melbourne
Edward Shead
Thomas Sheppy
Roger Holmes
widow Deane
Edward Vincent
widow Keniman
William Thrower
John Johnson
widow Gotterson

St Martin at Palace [continued]

George Tant
Titus Fulcher
widow Percivall
Robert Griggs
John Sammon
widow Hill
Henry Weston
Henry Pulham
George Lowes
Margaret Fuller
goodman England
Robert Thompson
Edward Havers
widow Fisher
Arnold Catlyn
Robert Wesson
Alexander Carle
Edmund Downinge
Margaret Thacker
Mary Grey
Robert Howton
Abraham Keniman
Ann Key
William Purdy
Thomas Church
Samuel Clarke
John Jary
widow Scot
widow Norton
Peter Hewitt
Margaret Fuller
goodman Wilde
Barnaby Symmonds

[90 Names]

E 179/338, f.29

St Martin at Palace [in Fyebridge Ward]

23 Mar 1670/1

Thomas Johnson

85

St Martin at Palace [continued]

George Amis
John Fenn
John Taylor
Robert Lyncorne
Mark Eatch
Richard Cupis
Thomas Spink
Thomas Holl
Robert Johnson
Michael Clarke
widow Wilson
widow Shinkfield
Ralph Greene
widow England
Edmund Rant
James Dey
John Scottowe
John Graves
Samuel Hewitt
Thomas Saddler
Amy Key
Nicholas Crowder
James Sowell
widow Beamond
Edward Humphry
Edward Parker or Parkins
George Acres
widow Denney

[29 Names]

E 179/336, f.65

St Martin at Palace

15 Feb 1671/2

Mary Harris
Robert Pulham
John Pomeffery
Frances Grims
widow Miller
Thomas Tomsson
Edward Eason

St Martin at Palace [continued]

William Mils
Thomas Tante
Robert Graves
Thomas Jarie
Charles Dewell
Thomas Curbye
William Maggs
Thomas Church
widow Fisher
Nicholas Viall
John Brees
William Trull
Richard Tills
widow Garwood
widow Ward
Richard Wels
John Elving
George Gaye
Samuel Dayson
Eli Emperer
widow Blyth
Lawrence Wittmore
Thomas Gayse
Richard Scotte
Stephen Sheppie
Nicholas Dixe
widow Springall
Thomas Norman
widow Elsegood
Edward Witmore
widow Willson
Thomas Bonie
John Goulding
Ann Dye
Richard Batting
Henry Lemman
Gregory Pierson
John Vinson
widow Milborne
John Shead
Thomas Shippye
Roger Homls
widow Deane
Edward Vincent

St Martin at Palace [continued]

widow Kineman
William Thrower
John Johnsons
widow Gotterson
George Tant
Titus Fulcher
widow Persivall
Robert Griggs
John Sammon
widow Hill
Henry Weston
Henry Pulham
George Lawes
Margaret Fuller
goodman Ingland
Robert Tomson
Edward Havers
widow Fisher
Bridget Cattlin
Robert Weston
Alexander Carlt
Edmund Downing
Francis Grime
good Giddings
Robert Houghton
Abraham Kineman
Amy Key
William Purdy
George Holl
Edmund Foulger
Samuel Clarke
Benjamin Rix
widow Scott
widow Norton
Peter Huitt
widow Fuller
Edmund Slipper
Richard Gray
Thomas Watson
Thomas Beasly
John Ridland
widow Wheatly
widow More
goody Mickleburrow

St Martin at Palace [continued]

Elizabeth Bristo
William Ingland
William Davy
George Levitt
widow Thurlethorpe
John Bird
John Waybeard
Robert Woolbread
Elizabeth Poule
Humphrey Rant
Mary Basham
Thomas Browne
Margaret Wenn

[108 Names]

E 179/336, f.66

St Martin at Palace

17 July 1672

John Burton
widow Percivall
Thomas Garwood
Benjamin Gosse
John Pomphrey
Francis Grimes
widow Miller
Thomas Tomson
Edward Eason
William Miles
Thomas Tant
Thomas Curby
William Maggs
Nicholas Viall
John Breese
William Trull
Richard Tills
widow Garwood
Richard Wells
John Elvin
George Gay
Samuel Dunson

St Martin at Palace [continued]

Eli Emperor
widow Blith
Lawrence Whittimore
Stephen Shippey
Thomas Norman
Amy Key
Thomas Spinkes
widow Godwell
William Balls
widow Harris
widow Fisher
Richard Gray
Thomas Jary
widow Beles
John Hushoye
Thomas Browne
John Danes
John Smyth
widow Elsegoe
Edward Whittmore
widow Wilson
John Golding
Richard Pattinge
Richard Borman
Henry Lemmond
Gregory Person
John Shead
Thomas Shippey
Roger Holines
widow Deane
John Vincent
Edward Vincent
widow Hineman
widow Thrower
John Johnson
widow Gotterson
George Tant
Titus Fulcher
widow Persivall
Robert Griggs
widow Hill
Henry Weston
Henry Pulham
Margaret Fuller

St Martin at Palace [continued]

Robert Tompson
Bridget Cattlin
Edmund Downing
Edmund Foulger
Samuel Clarke
Benjamin Rix
widow Scott
widow Norton
Edmund Slipper
Richard Gray
John Ridland
widow Wheately
widow More
widow Thirlethorpe
William Ingland
George Levitt
goodwife Mickleburrow
Elizabeth Bristo
widow Mason
Robert Pulham
Thomas Church
Richard Scott
Ann Dye
goodman England
widow Giddings
Peter Hewitt
Thomas Beasely
John Wheybeard
Elizabeth Poule
Mary Basham
Margaret Wenn
Samuel Clarke
Peter Leake
Daniel Read
John Sammon
Edward Havers
Alexander Carle
Thomas Balding
Charles Dovell
John Bird
Thomas West
Robert Gourney
John Whitmyr
Thomas Watson

St Martin at Palace [continued]

Thomas Roose
Catherine Fuller

[112 Names]

E 179/336, f.67

St Martin at Palace

10 May 1674

Benjamin Goss	1
John Pumfrie	1
Francis Grime	1
Thomas Tant	1
Thomas Kirby	1
William Maggs	1
Michael Viall	1
Richard Wells	1
John Elvin	1
Samuel Dawson	2
Eli Emperor	1
Lawrence Whitmore	2
Stephen Shippey	2
Thomas Norman	1
William Balls	2
Richard Gray	1
Robert Whitmore	1
John Goulding	1
Richard Patten	1
Henry Lemmon	1
Gregory Person	1
Thomas Shippey	2
Roger Holmes	1
John Vincent	1
Edward Vincent	1
John Johnson	1
Alexander Carle	1
Charles Dowell	2
Thomas Swatson	1
Thomas Parnell	1
William Curson	1
John Vere	1
Henry Everad	2

St Martin at Palace [continued]

Francis Strangleman	2
Thomas Balding	2
William Thrower	1
goodman Pestell	1
Abraham Kineman	2
Nathaniel Wife	1
Thomas Copling	1
William Salter	1
Joseph Salter	1
William Boecroft	2
Edmund Loveday	1
goodman Raydon	1
John Wild	1
Jonas Seggin	2
Anthony Bacon	1
Andrew Foker	1
George Gay	1
John Ridland	2
widow Barber	1
widow Elsegoe	1
widow Persivall	1
widow Miller	1
widow Garwood	1
widow Blith	2
widow Harris	1
widow Fisher	1
widow Wilson	1
widow Deane	1
widow Kineman	1
widow Sleaman	1
widow Gotterson	2
widow Fulcher	2
widow Hill	1
widow Fuller	1
widow Scott	1
widow Norton	1
widow Wheately	1
widow More	1
widow Clarke	1
widow Thirlethorpe	1
widow Halfeknights	1
widow Mason	1
widow Mickleburrough	2
Bridget Cattling	2

St Martin at Palace [continued]

Mary Basham	1
Margaret Wen	1
Elizabeth Poole	2
widow Fuller	1
widow Tomson	2
John Breese	2
Robert Grix	2
Henry Weston	1
Henry Pulham	1
Thomas Tant, jun.	1
Edmund Downing	2
Edward Foulsir	1
Samuel Clark	1
Benjamin Rix	2
William Ingland	1
George Leavick	1
Robert Pulham	1
Richard Scott	1
goodman Ingland	2
Thomas Beasly	1
John Whybeard	1
Peter Leake	1
John Bird	1
John Whittmore	1
Daniel Read	1
Edward Havers	2
Elizabeth Garnegoe	1
Elizabeth Bristo	1
widow Giddings	1
widow Hickling	2

[107 Names]

E 179/338, f.30

St Mary Coslany

4 Feb 1670/1

James Safely
Roger Youngs
Aaron Brooke
Nicholas Pike
William Harridence

St Mary Coslany [continued]

Robert Uttinge
Edmund Henburrow
Ann Wood
Toby Bensley
John Curby
William Cubitt
Michael Lankhorne
widow Webb
widow Gathercoale
Thomas Buxton
Joseph Curby
widow Wilkenson
widow Rantt
John Umphrey
Robert Springall
Ann Pickerall
Ann Church
Augustine Read
Moses Head
Elizabeth Porter
widow Wharley
Frances Beake
Mary Porter
Ann Eldred
Nicholas Swettman
Martin Land
Robert Watson
Rachel Johnson
widow Munns
Thomas Glavin
Richard Ebbs
widow Miles
William Land
widow Hone
Susan Titter
Judas More
Thomas Loads
Isaac Goss
Thomas Finck
John Cooper
John Richarson
John Mayden
old Kinebrooke
John Brady

St Mary Coslany [continued]

widow Burringham
goodwife Miles
Thomas Cupis
Thomas Wife
widow Brooke
widow Brooke
John Mayden
widow Bartrum
John Bussey
William Carter
John Brady
widow Clarke
Bartholomew Mills
widow Watson
Charles Lacey
Ann Larrowd
widow Key
Daniel Clarke
Edward Coates
John West
widow Ellis
George Kactham
Elizabeth Dade
Daniel Cluse
Frances Coates
Robert Hubeart
Daniel Cluse
Anthony Hipper
widow Thulthorpe
Bridget Deareing
Robert Richerson
Ann Newton
widow Cushin
Robert Huberd
Michael Croplett
William Woolfe
widow Cushin
widow Wattson
Henry Knights
widow Stuff
Thomas Brady
John Atthill
widow Hart
Robert Deacon

St Mary Coslany [continued]

old Riches
Thomas Watters
widow West
widow Titter
widow Hart
goodman Crome
widow Pollerd
Simon Hart
John Mowfree
John Graves
John More
widow Munns
widow Neave
Robert Damm
goodman King
John Armes
John March
John Jempson
Nicholas Chest
widow Butler
widow Miles
William Whight
Ambrose Mallowes
good Cotten
widow Everitt
Abraham Quinten
widow Armes
widow Everitt
widow Stonn
Abraham Mace
Edmund Pillgrum
Richard Stigall
good Beecroft
widow Rookewood
widow Studley
Roger Youngs
John Parker
James Browne
Elizabeth Clippin
William Tills
Robert Tennant
widow Brett
Peter Dale

St Mary Coslany [continued]

John Tills
Frances Green
William Fletcher

[139 Names]

E 179/336, f.68

St Mary Coslany

8 May 1672

widow Gathercole
widow Webb
Michael Lanchorn
Edward Himborow
Tobias Bensly
Robert Uton
widow Woods
John Curby
Nicholas Picke
widow Sowell
William Mayes
Roger Youngs
John Till
widow Cliffen
widow Till
John Wixly
widow Brett
Peter Dale
Richard Stigall
William Flecher
widow Weeds
William Harnese
widow Rookwod
Richard Sparke
John Scot
widow Safley
William Studly
John Parker
Edmund Pilgram
James Browne
widow Haridence
widow Everit

St Mary Coslany [continued]

John Page
widow Nun
widow Armes
Abraham Mace
William Allin
Abraham Quinton
Ambrose Malos
Matthew Miles
John Jemson
Nicholas Chest
John March
widow Buttler
John Doliman
widow Brooke
John Armes
Thomas King
Thomas Geedg
John Graves
Humphrey Neave
Thomas Whiteker
John More
John Crooke
widow Munes
widow Daues
John Morferey
Thomas Crome
widow Polord
Simon Hart
widow Hart
John Sadler
Robert Riches
John Hill
John Titter
William Burges
John Norfor
Thomas Brady
widow Stafe
John Bates
Henry Knits
John Gedge
Robert Dam
George Larrawnce
Robert Hubert
widow Ellis

St Mary Coslany [continued]

Daniel Cluse
Elizabeth Dade
Robert Hubert
widow Kitchum
Francis Coats
Thomas Greene
widow Key
Charles Lacey
Bridget Dearing
widow Watson
Bartholomew Wilis
John Read
widow Clarke
Aaron Brooke
Henry Adoms
John Busell
Thomas Low
William Bartrem
widow Barningham
John Jacks
Margaret Wrench
Thomas Mills
Matthew Freeman
Thomas Wilde
Thomas Cupis
widow Brooke
John Brady
widow Kiningbrook
Abraham Daniell
John Cooper
Thomas Finke
William Carter
John Maiden
John Richis
Sarah ...ling
widow Titter
widow Hone
widow Fuller
widow More
Thomas Loods
Isaac Gose
Richard Tubey
William Lond
John Purdey

St Mary Coslany [continued]

Thomas Glavin
widow Miels
Michael Harison
Richard Ebbs
Martin Lond
widow Witherick
Timothy Gouldknop
Nicholas Swetman
Mary Porter
Richard Lewes
John Sharpin
widow Eldred
Moses Head
Daniel Swetman
Augustine Read
Ann Church
Ann Pickerill
Thomas Brurerwood
John Umpherey
Richard Witom
widow Wharlow
widow Cushing
widow Haridence

[143 Names]

E 179/336, f.69

St Mary Coslany

12 Sep 1672

widow Gathercole
widow Web
Michael Lanckthorn
Edward Himborrow
Toby Bensly
Robert Utton
widow Brooke
John Curby
Richard Puckle
goodman Cubit
Nicholas Picke
William Mayes

St Mary Coslany [continued]

goodman Watson
Francis Greene
Roger Youngs
William Allen
Robert Duncks
John Till
widow Cleffen
widow Till
widow Brett
Peter Dale
Joseph Curby
Richard Stigall
William Fletche
widow Weeds
William Harnes
widow Rookwod
Richard Sparke
John Scot
widow Safly
William Studly
John Parker
Edmund Pilgram
widow Everit
widow Stone
John Page
widow Nun
widow Armes
Abraham Mace
Abraham Quinton
James Browne
Ambrose Mallos
good Dollaman
Matthew Miles
John Jemson
Nicholas Chist
John March
widow Buttler
John Armes
Thomas Gedg
Thomas King
widow Hart
Humphrey Neve
Thomas Whitaker
widow Hone

St Mary Coslany [continued]

John More
widow Dawes
Daniel Swetman
widow Muns
John Mofery
Thomas Crome
widow Pollard
Simon Hart
John Sadler
John Hill
John Titter
William Burges
William Colman
John Norfor
Thomas Bradey
John Bates
Henry Knights
widow Cushing
John Gedg
good Lee
Robert Dame
widow Stafe
Robert Hubert
George Larrance
widow Cott
goodman Humall
goodman Hubert
Daniel Cluse
Thomas Beady
Francis Cotes
Thomas Greene
widow Ellis
Charles Lacey
Elizabeth Key
widow Watson
Thomas West
Bartholomew Willis
Henry Adams
Aaron Brooke
John Read
Henry Brady
John Busell
Thomas Low
William Bartrem

St Mary Coslany [continued]

widow Barnigham
John Jacks
Margaret Wrench
Thomas Mills
Matthew Freeman
Samuel Wilde
Ann Brooke, widow
John Brady
widow Kinebrooke
Abraham Daniell
William Carter
John Cooper
Thomas Fincke
John Mayden
John Richer
Mary Starling
widow Titter
widow Hone
Thomas Lodes
William Studly
widow Sowell
Isaac Gose
William Lande
John Purdy
Thomas Glavin
widow Miles
Michael Harison
Richard Ebbs
Martin Lande
widow Witherick
Timothy Gouldknop
Nicholas Swetman
Mary Porter
Richard Lewis
John Sharpin
widow Eldred
James Tomson
Moses Head
Rebecca Porter
Augustine Read
Ann Pickerill
Thomas Brotherhood
John Umphery
Richard Wittham

St Mary Coslany [continued]

widow Howard
widow Rant
widow Wharlow

[147 Names]

E 179/336, f.70

St Mary Coslany

[undated ?late 1673 or early 1674]

widow Garthercole	1
John Pearson	1
widow Weebe	1
Sarah Dobes	1
good Lanthorn	2
good Cubet	1
good Curby	1
good Bensly	1
good Summers	1
good Hutten	1
good Mickelborrow	1
good Pick	1
good Fosbrook	1
widow Harredence	1
widow Whorlo	1
good Dunks	1
good Allen	2
good More	1
good Mais	1
good Youngs	1
good Greene	1
good Dale	2
good Wilson	1
widow Bret	2
widow Till	1
good Allen	2
good Till	2
good Blogg	1
good Stutly	1
widow Safly	1
good Chandler	1

St Mary Coslany [continued]

widow Rookwood	1
good Sparke	2
good Daines	2
widow Weeds	1
good Scot	1
good Fletcher	1
good Stigall	1
good Parker	1
widow Evefret	2
good Page	1
widow Armes	1
good Mace	2
good Quinton	1
good Dallaman	1
good Browne	1
good Buttul	1
good Gemson	1
good March	2
good Chest	1
good Riall	1
good Plesents	1
good Mallows	1
good Mills	1
good Armes	1
good Geedg	1
good Douson	1
good Swetman	1
widow Hart	1
good Neave	1
widow Hone	2
William Daus	1
good Whettecar	1
widow Daus	2
good Graves	1
good Crome	1
good Hart	1
widow Pollard	1
good Moffrey	1
good Sadler	1
widow Richs	1
good Titter	1
widow Burges	1
good Munser	2
Thomas Brady	2

St Mary Coslany [continued]

good Norfer	1
good Knights	1
good Bats	1
widow Eldred	2
John Geedge	1
good Lee	1
good Pilgrom	1
widow Drew	1
good Cot	2
good Greengol	1
good Dam	1
good Hubert	1
good Clus	1
widow Elles	1
widow Coats	1
widow Kethen	1
good West	1
good Dam	2
widow Watson	1
good Welles	1
good Adams	2
good Brook	1
good Read	2
Henry Brady	2
good Agges	1
Mary Hood	1
good Battrom	1
Margaret Wrentch	1
widow Barnegham	1
good Coupes	1
good Mels	2
good Wild	1
widow Brook	1
good Brady	1
widow Kennebrook	1
good Danill	1
good Cooper	1
widow Cleffen	1
widow Ston	1
good Maiden	1
good Studly	1
good Lods	1
good Goos	1
good Jackson	1

St Mary Coslany [continued]

widow Titter	1
widow Dehon	1
good Land	1
good Glffen	1
good Purdy	1
good Harroson	1
widow Mils	1
good Ebbes	1
good Land	2
widow Wethereck	1
good Tomson	1
good Lewes	1
good Swetman	1
Mary Porter	2
good Goudknop	1
good Head	1
good Read	2
widow Pickrell	1
Ann Church	1
good Brotherhood	1
good Wittom	1
good Humfrey	1
good Watson	2
widow Wharlo	2
good Sharpen	2
widow Howard	1
old Sparke	2

[146 Names]

E 179/338, f.31

St Michael at Plea

8 Mar 1670/1

John Cooper, jun.
widow Beacon
John Brandon
old Ligburrow
John Avers
James Smith
widow Comfitt
John Crocth

St Michael at Plea [continued]

John Linsey
widow Croth
widow Smith
John Hall
Martha Kemp
Henry Mussum
Henry Wells
widow Haris
Thomas Clarke
Alice Bleese
Edward Burrowes
John Cooper, sen.
widow Armes
William Tomson
John Crobden
William Spark
a vacant house
Thomas Hood
John Ellis
John Holden

[27 Names]

E 179/336, f.71

St Michael at Plea

20 Apr 1672

John Cooper
widow Bliss
Thomas Clarke
William Tomson
widow Baker
Elizabeth Woller
widow Cropden
Thomas Ellis
goodman Sparke
Michael Bouroughs
Francis Picke
John Crotch
Samuel Smith
John Cooper, jun.
George Lickbourgh

St Michael at Plea [continued]

John Lindly
Cicely Couell
Robert Scarry
Thomas Hoode
John Havers
John Hall
widow Kempe
James Smith
widow Crotch
James Chapman
Henry Masham
Henry Wells
Richard Clarke

[28 Names]

E 179/336, f.72

St Michael at Plea

24 July 1672

Francis Picke
Mary Kitbe
John Cooper
widow Bliss
Thomas Clarke
William Tompson
widow Baker
Eli Waller
widow Cropden
Thomas Ellis
good Sparke
Michael Burrough
John Crotch
Samuel Smith
John Cooper, jun.
George Lickburgh
John Lindly
Cicely Couell
Robert Scerry
Thomas Hoode
John Havers

St Michael at Plea [continued]

John Hall
widow Kempe
James Smith
widow Crotch
James Chapman
Henry Wells
Richard Clarke
John Horne

[29 Names]

E 179/336, f.73

St Michael at Plea

18 Feb 1673/4

Mary Kidby	1
widow Bliss	2
Thomas Clark	1
John Cooper, sen.	2
William Tompson	1
widow Baker	1
Elizabeth Waller	2
widow Cropden	1
Thomas Ellis	1
Elizabeth Sparke	2
Michael Burrow	1
John Crotch	2
Samuel Smith	2
John Cooper, jun.	1
George Ligburrow	1
Francis Pike	1
John Lindly	1
Cicely Cowell	1
Robert Skerrey	1
John Hall	2
widow Kemp	1
James Smith	2
widow Crotch	1
James Chapman	1
Henry Wells	2
Richard Clarke	1
Thomas Hoode	1

St Michael at Plea [continued]

John Saffry	1
John Haves	1

[29 Names]

E 179/338, f.32

St Michael at Thorn

20 Mar 1670/1

John Gibson, cook
Susan Harmon
Thomas Wissman
Thomas Burrell
Titus Aubery
William Nuwark
widow Gregory
William Morgen
John Blak
Augustine Pearse
Thomas Oakes
John Pike
John Houell
Ann Smith
Jasper Brime
Amy Couell
Gregory Newhouse
William Adames
Christopher King
Thomas Clamtree
William Wife
John White
Robert Gregory
John Cordey
William Smith
Seth Perker
John Numan
John Watts
James Miles
widow Bretingem
Jere... Scott
John Gedg
John Pettet

St Michael at Thorn [continued]

Thomas Watts
Robert King
William Sheringem
William Watts
Samuel Penney
Edmund Whitte
William Baxter
Francis High
William Deeker
John Lines
Sarah Townsend
Philip Thurton
Roger Tayler
John Tagney
John Blakmore
Thomas Spanton
Edmund Fellsted
Ann Rutter
Thomas Armsted
Thomas Watts
Thomas Carr
William Austin
Robert Frank
Matthew Heath
widow Randall
widow Tudneham
Jane Persely
Ann Persely
Richard Stinpson
widow Wymer
John Akers
Thomas Harper
Henry Peck
Mary Tey
Michael Smith
Francis Barton
Thomas Dorby
John Curtius
Samuel Midleton
John Goodall
Henry Colintun
John Shinkfild
Richard Punder
Robert Eagleston

St Michael at Thorn [continued]

goodman Eaveret
old Hodkins
widow Mathies
Robert Bretinham
Edward Stimson
Anthony Camplin
Henry Rivers
Samuel Peney
John Harker
William Cooke
John Poyt
Cicely Wister, widow
Richard Townsend
widow Brand
Edmund Heringe
Thomas Townsend
Thomas Alexsander
Dorothy Hocknell, widow
Henry Wright
widow Clarke
widow Roads
William Godffrey
Luke Hill
Daniel Fitt
Edward Strangways
John Camplin
widow Hall
George Downing
Augustine Booty
Roger Hocknell
John Ransom
Thomas Rose
widow Pettman
widow Barton
Thomas Durrant
Elizabeth Fisher, widow
Robert Bedingfild
Henry Alldersun
widow Allderson
Thomas Goodwin
Benjamin Fisher
Elizabeth Hayam, widow
Henry Bayly, jun.
Bennett Numan

St Michael at Thorn [continued]

William Cley
Henry Bayly, sen.
Edmund Hill
John Foster
goodman Bone
Adam Dickerson
goodman Robinson
William Bayly
Robert Mosse
John Gedg
widow Carr
William Semons
Robert Jell
widow Bayly
Nicholas Everat
Jane Georg
Jacob Thurston
Jane Feby, widow
Henry Cockett
Christopher Moore
Truth Cooke, widow
Thomas Bemont
Edward Ringall
John Wattson
William Money

[146 Names]

E 179/337, f.12

St Michael at Thorn

[blank] May 1672

John Gibson	2
Susan Harmon	2
Thomas Wiseman	1
Thomas Burrell	2
Titus Abery	2
widow Grigory	1
William Morgan	1
Augustine Peirce	1
Thomas Oakes	1
John Pike	1

St Michael at Thorn [continued]

John Hooell	1
John Gayes	1
Ann Smith	1
Joseph Brine	1
Ann Couell	1
Gregory Newhouse	2
William Adams	1
Christopher Kinge	2
Thomas Clamtree	1
William Wife	2
Robert Grigory	1
John Caudy	2
William Smith	1
Robert Jell	1
widow Baly	1
Nicholas Everett	1
James George	1
Jacob Thirston	1
Joan Philliby	1
Henry Cockett	1
Seth Brity	1
John Newman	1
John Watts	2
Isaac Miels	2
John Geedg	2
Robert Hart	1
John Pettitt	1
Thomas Watts	1
Robert King	2
widow Sheringham	1
Edward Bassell	2
Samuel Penny	2
Edmund White	2
William Baxter	2
William Diker	1
Thomas Dawes	2
Sarah Towsend	2
Philip Thurston	1
Roger Tayler	2
Edward Short	1
John Mins	2
Ann Rutter	2
Thomas Armestead	2
Thomas Watts	1

St Michael at Thorn [continued]

Christopher More	1
Thomas Bemant	1
Thomas Sutton	1
widow Cooke	1
Edward Ringall	1
John Wattson	1
John Foster	2
Adam Dickerson	1
Thomas Carr	1
William Asten	1
John Frank	1
Matthew Hearth	2
widow Randale	1
widow Tuddinham	1
Jane Parsley	1
Ann Parsley	1
widow Wymer	1
John Arcres	1
Thomas Harper	1
Henry Peck	1
Mary Tye	1
Michael Smith	1
Francis Burton	1
Thomas Darby	1
John Curtis	1
Samuel Medellton	1
John Goodale	1
Henry Collinton	1
John Shinkfeld	1
John Nunn	1
Robert Eglestone	2
Nicholas Everitt	1
Thomas Pembrook	1
widow White	1
Edmund White	2
old Hodgkin	1
widow Matthers	1
Thomas Harper	1
Edward Stimpson	1
Anthony Campling	1
Henry Rivers	1
John Harper	1
William Cooke	2
John Poyt	1

St Michael at Thorn [continued]

Cicely Wisiter	2
Richard Towsend	1
widow Brand	1
Edmund Hering	2
Thomas Alexander	1
widow Hocknell	2
Henry Write	2
widow Clark	1
widow Roads	1
William Godfrey	1
Luke Hill	1
Daniel Fitt	2
Edward Stranguish	2
John Campling	2
widow Viper	1
George Downing	2
Henry Balye	1
Roger Hacknell	1
John Ransom	1
Thomas Rose	1
widow Pettman	1
Richard Matt...	1
Thomas Durrent	1
widow Fisher	1
widow Alderson	1
Thomas Goodwin	1
Ann Fisher	1
Elizabeth Heyham	2
Henry Jefreys	2
widow Skitter	1
Bennett Numan	2
William Clye	2
Edmund Hill	2
Henry Collington	1
Richard Dallison	1
Robert Phebe	2
George Moss	2
Thomas Robinson	1
widow Carr	2
John Gedg	2
William Sammon	1
John Blackmore	1
Thomas Gregory	1
John Cordy	1

St Michael at Thorn [continued]

Robert Cordy	1
Jacob Thurston	1
James Jorg	1
widow Tuddintom	1
widow Balye	2
good Milles	1
William Balye	1
good Lawes	1
good Stanton	2
Jasper Brime	1
Joseph Hurn	1
Matthew Sherwood	2
Robert Felltrop	1
Edmund Buskerd	2

[156 Names]

E 179/336, f.74

St Michael at Thorn

28 Feb 1672/3

John Gibson
Susan Harman
Thomas Wiseman
Thomas Burrell
Titus Abery
widow Grigory
William Morgan
Augustine Peirson
Thomas Oaks
John Pike
John Howell
John Gayes
Ann Smith
Joseph Brine
Ann Couell
Gregory Newhowse
William Adams
Christopher King
Thomas Clamtree
William Wife
Robert Grigory

St Michael at Thorn [continued]

John Caudy
William Smith
Robert Joll
widow Bayly
Nicholas Everett
James George
Jacob Thirston
Joan Philiby
Henry Cockett
Seth Britie
John Newman
John Watts
Isaac Miles
John Gedg
Robert Hart
John Pettett
Thomas Watts
Robert King
widow Sheringham
Edward Bossell
Samuel Penny
Edmund White
William Baxter
widow Diker
Thomas Dawes
Sarah Townsend
Philip Thirton
Roger Tailor
Edmund Short
Ann Rutter
Thomas Armsted
Thomas Watts
Christopher More
Thomas Bemont
Thomas Sutton
widow Cooke
Edward Ringall
John Wattson
John Foster
Adam Dikerson
Thomas Carr
William Asten
John Frank
Matthew Heath

St Michael at Thorn [continued]

widow Randall
widow Tudenham
Jane Parsly
Ann Parsly
widow Wymer
John Acres
Thomas Harper
Henry Peck
Mary Tye
Michael Smith
Francis Burton
Thomas Darby
John Curtis
William Middleton
John Goodale
Henry Collington
John Shinkfield
widow Petman
Richard Man
widow Alderson
Thomas Goodwin
Henry Jefreys
widow Skitter
Bennett Newman
William Cley
Edmund Hill
Henry Collington
Richard Dalleson
Robert Phebey
George Moss
Thomas Robingson
widow Carr
John Gedg
William Samon
John Blackmore
Thomas Grigory
John Cordy
John Nunn
Robert Halston
Nicholas Everett
Thomas Pembroke
widow White
Edmund White
old Hodskin

St Michael at Thorn [continued]

widow Matthews
Thomas Harper
Edmund Stimson
Anthony Camplen
Henry Rivers
John Harper
William Cooke
John Poyt
Cicely Wisister
Richard Townsend
widow Brand
Edmund Hering
Thomas Allexsander
widow Hocknell
Henry Write
widow Clarke
widow Roades
William Godfrey
Luke Hill
Daniel Fitt
Edward Strangway
John Camplen
widow Viper
George Downing
Henry Baily
Roger Hocknell
John Ransome
Thomas Rose
Thomas Durrant
Elizabeth Fisher
Ann Fisher
Elizabeth Heigham
Robert Cardy
Jacob Thirston
widow Tuddinton
widow Baily
goody Miells
William Baly
goody Lawes
goody Stanton
Jasper Brine
Joseph Harne
Matthew Sherwood
Robert Felltrop

St Michael at Thorn [continued]

Edmund Busberd

[154 Names]

E 179/336, f.75

St Michael at Thorn

20 Nov 1673

John Gibsonn	1
Susan Harman	1
Thomas Wiseman	1
Titus Abbery	2
widow Gregory	1
Cooper Leigh	1
Augustine Person	1
John Howell	2
Christopher Rymer	2
Jasper Brime	1
Gregory Newhowse	1
William Adams	1
Thomas Symonds	2
Christopher Kinge	2
Thomas Clamtree	1
Robert Gregory	2
old Blackamore	1
goodman Foster	1
widow Gell	2
widow Baly	1
Nicholas Everett	1
James George	2
widow Pheby	1
Robert Philby	2
Henry Cockett	2
John Newman	2
John Gedge	2
John Pettet	1
widow Watts	1
Edmund Hill	1
Edward Bossell	1
Samuel Penny	2
Edmund White	2
William Baxter	1

St Michael at Thorn [continued]

widow Decker	1
Thomas Daues	2
Sarah Townsin	1
Philip Thirton	2
Roger Taylor	1
Edward Short	2
Nicholas Randell	1
Thomas Armstead	1
Thomas Watts	2
Christopher Moore	1
Thomas Bowment	1
widow Cooke	1
Edward Ringall	1
John Wattson	1
John Foster	2
Adam Dickersonn	2
Thomas Carr	2
William Austine	1
John Franke	1
Matthew Hoth	1
widow Randell	1
widow Tuddenham	2
Jane Parsly	1
widow Wymer	2
Thomas Harper	1
Henry Peck	1
Michael Smyth	1
Francis Burton	1
Thomas Darby	2
Richard Pully	1
John Goodale	1
Henry Collington	2
John Shinkfeild	2
widow Petman	1
Richard Mann	1
widow Alderson	2
'Xestis' Skinner	1
Henry Jeffry	2
widow Skitter	1
William Cly	1
Henry Collington, jun.	1
Richard Dallison	1
George Moss	1
Thomas Robinson	1

St Michael at Thorn [continued]

widow Carr	2
William Salmon	1
Thomas Gregory	1
John Cordy	2
John Nunn	1
Robert Egleston	1
old Hogskin	1
Sarah White	1
widow Matthew	1
William Cooke	2
John Poyte	1
widow Wissiter	2
Richard Townsend	1
John Willis	1
widow Brand	1
Thomas Alexander	2
widow Hocknell	1
Henry Wright	1
widow Clarke	1
widow Roads	1
William Godfry	1
Luke Hill	1
Daniel Fitt	1
Edward Stranguish	2
John Camplin	1
John Adkins	1
Augustine Kempe	1
Henry Baly	1
Roger Hocknell	2
John Ransom	1
Thomas Rose	1
Thomas Durrant	1
Elizabeth Fisher	1
Ann Fisher	1
Henry Baly, sen.	1
Robert Cawdy	1
good Crawly	1
widow Tuddenham	1
William Baly	1
old Miles	1
good Lay	1
Robert Falthorpe	1
Matthew Sherwood	1
Thomas Hood	1

St Michael at Thorn [continued]

John Frost	1
Edmund Buskin	1
Anthony Camplin	1
Gilbert Barker	1
Edward Camplin	1
John Wyth	1
Thomas Burrell	1
George Downinge	2
Cornelius Browne	1
Peter Everet	1
goodman Hall	1
Margaret Browne	1
Margaret Burman	1
good Scott	1
John Colman	1
William Firman	2
Samuel Boldrew	1
William Lay	1
goodman Rant	1
widow Arch	1
William Morgin	2
William Manser	1
William Mony	1
Benjamin Fisher	2
widow Burrell	1
Thomas Goodman	1

[148 Names]

E 179/338, f.33

St Michael Coslany

7 Mar 1670/1

John Head
Daniel Cooper
John Jarram
John Lynsey
Richard Hansell
John Poppey
John Goss
John Wake
Adam Brickham

St Michael Coslany [continued]

Henry Harpoole
widow Grey
widow Cockidiy
James Freeman
Daniel Clarke
widow Scot
Joseph Shepard
widow Deacon
John Neale
Thomas Hansell
William Pyke
Daniel Ebbets
Francis Morley
Edward Gouldknop
Philip Sparrow
Stephen Adcock
Thomas Holmes
Francis Copping
John Sayer
John Hansell
widow Deacon
John Allen
Zachariah Knights
Nathaniel Garrod
John Sharpin
widow Fletcher
widow Braban
good Jeams
Edward Burrough
widow Goss
goodman Gary
Abraham Hansell
Philip Greengole
Thomas Wade
Samuel Sadler
widow Breviter
Samuel Witherell
Robert Sparrow
widow Parker
widow Cooper
William Atkins
William Lawrence
John Palmer
Catherine Starchy

St Michael Coslany [continued]

John Hastings
Thomas Athey
William Atkins, sen.
Sarah Witherly
widow Gunton
Walter Smith
Benjamin Bloome
widow Barlo
Richard Myles
Sarah Dobbs
Sarah Ebbs
Robert Poynter
Matthew Camstead
Dinah Lister
Thomas House
John Jarram
good Bloome
Nathaniel Barlow
widow Beake
Richard Callow
George Hawkings
widow Waller
John Whitlock
Anthony Collings
widow Hill
John Summers
Elias Boyce
Samuel Violl
Robert Cole
... Thyrtickle
widow Connys
widow Corbet
John Jarram, sen.
William Bond
Richard Burrell
... Mickleburgh
Margaret Yongman
Peter Beake
widow Moss
Rose Joyce
John Davy
Edmund Cooper
William Foster
Henry Hampton

St Michael Coslany [continued]

Susan Pile
widow Kinderley
William Créttings
William Knights
Jonas Jonson
widow Sandevill
John Danyres
good Clarke
Thomas Garrod
Susan Garrod
widow Jerson
Peter Barker
Thomas Sergerson
William Cooke
Richard Beavis
John Poynter
William Spernall
Richard Rock

[115 Names]

E 179/336, f.76

St Michael Coslany

13 May 1672

Joan Head
John Jarram, jun.
William Foster
Daniel Cooper
widow Moy
goodman Lynsey
Richard Hansell
Robert Coule
Thomas Summers
Thomas Wake
widow Gray
Daniel Clarke
goodman Burton
widow Scott
goodman Mollet
Anthony Collings
John Neale

St Michael Coslany [continued]

William Peeke
Philip George
Francis Morley
Robert Sparrow
Philip Sparrow
John Allen
Stephen Adcock
John Sayer
widow Tayler
John Hansell
Moses Clarke
Thomas Hansell
Daniel Ebbitts
Stephen Jepps
William Lynstead
Zachariah Knights
Nathaniel Garwood
John Sharpin
Thomas Passifield
Edward Parrish
widow Deacon
Joseph Cutlock
Robert Deacon
Michael Woofe
Edward Burrowes
Thomas Homes
Mary Jarry, widow
widow Foaker
Samuel Sadler
Thomas Beanes
John Palmer
John Godfrey
William Braban
goodman Foulsham
goodman Edger
Samuel Witherill
widow Parker
Margaret Rootley
widow Thirston
William Cooper
goodman Joyce
John Hadden
Catherine Starkey
Philip Sparrow

St Michael Coslany [continued]

Mary Kemp, widow
widow Witherill
William Adkins
William Johnson
William Adkings, tyler
Robert Gunton
Robert Key
Richard Mills
Anthony Last
Matthew Ringstead
Robert Poynter
Robert Berney
Sarah Dobbs
Palfreyman Knights
goodman Brooke
goodman Hewit
Walter Smyth
Robert Crow
Thomas Howes
Elizabeth Meares, widow
William Lawrance
Richard Norrice
James Wilkerson
John English
John Wenn
John Meares
Edmund Powell
goodman White
goodman Eatton
goodman Risbrough
Thomas Helmes
James Vincent
Peter Gibson
John Whitlocke
widow Hill
John Summers
Henry Bird
Edward Mollet
Thomas Folkner
Elias Boyce
Samuel Watson
widow Corbit
John Jarram, sen.
Peter Verbeake

St Michael Coslany [continued]

Francis Bond
Margaret Youngman
Jonas Davey
Esther Dogg
Matthew Micklebrough
Robert Walstone
widow Waller
widow Munns
Henry Hampton
widow Cooper
Edmund Cooper
Henry Lawes
John Leasingham
John Thirtickle
widow Kenderly
Hugh Kenderly
Bernard Lister
widow Knights
Thomas Johnson
widow Sandafield
John Daynes
Thomas Watts
widow Fletcher
John Ireson
John Poppey
Peter Barker
Richard Rock
Richard Beavis
William Cooke
Thomas Sergeson
goodman Wharle
William Sparrell

[137 Names]

E 179/336, f.77

St Michael Coslany

28 Aug 1672

John Head
John Jarram, jun.
William Foster

St Michael Coslany [continued]

Daniel Cooper
goodman Lynsey
Richard Hansell
Robert Coule
Thomas Summers
Thomas Wake
widow Gray
John Headly
Daniel Clarke
Joseph Shepheard
Moses Clarke
goodman Barton
widow Scott
goodman Mollet
widow Kempe
Anthony Collings
John Neale
William Peeke
Francis Morley
Robert Sparrow
Philip Sparrow
John Allen
Stephen Adcock
Philip George
John Sayer
widow Tayler
John Hansell
Thomas Hansell
Daniel Ebbitts
Stephen Jepps
William Linstead
Zachariah Knights
Nathaniel Garwood
Jeremiah Toukley
John Sharpin
Thomas Passifield
Edward Parrish
widow Deacon
Joseph Cutlocke
Robert Deacon
Michael Woofe
Edward Barrowes
Thomas Homes
Mary Jary, widow

St Michael Coslany [continued]

widow Foaker
Samuel Sadler
Samuel Witherill
goodman Titlow
Thomas Benes
John Godfrey
William Braban
goodman Foulsham
goodman Edger
widow Parker
Margaret Rootley
widow Thirston
William Cooper
goodman Joyce
John Hadden
Catherine Starkey
Philip Sparrow
widow Witherly
William Adkins
William Johnson
William Adkins, tyler
Robert Guton
Robert Key
Richard Mills
Matthew Ringstead
Robert Poynter
Robert Berney
Sarah Dobbs
Palfreyman Knights
goodman Brooke
goodman Hewit
Thomas Howes
Elizabeth Meares, widow
William Lawrence
Richard Norrice
goodman Bigott
goodman Smyth
goodman Risbrow
Robert Crow
John English
John Wenn
John Meares
Edmund Powell
goodman White

St Michael Coslany [continued]

goodman Eatton
Thomas Helmes
James Vincent
Peter Gibson
John Whitlock
widow Hill
John Summers
Henry Bird
Edward Mollet
Thomas Folkner
Elias Boyce
Samuel Watson
Thomas Wattson
widow Corbit
John Jarram, sen.
Peter Verbeake
Francis Bond
Margaret Yongman
Jonas Davy
Esther Dogg
Matthew Micklebrough
Robert Walstone
widow Waller
widow Munns
Henry Hampton
widow Cooper
Edmund Cooper
Henry Lawes
John Leasingham
John Thirticle
widow Kenderly
Hugh Kenderly
Bernard Lister
widow Knights
Thomas Johnson
widow Sandafield
Thomas Watts
John Daynes
widow Fletcher
John Ireson
John Poppey
Susan Garwood
Peter Barker
Richard Rock

St Michael Coslany [continued]

Richard Beavis
William Cooke
Thomas Sergeson
goodman Wharle
William Sparnell
James Wilkerson

[141 Names]

E 179/336, f.78

St Michael Coslany

15 Apr 1674

John Head	2
John Jarram, jun.	
William Foster	
goodman Lynsey	2
Richard Hansell	
Thomas Wake	
widow Gray	
John Headley	
Daniel Clarke	2
Joseph Sheppard	2
Moses Clarke	
Robert Coule	
John English	2
Anthony Collings	
John Neale	2
Daniel Ebbitts	2
Robert Sparrow	
Philip Sparrow	
Francis Morley	
Stephen Adcock	
Philip George	
widow Bossell	
John Sayer	2
Samuel Sadler	2
widow Tayler	2
John Hansell	2
Thomas Hansell	1
Samuel Wissiter	
Stephen Jepps	

St Michael Coslany [continued]

John Sharpin	
Jeremiah Toakley	
William Harnes	
Clement Lemman	
Thomas Passifield	
goodman Palmer	
Edward Parrish	
John Allen	2
widow Kempe	
Zachariah Knights	2
William Linstead	2
Joseph Cutlock	
Michael Wooffe	
John Wignall	
Edward Burrowes	
Thomas Homes	2
widow Moy	
widow Scott	
widow Garry	
Samuel Witherill	
Robert Berney	2
widow Parker	2
William Cooper	2
Margaret Rootley	
widow Thirston	
goodman Baldwyne	
Catherine Starkey	
Edmund Powell	2
Philip Sparrow, jun.	
William Adkins, sen.	
widow Witherley	2
Robert Gunton	
Robert Key	
Richard Myles	
Matthew Ringstead	
Robert Poynter	
Walter Smyth	
Elizabeth Meares	
Robert Bately	
Richard Norrice	
John Wenn	
Thomas Risbrough	
goodman White	2
Henry Benceley	

St Michael Coslany [continued]

Sebastian Johnson	
Thomas Elmes	2
James Vincent	
Peter Gibson	
John Hewett	
widow Hill	
John Summers	2
John Hadden	
goodman Brabant	
Elias Boyce	
Samuel Watson	
Thomas Watson	
Edward Mollet	
James Wilkerson	
John Jarram, sen.	
widow Deacon	2
Peter Beake	
Francis Bond	
Margaret Youngman	
Jonas Davy	
Henry Lawes	
goodman Tayler	
goodman Blyth	
goodman Daynes, com...r	
widow Waller	
John Witherley	
widow Woolnough	
William Adkins, jun.	2
Henry Hampton	
widow Cooper	
Edmund Cooper	
John Leasingham	2
Elizabeth Kenderley	
John Thirticle	
Hugh Kenderley	
Bernard Lister	
widow Knights	
Thomas Johnson	
widow Sandafield	
John Daynes	
Thomas Watts	
John Ireson	
Peter Barker	
widow Fletcher	

St Michael Coslany [continued]

Richard Beavice	
Thomas Sergesson	
goodman Cooke	
Priscilla Gilman	
John Beake	
Richard Rock	
goodman Bracenett	
John Athill	
Robert Walstine	
goodman Fockner	
widow Foaker	
Henry Bird	
goodman Eaton	2
goodman Bennall, jun.	
goodman Keddall	
William Lynstead	2
Sarah Lawes, widow	
John Poppey	
widow Allen	
goodman Beecroft	
widow Barritt	
goodman Adkins, tyler	
goodman Pantrey	

[140 Names]

E 179/338, f.34

St Paul

16 Feb 1670/1

Nicholas Denny
Peter Fever
Thomas Salmon
widow Bassett
Ralph Kidd
Richard Newarke
Edmund Smyth
George Metcalfe
Robert Lowe
Thomas Pawe
Alice Flattman
Simon West

St Paul [continued]

Nicholas Carr
Susan Blooker
Thomas Norton
James Downinge
William Saddler
William Grundy
widow Saddler
Philip Brady
Robert Carter
Geoffrey Foster
Ralph Hudson
widow Reeve
Robert Read
John Burdocke
Robert Nobbs
Robert Parmenter
Erasmus Havers
Richard Ringhall
widow Wood
Robert Parker
Robert Nevill
widow Hovell
Thomas Crotch
widow Polley
Paul Cooke
John Syer
Robert Harman
John Reeve
Henry Parker
Henry Crotch
old Heasle
Thomas Godfry
Thomas Johnson
Abraham Rickey
Richard High
Timothy Haddowe
Lewis France
Edmund Starlinge
Diana Fuller
Thomas Cockmane
Nicholas Margate
Timothy Baldwyn
Oliver Brandwood
John Barker

St Paul [continued]

Edward Preston
Robert Grand
Nicholas Carr
John Rant
William Hill
John Kempe
John Short
Thomas Loftley
Oliver Brandwood, jun.
Peter Say
William Stillyard
James Salenger
William Richardson
Francis Cadie
widow Jex
Thomas Symonds
John Cooke
Thomas Tapper
James Aldredge
William Holbecke
Thomas Plumbe
Henry Clapperson
Francis Kempe
John Ballinster
Henry Butcher
Arthur Moulton
Richard Lindsey
John Cockman
William Parish
Philip Volley, jun.
widow Micleborough
Robert Cleare
George Grey
Philip Volley
William Abbott
Henry Parker
Thomas Clarke
Randolph Wigginton
John Read
John Kempe
William Newton
Zachariah Mayhu
Robert Morrant
Thomas Fuller

St Paul [continued]

Susan Cockade
Samuel Beavis
Humphrey Lane
William Beamond
Francis Woods
William Thompson
Robert Thompson
Robert Howard
Peter Cornelds
John Wolterton
Isaac Rickey
Thomas Moy
Richard Hudson
Clement Crowe
William Chappman
William Bayes
Thomas Hardy
Walter Beamond
John Billney
John Cotten
John Pecke
John Tapper
William Cooke
Robert Leach
John Read
Thomas Mayes
widow Eagle
Francis Balls
George Tubby
Christopher Baldinge
widow Stasey
John Carter
John Woodcock
Joseph Meeke
Samuel Murrell
William Johnson
John Iverson
Samuel Mare
widow Pawe
John Rouse

[140 Names]

E 179/336, f.79

St Paul

1 May 1672

Robert Neuill
widow Nouell
Thomas Croch
widow Pelley
Paul Cooke
John Syer
Robert Harman
John Reeve
Henry Parker
old Heasell
Thomas Godfrey
Thomas Johnson
Abraham Rickey
Richard Hickes
Timothy Hadow
Lewis Franse
Edmund Starlinge
Daniel Fuller
Thomas Cockeman
Nicholas Margate
Timothy Baldwing
Oliver Brandwod
John Barker
Edward Presson
Robert Grand
Ralph Hudson
Nicholas Care
John Rant
William Hill
John Kemp
John Short
Thomas Leasey
Oliver Brandwod, sen.
Peter Say
William Stilliard
James Sillinger
William Richerdson
Frank Cadie
widow Jex
Thomas Symonds

St Paul [continued]

John Cooke
Thomas Tapper
James Aldredge
William Holdbacke
Thomas Plumbe
Henry Claperson
Frank Kemp
John Ballister
Henry Barker
Arthur Mullton
Richard Linsey
John Cockman
William Parish
Philip Voley, jun.
widow Micklborugh
Robert Cleare
George Gray
Philip Voley, sen.
William Abbot
Henry Parker
widow Clarke
Randolph Wiginton
John Read
John Kemp
William Newton
Zachary Mahew
Robert Morrant
Thomas Fuller
widow Cockade
Samuel Bevis
Humphrey Lane
William Bewment
Frank Wood
William Thompson
Thomas Thompson
Robert Howard
Peter Corneale
John Wolterton
Isaac Rickey
Thomas Mayes
Clement Crow
William Chapman
Thomas Hardie
Walter Bewmet

St Paul [continued]

John Billney
John Cotton
John Pecke
John Tappar
William Cooke
Robert Leach
John Read
Thomas Moyes
widow Eagle
Frank Balls
George Tubby
Christopher Boldinge
widow Stacey
John Carter
John Woodcoke
Geoffrey Meeke
Samuel Murrell
John Bustocke
goodman Cookoe
Robert Blyth
R[?ichard] Hye
Richard Deney
Peter Feaver
Thomas Sammon
widow Basset
old Low...ings
Richard Newwork, sen.
Edmund Smith
Gregory Mettcalf
Robert Low
Thomas Pow
widow Pow
Alice Flattman
Simon West
Richard Carre
Susan Blocker
Thomas Nortton
widow Sadler
William Grondy
widow Sadler, jun.
Philip Bradie
Robert Cartter
Geoffrey Foster
... Ayers

St Paul [continued]

Ralph Hudsson, sen.
widow Reeve
Robert Head
John Burdoke, sen.
Robert Nobbs
Robert Parmenter
old Havers
Richard Ringall
widow Wood, sen.
Robert Parker
Jacob Rustinge
John Godfery
Lawrence Coman
Andrew Stone
Henry Butcher

[143 Names]

E 179/336, f.80

St Paul

14 Sep 1672

Robert Newell
widow Newell
Thomas Croch
widow Pelly
Paul Gooch
John Syser
Robert Harman
John Reeve
Henry Parker
old He[?as]ell
Thomas Godfrey
Thomas John Johnson [*sic*]
Abraham Rihes
Richard Hach
Timothy Haddow
Lewis Feron
Edmund Starlinge
Daniel Fuller
Thomas Cockman
Michael Moris

St Paul [continued]

Simon Balldinge
Oliver Bundwood
John Barker
Edmund Presston
Robert Grand
Ralph Hudson
Nicholas Carr
John Rant
William Hill
John Kemp
John Short
Thomas Leasey
Oliver Brandwood, sen.
Peter Say
William Stiylayad
Samuel S...illinger
William Richardson
Frank Kadie
widow Jex
Thomas Symonds
John Kooke
Thomas Cooper
James Alldred
William Houldbacke
Thomas Plumer
Henry Clapperson
Frank Kemp
John Bollite
Henry Barker
Arthur Moulton
Richard Leasey
John Cockman
William Parris
Philip Wolby, jun.
widow Mickleborugh
Robert Cleare
Grey & Wolby, jun. [sic]
Abott & Barker
Clark & Wiginton
Read & Kempe
Newton & Wallker
Warent [&] Fuller
Cockend & Beavis
Lane & Bement

St Paul [continued]

Woods [&] Thompson, sen.
Robert Thompson
Robert Howard
Peter Cunwell
Wolterton & Riches
Mayes & Crow
Clopham & Hardie
Beament & Billy
Cotton [&] Pecke
Caper & Cooke
Leach & Read, sen.
Thomas Moseyes
William Eagle
Frank Bull
Gregory Tubby
Christopher Baldy
William Stacy
John Cotton
Woodcoke & Meeke
Murle & Bustocke
goodman Cock, jun.
Blyth & Hicks
Richard Denney
Peter Feiver
Thomas Leamon
Bassey & Lowlinge
Richard Neworth
Medcalfe & Smith
Low & Perr
widow Pow
Flatman & West
Carr & Blocker
Thomas Nortton
widow Sadley
widow Grondy
widow Sadler, jun.
Bradie & Corker
Geoffrey Foster
Archer & Reeve
Ralph Hudsson, sen.
Robert Stead
John Burdocke, sen.
Robert Nobs
Robert Parmenter

St Paul [continued]

old Harris
Richard Ringall
widow Woods, sen.
Robert Parker
James Rustinge
John Godfery
Lawrence Coman
Andrew Ston
Henry Bucher
John Coyman, jun.

[118 lines; 144 names]

E 179/336, f.81

St Paul

10 Mar 1673/4

Robert Nevill	1
Thomas Croch	1
widow Pelly	1
Paul Cooke	1
John Sier	1
Robert Harman	2
John Reeve	1
Thomas Godfry	2
William Jonsons	1
old Riches	1
Timothy Haddew	2
Lewis France	2
Edward Starling	1
Thomas Fuller	1
Oliver Brangall	2
Thomas Cockman	1
John Barker	1
Robert Grand	1
Ralph Hudson	2
Nicholas Carr	1
William Parish	1
John Kemp	1
John Leasy	1
Oliver Brangall, sen.	2
Peter Say	1

St Paul [continued]

William Stilliard	1
James Sillinger	1
John Cooke, sen.	1
James Alldrege	1
Thomas Plumer	1
Henry Claphamson	1
William Houldback	1
Frances Kemp	1
Arthur Moulton	1
John Cockman	1
Robert Cleare	1
George Grey	1
old Abbetts	1
old Wigginton	2
John Walker	1
old Read	1
widow Cockedy	1
Samuel Bevis	1
widow Lane	1
old Beamont	1
Robert Howard	1
Woods & Tompson	1
John Wolterton	2
... Bement	1
John Cotton	1
John Cooke	1
widow Eagle	2
Francis Balls	1
George Tubby	1
Christopher Baldin	2
goodman Cooke	2
Henry Bucher	1
John Woodcocke	1
widow Blith	1
William Flatman	2
Carr & Blocker	1
William Smith	2
Thomas Norton	1
widow Sadler	1
Thomas Jonsons	1
William Grundy	1
Philip Brady	2
Jeremiah Foster	1
John Reeve	1

St Paul [continued]

John Burdock	1
widow Parmenter	1
Richard Ringall	1
widow Woods	2
Andrew Stone	1
James Downing	1
Thomas Rix	1
Thomas Davy	1
Edward Py	1
Henry Harrison	2
Edward Osborn	1
Thomas Loftis	1
Peter Ricky	1
Timothy Baldin	1
John Cooke, jun.	2
John Butteris	1
Joseph Meeke	1
Harman Rogers	1
William Gimson	1
Robert Morrent	2
Simon West	1
John Tapper	1
William Chapman	2
John Miller	1
Jacob Ruston	1
Zachary Mayhew	1
John Kempe	1
Richard Linsey	1
widow Reeve	1
old Kidd	2
John Rofe	1
Erasmus Havers	1
Abraham Sheperd	1
widow Jarvis	1
Mary Pa...	1
Peter Cunwell	1
Peter Heittes	1
Walter Bemant	2
Francis Woods	1
goodman Moore	2
William Rant	1
Robert Flecher	1
John Read	1
widow Clarke	1

St Paul [continued]

old Nicolls	1
James Taylace	1
old Moy	1
old Carr	1
old Watson	1
goodman Bretton	2
old Hudson	1
William Hill	1
William Poule	1
Richard Newark	1
old Samond	1
old Shead	1
Ralph Kidd	1
Thomas Watts	1
John Peck	1
Gregory Madcafe	1
John Leasy	1
Thomas Poye	1
Jonathan Parker	1
Peter Fever	1
Philip Verle, sen.	2
Philip Verle, jun.	1
John Shortt	1
Robert Tompson	1
Michael Clarke	1
Thomas Maies	1
Michael Morris	1
widow Stacy	2
Henry Barker	1
Richard Cookooe	1
goodman Crow	2
goodman Shreeve	1
widow Adkins	1
goodman ...ordly	2

[147 Names]

E 179/338, f.35

St Peter Hungate

23 Mar 1670/1

Thomas Gostlinge

St Peter Hungate [continued]

John Hast
Robert Moore
Henry Everard
Thomas Scarfe
George Curtis
widow Row
widow Nockols

[8 Names]

E 179/336, f.82

St Peter Hungate

17 Feb 1671/2

Thomas Gosling
John Hast
Robert More
Thomas Scarfe
George Curtis
widow Row
widow Knockals
William Adkins
Augustine Alldred
widow Church

[10 Names]

E 179/336, f.83

St Peter Hungate

17 July 1672

Thomas Scarfe
widow Nockles
widow Row
Thomas More
Thomas Gosling
John Hast
George Curtis
William Adkins

St Peter Hungate [continued]

widow Church
Augustine Aldred

[10 Names]

E 179/336, f.84

St Peter Hungate

8 May 1674

Thomas Scarfe	2
widow Nockles	1
widow Row	1
Thomas More	1
George Curtis	2
widow Church	1
Augustine Aldred	2
widow Goselling	2

[8 Names]

E 179/338, f.36

St Peter Mancroft

21 Feb 1670/1

William Whamsley
Andrew Wilkinson
Charles Rutter
Grace Stanford
Edward Bucke
William Browne
Mary Jary
Edward Bozell
Richard Curtis
Valentine Cutball
John Fitts
John Bush
Joan Symonds
Jonas Wrench
James Chapman
Michael Barnard

St Peter Mancroft [continued]

George Wen, sen.
John Bourne
George Wen, jun.
William Howlands
Anthony Howgell
John Browne
John Baxter
John Basterd
Elizabeth Daynes
Thomas Parker
Richard Woods
widow Parr
widow Tucke
Ann Lawes
widow Emperor
John Wright
Simon Ward
John Clayborne
Elizabeth Haygrave
Ann Thompson
Thomas Ebbs
William Cooke
William Rookewood
Thomas Meed
widow Lambert
Ralph Deacon
Edward Single
John Wilde
John Hamond
John Stannard
John Madwell
widow Bainard
John Brooke
John Smith
Peter Smith
Edmund Wilde
Richard Lowes
William Greenacre
Anthony Watters
Nicholas Hobert
Thomas Cooke
widow Baker
goodman Webster
widow Heaslewood

St Peter Mancroft [continued]

Marmaduke Low, sen.
Thomas Barker
Joseph Langley
John Dunn
Robert Keepis
William Sebbe...
William Green
Robert Lasebrooke
Abraham Browne
Catherine Pestle, widow
widow Warnes
widow Clarke
widow Bircth
Roger Gayward
Robert Thornton
William Crome, mason
William Pinder, a binder of
  books
John Roote, carpenter
John Baxter, tailor
John Hamond, tailor
Richard Sanders, mason
Marmaduke Low, smith
Margaret Parson
Ann Roote
Robert Claborne, sen.
Catherine Baston, widow
Mary Milborne, widow
Joan Padge, widow
William Sherive
widow Laws
Catherine Bastard
John Jeake
Francis Gedney
James Buddell
Thomas Wymer, gl[azier]

[95 Names]

E 179/337, f.13

St Peter Mancroft

3 Apr 1672

St Peter Mancroft [continued]

George Tayler
widow Clarke
William Wamsly
Andrew Wilkeson
Charles Rutter
Grace Stanford
Thomas Wymer
Edward Buckell
William Boone
Edward Bosell
Ann Roate
Richard Curtis
Valentine Cutball
John Fitts
John Bush
widow Selby
Joan Simonds
Marmaduke Low, jun.
Jonas Wrench
James Chapman
John Mason
widow Lawes
George Wenn, jun.
William Howlings
Anthony Higgin
John Browne, sen.
John Baxter
John Bastard
Elizabeth Dawes
Alice Barnard
George Wenn, sen.
James Budwell
Thomas Parker
Richard Woods
widow Parre
widow Tucke
Catherine Bastum
Ann Lawes
Catherine Bastard
widow Heaslewood
John Pace
Francis Gedney
Francis Emperor
Richard Claborne

St Peter Mancroft [continued]

John Wright
Simon Ward
widow Milborne
John Claborne
Elizabeth Hargrave
Ann Thomson
Thomas Ebbes
Richard Lawes
goodman Stubbes
John Hammont
Joan Page, widow
Nicholas Hobart
Anthony Waters
William Greenaker
Thomas Cooke
widow Baker
goodman Webster
Marmaduke Low
Thomas Barber
Joseph Langley
John Browne
widow Parson
Robert Keepis
William Green
Robert Lasworth
Abraham Browne
widow Pestell
widow Warnes
widow Birch
Roger Goward
Robert Thornton
William Shreefe
William Wright
goodman Hammont
Mary Person
William Cooke
William Rockard
John Roate
Richard Sanders
Thomas Meade
widow Lambert
Ralph Debton
William Crome
Edward Stringell

St Peter Mancroft [continued]

John Wild
William Pinder
John Stainard
John Madwell
widow Banyard
John Brooke
John Smyth
Peter Smyth
Edmund Wilde

[97 Names]

E 179/336, f.85

St Peter Mancroft

23 Mar 1672/3

George Taylour
William Wanesley
widow Clarke
Andrew Willison
Charles Rutter
Grace Sampford
Thomas Wyener
Edward Buckell
William Boone
Edward Bossell
Ann Roote
Richard Curtis
Valentine Cuttkall
John Fitts
John Bush
widow Gelby
James Symonds
Marmaduke Low, jun.
Jonas Wrench
James Chapman
John Mason
widow Lawes
George Wenn, jun.
William Howlings
Anthony Higgon
John Browne, sen.

St Peter Mancroft [continued]

John Baxter
John Bastard
Elizabeth Lawes
Alice Bernard
George Wenn, sen.
John Budwell
Thomas Parker
Richard Woods
widow Parr
widow Tucke
Catherine Baston
Ann Hawes
Catherine Bastard
widow Houzlewood
John Pace
Francis Gedney
Francis Emperour
Richard Clabourne
John Wright
Simon Ustard
widow Millbourne
John Claborne
Elizabeth Hargrave
Ann Tompson
Thomas Ebbs
Richard Lawes
good Stubbs
John Hamond
widow Paye
Nicholas Hubart
Anthony Waters
William Greeneaker
Thomas Cooke
widow Baker
goodman Webster
Marmaduke Low, sen.
Thomas Barker
Joseph Langley
John Browne
widow Parson
Robert Ropps
William Greene
Robert Hasworth
Abraham Browne

St Peter Mancroft [continued]

widow Pestill
widow Warnes
widow Spinke
widow Goward
Robert Thurston
William Shreeve
William Wright
good Hamond
Mary Parson
William Cooke
William Rockland
John Roote
Richard Sanderson
Thomas Mede
William Lambert
Ralph Depton
William Crome
Edward Stringall
John Needs
William Pinder
John Stanard
John Muddwell
widow Baynyard
John Brooks
John Smyth
Peter Smyth
Edward Wilde
Robert Armiger
Benjamin Brockden

[99 Names]

E 179/336, f.86

St Peter Mancroft

14 Oct 1673

William Wainsly
widow Clarke
Andrew Willison
Charles Rutter
Grace Stanford
Thomas Wiggener

St Peter Mancroft [continued]

Edward Buckill
William Boone
Edward Bosell
Ann Roote
Richard Curtiss
Valentine Cutkall
John Fitts
widow Golbey
James Simonds
Marmaduke Low, jun.
Jonas Wrench
James Chapman
George Wenn, jun.
William Howlings
Anthony Higgon
John Browne, sen.
John Bastard
Elizabeth Lawer
Alice Basterd
George Wenn, sen.
Thomas Parker
Richard Woods
widow Parr
widow Tuck
Catherine Baston
Ann Haws
Catherine Basford
widow Hezelewood
John Pace
Francis Gedney
Frances Emperour
Robert Claborne
John Wright
Simon Ustard
widow Milborne
John Claborne
Elizabeth Hargrave
Ann Tompson
Thomas Ebbes
Richard Lawes
John Hammonds
widow Sego
Nicholas Hubert
Anthony Warters

St Peter Mancroft [continued]

William Greenaker
Thomas Cooke
widow Baker
good Webster
Marmaduke Low, sen.
Thomas Baker
John Browne
widow Pearson
Robert Peepes
William Greene
Abraham Browne
widow Pestell
widow Warnes
widow Goward
Robert Thirston
William Shreeve
good Hammand
Mary Pearson
Richard Sanderson
William R...d
John Baxter
Thomas Mead
William Lambert
Ralph Dixton
William Croome
Edward Stringall
John Needs
John Stanard
John Mudwell
widow Banyard
John Brooke
John Smith
Peter Smith
Edward Wild
Benjamin Brockden
William Rockland
widow Smitter
widow Burgh
good Hugell
widow Collman
Simon Ward
Matthew Jarry
John Dearne
Mary Glasbrooke

St Peter Mancroft [continued]

good Jary
goody Buck
Joan Weak
goodman Thornton
Robert Arminger
widow Scarfe
John Peckitt
William Salvy
John Shukford
Thomas Banfather

[104 Names]

E 179/338, f.37

St Peter Parmentergate

12 Mar 1670/1

widow Gary
Joseph Wooley
Ursula Tooly
Henry Hoofflett
Philip Willson
widow Crook
Robert Senior
John Overinge
widow Dix
Samuel Gayton
John Finch
Henry Downes
Henry Broughton
Stephen Robinson
Richard Tite
Robert Sharping
widow Kiffin
John Sammon
John Gayton, jun.
George Pute
Ann Hardinge
Robert Pitcher
widow Steward
widow Gayton
John Gayton, sen.

St Peter Parmentergate [continued]

widow Walbey
widow Spurlinge
John Booth
Christopher Sparnell
John Kempe
widow Fittin
Christopher Steward
William Clarke
Henry Marsham
Thomas Rodrom
goodman Whitbey
Henry Howe
goodwife Sparrow
John Hewitt
Richard Myles
Robert Bell
widow Thompson
Samuel Coole
widow Appleby
Mary Anderson
Thomas Warrant
goodman Delfe
Robert Aubere
widow More
Richard Holden
John Harman
John Baly
Robert Badly
widow Crowe
widow Dey
Mary Barnes
William Beales
widow Weld
R William Wattes [sic]
William Reeve
Francis Osbourne
John Newes
Edward Stacy
Mary Gafford
Samuel Barlowe
Thomas Burrage
Philip Pick
widow Herrington

St Peter Parmentergate
[continued]

Henry Sparke
Richard Holt
Stephen Hunter
John Tooly
Simon Howard
Thomas Arnold
John Peckett
Richard Smith
John Baxter
Elizabeth Lambath
Richard White
widow Ayres
John White
goodman Sammon
John Constable
John Root
John Chappman
William Fell
John Dix, jun.
Henry More
Nicholas Browne
Richard Ricebrooke
widow Edmunds
widow Man
Thomas Hoode
Thomas Marten
Peter Lilly
John Earle
widow Jacoms
William Browne
Luke Martins
Francis Collman
widow Graves
Thomas More
widow Deane
Richard Clayton
Robert Rounde
George Hill
widow Starlinge
Christopher Stacy
Robert Taylor
widow Jordan
Robert Rush

St Peter Parmentergate
[continued]

Ralph Dexter
widow Shinkfield
Ann Roe
James Moss
Ambrose Bycroft
widow Browne
widow Gardner
Thomas Barney
Esther Wright
Robert Fletcher
widow Gouch
widow Hoth
Joseph Jay
widow Townsend
widow Emens
James Pleasant
widow Jeames
Jeremiah Ogden
Thomas Fellow, jun.
Joseph Myles
Stephen Crotch
Clement Barton
Robert Bunsdale
John Mortemy
Nicholas Comfitt
Thomas Maine
Ann Gibbs
William Roe
Thomas Darney
William Balliston
John Darney, jun.
John Dix, sen.
Thomas Callowe
John Rant
Robert Bone
John Greenwood
Edward Knites
Edward Lawes
Jacob Herd
William Riches
William Carlton
Robert Webster
John Loftie

St Peter Parmentergate
[continued]

Robert Bowman
widow Adams
Thomas Mannell
Thomas Freeman
goodwife Finch
widow Miller
John Lowe
Amy Everett
John Wickom
John Rush
Samuel Rush
Richard Fox
Gregory Carter
Robert Pagett
Richard Sugett
John Deacon
Joseph Southen
widow Starlinge
Robert Sharpinge
widow Kitchin
Thomas Ryall
Thomas Rand
James Hood
Leonard Reeve
Richard Moss
Robert Steele
James Holl
widow Skipp
Matthew Coates
widow Crickett
Thomas Carr
Adam Wilson
Thomas Grigorie
John Ogle
widow Wyer
William Motimore
Edmund Mortemy
Roger Burr
Stephen Robertson
Ann Bracy
Robert Ratsey
Thomas Wells
Leonard Reeve

St Peter Parmentergate
[continued]

Henry Stacey
Thomas Peck
John Oager
Edward Nickerson
Ann Wisiter
widow Wisiter
Edward Burton
Matthew Rutter
John Jackson
Peter Wacker
Elizabeth Freeman
goodman Phillipps
Thomas Sider
John Neslin
Ellen Shinkfield
Thomas Deane
Henry Webster
widow Kettle
widow Mason
widow Mason
widow Ringe
goodman Delfe
Robert Rant
widow Spanton
Joseph Smith
Samuel Berry
Thomas Collins
Thomas Osban
Francis Osban
Mary Spall
George Ellis, sen.
widow Cowsen
William Hall
Blyth Rix
Christopher Graves
Richard Carlton
John Blackmore
Michael Gamball
widow Dalliston

[236 Names]

127

E 179/336, f.87

St Peter Parmentergate

26 Apr 1672

widow Garry
Joseph Woley
widow Tooley
Henry Hafflet
Philip Willson
widow Crooke
Robert Senior
John Overing
widow Dix
Samuel Tyton
John Finch
Henry Downes
Henry Broughton
John Wells
Stephen Robrtson
Richard Tyte
Robert Sharping
widow Kiffinge
John Sammon
John Gayton
George Depute
Ann Hardinge
Robert Pichard
widow Steward
widow Gyton
John Gyton, sen.
widow Walby
widow Sharpen
John Booth
Thomas Sparnell
John Kemp
widow Fitten
Christopher Steward
William Clarke
Henry Masham
Thomas Ruderum
widow Whitby
widow Salter
widow Miller
widow Sparum

St Peter Parmentergate
[continued]

John Hewitt
Richard Myles
widow Bell
widow Thompson
Samuel Cole
widow Appleby
widow Anderson
Thomas Warrant
widow Delf
widow Ouldum
Robert Arbere
widow Morr
Richard Houlden
John Harman
John Balley
Robert Balley
widow Crow
widow Dye
widow Barnes
William Beales
widow Wells
William Watts
Richard Monny
William Reeve
Frank Ossborne
John Newes
John Augur
Edward Stacey
widow Gaffory
Samuel Barlow
Philip Puttocke
widow Herington
Henry Sparke
Richard Hoult
Stephen Hunter
William Fellow
John Tooley
Simon Howard
Thomas Arnold
Thomas Be...
Richard Smith
John Baxtor
widow Lambeth

St Peter Parmentergate
[continued]

Richard Whitte
widow Arnes
John White
goodman Sammon
John Cunstable
John Roote
John Chapman
William Fell
John Dix, jun.
Henry Morre, sen.
Richard Browne
Richard Rysbroke
widow Edmonds
widow Man
Thomas Hood
Thomas Wharton
Peter Lillie
John Earle
widow Jacom
William Browne
Luke Marten
Frank Coleman
Peter Whitte
widow Graves
Thomas Morre
widow Deane
Richard Clayton, sen.
Robert Pond
Samuel Balley
George Still
widow Starlinge
Christopher Stacey
Robert Taylor
widow Jordan
Robert Rush
Ralph Dexter
widow Shinkfield
widow Roe
James Moss
Ambrose Bycroft
widow Browne
widow Gardener
Thomas Barney

St Peter Parmentergate
[continued]

widow Wright
Robert Flecher
widow Gosh
widow Hoth
Joseph Say
widow Townsend
widow Eme[?ns]
James Pleasens
widow James
Jeremiah Ogden
Thomas Felow, jun.
Joseph Myles
Stephen Croch
Clement Barton
Robert Bunsdell
John Morttinge
Nicholas Comfitt
Thomas Maine
Amy Gibbs
William Roe
Thomas Darney
William Balliston
John Darney, jun.
John Dix, sen.
Thomas Callow
John Rant
Robert Boone
John Greenwood
Edward Knigts
Edward Lawes
Jacob Stead
William Riches
William Calton
Robert Webster
William Gayffor
John Loftes
Robert Bowman
widow Adhams
Thomas Mannell
Thomas Freman
goodwife Huish
goodman Gamble
John Lowe

St Peter Parmentergate
[continued]

widow Everetts
John Wickam
John Rush
Samuel Rush
Richard Fox
Gregory Carter
Robert Pagett
John Deacon
Joseph Soulden
widow Starlinge
Robert Sharpinge
widow Kichinge
Thomas Ryall
Thomas Pond
James Hood
Leonard Reeve
Richard Moss
Robert Steele
James Holl
widow Skipe
Matthew Coats
widow Cricket
Thomas Carre
Adam Willson
Thomas Grigory
John Ogle
widow Wyer
William Mottimer
Edward Morttimer
Roger Burr
Stephen Dobson
widow Brasey
Robert Brasey
Thomas Wells
Leonard Reeve
Henry Stacey
widow Pecke
John Ouger
Edward Nickerson, sen.
widow Wissester
Ann Wissetter
Edward Burton
Matthew Rutter

St Peter Parmentergate
[continued]

John Jackson
Peter Warker
widow Freman
widow Phillops
Thomas Syder
John Neslinge
Ellen Shinkfeild
Thomas Deane
Henry Webster
widow Kettle
widow Mason
widow Kinge
goodman Delf
Robert Rant
widow Spanton
Joseph Smith
Samuel Berey
Edmund Wattson
Thomas Collings
Thomas Ossborne
Frank Ossborne
Mary Spall
George Ellis, sen.
Timothy Aberey
widow Custings
William Shaw
Blyth Rix
Christopher Graves
Richard Curston
John Blackmore
Michael Gamble
widow Dallison
Mary Barnes
widow Man, sen.

[246 Names]

130

E 179/336, f.88

St Peter Parmentergate

11 Sep 1672

Simon Haward
Stephen Hunter
John Dix
John Tooly
Richard Holte
John Overing
widow Dix
Henry Sparke
widow Herinton
Thomas Fellow, sen.
John Blakamore, sen.
Edward Stacy
Nicholas Reaman
Robert Fellow
William Gayford
Thomas Arnold
Thomas Toll
Richard Smith
John White
Joseph Ayers
Richard White
John Baxter
widow Sparrow
widow Glading
Thomas Ruddrum
Edmund Mortimer
Richard Miles
John Huett
Richard Stimson
widow Appelbey
widow Bell
Esther Goodman
James Waston
Peter Harper
widow Kempe
Alice J...an
Thomas Warrant
William Hall
John Harmon
John Balife

St Peter Parmentergate
[continued]

widow Crow
Philip Dike
William Clarke
Robert Wetherly
Robert Godferey
widow Houlden
widow Sharpenton
Timothy Abree
Bartholomew Carter
Edmund Webster
John Augur
Frances Osburne
Mary Barnes
Robert Dicher
William Mony
widow Margerum
widow Dey
Thomas Gayford
widow Walbey
George Pute
John Giton
Christopher Steward
John Finch
widow Ayers
widow Gitton
William Beales
John Wells
Ann Hardy
Robert Chilvers
Henry Downes
Thomas Osburne
widow Fox
Stephen Roberson
Henry Browton
William Browne
William Callow
James Holl
widow Everitt
William Watts
John Burges
Samuel Berrey
James Lane
Samuel Meddelton

St Peter Parmentergate
[continued]

Thomas Sidewell
Henry Webster
Thomas Collings
Philemon Hamling
widow Mason
widow Wilkes
widow Chapman
Ellen Lenegur
Edmund Wattson
Richard Caltron
William Mortimer
widow Skipe
William Barney
widow Sargent
William Balistone
John Robines
George Ellis, sen.
George Ellis, jun.
Robert Free
John Kempe
Edmund Hines
George Sharpen
widow Mason
Godfrey Munford
John Jakeson
Peter Walker
widow Freman
Joseph Smith
Robert Steele
widow Carter
Edward Burton
Margaret Rutter
Henry Porter
widow Hawes
widow Pinner
Edward Nicerson
Thomas Carr
Henry Stacey
Henry Banfather
Roger Burr
Timothy Drury
widow Edmonds
Thomas Well

St Peter Parmentergate
[continued]

widow Well
Audrey Hart
Henry Booty
Leonard Reave
Frances Burton
Luke Marten
Charles Linsey
Matthew Coots
widow Fiddan
John Ogell
William Reave
Adam Willson
Robert Just
widow Haddon
John Gray
Abraham Wyer
Joseph Glister
widow Man
Robert Paggett
John Rand
widow Kiching
John Lowe
Joseph Soulden
John Decon
Robert Johnsons
Thomas Riches
widow Starling
Thomas Crow
William Lam
John Cooper
Thomas Royall
Thomas Willis
John Daney, sen.
John Blakamore, jun.
Martin Hooke
John Daney, jun.
John B[?oo]th
John Rante
John Mason
Henry Carr
Edmund Lawes
John Davy
Christopher Graves

St Peter Parmentergate
[continued]

John Grenwoods
Henry Wisester
John Dix, jun.
Thomas Daney
Robert Collinton
William Caltron, sen.
James Mose
Margaret Heard
John Finch
Michael Gambell
Thomas Freman
George Adcoke
Thomas Barnard
John Lofty
John Vines
William Hodgkine
Roger Kente
widow Smith
William Browne
Robert Ruch
William Shinkfild
Ralph Dexter
Brian Quintom
John Turner
Christopher Stacy
Robert Tayler
widow Jurden
John Hansell
Samuel Baly
Samuel Gyton
George Hill
Richard Clayton
Thomas Deane
widow Deane
Henry Albey
widow Lesinge
Frances Coleman
Robert Reve
William Haward
widow Gayford
widow Chapman
John Earle
Thomas Murton

St Peter Parmentergate
[continued]

widow Man
Richard Rusbrooke
Henry More
William Fell
Peter Lilly
Thomas Barney
widow Webster
Thomas Hood
Thomas Maine
Thomas Rusbrooke
Stephen Chroch
Roger Stanton
Benjamin Riches
John Wickham
Thomas Fellow, jun.
Mary Anderson
Thomas Mortimer
widow Jay
Robert Badly
widow Gardener
Jeremiah Ogden
Robert Flecher
James Pleasence
widow Gooch
widow Hoath
Ann Baker
Isaac Hansell
John Anderson
Richard Sammon
John Bucknam
John Newhouse
John Roote
John Cunstabell
Robert Auberee
Edmund Rippon
Peter White
Ambrose Becrofte
Mary Browne
Robert Sinyard
widow Gary
Henry Ufflett
Gabriel Plumer
Thomas Flowers

St Peter Parmentergate
[continued]

widow Tooly
John Coots
widow Pinchen

[258 Names]

E 179/336, f.89

St Peter Parmentergate

13 Apr 1674

widow Crow
Philip Pike
John Baly
Joseph Burger
widow Holden
John Freeman
William Fox
John Harman
widow Moore
William Hall
Joseph Page
James Beck
widow Cempe
Peter Harper
widow Tomson
widow Applebee
James Westo
Robert Gray
Richard Miles
Robert Mittin
widow Goodman   2
Thomas Durrant
Christopher Tomas
Robert Clarke
Thomas Hood
William Fox
Thomas Warren
Edmund Sliper
John Baxter   2
Richard Smith
John Dix

St Peter Parmentergate
[continued]

John Tooly
Simon Hayward
Stephen Hunter
widow Dix
Richard Holt
Henry Sparke
widow Herington
Thomas Toll
Thomas Fellow
William Cowel
John Wite
Stephen Haires
widow Crow
Nicholas Reaman   2
widow Sparrow
Edward Stasy
Francis Osborne
John Oger
Jane Malton
Robert Pitcher
Thomas Machen
Peter Moyes
William Leads
widow Dye
John Bouth
Thomas Gaifer
widow Walby
widow Sharpin
Robert Fellow
George Pute
Christopher Steward
John Guiton
Samuel Guiton   2
widow Guiton
John Finch   2
widow Haires
John Welles
Henry Canuwell
Peter Reason
Robert Chilvers
Robert Drury
Henry Broghton
Stephen Roberson   2

St Peter Parmentergate
[continued]

Henry Dounes
Robert Segoe
Thomas Osborne
James Holl
Gregory Carter
William Calloway
widow Stanhawe
Thomas Copland   2
Joseph Agers
John Cooper
Thomas Carver
widow Fittin
Nathaniel Coats
Charles Linsy
John Condly
John Gray
Abraham Wire
Robert Just
Joseph Plister
widow Haddon
Henry Morrend
William Reve
widow Wells
Thomas Wells   2
Leonard Reve
widow Edmonds
Henry Reve
Thomas Springall
Thomas Nunn
Roger Burr
Robert Poston
Robert Reve
Francis Burton
Henry Banfether
Thomas Barny
Henry Booty
Catherine Kempe
Timothy Drury
William Watts
Audrey Hart
Thomas Rush
Thomas Royall
Robert Steele

St Peter Parmentergate
[continued]

Edward Burton
Augustine Medcap
Edward Neckerson
Thomas Car...
widow Pinder
Henry Wood
William Bunn
widow Hawes
Peter Waker
widow Freeman
widow Bastanee
Godfrey Munford
John Jackson
Robert Coolings
Thomas Carr
George Sharpington
George Adcock
George Ellice
George Ellice
John Roberds
William Balliston
widow Skip
William Mortimie
widow Sargant
Richard Yorke
widow Gould
widow Wilkes
widow Mason
widow Chapman
Richard Carlton
Thomas Sider
Henry Webster
John Nesland
Robert Johnson
Edmund Gosland
Edmund Wattson
Thomas Scot
Samuel Middlton
John Burgis
John Cempe
William Watts
Richard Bowman
Joseph Smith

St Peter Parmentergate
[continued]

Thomas Peck
Michael Cumball
John Low
John Rand
Robert Paggitt
John Dacon
Joseph Solden
widow Man
widow Wilson
William Barn
Thomas Barber
widow Starling
widow Skiles
Edward Harper 2
widow Gibbs
Stephen Uflett
Thomas Willis
Henry Wisester
John Hewit
Anthony Numam 2
Thomas Dany
widow Moss
John Dany
John Graves
John Davy
William Carlton
John Dany
John Greenwood
Edmund Lawes
George Lindly
Brian Quintin
widow Blackamore 2
Augustine Person
Peter Lillie
John Finch
Edward Crosfield
William Clarke
Edward Elby
Richard Burnum
Francis Clarke
John Lofty
William Hodskin
John Duing

St Peter Parmentergate
[continued]

John Turner
William Browne
widow Smith
Robert Rush
Edmund Mortimie
Richard Booth 2
Thomas Shingfield
John Dix
widow Jording
Thomas Okes
widow Browne
William Fell
Thomas Murton
John Earle
Thomas Hood
James Nunn
John Browne
Henry Moore
widow Man
Thomas Rusbrooke
George Hill
widow Browne
John Hansell 2
Richard Claydon
Thomas Deane
Samuel Baly
widow Deane
John Hood
widow Leasing
Francis Colman
William Browne
widow Hewit
Robert Abree
widow Gaifer
Robert Sinyard
Robert Taylor
John Newhouse
widow Buckingham
Robert Samond
John Cunstable
Stephen Croch
Thomas Maine
Thomas Fellow

St Peter Parmentergate
[continued]

Thomas Clup
Roger Stantin
Mary Anderson
widow Howard
Benjamin Riches
Thomas Mortimie
William Howell
William Gary
Robert Badly   2
John Budery
Thomas Cunstable
Jeremiah Ogden
widow Hansell
widow Hoath
widow [?Wr]ight
Robert Fletcher
Ann Baker
widow Bowman
Edmund Kippin
Thomas Gardiner   2

[266 Names]

E 179/338, f.38

St Peter Southgate

13 Mar 1670/1

Robert Hye
William Gegg
widow Hurne
William Cotten
James Nunn
William Phillips
Job Barnes
Roger Linsey
James Vines
Charles Stevens
James Barlow
Nicholas Salter
James Fitt
widow Mayes

St Peter Southgate [continued]

John Nicksonne
Richard Harwood
Robert Smith
widow Devill
widow Buntin
Thomas Turner
Richard Worminger
Oliver Bunn
Richard Rudd
Nicholas Turner
Thomas Larman
William Worminger
widow Albro
William Nobs
Ralph Turner
Thomas Thorlow
James Cooper
widow Holland
William Sherwood
widow Puntt
Ambrose Pagg
Robert Worminger
widow Green
Arthur Sherman
William Dunkes
Christopher Andersonne
Thomas Chamberlin
William Mace
widow Loudy
Nathaniel Gouldin
Robert Crisnall
Richard Beasly
Elizabeth Lemmon
William Paggett
John Youngs
Thomas Stacy
John Turner
Richard Dawsonne
John Bradford
John Burton
William Nobs
Thomas Fox
widow Green
Richard Hoath

St Peter Southgate [continued]

Thomas Hogdkins
Thomas Woodgard
George Blancher
Alexander Burgis
Susan Beare
Joseph Goold
widow Gray
widow Digby
William Gedg
George Paggett
William Franklin
Richard Turner
John Sharpe
John Baker
Joseph Shinkfild
widow Shinkfild
Christopher Stuard
George Halftonne
Elizabeth Winkfild
Richard Powell
widow Wing
Richard Thurkittell
goodman Skarfe
Augustine Swadock
William Evins
Thomas Balliston
John Durrant
Matthew Steward
Thomas Pamment
Nicholas Salter
Thomas Bucher
Esther Tompsonne
goodman Mayes
James Newby
widow Basly
widow Cock
Philip Rysine
widow Balding
widow Harvy
Richard Brome
widow Knowles
George Picher
widow Playne
John Rissin

St Peter Southgate [continued]

goodman Howlins
widow More

[104 Names]

E 179/336, f.90

St Peter Southgate

12 Apr 1672

Robert Hey
Peter Moer
John Risen
widow Hunne
widow Gagge
James Nunne
Nicholas Salter
James Barly
Charles Stephen
Thomas Turnes
William Cotton
Charles Phillips
Job Barnes
George Picher
Roger Lingey
James Vines
Richard Harwod
Thomas Buckes
James Fitt
Robert ...
Richard Brame
Richard Warmenger
widow Green
Rose Maies
Oliver Bunn
John Mixon
Richard Rud
William Warmenger
Ambrose Pagge
Robert Wamenger
George Hailston
Jean Bunton
Augustine Swadd

St Peter Southgate [continued]

Ann Swallbing
Nicholas Turner
Thomas Leamon
Thomas Leasey
widow Holand
widow Jone
Ralph Turner
William Euins
Charles Andosen
widow Punt
Matthew Stuard
widow Loufdey
Nathaniel Goulden
Robert Crisnoll
Thomas Chambrlin
Richard Beasly
Thomas Thurlow
widow Leaman
Thomas Paymet
Nicholas Salter
William Nobes
William Pagget
...am [?John] Yonges
John Turner
Richard Darson
John Burton
Thomas Baleston
John Bradfuard
Esther Tomson
Thomas Foox
John Maies
James Neube
Gregory Barker
widow Green
Thomas Hodgking
Thomas Woodgward
Susan Beare
Luke Shearman
Joseph Smith
John Miller
Robert Barnood
Mary Degbey
Ann Gray
widow Goulding

St Peter Southgate [continued]

Richard Hoth, jun.
William Gegge
widow Basey
Alexander Burges
widow Coock
William Franklin
John Sharp
George Pagget
Richard Turner
John Baker
Joseph Shukfild
Richard Thirkettle
Christopher Scarfe
widow Wingfild
James ...e
widow Winge
Richard Pouell
John Durent
William Nobbe
widow Shinkfild
Richard Thurckitel
Michael Scarfe
widow Danill
William Franklin
widow Bolden
widow Plaine
John Hoaking
widow Knowels
William Soutter
Simon Ollyett
widow Ossbard

[108 Names]

E 179/336, f.91

St Peter Southgate

10 Feb 1672/3

Robert Hye	1
widow Harvie	1
William Cottin	2
Roger Linsie	

St Peter Southgate [continued]

James Vines
John Pindalow
Robert More
Nicholas Saltar
William Phillips
Job Barnes
Frances Elderton
widow Mayes
John Nickson
Richard Harod
widow Davell
widow Bursin
Thomas Turner
Richard Warminger
Oliver Bunn
Edmund More
Nicholas Turner
William Worminger
Thomas Harmun
widow Alborow
John Cristin
Ralph Turner
widow Hollond
Thomas Dewson
Richard Bowman
Edmund Harod
Christopher Stuard
widow Punt
William Folliw
James Suffell
Christopher Andarson
Robert Lansalot
William Mase
Robert Worminger
Robert Crisnall
Richard Basely
William Pagget
Elizabeth Leaman
Bartholomew Goulder
John Youngs
John Bradfer
John Turner
Richard Doorson
William Nobes

St Peter Southgate [continued]

goody Buttrie
Christopher Brum
widow Digby
John Durrunt
Thomas Woodger
Matthew Wooddie
'Meg' Turner
William Gage
Thomas Hogkines
Richard Harth
George Blancher
Susan Beare
Alexander Burgis
John Miller
Joseph Guld
widow Gray
William Gege
John Ovaren
George Pagget
Thomas Horth
Robert Nockales
George Balston
John Sharpe
John Bacur
Joseph Shinkefild
widow Shinkefild
Matthew Stuard
Henry Dye
Frances Spareman
widow Wing
Richard Thurketell
goody Scarfe
Paul Deker
William Eiuins
William Nobs
Thomas Fox
Benjamin Thurketell
Thomas Pammant
Richard Poull
widow ...y
William C...ll
James Newby
William Mayes
Thomas Bucher

St Peter Southgate [continued]

Nicholas Saltar
Richard Brume
William Jonsones
Philip Rison
widow Semmons
Charles Stevenes
Richard Turner
George Picher
Frances Gidney
John Rison
widow Playne
widow Moore
widow Knoules

[105 Names]

E 179/336, f.92

St Peter Southgate

6 May 1674

widow Starvey	1
William Colten	1
Roger Linsey	1
widow Holland	1
Robert Moore	1
Nicholas Saffer	1
William Phillops	1
Job Barnes	1
Francis Elderton	1
widow Wiges	1
widow Broome	1
mother Harvy, widow	1
widow Balderey	1
James Clough	1
widow Devell	1
widow Burton	1
Thomas Turner	1
Richard Warmeger	1
Oliver Bunn	1
Nicholas Turner	1
William Warmiger	1
widow Alborrough	1

St Peter Southgate [continued]

John Christian	1
Ralph Turner	1
widow Holland	1
Thomas Dewson	1
Richard Bowman	1
Christopher Stewart	1
John Metcalfe	1
William Salter	1
Joseph Shinkefeild	1
Christopher Anderson	1
John Cutter	1
widow Maze	1
Robert Worminger	1
Robert Cresnall	1
Richard Baseley	1
William Pagett	1
Elizabeth Lemmon	1
Bartholomew Goulder	1
John Youngs	1
John Bradfer	1
John Turner	1
Richard Dawson	1
William Nobbs	1
old Buttery	1
Christopher Brome	1
widow Digby	1
John Durrant	1
Thomas Woodger	1
Matthew Woodye	1
… Turner	1
William Gedge	1
Thomas Hodgkines	1
Richard Horth	1
George Blancher	1
Susan Beare	1
Alexander Burges	1
John Miller	1
Thomas Woodyard	1
widow Gray	1
William Callingworth	1
John Overing	1
George Pagett	1
Thomas Hoth	1
Robert Nokholds	1

St Peter Southgate [continued]   E 179/338, f.39

George Halster	1
John Sharpe	1
John Staver	1
widow Shinkefield	1
Matthew Steward	1
Henry Dye	1
Francis Spareman	1
widow Wing	1
Richard Thirkettle	1
widow Skarfe	1
Paul Dicker	1
William Ewens	1
William Nobbs	1
Thomas Fox	1
Benjamin Thirkettle	1
Thomas Pament	1
Richard Edwards	1
William Tompson	1
Thomas Symonds	1
James Newby	1
William Mayes	1
John Brigg	1
Thomas Bucher	1
Nicholas Foster	1
Richard Browne	1
James Newby	1
Nicholas Salter	1
William Johnsons	1
Philip Ryson	1
widow Semmonds	1
widow Stephens	1
George Read	1
Francis Gidney	1
John Ryson	1
widow Moore	1
widow Knowles	1
William Pyndelow	1
Thomas Riches	2
widow Sheringham	1
John Baker	1
Edward Shearewood	1

[107 Names]

St Saviour [in Fyebridge Ward]

[undated ?early 1671]

Ellen Thompson
widow Dingle
Roger Gibson
John Demoline
Elisha Kineman
widow Beverly
Christopher Cooke
Peter Kiniman
John Hewit
John Warner
widow Tasey
widow Ringall
widow Thompson
James Parnell
Thomas Allyn
John Molden
George Beckwith
Richard Dey
William Collyn
widow Wilson
widow Sowell
Edward Warnes
Penelope Thirston
widow Dowsinge
widow Ba...es
widow Barton
Thomas Leath

[27 Names]

E 179/338, f.40

St Saviour [in Colegate Ward]

15 Feb 1670/1

widow Drome
Edmund Monford
Charles Gringale
widow Barton

St Saviour [continued]

Zachariah Mayhew
5 Alms Houses
widow Tace
William Adams
John Broombe
John Spinsbee
Elizabeth Kerey
widow Camplin
Roger Robinson
Thomas West
widow Inman
John Hogg
Henry Sharpe
Robert Pickerill
John Inman

[19 Names]

E 179/336, f.93

St Saviour [in Fyebridge Ward]

20 Apr 1672

Ellen Tompson
widow Dingle
Roger Gibson
John Demoline
widow Beaverly
Peter Kinaman
John Warner
widow Tase
James Parnall
Thomas Allen
John Maulden
George Beckwith
Richard Dey
William Collens
widow Wilson
widow Sewell
Edward Warnes
Thomas Leath
John Hunt
William Beecraft

St Saviour [continued]

Christopher Cooke
widow Tompson

[22 Names]

E 179/336, f.94

St Saviour [in Colegate Ward]

20 Apr 1672

John Brombe
John Inman
Roger Roberson
Thomas West
goodman Hogge
goodwife Barton
goodman Shinking
the Alms Houses
John Spinsby
widow Inman
William Fakner
widow Dromer
Edmund Munford
Charles Cogwell
Zachary Mayhew
widow Camplin
Henry Sharpe
Robert Pickrin

[18 Names]

E 179/336, f.95

St Saviour [in Fyebridge Ward]

16 Aug 1672

John Moline
Thomas Leath
John Warner
Thomas Rix
James Parnall

St Saviour [continued]

Thomas Allen
John Baliston
widow Dingle
widow Beaverly
George Beckwith
William Collens
goodman Becraft
Edward Warnes
Richard Dey
widow Wilson
John Moldin
Peter Kinaman
widow Sewell
Richard Tite
John Harman
William Pecke

[21 Names]

E 179/336, f.96

St Saviour [in Colegate Ward]

31 Aug 1672

Thomas West
Roger Roberson
goodman Hogg
John Inman
John Brombe
John Spinsby
widow Tasy
widow Micklburrow
widow Jell
widow Bookes
William Adams
widow Inman
William Faskner
Edmund Munford
widow Barton
Henry Sharpe
Robert Pickrin

[17 Names]

E 179/336, f.97

St Saviour [in Fyebridge Ward]

18 Apr 1674

Thomas Leath	1
Peter Kinaman	2
John Demoline	1
widow Beaverly	1
John Huith	1
John Warner	2
John Spinsly	2
Eli Catew	1
James Parnall	2
Edward Warnes	1
widow Wilson	1
widow Sewell	1
goodman Dey	2
John Baliston	1
goodman Moltier	1
William Collings	1
Adam Prix	1

[17 Names]

E 179/336, f.98

St Saviour [in Colegate Ward]

3 May 1674

John Inman	1
John Broome	1
John Hogg	2
Thomas West	1
widow Inman	1
William Feakner	1
widow Taze	1
Robert Pickeringe	2
the 6 widows in the Alms Houses	
Edmund Munford	2
widow Barton	1
Henry Sharfe	1
goodman Ransham	2

144

St Saviour [continued]

Peter Shinquin	1
John Fremon	1
Benjamin Gunton	1
Jane Dremee	1
Abraham Dremee	1
Isaac Ricky	1
John Blunden	1
goodman Nicolls	1

[21 Names]

E 179/338, f.41

St Simon and St Jude

14 Dec 1670

Robert Trewe
Nicholas Thompson
Robert Graves
Charles Rewe
Alexander Cotten
Thomas Harrison
James Bullard
Wentworth Antell
Thomas Harman
Diana Linge
Richard Harvey
Thomas James
Thomas Robinson
widow Hansell
Edward Bacon
Thomas Tills
Thomas Hedgman
widow Harmon
Samuel Sparham
John Pooley
Edward Beavis
Henry Smyth
Thomas Harper
Thomas Symonds
widow Hubbard
Nathaniel Wife
Nicholas Balls

St Simon and St Jude
[continued]

[27 Names]

E 179/336, f.99

St Simon and St Jude

15 Feb 1671/2

Robert True
Nicholas Tomson
Charles Reve
Alexander Cotton
Thomas Harriss
James Bullerd
Wentworth Antell
Thomas Harmon
Diana Lang
Richard Harvy
Thomas James
Thomas Robinson
widow Hansell
Edward Bacon
Thomas Tills
Thomas Hedgman
widow Harmon
Samuel Sparrum
John Coely
Thomas Fiddiman
Henry Smith
Thomas Harper
Thomas Simonds
widow Hubberd
Nathaniel Wiffe

[25 Names]

E 179/336, f.100

St Simon and St Jude

17 July [blank ?1672]

Robert Trew

St Simon and St Jude
[continued]

Nicholas Tompson
Charles Reeve
Alexander Cotton
Thomas Harrice
Wentworth Antell
James Bullard
Thomas Hermon
Diana Ling
Richard Harvey
Thomas James
Thomas Robbeson
Edward Backon
Thomas Tyles
Thomas Hedgman
widow Harman
Samuel Sparrom
John Cooley
Henry Smith
Thomas Harper
Thomas Simons
widow Hubbord
Thomas Fiddemon
Robert Graves
John Dixeley
John Dunningston
widow Brooke
Nicholas Beales

[28 Names]

E 179/336, f.101

St Simon and St Jude

18 Feb 1673/4

Robert Trew	2
good Hedyman	1
widow Hubart	1
Thomas Symonds	2
good Bacon	2
widow Harman	1
Thomas Robinson	1

St Simon and St Jude
[continued]

Thomas Tyles	1
Alexander Cotton	2
Nicholas Tompson	2
Richard Harvey	1
widow Lyster	2
goodman Sparrow	1
widow Smith	1
goodman Pooly	1
goodman Harper	1
Robert Graves	2
Thomas Harman	1
Nicholas Balls	1
Thomas James	2
Thomas Fideman	1
widow Brooke	1
James Bullard	1
Thomas Harris	2

[24 Names]

E 179/338, f.42

St Stephen

[undated ?early 1671]

widow Seely
John Seaman
John Church
William Martin
Sarah Witherby
John Pratt
John Allyn
Samuel Reigham
Thomas Curson
John Secker
Robert Ruddall
William Brooke
John Wallington
William Stiles
James Reyner
widow Rushbrooke
Abraham Lambe

St Stephen [continued]

widow Carr
Oliver Burcham
Richard Turner
Robert Soames
William Chapman, sen.
widow Potter
John Collison
widow Stoneham
Susan Reeve
Richard Sparrowe
Thomas Mann
Ralph Pantre
Thomas Secker
widow Leavocke
Joan Fuller
Ann Thurlowe
Joan Feake
Henry Secker
Robert Wilde
Thomas Smith
Hugh Browne
Richard Barker
John Jenkingson
Richard Norgate
William Warrants
goodman Harvy
Stephen Johnson
Robert Jefferys
Richard Cooke
Robert Armestead
John Munns
Alice Hodges
goodman Greene
Mary Good
William Dussing
goodman Lake
John Jordan
widow Rogerson
Thomas Eldred
Robert Barber
Thomas Love
John Spratts
Elizabeth Dye
Henry Fothergell

St Stephen [continued]

Robert Suffelld
Grace Beckett
Francis Studd
John Ems
widow Smith
John Smith
George Martin
Silvanus Hodges
John Calloway
Robert Barber, jun.
Thomas Tillney
widow Clay
Thomas Collin
Richard Holland
Jeremiah Becke
John Thacker
Henry Curson
Samuel Leason
Elizabeth Gillmore
John Warren
Robert Tiler
Lawrence Moseley
William Chapman
widow Dudley
Edward Lyonell
John Tompson
Thomas Tompson
William Clarke
Joseph Nobbs
Nicholas Auborne
John Tuttill
John Mann
Richard Guns
John Potter
widow Burton
Edmund Balldwin
widow Allison
Samuel Whiten
widow Spill
Thomas Adkins
Richard Turner
William Stiles
goodwife Bell
goodwife Smith

St Stephen [continued]

goodman Fryer
widow Oliver
Henry Valentine
Francis Moulson
John Bery
George Hales
John Rusting
Isaac Thacker
Samuel Baldrowe
widow Elliott
widow Wells
John Sullman
John Titler
John Prittman
widow Durrant
Philip Lucas
widow Deye
Elizabeth Pilkington
John Barker
widow Scott
Thomas Rawlinge
John Fothergell
widow Juby
John Carr
John Johnson
Robert Tillney
good Nicherson
widow Reynollds
Nicholas Julier
James Nicholls
Mary Skipp
Edmund Woods
Frances Sidnor
widow Eaton
Adam Crotch
Frances Duberson
Robert Woodcrofte
Abraham Lambe
Thomas Woollmer
widow Cleare
Island Barber
widow Woods
widow Brooke
John Deye

St Stephen [continued]

Robert Browne
John Percivall
John Sharlowe
Thomas Tiler
goodwife Bell
Stephen Segens
widow Godsworth
Peter Fullchis
Edward Tuttill
goodwife Bell
widow Carr

[160 Names]

E 179/337, f.14

St Stephen

11 Apr 1672

Robert Brettingham
John Titter
widow Sealy
John Seamons
William Marttin
Stephen Seagood
Sarah Witherby
John Pratt
widow Dodsworth
John Alling
James Raynor
Thomas Curson
John Seacker
Robert Ruddall
William Brookes
John Warllinton
James Ragham
widow Rushbrooke
Abraham Lambe
Peter Fullches
Elizabeth Carr
Oliver Burchham
Richard Turner
Robert Soomes

St Stephen [continued]

William Chapman, sen.
widow Pootter
John Collowson
widow Stonham
Susan Reeve
Richard Sparow
Thomas Mann
widow Ellitt
widow Welles
John Sullman
John Prittyman
Ralph Panttry
Thomas Seacker
Edward Tuttell
widow Bell
widow Leavitt
John Fuller
Ann Thurllow
Joan Feake
Henry Seacker
Robert Willde
Thomas Smith
Hugh Browne
Richard Barker
John Jenkinson
Richard Norgitt
William Woron
goodman Harvy
Isaac Battes
Robert Jeeffrys
Richard Cooke
John Doobson
Robert Armsted
John Minis
Alice Hodgges
goodman Grenn
Mary Good
William Dusen
goodman Lake
William Rutter
John Jorden
Isaac Bllomfelld
widow Rodgerson
Thomas Ellderid

St Stephen [continued]

Robert Barber
Thomas Love
John Spratt
Henry Fothergell
Robert Suffelld
widow Carr, sen.
Grace Beckitt
widow Duront
Francis Studde
John ...ins
widow Smith
John Smith
George Marling
John Calloway
Robert Barber, sen.
Thomas Tillny
widow Clay
Thomas Collings
Richard Hollond
Jeremy Becke
John Thacker
Henry Curson
Samuel Leason
John Woron
Elizabeth Gillman
Robert Tyller
Lawrence Morsly
William Chapman
widow Dudley
Edward Lionell
John Tompson
Thomas Tompson
William Blacke
Joseph Noobs
Nicholas Awborn
John Tuttell
John Mann
Richard Gunnes
John Potter
widow Burtton
Edmund Boollden
widow Alleson
Samuel Whiting
widow Spill

St Stephen [continued]

Thomas Atkins
Richard Turnor
William Stylles
goody Bell
goody Smith
goodman Fryer
widow Olliver
Henry Vallintin
Francis Mallster
John Beary
George Halles
John Rusting
Isaac Thacker
Samuel Balldre
widow Baster
Philip Lucas
widow Dey
widow Pillkinton
John Barker
widow Scott
John Fothergell
widow Jubby
John Carr
John Jonsons
Robert Tillny
goodman Nickerson
widow Ranolles
Nicholas Jullyer
James Nickolles
Mary Skippe
Edmund Woods
Francis Siddnor
widow Eatton
Francis Dickinson
Adam Crotch
Robert Woodrufe
Abraham Lambe
Thomas Woolmer
widow Clear
Island Barber
widow Woods
widow Broocke
John Day
Robert Browne

St Stephen [continued]

John Parcivall
John Sharllon
Thomas Tyller
widow Bell
Robert Hunn
Margaret Tompon, widow
Thomas Thacker

[163 Names]

E 179/336, f.102

St Stephen

14 Feb 1672/3

Robert Bretingham
John Tyller
widow Seally
John Seaman
William Marttin
Stephen Seagood
Sarah Witherby
John Pratt
widow Dodsworth
John Alling
James Rayner
Thomas Secker
Robert Ruddall
William Brooke
John Warlinton
James Ragham
widow Rushbrooke
Abraham Lambe
Peter Fullcher
Elizabeth Carr
Oliver Burcham
Richard Turner
Robert Somes
William Potter
Thomas Creson
John Colison
widow Stanham
Susan Reve

St Stephen [continued]

Richard Sparough
Thomas Munn
widow Ellitt
widow Welles
John Sullman
John Prittyman
Ralph Panttery
Thomas Secker
Edward Tuttell
widow Bell
widow Levett
John Fuller
Ann Thurlow
John Feake
Henry Secker
Thomas Smith
Robert Willee
Hugh Browne
Richard Buxtton
John Jenkenson
Richard Norgatt
William Worron
goodman Harvy
Isaac Battes
Robert Jeferis
Richard Cooke
John Dobson
Robert Armsted
John Mines
Alice Hodges
goodman Grenn
Mary Good
William Dusing
goodman Leake
William Rutter
Isaac Blumfelld
widow Rodgerson
Thomas Ellderid
Robert Barker
John Sprutte
Henry Forthergell
Robert Sufelld
widow Carsor
widow Durente

St Stephen [continued]

Francis Stedd
John Rines
widow Smith
John Smith
George Marttin
Robert Barkerson
Thomas Tyllney
widow Skaye
Richard Holland
Jeremy Becke
John Thacker
Henry Curson
Samuel Leason
John Worrofor
Elizabeth Gillman
Robert Tyller
Lawrence Morselly
William Chapman
William Duddelly
John Tompson
Thomas Tompson
William Blake
Joseph Nobbs
William Chapman, sen.
John Jorden
Thomas Love
Grace Beckitt
John Dallowaye
Thomas Collings
Edward Leonell
Nicholas Auborn
John Tuttell
John Mann
Richard Gunnes
John Poottor
widow Burtton
Edmund Bolldin
widow Allison
Samuel Whitting
widow Spill
Thomas Attkinson
Richard Turnor
William Stilles
widow Bell

St Stephen [continued]

widow Smith
goodman Fryer
widow Olliver
Henry Vallintin
Frances Mallster
John Beary
George Halles
John Dustin
Isaac Thaker
Samuel Balldre
widow Buster
Philip Lucus
widow Dayes
widow Pilkinton
John Barker
widow Scott
John Forthergell
widow Jubby
John Carr
John Jonson
Robert Tylney
goodman Nyckerson
widow Renoulds
Nicholas Fuller
James Nickolls
Mary Scype
Edmund Woods
Francis Sidnor
widow Eatton
Francis Dickinson
Adam Crottch
Robert Wodrofe
Abraham Lambe
Thomas Wollmer
widow Clear
Island Barker
widow Woods
widow Browkes
John Daye
Robert Browne
John Parsefull
John Shallow
Thomas Tyller
widow Bell

St Stephen [continued]

Robert Hunn
widow Tompson
Thomas Thaker
Ann Beart, widow

[164 Names]

E 179/336, f.103

St Stephen

12 Mar 1673/4

Robert Brettingham	1
Robert Tyler	1
widow Sealey	1
John Seaman	1
William Watling	1
Stephen Seagood	1
Samuel Witherley	1
John Pratt	1
James Rayner	1
Thomas Secker	1
Robert Ruddin	1
William Brookes	1
John Wallington	2
James Raggum	1
widow Rushbrooke	1
Peter Fulchers	1
Elizabeth Carr	1
Oliver Burcham	1
Richard Turner	1
Robert Soames	1
John Potter	1
Henry Curson	1
John Collyson	1
widow Stannu...	2
Susan Reve	1
Richard Sparrow	1
Thomas Munn	1
widow Ellitt	1
Bartholomew Smith	2
John Allen	1
widow Wells	1

St Stephen [continued]

John Sulman	1
John Prittiman	1
Thomas Secker, sen.	1
Edward Tuttell	1
Joan Fuller	1
Ann Thurlow	1
Henry Secker	2
Thomas Smyth	1
Robert Wylee	1
widow Stockes	2
Hugh Browne	1
[?Richard] Buxton	1
John Jenkinson	1
Richard Norgate	1
William Worron	1
widow Harvy	1
Isaac Bates	2
Robert Jefferys	1
Richard Cooke	1
John Dobson	1
Robert Armstead	1
Alice Hodges	1
Thomas Grene	1
Mary Good	2
widow Leake	1
widow Rodgerson	1
Thomas Eldrid	1
Robert Barker	1
Henry Folthergill	1
goodman Styles	2
Francis Studd	1
John Grimes	1
widow Smith	2
John Smith	1
Thomas Tilney	2
Richard Holland	1
Geoffrey Beck	1
John Thacker	1
Samuel Leasy	2
John Burroughs	1
Elizabeth Guilmer	1
Lawrence Morsly	1
John Thompson	1
Thomas Thompson	1

St Stephen [continued]

William Bleake	1
William Chapman	1
Thomas House	2
Grace Beckitt	1
John Lovell	2
Dionisius Greenfed	2
Michael Croch	1
goodman Scott	1
Abraham Lambe	1
old Panterey	1
widow Bell	2
… Levit	1
John Feates	1
William Dussing	1
William Rutter	1
Isaac Blumfield	1
widow Rogerson	1
widow Carser	1
widow Durrant	1
George Marten	1
Robert Barkerson	1
widow Slabbs	1
John Nobbs	1
John Dalleway	1
Thomas Collings	1
Joseph Tuttell	1
Nicholas Aburne	1
John Potter	1
widow Burton	1
widow Smith	1
Abraham Lambe	1
widow Wolmer	1
widow Oliver	1
widow Eldred	1
John S…	1
widow S…ll	1
John Mann	1
Richard Gunns	2
Edward Baldin	1
widow Allyson	1
widow Spil[?l]	1
John Atkison	1
William Styles	1
goodman Fryer	1

St Stephen [continued]

Henry Vallentine	1
Francis Molster	1
John Berry	1
George Hales	2
John Dustin	1
Isaac Thacker	1
Samuel Baldery	1
Philip Lucas	1
Elizabeth Pilkerton	1
John Barker	1
John Folthergill	1
widow Juby	2
John Carr	1
… Johnsons	1
Robert Tilny	1
goodman Nickerson	2
widow Rennolds	1
James Nicholls	1
Edmund Woods	1
Francis Sidnor	1
widow Eaton	1
Francis Dickerson	2
Adam Crotche	1
Robert Woodwards	1
widow Cleare	1
John Browne	1
John Persivall	1
widow Sherlow	1
Robert Hunn	1
widow Thompson	2
Thomas Thacker	1
Martha Wells	1
Bridget Stuart	2
widow Nelson	1
Isabel Smyth	1
goodman Butler	1
widow Chamberlin	1
widow Lincoln	1
William Rushbrooke	2
Richard Barfurr	1
John Polter	1
widow Burton	1
Francis Stead	1
Robert Holland, sen.	1

St Stephen [continued]

[163 Names]

E 179/338, f.43

St Swithin

[undated ?early 1671]

widow Rodwell
widow Baxter
John Notter
Abraham Douty
Samuel Bryant
John Swanson
Thomas Hurlond
John Rudrum
John Goshen, jun.
John Goshen, sen.
Francis Horne
Thomas Bannister
Alice Willd
John Parson
Thomas Tunnill
John Francis
John Tompson
Thomas Allen
William Jarrum
Robert Fiddeman
Abraham Clarke
Joanna Larrold
goodman Blomfeild
Arthur Blomfeild
John Sad
Elizabeth Mandy
widow Baxter
goodman Bunn
Emanuel Bryant
Richard Seele
John Roberson
Thomas Foster
Robert Francum
Thomas Scarlet
widow Munement
Matthew Woods

154

St Swithin [continued]

Ann Stantin
widow Man
Francis Cossey
Thomas Long
Thomas Chapman
goodman Pree
James Harsicle
widow Stone
Charles Emerson
Richard Tuney
Thomas Swift

[47 Names]

E 179/337, f.15

St Swithin

18 Mar [blank ?1671/2]

James Pree
John Odder
John Goshan
Josiah Spratt
Abraham Douttie
John Portter
Nicholas Man
Robert Wattlin
Thomas Howard
Richard Selee
Thomas Swift
Daniel Wright
Clement Hubbard
John Tompson
Thomas Allin
Frances Horne
William Care
Thomas Ogger
Matthew Woods
Thomas Scarlett
goody Frances
John Brett
John Hagon
Ralph Whright

St Swithin [continued]

Charles Jarrum
Edward Curttis
John Lese
Robert Whimer
Jacob Stibborne
Nicholas Burne
Frances Coffie
William Barker
James Harsickle
Thomas Longe
widow Balstone
widow Mandue
widow Bradly
widow Browne
widow Bush
widow Broughton
Robert Booman
Thomas Sad
Robert Ruddrum
widow Warman
Arthur Blumfield
widow Frances
widow Wields
Peter Heires
Peter Scarfe
widow Man
goodman Stillard
Frances Forster
Thomas Britty
Richard Caper
Thomas Tunney
goodman Passiver
Mary Roddwell
goodman Annis
George Tompson
widow Tunney
Sarah Barker
John Tayler
Richard Bosell

[63 Names]

E 179/336, f.104

St Swithin

18 July 1672

Richard Cooper
widow Tunny, sen.
John Porter
John Odder
Joseph Spratt
Thomas Howard
Margaret Broughton
William Carr
George Tompson
Thomas Swift
Thomas Ogyure
John Gushen
Charles Jarrome
Nicholas Man
Thomas Allen
Thomas Styllyard
Ralph Wright
Jacob Stybbin
John Hakeny
Richard Boswell
William Barker
Lydia Bradly, widow
Elizabeth Mandy, widow
Matthew Woods
Thomas Sadd
Nicholas Burne
Sarah Barker
David France
Susan Blumfeild
Mary Ballingston
Francis Horne
Thomas Long
Thomas Skarles
widow Browne
Robert Bowman
John Witherly
Peter Skarfe
Robert Robinson
John Taylor
widow Tunny

St Swithin [continued]

Peter Heires
Richard Caper
Samuel Dye
Edward Curtis
James Hassickle
Mary Roddell
Robert Watlyn
Daniel Wright
John Tompson
Robert Ruddrome
James Pree
Richard Seely
goodman Pearse
Clement Hubbard
John Brett
Edward Tempell
widow Bush
Francis Foster
Thomas Bryty
goodman Passifull
Charles Annis
Abraham Dowly

[62 Names]

E 179/336, f.105

St Swithin

8 May 1674

Edward Curtis	2
Robert Watling	2
Robert Peine	1
Clement Hubbard	1
widow Broughton	1
Thomas Allen	1
Ralph Wright	2
widow Wright	1
Mary Rodwell	1
Robert Rudram	2
Daniel Barny	1
widow Daniell	1
widow Baliston	1

St Swithin [continued]

Francis Horne	1
John Brett	1
John Swanson, sen.	2
John Goshen	1
Thomas Swift	1
John Tompson	1
John Porter	2
widow Barker	1
Charles Jerome	1
widow Mandey	1
William Carr	1
widow Bradley	1
George Tompson	2
Nicholas Foster	1
John Swanson, jun.	1
Matthew Dyn	1
William Cudball	1
Thomas Augur	1
Martin True	1
widow Walfmond	1
widow Tunny	1
widow Tunny	1
widow Blomfeild	1
James Hasickle	2
Jacob Stebbon	2
Charles Annis	1
Thomas Howard	1
John Passifull	1
Samuel Dye	1
John Witherill	1
Edmund Gunton	1
Joseph Sprat	1
John Taylor	1
Richard Cowper	2
Thomas Tillead	1
widow Man	1
widow Brown	1
widow Vipers	1
widow Francis	1
David France	1
widow Bush	1
Thomas Scarlett	2
widow Wild	1
Thomas Long	1

St Swithin [continued]

Richard Middlebrooke	1
Thomas Sadd	2
Richard Boswell	2
Thomas Aldredge	1
Robert Bowman	2

[62 Names]

E 179/338, f.44

Trowse Millgate, Bracondale & Carrow

18 Feb 1670/1

James Cluse
widow Mann
Edward Bunn
Henry Elmy
Edward Church, sen.
widow Bolton
Edward Church, jun.
Mary Buntinge
widow Jarey
Henry Shreve
John Allesander
Jacob Baker
Anthony Bayliffe
widow Pettegre
John Tompson
Dennis Hunt
John Castilowe
widow Durrant
Tobias Allen
Jacob Humerstone
Elizabeth Bally
widow Clarke
Henry Symonds
Robert Shreve
John Godfery
Robert Cadle
Daniel Felsteade
Robert Stone
George Pettegre

Trowse Millgate, Bracondale & Carrow [continued]

John Porter
Edmund Dey
John Gaye
widow Cragge
Pettigrew Weaves
Edward Randall
Samuel Burton
Samuel Olyet
Daniel Parke
good Crabtre

[39 Names]

E 179/337, f.16

Trowse Millgate

22 Mar 1671/2

widow Mann	1
Edward Bun	1
John Dody	1
Edmund Church	1
widow Boulton	1
Edward Church, jun.	1
Mary Bunton	1
Thomas Subburn	1
widow Jary	1
Henry Chreve	1
John Allexanders	1
Jacob Baker	1
Anthony Baleffe	1
John Ballden	1
John Tompson	2
John Pitling	1
widow Durrent	1
Tobias Allen	1
John Ransom	1
Jacob Hembestone	1
John Heslup	1
William Baker	1
widow Clark	1
Henry Semons	1

Trowse Millgate [continued]

Robert Shrefe	2
John Godfrey	1
Thomas Benefeld	1
Richard Deny	1
Robert Cadle	1
Robert Stone	1
George Petegriue	1
Edward Day	1
John Gay	2
widow Crag	1
Pettigrew Weavers	1
widow Crabtree	1
Edward Randale	1
David Parke	1
Thomas Balistone	1
Thomas Riches	1
John Leveritt	1
Thomas Barne	1
Thomas Fering	1
Thomas Festead	2
widow Wats	1
Tobias Allen	1

[46 Names]

E 179/336, f.106

Trowse Millgate

27 Aug 1672

Toby Alene
Jacob Baker
William Baker
John Boules
Thomas Bunn
Robert Shriefs
John Godfriey
Samuel Boules
Thomas Browne
William Palmare
Thomas Richards
John Gay
Joseph Dey

Trowse Millgate [continued]

E 179/336, f.107

Trowse Millgate, Bracondale & Carrow

31 Dec 1673

widow Crake	
Ann Backer	
Robert Cadly	
Robert Stone	
Thomas Barney	
George Petygre	goody Bunn 1
goodman Rogers	widow Bunton 1
Edward Randle	Edmund Church 1
widow Crabtree	John Dawdy 1
goodman Lineicke	Thomas Sabberne 1
widow Cardle	Henry Shreife 1
John Balstone	widow Jery 1
John Parke	John West 1
Robert Browne	William Seaman 1
Edward Bunns	John Hansell 1
widow Molete	John Hardey 1
Edward Church, sen.	John Piteling 1
John Gadey	good Coppling 1
Thomas Subbone	Richard Denny 1
widow Garey	widow Day 1
Henry Shrf	Thomas Jeferis 1
William Semans	John Adcock 1
Richard Bolden	widow Church 1
widow Alexander	widow Durrant 1
widow Picklen	Anthony Beiyliffe 1
Anthony Balfs	John Ranson 1
John Tomsons	Samuel Cullyer 1
Richard Deney	Jacob Humberstone 1
Thomas Benifilds	John Haslewood 1
John Alcocke	William Baker 1
Edmund Church	widow Clarke 1
widow Durant	widow Adcock 1
John Ransom	John Susoms 1
Jacob Humerstone	Robert Sheriffe 1
John Fellips	John Godfre 1
widow Clarke	Richard Baldwin 1
widow Man	good Liniker 1
	Thomas Ballestone 1
[50 Names]	widow Cardle 1
	John Bowles 2
	Thomas Bunn 1
	John Parke 1
	William Hogges 1
	Thomas Pettitt 1

Trowse Millgate, Bracondale & Carrow [continued]

Thomas Riches	2
Samuel Bowels	1
William Palmer	1
John Gay	1
Joseph Dey	1
widow Cragge	1
Ann Baker	1
Robert Cardle	1
Robert Stone	1
Thomas Barney	1
George Pettegree	1
good Rogers	1
Edward Randle	1
widow Craptree	1

[53 Names]

Great Yarmouth

E 179/338, f.45

First North Ward

10 Feb 1670/1

John Copland	1
Thomasine Thompson, widow	1
widow Sturly	1
Ann Thompson, widow	1
widow Hagon	2
Henry Pembrooke	2
widow Scottaway	1
Judith Fox, widow	1
Robert Grubb	1
Robert Saule	1
James Harwood	1
widow Reeve	1
William Fowler	2
Mary Hallaway	1
Anthony Calfe	1
widow Horsely	1
widow Pomfrett	1

First North Ward [continued]

John Flowerday	1
William Denny	1
Winifred Carre	1
William Emmes	1
widow Browne	1
Thomas Smyth	1
widow Wilson	1
widow Fish	2
Isabella Kilby	1
Edward Tillny	2
widow Allen	1
Robert Midleton	1
Alms Houses outside the North Gates	10
Robert Harward	1
Alms Houses in the ...ampe Row	27
Thomas Smyth	1
Henry Jackson	2
John Drake	2
Norman Clymas	2
widow Johnson	2
Thomas Drake	1
Israel Warde	1
Robert Stward	1
Grace Walker, widow	1
Robert Smyth	2
widow Lacy	1
William Smyth	1
Scudamore Biggs	1
Benjamin Bell	1
widow Croome	1
Timothy Pinchinge	2
Joseph Godfrey	2
Thomas Packe	2
Edward Nicholls	2
Thomas Norton	1
widow Haste	1
James Davey	2
widow Johnson, jun.	1
John Smyth	2
widow Johnson, sen.	2
widow Mathewes	1
John Smyth	2

First North Ward [continued]

Nicholas Kinge	1
Thomas Mann	2
Theodore Bathurst	2
Thomas Bambridge	2
John Arminger	2
Robert Illbertt	1
Nicholas Tursey	1
Benjamin Clefton	2
widow Towne	1
widow Harley	1
Robert Trunchinge	1
widow Goldinge	1
widow Oult	1
Thomas Fancie	1
widow Pritty	2
Richard Haridance	1
Nicholas Wortely	2
Thomas Neave	1
Philip Rust	1
Thomas Tyte	2
Thomas Harvy	1
Thomas Rocken	1
widow Rose	1
Thomas Warde	1
widow Gay	2
Mark Yell	1
John Brett	2
Ralph Silver	1
Richard Creede	2
Thomas Smyth	1
Robert Hastens	1
Peter Candler	1
Christopher Ryall	1
widow Markeall	1
Mark Wheeler	2
Richard Pearson	1
John Seale	1
widow Woods	1
Alms Houses at the Pudding Gates	59
Elizabeth Johnson, widow	1
Robert Cully	2
Benjamin Horsley	1
Matthew Cocke	1

First North Ward [continued]

John Story	1
Joseph Jay	1
John Smyth	2
Edward Singler	1
Paul Leech	1
Prudence Fuller, widow	1
Alms Houses in the Condge	16
Roger Ruttler	2
Alms Houses about the Churchyard	5
Susan Childresse	1
John Dyer	2
Elizabeth Lambert	1
John Beare	1
widow Comeman	1
John Allen	1
John Disney	2
Robert Capon	2
William Brigham	1
widow Arnold	1
Isaac Allen	1
widow Hubard	1
Richard Swift	2
Robert Greene	1
widow Browne	2
widow Batcheldor	1
... Piggot	2
widow Teasdell	2
Henry Bellett	2
Samuel Mason	1
Susan George	1
Robert Newman	2
Joseph Fisher	2
Joshua Palmer	2
widow Wright	1
widow Garrard	1
John Murrible	2
widow Ellsey	1
Thomas Dowe	1
Grace Walker	1
widow Lanthorne	2
Benjamin Cheston	1
Robert Pearson	2
William Eldridge	1

First North Ward [continued]

Alexander March	1
Jeremiah Browne	1
Christopher Cooke	2
John Todd	1
Thomas Todd	1
widow Buttolph	1
widow Plumstead	1
James Elgate	2
Thomas Fiske	1
widow Wilde	1
widow Wade	1
William Martine	1
Thomas Cubitt	1
John Woods	1
John Cubitt	2
Andrew Ringer	1
Sarah Watts	1
Martin Salmon	1
Gabriel How	1
Henry Manclarke	2
Bartholomew Walker	2
widow Coleman	1
John Saule	2
Thomas Hinderwell	1
James Moss	1
John Huggens, jun.	1
William Barefoote	1
James Taylor	1
Philip Langston	1
widow Gibbs	1
Joseph Youngman	1
widow Wynn	1
Catherine Kinge	1
Dorothy Margeson	1
widow Fuller	1
widow Wilson	1
Thomas Seagoe	1
Margaret Ives	1
Robert Payne	1
widow Paynter	1
Thomas Payne	1
Sarah Tyres	2
Robert Palmer	1
John Gitter	1

First North Ward [continued]

John Bunn	1
Elisha House	1
William Cooper	2
widow Leacocke	1
Robert Quintree	2
John Bowman	1
Christopher Brettnell	2
widow Fleman	1
Edward Jecks	1
widow Howard	1
widow Lambert	1
William Aldridge, sen.	1
widow Riches	1
widow Hurst	1
Robert Watson	1
widow Acorne	1
Edward House	2
widow Stocken	1
Robert Bell	1
Robert Giffen	1
George Warde	2
Thomas English	1
Mary Oliver	1
Samuel Manninge	1
Martin Bocken	1
Henry Hardinge	2
Robert Garnies	2
Mary Claxton	1
widow Jordan	1
Nicholas Morley	1
Joseph Palmer	1
Andrew Wortely	2
John Fowler	1
widow March	1
Henry Archer	1
Thomas Mills	1
Richard Wallden	1
Francis Bates	1
Nathaniel Leacocke	1
widow Stowman	1
Elizabeth Becker	2
John Bishope	1
Robert Watts	2
Philip Fiske	2

First North Ward [continued]

John Bearte	2
widow Adams	1
Thomas Smyth	1
Robert Swann	1
Robert Johnson	1
Thomas Fitter	1
John Teasdell	1
John Todd	1
John Whitleton	1
Henry Jellett	2
Richard Rumsey	2
William Boyce	1
Margaret Warde, widow	1
widow Leacocke	1
Sarah Couldham	1
William Cooper	2
widow Hurst	1
widow Thompson	1
widow Johnson	2
John Carter	1
Richard Cowson	1
Joh... ...st	2
Roger Kempe	2
William Mustance	1
Thomas Vickerman	1
widow Cater	1
Jacob Crowe	2
... Durrant	2
Ann Browne	1
Mary Cobb, widow	1
Joseph Browne	1
Mary Brigham, widow	1
John Bayfeild	2
John Hastens	1
John Hardinge	2
Elizabeth Shorte	1
Edward Whittleton	1
William Emmes	1
Elizabeth Bodham, widow	1
Henry Dunn	2
widow Burges	1

[269 Names]

E 179/337, f.17

First North Ward

30 Aug 1672

Anthony Colfe
John Copeland
Thomasine Tompson
widow Starly
Henry Newell
Joseph Hollond
Ann Tompson
widow Hagon
Henry Penbrook
widow Scotteway
widow Fox
William Willsby
Robert Grabell
Robert Saule
James Harwood
widow Reve
Joseph Chapman
Mary Hollaway, jun.
William Flower
Mary Holloway, sen.
John Martin
John Nutt
widow Horsly
widow Pomferit
John Flowerday
William Denny
Winifred Clare
William Simes
widow Browne
Thomas Smith
widow Winson
widow Fish
Henry Jackson
widow Allin
Robert Midelton
Robert Harmer
Edward Tillny
Thomas Smith
Anthony Gloster
Isabel Rasba

First North Ward [continued]

Thomas Dreake
Israel Wade
Robert Steward
John Drake
Norman Clemins
widow Jonson
Robert Smith
Grace Waller
widow Hatch
William Smith
Scudamore Puggs
Timothy Pinchin
Philip Harriston
Benjamin Bell
Francis Bates
Thomas Norton
widow Crone
widow Jonson, jun.
Joseph Godfrey
Thomas Pack
widow Mathews
Edward Nicholas
John Smith
Nicholas King
widow Jonson, sen.
Robert Ileburt
Robert Whitelead
Thomas Wann
Nicholas Jarsey
widow Towne
Theodore Backhurst
widow Horly
Robert Tounching
widow Golding
widow Cubit
Thomas Fancy
Richard Hindence
Thomas Neave
Thomas Banburdge
Philip Rust
John Arminger
Benjamin Clifton
widow Pritty
widow Hartly

First North Ward [continued]

Thomas Bosken
widow Rose
Thomas Ward
Mark Gell
Ralph Silver
Thomas Smith
Robert Hastings
Nicholas Wortly
Thomas Tite
widow Gay
Peter Candler
Christopher Rabilla
widow Markhall
Richard Pearson
Nathaniel Lacock
John Bret
John Seale
Richard Woods
Richard Creed
Elizabeth Jonson
Benjamin Horsly
John Smith
Mark Wheeler
John Story
Joseph Jay
Robert Cully
Thomas Ranalls
Ralph Ginne
Paul Leech
Prudence Fuller
Edward Angler
Susan Childirhouse
John Dyer
Elizabeth Lambord
John Disny
John Beare
widow Coman
John Allin
William Bucknam
widow Arnold
Isabel Allin
Robert Capman
Richard Swift
widow Hubard

First North Ward [continued]

Robert Gixin
widow Browne, sen.
John Bigget
widow Bachelder
Samuel Mason
widow Tisdall
Susan George
widow Wright
widow Garret
Henry Bellit
widow Elsy
Robert Newman
Joseph Fisher
Joseph Palmer
Thomas Dow
Grace Walker
John Murribly
Benjamin Cleston
Robert Pearson
William Eldrid
Alexander Marsh
John Tod
Thomas Tod
widow Stowman
widow Lanthorn
Thomas Goodwell
widow Plumstead
Thomas Fisk
Robert Pearson
Christopher Cook
widow Wild
widow Wade
William Martin
Thomas Cubit
John Woods
Andrew Ringer
Sarah Wates
Martin Salmon
Gabriel How
James Elgat
widow Coleman
John Cubit, sen.
Henry Manclark
Bartholomew Walker

First North Ward [continued]

John Sella
Thomas Hinderwell
Joseph Holland
James More
John Huggins, jun.
William Barfoot
Jane Tayler
Philip Langston
Samuel Gibs
Matthew Cock
John S...ach
Joseph Wengman
Roger Botler
widow Wyn
Catherine King
widow Hast
Dorothy Maston
widow Fuller
Henry Newell
Alexander March
widow Jonson
Edward Tillny
Robert Jacob
Ralph Gimne
Israel Blackbourn
widow Willson
Thomas Sego
Sarah Tyre
Margaret Ives
Robert Pene
William Cooper
widow Pointer
widow Benton
John Godson
John Rose
Robert Palmer
John Gutter
Thomas Bunn
Elisha Howse
widow Lecock
Robert Camtree
John Dowman
widow Fleming
Christopher Buttwell

First North Ward [continued]

Edward Jeekes
widow Howard
widow Lambond
William Aldridg, sen.
widow Riches
widow Hust
Edward House
Edmund Wright
Edward Emerson
widow Howard
Amy Wright
John Baly
Robert Watson
widow Acorn
George Ward
widow Sleckin
Robert Bell
Robert Giffen
Thomas Inglish
Mary Wellphir
Henry Harding
Samuel Maning
Joseph Haine
George Dowseing
Thomas Rump
goody Hagon
Martin Backin
Robert Haris
Mary Claxton
Andrew Wortly
widow Jordan
Isaac Morly
Joseph Palmon
John Flower
Jacob Cron
John Smith, sen.
Sarah Newby, jun.
John Turner
Robert Riches
William Boyce
Richard Colse
widow March
Henry Archer
Thomas Miles

First North Ward [continued]

Richard Walden
Elizabeth Baker
John Balton
widow Stowman
John Boship
John Standly
Robert Watters
widow Adams
Thomas Smith
Robert Swan
Philip Fiske
Robert Jinson
Thomas Fitter
John Tisdell
John Todd
John Whitelton
Henry Goblet
Margaret Wade
Richard Rumse
widow Lacock
Sarah Coldham
widow Hust
William Cooper
widow Jonson
widow Tompson
Thomas Hurst
John Carter
Richard Cosin
William Mustent
Roger Cemp
Thomas Rump
Thomas Vickerman
Mrs Allin
Henry Herredin
Edward Costerdin
John Goblet
Thomas Winell
Henry Fleman
widow Bodham
Robert Watson
George Wade
John Goodson
John Heydon
Francis Wates

First North Ward [continued]

John Cubit
John Stanly
John Smith
widow Cane
Ann Wight
widow Howard
Mrs Myth
William Tompson
Peter Candler
Thomas Norton
John Spanton
widow Allin
widow Mally
Francis May

[318 Names]

E 179/337, f.18

First North Ward

16 Feb 1673/4

Anthony Colfe	1
John Copeland	2
Thomas Tompson	1
widow Starly	1
Henry Newell	2
Joseph Holland	1
Ann Tomson	1
widow Hagon	2
Henry Pembrooke	1
widow Scottoway	1
widow Foxe	2
William Wilsby	1
Robert Grabell	1
Robert Saul	2
James Harwood	1
widow Reeve	1
John Chapman	2
Mary Halloway	1
William Flower	1
Mary Hollaway, sen.	1
John Martin	2

First North Ward [continued]

widow Tusly	1
widow Rumfert	2
John Flowerday	1
William Denny	2
William Clare	1
William Simes	1
widow Browne	2
Thomas Smith	1
widow Winson	1
widow Fierly	1
Henry Jackson	1
widow Allen	1
Robert Midleton	1
Robert Harmer	2
Edward Tilling	2
Thomas Smith	1
Isabel Rose	1
Thomas Drake	2
Isabel Wade	1
Robert Steward	1
Norman Clement	2
widow Sanson	1
Grace Waller	2
widow Hutch	1
William Smith	2
Scudamore Biggs	1
Timothy Pintchin	1
Philip Harrison	2
Benjamin Bell	1
Francis Bates	1
Thomas Norton	1
widow Crane	2
widow Johnson, jun.	1
Joseph Godfrye	1
Thomas Baske	1
widow Mathews	2
Edward Nichols	1
John Smith	1
Nicholas King	1
widow Johnson, sen.	2
Robert Illbart	1
Robert Whitlock	1
Thomas Winne	1
Nicholas Jarsye	2

First North Ward [continued]

widow Towne	1
Theodore Backhouse	1
widow Harly	1
Robert Townsling	2
widow Goulding	1
widow Cubitt	1
Thomas Fancy	1
Richard Hindresse	2
Thomas Neave	1
Oliver Rust	1
John Armeger	2
John Clifton	1
widow Grime	1
widow Hartly	1
Thomas Bosken	2
widow Rosse	1
Thomas Ward	1
Mark Gell	1
Ralph Silver	2
Thomas Smith	1
Robert Hasting	1
Nicholas Wortly	2
Thomas Tite	1
widow Gaye	1
Peter Candler	1
widow Nicholls	2
Robert Dowsing	1
Nathaniel Leacock	1
John Brett	1
John Spaul	1
Richard Ward	2
Richard Creed	1
Elizabeth Johnson	1
Christopher Rabilla	2
Adam Adams	2
William Mustins	1
widow L...	1
goodman Roberson	1
widow Had	1
Roger Kemp	1
Thomas Witting	1
Benjamin Horsly	1
John Smith	1
Mark Wheeler	1

First North Ward [continued]

John Story	1
John Jaye	1
Robert Cullye	2
Thomas Reynolds	1
Joseph Gyme	1
Paul Leech	1
Prudence Fuller	1
Edward Angler	1
Susanna Childresse	2
John Dye	1
Thomas Lambard	1
John Dising	2
John Beare	2
widow Coman	1
John Allen	1
William Bucknam	1
widow Arnold	1
Francis Allen	2
Robert Chapman	2
Richard Wright	1
widow Halieards	1
Robert Grixen	1
widow Brewer, sen.	2
John Biggett	1
widow Buckleder	1
Samuel Mason	2
widow Tesdell	1
Susan George	1
widow Wright	1
widow Gerritt	1
Henry Billitt	2
widow Elsye	2
Robert Newman	1
Joseph Fieler	1
Joseph Palmer	1
Thomas Dowe	1
John Murrell	1
Benjamin Clesson	1
Robert Parson	2
William Eldridge	1
Alan Marsh	1
John Bad	1
Thomas Tod	2
widow Scowman	1

First North Ward [continued]

widow Lamthorne	2
Thomas Goodwell	2
widow Plumsted	1
Thomas Fiske	1
Christopher Cooke	1
widow Wills	1
widow Wade	1
William Martins	1
Thomas Cubitt	1
John Wood	2
Andrew Ringer	1
Sarah Watts	1
Marian Sadman	1
Gabriel Howe	2
James Elgate	1
widow Colman	1
John Cubitt, sen.	2
Henry Manclarke	1
Bartholomew Walker	1
John Sealye	1
Thomas Hindwell	1
Joseph Holland	2
James More	1
John Huggin, jun.	1
William Barefoote	2
Jane Taylor	1
Philip Langston	1
Samuel Gilles	1
Matthew Cock	2
John Stark	1
Joseph Wingman	1
Roger Butler	1
widow Winne	1
Ralph King	2
widow Hust	1
Dorothy Maston	1
widow Huller	2
Henry Nickwell	1
widow Johnson	2
Edward Tilling	1
Robert Jacob	1
Rachel Gymer	1
Israel Blackburne	2
widow Wilson	1

First North Ward [continued]

Thomas Segoe	1
Sarah Tyre	1
Mary Jaye	1
Robert Penn	2
William Cooper	1
widow Pointer	1
widow Benton	1
John Godson	1
widow Molly	1
John Rose	2
Robert Palmer	1
John Gutter	1
Thomas Bunn	1
Elizabeth Howes	1
widow Leacocke	2
Rose Cumfrey	1
John Pooreman	2
widow Flemin	1
Christopher Buttwell	2
Edward Jeesep	1
widow Howard	2
widow Lambard	1
widow Pawlin	1
widow Hust	1
Edward Howes	1
Edward Wright	2
Edward Emerson	1
widow Howard	1
Anthony Wrighe	2
John Balye	1
Robert Watson	2
widow Acorne	1
Godfrey Ward	1
widow Sleakin	1
Robert Bell	2
Rose Gisnitt	1
Thomas English	1
Mary Wollfare	2
Henry Harding	1
Samuel Manning	1
Joseph Home	1
Godfrey Dowe, sen.	1
Thomas Runry	2
goody Huggin	2

First North Ward [continued]

Martin Barkin	1
Robert Harris	1
Mary Claxton	1
Andrew Wurtly	2
widow Jordan	2
Isaac Morly	1
John Flower	1
Jacob Crane	1
John Smith, sen.	2
Sarah Newell, sen.	1
John Tunre	1
Robert Riches	1
William Booth	1
Richard Colfe	2
widow Maske	2
Henry Archer	1
Thomas Miles	1
Richard Walden	1
Ellen Baker	2
John Balton	2
widow Stoneman	1
John Bishop	1
John Stanly	1
Robert Waters	2
Thomas Dowe	2
Thomas Smith	1
Robert Swane	1
Oliver Firke	1
Robert Jinson	2
Thomas Fitter	1
John Tisdell	1
John Todd	2
John Whittleton	2
Henry Goblett	1
Mary Wade	1
Sarah Coldham	1
widow Hust	1
widow Tompson	2
widow Johnson	2
Thomas Hurst	1
John Carter	1
Richard Cosin	1
William Mustard	1
Roger Kemp	1

First North Ward [continued]

Thomas R[?ump]	1
Thomas Vickerman	2
M... Allen	1
Henry Herreden	1
Edward Costerton	1
John Gorbett	2
Thomas Winell	1
Henry Flemin	2
widow Bodham	1
Robert Watson	2
Grace Wade	2
John Goodson	1
John Heydon	1
Francis Wutte	2
John Cubitt	1
John Stanly	2
John Smith	1
widow Cane	1
Ann Wright	2
widow Howard	1
widow Mash	1
William Tomson	1
Peter Candler	2
John Spanton	1
widow Allen	1
widow Molly	2
Francis Moy	1
John Woods	2
Thomas Cooke	1
John Fisher	2
Thomas Hagon	2

[316 Names]

E 179/338, f.46

Second North Ward

2 Mar 1670/1

Robert Ranalls	2
William Martans	1
John Weldon	1
Thomas Thorpe	1

NORFOLK HEARTH TAX EXEMPTIONS

Second North Ward [continued]

Richard Moll	1
Mary Cooke	1
John Lambard	2
John Jacob	1
William Brouton	2
Henry Scarr	2
widow Davie	1
Edmund Sceldon	1
Richard Dye	1
widow Ladstone	1
Edward Flaxman	1
John Corpe	1
John Antle	1
widow Scurbrow	1
Thomas Leake	2
Elizabeth Searles	2
widow Chandler	1
John Creasy	2
John Dye	2
William Reeve	1
widow Bishope	1
Thomas Tittly	1
William Hagon	1
John Pagget	1
widow Dauson	1
John Gilbard	1
Titus Harwood	1
widow Sweetlad	1
John Willes	1
widow Rusalls	1
Thomas Eaton	1
widow Pearson	2
Stephen Scofen	2
widow Miner	1
widow Titsall	1
Thomas Clarke	1
George Goodson	2
John Dow	1
Francis Hardinge	1
Christopher Claxton	1
widow Browne	1
widow Gorball	1
Nathaniel Pusly	1
widow Eives	1

Second North Ward [continued]

Mary Rosse	1
widow Griges	1
John Stimpson	1
Thomas Jorden	1
Phineas Winter	1
Stephen Sharpe	1
John Garrad	2
widow Comer	1
widow Maning	1
Thomas Roabs	1
widow Feild	2
widow Angle	1
widow Browne	1
Thomas Watsonne	1
Lydia Hoult	1
William Ashly	1
John Robenson	1
Catherine Turner	1
Titus Pagget	1
Robert Mimes	1
Friend Nuell	1
John Towne	1
William Bussy	1
Geoffrey Love	1
widow Page	1
widow Pilgram	1
widow Hastings	1
widow Lankester	1
widow Prier	1
Mary Mered	1
Benjamin Tompson	1
John Milles	1
Daniel Bond	1
John Browne	1
John Leake	1
widow Robarts	1
Robert Parrish	1
Robert Hearne	1
John Denny	1
Ambrose Pamer	1
Robert Hassell	1
Thomas Shreeve	2
widow Watsonne	1
widow Wakman	1

NORFOLK HEARTH TAX EXEMPTIONS

Second North Ward [continued]

widow Sturges	2
Robert Birelengam	2
Isaac Cross	1
widow Jenny	1
widow Watsonne	2
Peter Witchengam	2
William Nichols	1
Robert Clay	1
widow Scofen	1
John Ward	1
goodman Warnes	1
John Gay	1
Harman Teale	1
Robert Whitte	1
widow Midow	1
John Sympson	1
Ambrose Eives	1
goodman Crow	1
John Goblet	1
Thomas Comfort	1
widow Grant	1
Patrick Clinch	1
John Rangham	1
John Boolman	1
John Dowsing	1
William Bell	1
Thomas Corke	1
widow Jenn	1
widow Pilesto	1
Christopher Smith	1
Robert Chay	1
widow Scofen	2
Clement Warnes	1
William Widow	2
Harman Skele	1
widow Alexander	1
Adam Drake	2
Thomas Inthols	2
widow Walpoole	1
Thomas Hamon	1
widow Holmes	1
widow Page	1
widow Lindo	1
widow Monford	1

Second North Ward [continued]

widow Dowson	1
Frances Fosdicke	1
John Ellet	2
Robert Clarke	2
John Lutter	1
Ann Cooper	1
Dorothy Jones	1
Daniel Solomon	1
William Palmor	1
Isaac Larrad	1
Mary Jonson	1
Peter Macklinge	1
Nicholas Payne	1
William Caston	2
Richard Metcalfe	1
Margaret Pey	1
Robert Watson	1
widow Lindo	1
John Hansell	1
Nicholas Payne	1
Vincent Stimpson	1
Thomas Williams	1
Robert Eimson	1
William Salter	1
Lawrence Ferman	1
John Charlton	1
Nease Harras	1
widow Lancaster	1
Hosea Vinsent	1
widow Worts	2
widow Ascew	1
Ellis Angell	2
Thomas Scapes	2
John Buxton	1
John Huett	1
goodman Martans	1
Hugh Horget	1
James Adkins	1
Thomas Pamer	1
Leonard Dobbes	1
James Jarvies	1
John Claxton	2
William Hagon	1
widow Neuell	1

Second North Ward [continued]

Thomas Arminger	1
John Tompson	2
Prudence Barnes	1
Thomas Sugat	1
Thomas Cock	1
William Baulder	1
Robert Clarke	1
Simon Overton	1
Thomas Marshman	1
James Midew	2
widow Garred	2
widow Tilles	2
William Linstead	1
William Reeve	1
Richard Symons	1
Ezda Cossens	1
John Turner	1
widow Shackell	1
James Margram	1
John Bucher	1
Theobald Moy	1
Richard Church	2
Simon Riches	1
Samuel Doady	1
John Wilmanson	2
Edmund Foster	1
William Stimson	2
James Streeke	2
A... Smitson	1
William Leaghton	1
William Pell	1
Theodora Reamy	1
Samuel Douson	1
William Heasell	2
Henry Pey	1
widow Rolfe	1
Francis Smith	1
good Rivet	1
widow Pearson	2
Thomas Thurse	2
Edmund Jacob	1
Stephen Gardner	2
Robert Reve	1
William Bell	2

Second North Ward [continued]

widow Cammant	1
Samuel Lindo	1
Rachel Banes	1
Nicholas Bishope	2
Samuel Dix	1
widow Coock	1
Alexander Cuspe	1
John Seago	1
Henry Flemon	1
Christopher Smith	1
Thomas Crane	1
Edmund Rud	1
John Suffam	1
widow Pratt	2
Francis Spenson	2
widow Starke	1

[240 Names]

E 179/337, f.19

Second North Ward

16 Aug 1672

Ambrose Palmer
John Dennis
Robert Parrish
William Browne
David Bond, jun.
John Browne
Giles Robertson
Stephen Coffen
Thomas Crane
William Huggins
goodman Harwod
John Pagit
John Gilbert
Thomas Dulingham
goodwife Denny
Thomas Roals
Thomas Casberie
John Gillingwater
widow Bateman

Second North Ward [continued]

Ralph Burly
Thomas Rannols
John Fleetwood
Robert Clay
widow Gennings
Edmund Cusle
Isaac Rosse
Simon Johnson
John Ward
John Huggins
Friend Newell
Titus Padgit
widow Holt
widow Wotton
widow Jennis
widow Shackle
Thomas Walker
Robert Gorbell
Thomas Hodges
Kenneth Kirby
Abraham Wolpole
Nicholas Bussey
widow Witton
widow Russels
Titus Harrod
widow Sweetlad
Joseph Sparham
Philip Glover
Edmund Skelden
Richard Dye
Edmund Flaxman
widow Titsell
Frances Gladston
Thomas Peabody
John Miller
Christopher Claxton
John Gilbert
William Drew
Nathaniel Randall
Thomas Tittly
widow Shreeve
Frances Frostick
John Padit
William Lightfoot

Second North Ward [continued]

Frances Bowen
Samuel Dix
John Dawson
William Scarbrough
John Jacob
William Martin
John Madline
Thomas Tharp
George Bottall
Richard Moll
Joseph Claxton
William Currell
John Archer
Edmund Foster
Thomas Camell
William Browne
widow Wethers
widow Suffild
Thomas Comfort
John Grasham
Thomas Ranals
Mr Bromwell
Matthew Thurton
John Garwood
widow Browne
John Luther
John Butcher
George Morter
Hugh Jones
Peter Mackline
widow Palmer
Leonard Dobbs
John Williams
James Atkins
Samuel Daudy
widow Streck
Thomas Huit
widow Newell
Hugh Norgate
William Hagon
Robert Bird
widow Smith
William Yell
Theobald Morly

Second North Ward [continued]

Ann Cooper
widow Lecock
widow Barnes
Theodora Raimer
widow Gillin
Isaac Larwood
John Bulman
widow Johnson
Roger Battler
widow Baldry
Samuel Dowson
John Hanson
Robert Clark
Thomas Marsham
William Heasell
Nicholas Payne
Henry Pey
Simon ...enffer
widow Myles
John Wallis
Mary Thornbrough
John Garrit
Thomas Sugit
Jonathan Wrangham
Edmund Hodge
William Sowell
John Evrit
Thomas Thesdell
widow Thempson
widow Huggins
John Antell
widow Midleton
John Kempe
Thomas Wand
Thomas Gooch
James Trundle
widow Tayler
widow Thurkle
widow Reade
goodwife Pumphrey
Frances Smith
goodwife Thurss
widow Emmerston
widow Midows

Second North Ward [continued]

Michael Bushop
John Rivit
widow Sallter
James Margram
John Palmer
Robert Ellis
Thomas Arminger
widow Camplin
widow Marshall
widow Garrit
William Ollie
widow Crowe
widow Preston
Robert Edwords
Joseph Dowson
widow Tills
Clare Threat
Edward Jex
Alice Harris
Richard Symons
William Reeve
widow Lamkester
William Gardner
William Linstead
Nicholas Hollibone
Vincent Fossie
Henry Hudson
William Roe
widow Bond
widow Curspe
widow Tayler
John Turner
widow Camell
widow Ascue
John Callow
William Burton
Thomas Eatton
Ambrose Eives
widow Allixander
widow Cork
William Meann
widow Griggs
Robert White
Harman Tale

Second North Ward [continued]

John Evfret
Christopher Claxton
John Miller
widow Smith
goodman Jolly
Frances Bowen
Mark King
widow England
Richard Hollibone
Robert Leaverick
Robert Edwards
John Smith
Robert Thirtle
Clement Warnes
widow Bucksher
John Grant
John Ward
widow Scoffen
John Gresham
Edward Church
John Browne
Robert Clay
John Hale
Margaret Stark
widow Genn
Margaret Willson
Isaac Rosse
widow Fenn
John Corp
widow Pratt
widow Sturges
James Milles
William Lavender
widow Wattson
Michael Harrison
Thomas Palmer
Thomas Jurdon
Frances Harman
Sampson Balls
Robert Burlingham
Phineas Winter
John Borrow
Peter Witchingham
Stephen Sharp

Second North Ward [continued]

William Hasnell
John Browne
Richard Welden

[242 Names]

E 179/337, f.20

Second North Ward

17 Feb 1673/4

John Dennis	1
Ambrose Palmor	1
Robert Parris	2
William Pound	2
David Bond, jun.	2
John Browne	1
Giles Robinson	2
John Gilbert	1
Thomas Dallinigat	2
widow Deime	1
Thomas Roales	2
Thomas Custberus	1
John Gillingwater	2
widow Batman	1
John Archer	2
Edward Trotter	1
Thomas Camell	2
William Browne	1
widow Witheres	1
widow Sufeild	1
Thomas Comfort	2
John Grossinns	1
Thomas Raynolds	2
widow Bromell	2
Matthew Thirton	1
John Garwood	2
William Browne	1
John Luther	1
John Bucher	1
George Morter	1
Hugh Joanes	1
Mary Thornborgh	1

NORFOLK HEARTH TAX EXEMPTIONS

Second North Ward [continued]

John Gurnell	1
Thomas Suggall	2
James Wingham	2
Edmund Hodg	1
widow Lowell	1
John Everit	2
Thomas Tasdell	1
Thomas Thompson	1
Thomas Hoogans	1
Ralph Edwards	2
Ann Cooper	1
widow Lacock	2
Esther Coffin	1
widow Crane	2
William Huggines	1
widow Harwood	2
John Pagett	1
John Ward	1
John Huggins	2
Friend Newill	1
Titus Paggett	1
William Wholl	1
Peter Mackling	1
widow Palmor	1
Leonard Dobs	1
John Willames	2
James Adbines	1
Samuel Dadey	1
widow Strick	2
Thomas Winter	1
widow Newell	2
Hugh Norgat	1
William Hagon	1
Robert Bird	1
widow Smith	1
William Gell	2
William Morley	1
William Wootton	1
widow Jnney	1
widow Shackell	2
widow Gorbell	1
Thomas Waller	1
widow Midlem	1
John ...itle	2

Second North Ward [continued]

John Cemp	1
Thomas Wand	1
Thomas Gooch	2
James Trundell	1
widow Tayler	1
widow Thirkettell	1
widow Leache	1
widow Pomfrey	2
Francis Smith	2
widow Thurse	1
widow Barnes	1
Thomas Ramor	1
widow Gillin	1
Ralph Barley	1
Thomas Ranolds	1
John Fletwood	1
Robert Clay	2
widow Ginins	1
Edward Cash	1
Isaac Roase	1
Simon Johnson	2
Thomas Hodges	1
Henry Kieby	2
Isaac Larwod	1
John Bulman	2
widow Johnson	1
Roger Butler	1
widow Baldre	1
Samuel Dauson	2
John Hamsin	1
Robert Clarke	1
Thomas Marshman	2
William Peasell	1
Nicholas Panie	1
Henry Pyd	2
Simon Ossier	1
widow Milles	1
John Wallis	1
Thomas Cranne	1
Thomas Proston	1
John Dadell	1
William Lightfoot	1
Francis Browne	2
widow Emerson	1

Second North Ward [continued]

widow Meadows	1
Matthew Buship	2
John Rivett	1
widow Salter	1
James Morgan	2
Abraham Wolpool	1
widow Horner	2
Edmund Skeldan	2
Francis Glodgen	2
John Gillert	1
Robert Ellis	1
widow Garnis	1
widow Olly	2
widow Green	1
widow Lancaster	1
Edward Bond	1
widow Cursp	1
widow Taylor	1
William Neave	2
widow Grigs	1
Robert White	1
Horner Toole	2
John Humfrey	1
Christopher Claxton	1
widow Ingland	2
Richard Hollowbon	1
John Grant	2
John Ward	1
Mary Stork	1
widow Gann	2
Maurice Wilson	1
Thomas Palmor	2
Thomas Jorden	1
Stephen Sharp	1
Nicholas Bosle	1
widow Swetlad	1
Richard Dye	1
Thomas Sebody	1
Michael Drew	2
Thomas Armiger	2
Joseph Dawson	1
widow Tills	1
William Gardner	2
William Linsted	1

Second North Ward [continued]

John Turner	2
widow Gammon	1
widow Asben	1
John Miller	1
widow Smith	2
widow Tooly	1
Francis Daney	2
Thomas Titley	1
widow Shreives	1
Robert Leverick	2
Robert Edwards	1
widow Leoland	2
John Gressam	1
Isaac Roase	2
widow Fenn	1
John Corp	1
Francis Harman	1
Samuel Calley	2
William Haswell	1
widow Wittin	1
Joseph Sparham	1
Edmund Flaxman	1
John Miller	2
Nathaniel Randall	1
widow Campling	1
Clare Threat	1
Edward Jeeks	2
Nicholas Holberton	1
Vincent Croase	2
John Callo	2
William Burto	1
Thomas Eaton	1
Francis Frosduit	2
Samuel Dix	1
John Dawson	1
William Skorbrow	2
John Jacob	1
William Martin	1
John Madlin	1
John Smith	1
Robert Thirtell	1
Edmund Church	1
John Browne	1
widow Prat	1

Second North Ward [continued]

widow Sturgis	2
James Myler	2
Robert Burlingham	1
Phineas Winter	1
John Browne	2
widow Russell	1
Thomas Glover	1
widow Titsell	1
Christopher Claxton	1
John Palmer	1
widow Mushall	1
Alice Harrwod	1
Richard Symons	1
Henry Hodson	1
William Bone	2
Ambrose Ives	1
widow Allexender	1
widow Corpe	1
Theodore Sharp	1
George Bodell	2
Richard Moall	1
Joshua Hoxon	1
William Currell	1
Mark King	1
Clement Warnes	1
widow Bricksher	1
Robert Cley	2
John Hollis	1
William Lavender	1
widow Watson	1
Michael Harrison	1
John Dorrin	1
Peter Wichinham	2
Richard Walden	1

[242 Names]

E 179/338, f.47

First North Middle Ward

6 Mar 1670/1

Edmund Waters	1

First North Middle Ward
[continued]

James Lee	1
widow Cooper	1
Samuel Postle	1
William Yewell	1
widow Waymore	1
John Bristo	1
Richard Cox	1
John Lee	1
Nathaniel Simonds	1
widow Bond	1
goody Dow	1
John Tytus	1
Francis Smithson	1
John Barber	2
widow Granedell	2
Nicholas Holman	1
Jonathan Wheely	2
Richard Smith	1
Andrew Secker	1
Hannah Willd	1
Daniel Disly	1
William Burr	1
widow Tompson	1
Joseph Smith	1
Robert Fickling	1
William Candler	1
Richard Sallter	1
widow Lawson	1
Humphrey Waynflet	1
widow Greeves	1
Edward Holley	1
Daniel Jackson	1
John Lawes	1
John Banger	1
William Woods	1
Margaret Skipp	1
widow Hortly	1
Ellen Cully	1
Mary Pinchinge	1
Thomas Philips	1
Thomas Bristow	1
William Matchet	1
Valentine Littlewood	1

First North Middle Ward
[continued]

Thomas Whight	1
Henry Bootes	1
William Wigget	1
Richard Harrison	1
widow Bines	1
Andrew Pegg	1
Giles Pyles	2
widow Tennent	1
widow Whittinge	1
William Bigsby	1
John Jones	1
Thomas Woodroff	1
widow Lecock	1
widow Buttell	1
Richard Nightingel	1
Robert Hamond	1
Henry Tayler	1
George Hastings	1
widow Lyon	1
John Tayler	1
William Little	1
Samuel Ward	1
Robert Wakefield	1
Edward Clarke	1
widow Mason	1
John Anyson	1
Thomas Robeson	1
widow Townsen	1
widow Collings	1
Edward Hall	1
John Allen	1
John Wills	1
Bartholomew Roddyck	1
John Hall	1
Francis Towsel	1
Abraham Taucks	1
John Lee	1
Elizabeth Curtis	1
widow Browne	2
John Edwards	1
widow Call	1
widow Love	1
Catherine Cutbard	1

First North Middle Ward
[continued]

widow Gellingwater	2
Sarah Brocke	1
John Boles	2
John Person	1
a house in the Deanes	2
pest house	1
a washhouse	2
Thomas Oldman	1
Richard Waters	1
Edward Warnes	2
Francis Tompson	1
Mary Ranalls	1
James Firmen	1
Thomas Smith	1
John Purviss	1
Richard Ward	1
Isaac Wenn	1
John Ranells	1
William Askue	1
George Palmer	1
George Holmes	1
Thomas Abes	1
John Harve	1
widow Wilkenson	1
Richard Cellby	1
Thomas Lambard	1
William Dep	1

[144 Names]

E 179/337, f.21

First North Middle Ward

26 Aug 1672

Edmund Waters
James Lee
widow Cooper
widow Randall
Samuel Postall
William Yewell
widow Marsham

First North Middle Ward
[continued]

John Bristo
John Lee, jun.
Richard Cooke
Matthew Seaman
widow Borrit
widow Bond
Thomas Willyams
widow Dowe
John Titus
Francis Smithson
John Barber
widow Grundall
Nicholas Hollman
Jonathan Wheeler
Richard Smith
Andrew Seecar
Henry Wild
Daniel Disly
John Lee, sen.
widow Ewill
widow Watson
William Burr
John Pouse
Joseph Smith
William Martin
William Chandler
Robert Hicklin
Richard Salter
widow Laws
widow Greives
Ann Row
widow Bragg
Humphrey Winkfeild
Edward Stolly
William Candler
Daniel Jackson
John Laws
John Banger
Giles Ryle
widow Brath'ms
widow Hartly
Ellen Cully
William Woods

First North Middle Ward
[continued]

Thomas Philips
Thomas Bristo
William Matchet
William Litlewood
Thomas White, sen.
Mary Pinching
Henry Buts
Mary Skip
widow Jenkeson
Richard Harrison
widow Bines
Andrew Digg
widow Tennat
Thomas Whiteing
John Hartly
Edward Warnes
William Bigsby
John Johns
Thomas Woodroof
John Pierson
widow Cutler
Richard Nightingall
Robert Hammond
William Yellows
widow Lyne
John Taylor
William Litle
Samuel Ward
Robert Wakefeild
Robert Clarke
widow Watson
widow Gildinwater
Thomas Robeson
widow Townsend
widow Collins
Edward Hall
John Allin
Robert Rodrick
John Hall
John Leeds
Elizabeth Curtis
John Edwards
widow Love

First North Middle Ward
[continued]

Bartholomew Culbert
Sarah Barker
John Dawson
Thomas Oldman
Richard Waters
Francis Touson
Richard Ward
Henry Winn
John Bowles
George Palmer
George Helmes
Thomas Abs
William Wigget
John Lane
widow Willings
Richard Nightengall
Thomas Walker, jun.
Thomas Walker, sen.
Richard Selly
John Balls
Thomas Lambert
widow Lemon
William Deeper
William Tompson
Henry Yewell
Joseph Holland
Robert Jacob
Joseph Jonson
Richard Mons
widow Bready
William Martins
widow Foltrick
John Mays
Thomas White
widow Browne
widow Warner
James Willson
Robert Allin
Stephen Clarke

[132 Names]

E 179/337, f.22

First North Middle Ward

16 Feb 1673/4

Edmund Waters	1
James Lee	2
widow Coopr	1
widow Randall	1
Samuel Postall	1
William Yewall	2
widow Markham	1
John Bristo	1
John Lee, jun.	1
Richard Cook	2
Matthew Seaman	1
widow Barret	1
widow Bond	1
Thomas Willyams	2
widow Dow	1
John Tytus	2
Francis Smithson	2
John Barber	1
widow Grundell	1
Nicholas Hollman	1
Jonathan Wheeler	2
Richard Smith	1
Andrew Seacker	2
Henry Wild	1
Daniel Disly	1
John Lee, sen.	2
widow Ewill	1
widow Watson	1
William Bur	1
John Pouse	1
Joseph Smith	2
William Martins	1
William Chandler	1
Robert Hickel[?in]	2
Richard Salter	1
widow Lawes	1
widow Greives	2
Ann Row	1
widow Brag	2
Humphrey Winkfeild	1

First North Middle Ward
[continued]

Edward Stooly	1
William Chandler	1
Daniel Jaxson	2
John Lawes	1
John Bange	2
Giles Pyles	1
widow Breathames	1
widow Hartly	1
Ellen Cully	1
William Woods	2
Thomas Phillips	1
Thomas Bristo	1
William Matchet	1
William Litlewood	2
Thomas White, sen.	2
Mary Pinchin	1
Henry Buts	1
Mary Skip	2
widow Jenkson	1
Richard Harreson	2
widow Bines	1
Andrew Digg	1
widow Tinnent	2
Thomas Whiteing	1
John Hartly	2
Edward Warnes	1
William Digly	2
John Johnes	2
Thomas Woodrof	1
John Peirsson	2
widow Cutler	1
Richard Nightengal	1
Robert Hammond	1
William Yellows	2
widow Lyne	2
John Taylor	1
William Litle	1
Samuel Ward	1
Robert Wakefeild	1
Robert Clarke	2
widow Watson	1
widow Gildingwater	2
Thomas Robeson	1

First North Middle Ward
[continued]

widow Townsend	1
widow Collins	2
Edward Hall	1
John Allen	1
Robert Rodrick	2
John Hall	1
John Leeds	2
Elizabeth Curtis	1
John Edwards	2
widow Love	1
Bartholomew Cutbert	1
Sarah Clarke	1
John Dawson	1
Thomas Oldman	1
Richard Waters	2
Francis Towsin	1
Mary Ranolls	2
Richard Ward	1
Henry Wi[?nn]	2
John Bowles	1
George Palmer	2
Thomas Abbs	1
William Wiggot	2
John Lane	2
widow Wilking	1
Richard Nightengal	2
Thomas Walker, jun.	1
Thomas Walker, sen.	2
Richard Sebby	1
John Balls	2
Thomas Lambert	1
widow Lemmon	1
William Deeper	1
William Tompson	2
Henry Yewell	1
Joseph Holland	1
Robert Jacob	2
Joseph Jonson	1
Richard Mons	2
widow Bready	1
William Martin	1
widow Fostrick	1
John Mayes	2

First North Middle Ward
[continued]

widow Brown	1
widow Warner	1
James Willsin	2
Robert Allen	1
Stephen Clark	2

[131 Names]

E 179/338, f.48

Second North Middle Ward

[blank] March 1670/1

William Willisea	2
John Doughty	2
Elizabeth Passufant	1
John Pute	1
William Martins	1
Richard Gillings	2
Peter Wittem	1
Bartholomew Pratt	1
goody Fish	1
widow Ward	1
Walter Padgett	1
John Wilson	1
Thomas Ward	1
Philip Fish	1
goody Turner	1
William Dale	2
goody Boyce	1
Robert More	1
widow Reynolds	1
goody Swamburrow	2
widow Smith	1
widow Kendall	1
Ann Feack	1
goodman Fisher	2
goody Bushop	1
widow Condlye	1
widow Hurne	1
goodman Roberts	1
goody Foreman	2

Second North Middle Ward
[continued]

Thomas Rush	1
widow Hammond	1
William Jermys	1
widow Mashman	1
widow Currey	1
William Wilson	2
widow Clossell	1
Tobias Beales	1
Anthony Snowdin	1
Ann Allison	1
widow Eldridge	1
William Smith	2
Jonas Che[?ny]	1
William Scarburow	1
Thomas Driver	1
goodman Padgit	1
Thomas Hill	1
Thomas Feriman	1

[47 Names]

E 179/337, f.23

Second South Mid Ward

[sic; but the names are those of the Second North Middle Ward]

30 Aug 1672

William Willson
Elizabeth Plasant
John Doughty
John Pate
William Martin
Richard Gillions
Peter Witty
William Willose
Margaret Flat
widow Fretter
Robert Brease
James Pidgeon
Bartholomew Prat

Second North Middle Ward
[continued]

widow Fish
Edward Ward
Walter Pagit
John Willson
Thomas Ward
William Coman
Anthony Towell
Philip Fish
widow Turner
widow Dale
widow Boyce
widow Godson
widow Wray, sen.
widow Wray, jun.
Gabriel Winson
Robert More
widow Rainolds
widow Swanbourgh
widow Smith
widow Randall
Ann Harth
Thomas Miller
... Fisher, sen.
Edward Mack
widow Fisher
widow Candler
widow Hearne
widow Robarts
widow Foreman
Samuel Ball
John Milleson
Henry Adkins
William Denny
John Blackwood
John Steephens
Thomas Rash
widow Hammond
widow More
William Jarmy
William Mashman
William Cary
William Jonson
William Crossell

Second North Middle Ward
[continued]

William Newton
Tobias Beales
Anthony Snowden
Ann Allison
William Aldridg
Jonas Cheny
William Smith
William Scarborow
Thomas Drury
goodman Pagget
Thomas Hall
Thomas Ferreman
John Pute
widow Rimshire
John Ellis
Robert Watlin
Thomas Peagon
John Crapp
widow Leage
Ann Foakes
widow Coffin
Richard Poasey
Thomas Budwell
widow Parkin
Bartholomew Brant
widow Wollton
James Heaselwood
Richard Jolands
widow Eldridg
widow Turner
widow Smith
John Hall
John Fisher, jun.
widow Ford

[90 Names]

E 179/337, f.24

Second North Middle Ward

[?20] Mar 1672/3

William Wilson
Elizabeth Pursevant
John Dowghty
John Pote
William Martyn
Richard Gillins
Peter Witty
Bartholomew Prat
widow Fish
Edward Ward
Walter Pagget
John Wilson
Thomas Ward
Philip Fish
widow Turner
widow Dale
widow Boyce
Robert Moore
widow Reynolds
widow Swanburgh
widow Smyth
widow Randall
Ann Hearth
old Fisher
widow Candler
widow Herne
widow Roberts
widow Foreman
Thomas Rush
widow Hamond
widow Moore
William Jermy
William Mashman
William Carey
William Johnson
William Crosswell
Tobias Beales
Anthony Snowden
Ann Allyson
William Eldridge

Second North Middle Ward
[continued]

Josiah Cheny
William Smyth
William Scarburgh
Thomas Drury
goodman Paggit
Thomas Hall
Thomas Ferryman
John Putt
widow Kinishrer
John Ellis
Robert Watlyn
Thomas Peyon
John Cripp
widow Legge
Ann Feakes
widow Coffyn
Bartholomew Brine
widow Walton
James Heaslewood
Richard Josand
widow Eldridge
widow Turner
widow Smyth
John Hall
goodman Fisher
widow Ford

[66 Names]

E 179/337, f.25

Second North Middle Ward

4 Feb 1673/4

widow Ra...ens	1
Matthew Bush	2
goodman Fisher	1
widow Hurst	1
widow Crow	1
goodman Skollar	2
Thomas Comby	2
John Bustings	2

Second North Middle Ward
[continued]

John Hall	1
Henry Gills	1
goodman Fish	2
goodman Skarborough	1
widow Rimsher	2
widow Watlinge	2
widow Ford	1
goodman Shippie	1
goodman Potter	1
widow Carr	2
Thomas Pigeon	2
widow Hammond	1
Thomas Ferriman	1
William Martins	2
Thomas Hollond	2
Anthony Snordin	1
widow Hill	2
widow Feaver	1
Bartholomew Tailer	2
John Warterson	2
Alms Houses	16
old Cendall	1
Thomas Dicksin	2
Edward Gooch	1
Richard Gillens	2
widow Fish	1
widow Ward	2
widow Willsin	2
widow Turner	1
Peter Whitfild	1
Ann Heath	1
John Dowty	1
good Palmer	2
widow Corpen	2
John Durham	1
widow Wardin	2
Thomas Gilburd	2
widow Hill	1
Thomas Driver	1
Thomas Archer	1
widow Pute	2
Thomas Goldsworth	2
goodman Lows	1

Second North Middle Ward
[continued]

Ann Fisher	2
widow Dicksin	1
Robert Mallit	1
widow Eldridge	2
Robert Turner	1
widow Hill	1
widow Padgit	2
widow Ward	2

[59 Names]

E 179/338, f.49

First South Middle Ward

2 Mar 1670/1

William Blasey	2
Mary Hosk, widow	1
widow Torner	1
widow Boyes	2
widow Heasellwod	1
widow Golt	1
widow Breadcock	1
widow Richman	1
Joseph Oldred	1
widow England	2
Richard Payenter	1
Robert Margesen	1
widow Dadey	1
widow Laborne	1
William Robards	1
Joseph Writt	1
Edmund Fittam	1
Mary Shovell	1
widow Abell	1
John Hastons	1
Edmund Cads	1
widow Whitt	2
William Lee	1
Christopher Powell	1
William Boott	2
widow Turner	1

First South Middle Ward
[continued]

John Hipking	2
widow Sandiell	1
John Muerell	1
widow Bell	1
Thomas Dickes	1
Frances Wacker	1
John Custings	2
Roger Towsand	1
Daniel Curtis	2
goodman Stepen	1
Ann Payet, widow	2
widow Satson	1
John Die	2
John Harmer	1
Valentine Pamer	2
Stephen Allt	2
Ralph Gesper	1
widow Larnce	1
Thomas Woots	1
widow Man	1
widow Purgall	1
Christopher Piner	1
widow …illes	1
Simon Johnson	2
John Foster	2
Stephen Tomes	1
Joseph Carter	1
widow Hill	1

[54 Names]

E 179/337, f.26

First South Middle Ward

27 Aug 1672

William Blasie	2
widow Mason	1
William Lee	1
William Elles	2
Elizabeth Skip	1
Mary Preston	1

First South Middle Ward
[continued]

Joseph Aldridg	1
widow Hill	2
widow Hooke	1
widow Daudy	1
widow Bell	1
John Muriell	1
Robert Margeson	1
widow White	2
William Butt	2
widow Mathews	1
widow Essex	1
David Erington	1
Thomas Huss	1
Robert Lilly	1
Thomas Dixson	1
Francis Waker	1
widow Richman	1
Joseph Write	1
John Tompson	1
John Custens	2
widow Bleeder	2
Stephen Hoult	2
widow Laban	1
Richard Dye	1
widow Golt	1
Thomas Parson	1
widow Dixson	1
Ralph Jesper	1
widow Hope	1
widow Dye	1
widow Laurenc	1
widow Able	1
Edward Eades	1
widow Hastens	1
widow Tompson	1
Daniel Curtis	2
widow Paine	2
George Sutten	1
John Foster	2
Thomas Casemonde	1
Christopher Powell	1
Tobias Butcher	1
William Giles	1

First South Middle Ward
[continued]

Alice Yoke	1
widow Heaselwood	1
Simon Johnson	2
Thomas Woorts	1
Samuel Man	1
John Nolbro	2
widow Turner	1
widow Trotter	2
James Robinson	1
Christopher Lowe	1
widow Keelin	2
John Boyce	1
Elizabeth Hastens	1
Stephen Thomas	1
John Smith	1
Richard Lovell	1
Christopher Spenten	1
Roger Townsend	1
Thomas Smith	1

[68 Names]

E 179/337, f.27

First South Middle Ward

15 Feb 1673/4

William Blasse	1
widow Mason	1
William Lee	1
Simon Johnson	1
Tobias Smith	2
John Morre	1
George Beare	1
William Butt	1
widow Hill	2
widow Hook	2
widow Jarrow	2
John Marvell	2
Robert Margesen	1
widow White	1
widow Dobson	2

First South Middle Ward
[continued]

John Smith	1
widow Hirington	2
Samuel Noble	1
Robert Liley	1
William Burton	1
Frances Waker	2
widow Richman	2
Joseph Write	1
John Tomson	2
John Custens	1
widow Bleder	2
Stephen Hoult	1
widow Labon	2
widow Goalt	2
widow Dixsen	1
widow Jesper	1
widow Dey	1
widow Laurance	1
widow Able	2
Edward Cade	1
widow Hastens	2
widow Haslewood	1
Daniel Curtis	2
John Hosler	1
Thomas Casement	2
Christopher Pouell	1
Tobias Bucher	1
Alice Yoake	1
John Albro	2
widow Troter	2
Elizabeth Hasten	1
Christopher Spanton	1
John Hivington	2
James Jeelle	1
John Waringer	1
William Berton, sen.	1
widow Weeds	1
Thomas Parson	1
Henry Thomson	1
Richard Dey	1
widow Wattson	1
Edward Matchet	1
William Gilliens	2

First South Middle Ward
[continued]

widow Rainewater 'vac'	2
Thomas Pamer	1
William Liddle	1
Bartholomew Grant	1
goodman Plafer	1
widow Budwell	1
Edward Turner	1
William Egleton	1

[66 Names]

E 179/338, f.50

Second South Middle Ward

2 Mar 1670/1

Thomas Carter	1
Michael Sadler	1
William Adkins	2
Robert Daynes	1
widow Dunmarke	1
widow Dobson, elder	2
Philip Miner	2
Theophilus Downing	2
Robert Scoller	1
William Willson	1
Richard Boyse	1
widow Bott	1
Catherine Parston	1
Elizabeth Aldred	1
Thomas Cads	1
John Davis	1
widow Lawrence	1
widow Goodwin	1
John Herington	1
widow Eagle	2
Benjamin Woods	2
widow Frost	1
Robert Crockett	2
widow Clarke	1
widow Chalton	2
John Eaton	1

Second South Middle Ward
[continued]

Clement Mathes	1
Thomas Raynolds	1
Daniel Croft	1
John Hickmer	1
John Hutcherson	1
Robert Simonds	2
William Singler	1
Thomas Brackett	1
widow Furman	1
Benjamin Crow	1
widow Bradcocke	1
Benjamin Smith	1
widow Giles	1
widow Lockwood	1
widow Wattson	1
Geoffrey Bradcocke	1
Mary Masters	1
Peter Bretinger	1
Henry Herrington	1
widow Swansan	1
Thomas Haymer	2
widow Horney	1
William Burton	2
Michael Huton	2
John Stubbs	2
Robert Lofte	1
widow Drowne	1
widow Dobson, jun.	1
Samuel Franckes	2
James Crosekeys	2
widow Cliffing	1
widow Bleeder	1
John Ward	1
John Holton	2
widow Fish	1
Elizabeth Burgesse	1
widow Norton	1
widow Dobson	1
Richard Chip	2
Henry Scoffing	1
Richard Swaine	1
widow Budwell	1
Robert Fleman	1

Second South Middle Ward
[continued]

Thomas Hickson	2
John Munement	1
John Rider	1
John Hutcherson	1
widow Robertson	1
John Swiggett	2
Robert Metherell	1
Robert Cooper	2
James Lanthorne	1
John Houghteway	1
Catherine Parson	2
John Atcherson	1
widow Sharp	2

[82 Names]

E 179/337, f.28

Second South Middle Ward

3 Sep 1674

Abraham Norton	2
widow Griffin	1
Thomas Turnor	2
widow Burton	1
widow Eagle	1
Stephen Thomas	2
widow Sharpe	2
John Taylor	2
Elizabeth Crosse	1
widow Holloway	1
Roger Barcham	1
James Wilson	2
widow Swanskin	1
widow Holland	1
Robert Cooper	2
Elizabeth Church	1
widow Jarvis	2
John Kettle	1
widow Cooper	1
William Wigget	2
Francis Howard	2

Second South Middle Ward
[continued]

Richard Lovell	2
William Rounse	1
widow Hovell	2
Thomas Masters	1
Adam Drake	1
William Clifton	1
Edmund Boldman	2
Jonathan Wealy	2
William Adkins	1
widow Denmarke	1
widow England	2
widow Locker	2
Richard Boyse	2
widow Turnor	1
Benjamin Adkins	1
John Erington	1
widow Jasper	1
Simon Johnson	2
Mary Bott, widow	1
widow Goodnings	2
widow Erington	2
Henry Handson	1
widow Goodson	2
widow Crispe	2
widow Cades	1
Michael Middleton	2
Richard Lovell	1
John Taylor	1
John Gaton	2
widow Burrell	2
widow Chalton	2
Robert Grogget	1
widow Sharpe	2
widow Breadcock	1
Benjamin Smith	1
Benjamin Crow	2
Robert Seaman	1
widow Firman	2
Edward Macke	1
William Page	2
William Fish	1
John Hawkes	1
John Spanton	1

Second South Middle Ward
[continued]

John Hickmote	1
John Hattinson	2
Philip Miner	2
widow Miller	1
Hugh Crowfoote	1
widow Nunn	1
widow Spicer	2
Peter Breginere	1
John Pross	1
W Scoffing	2
widow Wray	1
Thomas Hayham	2
Richard Harwood	1
Michael Sadler	2
William Ginn	2
Robert Loft	1
Michael Huton	2
widow Chipp	2
widow Sharpe	1
widow Nobson	1
Stephen Calme	2
Walter Tabor	2
Henry Scoffing	1
widow Turnor	1
Oliver Hall	2
Ann Wright, widow	2
widow Bell	1
William Ward	2
widow Greene	1
Thomas Poll	2
William Silvers	1
George Hope	1
Robert Flemen	2
Thomas Bottle	2
widow Budwell	1
Richard Foreman	1
Edward Youngs	2

[101 Names]

E 179/338, f.51

First South Ward

7 Mar 1670/1

widow of Benjamin Herring	2
Rose Bennet	2
Henry Ward	1
Richard Atkeson	1
Margaret Spencer	1
widow Capell, jun.	1
Abigail Tod	1
Elizabeth Robinson	1
Robert Moone	1
Magnus Harrison	1
Henry Wilson	1
widow Capell, sen.	1
widow Allen	1
William Lucock	1
William Nichols	1
John Nobbs	1
Mary Burton	1
Edmund Jeffris	1
Samuel Smith	1
widow Pharrow	1
John Piggen	1
Henry Arnold	1
John Parson	1
Thomas Hales	1
Mary Page	1
Thomas Cove	2
Henry Hamborough	1
Samuel When	1
William Wood	1
widow Ward	2
widow Attkins	2
Robert Baley	2
widow Kent	2
Nurse Deborah	1
Robert Berry	1
William Allman	1
Richard Garret	1
Edmund George	1
Dorothy Foreman	1
Thomas Manthorpe	1

First South Ward [continued]

John Holland	1
Richard Neave	1
widow Gibson	1
widow Cooper	1
James Masham	1
goodman Stone	1
Thomas Balls	2
widow of Nathaniel King	2
widow of Thomas King	1
widow Wilson	2
widow Spanton	1
widow Davey	1
widow Garwood	1
John Wasen	1
James Boyce	2
Rose Crane	1
Isaac Dent	1
widow of Michael Dent	1
widow Coxson	1
Edward Mat[?chet]	1
George Saunders	2
widow Palling	1
widow Trundle	1
goodman Johnson	1
goodman Brock	1
goodman Mason	1
John Rose	1
widow Loveridge	1
William Cock	1
John Waters	1
John Gray	2
widow Wyet	1
widow Townson	2
Henry Newell	1
widow Gabriell	1
widow Purdy	1
Henry Stevens	1
widow Ems	1
Susan Kendall	1
widow Cobb	1
Robert Cross	1
widow Wilson	1
widow Chapman	2
widow Smith	2

First South Ward [continued]

Robert Duck	1
widow Mattock	1
Robert Beacon	1
widow Linsea	1
Thomas Howard	2
Thomas Whitson	1
widow Wilkinson	1
widow Pestell	1
goodman Life	1
widow Jay	1
widow Ashly	1
goody Scarborough	1
Matthew Wilson	1
Thomas Lee	1
Thomas Penny	1
Geoffrey Batts	1
William Woodjer	2
John Hopkins	2
widow Annis	1
Samuel Rope	1
John Kent	1
Robert Wily	1
George Woolling	1
widow Motts	1
Benjamin Cann	1
Richard Lad	2
Thomas Surry	2
James Grigs	2
John Whittecar	1
Samuel Huggins	1
in a town house	4
at the Fort	3
widow Curtis	1
Edmund Jay	1
Emma Rose	1
William Draper	1
John Bennet	1
John Hansell	1
Francis Ditcham	1
John Hall	1
widow Moone	1
Joseph Eagle	1
William Campthorne	1
Francis Arnold	1

First South Ward [continued]

Catherine Hakeney	1
Richard Kippen	1
Andrew Swan	1
Samuel Write	1
Richard Tod	1
Richard Tubbin	1
John Morly	1
Cornelius Johnson	1
Henry Watterson in the Deans	1
widow Coulson	1
Robert Gibson	2
Thomas Borne	1
Thomas Hill	1
Henry Foster	1

[140 Names]

E 179/337, f.29

First South Ward

2 Sep 1672

widow Heiring	1
Rose Bennit	1
Henry Ward	1
Richard Attkinson	1
Margaret Spencer	1
widow Capell, jun.	2
Abigail Todd	1
widow Benet	2
Ellis Robinson	1
Robert Moone	1
Magnus Harison	2
Henry Willson	1
widow Capell, sen.	1
widow Allen	1
William Leacock	2
William Nicholas	1
John Nobbs	1
Mary Burton	1
Edmund Jefferies	1
Samuel Smith	2

First South Ward [continued]

widow Farrow	2
John Piggen	1
Henry Arnould	2
widow Tomnson	1
widow Buckingham	2
Thomas Halles	1
Mary Pagge	1
Thomas Conne	1
Henry Hanbrough	2
Samuel Wheane	1
widow Ward	1
widow Askines	1
Robert Bally	1
widow Gibbson	2
Nurse Deborah	1
widow Leak	1
William Allman	2
Richard Garrat	2
Edmund George	1
Dorothy Freeman	2
Thomas Manthorp	1
John Holland	1
Richard Neale	2
widow Cooper	1
widow Masham	2
goodman Stone	1
Thomas Balls	2
widow King	1
William Willson	1
widow Craggs	1
widow Spenton	1
widow Davie	2
widow Griffen	1
John Wasey	1
Jeremiah Boyce	1
Rose Crane	1
Isaac Dentt	2
widow Coxson	1
William Nobbs	1
Edward Mattshell	2
George Sanders	1
widow Paulling	2
widow Trundell	1
Cornelius Johnson	2

First South Ward [continued]

Henry Newell	1
John Rose	2
widow Loveridge	1
William Cocke	1
John Wattes	1
John Gray	1
widow Wiatt	2
Benjamin Crane	1
Samuel Huggines	2
widow Townson	2
Thomas Tittly	1
Edmund Caffe	2
widow Gabrill	2
widow Perey	1
Henry Stephenes	1
widow Emes	1
Susan Kendell	2
widow Cobb	1
Robert Crose	1
widow Willson	2
widow Chapman	1
widow South	1
Robert Duck	2
widow Mattocck	1
Thomas Mann	1
Robert Baccon	2
widow Linca	1
Thomas Whitson	2
widow Willkson	1
widow Pestell	1
John Life	2
Thomas Howard	1
widow Jay	1
Samuel Roper	1
John Hopkines	2
John More	1
widow Ashley	1
goodman Scarbrough	2
Margaret Willson	1
Thomas Lee	1
Thomas Penney	1
Geoffrey Bettes	1
widow Annis	2
John Kent	2

First South Ward [continued]

Robert Willson	1
William Woodiere	1
George Wollen	1
widow Mattes	1
John Benett	2
widow Curtis	1
Edmund Jay	1
Edmund Rose	1
William Draper	1
John Hansell	1
Francis Dicham	2
John Hall	1
widow Moone	2
Joseph Eagle	1
James Grigges	1
William Kempthorn	1
widow Warde	2
Nicholas Browning	1
John Tomson	2
Catherine Hakney	1
John Haris	1
Richard Kippin	2
Andrew Swan	1
Thomas Burton	1
Samuel Wright	1
Richard Todd	1
Richard Tubine	2
John Morly	2
Henry Watterson	1
widow Coulson	1
Thomas Brone	1
Robert Gibbson	2
Thomas Hill	1
Henry Forister	1
James Allison	1
William Knites	1
widow Springall	2
John Mann	2
Thomas Sutton	1
Thomas Bashfeiled	1
Davy Hunn	1
Nicholas Halles	1
Robert Moone	1
widow Cooper	1

First South Ward [continued]

John Sherrin	1
Robert Cooke	1
William Stookes	1
widow Linkly	1

[156 Names]

E 179/337, f.30

First South Ward

12 Feb 1673/4

widow Sherin
Rose Bennit
Henry Ward
Richard Attkinson
Margaret Spencer
widow Cassell, jun.
Abigail Tode
widow Bennett
Ellis Robeson
Robert Moone
Magnus Hawson
Henry Willson
William Capieson
widow Allen
William Lacock
William Nicholas
John Nobs
Mary Burton
Edward Jefferey
Samuel Smith
widow Fancy
John Piggon
Thomas Arrold
widow Tompson
widow Buckingham
Thomas Halles
Mary Page
Thomas Crow
Henry Harborow
Samuel Wheame
widow Adkins

First South Ward [continued]

Robert Baly
widow Gibson
Nurse Debeta
widow Leak
William Allman
Richard Gairett
Edward Gorge
D[?orothy] F[?reeman]
Thomas Manthorpe
John Holland
Richard Noale
widow Cooper
widow Massam
good Stone
Thomas Baley
widow King
William Willson
widow Cragg
widow Spanton
widow Davey
widow Griffin
John Wasey
Je[?remiah] Boyce
Isaac Dent
widow Copson
William Hobbs
Edward Matsell
George Sanders
widow Paulleing
widow ...undall
Cornelius Johnson
Henry Newell
John Rose
widow Lovrage
William Cock
John Watts
John Gray
widow Viall
...en [? Benjamin] Crane
Samuel Huggain
widow Townsen
John Fittly
Edmund Case
widow Gabrell

First South Ward [continued]

widow Penny
... Stephens
widow Emes
Susan Kendall
widow Cobb
Robert Ceasey
widow Willson
widow Chapman
widow South
Robert Duck
widow Mattock
Thomas Man
Robert Bettom
widow Lindsa
Thomas Whittson
widow Willson
widow Pestall
John Life
John Howard
widow Jay
Samuel Rope
John Hopkin
John More
widow Ashby
goody Scarbrow
Mary Willson
Thomas Lee
Thomas Penny
Geoffrey Beetes
widow Annis
John Kent
Robert Willson
William Woodiere
George Woollen
widow Mates
John Bennitt
widow Curtis
Edmund Gay
William Rose
William Draper
John Hansell
Francis Dicham
John Hall
widow Moore

First South Ward [continued]

Joseph Eagle
James Hinges
William Kempthorn
Michael Browneing
John Thomson
Catherine Hakny

[125 Names]

E 179/338, f.52

Second South Ward

[undated ?early March 1670/1]

widow Gooch	1
widow Richmond	1
Daniel Morey	1
Catherine Hackon	1
widow Eddey	1
Davy Hovell	1
widow Richis	2
Thomas Hollond	1
Daniel Lion	1
Jonas Anderson	1
Thomas Bulbrock	1
William Shincon	2
William House	1
Gilbert Woogget	2
William Sad	1
widow Wilcock	1
Robert Stevens	1
widow Decker	2
widow Perreman	2
widow Spiser	1
Thomas Hamblin	1
widow Sanders	1
widow Husin	2
widow Cummins	2
widow Wod	1
Susan Pasey	1
widow Pamer	1
widow Watson	2
William Nightley	1

Second South Ward [continued]

Elizabeth Lovday	2
Thomas Neale, sen.	1
Thomas Neale, jun.	1
Job Bunnell	1
widow Tiles	1
Susan Rusells	2
John Harmer	2
Robert Tuley	1
Vincent Stimson	2
Robert Skarfe	1
Nicholas Harrison	1
widow Cock	1
widow Laborn	1
widow Norton	1
Ann Grim	1
Christopher Vines	1
widow Clarck	1
widow Dickson	1
Robert House	2
John Clarck	1
Edmund Crisp	2
widow Kempe	1
widow Bobbit	1
widow Dason	1
Evan House	1
George Fox	1
William Barron	1
widow Golt	1
John Kemey	1
Edmund Norton	1
Arthur Wild	2
widow Wilkeson	2
John Burrowes	1
Edward Childe	1
widow Richeson	1
Edmund Prittey	1
Egebill Bart	1
William Pammer	1
Henry Skot	2
Thomas Burtton	1
widow Cursp	1
Thomas Balles	2
widow Clarck	2
William Buship	2

Second South Ward [continued]

John Buckman	1
Sarah Mallous	1
widow Shincon	1
Richard Fish	1
Mary Ogdin	1
John Murell	2
Thomas Lankester	1
Francis Clear	2
Simon Hurs	2
Ann Butter	1
John Sims	2
Edward Tims	1
Robert Browne	2
John Ockley	1
widow Allin	1
Frank Becket	1
Thomas Ma...hells	2
widow Lee	1
widow Robards	1
widow Johnson	1
William Batman	1
Richard Crowne	1
John Rose	1
Thomas Pritey	1
widow Cades	1
Mary Rannells	1
widow Riner	1
Thomas Rust	1
William Jolley	1
Benjamin Culpit	1
Esther Elvin	1
widow Hovell	1
widow Eacherd	1
widow Linnis	2
widow Lovrig	1
Joseph Gorge	1
widow Kendell	1
Oliver Rope	1
Robert Bucksher	2
Thomas Bets	1
widow Clarke	2
Jeremiah Peasey	2
Daniel Lion	2
Andrew Gurd	2

Second South Ward [continued]

widow Jarmin	1
Mary Barnes	1
George Cutting	1
John Die	1
Catherine Hamblin	1
William Eglinton	1
Roger Watson	1

[124 Names]

E 179/337, f.31

Second South Ward

30 Aug [blank ?1672]

Thomas Bullbroke	2
William Shinkin	1
widow Riches	1
William Huldan	1
Gilbert Wodgate	2
William Sadd	2
William Willcock	2
Robert Steevens	1
widow Peckar	1
widow Parmer	1
widow Spicer	2
widow Huson	2
Thomas Hamblins	2
widow Cummins	2
widow Nudd	1
widow Watson	1
widow Perce	1
Susan Peache	1
widow Parmer, sen.	1
William Rinthor	1
Thomas Neale, sen.	2
Thomas Neale, jun.	1
John Bunell	1
Eli Lubda	2
widow Tills	1
Susan Russells	1
John Harmson	1
Robert Tally	2

Second South Ward [continued]

Vincent Stimpson	2
Robert Skarfe	1
Nicholas Harrison	2
widow Cock	1
widow Labourn	1
Giles Vinyard	1
William Bateman	2
widow Ratman	1
Daniel Lyon	2
Catherine Hagon	1
widow Edgar	1
Thomas Holland	2
Diana Howell	1
Simon Larst	1
John Symes	1
Robert Gold	2
Philip More	2
John Hemblin	2
widow Norton	1
Ann Crime	1
Robert Hause	1
Christopher Winse	1
widow Clark	1
widow Dixon	1
John Clarke	1
widow Ramp	2
widow Bobit	2
widow Dafer	1
Edmund House	1
George Fockes	1
William Burron	1
widow Goult	1
John Camy	1
widow Norter	1
Thomas Swanborough	1
Robert Wafer	2
John Bourroughs	1
widow Willkeson	1
Edward Child	1
John Nichols	1
widow Kitson	1
Edmund Pretty	2
Abigail Prat	2
John Randall	1

Second South Ward [continued]

William Palmer	1
Henry Scatte	1
John Burton	1
Thomas Bowles	2
widow Clarke	2
William Bishop	1
John Bucknam	1
Sarah Mallows	1
widow Shinkin	1
Hannah Ogan	1
widow Curspe	1
John Morll	2
Thomas Lambertes	1
widow Cleare	1
Ann Barton	1
Edmund Tinse	1
Robert Browne	1
Robert Peny	1
William Stewards	1
John Oakly	1
John Woolen	2
widow Allin	1
Francis Bakar	1
widow Griffin	1
Thomas Nuttle	1
widow Lee	1
widow Robarts	2
widow Janson	2
Richard Browne	1
John Rose	1
Thomas Pettny	1
William Steward	1
widow Cadeys	1
Mary Ranolls	1
widow Kener	1
Thomas Roust	2
Benjamin Cullpen	1
Gilbert Grice	1
Edmund Kener	1
Thomas Smith	1
Arthur Allin	2
widow Hewell	1
widow Artler	1
widow ...ynes	1

Second South Ward [continued]

widow Leverage	1
John Jorge	2
widow Cendale	1
Oliver Roper	2
Robert Bucher	2
Thomas Betts	1
Simon Carsp	1
Richard Goodwins	2
John Rounse	2
widow Heynes	1
John Pye	1
John Winter	2
Samuel Manthorp	2
Thomas Hodg	1
William Suggat	1
Stephen Fisher	1
William Ingland	1
Samuel Hagon	2
Andrew Gunde	2
widow Carman	1
widow Barry	1
George Cutter	1
John Dye	1
Catherine Hemblin	1
William Engelton	1
Richard Gillins	1
Roger Watson	1
Stephen Suffeild	1
widow Homes	1
Robert Hill	2
Thomas Chruspe	2
John Peny	1
widow Sanders	1
Simon Dunkin	2
widow Clarke	1
widow Cumming, sen.	2

[152 Names]

E 179/337, f.32

Second South Ward [continued]

Second South Ward

17 Feb 1673/4

Roger Baily	2	Richard Fish	2
William Rous	2	Joseph George	2
David Hovell	1	Edmund Holmes	1
John Standford	1	John Bucknam	1
Robert Becon	1	William Bishop	1
widow Greshum	1	widow Nudds	1
widow Ryner	1	widow Richardson	1
Robert Wyley	2	widow Griffin	2
Ann Knights	2	widow Daines	1
William Bateman	1	Thomas Balls	2
widow Johnson	2	Francis Jolly	1
John Rose	2	Samuel Wenn	1
widow Pretty	1	widow Scott	1
widow Blogg	1	Valentine Palmer	1
John Nicholson	2	Thomas Braff	1
Simon Hurst	1	Richard Parker	1
widow Maddock	1	Edward Child	2
George Penny	1	John Rose	2
widow Thornborrow	1	Thomas Whitaker	1
Thomas Swanborrow	2	Samuel Smith	1
John Okley	1	widow Fish	2
Edward Tims	1	widow Wilkenson	1
widow Loverage	1	George Fox	1
widow Cleer	2	Mark Wright	1
widow Comfort	2	widow Dawson	1
Oliver Rope	1	Henry Pierson	2
widow Kendall	1	William Marden	2
Robert Seaman	2	widow Winter	2
Thomas Betts	1	Ezechias Harris	1
widow Eachards	1	widow Clarke	
widow Lennes	2	Jeremy Pacy	2
William Shinking	1	widow Bobbitt	2
Hannah Garett	1	Richard Perrott	1
Thomas Maylen	1	Francis Wilkins	1
widow Lee	1	widow Wale	1
John Murrell	1	Ralph Hymus	2
William Palmer	1	Simon Cuspe	1
Thomas Lancaster	1	John Clarke	
widow Claxon	1	Richard Edwards	2
Mary Hogden	1	widow Goodings	1
		widow Nutt	1
		Mary Smith	1
		Robert Hows	2
		Thomas Warns	1

Second South Ward [continued]

John Burcham	1
Samuel Manthorpe	
Robert Paine	1
widow Golt	2
Arthur Wilde	2
widow Kemp	1
Richard Vines	1
John Coultson	1
Robert Tooley	2
Richard Haes	2
Robert Skarf	1
John Day	1
widow Chaddock	1
Samuel Dy	2
Mary Urin	2
widow Lawson	1
Luke Boyce	2
Benjamin Motts	1
Joseph Eagle	1
widow Edgar	2
widow Cheny	1
widow Commings	1
John Harman	1
John Harman	1
William Egleton	1
Francis Eats	1
Thomas Neale	2
John Setchell	1
Roger Watson	2
widow Rope	1
Michael Pulham	1
widow Barns	1
Lawrence Peterson	1
widow Deeker	1
Thomas Hambleton	2
widow Cuspe	1
Matthew Weeds	1
widow Tasker	1
Robert Hill	1
William Loads	1
Robert Stevens	2
James Wood	1
widow Burton	2
widow Fenn	1

Second South Ward [continued]

John Burgis	1
Daniel Lyon	1
Thomas Holland	1
Robert Gold	2
... Wright	1
William Hows	1
William Laws	1
John Chapman	1
widow Sims	
widow Shinking	1
widow Richmond	1
Peter George	2
John Lawrence	1
Peter Bucknam	1
Thomas Hodge	1
George Cutting	1
widow Ead	2
widow Howlett	1
Gilbert Woodgate	
William Sad	1
John Smith	1
William Smith	2
William Tompson	1
widow Gooch	1
Francis Becker	1
John Shale	1
widow Gooch	1
John George	2

[156 Names]

King's Lynn

E 179/338, f.53

Chequer Ward

6 Mar 1670/1

Robert Mason
George Fenning
John Johnsons
Richard Edwards
widow Basham

Chequer Ward [continued]

Jonas Cobb
widow Smyth
Henry Nelson
William Vynyard
Richard Clarke
Richard Shipp
Peter Middleton
George Jackson
Christopher Croxson
Matthew Norffer
Richard Bridge
John Davison
Thomas Rawling
William Ansell
Henry Cottle
widow Mills
John Turner
Robert Wright
John Coe
widow Curtis
John Burton
Richard Stroud
Lionel Rawling
John Dixon
Samuel Townsend
John Crosse
Michael Adams
John Scott
John Parke
William Kinsman
Robert Feilding
Richard Read
Robert Harrison
widow Symes
William Garritt
George Grinings
widow Dunn
Thomas Sherman
Thomas Whitt
Rose Jordan
Francis Vincent
Michael Cutbert
John Brady
widow Skiner

Chequer Ward [continued]

Thomas Johnson
Priest Holman
Henry Callibert
Joseph Whitfoot
George Barnard
John Shelton
Henry Wilson
David Nodd
Thomas Johnson, jun.
Robert Rowson
Thomas Hill
Thomas Bayly
Bartholomew Pheborne
Anthony Furthergili
Daniel Widdowson
George Clarkeson
Ralph Sandy
widow Bayly
William Catling
Henry Meare
John Spurne
Thomas Fincham
Nicholas Wild
Thomas Hubbeard
Thomas Wilton
Robert Lone
widow Richarson
William Whittricke
William Rix
Abraham Henderby
James Leech
Robert Troth
John Bradly
William Ives
Joseph Stapler
James Foster
Henry Mew
Richard Denny
John Nobbs
Thomas Fincham, jun.
Richard Ranalls
Francis Brenton
Benjamin Postle
Thurston Hattfeild

Chequer Ward [continued]

widow Rivers
widow Read
John Wollis
Edmund Bacon
Thomas Wilson
William Andrewes
John Hoogin

[100 Names]

E 179/335, f.843

Chequer Ward

1 Mar 1671/2

Robert Mason
John Johnson
William Doubte
widow Smith
Robert Coder
Henry Woods
George Jackson
Daniel Midellton
Richard Bridges
Matthew Narfor
John Dawson
William Hancell
Thomas Rolling
George Tomson
John Flecher
Lionel Rolling
John Crose
widow Fillips
widow Curtis
Robert Say
John Carle
Francis Vinceson
John Parke
William Rall
James Parke
widow Dickson
Henry Man
John Tailor

Chequer Ward [continued]

John Burton
Jonathan Spauldin
Richard Reede
Robert Heinson
Richard Rennolles
Michael Adames
Henry Coleton
William Gent
Luke Thornton
Thomas Gillines
widow Donn
Thomas Sherman
widow Cole
John Hugines
Michael Cutbert
John Brade
James Foster
Thurston Hatfeild
William Bacon
widow Reede
John Vallis
widow Basham
Richard Clarke
widow Dure
widow Skiner
George Fening
Henry Widison
Joseph Whitwith
Edward Willson
Thomas Johnson
Thomas Hill
Richard Ship
widow Bernard
Richard Browne
James Mason
Thomas Palmer
Robert Rainer
Samuel Widison
John Spurne
Thomas Rowell
Bartholomew Fabon
widow Waselbe
John Rikes
Henry Rikes

Chequer Ward [continued]

Thomas Hubert
William Whitwith
Abel Henderbe
John Bradle
Thomas Avis
James Lech
William Iwory
William Challon
Robert Troth
Henry Nelson
William Blade
Ralph Sandy
widow Andues
John Townend
George Borrowes
Benjamin Postle
John Mobs
Thomas Fincham
Thomas Bayly
widow Balls
John Burton
Joseph Stabler
widow Reames
widow Barcock
widow Holland
widow Folly
Roger Sneth
Edmund Donne
William Fabon
widow ...ase

[102 Names]

E 179/337, f.33

Chequer Ward

21 Feb 1672/3

Robert Mason
George Feilding
John Jonsons
Richard Edwards
widow Basham

Chequer Ward [continued]

Josiah Cobb
widow Smith
Henry Nellson
William Vinyard
Richard Clarke
Richard Skip
Peter Midleton
George Jackson
Christopher Croxon
Matthew Narfer
Richard Bridge
John Dawson
Thomas Rawleing
William Annsell
Henry Cettle
widow Mylles
John Turner
Robert Wright
John Coe
widow Curtis
John Burton
Richard Stroud
Lionel Rawleing
John Dixin
Samuel Townsend
John Cross
Michael Adhams
John Scott
John Parke
William Lyndsman
Robert Feilding
Richard Read
Robert Haunson
widow Symes
William Garret
George Grimege
widow Dunn
Thomas Shearman
Thomas White
William Cole
Joseph Jordan
Francis Vincent
Michael Cutbert
John Brady

Chequer Ward [continued]

widow Skinner
Thomas Jonson
Priest Hollman
Henry Callibert
Joseph Whitefoot
Henry Sheeffeild
John Shelton
Henry Willson
Da[vid] Nods
Thomas Jonson
Robert Rowson
Thomas Hill
Thomas Bigly
Anthony Furthergill
Bartholomew Phebourn
widow Dowson
George Clarkson
Ralph Sandy
widow Baly
William Cating
Henry Meare
John Spurne
Thomas Avis
Thomas Fincham
Nicholas Wild
Thomas Hubbard
Thomas Wilton
Robert Lone
widow Richarson
William Whittrick
William Rix
Abraham Hindsly
James Leech
Robert Troth
William Ives
Joseph Stapler
James Foster
Henry Mew
Richard Denny
John Nobs
Thomas Fincham, jun.
Richard Ranalls
Francis Breton
Thurston Hatfeild

Chequer Ward [continued]

widow Rivers
widow Read
John Wallis
Henry Woods
Thomas Willson
William Andrews
John Hoogan
Robert Hallyard
William Rively

[102 Names]

E 179/337, f.34

Chequer Ward

[blank] Sep 1674

Robert Masson
George Feilding
John Johnson
Richard Edwards
widow Basshom
John Cobe
widow Smith
Henry Nettelton
William Vinard
Richard Clarck
Peter Meddelton
George Jackson
Christopher Cockson
Matthew Norfolck
Richard Bridgs
John Dosson
Thomas Rolling
William Hanssell
Henry Kettell
widow Mills
John Turner
Robert Wright
John See
widow Curttes
John Burtton
Richard Stroud

Chequer Ward [continued]

Lionel Rolling
John Deckson
Samuel Tounssend
John Crose
Michael Adoms
John Scott
John Backer
William Lyndsmon
Robert Felding
Richard Read
Robert Hamson
widow Symes
William Garrett
George Greenage
widow Dunn
Thomas Sharman
Thomas Whitt
William Coale
Joseph Jordan
Francis Vincent
Michael Cutbert
John Brady
widow Skiner
Thomas Jonson
Priest Hollman
Henry Callibeit
John Whittred
Henry Sheffeild
John Shelton
Henry Willson
David Nods
Thomas Jonson
Robert Rowson
Thomas Hill
Thomas Bagly
Anthony Forthgill
Bartholomew Faborne
widow Dorsson
George Clackson
Ralph Sande
widow Balle
William Curtting
Henry Meare
John Spourne

Chequer Ward [continued]

Thomas Avis
Thomas Fincham
Nicholas Wild
Thomas Hubbard
Thomas Willton
Robert Loane
widow Robeson
William Whiterick
William Ricx
Abraham Hansly
Jonas Leech
Robert Gooch
William Ives
Joseph Staplor
James Foster
Henry Mew
Richard Denney
John Nobs
Thomas Fincham, jun.
Richard Ranalls
Francis Bretton
George Robson
Thurston Hattfeild
William Ravin
Thomas Read
John Wallis
Thomas Wallson
William Androws
John Hoogan
Robert Hill
William Rively
widow Nessline
Edward Tomson
Henry Ward
Matthew Norfolk
Henry Scelton
John Walson
Thomas Gillanes
Thomas Sheared
John Willby
'Swenten' Staford
William Leaster
Henry Hosencraft

Chequer Ward [continued]

[113 Names]

E 179/338, f.54

Jew's Lane Ward

14 Dec 1670

widow Revely
Joseph Eldrege
widow Foreman
Edmund Dallimore
Walter Boyce
Edmund Drinkmilke
widow Greene
Edmund Boney
William Johnson
William Harrison
Richard Sowerman
William Duncon
Richard Bishup
widow Page
widow Emanc
Henry Hether
Francis Hill
Thomas Cobb
widow Banton
John Barker
Henry Coverley
Richard Bates
John Bagley
Seth Cleares
widow Coats
William Keeth
Thomas Scotten
Charles Browne
Judith Brevester
John Pampe
Anthony Athow
widow Evered
widow Hammond
James Thacker
Robert Cooke
Henry Lech

Jew's Lane Ward [continued]

widow Everson
Thomas Westgate
William Murton
Robert Turfe, jun.
Robert Barber
widow Swann
Thomas Aldrege
Thomas Lee
John Clarke
William Tayler
Henry Andrwes

[47 Names]

E 179/335, f.840

Jew's Lane Ward

29 Dec 1671

Thomas Lee
Roger Gant
Henry Leach
Thomas Wesgate
widow Everson
Robert Cooke
Nathaniel Barvell
widow Swann
Robert Barber
widow Reively
Thomas Gosslyn
Walter Boise
widow Drinkemilke
widow Greene
Edmund Boone
widow Harrison
Richard Sowerman
William Dunkin
Thomas Ross
Richard Bishope
widow Page
widow Fuller
widow Emes
widow Howell

Jew's Lane Ward [continued]

Francis Hill
Thomas Cobb
widow Banton
John Barker
John Carsey
widow Chapman
William Gurlyn
Robert Frost
Henry Emorly
widow Ross
Seth Cleares
widow Coates
William Keeth
Thomas Scotting
widow Redie
John Pampe
Richard Betts
John Everitt
John Wesgate
William Murton
widow Foreman
James Thacker
old Spann
Edmund Crispe
Thomas Penney
Nicholas Carr

[50 Names]

E 179/337, f.35

Jew's Lane Ward

19 Feb 1672/3

Thomas Lee
Roger Gaunt
Henry Leech
Thomas Westgate
widow Everson
widow Cooke
widow Barvell
John Browne
Edmund Crispe

Jew's Lane Ward [continued]

John Hawes
widow Swann
widow Reveley
widow Drinkmilke
widow Gremer
Edmund Boney
George Partington
Richard Sowerman
William Dunkin
Richard Bishop
widow Page
widow Fuller
Thomas Cooke
widow Banton
John Barker
John Gersey
Henry Coverley
widow Rose
widow Chapman
Robert Froste
Seth Cleares
widow Coates
William Keeth
John Turner
Thomas Scotting
widow Reeder
John Pompe
Richard Betes
Joan Everett
James Thacker
Robert Elsdine

[40 Names]

E 179/337, f.36

Jew's Lane Ward

[undated ?Sep 1674]

Thomas Lee
Henry Leech
Thomas Westgate
Roger Gaunt

Jew's Lane Ward [continued]   E 179/338, f.55

widow Cooke   **Kettlewell Ward**
widow Barvell
John Browne   14 Dec 1670
widow Reveley
John Eckles   Francis Lates
widow Gremer   widow Murton
John Dalison   Francis Bell
Edmund Booming   John Williamson
George Partinton   Walter Marvell
Richard Sowerman   John Youngs
William Dunkin   Thomas Ellerd
Richard Bishop   Francis Hales
widow Page   John Wilson
Thomas Cobb   John Browne
widow Banton   John Batley
Thomas Rose   Roger East
Henry Heather   John Jones
Henry Coverly   Thomas Fennill
Thomas Greve   William Bowell
Robert Bull   John Baxter
John Bagly   Francis Evenall
Robert Frost   William Burton
Seth Cleares   William Batt
widow Coates   widow Hoames
Richard Betts   George Pertinton
John Pompe   Robert Standelow
William Keath   Roger Knott
Thomas Skotting   John Dolton
widow Everett   Thomas Pond
James Thacker   John Cattricke
Edmund Crispe   William Killing
Susan Swane   Charles Browton
widow Rose   Thomas Hall
widow Emons   Ann Bakon
widow Reader   William Bake
widow Chapman   widow Bowldre
Robert Elsding   Nathaniel Dunkister
widow Gay   George Dewell
                                    widow Rawlins
[42 Names]   widow Mason
                                    Lubell Cubitt
                                    Andrew Dill
                                    Martin Rose
                                    widow Masters

Kettlewell Ward [continued]

Francis Hayles
Thomas Mtchill
Roger Rucket

[43 Names]

E 179/335, f.845

Kettlewell Ward

20 Dec 1671

Alms Houses
Frances [?]Coates
John Willyamson
widow Brett
William Pice
Thomas Burton
Thomas Ellards
Robert Williamson
John Dollton
John Eatrich
John Watson
Walter Marvill
Robert Rollit
Frances Hales
Nicholas Wiles
Roger Knot
William Batly
Thomas Finne
Andrew Dillingem
William Bower
John Baxter
William Burten
William Bates
Robert Standelow
widow Rolin
Lubell Cipitt
Richard Barker
Samuel Maris
John Goules
William Michell
John Willson
Henry Lawrence

[31 Names]

E 179/337, f.37

Kettlewell Ward

20 Feb 1672/3

John Willyamson
Walter Marvell
Thomas Ellard
Francis Hagles
John Bilby
John Willson
John Dalton
Thomas Fennyll
Charles Browton
Roger East
Roger Buckett
widow Mason
John Bately
John Caterick
William Killing
Francis Evenall
Henry Lawrance
… Mi…
John Joanes
Thomas Hall
John Youngs
Thomas Pond
John Browne
William Bowell
Francis Hales
Andrew Dill
Martin Rose
Walter Marvell
George Dewell
John Baxter
Francis Sharp
Francis Bell
Nathaniel Dunkester
Ann Bacon
George Partington
William Burton
Robert Standelow
widow Bowledre

Kettlewell Ward [continued]

Roger Knott
widow Masters
William Bake
William Batt
Lubell Cubitt
Robert Raylett

[44 Names]

E 179/337, f.38

Kettlewell Ward

2 Sep 1674

Roger Knot
John Watson
Richard Sunson
Robert Wellmson
Walter Marsell
Thomas Ellord
L[?ube]ll Cubuit
Th[?omas] Halls
Samuel ...es
Nicholas Wills
Richard Cellt
George Duell
Edmund Gremson
Thomas Rouell
William Batlley
Nathaniel Balley
Thomas Thakirr
Thomas Fenney
Henry Effenns
John Wesencrafft
John Wesgkit
Aaron Brit
Richard Barker
John Bakstorr
Matthew Coperr
Edward Richard...conn
Nathaniel Donstarr
John Dell
William Jervis

Kettlewell Ward [continued]

Thomas ...morr
Francis Esnall
John Payn
George Wellson
John Billy
John Dallton
John Willson
Roger East
Henry ...ons
Thomas Hall
Francis Hales
widow Bowledre
widow Baker
widow Batt
Ann Bacon
George Partington

[45 Names]

E 179/338, f.56

New Conduit Ward

6 Mar 1670/1

William Leddington
Thomas Grayes
Ivan Wilkcocke
Rose Marres
John Bladworth
William Wright
Thomas Mobb
Nathaniel Jay
Alice Sanders
old Joan
William Bottome
widow Hutton
George Carman
John Worme
John Carsey
Henry Mason
John Downeing
Elias Knights
Thomas Ouldman

New Conduit Ward [continued]   E 179/335, f.818

New Conduit Ward

John Lee
widow Pemington
widow Blackwood   1 Mar 1671/2
widow West
James Gunn   Thomas Gray
Ann Towers   Richard Browne
Israel Curle   Ann Mears
widow Rayner   Christopher Croxon
William Wilkenson   William Wright
widow Richardson   William Bassett
James Graves   Nathaniel Gay
Francis Gant   William Bottom
Henry Castle   William Read
widow Coleman   John Worme
Thomas Barnard   Michael Crane
widow Chapman   John Bladworth
William Pearson   Robert Walker
Marmaduke Bootflour   Elias Knight
Matthew Ebden   John Raiper
widow Gamble   Stephen Hill
John Eatton   William Lister
John Jay   widow Penistone
widow Hall   widow Keamer
John Cragg   widow West
Matthew Silver   George Carman
Thomas Godbold   widow Blockwood
John Haynes   Israel Curle
Thomas Smyth   John Downing
John Taylour   John Graves
widow Coe   William Wilkinson
widow Hammond   William Maud
John Berman   Henry Castell
Nicholas Cathpoole   Elizabeth Richerson
widow Voucher   William Lemon
William Bush   Joan Chapman
Thomas Walker   Thomas Barnwell
Thomas Grandger   widow Tiffin
John Clarke   widow Dane
Thomas Gay   Henry Mason
Richard Brown   widow Gamble
widow Keemer   Thomas Godboul
widow Vann   John Eaton
                         Edward Johnson
[61 Names]   Thomas Mobb

New Conduit Ward [continued]

Ann Towars
John Joay
Ann Hunt
John Cragg
Matthew Silver
John Hains
Ellen Cannum
John Taylor
widow Coe
widow Hamon
Robert Sole
widow Voucher
widow Bell
widow Walker
Nicholas Catchpoole
William Bush
John Lee
widow Gay
Robert Hardwitt
widow Coleman
Mary King, widow
Peter Jackson
widow Martin

[63 Names]

E 179/337, f.39

New Conduit Ward

[undated ?Feb 1672/3]

Thomas Gray
Richard Browne
John Wild
Ann Mears
Christopher Croxon
William Wright
William Bassett
widow Brittan
Sherwood Day
Nathaniel Gay
William Bottom
Robert Hardy

New Conduit Ward [continued]

John Rivett
John Bladworth
John Raiper
Thomas Coppla
William Case
Robert Walker
Stephen Hill
widow Sendall
widow Peniston
widow West
widow Blockwood
widow Keamer
widow King
widow Vanne
John Downing
widow Rainer
Israel Curle
George Carman
John Graves
William Willkinson
Samuel Neale
William Lemon
Ellen Everitt
Henry Castell
widow Coleman
Thomas Barnwell
widow Tiffin
William Person
Henry Mason
widow Shepard
John Jay
John Ebden
widow Gamble
John Warlington
Thomas Godboll
John Eaton
Isaac John
Thomas Bancraft
Ann Hunter
John Cragg
Matthew Silver
John Hains
widow Coe
widow Hamond

New Conduit Ward [continued]

John Taylor
Thomas Smith
Robert Sole
Robert Beckham
widow Voucher
widow Martin
Robert Hardwitt
John Bush

[64 Names]

E 179/337, f.40

New Conduit Ward

2 Sep 1674

Thomas Gray
Richard Browne
John Wild
Ann Ma... [? Mears]
William Wright
William Basett
widow Preston
Sh[?erwood] Day
Nathaniel Gay
William Bottom
Robert Hardy
John Rivett
John Bladworth
John Reaper
William Case
Robert Walker
Stephen Hill
widow Sendell
widow Peniston
widow West
widow Blackwod
widow Keepie
widow Kinge
widow Vane
John Dowing
widow Rand
Israel Curle

New Conduit Ward [continued]

George Carman
John Graney
William Willkeson
Samuel Neale
William Lemon
Elizabeth Everat
Henry Casell
widow Coleman
Thomas Barnwell
widow Tiffen
Henry Mason
widow Shepard
John Jay
John Elden
widow Gambell
John Wartington
Thomas Godbould
John Eaten
Francis Fenn
Thomas Bancraft
Ann Hunter
John Crag
Matthew Sillveres
John Heines
widow Bee
widow Hanand
John Tayler
John Smith
Robert Sole
Robert Bockham
widow Vocher
widow Marten
Robert Hardwit
John Burch
Christopher Proxson
Thomas Copila
William Prasen

[64 Names]

E 179/338, f.57

North End Ward

14 Dec 1670

Francis Smith
Robert Farrow
Joseph Hill
John Bowell
widow Gant
widow Toone
Robert Sharpe
Thomas Chambars
Peter Marlow
John Eagle
Thomas Kendall
Bartholomew Collins
widow Money
Thomas Drake
widow Parke
Nathaniel Baley
… Heaslewood
John Platfoote
George Hall
William Weabe
John Murrell
Henry Barness
goody Palmer
James Cooper
Richard Hardingham
George Clements
Thomas Bond
Mary Curreson
Samuel Fenn
Robert Accope
widow Tee
Thomas Bridges
widow Clarke
John Goss
widow Raches
William Ashbey
Daniel Indgrame
widow Woods
John Dosen
Thomas Bucke

North End Ward [continued]

widow Andrewes
Richard Johnson
Henry Hall
widow Murton
widow Deane
Stephen Mathews
George Ingram
Theophilus Trundle
Thomas Good
widow Waller
widow Woodcocke
widow Murrell
John Payne
John Bridges
George Lee
widow Gold
Francis Lane
Robert Hollis
Christopher Stimpson
Henry Scott
William Haycocke
widow Corry
Thomas Bone
widow Bone
Francis Tee
George Burrowes
widow Armitage
Thomas Drake
James Mallett
widow Monke
John Roberts
John Dallison
John Foster
William Gray
widow Middus
Thomas Exleby
Walter Aubeney
Edmund Flower
widow Lee
Richard Tizard
Michael Dunken
widow Noone
Robert Coppin
widow Money, jun.

North End Ward [continued]

John Parke
William Bridgstocke
William Balsome
John Barfoote
Thomas Midleton
William Barber
widow Dunkine
James Mumford
widow Graves
Walter Boyce
widow Mindham
John Randall
Hugh Darby
John Pall
widow Phillips
widow Rossen
William Lambe
William Randall
John Browne
Andrew Toby
Francis Pike
widow Ancient
Mary Boone
John Midleton
widow Gurden
widow Turner
Ralph Grundy
John Starling
widow Hendry
John Eaton
Thomas Clayton

[115 Names]

E 179/335, f.819

North End Ward

12 Dec 1671

Frances Smith
Robert Farrowe
John Bouell
widow Wouds

North End Ward [continued]

widow Gant
Thomas Kendall
Walter Aubeny
Robert Sharpe
Peter Marly
John Foster
Bartholomew Collings
Thomas Chambers
John Eagell
W John Ashly [sic]
Robert Coppen
William Randell
William Brigstock
widow Mony
widow Tee
Frances Pike
Nathaniel Baly
Thomas Drake
Thomas Good
widow Park
widow Woods
Joseph Hill
Thomas Buck
widow Andrus
John Midelton
Humphrey Faudalow
James Coppen
William Ashby
John Platfor
Daniel Engrime
Richard Johnson
William Weab
Henry Hall
George Engrame
John Paine
widow Clarke
Thomas Bridges
widow Hendry
John Eatten
George Hall
widow Cory
John Bridges
William Boone
Robert Holles

North End Ward [continued]

Henry Barnes
widow Middus
Richard Hardingam
John Gos
Frances Heselwod
Robert Accop
George Climones
widow Corrisson
widow Riches
Samuel Fenn
widow Rossonn
widow Deane
Stephen Mathes
William Lamb
widow Anchant
Theophilus Trundell
widow Murrell
Mary Boone
John Dossen
William Rainer
widow Lee
George Burrowes
John Starling
Frances Lane
John Murrell
Christopher Simson
widow Boone
Henry Scott
James Mallet
widow Murton
George Lee
Thomas Boone
Frances Lee
William Haycoke
widow Armetage
widow Goold
widow Mounke
widow Turner
widow Woodcoke
Thomas Exelbe
William Gray
widow Garnes
Andrew Tobey
John Allcoke

North End Ward [continued]

Thomas Midringame
widow Gould
James Munfer
Michael Dunken
John Murell
Roger Resston
John Dallisson
John Parke
Richard Tisserd
William Willson
Michael Kemer
widow Anchant
William Bolsonm
William Barber
widow Mindonm
Henry Pall
William Walker
John Randell
widow Dunken
Hugh Darby
widow Waller
widow Nonne
widow Sandy
John Parke
Edmund Flouer
John Barffot
John Barber
widow Jarden
John Broune
Thomas Clayden
Edmund Richerson
widow Philloups
John Roberds
Ralph Grundy
William Gray

[127 Names]

E 179/337, f.41

North End Ward

23 [blank ?Feb] 1672/3

Frances Smith
Robert Farrowe
John Bouell
widow Wouds
widow Gant
Thomas Randell
Walter Aubeny
Robert Sharpe
Peter Marly
John Foster
John Eagell
Thomas Chambers
Robert Coppen
William Randall
William Bridgstock
widow Mony
widow Tee
Frances Pike
Nathaniel Baly
Thomas Drack
widow Parck
widow Wouds
Thomas Buck
Joseph Hill
widow Andrus
John Midelton
Humphrey Faudalow
James Copper
William Ashby
Daniel Engrem
Richard Johnson
William Weab
George Ingrames
John Payne
widow Clarke
Thomas Bridges
widow Hendry
John Eatton
George Hall
widow Cory

North End Ward [continued]

John Bridges
widow Boone
Henry Barnes
widow Midus
Richard Hardingam
John Gos
Frances Hesselwoud
Robert Accope
George Climens
widow Currisson
widow Riches
Samuel Fen
widow Rossonn
widow Deane
Stephen Mathues
William L[?a]mb
widow Anchant
Theophilus Trundell
widow Murrell
Mary Bounes
William Raner
widow Lee
John Starling
Frances Lane
John Murrell
Christopher Simson
widow Boune
Henry Scott
James Mallit
widow Murton
George Lee
Thomas Boone
Frances Tee
William Haycoke
widow Armetage
widow Goold
widow Turner
widow Woodcoke
Thomas Exelsby
William Gray
widow Garnes
Andrew Toby
John Allcoke
Thomas Mid[?er]ingame

North End Ward [continued]

widow Gould
James Munfore
Michael Duncken
John Murell
Roger Reston
John Clarke
Richard Tissend
William Willson
Michael Kemer
widow Anchant
William Bolsonm
William Barber
widow Mindonm
Henry Boll
William Walker
John Randell
widow Duncken
Hugh Darby
widow Waler
widow None
widow Sandy
John Parke
Edmund Flouer
John Barfoott
John Barber
widow Garden
John Broune
Thomas Clayden
Edmund Richerson
John Roberds
[?Ralph] Grundy
William Gray

[116 Names]

E 179/337, f.42

North End Ward

2 Sep 1674

widow Dove
Francis Smith
Robert Farrow

North End Ward [continued]

John Bowell
widow Woods
widow Gant
Thomas Randall
Walter Aubony
Robert Sharp
Peter Marly
John Foster
John Eagle
Thomas Chambers
Robert Coppin
William Randall
William Brigstock
widow Mony
widow Tee
Francis Pike
Nathaniel Baly
Thomas Drake
widow Derrik
widow Wouds
Thomas Buck
Joseph Hill
widow Andrews
John Midleton
Humphrey Fadelow
James Cooper
William Douffen
William Ashly
Daniel Egrim
Richard Jonson
William Weeb
George Ingram
John Paine
widow Clarke
Thomas Bridges
widow Hodges
John Eaton
George Hall
widow Cory
John Bridges
widow Boone
Henry Barnes
… Meadows
Richard Hardingham

North End Ward [continued]

John Goss
Francis Heaslewood
Robert Accop
George Clemence
widow Riches
widow Carrison
Samuel Fenn
widow Roseman
widow Deane
Stephen Mathews
William Lamb
widow Anchent
Richard Ellwood
Theophilus Trundle
widow Murrell
Mary Boone
widow Rainer
widow Lee
John Starling
Francis Lane
John Murrell
Christopher Simpson
widow Boone
Henry Scott
James Mallet
widow Murtton
George Lee
William Whitehead
Thomas Boone
widow Munford
Nicholas Dunkin
John Murry
Roger Royston
John Clarke
Richard Lisard
William Willson
Michael Keemer
widow Andrews
William Ballsonn
William Barber
widow Mardam
Henry Voll
William Walker
John Randall

North End Ward [continued]

Richard Dunkin
Hugh Derby
widow Walker
widow Norris
widow Sandy
John Park
Simon Hower
John Barford
John Barber
widow Goodwyn
John Brown
Thomas Clayton
Edmund Rouldston
John Robart
William Grey
Stephen Ga...
Francis Tee
William Haycok
widow Armitage
widow Gold
widow Turner
widow Woodcok
Thomas Exelsbe
widow Garner
Andrew Toby
John Allcock
Thomas Mideringham
William Gold

[119 Names]

E 179/338, f.58

Paradise Ward

6 Mar 1670/1

Thomas Burton
Isaiah Bright
James Farewell
William Bulman
widow Wilson
widow Smith
widow Claxon

Paradise Ward [continued]

Ann Green
Edward North
widow Rastricke
Henry Humpheys
John Wilkerson
John Holloways
Isaac Winge
Edward Simmons
John Bibby
John Walson
widow Fiske
widow Gage
James Blogg
John Smith
John Hall
widow Beverly
Nicholas Powell
John Lybby
George Gray
Thomas Wildman
Robert Howard
widow Gray
widow Bottom
Robert Smith
John Callington
Edmund Reedy
widow Cocksedge
Edmund Grimson
Edmund Werdinge
John Somes
Robert Stangrame
John Osborne
Robert Faulkner
Samuel Cullings
widow Eames
widow Starkine
Isaac Fenn
Roger Symons
Emanuel Adomson
John Bishop
John Honey
John Gold
widow Alcocke
Robert Mudd

Paradise Ward [continued]

widow Osborne
George Deueing
John Springall
Richard Barker
Jonathan Ashly
John Barnard
John Morris
Thomas Wing
John Fox
Richard Rudd
William Skerfe
John Laxly
Henry Widdowson
James Browne
widow Partin
Robert Beard
Thomas Murton
John Stoneham
Richard Swanson
Charles Browne
James Dunn
John Bishop, jun.
John Barnard, sen.
Robert Hullyard
Hugh Shone
widow Hokins
John Tenant
Robert Baker
John Towers
George Ravis
John Robinson
Thomas Bishop
William Mortimore
widow Byfield
John Bruyhys
James Brown
Roger Blackwood
Moses Hart
Mary House
widow Grewe
Richard Symons
George Tompson
Ann Hunter
John Hopp

Paradise Ward [continued]

widow Brown
Edward Jackson
Samuel Wythe
widow Gould
John Cobb
John Grey

[101 Names]

E 179/335, f.832

Paradise Ward

5 Feb 1671/2

widow Dosen
Thomas Borton
Isaiah Brite
James Farnell
William Welson
Edward Northe
widow Restrek
Henry Omfry
William Bolman
John Wilkeson
John Halowayes
Isaac Wenge
Edmund Semens
John Bolby
widow Fiske
James Bloge
John Smeth
Nicholas Poule
John Hall
widow Bfley
Anthony Athow
Robert Houard
Thomas Wilman
Roger Semens
Robert Smeth
widow Scote
George Anderson
… Abres
Edmund Gremson

Paradise Ward [continued]

John Somes
Robert Stangrome
John Osbon
John Rensted
Robert Fokner
Samuel Colens
widow Omes
George Paues
Jude Breuster
John Doulton
John Hope
widow Botoham
widow Accoke
George Deuell
widow Osbon
John Welles
George Starkens
William Colet
Martin Rose
Thomas Breges
Jonathan Ashley
John Barnod
George White
John Bosse
William Heuet
Thomas Wenge
John Watson
John Nockles
Nicholas Carpe
John Yaxley
John Wenckly
widow Kinge
widow Cote
widow Broune
widow Steward
John Gray
Richard Codde
William Waite
Henry Shone
widow Barenson
widow Meakens
George Este
Richard Hoberd
Daniel Foster

Paradise Ward [continued]

Richard Roberson
Robert Noton
Richard Swanson
John Busup
Francis Roberson
widow Broune
Edmund Gackson
Robert Rayment
widow Parton
Thomas Moulton
John Stonham
John Edwords
Francis Gente
William Makens
Robert Barker
John Barned
widow Wilkson
widow Mesterd
widow Skener
Roger Blockwod
William Weleson
Thomas Godboult
widow Goolsmith
widow Co...
Robert Mode
Richard Clore
Richard Clerolle
John Roberson
widow Bouer
George Busup
George Gray
William Bafley

[105 Names]

E 179/337, f.43

Paradise Ward

[undated ?Feb 1672/3]

Thomas Burton
James Faruell
William Wilson

Paradise Ward [continued]

Edward Northe
widow Restret
James Moarde
Henry Omfry
William Bulman
John Wilkeson
John Halawas
Isaac Wenge
Edmund Semens
John Belby
William Adde
widow Feske
James Bloge
John Smeth
Nicholas Poule
John Halle
widow Beffley
Anthony Athow
Robert Howard
Thomas Wilman
Roger Semens
John Pise
Robert Smeth
widow Scote
George Anderson
Edmund Gremson
widow Chockhead
John Somes
Robert Stangrome
John Osbon
John Renstead
Robert Foknor
Samuel Colens
widow Omese
Lubell Ceubet
Samuel Morde
George Paues
Jude Bruster
John Doulton
Roger Notte
John Hope
widow Arcoke
George Deuell
widow Osbon

Paradise Ward [continued]

Robert Mode
John Welows
George Starken
William Colett
Martin Rose
Thomas Breges
Jonathan Ashley
John Barnod
George Witte
John Bose
William Heuet
Thomas Wenge
George Gray
John Neckelson
Nicholas Carpe
John Yaxly
Thomas Goodboult
John Wenckly
widow Codde
widow Coinge
widow Browne
widow Stoneham
John Gray
Richard Codde
William Wiatte
Henry Shone
widow Harson
widow Makens
George Este
Robert Hobert
Daniel Foster
Robert Roberson
Robert Noten
Richard Swanson
John Busup
Francis Roberson
widow Browne
Edmund Gaxson
Robert Rayment
widow Partonn
John Stonham
John Edwards
Francis Gante
William Makens

Paradise Ward [continued]

Robert Baker
John Barned
widow Wilkson
widow Mastors

[95 Names]

E 179/337, f.44

Paradise Ward

2 Sep 1674

widow Dosen
Isaiah Brite
James Farell
James Moade
William Wilson
Edward Northe
widow Restocke
Henry Omfrey
William Bulman
John Wilekson
John Halowas
Isaac Wenge
Edmund Semens
John Belby
John Cane
widow Feske
James Bloge
John Smeth
Nicholas Poule
John Holle
widow Befley
Anthony Attow
Robert Houard
Thomas Wilman
Roger Semens
Robert Smethe
widow Scote
George Anderson
Edmund Gremson
Robert Stangrome
John Osbon

Paradise Ward [continued]

John Rensted
Robert Fokner
Samuel Colens
widow Omese
William Couke
John Welson
John Dowlton
Roger Semens
James Browne
John Hope
Thomas Bourton
widow Ackoke
Robert Mode
widow Osbon
John Welles
William Kelet
Martin Rose
Thomas Breges
Joan Ashley
John Barned
George White
John Bose
widow Heuete
Thomas Wenge
John Neckles
Nicholas Carpe
John Gaxsley
John Weakley
widow Ceede
widow Browne
John Browne
widow Stonham
John Gray
Richard Ceede
George Belby
William Weait
Henry Shone
widow Hareson
widow Ransom
widow Makens
widow Smethe
George Este
Robert Hobert
Daniel Foster

Paradise Ward [continued]

Robert Roberson
Robert Noten
Richard Swanson
John Busup
Francis Roberson
widow Browne
Edward Gaxson
Robert Rayment
widow Parten
Thomas Moulton
John Stonham
John Edwards
Francis Gente
widow Makens
Robert Baker
John Barned
widow Welkson
widow Mestors
widow Skener
William Spane
George Paues
Richard Secker
George Greg
Roger Blockewod
William Wilkson
Augustine Plesgers
John Benett
widow Hales
John Welleby

[104 Names]

E 179/338, f.59

Sedgeford Lane Ward

[blank] Dec 1670

widow Bootflower
Robert Rayner
William Day
William Woodham
widow Feake
Peregrine Taylor

226

Sedgeford Lane Ward
[continued]

Robert Hutchinson
Mary Read
widow Buckwood
John Powell
Richard Partinton
John Randall
widow Ogle
widow Stimpson
Henry Dawson
John Manfeild
Frances Houlton
John Selfe
Catherine Mason
William Dunkyn
William Cocke
John Oxburrow
Roger Tyson
widow Outlaw
George Newton
Humphrey Page
Robert Gibson
John Playne
John Bishopp
Henry Smith
widow Blogge
Thomas Curtis
John Martine
Matthew Walker
William Jarrett
William Gore
Susan Backhouse
John Collins
widow Bright
Edward Dewse
Stephen Gall
widow Rawlyn
widow Gritt
widow Ball
Joseph Gibson
widow Bussy
John Soames
John Watson
widow Bully

Sedgeford Lane Ward
[continued]

John Jay
John Silly
Robert Alderton
Moses Hart
Cicely Marriott
widow Porter
William Howlett
widow Osborne
Robert Dempster
widow Sapton
Robert Wright
Ralph Claydon
James Barcock
Ann Crispe
John Markham
widow Buxton
Joan Mellsopp
Elizabeth Clarke
Roger Blockwood
John Anderson
Samuel Roseby
John Edwards
widow Gamble
Thomas Balls
widow Burly
Robert Frankelyn
widow Woollen
Thomas Tisborow
George Winson
Thomas Markeham
John Myas
widow Disborow
William Buing
John Buckland
Robert Harrison
John Jay
Thomas Moulton
Lawrence Graves
John Wallowyn
Ann Bird
Robert Goodlad
John Edwards
Arthur Howes

Sedgeford Lane Ward
[continued]

E 179/335, f.841

Sedgeford Lane Ward

Thomas Makin
Daniel Dennison
William Wiborow
John Sadler
John Willis
Thomas Wallinton
William Wallowyn
John Smith
James Davy
John Harrald
John Randall
John Newman
widow Sherrald
widow Read
Charles Randall
Roger Dunne
Lawrence Myers
Roger Bunting
Edward Baker
Henry Colten
Robert Blacke
Henry Masters
Ann Jubbes
John Tyson
town houses (two)
Charles Burroughs
Robert Slater
Robert Wallinley
William Bennett
William Edwards
Roger Bunting
Robert Backhouse
Thomas Willowby
town houses (six)
Robert Gosling
John Parre
Robert Dearing
town & pesthouses (fifteen)

[127 Names]

26 Mar 1672

widow Bootflowre
Robert Rayner
William Day
widow Bathues
Thurston Hadfiield
William Wodhamm
widow Foce
William Wilbeson
William Harrimann
Ann Rollins
Ralph Poulee
Mary Reade
Richard Portingeton
widow Sargeant
Edward Frost
widow Ogell
John Randall
William Stimpsonn
Henry Dausonn
John Manafield
widow Crampton
William Neewe
Francis Holtone
John Selfe
William Bullinge
widow Hamsonn
Catherine Mason
William Dunkin
widow Cocke
John Oxborrow
Roger Tisin
widow Outlaw
George Newton
Humphrey Page
Robert Gibsonn
widow Wallowing
John Plaine
John Bushope
Henry Smith
widow Bloge

Sedgeford Lane Ward
[continued]

Thomas Certes
Thomas Wallington
William Wallowinge
John Sadler
John Harold
John Randall
John Newman
John Hampson
widow Shewde
widow Read
Charles Randall
John Murtonn
Matthew Wilker
William Garrett
widow Goore
John Collinges
widow Brighte
Edward Duse
William Neeve
Henry Rollins
widow Garrett
widow Bull
Joseph Gipsonn
widow Bushope
John Coms
John Watsonn
John Joyye
widow Bullinge
John Jay
William Bullinge
John Jay
John ...ille
Roger Doone
Lawrence Moyas
Roger Buntinge
Edward Barker
Henry Cotton
Robert Blacke
Henry Masters
Ann Jolls
John Tisin
a town house
Charles Berrous

Sedgeford Lane Ward
[continued]

Robert Aldertonn
Moses Hart
Susan Mullett
widow Porter
widow Howlit
William Woodes
widow Osborne
Robert Demster
Robert Right
Thomas Hopekins
Ralph Claidane
James Barcocke
Ann Crispe
John Marb...
widow Bukstonn
Joan Miksope
Elizabeth Clarke
widow Blobwood
John Adersonn
Samuel Rosbye
John Edwards
widow Cambell
Thomas Bull
widow Berlie
Robert Frankling
widow Wallinge
Thomas Tisberrow
George [?Win]son
Thomas Marckhamm
John Moyas
widow Disborrow
widow Berrey
John Buckland
Robert Harrisonn
John Jay
Thomas Moultonn
Lawrence Graves
John Wallowinge
Ann Bird
Robert Goodlad
John Edwards
Arthur Houss
Daniel Dausonn

Sedgeford Lane Ward
[continued]

widow Rayner
widow Wyberrow
John Calder
John Miles
Robert Salter
Robert Walmly
William Briant
William Edwards
Robert Bunting
Robert Backhouse
Thomas Wallowinge
Robert Gase
Robert Darndy
town houses & pesthouses   15

[139 Names]

E 179/337, f.45

Sedgeford Lane Ward

21 Feb 1672/3

Robert Rainer
widow Bootflower
William Day
William Woodham
widow Feake
Peregrine Taylor
Robert Hutcheson
Mary Read
widow Buckwood
John Pool...
Richard P[?or]tington
widow Oagle
John Randall
widow Steavenson
Henry Dawson
John Manfeild
Francis Houlton
John Selfe
William Bulling
widow Hensin

Sedgeford Lane Ward
[continued]

Catherine Mason
William Dunkin
William Cooke
John Oxborrow
Roger Tyson
widow Outlaw
George Newton
John Lashly
Humphrey Page
Robert Gibson
John Plaine
John Bishop
Henry Smith
widow Blogg
Thomas Curtis
John Martin
Matthew Walker
William Garrett
widow Goare
Susan Backhouse
John Collins
widow Bright
Edward Dewce
Stephen Gall
widow Rawleing
widow Garrett
widow Ball
Joseph Gibson
widow Bus[?se]y
John Soames
John Watson
widow Bully
John Jary
John Seely
Robert Allderton
Moses Hart
Cicely Marriott
widow Porter
widow Howlett
widow Osbourn
Robert Dempster
good Hopen
Robert Wright

Sedgeford Lane Ward
[continued]

Ralph Claydon
James Barcock
Ann Crispe
John Markham
widow Buxton
Joan Milksak
Elizabeth Clark
Roger Blackwood
John Oderson
Samuel Roseby
John Edwards
widow Hampton
John Balls
widow Burly
Robert Franklyn
widow Woollen
Thomas Teasborow
George Winson
Thomas Markham
John Mias
widow Disborow
widow Brien
John Buxlan
Robert Harrison
John Jary
Thomas Moulton
Lawrence Graves
John Wollowing
Ann Bird
Robert Goodlad
John Edwards
Arthur Hews
Thomas Makins
Daniel Tompson
William Wyborow
Nicholas Dix
John Sadler, sen.
John Wilby
Thomas Wallington
William Wallinham
John Sadler, jun.
John Randall
widow Shrewall

Sedgeford Lane Ward
[continued]

widow Read
Charles Randall
Roger Dunn
Lawrence Mias
Roger Buntin
Edward Baker
Henry Cattin
Robert Black
Henry Masters
Ann Jabbs
John Preston
Charles Burrows
Robert Salter
John Denny
John Newman
Robert Walmsby
[?William] Bryent
William Edwards
Robert Buntin
Robert Backhouse
Thomas Willoby
Robert Gosslin
Robert Dereing

[129 Names]

E 179/337, f.46

Sedgeford Lane Ward

2 Sep 1674

Robert Raynor
widow Bootflower
widow Daye
William Woodham
widow Feake
William Taylor
Robert Hutcheson
Mary Read
widow Blacke
John Proly
Richard Pirtingham

Sedgeford Lane Ward
[continued]

widow Oagle
John Randall
widow Steevenson
Henry Dawson
John Manfield
Francis Houlton
John Selfe
William Bulling
widow Hinson
Catherine Masson
Ann Dunkin
William Cooke
John Oxbourrough
Roger Tison
widow Outlaw
George Newton
John Lashly
Humphrey Page
Robert Gibson
John Plain
John Bishop
Henry Smyth
widow Blog
Thomas Curtice
John Martin
Matthew Walker
William Garrard
widow Goar
widow Backhouse
John Collann
widow Bright
Edward Duce
Stephen Gall
widow Rawlin
widow Garrard
widow Bell
John Gibson
widow Busting
John Somes
John Watson
widow Burly
John Saye
John Seely

Sedgeford Lane Ward
[continued]

Robert Alderton
Moses Hart
Cicely Marriott
widow Porter
widow Howlett
widow Osbourn
Robert Dempter
good Hopen
Robert Waight
Ralph Clayden
James Barwick
William Crisp
John Markham
widow Broxton
Joan Milksop
Edward Clark
George Blackwood
John Edwards
John Oderson
Samuel Roseby
widow Hampton
John Bull
widow Burly
Robert Franklin
widow Woollton
Thomas Teasborow
George Wanson
Thomas Markham
John Mias
widow Disborrough
widow Browne
John Boxham
Robert Harison
John Saye
Thomas Moulten
Lawrence Grays
John Wollowing
William Bird
Rowland Goodland
John Edwards
widow Hews
Thomas Makins
Daniel Stepson

Sedgeford Lane Ward
[continued]

Ann Wisborrow
Nicholas Dixe
John Sadler
John Wilby
Thomas Wollinton
William Willingham
John Sadler
John Randell
widow Sherwood
widow Read
Charles Randell
Roger Dunn
Lawrence Miers
Roger Bunton
Edward Baker
Henry Cotton
Robert Blacke
Henry Masters
Ann Jablis
John Presson
Charles Burrows
Robert Salter
John Deny
John Newman
Robert Walmsby
William Briant
William Edwards
Robert Bunton
Robert Backhous
Thomas Williby
Robert Gosslin
Robert Dearing

[129 Names]

E 179/338, f.60

South Lynn Ward

6 Mar 1670/1

Simon Smith
John Specke

South Lynn Ward [continued]

William Medcalfe
Matthew Gadge
Thomas Howlet
Thomas Davyis
Thomas Smith
widow Barvell
George Goodbourne
Thomas Appleyard
William Pilch
Joseph Trundle
widow Tompson
John Smith
William Bowles
Thomas Goodbourn
Robert Clapman
Thomas Clarke
widow Scotrill
William Wellin
Thomas Springall
John Plane
widow Grimes

[23 Names]

E 179/335, f.842

South Lynn Ward

26 Feb 1671/2

widow Grime
John Plaine
Thomas Springall
widow Wellin
widow Scotterill
Thomas Clarke
John Smith
William Pilch
widow Childeris
Thomas Apleyard
Mary Howlet
Simon Smith
John Specke
William Bowles

South Lynn Ward [continued]

Thomas Cutbonn
widow Jone
widow Bowles
William Bolsum
Thomas Davie
Matthew Gage
Robert Clapham
John Sherrid
William Wellin

[23 Names]

E 179/337, f.47

South Lynn Ward

8 Feb 1672/3

widow Grime
John Playne
Thomas Springall
widow Wellyn
widow Scotterill
Thomas Clarke
John Smyth
William Pilch
widow Childers
Thomas Apleyard
Mary Howlet
Simon Smyth
John Speck
William Bowles
William Bolshum
Thomas Davy
Matthew Gage
Robert Clopham
Joseph Trundle
John Shre...d
widow Joom
widow Bowles
William Wellem

[23 Names]

E 179/337, f.48

South Lynn Ward

2 Sep 1674

widow Grime
John Plaine
Thomas Springall
widow Wellin
widow Scotterill
Thomas Clarke
John Smith
William Pilch
widow Childers
Thomas Apleyard
Mary Howlett
Simon Smith
John Speck
William Bowles
William Bassum
Thomas Davy
Matthew Gage
Robert Chapman
Joseph Trundle
John Sherwood
William Wellin
widow Iron
widow Bowles

[23 Names]

E 179/338/1, f.61

Stonegate Ward

6 Mar 1670/1

Moses Hartt
William Goodger
Robert Clements
widow Browne
John Croxson
widow Hammon
John Munford
Elizabeth Baker

Stonegate Ward [continued]

William Bogg
William Collings
Winifred Gurling
Adam Curtis
Francis Cranne
John Babram
Walter Walker
widow Hartt
Elizabeth Furnis
Michael Whittington
Christopher Herring
widow Gray
Robert Masters
Robert Jarvis
Zachariah True
Thomas Peach
Edward Wright
widow David
Humphrey Johnson
widow Carlton
Matthew Hartt
William Mancer
widow Gabbs
Robert Antient
George Paynter
Richard Bradley
John Horner
Edward Taylour
widow Biggland
Catherine Carter
Charles Porter
Christopher Impin
John Bayley
Seth Soames
William Wright
widow Squire
Giles Hunt
John Perkis
John Paiton
widow Emperor
Leonard Walkinton
widow Twidey
Osborne Wood
George Haypresse

Stonegate Ward [continued]

widow Baycocke
Francis Runton
widow Acres
Richard Manfeild
Matthew Haigett
John Houching
Arthur Cooke
Thomas Rootlatch
widow Andrewes
Maurice Barnard
Edward Margerum
Clement Hopkins
widow Vasty
Nicholas Oxborrow
Thomas Bowden
Truth Ellot
Edward Wilkinson
widow Dueill
William Newson
John Kendall
Thomas Charington
John Thorpe
William Ives
Robert Popple
widow Drough
William Pinner
Thomas Archer
Stephen Wardell
Robert Vallinton
Joseph Whittington
John Silvers
Nicholas Croford
James Carlesse
John Harrison
Stephen Gall
widow Sargent
William Glower
John Harrison
Robert Narborrough
Henry Wheler
Thomas Reney
Richard Killingwood
Robert Gosling
Henry Gurdleston

Stonegate Ward [continued]

Isaac Smyth
William Wilcher
Thomas Mitting
widow Crimity
widow Harrison
James Whittington
widow Evisom
John Sherwood
Nathaniel Arger
Elizabeth Wrinch
John Graves
John Towers
Robert Martine
Richard Hurtt
Edmund Vincent
Joseph Smyth
Francis Moore
widow Jackson
Edmund Godard
Edward Jackson
Richard Lightfoote
John Cooke
Robert Smyth
Thomas Whitte
Everett Farthing
Thomas Williamson
George Burton
widow Bayley
John Gates
Robert Powell
widow Master
William Thurston
Thomas Wilkenson

[129 Names]

E 179/335, f.831

Stonegate Ward

21 Mar 1671/2

Walter Walker
Elizabeth Gray, widow

Stonegate Ward [continued]

William Gray
Robert Clemence
Francis Crane
John Babrum
Moses Hartt
Thomas Hartt
John Croxson
Barbara Woodrow
widow Baycock
Thomas Clarke
William Bogg
William Collens
John Briges
Thomas Peach
John Morres
Thomas Archer
Henry Smith
Francis Baker
John Gates
James Carles
widow Empson
Thomas Smith
Edmund Godard
Thomas Smith
Richard Hartt
Matthew Hartt
Richard Lightfoote
William Manser
Mary Feake, widow
John Squire
Edward Wright
John Harrison
Christopher Empin
Thomas Mobb
William Thurston
Samuel Drought
Humphrey Johnson
Edward Vincent
widow Simms
George Burton
John Horner
Edward Margerum
Thomas Boudin
Thomas Kerrey

Stonegate Ward [continued]

Robert Vallintine
Joseph Smith
Bartholomew Pinner
Stephen Wardell
widow Daniell
William Wright
George Kendell
Iillia Iives [sic]
John Huchin
widow Bradly
Arthur Cooke
Osbert Woods
widow Pople
William Cobb
widow Twidde
William Edmunds
Matthew Hargit
John Bayley
Mary Priest
Giles Hunt
William Fitt
widow Bayley
John Payton
Edward Wilkinson
Truth Ellet
John Silvers
widow Hopkins
widow Graves
Richard Wilson
Robert Edwards
John May
Robert Gosling
George Haires
Francis Moore
widow Acres
John Towler
Nathaniel Arger
William Wilshire
widow Wrinch
widow Hamon
Thomas Cherington
widow Crumity
widow Browne
widow Bigland

Stonegate Ward [continued]

John Thorpe
Thomas Renney
Henry Wheeler
Robert Narborow
William Newsum
John Oxenborow
Thomas Jolls
William Glover
John Harrison
Nicholas Crofer
Osbert Shingfield
John Cannome
George Painter
Maurice Barnard
widow Race
widow Gabbs
Thomas Done
Zachariah Trew
Henry Deane
widow Jackson
Seth Somes
widow Hartt
Joseph Whitington
Leonard Walkington
Robert Jarvice
Thomas Williamson
Henry Girdleston
widow Hartt
widow Furnis
widow Tylson
Nicholas Whittington
Robert Masters
Thomas White
John Munford
widow Barnard
Stephen Galle
Isaac Smith
widow Carleton
widow Squire
John Cooke
Charles Porter
Edward Tayler

[132 Names]

E 179/337, f.49

Stonegate Ward

21 Feb 1672/3

Elizabeth Gray
William Guger
Robert Clemens
Francis Crane
John Babram
Moses Hart
Thomas Hart
Barbara Wodrow
widow Baycock
Thomas Peace
widow Morris
Thomas Archer
Henry Finch
Francis Baker
John Gates
James Carles
widow Impson
Thomas Smith
Edmund Goddard
Thomas Smith, sen.
Richard Hart
Richard Lightfoot
Matthew Hart
William Mansir
Mary Feake
John Squier
Edward Wright
Christopher Impin
Thomas Mobb
William Thurston
Samuel Drought
Humphrey Johnson
Edward Vinson
widow Simes
George Burton
John Horner
Edward Margerum
Thomas Bowdon
Thomas Berry
Robert Vallentine

Stonegate Ward [continued]

Joseph Smith
Bartholomew Pinner
Stephen Wardel
widow Danill
William Wright
George Kendall
William Ives
John Huchin
widow Bradley
Arthur Cooke
John Whattum
Osbert Woodes
widow Poppell
William Cobb
William Edmunds
Matthew Harstote
Edmund Davy
John Baly
Giles Hunt
William Fitt
widow Bagly
John Pittom
Edward Wilkinson
Truth Elliet
widow Hopkins
widow Gurlyn
Richard Wilson
Robert Edmunds
John May
John Taylour
Nathan Argier
William Wilshire
widow Wrench
widow Hamond
Thomas Kerrington
widow Cromety
widow Browne
widow Bigland
John Thorpe
Thomas Renney
Henry Wheler
Robert Narborow
William Newson
John Oxborrow

Stonegate Ward [continued]

Thomas Jowles
William Glover
John Harrison
Nicholas Crafer
Osbert Shinfeild
John Cannum
George Painter
Maurice Barnard
widow Rowse
widow Tilson
widow Gabbs
Thomas Donn
widow Plain
Thomas Whiteseed
Zachariah Trew
widow Jackson
Seth Somes
widow Hart
Joseph Whittington
Leonard Walkinton
Robert Jarvis
Thomas Williamson
Henry Girleston
widow Hart
widow Furnis
Nicholas Whittington
Robert Masters
John Kerres
John Munford
widow Barnard
Stephen Gall
Isaac Smith
widow Carlton
widow Squier
John Cooke
Charles Porter
Edward Taylor
George Hayrs
Francis Giles
widow Umphry
Charles Warwick
Adam Curtis
Thomas Gray
Thomas Harriman

Stonegate Ward [continued]

Joseph Trundell

[129 Names]

E 179/337, f.50

Stonegate Ward

2 Sep 1674

Eli Gray	2
Edmund Guger	1
Robert Clement	1
Francis Crame	2
John Babram	2
Moses Hart	1
Thomas Hart	1
Barbara Woodrow	1
widow Bacock	1
Thomas Pearce	1
widow Morris	2
Thomas Archer	2
Henry Finch	2
Francis Baker	2
John Gates	1
Charles Porter	2
Edward Taylor	1
George Hayres	2
Francis Gyles	1
widow Humphry	2
Charles Warwick	1
Adam Curtis	1
Thomas Gray	2
Thomas Harman	1
Joseph Trundle	2
Maurice Barnard	1
widow Rouse	2
widow Tilson	1
widow Gabbs	1
Thomas Dun	1
Zachariah True	1
widow Jackson	2
Seth Soames	1
widow Hart	2

Stonegate Ward [continued]

James Carles	2
widow Imprer	1
Thomas Smith	2
Edmund Goddard	1
Thomas Smith, sen.	2
Richard Hart	1
Richard Lightfoot	1
Matthew Hart	2
William Manser	1
widow Feake	1
John Squir	1
Edward Wright	1
Christopher Impin	1
Thomas Mobe	1
William Thurston	1
Samuel Drought	2
Edward Vincent	2
widow Symes	1
George Burton	1
John Horner	1
Edward Margerim	2
Thomas Bouden	2
Thomas Berry	1
Robert Valintin	1
Joseph Smith	1
Bartholomew Pinner	1
William Wordell	1
William Danniell	1
William Wright	1
George Kendall	1
William Ives	1
John Huchin	1
William Bardly	1
Arthur Cooke	2
John Whittun	1
Osbert Woods	1
widow Popell	1
William Coll	1
William Edmuns	1
Edmund Davy	
John Baly	1
Giles Hunt	1
William Fitt	2
John Pittum	1

Stonegate Ward [continued]

Edward Wilson	1
Truth Elliot	1
widow Hopkins	1
widow Gurlin	1
Richard Wilson	1
Robert Eedmuns	1
John May	2
John Taylind	2
Nathaniel Argeair	1
widow Wrench	1
widow Hammon	1
Thomas Kerington	2
widow Cromity	1
widow Browne	1
widow Bigland	1
John Thorp	2
Thomas Renny	1
Henry Wheler	1
Robert Narbrough	2
William Newson	2
John Oxborrow	1
Thomas Jowles	1
John Harrison	2
Nicholas Crafer	1
Osbert Shinfeild	1
John Cannum	2
George Panter	1
widow Plane	2
Joseph Whittington	1
Robert Jarvis	2
Thomas Williamson	2
Henry Gurledston	1
widow Hart	1
widow Furnis	2
Richard Whitington	2
Robert Masters	1
John Kerry	2
John Munford	2
widow Barnard	2
Henry Gall	1
Isaac Smith	1
widow Carlton	2
widow Squier	2
John Cooke	1

[122 Names]

E 179/338, f.62

Trinity Hall Ward

14 Dec 1670

William Oldcorne
Robert Pinner
Arthur Yates
James Dickeson
Guy Joanes
John Swifte
Catherine Morres
widow Smith
Francis Cowyard
William Blinkhorne
John Richardson, sen.
William Cace
William Mason
Anthony Hewerson
widow Cobb
widow Greene
Rowland Morres
Robert Curtis
John Foster
widow Nickolls
John Eeveringham
widow Miles
Elizabeth Walker
Edward Minns
widow Dent
Thomas Muny, sen.
Robert Scott
Henry Pinner
widow Sandie
widow Gambell
Diana Coxson
John Betts
Thomas Palmer
Ann Flower
widow Doyson
William Landage
widow Nods
Thomas Rame

Trinity Hall Ward [continued]

widow Lynes
Thomas Coward
Ann Rudducke
widow King
Richard Buckes
widow Pinner
Fortune Banister
Robert Landage
Robert Wilson
Edward Silvers
John Wise
Robert Hambline
Francis Rost
widow Collens
widow Gidney, sen.
Thomas Bradshaw
widow Allen

[55 Names]

E 179/335, f.839

Trinity Hall Ward

29 Dec 1671

Thomas Smith
William Mason
John Sueft
Catherine Moris
widow Gell
Guy Gones
Dinah Coxson
Martin Yats
Robert Pmer [?Palmer]
Francis Coueard
William Reding
Edward Pattreg
William Dentt
widow Piner
William Martimor
widow Foster
Robert Radly
Robert Landiedge

Trinity Hall Ward [continued]

John Betts
Elizabeth Sley
widow Chambres
William Ouldkorne
Thomas Flower
Thomas ...
William Landidge
David Nods
William Elis
widow Lines
John Bilingham
Edward Whittingtan
Thomas Cleals
William Brooks
William Walling
Robert P[?inner]
Edward Mins
John Wild
Richard Slinger
Robert Blinkhorne
John Evringam
Edward Scilvers
Matthew Eldon, sen.
Matthew Eldon, jun.
Thomas Mony, jun,
Edward Sumers
William Loyston
Thomas Mony, sen.
John Wise
widow Gidny
Robert Willson
John Richardson, sen.

[50 Names]

E 179/337, f.51

Trinity Hall Ward

19 Feb 1672/3

John Richardson, sen.
William Case
widow Coll

Trinity Hall Ward [continued]

Anthony Hewerston
Francis Rost
Robert Hamblin
widow Collis
widow Greine
Rowland Morris
Thomas Bradshaw
Robert Curtis
John Foster
widow Nichleson
John Everingham
widow Myles
James Dixeson
Richard Singall
widow Smith
widow Dent
Thomas Mony, sen.
Diana Coxon
Grace King
Ann Flower
Henry Piner
widow Sandy
widow Gamble
Francis Coward
Arthur Yates
Robert Piner
James Dickenson
George Jones
Eli Walker
Catherine Morris
Thomas Coward
Edward Mines
John Betts
William Oldcorne
Thomas Palmer
widow Davison
William Landitch
widow Nods
Thomas Ram
widow Lynes
widow Allen
Francis Rost
Ann Ruddock
Richard Backus

Trinity Hall Ward [continued]

widow Priner
Robert Landitch
Fortune Banister
Edward Silvers
Robert Scott
Edward Mines
Robert Willson
widow Gidny
John Wise
John Swift

[57 Names]

E 179/337, f.52

Trinity Hall Ward

2 Sep 1674

John Richerson, sen.
widow Coll
Anthony Hewison
Francis Rust
Robert Hamblin
widow Collis
widow Grinn
Rowland Moris
Thomas Bradshaw
Robert Curtice
John Foster
widow Nickison
John Everinham
widow Miles
James Dickson
Richard Singell
widow Smyth
widow Dent
Thomas Mony
Dinah Coxen
George King
Ann Flower
Henry Pryer
widow Sandy
widow Gamble

Trinity Hall Ward [continued]

Francis Edwards
Anthony Gates
Robert Pinner
James Dickison
Guy Joans
Elizabeth Walker
Catherine Morris
Thomas Edwards
Edward Mins
John Bell
William Oldcorne
Thomas Palmer
widow Dawson
William Landeg
widow Hoge
Thomas Ram
widow Lynnes
Francis Ros
Ann Ruddock
Richard Backhous
widow Pinner
Robert Landich
Fortune Dannister
Edward Silvers
Edward Mines
Robert Wilson
widow Kedney
John Wise
John Swift

[54 Names]

Thetford

E 179/338, f.63

Bailey End Ward; St Cuthbert

25 Jan 1670/1

widow Goodale
William Tucke
John Martin
widow Graves

Bailey End Ward; St Cuthbert
[continued]

Thomas Mathum
widow Johnson
Henry Poole
widow Ward
widow Sparrow
Thomas Pigg
widow Baxter
Francis Pigg
widow Bell
Edward Barton
widow King
John Browne
widow Bilham
widow Reeve
Thomas Mash
widow Shred
William Madder
Francis Say
Barbara Tooley
Nicholas Fen
Abraham Faukes
John Shreid
Isaac Fauks
John Couldham
William Eldred
William Coldham
Henry Barret
Robert French
Robert Lyncolne
William Wright
widow Whitehand
Richard Roafe
John Roberts
Richard Sayer
Thomas Baxter
James Laurence
Thomas Briant
Barbara Tomson
Thomas Atmeere
Thomas Godsall
Robert Funnell
widow Dillingham
Christopher East

Bailey End Ward; St Cuthbert
[continued]

Christian Taxton
John Everard
John Thaxton
J...
Edmund Garnham
widow Cotton
widow Howlett
Peter Whiting, jun.
William Rushbrooke
Henry Carter
William Newell
William Scott
Thomas Wrettum
William Osbond
Richard Stegold
William Mobbs
widow Grengrass
John Baxter
Frances Winter
Richard Pannell
widow Moore
Peter Bacon
widow Dent
William Newell
Walter Newton
John Goodwin
John Cowles
John Parfret
Robert Elden
Stephen Stackwood
Samuel Cocke
Frances Gawdy
John Newell
Michael Starlinge
Thomas Duckling
widow Warwick
Thomas Scott
Richard Stevenso
Martha Edmunds
Ralph Stegold
Elizabeth Plumme
widow Herne
widow Mathum

Bailey End Ward; St Cuthbert
[continued]

widow Wretham
John Lambert
Amy Newell
Edward Ma...y
John Roberts
Peter Whiting, sen.
Matthew Lacke
Edmund Lacke

[98 Names]

E 179/335, f.686

St Cuthbert

18 Mar [1671/2]

William Newell
widow Scott
Thomas Enill
William Osbone
Richard Stegall
William Mobbs
widow Shreed
... Greenegrase
John Baxster
Francis Winter
Richard Pannell
Peter Bacon
widow Dent
widow Newton
Thomas Thaxsons
widow Colton
widow Johnshons
... Stannell
John Harrald
Robert Bazely
Peter Whitting
William Risbrocke
Henry Carter
John Martine
William Tuck
widow Graves

St Cuthbert [continued]

Henry Poole
Thomas Mathum
Ralph Stegall
Thomas Monings
Thomas Wretham
widow Ward
Amos Newell
Peter Whitinge
Matthew Lacke
Edmund Lacke
William Wright
... Whitehand
John Roberts, tailor
Richard Sayer
widow Sparrow
Thomas Baxster
James Lawrence
Thomas Bryant
Barbara Tomshon
Thomas Atmeare
widow Baxster
Thomas Godsoale
widow Willingham
Christopher East
Christian Thaxsons
John Gooding
John Cowles
John Parfitt
Robert Eldine
Stephen Stacwood
Samuel Cocke
Michael Starlinge
John Newell
widow Warrick
Thomas Scott
Thomas Pigg
Thomas Duckline
William Mader
widow Goodale
Matthew Edmonds
John Lambard
widow Wretham
widow Mathum
Elizabeth Plum

St Cuthbert [continued]

William Shreed
Nicholas Fenn
Francis Pigg
widow Bell
Edward Barton
widow Kinge
John Browne
widow Billam
widow Rutter
widow Reve
Thomas Mash
Abraham Fa[?uk]es
John Shreed
Isaac Facks
John Couldham
William Eldrid
William Couldham
Robert French
Robert Lincolne
John Poole
widow Funnell
Richard Rofe
Thomas Friet
Robert Say, sen.

[94 Names]

E 179/336, f.108

Bailey End Ward; St Cuthbert

4 Sep 1672

John Harold
widow Newell
widow Scot
Thomas Innell
William Osborne
Richard Stiggold
widow Shred
John Baxter
Francis Winter
Richard Pannell
Peter Bacon

Bailey End Ward; St Cuthbert [continued]

widow Dent
widow Newton
Thomas Thaxton
widow Johnson
Robert Bazeley
Peter Whiting, sen.
William Rusbrooke
Henry Carter
John Martin
William Tuck
widow Graves
Henry Poole
Thomas Mathom
widow Stiggoll
Thomas Munnings
Thomas Wretham
widow Ward
Amos Newell
Peter Whiting, jun.
Edmund Lack
William Wright
… Whitehand
John Roberts
Richard Sayer
widow Sparrow
Thomas Baxter
James Lawrence
Thomas Briant
Barbara Tompson
Thomas Atmeare
Thomas Godsall
widow Dillingham
Christopher East
Christian Thaxton
John Gooding
John Cowles
John Perfits
Robert Elden
Samuel Cock
Michael Sterling
John Newell
widow Warwick
Thomas Scot

Bailey End Ward; St Cuthbert
[continued]

Thomas Pigge
Thomas Duckling
William Madder
widow Goodall
Matthew Edmunds
widow Rutter
John Lambert
widow Mathom
Elizabeth Plumme
widow Shred
Nicholas Fenne
Francis Pigge
Thomas Friet
widow Bell
Edward Barton
widow King
John Brown
widow Billam
widow Reeve
Thomas Mash
Abraham Foakes
John Shred
Isaac Fakes
John Coldom
William Eldred
William Coldom
Robert French
Robert Say, sen.
John Poole
widow Funnell
Lydia Wretham
William Stanhill
wife of Cornelius Johnson
Richard Rolph
widow Cotton
Luke Waller

[90 Names]

E 179/336, f.109

Bailey End Ward; St Cuthbert

7 Nov 1673

John Harrold
widow Newell
widow Scott
Thomas Innall
William Osborne
Richard Stiggall
widow Shreed
John Baxter
Francis Winter
Richard Pannell
Peter Bacon
widow Dent
widow Newton
Thomas Thaxton
widow Johnson
Robert Bazely
Peter Whiting
William Rushbrooke
Henry Carter
widow Martin
William Tuck
widow Graves
widow Fincham
John Poole
Henry Poole
Thomas Matham
widow Steggall
Thomas Munnings
Thomas Wretham
widow Ward
Amos Newell
Peter Whitinge
Edmund Lack
William Wright
… Whitehand
John Coldham
Richard Sayer
widow Sparrow
Thomas Baxter
Thomas Bryant

Bailey End Ward; St Cuthbert
[continued]

James Lawrence
Barbara Tompson
Thomas Atmeare
Thomas Godsall
widow Dillingham
John Gooding
John Cowles
John Parfritt
Robert Elden, sen.
Robert Elden, jun.
Edmund Massey, jun.
Robert Mosh
Richard Moore
Samuel Cock
Michael Starling
John Newell
widow Warwick
Thomas Scott
Thomas Pigge
Thomas Ducklin
William Madder
widow Rutter
John Lambert
widow Matham
Elizabeth Plumme
William Shred
Nathaniel Fenne
Francis Pigge
Edmund Barton
John Andrews
John Browne
widow Billom
widow Reeve
Thomas Mash
Abraham Fakes
John Shred
Isaac Fakes
widow Eldred
William Coldham
Robert French
Robert Lincolne
Thomas Friett
widow Funnell

Bailey End Ward; St Cuthbert
[continued]

Cornelius Johnson's wife
William Stanhill

[85 Names]

E 179/338, f.64

Bridgegate Ward; St Peter

23 Jan 1670/1

Richard Bret
Robert Salsby
William Tomson
John Toley
widow Cocke
Alice Cunstable
widow Gaudy
George Salsby
John Sprinkfield
widow Wilie
Robert Poynton
widow Cambridge
widow Batteley
Robert Salsbie, sen.
William Garnham
Mary Bambidge
widow Sparaw
Catherine Gooding
John Tayler
John Frost
James Morris
John Bambridge
Henry Jonson
Edmund Day
widow Clay
John Mays
John Yellopp
Edmund Deake
John Garnham
widow Poole
widow Mash
Francis Rothersham

Bridgegate Ward; St Peter
[continued]

William Cocke
Thomas Sprinkfield
Thomas Rishbrooke
William Stubinge

[36 Names]

E 179/335, f.463

St Peter

19 Mar 1671/2

Thomas Bidwell
John Tooley
George Salisbury
Robert Salisbury
widow Gawdy
Francis Eliner
William Sprinkfield
William Roughlt
Augustine Howlet
widow Cock
William Tyler
Robert Salisbury
John Sprinkfield
widow Bambridge
widow Bateley
widow Sparrow
Alice Constable
widow Fuller
Edmund Bell
Edmund Drake
James Drinkmilk
Richard Gill
Richard Gill
widow Wylie
John Frost
Edmund Day
John Mayes
Henry Johnson
Thomas Sprinkfield
widow Pooley

Bridgegate Ward; St Peter
[continued]

John Rowse
John Bambridge
Yellop's wife
widow Mobbs
widow Tompson
widow Ward
widow Sprinkfield
William Tompson
Robert Poynton
Francis Rotherham
John Fuller
William Garnham
John Garnham
John Taylor
widow Mash
widow Tomson

[46 Names]

E 179/336, f.110

Bridgegate Ward; St Peter

4 Sep 1672

Edmund Bell
Thomas Bidwill
John Toley
George Salsby
widow Seamer
Francis Elener
William Sprinkfild
William Wrought
Augustine Howlett
widow Cock
William Tyler
Robert Salsby, sen.
John Sprinkfild
widow Bambridge
widow Cambridge
widow Batteley
widow Sparrow
Robert Tomson

Bridgegate Ward; St Peter
[continued]

Edmund Drake
James Drinkmilke
Richard Gill
widow Wilie
John Frost
Edward Day
John Mays
Henry Jonson
Thomas Sprinkfild
widow Pooley
John Rowse
John Bambridge
Yollop's wife
widow Mobbs
widow Ward
widow Tomson
widow Sprinkfeld
William Tomson
Robert Poynton
Francis Rutherham
old Garnham
widow Mast
John Tayler
John Garnham
John Rutherham
Richard Gill
John Fuller
Robert Salsby

[46 Names]

E 179/336, f.111

Bridgegate Ward; St Peter

7 Nov 1673

Thomas Bedwell, sen.
John Tooley
George Salsby
Robert Salsby, sen.
widow Cambridge
William Sprinkfield

Bridgegate Ward; St Peter
[continued]

William Rowlt
Augustine Howlett
widow Cock
William Tyler
Robert Salsby, jun.
widow Seamour
William Stubbins
John Sprinkfield
widow Bambridge
widow Bately
widow Sparrow
Robert Tompson
Edmund Bell, sen.
Edmund Bell, jun.
Edmund Drake
James Drinkmilke
Richard Gill, sen.
Richard Gill, jun.
widow Wylie
John Frost
Edmund Day
John Mays
Henry Johnson
Thomas Sprinkfield
widow Poley
John Rowse
John Bambridge
Yellop's wife
widow Mobs
widow Tompson
widow Ward
widow Sprinkfield
William Tompson
Robert Poynton
Francis Rudrham
John Fuller
William Garnham
John Garnham
John Taylor
William Mosse
widow Mash
John Rudrham
George Sterne, jun.

[49 Names]

The rest of Thetford - the parish
of St Mary - lay in Lackford
Hundred in the County of
Suffolk

INDEX OF NAMES

Alderson (Allderson, Alldersun) Hy 100; Tho 4; wid 100, 102-3, 105

Alderton (Aldertonn, Allderton) Robt 227, 229-30, 232; Tho 2-3

Aldred (Alldred, Alldrid, Oldred) Augustine 57, 119-20; Eliz 190; Jas 116; Jos 187; Wm 37, 59 (2); goodman 4

Aldredge, Aldrege *see* Aldridge

Aldrich Robt 30

Aldridge (Aldredge, Aldrege, Aldridg, Aldrige, Alldrege, Alldrge) Jas 113, 115, 118; Jos 188; Nich 69; Tho 157, 208; Wm 58, 162, 166, 185; wid 30, 69, 71

Aldrush Jas 41

Alen, Alene *see* Allen

Alexander (Alexsander, Allesander, Allexanders, Allexender, Allexsander, Allixander) Jn 157-8; Tho 100, 102, 104-5; wid 159, 172, 175, 179

Allcock, Allcoke *see* Alcock

Allden *see* Alden

Allderson, Alldersun *see* Alderson

Allderton *see* Alderton

Alldred *see* Aldred

Alldrege, Alldrge *see* Aldridge

Alldrid *see* Aldred

Allen (Alen, Alene, Allenn, Allin, Alline, Alling, Alliny, Allni, Allyn) Arthur 200; Edw 28-9; Francis 59, 168; Hy 13, 15, 18 (2); Isaac 161; Isabel 164; Jn 106, 108-9, 111, 146, 148, 150, 152, 161, 164, 168, 180-1, 183; Lancelot 32, 60-61; M. 170; Robt 182, 184; Sam 23-5; Tho 142-4, 154-6; Tobias 157-8; Toby 158; Wm 16, 19, 60-61, 64, 92, 94; good 95; goodman 4; Mrs 166; wid 2, 30, 31 (2), 32, 45, 48, 53-5, 112, 160, 163, 167 (2), 170, 192, 194, 196, 198, 200, 241-2

Allerd Geo 78

Allesander *see* Alexander

Alleson *see* Allison

Allexanders, Allexender, Allexsander *see* Alexander

Allin, Alline, Alling, Alliny *see* Allen

Allison (Alleson, Allyson) Ann 184-6; Jas 195; wid 147, 149, 151, 153

Allixander *see* Alexander

Allman Wm 192, 194, 196

Allni *see* Allen

Allt Ste 188

Allyn *see* Allen

Aloys (Alouys, Aloyc, Aloye, Aloyes, Aloyse, Loyce, Loys, Loyse) Abraham 70, 71 (2), 72; Edm 24-5; Isaac 69-72, 74-5; Jeremiah 70; Jn 70-2; Nathaniel 58-9

Ambrook (Ambroock, Ambruck) Tho 65-7

Ames (Ameis, Amis, Amos, Amys) Edw 41, 43, 44 (2); Geo 86; Lydia 2; Margt 77; Pet 36-8; Tho 25; Wm 23, 25; wid 36

Ancient (Anchant, Anchent, Antient) Robt 235; wid 217-21

Anderson (Adersonn, Andarson, Andersonne, Andosen, Oderson) Chas 139; Christopher 137, 140-1; Geo 223-5; Hy 24-6; Jn 133, 227, 229, 231-2; Jonas 197; Mary 125, 133, 137; wid 128

Andrews (Andrewes, Androes, Androws, Andrus, Andrwes, Andues) Christopher 14, 16, 20, 42-4; Hy 208; Jn 77, 83, 248; Robt 78, 80-1, 83; Wm 204, 206-7; wid 78, 205, 216-7, 219-21, 235

Angell (Angle) Ellis 172; Jn 36; wid 36-9, 171

Anger wid 33 (2)

Angle *see* Angell

Angler Edw 164, 168

Annis Chas 156-7; goodman 155; wid 193, 195, 197

Annison (Anyson) Jn 180

Annsell, Ansell *see* Hansell

Antell (Antle) Jn 171, 175; Wentworth 145 (2), 146

Antient *see* Ancient

INDEX OF NAMES

Antle *see* Antell
Anyson *see* Annison
Apleyard *see* Appleyard
Appleby (Appelbey, Applebee) wid 125,
128, 131, 134
Appleyard Tho 233 (2), 234 (2)
Arbere *see* Aubrey
Arbor Ann 53
Arch wid 106
Archer (Archar) Archer & Reeve 117;
Ann 56; Hy 162, 166, 170; Jn 174,
176; Sam 11; Tho 187, 235-6,
238-9; good 55
Arcoke *see* Alcock
Arcres *see* Acres
Ardnold *see* Arnold
Arger (Argeair, Argier) Nathaniel
(Nathan) 236-8, 240
Armeger, Armenger *see* Armiger
Armes Jn 25-6, 91-2, 94; Tho 25-6;
good 96; wid 91-2, 94, 96-7
Armestead *see* Armstead
Armetage *see* Armitage
Armiger (Armeger, Armenger, Arminger)
Christopher 36-8; Jn 161, 164, 168;
Robt 123, 125; Tho 173, 175, 178;
good 39
Armitage (Armetage) wid 216, 219-19,
221
Armstead (Armestead, Armsted) Robt
147, 149, 151, 153; Tho 99, 101,
103, 105
Arnald, Arneld *see* Arnold
Arnes wid 129
Arnold (Ardnold, Arnald, Arneld, Arnoll,
Arnould) Francis 193; Hy 192, 194;
Jn 77; Robt 13, 15, 18 (2); Tho 76,
79, 126, 128, 131; wid 161, 164,
168
Arrold Tho 196
Artler wid 200
Asben wid 178
Ascew, Ascue *see* Askew
Asen Wm 66
Ashby (Ashbey) Wm 216-7, 219; wid 197

Ashley (Ashly, Lashly) Joan 226; Jn 58-9,
230, 232; Jonathan 222-3, 225;
Margt 62, 64; Wm 171, 220; W.
John 217; wid 60-1, 193, 195
Ashminall (Ashmenal, Ashmenall)
Tho 65-6, 68
Askew (Ascew, Ascue, Askue) Wm 180;
wid 172, 175
Askines *see* Atkins
Askue *see* Askew
Asson Sarah 3
Asstine, Asten. Astinne *see* Austin
Atcherson Jn 191
Athey Tho 107
Athill *see* Atthill
Athow *see* Attoe
Atkeson *see* Atkinson
Atkins (Adbines, Adkings, Adkins,
Askines, Attkins) Benjamin 191; Hy
185; Jas 172, 174, 177; Jn 36-8,
105; Tho 147, 150; Wm 106-8,
110-12, 119, 190-1; goodman 112;
wid 60, 119, 192, 194, 196
Atkinson (Atkeson, Atkison, Attkinson)
Jn 153; Rd 192, 194, 196; Tho 151
Atmore (Atmeare, Atmeere) Tho 244-6,
248
Atterson wid 39
Atthill (Athill) Jn 91, 112
Attkins *see* Atkins
Attkinson *see* Atkinson
Attoe (Athow, Attow) Anthony 208, 223-5
Aubeney (Aubeny, Aubony) Walter 216-7,
219-20
Aubrey (Abbery, Aberey, Abery, Abree,
Arbere, Aubere, Auberee, Aubery,
Awbree) ... 68; Robt 125, 128, 133,
136; Timothy 130-1; Titus 99, 100,
102, 104
Aubony *see* Aubeney
Auborn, Auborne *see* Awborne
Auger (Augar, Augur) Jn 128, 131;
Tho 157; Wm 52
Augustine wid 1
Austea Robt 83

255

Baldwin (Baldin, Baldwing, Baldwyn,
　　Baldwyne, Balldwin, Bolldin,
　　Boollden) Edm 147, 149, 151; Edw
　　153; Rd 159; Timothy 113-4;
　　goodman 26, 111
　　see also Balding)
Baldy see Baldry
Bale Hy 50-51, 53
Baleffe see Bayliffe
Balenc see Ballance
Baleston see Balliston
Baley see Bailey
Balfs, Balife see Bayliffe
Baliston, Balistone see Balliston
Ball Sam 185; Tho 55; wid 227, 230
Ballance (Balanc, Balenc, Ballence,
　　Bollence) Jn 41-4; Tho 39, 40 (2)
Ballden see Bolding
Balldinge see Balding
Balldre see Baldry
Balldwin see Baldwin
Balle see Bailey
Ballence see Ballance
Balles see Balls
Ballestone see Balliston
Balley see Bailey
Ballingston see Balliston
Ballister (Ballinster, Bollite) Jn 113, 115-6
Balliston (Baleston, Baliston, Balistone,
　　Ballestone, Ballingston, Balston,
　　Balstone) Geo 140; Jn 144, 159;
　　Mary 156; Tho 138-9, 158-9; Wm
　　126, 129, 132, 135; wid 155-6
Balls (Balles, Bals) Francis 114, 118;
　　Frank 115; Jn 182-3, 231; Nich
　　145-6; Sampson 176; Tho 79, 81,
　　84, 193-4, 198, 201, 227; Wm 88-9;
　　wid 205
Ballsonn see Balsome
Bally see Bailey
Bals see Balls
Balsome (Ballsonn, Bassum, Bolshum,
　　Bolsonm, Bolsum) Wm 217-8,
　　220-1, 234 (3)
Balston, Balstone see Balliston
Balton Jn 166, 170

Baly, Balye see Bailey
Bambridge (Bambridge, Banburdge)
　　Jn 248-50; Mary 248; Tho 161, 164;
　　wid 249-50
Bancks see Banks
Bancraft Tho 214-15
Banes Rachel 173
Banfather (Banfether, Barnfather) Hy 132,
　　135; Tho 125; wid 80, 82
Banger (Bange) Jn 179, 181, 183
Banister see Bannister
Banks (Bancks, Bankes) Mary 26; Sam 6,
　　7 (2)
Bannister (Banister, Dannister) Fortune
　　241, 243 (2); Jn 69-71, 73; Tho 154
Banton wid 208, 209, 210
Banyard (Bainard, Baynyard) Tho 17, 19;
　　wid 120, 122-4
Barber (Barbor) Island 148, 150; Jn 10,
　　179, 181-2, 218, 220-21; Rd 17, 19;
　　Robt 15, 147, 149, 208; Tho 122,
　　136; Wm 14, 16-17, 19, 217-18,
　　220-21; wid 89
Barcer see Barker
Barcham see Burcham
Barck see Bark
Barcock (Barcocke) Jas 227, 229, 231;
　　wid 205
Bardly Wm 240
Barefoote see Barfoot
Barenson wid 223
Barfoot (Barefoote, Barffot, Barfoote,
　　Barfoott, Barford) Jn 217-8, 220-1;
　　Wm 162, 165, 169
Barfurr Rd 154
Bark (Barck, Barke) wid 51-2
Barker (Barcer, Berker) Abott & Barker
　　116; Edw 229; Frances 80; Francis
　　78, 82-3; Gilbert 106; Gregory 139;
　　Hy 115-16, 119; Island 152; Jn 8-10,
　　113-14, 116-17, 148, 150, 152, 154,
　　208-9; Mich 61-3; Pet 107, 109-10,
　　112; Rd 147, 149, 211-12, 222;
　　Robt 29, 151, 153, 224; Sarah
　　155-6, 182; Tho 121, 123; Wm 27,
　　155-6; wid 157

Buxton (Broxton, Buckston, Bukstonn,
    Buxtton) Christopher 48, 49; Jn 172;
    Rd 151, 153; Tho 90; goodman 49;
    wid 227, 229, 231-2
Bybrest (Bibrest, Bybress) Ann 67;
    wid 64, 66
Byce (Buise, Byse) wid 39, 40 (2)
Bycroft see Beecroft
Byfield wid 222
Byse see Byce

C...ll Wm 140
Cable (Cabel, Keble) Edm 45, 46 (2), 47;
    Jn 57-9
Cace see Case
Cacket see Cockett
Cade see Cades
Cademon wid 46
Cades (Cade, Cadeys, Cads) Edm 187;
    Edw 189; Tho 190; wid 191, 198,
    200
Cadie see Cady
Cadle, Cadly see Cardle
Cads see Cades
Cady (Cadie, Kadie) Eliz 60-61, 63;
    Francis 113; Frank 114, 116; wid 4,
    64, 76
Caffe Edm 195
Calder Jn 230
Caley (Cale, Calley, Caly) Hy 73-4, 76;
    Sam 178; Wm 8-10
Calfe (Calf) Anthony 160; Edw 11-12; Jn
    11 (2), 12-13, 36; Wm 58 (2), 59;
    wid 13
Call wid 180
Callaway see Calloway
Calley see Caley
Callibert (Callibeit) Hy 203, 206-7
Callington Jn 222
Callingworth Wm 141
Callow (Callo, Callowe) Jn 175, 178; Rd
    36, 107; Tho 126, 129; Wm 131;
    good 39; wid 38-9
Calloway (Callaway) Jn 147, 149; Rd 37;
    Wm 135
Callowe see Callow

Calme Ste 192
Calthorpe (Caltrup, Colthorp, Coltrup)
    Tho 22, 24-6
Calton, Caltron see Carlton
Caltrup see Calthorpe
Caly see Caley
Cambell wid 229
Cambridge wid 248-50
Camby see Canbey
Camell Tho 174, 176; wid 175
Cammant wid 173
Camp (Campe) wid 34 (2)
Campling (Camplen, Camplin, Campline,
    Kamplin) Anthony 100-01, 104, 106;
    Catherine 46; Edw 106; Jn 100, 102,
    104-5; Robt 45-6; Tho 17, 20; wid
    47, 61, 64 (2), 143, 175, 178
Campthorne see Kempthorne
Camstead Matthew 107
Camtree Robt 165
Camy Jn 199
Canam see Canham
Canbey (Camby, Candbey) Giles 30 (2),
    31
Candler (Condlye) Pet 161, 164, 167-8,
    170; Wm 179, 181; wid 184-6
    (see also Chandler)
Cane Jn 12, 225; wid 167, 170
Canham (Canam, Cannom, Cannome,
    Cannon, Cannum, Cunnon) Eliz
    60-3; Ellen 214; Frances 55, 57;
    Francis 53, 56; Geo 50-1, 52 (2); Jn
    237, 239-40
Cann Benjamin 193
Cannell (Cannells, Cannolds, Connalds,
    Cunnills) Geo 14, 16-17, 20
Cannom, Cannome, Cannon, Cannum see
    Canham
Canuwell Hy 134
Capell Edw 61-2; Jn 60; wid 192, 194
Caper Caper & Cooke 117; Rd 155-6
Capieson Wm 196
Capman, Capon see Chapman
Car see Carr
Car... Tho 135

INDEX OF NAMES

Certes *see* Curtis
Cettle *see* Kettle
Ceubet *see* Cubitt
Chace Christopher 67
Chaddock wid 202
Challon Wm 205
Chalton wid 190-91
Chambars *see* Chambers
Chamberlin (Chambelin, Chambrlin) Edm 7; Eliz 7; Tho 137, 139; wid 6-7, 154
Chambers (Chambars, Chambres) Ann 45; Edm 7; Edw 7; Jn 77, 80-81; Tho 47, 216-7, 219-20; wid 7, 242
Chambrlin *see* Chamberlin
Chandler Wm 181-3; good 95; wid 171 (*see also* Candler)
Chaplin (Chapline) Tho 75
Chapman (Capman, Capon, Chapmann, Chappman) Anthony 14, 16; Hy 77; Jas 23, 98, 120-22, 124; Joan 213; Jn 83, 126, 129, 167, 202; Jos 163; Nich 34, 35; Pet 64, 66; Rd 50 (2), 51; Robt 161, 164, 168, 234; Tho 155; Wm 114-5, 118, 147 (2), 149 (2), 151, 153; wid 17, 19, 37-9, 132-3, 135, 193, 195, 197; wid 209-10, 213
Charington (Cherington) Tho 235, 237
Charlton Jn 172
Chartwrite *see* Cartwright
Chay Robt 172
Cheny Jonas 184-5; Josiah 186; wid 202
Cherington *see* Charington
Chest (Chist) Nich 91-2, 94; good 96
Cheston Benjamin 161
Chettleburgh (Chetleburgh) Anthony 2
Child (Childe) Edw 198-9, 201; Tho 70, 72-3
Childerhouse (Childeris, Childers, Childirhouse, Childresse) Susan 161, 164; Susanna 168; wid 233-4
Chilvers Robt 131, 134
Chip (Chipp) Rd 190; wid 192
Chist *see* Chest
Chockhead wid 224

Chreve *see* Shreeve
Chrispe *see* Crisp
Christian (Christan, Christon, Cristen, Cristin) Jn 65-6, 140-1; wid 66-8
Chrithood *see* Critwood
Chroch *see* Crotch
Chruspe *see* Crisp
Chubb goodman 45
Church Ann 90, 93, 97; Edm 158, 159 (2), 178; Edw 157 (2), 158-9, 176; Eliz 191; Hy 32; Jn 146; Rd 173; Tho 36, 77, 80, 82-3, 85-6, 88; wid 119, 120, 159
Churchman Edw 6 (2), 7 (2)
Cinderland *see* Sinderland
Cipitt *see* Cubitt
Clabborn (Clabarn, Clabbon, Clabborne, Claborne, Clabourne, Clayborne) ... 44; Jn 2-3, 42, 44, 120, 122-4; Rd 121, 123; Robt 121, 124
Clackson *see* Clarkson
Claidane *see* Claydon
Clake wid 70
Clamtree Tho 99, 101-2, 104
Claperson *see* Clapperson
Clapham (Clapman) Robt 233-4
Claphamson, Clapison *see* Clapperson
Clapman *see* Clapham
Clapperson (Claperson, Claphamson, Clapison) Hy 113, 115-6, 118; Jeremy 78
Clarck *see* Clarke
Clare Wm 167; Winifred 163
Clarke (Clarck, Clark, Clerk) Clark and Wiginton 116; Abraham 74-6, 154; Adam 13, 15, 18; Dan 75, 91, 106-7, 109, 111; Edm 36; Edw 37, 180, 232; Eliz 227, 229, 231; Frances 65-6; Francis 136; Jas 65-6; Jn 11 (2), 14, 16, 30, 44 (2), 198-9, 201, 208, 213, 220-21; Mary 30; Mich 86, 119; Moses 108-9, 111; Rd 98, 203-6; Robt 10, 19, 71, 134, 172-3, 175, 177, 181, 183; Sam 85, 87-8, 90; Sarah 183; Ste 182, 184; Tho 75, 97, 98 (2), 113, 171;

Dallimore Edm 208

Dallinigat Tho 176

Dallison (Dalesen, Dalison, Dallisson, Dalliston, Dalleson, Dallesonne) Jn 210, 216, 218; Rd 65-6, 102-3, 105; wid 127, 130

Dallowaye (Dalleway) Jn 151, 153

Dalton (Dallton, Dollton, Dolton) Alice 60-1; Jn 210, 211 (2), 212

Dam (Dame, Damm, Dum) Godfrey 53, 57; Jn 32-4; Robt 91-2, 94; good 96

Dane wid 213

Danee Jos 69

Danell *see* Daniel

Danes *see* Daines

Daney *see* Darney

Dangerfe... goodman 64

Daniel (Danell, Daniell, Danill, Danniell), Danyell Abraham 93, 95; Benjamin 70-2; Robt 44; Ste 1; Wm 240; good 96; wid 139, 156, 237-8

Dannister *see* Bannister

Danny *see* Denny

Dany *see* Darney

Danyell *see* Daniel

Danyres *see* Daynes

Darby (Darbey, Derby, Dorby) Hugh 217-18, 220-1; Robt 41-4; Tho 99, 101, 103, 105

Darcy Jn 80; wid 82

Darndy Robt 230

Darney (Daney, Dany) Francis 178; Jn 126, 129, 132, 136; Tho 126, 129, 133, 136

Darson, Dason, Dasson *see* Dawson

Datey Jn 72

Datree *see* Delatree

Datte Jos 71

Daudy *see* Dady

Daue *see* Davy

Daues, Daus *see* Dawes

Dause *see* Dawsy

Dausen, Dauson, Dausonn *see* Dawson

Davell *see* Devell

Davey *see* Davy

David wid 235

Davie *see* Davy

Davis (Davies) Jn 10, 60-61, 190; goody 21

Davison Jn 203; wid 242

Davy (Daue, Davey, Davie, Davyis) Edm 238, 240; Jas 160, 228; Jn 70-2, 107, 132, 136; Jonas 109-10, 112; Jos 70; Pet 45-7; Tho 36, 68, 118, 233, 234 (2); Wm 87; goody 39; wid 65-7, 72, 74-5, 171, 193-4, 196

Dawbnye *see* Dabney

Dawdy (Dody) Jn 158-9

Dawes (Daues, Daus, Dawis) Chas 47; Eliz 121; Jn 27, 29, 62, 64; Tho 101, 103, 105; Wm 25, 96; wid 92, 94, 96

Dawney goody 22

Dawson (Darson, Dason, Dasson, Dausen, Dauson, Dausonn, Dawsen, Dawsun, Dayson, Dewsing, Dewson, Doliman, Doorson, Dorsson, Dosen, Dossen, Dosson, Doyson, Dunson, Durson) Dan 229; Edw 21, 69, 71-2; Hy 227-8, 230, 232; Jn 174, 178, 182-3, 204-6, 216, 218; Jos 178; Rd 24-6, 137, 139-41; Robt 72; Sam 85-7, 89, 177; Tho 23, 53, 56-7, 77, 140-41; Wm 25-6; goodman 22; wid 36, 83, 171, 198, 201, 207, 223, 225, 241, 243
(*see also* Dowsing)

Dawsy (Dause) Jn 78, 82

Day (Daye) Edm 248-50; Edw 158, 250; Hy 14, 16-17, 20; Jn 40, 150, 152, 202; Robt 2; Sherwood 214-15; Wm 226, 228, 230; wid 159, 231

Dayes wid 152

Daynes (Danyres, Dayne, Dayns) Clement 39, 40 (2), 41; goodman 112; Eliz 120; Hy 20; Jn 107, 109-10, 112; Robt 190; wid 80
see also Daines)

Dayson *see* Dawson

Deacon (Dacon, Decon) Jn 127, 130, 132, 136; Ralph 120; Robt 91, 108-9; wid 106, 108-9, 112

Dowlton *see* Doulton

Dowly *see* Doughty

Dowman Jn 165

Downeing *see* Downing

Downes (Dounes, Dowine) Edm 20-21; Edw 21-2; Hy 125, 128, 131, 135; Jn 39; Susan 1

Downing (Dowing, Downeing, Downinge) Edm 85, 87-8, 90; Geo 100, 102, 104, 106; Jas 113, 118; Jn 212-15; Mich 10, 54; Theophilus 190; wid 76, 79, 82-3

Dowsing (Douson, Dowseing, Dowsin, Dowsinge, Dowson, Dowzin) Christopher 38-9; Geo 166; Jn 172; Jos 175; Robt 70, 73, 168; Sam 173, 175; good 96; old 73; wid 142, 172, 206

(*see also* Dawson)

Dowty *see* Doughty

Dowzin *see* Dowsing

Doyle Tho 11

Doyson *see* Dawson

Drake (Drack, Dreake) Adam 172, 191; Edm 249-50; Jn 160, 164; Tho 160, 164, 167, 216-7, 219-20

Draper Tho 60-61, 63; Wm 193, 195, 197; goodman 64

Drayton Jn 8, 29

Dreake *see* Drake

Dremee (Drewmoy) Abraham 22, 145; Jane 145

Dremon *see* Deremon

Dremow Dan 77

Dreu *see* Drew

Dreury *see* Drury

Drew (Dreu) Jas 26; Mich 178; Rd 29; Wm 174; wid 96

Drewmoy *see* Dremee

Drewry *see* Drury

Drinckale *see* Drinkale

Dring (Dringe) Pet 20, 21 (2), 22

Dringlee ... 41-2

Drinkale (Drinckale, Drinkall) Matthew 17; Nathaniel 14, 16, 19

Drinkmilke (Drinkemilke, Drinkmilk) Edm 208; Jas 249-50; wid 208-9

Driver Tho 184, 187

Drome (Dromer) wid 142-3

Drought (Drough) Sam 236, 238, 240; wid 235

Drowne wid 190

Drury (Dreury, Drewry, Druery) Francis 14, 16; Robt 13, 15, 17-8, 134; Tho 185-6; Timothy 132, 135; wid 17

Dubbelday, Dubbledy *see* Doubleday

Duberry Tho 48

Duberson Frances 148

Dubleday *see* Doubleday

Duce *see* Dewce

Duck Robt 193, 195, 197

Duckett (Duckit, Durkett) Lancelot 70-1; Rose 62

Duckling (Ducklin, Duckline) Tho 244-5, 247-8

Duckman Jas 22

Duddelly *see* Dudley

Dudles Jn 4

Dudley (Duddelly) Wm 151; wid 147, 149

Dueill *see* Dewell

Dueing *see* Dewing

Duell *see* Dewell

Duete Jn 73

Duffield (Doffell, Duffeill, Duffeld, Duffell, Duffild) Humphrey 14, 16-17, 19; Wm 2-4

Duglis *see* Douglas

Duing *see* Dewing

Dulingham Tho 173

Dum *see* Dam

Dun *see* Dunn

Duncan (Duncken, Duncon, Dunken, Dunkin, Dunkine, Dunkyn) Ann 232; Mich 216, 218, 220; Nich 221; Rd 221; Simon 200; Wm 208 (2), 209-10, 227-8, 230; wid 217-18, 220

Duncks *see* Dunkes

Duncon *see* Duncan

Dune *see* Dunn

Dunken *see* Duncan

Elsegood (Elsegoe) wid 85-6, 88-9

Elsey (Ellsey, Elsy, Elsye) wid 161, 165, 168

Elvin (Ellvin, Ellwin, Elven, Elving, Elwin, Eulviny) Esther 198; Jn 8-10, 50, 85-7, 89; Robt 76, 79, 81, 83; Rog 15, 17, 20; Tho 51-2; Wm 23; wid 8, 25 (2)

Emanc *see* Emons

Emens wid 126, 129

Emerson (Emmerston, Emmirson) Chas 74, 76, 155; Edw 166, 169; wid 175, 177

Emes *see* Emms

Emmerston *see* Emerson

Emmes *see* Emms

Emmirson *see* Emerson

Emms (Eams, Emes, Emmes, Ems) Geo 23 (2), 25; Jn 23, 25-6, 52, 147; Wm 25, 58 (3), 59, 160, 163; wid 23, 193, 195, 197, 208

Emons (Emanc) wid 208, 210

Emorly Hy 209

Emperor (Emperer, Emperour, Emprer, Imprer) Chas 70, 73; Eli 86, 88-9; Frances 124; Francis 121, 123; Geo 85; Jn 40; Jos 39, 40 (2); wid 72, 120, 235, 240

Empin *see* Impin

Emprer *see* Emperor

Empson (Impson) wid 236, 238

Ems *see* Emms

Engelton Wm 200

England (Ingland) Geo 37; Wm 87-8, 90, 200; goodman 85, 87-8, 90; wid 86, 176, 178, 187, 191

English (Inglish) Jn 108, 110-11; Tho 162, 166, 169

Engrame, Engrem, Engrime *see* Ingram

Enill *see* Innall

Erington David 188; Jn 191; wid 191

Esnall Francis 212

Essex wid 188

Este Geo 223, 225-6

Eten *see* Eaton

Euins *see* Ewens

Eulviny *see* Elvin

Evefret *see* Everitt

Evenall Francis 210-11

Everad *see* Everard

Everade *see* Everitt

Everard (Everad, Evered) Abigail 30, 31 (2); Hy 89, 119; Jn 244; wid 208

Everat, Everate *see* Everitt

Evered *see* Everard

Everet, Everett, Everetts *see* Everitt

Everingham (Eeveringham, Everinham, Evringam) Jn 241, 242 (2), 243

Everitt (Eaveret, Everat, Everate, Everet, Everett, Everetts, Everit, Everits, Evefret, Everade, Evfret, Evrit) Amy 127; Eliz 215; Ellen 214; Joan 209; Jn 175-7, 209; Nich 100, 101 (2), 103-4; Pet 106; Wm 78, 82; goodman 100; wid 48 (2), 49, 84, 91-2, 94, 96, 130-1, 210

Everson wid 208-9

Evfret *see* Everitt

Evins *see* Ewens

Evisom wid 236

Evringam *see* Everingham

Evrit *see* Everitt

Ewell *see* Ewill

Ewens (Eiuins, Euins, Evins) Wm 138-40, 142

Ewill (Ewell) Tho 84; wid 181-2

Exleby (Exelbe, Exelsbe, Exelsby) Tho 216, 218-9, 221

Eyers (Heires, Heyers) Pet 20-1, 155-6 (*see also* Ayers)

Fabbes (Fabes) Tho 11 (2)

Fabon, Faborne *see* Pheborne

Facknam *see* Fakenham

Facks *see* Feake

Fadelow (Faudalow) Humphrey 217, 219-20

Fairweather (Farweather, Farwether, Fayther) wid 70-2

Fakenham (Facknam, Flacknam, Flakman) Edw 14, 16-17, 19

Fakes *see* Feake

Frumety *see* Fromantell

Fryer goodman 148, 150, 152-3

Fulcher (Fulchers, Fullcher, Fullches,
 Fullchis) Pet 148 (2), 150, 152; Tho
 32-4; Titus 85, 87-8; wid 89

Fuler *see* Fuller

Fullcher, Fullches, Fullchis *see* Fulcher

Fuller (Fuler) Warent & Fuller 116;
 Abraham 28-9; Catherine 89; Dan
 114, 116; Diana 113; Edw 6-7, 13,
 15, 18; Geo 11-12; Jas 29; Joan 147,
 153; Jn 149, 151, 249-50; Margt 85,
 87-8; Nich 152; Prudence 161, 164,
 168; Robt 61; Tho 70, 72-3, 78-9,
 81, 84, 113, 115, 117; wid 8, 9-10,
 87, 89-90, 93, 162, 165, 208-9, 249

Funnell (Funell) Robt 244; wid 41-4,
 246-8

Furman *see* Firman

Furnis Eliz 235; wid 237, 239-40

Furthergill *see* Fothergill

Fytt *see* Fitt

Ga... Ste 221

Gabbs wid 235, 237, 239

Gabriell (Gabrell, Gabrill) wid 193, 195-6

Gackson *see* Jackson

Gadey Jn 159

Gadge *see* Gedge

Gaes *see* Gaze

Gaff wid 75

Gafford, Gaffory *see* Gayford

Gage, Gagge *see* Gedge

Gaifer *see* Gayford

Gairett *see* Garrett

Galent *see* Gallant

Gall (Galle) Hy 240; Ste 227, 230, 232,
 235, 237, 239

Gallant (Galent, Gallent) Mich 28 (2), 29

Galle *see* Gall

Gallent *see* Gallant

Gallfe wid 74

Gamble (Gamball, Gambell) Mich 127,
 130, 133; goodman 129; wid 213-5,
 227, 241-3

Gammon wid 178

Gann wid 178

Gant (Gante, Gaunt, Gent, Gente) Francis
 213, 224-6; Mich 19; Rog 208-9;
 Wm 204; wid 216-17, 219-20

Garden (Gardine, Jarden) Jn 23, 25-6;
 wid 218, 220

Gardener *see* Gardiner

Gardine *see* Garden

Gardiner (Gardener, Gardner) Hy 67; Ste
 173; Tho 137; Wm 11, 175, 178;
 wid 126, 129, 133

Garett *see* Garrett

Garey *see* Jary

Gargill (Gargell, Gargen, Gargett,
 Gargile, Gargilt, Gargin, Gargirle,
 Gargitt) Jn 30, 32; Pet 15-17, 19; Rd
 45-6, 47 (2); Wm 19, 30, 33-4; good
 30-1

Garie *see* Gary

Garnegoe Eliz 90

Garner wid 221

Garnes (Garnies, Garnis) Robt 162; wid
 178, 218-19

Garnham Edm 244; Jn 248-50;
 Wm 248-50; old 250

Garnies, Garnis *see* Garnes

Garrad *see* Garrod

Garrard Wm 232; wid 161, 232

Garrat *see* Garrett

Garred *see* Garrod

Garren wid 23

Garrett (Gairett, Garett, Garrat, Garret,
 Garrit, Garritt, Gerritt, Gritt)
 Hannah 201; Jn 175; Rd 192, 194;
 Wm 203, 205, 207, 229-30; wid 4,
 65, 165, 168, 175, 227, 229-30
  (*see also* Garrod and Garwood)

Garrod (Garrad, Garred, Garrood,
 Garrowd) Abigail 3; Grizell 69; Jn
 171; Nathaniel 48, 106; Susan 107;
 Tho 24,107; wid 3, 173
  (*see also* Garrett and Garwood)

Garry *see* Gary

Garthercole *see* Gathercole

Garthorn (Gathorne, Gorthern) Rd 45-6

Garves, Garvis *see* Jarvis

Hewitt [continued]
Wm 223, 225; goodman 108, 110;
wid 14, 16, 48 (2), 77, 78 (2), 80,
82, 136, 226
Hews see Howes
Hewson (Hewerson, Hewerston, Hewison,
Hueson) Anthony 241-3; Jn 56
Hey see High
Heydon Jn 166, 170
Heye see High
Heyers see Eyers
Heyham see Heigham
Heymes Jn 61
Heynes see Haines
Hezelewood see Haslewood
Hickelin see Hicklin
Hickes see Hicks
Hickling (Hickelin, Hicklin, Hicklinge)
... 61; Philip 60, 62-3; Robt 181-2;
Tho 70-72; wid 90
Hickmer Jn 190
Hickmote Jn 192
Hicks (Hickes) ... 46; Blyth & Hicks 117;
Rd 114; wid 46
Hickson Tho 191
Hicling see Hicklin
Hideman (Hidman, Hydeman) Jn 32-4
Higgin (Higgon) Anthony 121-2, 124
High (Hey, Heye, Hye) Francis 99; Rd
113, 115; Robt 137-9; Wm 60-2, 64
Hilderstone goodman 83
Hill (Hell) Edm 100, 102-4; Francis
208-9; Geo 126, 133, 136; Jn 14,
16, 57-8, 64, 92, 94; Jos 216-17,
219-20; Luke 100, 102, 104-5; Robt
200, 202, 207; Rog 58-9; Ste
213-15; Tho 80, 82-3, 184, 194-5,
203-4, 206-7; Wm 113-14, 116,
119; wid 46 (2), 85, 87-9, 107-8,
110, 112, 187 (3), 188-9
Hilland see Holland
Himborow, Himborrow see Henburrow
Hindence see Harridence
Hinderwell (Hindwell) Tho 162, 165, 169
Hindresse see Harridence

Hinds (Hines, Hyndes, Hynds, Hynes)
Edm 132; Rd 30-1; Robt 31 (2); Tho
76, 81-2
Hindsly see Hinsley
Hindwell see Hinderwell
Hineman wid 88
Hines see Hinds
Hinges Jas 197
Hinsley (Hindsly) Abraham 206-7
Hinson see Henson
Hipking Jn 188
Hipper Anthony 91; wid 78-9, 81, 84
Hirington, Hivington see Herrington
Hoaking Jn 139
Hoames see Holmes
Hoaney see Honey
Hoath Edw 50-51, 53; Rd 137; Tho 68;
Wm 50-51, 53; wid 133, 137
Hobart (Hoberd, Hobert, Hubart,
Hubbert) Jas 74; Nich 50-51, 120,
122-3; Rd 223; Robt 225-6; Simon
47; Susan 74; wid 27-8, 146
Hobbs Wm 196
Hoberd, Hobert see Hobart
Hobson Elias 28
Hock Isabel 35
Hocknell (Hacknell) Dorothy 100; Rog
100, 102, 104-5; wid 102, 104-5
Hoddy Ann 20-21; Geo 22; Jn 21;
wid 21-2
Hodges (Hodg, Hodge, Hodgges, Hodgne,
Hoges, Hoghenet) Alice 147, 149,
151, 153; Edm 175, 177; Hy 79, 81;
Jn 10; Mark 42-3; Mercy 41, 44;
Silvanus 147; Tho 174, 177, 200,
202; wid 220
Hodgkin (Hodgkine, Hodgkines,
Hodgking, Hodkins, Hodskin,
Hogdkins, Hogkines, Hogskin) Tho
138-41; Wm 133, 136; old 100-1,
103, 105
Hodgne see Hodges
Hodkins, Hodskin see Hodgkin
Hodson Hodson and Julons (Hatson and
Julians) 55-6; Hy 179; Hugh 17-18;
Jn 20; wid 13, 15, 17-19

Matham (Mathom, Mathum) Tho 244-7;
   wid 244-5, 247-8
Mathes, Mathewes, Mathews, Mathies *see*
   Matthews
Mathom *see* Matham
Maththas wid 59
Mathues *see* Matthews
Mathum *see* Matham
Mathyes *see* Matthews
Matsell (Mattshell) Edw 194, 196
Matt... Rd 102
Mattes wid 195
Matthews (Mathes, Mathewes, Mathews,
   Mathies, Mathues, Mathyes,
   Matthers, Matthew) Clement 190;
   Mich 26; Pet 35; Robt 37-9; Ste
   216, 218-19, 221; wid 36, 100-01,
   104-5, 160, 164, 167, 188
Mattock (Mattoock) wid 193, 195, 197
Mattshell *see* Matsell
Maud Wm 213
Maufree wid 58
Maulby *see* Malby
Maulden *see* Malden
Maunden (Maundy) Ann 21-2
May Francis 167; Jn 237-8, 240
Mayden *see* Maiden
Mayes (Maies, Mais, Mase, Mays, Maze)
   Mayes & Crow 117; Jn 139, 182-3,
   248-50; Rose 138; Tho 114-15, 119;
   Wm 2-3, 92-3, 140 (2), 142; good
   95; goodman 22, 138; wid 137,
   140-1
Mayhew (Mahew, Mahewe, Mayhu,
   Mayhue) Jn 39; Sarah 78, 82, 84;
   Zachariah 24-5, 113, 143; Zachary
   115, 118, 143; wid 77
Mayle *see* Male
Maylen Tho 201
Mays, Maze *see* Mayes
Mead (Meade, Mede, Meed) Tho 120,
   122-4
Meadows (Middus, Midow, Midows,
   Midus) ... 220; wid 172, 175, 178,
   216, 218-9
Meakens *see* Makins

Meann Wm 175
Meare Hy 203, 206-7
Meares (Mears) Ann 213-15; Eliz 108,
   110-11; Jn 108, 110
Medcaf, Medcalf, Medcalfe, Medcap *see*
   Metcalfe
Meddelton *see* Middleton
Mede *see* Mead
Medellton, Medelton *see* Middleton
Medler (Medle, Medly, Midle) Rd 27,
   28 (2), 29; Tho 13, 15, 17, 20
Medleton *see* Middleton
Medly *see* Medler
Meed *see* Mead
Meek (Meeke) Woodcoke & Meeke 117;
   Geoffrey 115; Jos 114, 118; Rd 58-9
Melbourne *see* Milborne
Mellsopp *see* Milksop
Mels *see* Mills
Melton Mary 8; wid 8-10
Mendham (Mendum, Mendume) Eliz
   20-21; Jn 24-5; Jos 26; goody 21-2
Mercer (Messer) wid 2 (2), 3
Mered Mary 171
Messer *see* Mercer
Mesterd, Mestors *see* Masters
Metcalfe (Madcafe, Madcalfe, Medcaf,
   Medcalf, Medcalfe, Medcap,
   Mettcalf) ... 49; Medcalfe & Smith
   117; Augustine 135; Edw 48 (2), 49;
   Geo 112; Gregory 115, 119;
   Jeremiah 32-4; Jn 141; Rd 172; Tho
   50-3; Wm 233; good 5; goodman 5
Metherell Robt 191
Mettcalf *see* Metcalfe
Mew Hy 203, 206-7
Mi... ... 211
Mias *see* Myers
Michell *see* Mitchell
Mickleburgh (Mickelborrow,
   Micklborugh, Micklburrow,
   Mickleborough, Micklebrough,
   Mickleburrough, Mickleburrow,
   Micleborough) ... 107; Matthew
   109-10; good 95; goodw 88; goody
   87; wid 89, 113, 115-6, 144

Molster *see* Malster

Moltier goodman 144

Mone *see* Money

Mones Jeremiah 70

Money (Mone, Monny, Mony, Muney, Muny) Geoffrey 11; Jn 2-4, 38-9, 54, 56, 75; Rd 128; Robt 27; Tho 28-9, 65, 67, 241, 242 (2), 243; Wm 45-6, 53, 100, 106, 131; good 54; goodman 59; goody 55; wid 216-7, 219-20

Moneyment (Munement) Jn 191; wid 154

Monford *see* Munford

Monings *see* Munnings

Monke (Mounke) wid 216, 218

Monny *see* Money

Mons Rd 182-3

Mony *see* Money

Moone Robt 192, 194-6; wid 193, 195

Moore (Moer, More, Morr, Morre) Christopher 100-1, 103, 105; Edm 140; Francis 47-8, 60-1, 63, 236-7; Geoffrey 54-5, 57; Hy 126, 129, 133, 136; Jas 165, 169; Jn 60-1, 78-9, 91-2, 94, 189, 195, 197; Judas 90; Pet 138; Philip 199; Rd 248; Robt 6, 14, 16, 119 (2), 140-1, 184-6; Sam 17, 19; Sarah 62-3; Tho 119-20, 126, 129; good 95; goodman 118; wid 36-8, 60-1, 64, 67 (2), 68-9, 87-9, 93, 125, 128, 134, 138, 141-2, 185-6, 197, 244

Moote (Mute) Ste 53, 57

Morde (Moarde) Jas 224; Sam 224

More *see* Moore

Morey Dan 197

Morferey *see* Morphew

Morgan (Morgen, Morgin) Jas 178; Wm 99-100, 102, 106

Moris *see* Morris

Morley (Morly) Clement 20; Francis 106, 108-9, 111; Isaac 166, 170; Jn 194-5; Jos 54; Margt 69; Nich 162; Theobald 174; Wm 177

Morll *see* Murrell

Morly *see* Morley

Morphew (Mofery, Moffrey, Morferey, Mowfree) Jn 91-2, 94; good 96

Morr *see* Moore

Morrant (Morrent) Robt 113, 115, 118

Morre *see* Moore

Morrend Hy 135

Morrent *see* Morrant

Morris (Moris, Morres) Catherine 241 (2), 242-3; Jas 248; Jn 222, 236; Mich 116, 119; Rowland 241-3; wid 238-9

Morrold *see* Murrell

Morsly (Morselly, Moseley) Lawrence 147, 149, 151, 153

Mortema, Morteme, Mortemy *see* Mortimer

Morter Geo 174, 176

Mortimer (Martem, Martimor, Mortema, Morteme, Mortemy, Mortimie, Mortimore, Morttimer, Morttinge, Motimore, Mottimer) Edm 127, 131, 136; Edw 130; Jn 58, 126, 129; Robt 32 (2); Sam 65-8; Sarah 32-4; Tho 21, 33 (2), 34, 133, 137; Wm 127, 130, 132, 135, 222, 241

Mortone Jn 59

Morttimer, Morttinge *see* Mortimer

Mose *see* Moss

Moseley *see* Morsley

Moseyes Tho 117

Mosh Robt 248

Moss (Mose, Mosse) Francis 37, 39; Geo 102-3, 105; Jas 126, 129, 133, 162; Rd 66-7, 127, 130; Robt 100; Tho 36-7, 39; Wm 250; good 38; old 41-3; wid 107, 136

Mote *see* Mott

Motimore *see* Mortimer

Mott (Mote, Motts) Benjamin 202; Mary 47; Matthew 2 (2), 3; goodman 4; wid 48, 193

Mottimer *see* Mortimer

Mottley Tho 70-71

Motts *see* Mott

Moulson *see* Malster

Plumme *see* Plum
Plummer (Plumbe, Plumer) Gabriel 133;
    Tho 113, 115-6, 118; goodman
    40 (2)
Plumstead (Plumsted) Bartholomew 18;
    wid 162, 165, 169
Pmer *see* Palmer
Poasey Rd 185
Pointer (Poynter) Jn 107; Robt 107-8,
    110-11; wid 78, 165, 169
Pointing (Poynten, Poynting) Jos 31;
    wid 32
Polder (Pollder) Wm 21 (2)
Poley *see* Pooley
Poll Tho 192
Pollard (Pollerd, Polord) wid 91-2, 94, 96
Pollder *see* Polder
Pollerd *see* Pollard
Polley *see* Pooley
Polord *see* Pollard
Polter Jn 154
Pomfrey (Pomeffery, Pomferit, Pomfery,
    Pomfrett, Pomphrey, Pumfrie,
    Pumphrey) Jn 84, 86-7, 89; goodw
    175; wid 160, 163, 177
Pompe (Pampe) Jn 208, 209 (2), 210
Pomphrey *see* Pomfrey
Pond Robt 129; Tho 130, 210-11
Pool... Jn 230
Poole Eliz 90; Hy 244-7; Jn 246-7;
    wid 20-21, 248
    (*see also* Pooley; Powell
Pooley (Pally, Poley, Polley, Pooly,
    Poulee, Puley, Pulley, Pully) Chas
    80, 82; Jn 79, 82, 84, 145; Ralph
    228; Rd 34-5, 105; good 39, 73;
    goodman 70-1, 146; goody 44; wid
    113, 249, 250 (2)
    (*see also* Poole; Powell)
Pooreman Jn 169
Pootter, Poottor *see* Potter
Pope Wm 47
Popell, Pople, Poppell *see* Popple
Poppey *see* Poppy
Popple (Popell, Pople, Poppell) Robt 235;
    wid 237-8, 240

Poppy (Poppey) Jn 106, 109-10, 112
Porson wid 55
Porter (Portter) Chas 235, 237, 239; Eliz
    90; Hy 132; Jn 10, 76, 155-8; Mary
    90, 93, 95, 97; Matthew 39;
    Nathaniel 36-8; Rebecca 95; Vincent
    45, 46, 47; wid 79, 81-2, 227,
    229-30, 232
Portingeton, Portington *see* Partington
Portman Jn 50-53
Portter *see* Porter
Postle (Posle, Postall) Benjamin 203, 205;
    Robt 32; Sam 179-80, 182; Tho
    33 (2), 34
Poston Robt 135
Pote *see* Pute
Potter (Pootter, Poottor) Jn 58 (2), 59,
    147, 149, 151-3; Robt 9 (2), 10;
    Wm 73, 150; goodman 187; goody
    41-2; wid 43, 147, 149
Pouell, Poul, Poule *see* Powell
Poulee *see* Pooley
Poull *see* Powell
Pound Wm 176
Pouse Jn 181-2
Pow (Pawe, Poye) Tho 112, 115, 119;
    wid 114-15, 117
Powell (Pouell, Poule, Poull, Powl,
    Powle) Arthur 73; Christopher
    187-9; Edm 108, 110-11; Eliz 8708;
    Jas 26-9; Jn 48, 227; Nich 222-5;
    Rebecca 69, 71; Rd 72, 138-40;
    Robt 236; Tho 54, 57; Wm 119; wid
    69
    (*see also* Poole; Pooley
Poye *see* Pow
Poynten *see* Pointing
Poynter *see* Pointer
Poynting *see* Pointing
Poynton Robt 248-50
Poyt (Poyte) Hannah 53; Jn 100-101,
    104-5
Prasen Wm 215
Pratt (Prat) Abigail 199; Bartholomew
    184 (2), 186; Jn 146, 148, 150, 152;
    wid 14 (2), 16-17, 173, 176, 178

Rippon Edm 133

Risborow *see* Riseborough

Risbrocke *see* Rushbrooke

Risbrough, Risbrow *see* Riseborough

Rise Benjamin 61

Riseborough (Risborow, Risbrough, Risbrow, Rsbro) Christopher 34-5; Tho 111; goodman 108, 110

Risen, Riser *see* Rising

Rishbrooke *see* Rushbrooke

Rising (Risen, Riser, Rison, Rissin, Rysine, Ryson) Jn 138 (2), 141-2; Philip 138, 141-2; wid 34, 35 (2)

Riss wid 13

Rissin *see* Rising

Riston *see* Reston

Rively *see* Reveley

Rivers Hy 100-101, 104; wid 204, 206

Rivett (Rivet, Rivit) Jn 175, 178, 214-15; Robt 41-2; good 173; old 45

Rivins *see* Revins

Rivit *see* Rivett

Rix (Ricx, Rikes, Rixe) Benjamin 87-8, 90; Blyth 127, 130; Edm 45; Hy 204; Jn 204; Tho 118, 143; Wm 203, 206-7

Ro... Philip 2

Roabs Tho 171

Roades (Roads, Rodes) Rd 62; wid 100, 102, 104-5

Roafe *see* Rolfe

Roals (Roales) Tho 173, 176

Roase *see* Rose

Roate *see* Root

Robards *see* Roberts

Robarson *see* Robinson

Robart, Robartes, Robarts *see* Roberts

Robason Rog 32

Robbeson *see* Robinson

Robbins *see* Robins

Robenson *see* Robinson

Roberson *see* Robertson

Roberts (Rabards, Robards, Robart, Robartes, Robarts, Roberds) Jn 56 (2), 135, 216, 218, 220-1, 244, 245 (2), 246; Sarah 29; Tho 17, 20;

Roberts [*continued*]

Wm 187; goodman 84, 184; wid 171, 185-6, 198, 200

Robertson (Robarson, Robbesonn, Roberson, Robrson, Robrtson) Francis 224-6; Geo 1, 3 (2), 4; Giles 173; Hy 6-7; Jn 28 (2), 29, 71-2, 154, 224; Rd 224; Robt 28 (2), 29, 79, 81, 225-6; Rog 143-4; Rowland 75; Ste 127-8, 131, 134; Tho 55; goodman 168; wid 191

(*see also* Robinson)

Robeson *see* Robertson and Robinson

Robines *see* Robins

Robingson *see* Robinson

Robins (Robbins, Robines, Robkins) Geo 77; Jn 132; wid 5 (2)

Robinson (Robbeson, Robenson, Robingson) ... 54; Eliz 192; Ellis 194, 196; Geo 80, 82; Giles 176; Hy 7 (2); Jas 189; Jn 30, 70, 171, 222; Rd 20; Robt 18, 27, 78, 156; Rog 143; Ste 125; Tho 53, 56-7, 102-3, 105, 145-6, 180-1, 183; Wm 53, 69; goodman 100; wid 74-5, 207

(*see also* Robertson)

Robison *see* Robertson and Robinson

Robkins *see* Robins

Robrson, Robrtson *see* Robertson

Robson Geo 207; Robt 76

Rochester (Rochister, Roschester) Jn 70-2

Rock Rd 107, 109-10, 112; wid 23

Rockard *see* Rookwood

Rocken Tho 161

Rockland Wm 123-4

Roddell, Roddwell *see* Rodwell

Roddyck *see* Rodrick

Rodes *see* Roads

Rodgers *see* Rogers

Rodgerson *see* Rogerson

Rodrick (Roddyck) Bartholomew 180; Robt 181, 183

Rodrom *see* Rudderham

Rodwell (Roddell, Roddwell) Mary 155, 156 (2); wid 154

Roe *see* Row

Ruddock (Rudducke) Ann 241-3
Ruddrome, Ruddrum see Rudrum
Rudducke see Ruddock
Ruderam, Ruderum see Rudrum
Rudland (Rutland) Jn 5 (3), 6
Rudram, Rudrham, Rudrum see Rudrum
Rumfert wid 167
Rump (Ramp) Tho 166, 170; wid 199
Rumsey (Rumse) Rd 163, 166
Rungry see Wrongrey
Runry Tho 169
Runton Francis 235
Rusalls see Russell
Rusbrooke see Rushbrooke
Rusells see Russell
Rush (Rash) Jn 127, 130; Robt 126, 129,
    136; Sam 127, 130; Tho 135, 184-6;
    goodman 67
Rushbrooke (Ricebrooke, Risbrocke,
    Rishbrooke, Rusbrooke, Rysbroke)
    Rd 126, 129, 133; Tho 133, 136,
    249; Wm 154, 244-7; wid 146, 148,
    150, 152
Russell (Rusalls, Rusells, Russells,
    Russels) Jas 77, 79, 81; Rd 45, 46
    (2); Susan 198-9; wid 27, 171, 174,
    179
Russen (Russon) Tho 80, 82-3
Rust (Ros, Rost, Roust, Ruste) Dan 19;
    Francis 241-2, 243 (2); Jn 41-4,
    70-71, 73; Nathaniel 21-2; Oliver
    168; Philip 49, 161, 164; Sam 64,
    66; Tho 21 (2), 50-52, 198, 200;
    Titus 22
Ruster Jas 66
Ruston (Rusting, Rustinge) Jacob 116,
    118; Jas 117; Jn 148, 150; Tho 77
Rutherham see Rotherham
Rutland see Rudland
Rutter Ann 99, 101, 103; Chas 120-23;
    Jas 27, 29; Margt 132; Matthew
    127, 130; Tho 30, 31-2; Wm 60-61,
    63-4, 149, 151, 153; wid 246-8
Ruttler Rog 161
Ryall see Royal
Ryle Giles 181

Rymer Christopher 104
Ryner wid 201
Rysbroke see Rushbrooke
Rysine, Ryson see Rising

S... Jn 153
S...ach Jn 165
S...illinger Sam 116
S...ll wid 153
Sabberne see Sabborne
Sabberton (Saberton, Sabeton) Margt 7;
    Rd 64; Robt 63; wid 6, 7 (2), 65,
    67-8
Sabborne (Sabberne, Sabborn, Subbone,
    Subburn) Jas 3-4; Jn 4; Tho 158,
    159 (2); Wm 3 (2)
Saberton, Sabeton see Sabberton
Sadd (Sad) Jn 28 (2), 154; Tho 155-7;
    Wm 197, 199, 202
Sadler (Saddler, Sadley) Jn 14, 16-17, 19,
    92, 94, 228-9, 231, 233; Mich 190,
    192; Sam 106, 108, 110-11; Tho 86;
    Wm 113; good 96; wid 113, 115,
    117 (2), 118
Sadman Marian 169
Safely see Safely
Safery see Savory
Saffer (Saffear) Nich 141; Oliver 35
Saffery, Saffrey, Saffry see Savory
Safley (Safely, Safly) Jas 90; wid 92, 94-5
Safry see Savory
Saftly Jas 76
Salenger (Sillinger) Jas 113-4, 118
Salisbury (Salsbie, Salsby) Geo 248,
    249 (2), 250; Robt 248 (2), 249 (2),
    250 (2)
Sall, Salle see Saul
Sallett (Sallet) Wm 9 (2), 10
Sallmon see Salmon
Sallter see Salter
Salmon (Sallmon, Samman, Sammon,
    Samnon, Samon, Samond) Edm 49;
    Jn 85, 87-8, 125, 128; Martin 40,
    162, 165; Matthew 39, 40 (2);
    Mildred 60, 62; Rd 78, 80, 84, 133;
    Robt 39, 40 (2), 41, 136; Tho 18-19,

Sparkell Tho 77

Sparkes *see* Sparke

Sparnell (Sparnall, Sparrell, Spernall) Christopher 125; Jn 28 (2), 29; Robt 46; Tho 128; Wm 107, 109, 111

Sparough, Sparow *see* Sparrow

Sparram *see* Sparham

Sparrell *see* Sparnell

Sparrom *see* Sparham

Sparrow (Sparaw, Sparough, Sparow, Sparrowe) Jn 19; Philip 106, 108-11; Rd 147, 149, 151-2; Robt 106, 108-9, 111; Tho 18, 32; goodman 146; goodw 125; wid 131, 134, 244-50

Sparrum, Sparum *see* Sparham

Spaul (Spall) Jn 168; Mary 127, 130

Spaulden, Spauldin *see* Spalding

Speck (Specke) Jn 233-4

Spedding (Spedeing, Speding, Speeding) Wm 42, 43 (2), 44

Speed (Speede) Tho 81, 83

Speeding *see* Spedding

Spencer (Spenser) Margt 192, 194, 196; Robt 76, 78, 80; Tho 70-2, 80, 82-3; wid 52

Spenson Francis 173

Spenten, Spenton *see* Spanton

Spernall *see* Sparnell

Spicer (Spiser) wid 192, 197, 199

Spill wid 147, 149, 151, 153

Spink (Spinke, Spinkes, Spinks) Tho 53, 86, 88; wid 123

Spinsby (Spinsbee, Spinsly) Jn 143 (2), 144 (2); Robt 17, 20

Spiser *see* Spicer

Spitt Tho 80

Spolden, Spolding *see* Spalding

Spooner (Sponer) Robt 58-9; Tho 60-1; Wm 28-9

Spourne *see* Spurne

Spratt (Sprat, Spratts, Sprutte) Jn 147, 149, 151; Jos 156-7; Josiah 155

Springall (Springal, Springhall) Jn 36-7, 39, 222; Robt 28-9, 90; Sam 50-2; Tho 135, 233-4; goodman 27; wid 85-6, 195

Springer Jn 55

Springfield (Sprinkfeld, Sprinkfield, Sprinkfild) Jn 248, 249 (2), 250; Tho 249, 250 (2); Wm 249 (2), 250; wid 249, 250 (2)

Springhall *see* Springall

Sprinkfeld, Sprinkfield, Sprinkfild *see* Springfield

Sprunt (Spront) Christopher 54-5; wid 56

Sprutte *see* Spratt

Spurgin Tho 3

Spurlinge wid 125

Spurne (Spourne) Jn 203-4, 206-7

Squire (Squier, Squir) Jn 236, 238, 240; wid 235, 237, 239-40

Stabler Jos 205

Stacey (Stacy, Stacye, Stasey, Stasy) Christopher 126, 129, 133; Edw 125, 128, 131, 134; Hy 127, 130, 132; Tho 137; Wm 117; wid 11-13, 114-15, 119

Stackwood (Stacwood) Ste 244-5

Stacy, Stacye *see* Stacey

Staff (Stafe, Stuff) wid 91-2, 94

Stafford (Staford) 'Swenten' 207

Stainard *see* Stannard

Stalyard *see* Tillyard

Stamford (Sampford, Standford, Stanford) Francis 14-15, 18; Grace 120-3; Jn 201

Stanard *see* Stannard

Stanart Nathaniel 74

Standelow Robt 210-11

Standford *see* Stamford

Standly *see* Stanley

Stanford *see* Stamford

Stangroom (Stangrame, Stangrome) Robt 222-5

Stanham *see* Stoneham

Stanhawe wid 135

Stanhill Wm 247-8

Stanley (Standly, Stanly) Jn 166-7, 170

335

Torner *see* Turner

Tottnell (Totnell, Tottnett) Jn 21 (2), 22;
Martha 20; Matthew 21

Toukley *see* Tokeley

Touly *see* Tooley

Tounching Robt 164

Tounssend, Tousand, Touson *see*
Townsend

Tovell *see* Towell

Towars *see* Towers

Towell (Tovell) Anthony 185; Hy 43;
Jn 51-2; Robt 78-9, 81, 84

Towers (Towars) Ann 213-14; Jn 222,
236; wid 12-13

Towler Jn 237

Town (Towne) Jn 171; wid 161, 164, 168

Townsend (Tounssend, Tousand, Touson,
Townend, Townesend, Townsan,
Townsen, Townsin, Townsing,
Townsling, Townson, Towsan,
Towsand, Towsel, Towsend,
Towsin) Christopher 11, 12 (2), 13;
Francis 180, 182-3; Jas 3-4, 69,
70 (2); Jn 205; Rd 100, 102, 104-5;
Robt 168; Rog 188-9; Sam 203, 205,
207; Sarah 99, 101, 103, 105; Tho
100; wid 126, 129, 180-1, 183, 193,
195-6

Tracey wid 6

Tredaway (Theadaway) Jn 77;
goodman 83

Tredwell (Thredwell) Jn 78, 82

Treu, Trew, Trewe *see* True

Trollope (Trolley, Trollop, Trollup)
Eliz 60-1; wid 63-4

Troter *see* Trotter

Troth Robt 203, 205-6

Trotter (Troter) Edw 176; wid 189 (2)

True (Treu, Trew, Trewe, Tru) Edm 8,
9-10, 68; Eliz 36; Jn 4; Martha 53;
Martin 157; Robt 145 (3), 146; Wm
4; Zachariah 235, 237, 239 (2); Mrs
55-6

Trull Lancelot 32; Lawrence 32-3;
Wm 85-7; wid 34

Trunchinge Robt 161

Trundle (Trundell) Jas 175, 177;
Jos 233-4, 239 (2); Theophilus 216,
218-19, 221; wid 193-4

Tubby (Tubbin, Tubbine, Tubey, Tubine)
Geo 114-15, 118; Gregory 117; Rd
93, 194-5; Wm 74-5

Tuck (Tucke) Alice 58-9; Jn 76; Wm 243,
245-7; wid 17-18, 120-21, 123-4

Tuddenham (Tuddinham, Tuddintom,
Tuddinton, Tudenham, Tudneham)
wid 99, 101-5

Tuffin (Tufen, Tuffen, Tuffill, Tuffyn)
Catherine 2-3; Gilbert 3-4; Wm 2;
wid 2, 4

Tuley *see* Tooley

Tunell Jn 75

Tuney *see* Tunney

Tungate (Tungat) Jn 53, 55

Tunney (Tonny, Tuney, Tunny) Isaac 71,
73; Rd 29, 74-6, 155; Tho 75, 155;
wid 155-7

Tunnill Tho 154

Tunny *see* Tunney

Tunre *see* Turner

Turfe Robt 208

Turner (Torner, Tunre, Turnner, Turnor)
... 141; Catherine 171; Dan 32-4;
Edw 190; Hy 36-7; Jn 1-4, 133,
136-7, 139-41, 166, 170, 173, 175,
178, 203, 205-6, 209; Jos 42-4;
'Meg' 140; Nich 137, 139-41; Ralph
137, 139-41; Rd 138-9, 141, 147-8,
150 (2), 151-2; Robt 65-8, 82, 187;
Tho 137, 140-41, 191; goody 70,
184; wid 72, 73, 185 (2), 186 (2),
187 (2), 189, 191-2, 217-19, 221

Turnes Tho 138

Turnner, Turnor *see* Turner

Turrell *see* Tyrrell

Tursey Nich 161

Tush (Tushe) wid 41-4

Tusly wid 167

Tuttle (Tuttell, Tuttill) Edw 148-9, 151,
153; Jn 147, 149, 151; Jos 153

Twidde (Twidey) wid 235, 237

Tyce Robt 65, 67-8

Watts [*continued*]
    Robt 162; Sarah 14, 16-17, 162,
    169; Tho 8, 77, 99 (2), 101 (2), 103,
    105, 109-10, 112, 119; Wm 61-2,
    64, 99, 128, 131, 135; wid 42, 47,
    60-1, 104, 158
Wattson *see* Watson
Waybeard *see* Wheybeard
Waymore wid 179
Waynflet Humphrey 179
Weab, Weabe *see* Webb
Weait *see* Wyatt
Weak Joan 125
Weakley Jn 226
Wealy Jonathan 191
Weavers (Weaves) Pettigrew 158 (2)
Webb (Weab, Weabe, Web, Weeb,
    Weebe) Jn 37, 39; Wm 216-17,
    219-20; wid 90, 92-3, 95
Webster Edm 131; Hy 127, 130, 132, 135;
    Jn 62-3; Pet 50-52; Robt 126, 129;
    Wm 60-61, 69; good 124; goodman
    120, 122-3; wid 9, 10, 36, 133
Weeb, Weebe *see* Webb
Weeds Jn 13, 15, 17-18; Matthew 202;
    wid 92, 94, 96, 189
Weeke Sam 34
Weetherley *see* Witherley
Wegg (Wegge) Sam 33; Tho 30
Welch Jas 5
Weld wid 125
Weldon (Welden) Jn 170; Rd 176
Weleson *see* Wilkson
Welham (Wellham, Welloms, Wellum)
    Eliz 7 (2); Emma 7 (2); Tho 6
Welkson *see* Wilkson
Well *see* Wells
Welleby *see* Willoughby
Wellem *see* Wellin
Welles *see* Wells
Wellham *see* Welham
Wellin (Wellem, Wellyn) Wm 233,
    234 (2); wid 233, 234 (2)
Wellmson *see* Williamson
Welloms *see* Welham
Wellphir Mary 166

Wells (Well, Welles, Wels) Hy 97-8;
    Jn 55, 128, 131, 134, 223, 226;
    Martha 154; Rd 85-7, 89; Tho 127,
    130, 132, 135; Walter 30, 31-2;
    good 96; wid 128, 132, 135, 148-9,
    151-2
Wellson *see* Wilson
Wellum *see* Welham
Wellyn *see* Wellin
Welows Jn 225
Wels *see* Wells
Welson *see* Wilson
Welton Ann 73
Wen *see* Wenn
Wenckly Jn 223, 225
Wenge *see* Wing
Wengman *see* Wingman
Wenn (Wen, Wenne) Geo 120-4; Isaac
    180; Jn 108, 110-11; Margt 87-8,
    90; Sam 201; Tho 39; wid 75
Werdinge Edm 222
Wesencrafft Jn 212
Wesgate, Wesgkit *see* Westgate
Wesson *see* Weston
West (Waste) Flatman & West 117;
    Hy 11, 12 (2), 13; Jn 91, 159;
    Simon 112, 115, 118; Tho 88, 94,
    143, 144; good 96; wid 91; wid 213,
    214-15
Westgate (Wesgate, Wesgkit) Jn 209, 212;
    Tho 208 (2), 209
Weston (Waston, Wesson, Westo) Hy 85,
    87-8, 90; Jas 131, 134; Robt 85, 87
Wethereck *see* Witherick
Wetherell (Witherell, Witherill) Jn 157;
    Sam 106, 108, 110-11; Valentine 36;
    wid 108
Wetherley, Wetherly *see* Witherley
Wethers *see* Withers
Wethersett Tho 67
Wettman (Whetman) Jas 62; wid 60-61
Whall (Whalle) Hy 73-4, 76
Whalleron Hy 76
Whamsley *see* Wainsly
Wharle (Wharles) Francis 48;
    goodman 109, 111

INDEX OF PLACES

INDEX OF TRADES AND OCCUPATIONS

JACKET INFORMATION FOR HEARTH TAX VOLUMES

General

The fireplaces illustrated on the jacket come from various parts of England and Wales and reflect a wide social spectrum from the major gentry (Little Moreton Hall) to yeoman farmhouses (Valley Farm; Glencoyne). Unfortunately, few seventeenth-century fireplaces in small, single-hearth houses and cottages survive unaltered, and it has proved impossible to find suitable illustrations of them. However, the simple timber chimney and fireplace of Tŷ-Mawr, the brick one at Valley Farm, and the cooking hearth of Glencoyne, are typical of the period and could have been found in many smaller houses and cottages.

DESCRIPTIONS

Front jacket

Top Left

Little Moreton Hall, Cheshire. Decorative fireplace in the chamber over the porch. The house was owned by the powerful Moreton family, whose wealth was based on land. The fireplace is part of the late sixteenth-century additions to the medieval house. By the seventeenth century there were around twenty fireplaces. © Jeremy Milln.

Top Right

Wickens, Charing, Kent. Fireplace with plaster overmantel in the chamber over the parlour. The house was built around 1600 by the Dering family, who were minor gentry. Six hearths were charged in the hearth tax of 1664. © Sarah Pearson.

Bottom Left

Valley Farm, Flatford, Suffolk. A late-medieval yeoman's house; in the sixteenth century a brick fireplace and ceiling (now removed) were inserted into the open hall. By the late seventeenth century a second stack with one, or possibly two, fireplaces had been added to heat the adjacent cross wing. © John Walker.

Bottom Right

Tŷ-Mawr, Castell Caereinion, Montgomeryshire. An open-hall house built in 1461. In the sixteenth century a half-timbered fireplace was added, and later an upper floor inserted (now removed). Tŷ-Mawr means 'great house', and although probably a long-house, with animals at one end, and only one hearth in the 1660s, this was a dwelling of high status in the region. © Peter Smith.

Outside back jacket

Glencoyne Farm, Ullswater, Cumbria. A rare surviving open fire, complete with hearth furniture, set within a typical northern firehood. The large space was lit by its own window, to the right of this photograph of *c.*1900. The house received its present form in 1629. It was owned by a family called Harrison, one of whom was taxed on three hearths in 1674. Reproduced by courtesy of the Museum of Lakeland Life, Kendal, Cumbria.

MYSTERY ANIMALS
OF THE BRITISH ISLES

Kent

Neil Arnold

Typeset by Jonathan Downes,
Cover and Layout by orangecat-oh for CFZ Communications
Using Microsoft Word 2000, Microsoft , Publisher 2000, Adobe Photoshop CS.

Photographs © 2009 Neil Arnold except where noted

First published in Great Britain by CFZ Press

CFZ Press
Myrtle Cottage
Woolsery
Bideford
North Devon
EX39 5QR

ISBN: 978-1-905723-36-2

This book is dedicated to my dad, Ronnie, for all the journeys, memories, and advice.
To my mum, Paulene, for your strength, your caring and devotion.
And to my sister Vicki, for undying belief, understanding and precious encouragement.

I LOVE YOU ALL X

To
Michele & Steve
If you go down to the
woods today!

2011

The Mystery Animals of the British Isles

More years ago than I care to remember, my first wife bought me a birthday present. It was a book about the mystery animals of Britain and Ireland, and I devoured it avidly. When I finished, I was horribly disappointed. It had covered the mystery cats of the country in some depth, as it had done with the black dog legends, and a smattering of more arcane `things` (as the late, great Ivan T. Sanderson would doubtless have dubbed them) such as the Owlman of Mawnan, and the Big Grey Man of Ben McDhui. But there was *so* much that I knew that the author had simply left out.

Where were the mystery pine martens of the westcountry? Where were the Sutherland polecats? Where was the mysterious butterfly known as Albin's Hampstead Eye? This was an Australian butterfly, the type specimen of which was caught in a cellar in Hampstead (hence the name) but no-one knows how or why? Where were the butterflies, moths, birds and even mammals known from the British Isles on the basis of a handful of specimens only? And where were the local oddities; the semi-folkloric beasts only known from a specific location.

Although at the time I had no pretensions to being a writer, I started to collect information from around the country, and with the benefit of hindsight it is probably with my disappointment with my 27th birthday present that the seeds of what would eventually grow into the Centre for Fortean Zoology were planted.

Nearly twenty years later to the day, I was sat in my garden at the Centre for Fortean Zoology [CFZ] in North Devon, sharing a bottle of wine with my wife Corinna, and my old friends Richard Freeman and Mike Hallowell. The subject of my disappointing 27th birthday present came up, and someone suggested that we do our best to redress the balance. CFZ Press, the publishing arm of the CFZ, has become the largest dedicated fortean zoological publishers in the world, and we are now in the position to put my vague daydreams of a couple of decades ago into action. We decided that rather than trying to publish one enormous tome covering the mystery animals of the whole of the British Isles (which, by the way, geographically, if not politically, includes the Republic of Ireland, but excludes the Channel Islands) we would be much happier presenting this vast array of data in a series of books, each covering a county or two. Then we realised the enormity of what we were proposing: The series would probably end up being something in the region of forty volumes in length!

However, never ones to back away from a challenge, we decided to go ahead with the project, and now the first books in the series are being published.

We argued the toss for months over how we were going to format the series. For a long time we were intending to have a rigid format for all the books, somewhat akin to the Observer's books of the British countryside. But then we decided `No`. There are as many kinds of researcher as there are mystery animal, and it would - we felt - be more in keeping with the ethos of the CFZ, if we allowed each researcher to present his or her findings in their own inimitable style. The books, therefore, will reflect the character of the individual author.

Some will be poetic verging on mystical. Some will be matter of fact scientific. Some will be from the point of view of a naturalist, and some from the point of view of a folklorist. Some will be short, some will be long. Some will be full of scientific theorising, and some full of metaphysical speculation. But one thing is sure: Whoever gets one of these volumes for their 27th birthday present.....

.....They won't be disappointed!

Jonathan Downes
Director, Centre for Fortean Zoology
Woolfardisworthy,
North Devon,

CONTENTS

Blue Bell Hill bigfoot image created by Chris Eades. (p.374)

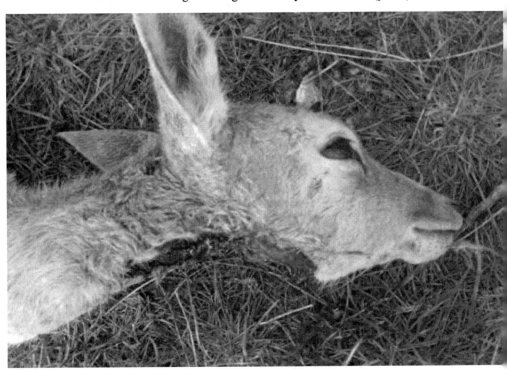

Deer kill Bethersden, Ashford 2005 (p. 245)

Introduction

"I still didn't really believe in the Beast. I mean, I believed in it in the dark at night, but not in the daytime on the bus."

'The Nature Of The Beast' – Janni Howker

I was born in Chatham, Kent in 1974. As I emerged into the world to two loving and wonderful parents, little did I realise that just a few miles away people were seeing strange animals in the local woodlands. I wasn't to get a taste of such mystery until the age of around nine when I was given a book written by Carey Miller entitled *Monsters & Mysterious Beasts* (Piccolo – published rather coincidentally in 1974) which tuned me on to a world of great mythical creatures, and other beasts that could well have had some reality or simply resided in some unknown and nightmarish place. Also around that time I watched a film that changed my life. *The Legend Of Boggy Creek* was a hazy American docu-drama directed by Charles B. Pierce, which concerned a strange hairy bipedal monster prowling the river bottoms of Arkansas in the U.S.A. It may have been the *BBC* that aired it, or I may have seen clips on VHS (a now extinct mechanical animal that used to eat video cassettes!) but it was that movie which sent my mind into a spiralling void of mystery and imagination. The thought that unusual critters, such as bigfoot may be roaming the wilderness of the world, (or even the back streets of the mind) sent me reeling, and I became fixated, especially at the intriguing and terrifying way that the film was made - almost as a documentary. It was as if it were a social commentary on something so eerily perplexing and unknown that, many years later has yet to be equalled in its undeniable reality. However, I didn't realise that other enigmatic, elusive, animals were being sighted just a few minutes from my home in Walderslade.

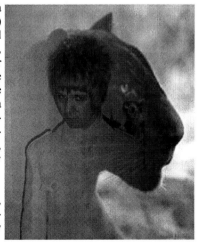

My family, particularly my grandad Ron, and father Ronnie, often read books on the unexplained, or fiction by such renowned authors as Dennis Wheatley, and as I grew up they

9

were a major influence on me. I would often hear tales from them regarding fishing trips into spooky woods, ghostly tales from the local lanes, and also friend-of-a-friend yarns concerning a Medway ghost known as the 'phantom hitchhiker' of Blue Bell Hill, near Maidstone. As a child, the thought that a female apparition was getting into cars and then disappearing was absolutely chilling. The area itself was, and still is, heavily wooded despite being sliced in half by a dual carriageway which is flanked by what is now known as Lower Blue Bell Hill and Upper Blue Bell Hill. Stories would often circulate amongst family members of a female figure walking the creepy, winding lanes, and on many occasions whilst returning from family trips at night, my father would stop the car, and tell me and my mother, Paulene, about the female hitchhiking phantom. This in turn would cause my mum to lock the doors and scream at my dad to drive away! All the while he would sit there, half-smirking at her distress as the flanking shadows encroached.

Even today the area still sends a shiver down my spine, and the reports of the ghostly girl still persist (although less frequently), making Blue Bell Hill one of the most intriguing haunted spots in the *world*, let alone Kent. However, the hitcher spectre is not the only mystery form to lurk around the dark corners. Over the past four-hundred years there have been accounts of ramblers encountering large animals on the bridle paths and in the undergrowth, which consists of steep quarries and ancient ruins. The most prominent of these ruins is Kit's Coty House, a burial chamber said to pre-date Stonehenge, which juts out mysteriously from the landscape like a monolithic set of goalposts! This monument, as well as various other stone anomalies date back to the Roman era, and many spooks and ghoulish stories often leak from the area and remain in our consciousness forever. So, at a very young age I became fascinated by this folkloric world, and a county steeped in history and mystique. I began to collect eyewitness reports of anything unusual that happened locally and gather anecdotal evidence, whilst always keeping an eye on matters worldwide, whether it was the latest swamp monster sighting, or ghostly account, but it was the monsters that intrigued so much and crept into my mind like a seeping gas. At times the mystery would become intoxicating, and so it was often so nice to break away from the clandestine universe of odd creatures and maybe play some football or watch crazy, psychedelic cartoons such as *The Banana Splits*; not forgetting that I was still only around ten years old at the time.

Every now and then in the local newspapers, such as the *Evening Post*, there would be snippets regarding slinking cat-like forms spotted around Kent. The stories appeared vague yet quirky, rather strange when you consider that during the early 1960s the Surrey 'puma' had been covered by a lot of UK press, and during the '80s the 'beasts' of Exmoor, in the southwest were starting to capture the imagination, and the phenomenon which would become tagged as the 'Alien Big Cat mystery', was all over the news. But local reporters *still* weren't grasping the Kent situation, and it wasn't until 1998 that on a local scale at least things really took off with regards to the press.

So, what were people seeing in the woods of Kent? Was it an escaped pet? A hoax, or misidentification? Or just the wild imaginations of people caught up in various anomalies that were popular at the time including ghost sightings and the UFO craze. Well, as a youngster I wasn't able to determine what species of animal were being sighted on the foggy lanes and rolling fields of a county that, to me anyway, seemed perfect habitat for *any* mysterious creature. Living in Walderslade, a small area in Chatham, I tended to take the vicinity of Blue Bell Hill for granted, for it was literally on my doorstep, and for a couple of years I'd been fixated by worldwide mysteries; the Yeti of the Himalayas, the Loch Ness monster of Scotland, and Bigfoot of British Columbia. But all of these mysteries were hazy, far-away forms that actually seemed out of the reach of investigation, and only viewable in crusty magazines such as *The Unexplained*; they lurked in inhospitable or inaccessible areas, whether it was the dense forests of Canada, or the twenty-six mile long Scottish loch with its black waters. However, I soon realised that something strange was happening locally, and not just in the misty woods of Blue Bell Hill, but countywide. Unfortunately, the press were not interested in taking on the subject of mystery animals as a separate issue, but instead were intent on keeping much of it confined to Blue Bell Hill. It struck an interesting chord with the public because of the other bouts of high strangeness. And, as you'll read in this book, the press just love a headline-making name, and story to match.

At the age of ten, I had to confine my studies to my local areas of Kent, where the rivers ran and the towns melted into one another. Hours of fishing at local lakes with my dad also became a passion. It was something else to trigger the imagination; the thought of not knowing what you were going to catch, and then - as the night drew in - the strange noises of the woodlands piercing the darkness, and then the whispered ghost stories leaked from the lips of uncles who pretended to be brave, and yet become huddled around the lamp light like frightened children. The rustle of a rat in the reeds would startle them as quite often my dad or grandad spun another yarn of a mystery sighting of another local creature or phantom. My dad might throw a stick into a tree, or my grandad would suddenly yell, causing a handful of rough 'n' ready, burly men to leap from their chairs and cower from the shadows. The mystery was around me all the time, not just on the lips of the storytellers but in the actual woods themselves. And so, I took it upon myself to bring these fables to the fore, to separate the myth from what I believed was a possible reality, and to be able to tell the stories myself... but as fact, because that's what these 'things' were, and still are. I knew it. I could feel it. And I hope that you, dear reader, with the evidence presented herein, will take the time to ponder just what is, and has been happening for hundreds of years, and something which has snowballed into a very real situation.

It's not just a Kent thing. It's a worldwide phenomenon. The fact that a variety of species of large cat is inhabiting Britain (and other parts of the world), and other strange, out-of-place, and even out of 'reality' creatures are also dwelling in the darkest corners, not only of our minds but in the woods too. However, whilst I will occasionally drift into other counties, and maybe even countries, I would like to focus on the mystery cats and other animals and unknown forms prowling the woods of Kent - the 'Garden of England'.

These are the animals with which I've been intrigued from a young age. Intrigued to such an extent that from the age of around fifteen I began to run Kent Big Cat Research; my own thorough investigation into monitoring evidence and eyewitness reports of large cats locally. This is a study that continues to this day as a love and dedication to chronicle as much information as possible on as many unusual species roaming the county. With this dedication I've been fortunate enough to see several large, exotic cats roaming the countryside, which I'll speak of within. I know they are out there, living and thriving healthily, yet, despite the hundreds of reports I receive each year, there are still many members of the general public who are not aware that these animals are inhabiting the local woodlands. This book aims to let those who are unaware, or even sceptical, learn more about the differing species this county offers, as well as their origins, habitat, diet and behaviour, and to separate the folklore from the facts. There are also those who are aware of these animals; they may have seen them themselves, but they need to know more, and hopefully this book will enable them to identify what they have seen, and also realise that their sightings are surprisingly common.

And there are the sceptics. Scepticism is healthy. There are many people who do not believe that animals such as puma and leopard can exist in counties such as Kent, or they may know of one or two sightings, and simply believe that such reports are of a select few cats recently released in the wilds. Again, this book will hopefully prove to the non-believers that these cats *do* exist, and in surprisingly large numbers. Unfortunately, some sceptics require evidence - such as a dead cat - to convince them, and even then they may simply feel that the corpse was from a one-off incident such as an escapee. The conflicts are numerous, which is why this book aims to present this mystery as a straightforward catalogue of eyewitness reports and evidence, as well as historical cases, and in-depth analysis of a situation that isn't a mystery at all, but a very real phenomenon that needs to be dragged from myth and perceived as fact; for the truth is *indeed* stranger than the fiction.

I hesitated for many years to write a book covering sightings in the county of Kent. Mainly because I was concerned with giving away too many locations where these cats prowl, and strongly believed - and still do - that they should be a protected population. I also felt that the thousands of witnesses that have come forward over the years deserved anonymity, and so in some cases names have been altered, and at times not even mentioned, and some locations only vaguely revealed. For me this is important, because the animals I am writing about here deserve their peace, and not the pursuit of hunters. Whilst they *must* be understood and accepted, they must also be *respected*, and so must the people who have reported their sightings, and given me their evidence, hence many fall-outs I have had with the press over the years when they've demanded personal details just to fuel their latest Hallowe'en story.

These animals are precious in our countryside, and so this book is dedicated to them in a way, as well as my loved ones.

This book also mentions other strange creatures reputedly haunting this rural abode. Many of these are certainly flesh and blood animals, released or escaped into the wilds. Reports date back centuries, and this book aims to catalogue each of those fascinating, quirky and intriguing reports. And then there are the incomprehensible things, and I say 'things' because they are not natural, and they deserve their own section because although I've never liked my research into exotic species to melt into the 'unexplained' as such, or 'supernatural' if you will, it is still down to me to cover a phantom menagerie too; a selection of surreal forms that legend relates. Such 'monsters' are not merely from the pages of some of the books I flicked through as a child, and neither did they come from the tongues of excitable friends eager to chill the spine. The fact is that there *are* some things out there more connected to the human psyche and cultural fear, than to the skies, rivers, fields and woods. Whether they are stalking us, or whether we as a race are accidentally bumping into them, we'll probably never know, but there has, for centuries, across the world, been sighted a whole gaggle of demonic and absurd apparitions; beasts and unbidden creatures, maybe from some ethereal void, or from the nightmares we've been brought up with and to fear. In 2007 I wrote a unique book on such creatures that had become known as 'zooforms', bizarre spectres seemingly having animal characteristics. The book, *Monster! The A-Z Of Zooform Phenomena* (CFZ Press) remains the world's only book to comprehensively list and explore a whole host of encounters with the weird and wonderful creatures of this, and other voids, which clearly are not flesh and blood, yet somehow remain embedded in our thoughts and the fabric of time we flitter through. The complex subject is obscure, and is neither paranormal, nor is it related to cryptozoology, which is the field within which to study unknown animals, rediscovered species and new species. 'Zooform Phenomena' was a term coined in the 1990s by monster-hunter Jonathan Downes who went on to publish my book. He created the controversial category simply to define, or hold within its grasp, the mind-boggling procession of 'animals' that were either a) ghostly in nature b) displaying qualities of supernatural or folkloric connection, or c) appearing as semi-mythical beasts, such as werewolves, but having a foothold in reality as we know it.

Whilst I, and many other children over time, have grown up with horror stories of fictional vampires and the like, not many will eventually indulge in research to actually discover that these traditional folk tales and fears have some credibility as actual forms that once existed, either as local bogeymen to prevent children from misbehaving, or as real woodland terrors that only appeared during the dead of night. Of course, many of us have grown up with parental talk of the `Tooth Fairy` who slips into the rooms of children who've recently lost a milk tooth, in order to replace the bloody shard with a shiny penny, or the `Sandman` who allegedly haunts the night with his large sack, and said to sprinkle sand into the eyes of kids during the hours of slumber. Many of these spooks and spectres, whether it's Father Christmas or the Yawning Man, or any other worldwide figure of lore, all have their meaning and motive either as sinister shadows that creep from the graveyards, or as magical beings who fly in on a sleigh. Over centuries these forms have become exaggerated, moulded by whichever society they haunt, and passed down through generations. We love - and at times fear them so much - because the mystery is around us always. Whether we choose to accept such monsters and fantasy into our life is another thing, but it's fair to say that over the course of many decades, such traditions and beliefs have gradually dissipated. No longer do we believe in fairies at the bottom of the garden, because such things have been replaced by new hopes and also new fears, and some of these are presented in this book, albeit as confusing and often terrifying apparitions, whilst others may echo the mystery we've always had instilled within our souls.

This book is not just about the mystery animals of Kent, but about mystery and our need for it in general. This is the book I've always wanted to write. These are the stories, the fables, the real accounts and whispers I craved as a child, and thankfully kept inside my heart and mind as I grew. To let go of such mystery and interest in the unknown would be a tragedy not for just for me, but for mankind in general, because in a world of often mundane routine, the human mind must also find a hunger for monsters instead of being driven by the banal world of commercialism in television, etc — whether it exists as the big fish that always eluded fishermen in the local lake, or the red-eyed phantom said to spook kissing couples at their own lover's lane. We crave that atmosphere, to snuggle as the storm rages, that crackling fire and the cosy yet unnerving tones of the ghost story teller, and we always have that need to look back over our shoulder as we take a stroll through the dark woods, because although we would be awfully frightened to see something, we don't really know what's out there, but you can guarantee that your mind will create something for you; a faceless entity, the sum of your greatest dread, the bogeyman, the window tapper.

In a way this book is almost an autobiography of my childhood fears and adult research, with little about me in-between. It will be my defining piece, because although I will write more, I know in my heart that this is the work I owe to myself, and to my county, and to all the strange things that reside within the air, woods, water, and minds. And hopefully it will stand as a unique chronicle to all that has gone before in this very weird county.

I hope you enjoy this book; it has been in my system for some twenty-odd years. It was worth the wait. And I sincerely hope it remains on the shelves of every library, dusty basement, avid collector, curious child, bookshop, next generation monster-hunter and also in the hearts and minds of others who seek their own personal mystery, and embark on the kind of quests I have.

So this is it, the only chronicle of its kind in relation to Kent, and proof also that when I was younger, even as a good footballer who promised so much, I simply had more belief in monsters than I did in myself. Whether you believe in such things only you can decide and all I can do is present the evidence, but, as the strange giant said to FBI Agent Dale Cooper in my favourite television show *Twin Peaks* from the 1990s, *"Don't search for all the answers at once..."*

Neil Arnold 2009

'...from boyhood...something in collocation of roofs and steeples and chimneys and brick walls formed contours touching deep viol-strings of ancestral emotion. I could tell that I was at the gateway of a region half-bewitched through the piling-up of unbroken time-accumulations; a region where old, strange things have had a chance to grow and linger because they have never been stirred up.'

The Whisperer In Darkness - H.P. Lovecraft

Lara the Lynx (p.17)

Part One
Setting the Scene

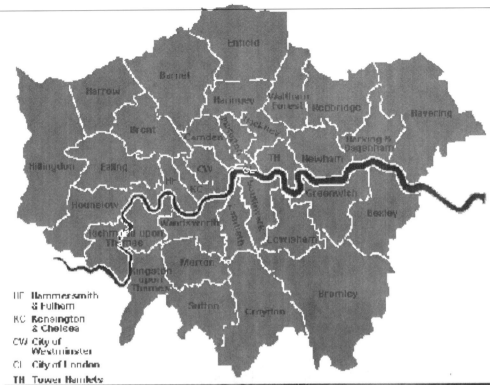

HF Hammersmith & Fulham

KC Kensington & Chelsea

CW City of Westminster

Cl City of London

TH Tower Hamlets

Neil Arnold with Channel Four Radio's Danny Robins (2005)

Cats around The Capital

'I stood there, cold, listening to the wind off the night moors. And maybe something else was listening. Something that kills hens and sheep and sometimes men....something that hears you, and comes closer... '

The Nature Of The Beast – Janni Howker

This is a transcript of a *'London Zoo Press Release'* – May 8th 2001:

London Zoo rescues a roaming European lynx from a Golders Green Garden. On Friday 4 May 2001, London Zoo received a call from the Barnet Borough Police based at Colindale Police Station, North London, requesting assistance with a big cat sighting in the Golders Green area.

A member of the public had seen an animal sitting on the wall of her back garden, which she initially thought was a leopard, as it had a spotted coat. London Zoo's Head Keeper of Big Cats, Ray Charter, and a colleague, Terry Marsh, were driven with a police escort to a residential area in Golders Green, where the cat had allegedly been seen in the large garden.

"*We get numerous calls at London Zoo reporting big cat sightings and so far all of them have proved incorrect – it usually turns out to be a large domestic cat*", commented Ray Charter. "*...so you can imagine my surprise when I bent down to look under the hedge expecting to see a large ginger Tom, only to be met by a much more exotic face!*".

After several attempts to catch the cat with a hand net in the large open area, it was finally contained in a smaller area under some steps of a nearby flat. Having assessed the situation, Ray decided to call London Zoo's Senior Veterinary Officer, Tony Sainsbury, who sedated the animal with a blowpipe. Once sedated, the animal was given a veterinary examination and was found to be a female European lynx of approximately 18 months.

"*The lynx was underweight, but in a fair condition*", says Tony Sainsbury.

"She is currently recovering in our hospital and we will do a full veterinary examination in the next couple of days. She seems to have a problem with her left hind leg which we will examine under anaesthetic."

The origin of the animal is still unknown.

"It is difficult to speculate where the animal came from", said Nick Lindsay, Senior Curator for London Zoo and Whipsnade Wild Animal Park. *"In order to own an exotic cat species you are required to have a Dangerous Wild Animal License from your local authority."*

There was some concern from local residents regarding the danger that was posed by this animal.

"If left alone it is unlikely that the animal would have harmed a person", continues Nick Lindsay. *"However, if it felt threatened or cornered it could give a nasty scratch or bite. It was more likely to be frightened than dangerous."*

DI Paul Anstee from the Barnet Borough Police says, *"The Police are extremely grateful that they had the back up of London Zoo's expertise in dealing with this unusual event."* The animal will remain in the care of London Zoo while she recuperates and her future is decided.'

This Is Local London - September 2001:

'Four months after being captured in a suburban back garden, the Beast of Barnet is alive and well at London Zoo.

A wild cat dubbed the 'Beast of Barnet', found in a Childs Hill garden back in May, has recovered well, according to London Zoo.

Times Group readers may recall how Potters Bar and South Mimms residents were forced to lock themselves in their own homes in September 1998 as police combed the area looking for a large catlike animal which had been sighted there earlier. There were also sightings of another 'Beast of Barnet' in the Bookman's Park area.

However, the captive lynx seems to be enjoying her new home, the big cat enclosure at London Zoo, having recovered fully from her ordeal.

Head keeper of London Zoo's big cat section, Ray Charter, said: *"We've called her Lara and she's the only lynx in the big cat enclosure here so we will not be breeding her. She's in good condition now."*

RSPCA inspector Dermot Murphy added: *"We haven't been able to find out who owned the lynx but believe it was privately owned. Unfortunately, there's been an increase in people owning exotic animals and we would warn anyone hoping to do this to think carefully as they are not ideal pets in the home."*

The inspector said it is an offence to hold an animal of this kind without license under the Government-enforced Dangerous Wild Animals Act.'

DANGEROUS WILD ANIMALS ACT 1976

Conditions subject to which the Licence is Granted.

1. While any animal concerned is being kept only under the authority of the Licence:

a)   The animal shall be kept by no person other than the person specified above.

b)   The animal shall normally be held at the premises specified on the licence.

c)   The animals shall not be moved from those premises without authorisation by the Borough Environmental Health Officer and shall not be moved except for the purpose of veterinary attention or to:

·   A zoological garden

·   A circus

·   Premises licensed as a pet shop under the Pet Animals Act 1951

·   A place registered pursuant to the Cruelty to Animals Act 1876 for the purpose of performing experiments.

Premises licensed to keep such animals under the provisions of the Dangerous Wild Animals Act 1976

d)   The person to whom the Licence is granted shall hold a   current insurance policy which insures him against liability for any damage which may be caused by the animals and the terms of such policy shall be approved by the Council.

2. The species and number of animals of each species which may be kept under the authority of the Licence shall be restricted to those specified on the licence.

3. Where snakes are kept the applicant shall provide to the satisfaction of the Borough Environmental Health Officer snake-proof wire screens to the window used for the ventilation of and the door to the room in which the animals are kept.

4. The animals shall be kept in containers constructed of materials and be so designed that they will not burn, shatter or collapse when involved in fire to the extent where animals could escape.

5. A properly constructed notice bearing the words 'WARNING - DANGEROUS ANIMALS' in 2 inch high block letters on a conspicuous background shall be securely affixed to the outside of the door of the room in which the animals are kept.

6. The door of the room in which the animals are kept shall be securely locked closed at all times when the animals are not being attended to.

7. In the case of snakes an antidote to the venom of the snakes shall be pro-

vided by the person to whom the Licence is granted and shall readily be available at all times including during transportation of the animals.

8. Transportation

a) Transportation of the animal shall only be undertaken in an approved stoutly made container so constructed that it will not shatter or collapse in the event of impact or fire and at all times secures that the animal shall not escape.

b) A properly constructed notice bearing the words 'WARNING – DANGEROUS ANIMALS' in one inch high block letters on a conspicuous background shall be securely affixed to the outside of the container in which the animal is kept.

c) Details of species of animal, availability of the antidote and the names and addresses of the consignor and consignee must be clearly displayed on the container.

d) The Licence holder shall ensure that all the above transportation requirements are complied with if the transportation of the animal is undertaken by a third person other than the consignor or consignee.

Despite the initial excitement of the lynx, many researchers concluded, and rapidly, that this particular animal had only been roaming free for a few days, if that, and clearly wasn't an elusive exotic caught by methodical research or even chance. Lara, had simply been sitting on a garden wall waiting to be fed, and only took off after two attempts to dart her and one sharp jab to her rear end. Some experts, including Mike Thomas of Newquay Zoo, believed that the lynx had been injured by a vehicle, which had damaged the poor animal's leg. It is very likely that the emaciated cat had only been feeding off scraps for a few days to get by. In an excellent little article written by Paul Crowther, entitled '*Lara The Lynx Of London Town*', which appeared in the Newsfile Xtra section of *Animals & Men* magazine, Issue 24, he asked, '*Why did it take so long for anyone to report seeing it?*', and added, '*The idea that a lynx could roam around London for approximately five days without anyone noticing it does beggar belief. If a lynx can roam around London without detection by the numerous people who live and work there, who is to deny that a similar exotic cat cannot survive and go unnoticed on Bodmin Moor for years!*'

The lynx was eventually transferred to Amneville Zoo, in France.

The Eurasian lynx (*L. lynx*) inhabits Northern Europe and East Asia, although many have been wiped out by hunters and fur trappers. By the mid-20th Century numbers had been greatly reduced, as have the forests which they inhabit. They can reach to over four feet in length and weigh up to eighty-five pounds. They were once indigenous to Britain, but it is generally accepted that they died out around four thousand years ago, although bones have been found in caves in Scotland which indicate that some of these animals may have lived here up until fifteen-hundred years ago. Scepticism arises to the possibility that such animals still linger on in the present day. However, I do not think this is impossible. Four thousand years is a very long time ago, but for an animal as elusive as the lynx, it's difficult to say exactly when it did die out, if it did at all. Some experts argue as to how these creatures eventually perished in the wilds of Britain. Some claim that the lynx simply died out due to climate change, but others prefer the theory which concerns humankind. It has been suggested that the lynx began to take the livestock from humans mainly due to the fact that men wiped out much of the lynx territory through deforestation. In turn, the lynx would come into farms and kill goats and sheep, which in turn angered the humans, who destroyed the cat.

These beautiful felids can inhabit rocky slopes, forest and open grassland, and even though such a cat can kill something up to four times its own size, in the United Kingdom, such a cat would feed on rodents, birds and rabbits. These creatures are easily recognisable by their short tails and tufted ears. Their coat can be of varied patterns, occasionally plain, but mostly rusty or greyish with a mottled effect.

In his booklet, *The Smaller Mystery Carnivores Of The West Country (CFZ Communications 1996)*, my friend, cryptozoologist Jonathan Downes, wrote of several lynx sightings dating back some few centuries. He wrote:

> '...*reports of lynx-like animals in Britain are not a modern phenomenon. The 16th Century author Ralph Holinshead wrote, 'Lions we had very many in the north parts of Scotland and those with manes of no less force than those of Mauretania; but how and when they were destroyed I do not yet read'. However, the most quoted reference to an early lynx sighting in Britain, came from the pen of William Cobbett, who was once described by English writer Sir John Verney as, '...farmer, writer, political commentator...', in his Rural Rides published in 1830. It is said that as a boy he observed a grey cat as big as a middle-sized spaniel dog whilst visiting Waverley Abbey somewhere between 1766 and 1770. On 27th October 1825 he took his son to the exact same spot where he'd seen the animal. His son, eleven-year old Richard measured the girth of the tree to some sixteen feet. Since then many have suggested that Cobbett saw a wildcat. One-hundred and thirteen years later, on 19th March 1938, also in Surrey, this time at Lightwater, an Irene Roberts wrote a letter to The Field magazine, to speak of the strange cries she was hearing outside her bedroom window of a night. Some of the cries, which she heard during the early hours of one July day, in 1937, were described as, '...of peculiar intensity, expressing, it seemed, mortal fear and physical pain'.*

However, Irene seemed quite knowledgeable of the sounds made by foxes or a rabbit being killed, but attributed these cries as from an unknown animal. Little did Irene realise that a quarter of a century later, these cries would manifest time and time again across the fields of Surrey, and many witnesses would come forward to report what was to become known as the 'Surrey Puma', the first 'big cat' headline.

The puma (*Puma concolor*), also known as the mountain lion, cougar, and in parts of America, the panther, is the largest of the lesser cats, which also include caracal, Canadian and European lynx , jungle cat, bobcat, and leopard cat. It is not a 'big cat', like the leopard, lion, tiger, and cheetah for it cannot roar, but instead lets out an eerie scream, which can travel for many miles across a valley and the rocky climbs where it roams in North, South and Central America. In some parts of the U.S.A. this animal is extremely rare, and has taken on the form of a ghostly, mythical felid, whilst in other areas, such as New Jersey, many sceptics argue against its existence, believing it was wiped from the map a century previous, despite modern days sightings of what the locals call the 'shadow' or 'ghost' cat. Rather strangely, there were probably more reports in Surrey, England, during the 1960s, than in a whole century in its native country!

In the United Kingdom the press often confuse the puma with the black 'panther', although the black 'panther' is simply a melanistic leopard - a darker form of the 'normal' leopard - which is no relation to the dark-tan coloured puma. The black puma is phenomenally rare; in fact only one specimen has ever been caught and that particular individual was debated. In parts of the United States many eyewitnesses are convinced that the black animals they are seeing are not black leopards, but melanistic, screaming pumas. Until one is captured, however, there will always be a strong degree of scepticism, especially when you consider that in many areas of the U.S.A. the puma is said to no longer exist, despite persistent reports. However, for sceptics and scientists to accept *normal* mountain lions it is hard enough, so for them to believe in black specimens is nigh on impossible. Some specimens in the United States have been found with very dark tan coats, but not black, or extremely dark as to look black, like that of the melanistic leopard. However, when a majority of the early reports of 'big cats' emerged in Britain during the middle to late 1900s, much confusion arose regarding species identification. Much of the public were unaware that leopards *could* be black, which is very understandable, and so if you take a stroll through many press reports - even today - regarding black cat sightings, many reporters will still describe witnesses as seeing a 'black, puma-like cat', instead of the black leopard, which we will talk more of later.

The puma is a reasonably large cat, and can reach over six feet in length. The young of the puma have spotted coats, and these spots gradually fade out. The tail of the puma, which is a wonderful balancing tool, can measure up to thirty inches. In parts of the United States they are feared as a threat to humans, although bees and dogs cause more deaths each year.

On 11th January 2004 *The Sunday Mirror* newspaper reported, '*Lion Kills A Cyclist*', and the story was echoed in *The People*, under the headline '*Girl Saved From Puma*', and also spread like wildfire across parts of the U.S.A. where the incident took place. *The Mirror* reported that, '...*a mountain lion was shot after mauling a man to death and dragging a woman one-hundred yards with her head in its mouth. Rangers hid near the body of cyclist Mark Reynolds, 35, waited for the lion to return to its prey and then killed it. The beast also attacked Anne Hjelle, 30, a fitness instructor. It pounced on her as she cycled with her friend, Deborah Nichols, in parkland outside Los Angeles. It sank its jaws into her head and dragged her one-hundred yards into a bush while Miss Nichols held on to her friend's legs. Miss Hjelle is now in a serious condition in a LA hospital.*

Describing last week's attack, Miss Nichols said: 'I held onto her and kept screaming and screaming. The lion just wouldn't let go of her face.'

One of the first ever recorded reports of the Surrey puma came from 1955 when a female witness, walking her dog near Abinger Hammer, discovered the grisly, half-eaten remains of a calf. She claimed, that after finding the gory mess, she was shocked to see a puma-like animal slinking out of sight. Four years after the sighting, during 1959, Mr Burningham, driving near Preston Candover in Hampshire, saw a large cat cross the road in front of his vehicle. He described the animal as being yellowish in colour, and the size of a Labrador dog, but with a cat's head. Its coat looked quite rough and its tail was long. Thankfully, the witness wasn't too dumbstruck to slow his vehicle and watch the animal for a short while, as it observed sheep in the adjacent field to the hedgerow in which it was sitting.

That same year a taxi-driver described seeing a 'lion', which leapt over a hedge in the vicinity of Tweezledown Racecourse, but things really began hotting up during the early '60s, when a huge flood of sightings bombarded the local newspapers, forcing the news crews and media hounds to wake up and take notice that some 'thing' was indeed out there stalking the fields. However, although 1963 is seen as the defining year in which the Surrey felid made its name, there were still handfuls of previous reports lurking around as anecdotal evidence.

A now defunct Surrey-related website page reported, on the '*Scare Bears & Other Creatures*' around Surrey, and mentioned an intriguing report from 1961:

'In 1961 golfers spotted a 'big black animal' (the first ever Surrey black leopard sighting I wonder?) in the autumn mist on Croham Hurst Golf Course. One man bravely moved closer to get a better view. He judged it to be a bear about three feet tall. It disappeared into the woods as the friends peered at it across the field. The golf club feared the animal might scare women and children, so police were called out, but a search revealed no trace of the mystery animal. Officers suggested it could have been a large dog, while Saint Bernards or dog badgers were put forward as solutions by some locals.'

Even more interestingly, the website went on to mention a 'big cat' escaping in Surrey, very early evidence that cats were present in the county, whether roaming free or circus-bound.

'In the 1920s 'Carmo Manor' in Shirley acted as the winter quarters of Carmo's Circus. The Great Carmo's menagerie was housed there, and the circus men would often wash the elephants in the old estate pond or take bears for exercise round the grounds. So when a woman rang the police station to report an escaped leopard the duty sergeant was on the point of organising a full-scale, armed leopard hunt. The creature had been seen to force its way through a hedge and then jump over a fence. Stopping a moment to check the facts, he rang Carmo's and found they had no leopards! This time, the twilight at dusk was accused of turning a Dalmatian into a vision of a leopard. The circus dog had apparently slipped out during training for a new act.'

It would be nice to prove these details as correct, and that it was indeed the circus dog that had escaped. One of the more popular theories on these wild cats roaming the British Isles is that they are generations spawned from cats that once escaped from the local circus or private collections. The Romans also had menageries dating back several centuries which we'll speak of later, and these would have included large cats such as the leopard. Strangely though, the normal spotted leopard, known for its rosette-marked coat, is rarely sighted in Britain, but melanistic leopards appear more common. Why is this so? Well, firstly, there is no difference between the two, they are the same animal, native to Africa and Asia. The black 'panther' is simply the name given to the darker form of the leopard, although darker coated versions are far more scarce in their homeland. This skin pigment, known as melanin, is a common condition known to occur in many felids, canids and other mammals such as squirrels, and is due to the changes in the agouti gene which controls banding of black and light areas on the hair shaft. Two normal parents can produce up to four young, and within this litter there can be melanistic individuals. However, melanistic parents can only produce black young, which is why reports of leopards in Britain only concern dark-coated cats, although the jaguar, very unlikely to roam Britain, can produce spotted young when two black parents produce. The black leopards are, in fact, a very dark brown, but from a distance look black. If these individuals are seen at closer quarters and under the right light conditions, the rosette pattern can be seen. However, there are an increasing number of eyewitnesses who describe what they believe are jet-black cats. A recessive gene in the melanistic leopard could, in fact, gradually phase out the rosette pattern, or increase the darkness of the coat to an almost jet-black colouration. It is claimed, through scientific research, that melanistic cats may be more resistant to diseases than their 'normal' coloured relatives. It's clear that in a majority of sightings regarding black cats, people are not merely seeing large feral cats, dogs or any other animal. They describe an animal able to stash prey up in trees. An animal that can reach over four feet in length, be of muscular build, and omit a deep, sawing cough noise and a double-barrelled snarl.

In Britain there is no evidence to suggest these animals are a danger

Roman carving of black leopard
from Rochester Guildhall Museum

23

to the public unless injured, provoked or cornered, and - so far - the attacks that have allegedly taken place, involving humans, are of dubious veracity. Some researchers argue that there are a selection of mystery black cat sightings which could point to a new species of British cat, something smaller than the leopard, but reports seem inconsistent, and also with regard to the possibility that such sightings of mystery British cats are of an unknown species. Zoologist Dr. Karl Shuker wrote, '...*I would be only too delighted and thrilled if a totally new species of large felid were to be discovered in Britain. As a zoologist surveying the possibility realistically my personal opinion of this is that its chances of success are gravely hampered by basic problems...To begin with, the British big cat would need to be nothing short of a shape shifter to account for the immense variety of felids reported – cats which are black, grey, every shade of brown, striped, spotted, with long legs, with short legs, with long tails, with short tails, with ear-tufts, without ear-tufts, which roar, which scream, which are of small dog size, which equal the size of the largest dog breeds etc, etc. Certainly no single non-domestic species of felid (indeed no wild mammal of any single species, known or unknown) could possibly exhibit so many markedly different forms...*'

Maybe this next fact is press-influenced, but it seems that a majority of Surrey puma sightings were of fawn-coloured animals. Was this because, quite simply, there were hardly any melanistic leopards around Surrey at the time, or because a hysterical public were only spotting the puma simply because the media had only informed them of such a cat, without ever mentioning other species?

Mr Ernest Jellett, who worked for the Mid-Wessex Water Board, was cycling near Heathy Park Reservoir at around 7:45 am on the day of 16th July 1962 when he saw a big cat with a flat face and big paws stalking a rabbit. Although at the time Mr Jellett described the creature he saw as something akin to a 'young lion cub', it seems clear that what he did in fact see was a small puma. In the December of '62 another water board employee saw the cat, and there were numerous other reports of a rabbit-coloured cat prowling the woods. Now, at the time, scepticism was rife. A majority of reports, even today, are not reported by some witnesses due to fear of ridicule, but there is more of an understanding and coverage of these sightings, with various research groups being set up to record the evidence of these exotic cats. During the 1960s - in fact, right up until the 1980s - a majority of sightings were not taken seriously. What didn't help was the fact that witnesses did not know what they were seeing, but this was, of course, natural. Nobody cycling down a country lane in Surrey expects to see a large cat - a big, slinking felid which they cannot recognise simply because all they are used to seeing are foxes and badgers.

So, this is where many of the 'lion' and 'young lioness' reports are born, but a majority of these must account for the puma. How do I know this? Well, quite simply put, there are no tigers, cheetahs or lions roaming the U.K., despite some of the more modern panics that have circulated, such as the Nottingham 'lion' scare, which took place in the 1970s, and others such as the lioness that was said to be on the loose in Winchmore Hill, north London, in March 1994 after eighteen independent reports emerged of a big cat with short golden hair and large padded feet. A helicopter buzzed the Palmers Green area, police staked the wooded areas out, and schoolchildren had to stay behind in class for fear of encountering the beast. Of course, no lion showed up, but left us asking the question as to who was the bigger danger, the mystery cat or the police? In fact, the only time such a lion would take to the countryside was if such a big cat had escaped from a zoo or a circus. Even then, such animals would be easier to trace, as they will seek larger prey; and also in the case of the lion, prowl open ground, whereas the animals we are dealing with in the British Isles are very elusive.

Reports snowballed into late winter, through to 1963, when a mysterious predator paid various visits to Bushylease Farm, between Crondall and Ewshot. Something silent had been spooking the farm dogs, and fleeting sightings of the slinking intruder often described it as tan-coloured. A huge hunt ensued for the creature during the summer of '63 after David Back spotted an animal laying by the roadside at 1am on the 18th July, at Shooter's Hill. One hundred and twenty-six policemen, accompanied by more than twenty dogs, alongside ambulance staff, and officials from the RSPCA, scoured more than 800 acres of land in the hunt for a cat they believed was a cheetah, despite no actual reports from the time describing such a thing! A complete waste of time and resources, as usual — and such a ridiculous attempt to flush out a cat was, unfortunately to be repeated time and time again, with the same results. This leads many to believe that, surely, these animals cannot exist if they are so clever as to evade hundreds of trackers.

Many of the sightings which emerged from 1964 were chronicled in Di Francis' superb book, *Cat Country (David & Charles 1983)*, and some read as follows:

> *27th September 1964 – 10:45 pm – a puma-like cat was sighted by a motorist at Loxwood. The next day on 28th September 1964 – 6:15 pm – a female witness observed a puma at Witley. Then, on 29th September 1964 – 6:45 am – a road worker in the Puttenham vicinity came face to face with a large cat.' There were also a couple of reports of a puma on October 3rd, and then, throughout October consistent eyewitness descriptions from Hascombe, Hindhead and Elstead, all reports describing a puma-like animal.*

However, some of the best documented sightings of the animal can be found in Marcus Matthews' excellent *Big Cats: Loose In Britain* book (CFZ Press 2007).

The following year Di Francis catalogued another consistent batch of reports, with one at Chiddingford where a female witness, tending to her horses, described how a 'big cat' had leapt over her head. During 1966 there were further reports from Puttenham, and Godalming also saw several sightings. Unfortunately, Di Francis only chronicles these reports as 'puma-like', so I am assuming that all these reports, which certainly reached over fifty during 1966, concerned fawn-tan coloured animals and not black cats which seemed pretty scarce, or were being ignored. As I have mentioned previously, the press often wrote of these sightings rather loosely. At the time many journalists would have been unaware of black leopard sightings, and many would have thought - in their ignorance - that a puma-like animal could well have been black. So it seems, a majority of these reports, from the early '60s, and on to the '80s, would have nearly always pertained to the 'puma-like' animals, despite the possibility that other animals were involved, including the lesser known cats such as the golden cat and jungle cat. Flick through any number of newspaper articles pertaining to cat sightings, and you'll notice a degree of ignorance from the journalists regarding identity of species, and so many headlines will only contain references to a 'big cat' - which is vague, to say the least.

During 1966, several motorists filed reports of large cat-like animals, especially in the Puttenham area. Many of these reports came from the summertime and into autumn. At Ash Green, on the morning of July 14th, a witness saw a big cat run into fields, and the same day, only three hours apart at Worplesdon, a witness observed a puma from just thirty yards away as it padded its way into the garden of the householder.

A puma was reported again during mid-August, this time at Cutt Mill. The police were spoken to regarding the sighting, although I'm unaware as to what action was taken. At Wormley, a few days after, another householder observed a large cat in the garden, but at Milford on 4th September 1966, a male witness was dumbstruck when a large cat sprang from a tree and sped off. Not only was this witness unaware that large, exotic cats were roaming the Surrey countryside, but also that they lay up in trees - a common trait of the leopard, which is a superb climber - where, in their countries of origin, they will stash prey in the branches of trees to avoid scavengers. Large cats, such as the puma and leopard, are agile predators, but despite having no fixed dens, unless to give birth, they will lay up wherever possible. Gardens, trees, churchyards, ruins, under cars…there's nowhere that a 'big cat' will not consider.

Many witnesses to large cats in Britain often describe grisly evidence in the form of half-eaten remains, often stashed up in trees, although smaller prey such as rabbits and pigeons are completely consumed with no real trace except for a few feathers and bones. The back legs of lambs have often been discovered in fields, as well as the remains of sheep, domestic cats, small dogs, deer and foxes. Sheep are usually half-eaten, cleanly devoured and rasped by the tongue of a large cat, and domestic cats have been found headless and stripped, foxes disembowelled, and even horses have been found, although alive, in some distress, bearing scratch marks on their flanks and bite marks to the throat. A large cat will not kill out of spite, or ravage like a dog; it will kill to survive. Traces of these animals are few and far between, a few carcasses here and there, a handful of dubious pugmarks which, unless very defined in mud or sand, are often smudged on bridle pathways, fields, and tracks; and there are also the scratch marks left on trees which, when found, are extremely impressive.

During September of 1966, many witnesses claimed to have found the paw-prints of big cats. These echoed similar evidence found in 1964 when, on September 7th, P.C. Bill Cooper was called out to investigate a strange set of impressions trailing across a field at Stileman's Racing Stables. The prints seemed to measure five inches across, and suggested that a heavy animal had made them. Unfortunately, after following the prints for half a mile, they disappeared into undergrowth. However, photographs were taken of the prints and examined by experts at London Zoo, who confirmed they had indeed been made by a large cat such as a puma. Unfortunately, a sceptical Dr. Maurice Burton suggested that the prints were made by a dog. What we must remember when looking at prints, as mentioned later, is that the dog does not retract its claws, but a large cat will. Claws may be thrown out to grip, but a majority of cat prints can be confirmed by the lack of claw marks. A puma was seen at Stringers Common on the evening of 22nd September 1966 by a woman out walking. There had been two other sightings earlier in the morning at Hog's Back. One of these concerned a motorist who had an impressive sighting of a brown cat, which was caught in the headlights as it slinked across the road.

The same animal was seen at Hog's Back in October of '66. Again, a motorist had caught the animal as it crossed the road, and before the year was out there'd been another handful of reports, and the rest of the decade was no different, with sightings coming from Wood Street and Thursley.

There were claims during the very late 1960s that a puma was shot and killed in the Surrey area, as well as Sussex and Hampshire. However, there is no proof of this, but if such an incident did occur then it is very likely that at the time the carcass would have been buried or burned.

Reports continued into 1968. Farnborough was an extremely active area. However, sometime during the '80s a rather vague critter was said to have been prowling Hackney Marshes, in East London although little appears to have been recorded regarding a creature that was described as being bear-like (see Section: *More Mystery Animals*)! Rather quirkily, English comedian Jasper Carrott and actor Robert Powell were to bring this obscure legend to the public eye, and out of the depths of obscurity, for an episode of their BBC series, *The Detectives*, in 1997.

Graham McKewan's important book pertaining to strange creatures, entitled *Mystery Animals Of Britain And Ireland(Hale 1985)* catalogues many eyewitness sightings touching the borders. One woman, Mrs Anne Stanette, described her encounter a decade later, in a letter, which happened in East Surrey:

> '*While I was out riding in Granger's Woods, Woldingham, in May 1978, I saw what I believe was a lion rush across the road in front of me. It ran from the Oxted side into thick bushes on the opposite side. It was about ten or twelve yards from me. It was a beige/light brown colour and had a small head in comparison with the rest of its body. (It had no shaggy mane).*'

Such a sighting, most definitely of a puma, proves how natural it was an occurrence, back then more so, for witnesses to wrongly identify the puma, as a lioness. At the time, much of the public, despite the spate of Surrey sightings, and also handfuls of sightings across Britain taking place, were familiar with the term 'big cat', but weren't quite sure exactly what 'cat' was roaming the countryside. A majority of animal documentaries, even today, cover the world of the lion. The puma is extremely elusive, and so footage is not as easy to come by, but back in the '60s people seeing beige cats often felt that they were seeing a lioness. However, the puma does have a small head in relation to its body, whereas the lioness is a much bigger animal, with a bigger, squarer head and its most distinguishing feature is its colouration, which is more of a sandy yellow colour. However, back then, and still, rather surprisingly in the present day, people do not - and did not - expect to see a large cat skulking around. And when they did spot one, the majority of people were probably unaware of what a puma looked like, unaware also that leopards can be black, unaware of the differing species actually out there, and so, in their minds, they probably put two and two together and guessed that they'd seen the only animal they really knew, the lion. However, two years previously in Nottingham - as mentioned earlier - several witnesses came forward to report what they'd described as, "…definitely a lion", roaming heavily populated areas. Even the Nottingham police were alarmed by the sightings and said that they were "…ninety-eight percent certain", that some kind of animal was out there. However, after many reports and countless searches, no lion was unearthed, but puma sightings in Nottingham, and other cities across Britain persisted.

From the New Forest area of Hampshire came several reports of a big, black animal, during the early 1970s. A John McPherson saw a massive cat cross the road in front of him on January 23rd 1973. In the September of 1976 three lions escaped from a circus at Epsom in Surrey, but were recaptured - but not before a horse was severely savaged by one of the large cats. A black cat with a very long tail was also seen in areas of Sussex during the summer of 1979, whilst five years later there were puma reports from Hertfordshire. Thankfully, one or two reports of large, black cats were filtering through to the press, proving that a variety of large animals were roaming the Home Counties. Unfortunately, the 1980s proved just as ignorant with regards to the coverage of the sightings. Reports were still consistent, possibly even more so, as any animal that may have been released during the 1970s after the introduction of the 1976 Animals Act, would surely be breeding if there were so many cats out there. Sceptics argued that the evidence was scarce which, in turn - to them anyway - meant that the animals were scarce too, but this didn't explain the numbers of animals being reported up and down the country. Unfortunately, the sceptics, and some of the journalists truly believed that there were just one or two escaped cats out there to be blamed for the hundreds of sightings which were now coming from parts of Scotland, the West Country, Midlands, Wales, parts of Ireland and down towards Kent and the Home Counties. The suggestion that just a handful of cats were the cause of all these sightings was quite simply more absurd than the mystery they were pursuing. And yet it still happens today. This is a typical problem with the media. Once an animal becomes the 'Beast of Exmoor', or the 'Surrey Puma', the finger is pointed at one animal, when in reality there could be anywhere between five and twenty cats out there - three to four species - yet they all become the local 'beast', something akin to the scenario of a werewolf movie.

During the 1970s, naturalist Maurice Burton concluded that all the reports of alleged large cats, which he had investigated, turned out to be fox, badger, deer, dog, otter and feral cats. Maybe it was conclusions like this that turned the 1980s into such a non-event for the Surrey 'big cat'. This lack of activity could also be blamed on another mystery felid, the 'beast' of Exmoor, which exploded into the '80s, and became the most popular headline-making 'big cat' in the business. However, reports still existed. In 1984 at Peaslake, hair samples believed to have belonged to a puma were analysed, and commented on as proof that a large cat was around Surrey. In the same year there were also sightings at Chiddingford and Witley Park, and in '85 regular reports from Esher, whilst Hertfordshire, Sussex and Kent were also providing several flaps of their own, proof that the animals roaming Surrey were indeed not responsible for the eyewitness reports in the neighbouring counties. During 1987 there were also rumours that a large cat, possibly a puma, was shot and killed near Greenwich Observatory, London.

The 1990s were indeed a popular time for sightings of exotic felids, and the puma of Surrey was often regurgitated when activity arose elsewhere in the U.K. Press interest was slightly more serious by the early to mid-'90s, and certainly more consistent, with reports featuring on the worldwide web, television and in the press on a weekly basis nationwide, and also worldwide, as strange reports of 'out of place' large cats filtered from Australia, the United States of America, Italy, New Zealand, France, Denmark, and even the Isle of Wight!

However, reports of the Surrey puma and other London-related cats decreased, but during 1993 a Mr Irvine saw a large cat at Hayes Common in Bromley, one of several reports from the outskirts of London that never reached the press. Mr Irvine was driving to work one morning at around 6:45 am when a char-coal-grey cat, with rosettes bleeding through the coat, bounded across the road ahead just fourteen feet away. The animal had a smallish head, a very long tail and small ears. At the time Mr Irvine thought this animal may have been an escaped Snow leopard. During 1975 a Clouded leopard escaped from Howletts Zoo in Canterbury, Kent. The cat was at large for eight months before it was shot and killed by a farmer whose lambs had been taken by the animal. However, in 1974 Fred Arnold saw a wild cat cross a road in Folkestone, not too many miles from Canterbury. Some say he described the animal as greyish in colour, with a yellow tint. The *Folkestone Herald* article of 1973 however, stated otherwise:

> '*Was it a puma the driver saw?*' – '*After a spell of two years has the mysterious puma returned to the Dover area? An animal was seen in the Tilmanstone area two years ago, at various times, by a number of witnesses. Some claimed it was a wild puma. Then it disappeared as suddenly as it arrived. Now another animal, possibly again a puma, has been sighted between Capel and Alkham, by Mr Fred Arnold as he drove along a country lane between the two villages. He claimed that the animal – about seven feet long – leapt from a bank, touched the centre of the road in front of his car, then leapt gracefully over the opposite bank and out of sight. Mr Arnold says the animal was covered in brown hair and was sleek and graceful. In 1972 a Peter Cookson, of Lympne, was driving during the early hours of a June morning when he too saw a yellowish animal, however he described it as having stripes!*'

One of the most impressive sightings came via website *Cryptozoology*, where, in 2005, witness Matt Beloof, wrote:

> '*I am a twenty-two year old male college student from California who visited England as a youngster about ten years ago (1995). While staying in England for about a month, we stayed in Oxford, Stratford and London.*
>
> *My sighting of a monstrous cat was in London of all places, not where you'd expect to see such a thing. We had switched homes with an English family (who loved California) and we had a great time staying in their home. They had a very bushy and unkempt backyard, but it was very large and appealing to look at – all surrounded by large fencing about six feet high.*
>
> *I was sitting in the backyard reading a pamphlet from the London Dungeons one evening (before sunset), and I heard a thump from the yard. I looked up and saw what appeared to be a large black panther or cat with abnormally illuminated yellowish-white eyes walking across the yard at a medium pace, staring at me the whole time. To my amazement it simply walked across the yard, and disappeared into some bushes and trees in the back cor-*

ner of the backyard. I told my parents but they thought I just imagined it. This was no house cat with which I have much experience. It was totally black, with the eyes mentioned above, about two-and-a-half to three feet at the shoulder and maybe four-to-five feet long. I had a deep feeling of discomfort and disbelief when I saw it. I watched it for at least six seconds or so...'

During the autumn of 1998 a sandy-coloured cat with a ring on the tip of its tail was sighted at South Mimms, Hertfordshire, and there were several sightings near Potters Bar, after which commenced another fruitless police search. This animal became the 'beast' of Barnet. By this time also, my own research into sightings in Kent and the southeast, had taken on its own snowball effect, with the 'beast' of Bluebell Hill, near Maidstone, being the local favourite, although since the '80s I'd filed reports, and looked into older cases. But by the time the '90s were over, I'd been consistently receiving weekly reports which transformed into a huge cabinet of data, which, when exhaustively studied proved that there were indeed more cats out there than I had first thought. Even with siphoning out some of the more dubious and vague reports, annually I was receiving over two-hundred eyewitness accounts of large cats roaming the countryside. But just how many *weren't* being reported?

Meanwhile, across the Thames – *'Four More Sightings Of The Beast Of Ongar'*, reported the *This Is Local London* website on Saturday 8th August 1998, claiming, *'...witnesses have told police the animal, seen three times in fields at Matchling Green, looked like a young panther. The most recent sighting was off Stanford Rivers Road, Ongar, last Wednesday.'*

Essex was certainly already on the map regarding sightings of large cats, but with years of reports coming from Exmoor and Bodmin from the West Country, and also Surrey, many other nationwide reports became either obscured, or simply forgotten.

In Essex the previous year, there'd been sightings of a 'big cat' around Wood End, but like so many others, the press merely obliterated any truth by stating the strangest 'facts'. One classic report as follows: 'Commenting on the Matchling Green sightings, PC Chris Caten said: *"..they said its tail was pantherish but it was not as big as they expected a panther to be'."* If this wasn't confusing enough, a local website reported, *"...confirmation that a 'big cat' is stalking the area came in February after an expert examined a goose, one of four savaged in attacks in Weald Bridge Road, North Weald. Claw marks on its body proved it was killed by a lynx or puma-sized animal."* So, we can see by these few sentences just how confusing these cat stories are painted to the public. We have a local policeman claiming that witnesses described to him a 'panther-ish' tail, whatever that is, and that the animal was, *"...not as big as they expected a panther to be"*, even though the report clearly states that the witnesses saw an animal resembling a young panther...which I'm assuming was in fact a black cat. We also have the confusion of the claw-marks on the body of the savaged geese which an expert claimed were made by a lynx, or a puma-sized animal! Well, which is it to be?

During September 1998 the cat of West Essex became the 'beast' of Bassett, and according to some websites, was identified as a Eurasian lynx, and even investigated on the BBC series *The X-Creatures*, presented by Chris Packham. He commented, *"About five-thousand years ago they* (the lynx) *would have been very common in Essex..."*, although the animal stalking the woods during 1998 was, in his words, *"...an escapee from a zoo or private collector."* Yet here was a man I'd worked with in the past who claimed that animals such as the black leopard were quite simply not inhabiting our woodlands, although he admitted that puma could survive!

PC Ross Luke claimed that sightings around Ongar had dated back to the mid-'80s, although there seemed to be some confusion between the sightings, as many reports seemed to describe a large black animal. Whatever the case, Mr Luke claimed that, "*We have a contingency plan; if the cat is ever cornered we would call up the Tactical Firearms Unit and it would be shot...dead.*"

During January 2001 a black leopard was sighted at Walthamstow, near marshland. The sleek felid was observed going through bins at 7:45 one evening by a woman sitting in her car waiting to pick up her son. Despite the fact that the animal came close to the vehicle, the witness described it only as fox-sized, but having a long tail, although in a statement to the press she claimed it was a 'huge animal'. The animal eventually slinked away toward Wickham Close.

On the 31st of January a report was filed concerning a Christmas sighting of the Ongar cat. Paul Ayton described how he was driving along Greenstead Road when he saw a large black animal, which at first he took to be a dog. The creature was walking alongside a hedgerow a few hundred metres away, but then headed towards the road. As the animal came closer, via a field, Paul noticed its feline gait. Eventually the witness slowed the car until just twenty yards away from the cat, before it slipped away out of sight alongside a house.

Thankfully, as of writing, these animals have eluded their pursuers and sightings of large cats still continue in Essex. Colchester, Witham, Clacton and Tiptree, have all been areas where large prowling felids have been sighted throughout 2006.

However, the strangest cat flap confusion regarding Essex, and in relation to Kent, took place during the 4th January 1975. According to reports in the *Daily Mail*, and *Weekly News*, an eight-week old 'panther' cub had been stolen from Colchester Zoo. However, the zoo never made the claim until a week later. On the 5th January angler Fred Lloyd was enjoying a day's fishing on the banks of the River Medway at East Peckham, when he was disturbed by a noise in the undergrowth. Much to his surprise a two-foot long 'panther' emerged from the bushes. The animal, which Fred took to be a cub, began to hiss at the shocked angler, but instead of facing the fisherman off with prowess and arrogance, the cat could only manage a comical tumble down the bank towards him. In a split second Fred bravely grasped the cat by the scruff of its neck and bundled it into his fishing box. He then packed his gear up and drove home, taking the peculiar find with him. According to reports, the cat ended up in a baby's playpen, which it attempted to destroy with its sharp claws.

After a short while Mr Lloyd phoned around the zoo parks but claimed that the response was of laughter and mockery. It wasn't until a day later that an RSPCA inspector could be bothered to turn up at Fred's house to take a look at the mystery cat that no-one had believed in. Much to his amazement, there it was, a baby leopard bundle, ready to be taken to a new home. Bizarrely though, Colchester Zoo then decided that the cat belonged to them and was in fact 'Zar', who was worth something in the region of six-hundred pounds. I'm not sure if the mystery cub ended up at Colchester Zoo. At the time, the RSPCA inspector said that before the zoo rang, the leopard was due to end up at Godstone in Surrey. Either way, one question must be asked. How could such an exhausted cat end up more than fifty miles away at East Peckham? Had someone stolen it and then let it go? Or did Mr Lloyd have a genuine encounter with a wild, British big cat cub?

'*Cat Brutally Murdered*' – 5th September 1998. *This Is Local London.*

'*A dead cat, with its head cut off, is the latest gruesome find in a series of bizarre attacks on animals across London. The cat was found with its head missing and most of its blood drained, in Main Road, Sidcup, last Thursday. It was removed by Bexley Council environmental health officers.*'

Several months ago another cat was found in a front garden of a house in Penshurst Avenue, Sidcup. Its head and tail had been removed. There was also a similar incident in Erith. A total of forty suspicious deaths among pets have taken place in the last ten months and the most common victims are domestic cats.

RSPCA inspector Nigel Shelton said: "*The number of cases of animals which have been decapitated or had limbs removed from their bodies is growing at an alarming rate and we would urge anybody with any information to contact us urgently.*"

An RSPCA spokesman said they had no idea of the motive behind the killings and said the widespread locations of the deaths made it likely that more than one person was involved. She said police were now following up the leads given by the public through the RSPCA's emergency hotline.

She added: "*At the moment, we have no hard facts about the person or people behind these attacks.*"

With the grisly, but seemingly unrelated cat-rippings making the local headlines, it was the turn of the Barnet 'beast' to rear its ugly head again, this time on September 25th 1998. Two policemen, Martin Stainton and Matthew Durkin, observed a cat which the press claimed was, '…*either a puma, cougar or mountain lion*', despite the fact that all three of these names belong to the same species of animal! And, in typical police fashion, a helicopter and twelve more policemen arrived on the scene to frighten off the animal.

There were between five and ten sightings of the Barnet prowler during the autumn months, and local inspectors claimed that the animal must have come from a private collection or been released on purpose, despite the nationwide sightings of similar animals.

By the 10th October 1998 the elusive yet harmless cat of Barnet had become known as the 'M25 Monster', and a report in the London press dated 31st October…yes, Halloween, described a '*Woman's Trauma Over Gruesome Cat Murder*':

'*A traumatised sixty-eight year old woman has warned pet owners to be extra vigilant after neighbours found her cat dumped in a garden with its head severed.*

Devastated pensioner Pamela Stockham of Caxton Road, Wimbledon, had been struggling to come to terms with the gruesome killing which happened sometime between October 15th and the 21st. Mrs Stockham first became worried when George – her pet of seven years – did not return to her house for twenty-four hours. The following day she targeted nearby roads with a leaflet campaign and put up posters in a bid to find her beloved cat. Just days later a neighbour in Garfield Road broke the news that George's body had been dumped in her garden. His head has not yet been found.

Mrs Stockham told *The Guardian*: '*I am still in absolute shock – I just can't believe it has happened. Who would do such a terrible thing? We know it's George's body because the description matches. He was black with white feet, tummy and neck and had white whiskers. I want to warn everybody who owns cats to be on their guard. The people who do these terrible things should be prosecuted – but right now I just want to kill them.*'

At the end of November *This Is Local London* claimed in an article that the strange cat killings had spread south, with ten rabbits also suffering the same fate as the many cats. Reports of dead cats circulated around Tottenham, Stepney and New Barnet when a dead cat was discovered on November 11th. Things then became even more serious when at the beginning of the December a psychiatrist was called in to draw up a profile of the London cat-ripper after claims that some forty animals had been slaughtered. A one-thousand pound reward was put up for the capture of the sadist but by December 19th 1998 someone or some 'thing' had struck again, this time in Twickenham, when an Eileen Tattershall lost her cat Bonkers. A neighbour found the dead cat, bereft of head and tail, but what was more sickening was how the RSPCA, during the April of 1999, attempted to solve the gory mystery. They claimed, after months of methodical and exhaustive research into the killings, that all of these deaths could be attributed to one killer – the car! An inspector told local press that post-mortems on the decapitated victims had proven that these poor animals had been killed on the road. Whilst other deaths could be attributed to scavengers such as foxes, dogs and even crows!

How the RSPCA came to such a conclusion is beyond me. Unless there are serial killing foxes, killer crows and knife-wielding dogs out there, I really couldn't, for the life of me, see how the victims could have their heads and tails removed, and the carcasses to be bereft of blood. And how a car manages this is also beyond me, and of course, what kind of car decapitates a domestic cat and then returns it to its home garden? The Met's wildlife liaison officer, Andy Fisher, also managed to come up with this classic statement: *"There has always been cats and there has always been traffic. What we don't know is why there has been a sudden increase in reports."* And what about the rabbits?

In the summer of '99 reporter Rob Bailey of the *Dartford Messenger* filed a sighting of a large cat in Orpington, at an area known as Badger's Mount. There had also been reports of large brown, as well as black, cats around Swanley, Darenth, up into Dartford and across in Sidcup where some of the domestic cat killings had taken place. All this was starting to take on a sinister yet familiar form. Was there really a twisted person out there severing the heads of domestic cats, or were these decapitations the work of a feline form? Or both?

Also, during this time, populations of cats across Kent, the outskirts of London, Sussex, Essex and Surrey were on the rise. A handful of large cats would soon become known as the Bluewater 'big cats', or as one newspaper dubbed them, the 'beasts' of Bean, whilst these territories would also cover Gravesend, in Kent, Sevenoaks, and further down in Tonbridge. All of a sudden it was difficult to monitor individual animals. There was an explosion to look at - a snowball effect that had been clouded by the media and their ability to confine certain cats to certain areas - when the fact of the matter was, there was an abundant population of varying species across the south.

On the 6th February 2001 a report was filed by the *Dartford Messenger* concerning a cat sighting near Bean, on the B255. A large animal leapt from a bank as Christine and Raymond Pearson approached in their vehicle. They described it as fawn in colour and around three feet long. However, sceptical Derek Gow of the *Herne Bay Wild Wood Discovery Park* stated, *"If there was a puma living in the local countryside there would be distinct signs, such as traces of their scent."*

What I found unusual about this statement was the fact that it exhibits such a disregard of the knowledge of the general public. People who see these animals are often unaware of what species of cat they are seeing, let alone the scent or signs they leave. For someone to be so dismissive on the grounds of lack of such obscure evidence is ridiculous.

On 17th August 2001 the cat beheadings hit the headlines again. For more than a year things had gone a little quiet, despite the fact that large cats were still being sighted at a record rate across the country, and many of these sightings had taken place in areas where domestic cats had previously been killed.

The head of a nineteen-year-old white cat was found in a back garden in Penge. Shortly after this incident the half-eaten remains of a Muntjac deer were found in the car park of the *South Bucks Star* offices, at High Wycombe. Was this a grisly prank? Well, judging by the state of the unfortunate victim, some large predator had feasted upon it over night and left the grisly, yet clean, remains behind. Trevor Smith, an animal expert who - coincidentally works alongside the CFZ on various projects - examined the carcass and told the press that, *"This is not the work of foxes. The animal's rib cage has been chewed off. It is very possible that this is the work of a big cat."*

According to Thames Valley Police a puma had been sighted at Wycombe Heights Golf Course just a fortnight previously. In 14th October 2001 *The Sunday Mirror* briefly covered a *'Puma On The Loose'* on the Hampshire-Surrey border. According to the report locals were blaming the disappearances of domestic cats on a large cat, thought to be a puma.

> *'Earlier this year (2002) whilst travelling on the M26 towards Surrey, about halfway along it, I was forced to slow down by slow moving traffic. I travel along this road every day to get to Surrey where I work. The position of the slow moving traffic was unusual as it starts to build up towards Junction 5, not at this particular spot. I slowly moved along until the traffic came to the cause of the delay.*
>
> *An animal had been hit and pieces of it were all over the road (all three lanes). I am used to seeing the bodies of dead animals on the roads of Kent. However, this was different. The animal seemed to have black fur. I immediately started thinking as to what it was. It was not a sheep or a fox. Not many things bother me like this did. It was a huge animal that had been hit, but I only caught a few seconds of the sight as I was forced to drive off.*
>
> *Do you know any information about this incident? I came to my own conclusion that it was a black cat.*
>
> *Thanks.*
>
> *Richard.'*

Little else seems to be known about this interesting incident. Although such events are few and far between they must surely happen on occasion. Smaller cats such as lynx and jungle cat have been picked up off the roads in Kent. In Brighton during the 1960s it was once reported that two or three black leopards caused a car accident as they casually strolled across a busy road one morning (see next chapter). However, many drivers who *do* hit animals such as these would probably drive off. Any cases that may have been reported would probably have been be cleared up by the RSPCA. Why this happens I am not sure. Do authorities fear mass hysteria from the public? In fact, would a press release by the authorities concerning the death of a 'big cat' be something akin to openly admitting that these 'mythical' animals do indeed exist? Would it be such a problem if these animals were accepted as part of a rural landscape? And if so, wouldn't that mean we could monitor them more closely rather than clandestinely investigate them? Unfortunately, the lack of official research and acknowledgment of these animals is far more baffling than the actual 'big cat' mystery itself!

Large tracks of a cat were found at the Wycombe Heights Golf Course in 2002, allegedly made by the animal known as the 'Bucks Beast'. More mutilated Muntjac deer were discovered in local forests and the press had a field day

> *'Is That Tiger Of Yours Licensed?'* – wrote the *Gravesend Messenger* on January 31st 2002.

'People who keep wild animals at home could face prosecution if they do not have license for them. The RSPCA is drafting new proposals calling for greater protection for captive wild animals.

The current law protects some, but not all potentially dangerous animals such as large constrictor snakes. Most owners do not apply for licenses, and escape annual inspections. Two years ago a poll found only thirty-four licenses in force in the south-east – far below the suspected actual number. Owners not aware of how to deal with and care for wild animals, could find them causing serious injury.'

Several reports of a large cat emerged from the Epping area, where geese were said to have been killed by a silent predator. Zoologist and friend Quentin Rose, at the time, examined a paw print found not far from Epping, but concluded it was made by a dog. The print simply looked large because it had been smudged in the mud. During the 1800s a coyote was found in the Epping area also, believed to have been released from a private collection that was imported via boat.

On the night of July 20th 2002, and again on August 1st, Bexley resident Stuart Campbell heard a strange scratching at his back door, which woke him. The man, who was a little concerned about the noises, and the safety of his three children, decided to contact the police and the RSPCA, but his call was never taken seriously. However, when he spotted a massive black cat in the Northumberland Heath area, his brother-in-law certainly took matters seriously because he'd seen it to. He described the animal has having shining eyes as he watched it from his bedroom window. The black intruder slinked around the garden in the darkness leaving the witnesses terrified.

Readers of the *News Shopper* in the Bexley area bombarded the news desk to report their own encounters with large, wild cats, with a majority describing a black animal, in contrast to the puma which was often reported in and around Surrey a few decades previous.

Bernice Fogherty saw an animal leap over a fence the previous year, at her home in Avenue Road, and there were also sightings in Erith and Eltham, as well as Welling and Belvedere.

A big, black cat was seen at Plumstead Common one month after Mr Campbell's sighting. Dave Loson watched the animal from the window of his flat as it prowled along Upton Road. He watched it for five minutes.

On 20th September 2002 the press asked, *'Is There A Richmond Beast?'* after a large paw print was found in a garden at East Sheen by Beverley Cooper, who contacted the *Twickenham Times*. Unfortunately, the print faded away before it could be verified. But, on the 25th it was alleged that the Plumstead 'panther' had been caught on film by Steve Gardiner who lives at Upton Road. According to the press this had been the sixth reported sighting in Woolwich and Bexley in just four weeks.

Mr Gardiner caught the cat on film as it strolled alongside his house. It was around 7:25 am when the witness watched the animal and was also aware that his security system had picked up the animal. Although the man described the animal as being around three feet long the image on the CCTV is nothing more than a hazy blob.

On 8th February 2003 a black cat, the size of a Labrador dog was sighted at Belvedere. Craig Lenney contacted me to say he'd watched the animal, from just seventy-metres away, cross the road, and head towards marshland at around 12:45 am. A few weeks later prints, which were claimed to have been made by a puma, were found and cast in the Crayford area. The prints measured over four inches wide and there were also sightings of a large, black animal at Princes Risborough.

The most unusual of all the reports to come from London and the surrounding areas emerged on 12th July 2003. Nick Allen, MSc FRAS, was staying at the *Tower Thistle Hotel*, next to Tower Bridge when he spied a strange cat from his window. The cat, according to Nick, was mooching around the taxi entrance to the hotel from the north end of London Bridge. He described the cat as, "...*over large, russet colour and had a brush on the end of its tail. It had very large and erect ears. I assumed it was an urban fox – but it wasn't – it was feline, far too big, and not canine in its behaviour.*"

"*What was odd,*" he added, "...*is that someone else thought it odd too. As it cowered in the undergrowth, a passing person noticed it and approached it. The animal ran off – and I saw the last of it as it ran away below past the restaurant window.*"

What was this extraordinary cat? Well, there is the possibility that Mr Allen had seen a lynx, as he never mentioned the tail being overly long. The brush could well have been the bobbed tail the lynx is known for, as well as the erect ears. The caracal (*C. caracal*), which are sometimes confused with the lynx, also have large, erect ears and are rust in colour, although the tail is longer and more slim. These beautiful felids are native to Africa and parts of Asia, and can reach up to around three feet in length. Another contender is the jungle cat (*Felis chaus*), also known as the 'swamp' or 'reed' cat, also native to Africa and Asia. The jungle cat, lynx and caracal could quite happily live in the U.K. The caracal and jungle cat, in their countries of origin, live on the fringes of human settlement, feeding off rats, birds, and mice, and can remain in these built-up areas without detection. The jungle cat is also able to breed with the domestic cat, and there have been many reports of animals resembling this cat across Britain, which makes for interesting hybrids. However, reports of the caracal are less common. Also, because these animals are smaller, monitoring sightings of them is nigh on impossible, which is why the animal seen near Tower Bridge has remained so elusive. And, until it is seen again, we'll never be able to put a true identity to it.

At the beginning of April, and certainly not a Fool's Day prank, the Bexley 'big cat' reared its head again. This time it was sixteen-year old Daniel Brown in Welling, who disturbed the creature as he let his own pet cat in through the back door. Daniel boldly shouted at the big, black cat that was squatting at the end of the garden and it leapt out of sight.

A year later residents of Barnehurst, in particular eighteen-year old Daniel Monck, and his sister Tracey, of Cheviot Close, were concerned about the animal. Rather oddly, the *News Shopper* said that Mr Monck described the animal as something akin to a large dog mixed with a sheep! The witness stated, "*It's too big to be an ordinary cat, it has a huge head and big paws and pointed ears.*"

The grandmother of Daniel, eighty-four year old Nell Hawes, also saw the animal and feared for her life around the time, and refused to go outside in case the creature was prowling around. Several neighbours reported that a large cat had been seen mooching around the dustbins and feeding off scraps.

On 20th of April a female witness, first name of Heather, saw a black leopard from her window. It was around 6:20 pm when something caught her eye rummaging around the undergrowth near the rail track nearby. The animal eventually slinked out of sight. The woman told me, "*I couldn't believe it when I saw the big cat. It wasn't the first time it had been seen in the area. My sister had seen it when she was visiting me about a year ago.*"

There are many sightings of large cats along railway lines, and there are several reasons for this. These animals use the lines for navigation, and many railway lines provide enough cover, especially at night, for a large cat to move from A to B in its territory. A lot of the sightings in built-up areas such as Bexley can be explained by the railroad theory. These lines often run along the back of gardens, so any large cat could lie up in a backyard over night after it has spent the evening hunting along the tracks. Also, there are many tracks in Britain which are not often used, or are maybe disused. Again, these animals can travel along these, and often remain out of view. We must also realise that the country is gradually being carved up by new land structures. Rail links are slicing their way through the countryside to enable easier ways of commuting, and many sightings do involve commuters who are gazing from their window admiring the countryside. The abundance of food along railway lines is also a major factor as to why these large cats roam there. Foxes, mice, rats, and rabbits provide a mini restaurant for the felids which stalk the rails.

During the early summer of 2004 several sightings emerged, from the Fawkham area, of a large black cat. One motorist observed a well-built melanistic leopard holding a rabbit in its mouth, and on Tuesday 29th June Mr Barton, driving on the M25 from Dartford to Swanley saw a large black animal walking across open fields towards a motor cross area. The one detail that caught Mr Barton's eye was the length of the animal's tail.

At 11 pm on the 12th July 2004 a witness encountered a puma in Bexley. The eye witness made a statement:

"I came out of an alley from Heath Road leading to Cold Blow Crescent and was faced with something sitting next to my car. At first I thought it was a fox, but when I approached it got up to move on and it looked like a big cat. It walked off up my neighbours drive, stopped and turned its head to look at me. When it saw I was still coming (I was walking up my footpath to my front door), it went to the next drive and again turned and stared. I looked at it for a good five minutes without either of us moving.

It definitely went up the drive it was standing on and through the gate which had been left open. I see a lot of foxes in Bexley and this definitely was not a fox. It didn't walk like a fox, it walked in a feline manner and was a sandy kind of colour – possibly a bit darker on the back. It was approximately three-foot long, not including the tail and when it was standing next to my car, its head was about level with the bottom of the window. Its face was quite wide. I didn't notice spots or stripes on it, but it was a little dark. I've had a quick look on the internet and it looks a bit like a lynx, especially the face, or it was something very similar."

This appears to describe a puma as there was no mention of a shorter tail, which the lynx has.
A Leatherhead resident claimed to have photographed a large brown cat which the press connected to sightings of the Surrey puma. Bruce Burgess, aged sixty, was surveying sites for an artificial lake, around Brook Willow Farm, Woodlands Road, when he snapped something in the distance near low branches. However, like so many other photographs of alleged big cats, this one also proved to be too fuzzy to determine what exactly was in the frame.

During October of 2004, albeit at Halstead, in Sevenoaks, a woman found her pet cat decapitated and bereft of its tail. The poor victim also had a large bite mark on its back. The shocked woman found her cat in her courtyard on the 26th at 8 am. Such a find merely added fuel to the fire that something more than a sinister human was around slicing and dicing moggies. Many fingers pointed to the so-called Otford 'panther', a large black cat seen for the last twenty or so years around Sevenoaks, although sightings date back almost a century.

The spring of 2005 kicked off with one of the most remarkable big cat stories ever to grace the pages of any newspaper. Anthony Holder claimed that he was attacked by a big, black cat during the early hours of 22nd March, whilst in his garden at Sydenham, a few miles from Penge. The witness claimed he was looking for his crying kitten at the bottom of his garden, which backs on to a patch of woodland, when the six-foot long predator leapt upon him. He told the press, *"All of a sudden I see this big black thing pouncing at me, knocked me flying. I just didn't know where I was, and the next thing there was this big black figure laying on my chest."*

Mr Holder, a father of three, allegedly suffered cuts and bruises after his encounter and was treated by paramedics. After the incident he ran indoors and 'phoned the police, but when they arrived at the scene there was no sign of the mystery attacker. Tony added, *"I could see these huge teeth and the whites of its eyes just inches from my face. It was snarling and growling and I really believe it was trying to do some serious damage. I tried to get it off but I couldn't move it, it was heavier than me. I was scared. I really thought my life was in danger but all I was worried about was my family. It was an absolute nightmare."*

Ashleigh, the fourteen-year old daughter of Mr Holder, claimed she had seen her father being attacked by the animal, and a local painter and decorator, Billy Rich, believed he saw the animal that afternoon, and a handful of other witnesses came forward to report possible sightings.

The Daily Mirror reported that the attacker sank its claws into Mr Holder's fingers and also swiped at his face, although no marks consistent with that of a leopard attack seemed evident.

As per usual a degree of hysteria boiled in the local community, with Sydenham Girls School closing, and police warning residents to stay indoors. *The Daily Mail* of Wednesday 23rd March 2005 claimed that, 'As Mr Holder was being treated by an ambulance crew in the street, he says he saw the beast again. "It was strolling past the back of the ambulance as if it didn't have a care in the world"*, said Tony.

Reports from the time seem inconsistent and several statements seem confused and the evidence does not add up to the possibility of an attack by a large cat. Whilst a cat, such as a leopard, may feel threatened if cornered, I do not see any reason to suggest that the witness was, in fact, attacked. Sightings have rarely come from Sydenham, and the injuries Mr Holder sustained are not consistent with marks that would be left by a leopard attack. The injuries were a 'bitten' finger, one minor five-inch scratch to the face and a cut wrist. Such an animal has extremely large and sharp claws which would lacerate deeply even if the swipe was merely to threaten rather than kill. Also, Mr Holder mentioned seeing the, *"...whites of the animal's eyes."* This is not consistent with the eye colouration of a leopard, which is more green-yellow when reflected in light, unless of course he was merely speaking figuratively. Even more dramatically, the police arrived on the scene in the form of an armed response unit armed with tasers, but failed to find the animal.

We can compare such an incident with the case of the South Harrow puma, which was owned by a local man in 1974 that often walked his prized pet through the local streets. However, on one occasion, during the November of '74, things got out of control. The owner in question casually strolled into the *Farm House* pub with his puma on a lead. After a short while several locals began to feel uncomfortable in the presence of the wild animal, and so the man was asked to leave. Although he complied with the requests of the staff and customers, the beast didn't, and - in turn - went berserk. The landlady at the time commented that, *"It took the man fifteen minutes to get the puma out of the pub and into his car, during which it tore off the man's glove and ripped open his hand"*. This was after it had caused severe damage to the chair upholstery in the public house, as well as damaging tables, smashing glasses and demolishing the bar in its frenzy. Then, the cat decided to shred the car seats, and the police were called to the scene where, after a short time, they towed both the vehicle and the aggravated felid away. Later, the man was charged with being drunk and incapable. But what happened to his cat?

In 1975 MP Peter Templemore claimed that, "*Someone sooner or later will get killed*", in response to a strange incident at Acton in London where an estranged husband dumped his puma in the back garden of his former home, with his wife and kids trapped inside the house screaming for help. The man left a note saying that he had nowhere else to put the cat, and it took the local police and RSPCA two hours to get the terrified family out of the house.

So, if Mr Holder really was attacked by a cat capable of shredding wood, smashing glasses, tearing car seat leather etc, etc, where were his injuries? Compare this also to cougar attacks in America, where people have been killed, and the same can be said for victims in Africa with reference to leopard attacks.

On 21st March 2005 a woman also saw a black leopard, this time in Sidcup. She was putting some washing out at around lunchtime when her garden fence began moving and she saw something black leap up. She phoned the RSPCA who took her details, but never seemed to follow the report up.

In 2002 a Gravesend man claimed he was slashed across the hand by a lynx after he disturbed it near his home. The cat was carrying a rabbit in his mouth and witness, Mr Cole, attempted to approach the animal, which at first he took to be a fox, in turn receiving a nasty set of scratch marks across his hand. Even this encounter at the time was treated with scepticism by some researchers, but the injuries Mr Cole sustained were far more horrific and in common with a 'big cat' attack than Mr Holder's. Mr Cole never blamed the attack on the animal, but instead stated he pretty much deserved it, the animal was merely retaliating after it felt threatened.

Borehamwood had a minor cat-flap during early April 2005 when several animal remains were found in fields near Berwick Road. The carcass of a swan was found by a six-year old boy, and his mother also claimed that various other animals had been discovered, half-eaten, as well as large paw prints. Chickens, ducks and foxes had allegedly been slain in the vicinity sparking rumours that a leopard or puma had been prowling around the neighbourhood. At the time sceptics claimed that the swan death may have been due to the power lines in the area, and that the poor bird had struck one of these whilst in flight. However, the other grisly remains discovered in the area seemed to suggest some kind of 'killing machine' was haunting the undergrowth.

Meanwhile, at Eltham around the same time, a devoured fox was found in the back garden of Laura Downes, who lives at Westmount Road. When she first went into her garden she found a dead fox which she didn't think was anything unusual, but one hour later when she returned, the fox had been stripped clean. The following day another eaten fox turned up, this time covered in maggots, suggesting this carcass was older. The terrified woman called the local Wildlife Officer who stated, "*It was horrendous. Whatever did that to the first fox did a good job. I've never seen anything like it. I was scared.*"

A female witness named Vicky saw a melanistic leopard in Ewell, Surrey, on 16th April 2005. She and her housemate were staring out of their kitchen window when something black caught their eye down the bottom of the garden. The animal had a feline gait and was as big as a medium-sized dog. The cat then disappeared into the neighbour's garden.

In May, one of the Surrey felids was caught on film at Winkworth Arboretum by Harry Fowler of Guilford. He shot the footage near Godalming two weeks after there was a report of a similar cat in a tree at Whitmoor Common. The cat on the film was pointed out to Mr Fowler by a female witness who spotted it near the boathouse at Phillmore Lake. The cat in the video is a rusty brown colour and roughly the height of an Alsatian dog. *Surrey Wildlife Trust* manager believed the animal in the film was a lynx, although it could also be a puma.

Shortly after the video footage was taken of the mystery cat, many Surrey residents called the press to report their sightings. Proof then that the Surrey puma and friends were still healthy, despite a decrease in Surrey sightings since the original flap. These current populations suggest that twenty to thirty years ago large cats such as the puma were indeed breeding, and there is also the small possibility that some cats are still being let go into the countryside to add to the already growing number.

Winchester's Marwell Zoo liaison officer Bill Hall commented, " *Personally I believe there may be a big cat somewhere but not leopards, and definitely not black ones.*" A very strange, almost amateurish view from a zoo officer! He continued however that, "*...I am quietly confident that a puma could survive.*" Whilst filming a programme in 2001, a Marwell zoo keeper also dismissed the possibility that leopards were in the wilds, claiming there'd be more signs of them. Naturally, his 'expertise' was required, but proved to be inaccurate. Those who look after large cats in zoo parks are not always qualified to say what's roaming the country; it's certainly a separate issue from their own level of expertise which often falters when commenting on sightings of large cats in the local wilds.

Mr Hall went on say, "*We get calls from people saying a big black animal jumped in front of the lights of their car, what do we think it was, and I say it was probably a Labrador dog.*" In my opinion, such a statement is a joke. Most witnesses know when they've seen a big black leopard, and I can't see why there would be an abundant population of stray, yet very uncharacteristically elusive black Labradors roaming the countryside. Mr Hall accepts that the puma could survive in Britain, but not the leopard despite the fact that menageries, and also private collections, housed both species of cat in equal measure, during the Victorian period and previously, up until today.

The 'beast' of Bexley was seen again in the May of 2005 by care worker Jim Hornby who works near Bexleyheath Broadway. At around 11 pm one night, whilst talking to his supervisor, something black caught his eye. A cat-like animal was creeping along on its belly near to Jim's car, as if it was stalking. The cat also seems to have left a calling card, a huge paw print which Mr Hornby discovered in a sandy area in the garden. The print measured five inches across.

I was contacted by nursing officer Nicole Webb regarding the sighting and the details she gave me were far more in-depth. She told me the following, "*Whilst on duty during May '05 I was stood talking to staff by an open door and saw what looked like a man on his hands and knees. We get a few intruders at the site, so myself and Jim went outside to tackle him. Jim was side on and I was behind what we quickly realised wasn't human. Our bowels emptied quicker than an enema could manage! All I saw was the back end, haunches and hockey-stick tail. A six-foot fence was cleared and it was gone. Jim's view was no better. He is a regular visitor, and we've heard him crashing out of a tree on to the roof of the mini-bus, leaving a big dent in the roof. We've witnessed the trees shaking violently on the most still of nights.*"

Surrey Advertiser 23rd May 2005:
'Comment – Is The Surrey Puma On The Prowl Again?'

Tales of unidentified animals roaming parts of Britain are not unusual - definitive proof of the existence of the Beast of Bodmin Moor and the Loch Ness Monster has been sought for years. While not having an enormous international profile, tales of the Surrey puma have become a local legend.

Our first recorded instance of a big cat sighting was more than 40 years ago when a Munstead workman, George Wisdom, saw a golden brown animal of around three to five feet in length while he was black-berrying one lunchtime. Plaster casts taken of the paw prints were said to be those of a 'large member of the cat family'. Sightings continued through-out the sixties, prompting headlines such as, "Puma could solve deer problem", "A plane may hunt the puma", "Green-keeper meets puma on the second tee" and the brilliant, "I trod on puma's tail - and hit its nose".

The story appeared to capture the imagination of Advertiser readers, as the many letters in its archives show. Photos of the beast started to appear as well, some blatantly domes-tic cats, others barely visible.Sightings in the 70s were few and far between compared to the preceding decade, and the paper even received this letter: "Sir-I am feeling horribly neglected; couldn't someone see me again soon? -Yours, etc. The Surrey Puma".

The 1980s were a non-event for the big cat, just like it was for the rest of us, and only a handful of stories made it into the paper. The '90s marked a glorious return, and pictures and sightings dotted the decade.After a short lull the beast has returned, and the myth lives on. One question though. No-one has claimed there is a breeding pair, how long do these cats live?

On 21st June 2005 the Bexley *News Shopper* reported another cat sighting, this time at CorralineWalk, Thamesmead. Belinda Bull was looking out of her living room window at around 9:30 pm, the previous week, when she spotted a large animal around some dustbins. Although she described the animal as hav-ing a massive head, big paws and a long tail, no description of colour was given.

A month after the sighting a fifteen-year old male from Farnham Road, Welling, saw a large cat whilst on his way home from a friend's house. It was around 10:00 pm on July 12th when he heard a rustling sound in the nearby bushes. As he strolled by he glimpsed a black cat in the undergrowth behind a metal fence. The witness called the police who followed up the report.

This Is Local London asked, '*Is A Panther Loose In Harpenden?*' after a sighting of a large cat on Octo-ber 3rd 2005. A woman walking her dog on Bower Heath Lane reported her sighting of, what the website claimed was a puma, to the police. A security firm in Hertfordshire believed they had caught the animal on CCTV in September although what became of this footage I do not know.

2006 was only eleven days old, when the press reported an early January encounter involving dog-walker John Costin who spotted a large cat at Churchfield Woods, in Bexley Village. The man was with his dog Mickey, when he observed an animal in long grass not far away. The cat, which he never got a clear look of, seemed to have a tortoiseshell pattern to its coat, and measured only around two feet at the most, from nose to rear. John never got a look at its tail but the animal seemed very wild, and he believed it must have been a lynx or a bobcat, which is slightly stockier than the lynx with a rust coat. However, the re-port of the animal didn't seem to be consistent with any other cat sightings, so the jury is still out on the matter.

One month after the strange cat sighting at Churchfield Woods, a *News Shopper* reader, Ms Cashnella, came forward to file a report of an animal which she saw some time during 2004. Her interesting letter read as follows:

'I too was a non-believer until I saw this cat for myself. Around two-and-a-half years ago I had a mare who was ready for foal and I went to check on her about 11:30 pm.

My horses are kept on Southmere Park, or, as some might know it, Erith Marshes.

There it was, stalking through the reed bed. It was about two feet in length and about eighteen inches high. I searched the internet to see if I could find out what I had seen and there it was, a jaguarundi. These cats come from South America and live in habitats ranging from semi-acrid scrubland to swamps. Its main prey are birds, rodents, rabbits and reptiles. Hence there is no savaging of domestic or wild animals or humans.

These cats can range from black to pale grey-brown or red in colour. They are about thirty-three inches long and weigh around ten to twenty pounds.'

This sighting was extremely intriguing, and certainly could've explained some reports of unusual cats around London. In fact, there are many eye witness reports nationwide which often remain inconsistent with the usual leopard, puma and lynx sightings, and this is because there are other, smaller species out there. Caracal, ocelot, and even jaguarundi reports do exist. Some of these cats may be individuals that have escaped from private collections or zoo parks, and a majority of times they are sighted, witnesses may well not know exactly what they have seen, unless they are quick to act like Ms Cashnella, who identified her marshland stalker via the internet.

Britain is a perfect habitat for a majority of large cats, and the smaller cats are even less likely to be seen. In fact, animals such as lynx can remain undetected for many years. We just do not know what cats are roaming our back yards at night, the variety really is surprising. The jaguarundi (*Puma yagouaroundi*) however, despite the Erith Marshes report, most certainly isn't the cat behind most of the sightings, because quite clearly it isn't a big enough animal. So, once again we go back to the puma and the melanistic leopard.

On 15th February *This Is Local London* claimed that the elusive 'beast' of Bexley had finally been photographed. Debbie Marshall of Crombie Road, Sidcup, snapped an animal whilst she was looking out of her bedroom window the previous weekend. A black animal lying in the grass caught her eye, so she reached for her digital camera, and took a photo as the animal mooched around the field. Unfortunately, despite a good description of the animal, the photograph is once again dubious, although most certainly shows a black object in the long grass quite a distance away, which Mrs Marshall estimated at around one-hundred feet. The photograph, which appeared in numerous newspapers over the course of a few days, appears to show the head and big shoulders of a black leopard skulking beyond the trees. This seems promising, although some sceptics argued that the image could be anything from a domestic cat to a black sack. Mrs Marshall claimed that her neighbour's pet cat was also in the field, yet looked around seven times smaller than the animal she'd photographed. However, despite the excitement of the witnesses, which included Mrs Marshall's three children, the photo has once again been filed alongside so many other 'big cat' pictures labelled under the 'maybe' category.

On May 30th 2006 *IC South London* reported on the '*Man To Keep Leopards In Back Garden*', with an exclusive report by Richard Porritt. The story concerned a Mr Todd Dalton, known locally as the Leopard Man of Peckham, due to his leopard mini-sanctuary which he'd constructed in his back garden. However, the man faced much fear and loathing from neighbours who believed that his animals were a threat to youngsters and so a ban was imposed, preventing him from keeping such animals. Mr Dalton, however, paid up to twenty-five thousand pounds to contest the decision and in May his ban was overturned after he dragged Southwark council through the courts.

Reporter Richard Porritt stated: '*After the hearing at Tower Bridge Magistrates' Court, Todd told the South London press he was, "...delighted", but the action had left him broke. "This appeal has cost me twenty-five thousand pounds and I am not applying for costs because I do not think the taxpayers should have to pay", said the internet entrepreneur.'*

According to the website, Mr Dalton had built large cages in his garden to house the leopards but councillors refused him permission to keep the animals despite the go-ahead from police and vets, and also working in compliance with the Dangerous Wild Animals Act.

On 11th June 2006 Clara Story, for *This Is Local London,* reported that another domestic cat had been found without its tail, this time in New Maiden, south-west London. At the same time, I received several reports from rural Maidstone of many domestic cats missing. One woman found the head of her pet cat on her patio one morning, a grisly find which befell another Maidstone resident some four years previously. Both witnesses had heard deep growling and a heavy rustling in the bushes the previous night.

The attack on the domestic cat in New Maiden was once again blamed on a knife-wielding psychopath due to the cleanliness of the wound. The poor cat probably died of a heart attack.

So, large sandy-coloured cats roaming Bexley, black 'panthers' slinking through back gardens of Sydenham, and large eared felids mooching through the capital. Just how did they get there? Well, the most common theory, which you'll read much about in this book, does concern exotics purchased during the mid 20th Century which may have been released during the 1960s and '70s, and after. Could cats obtained and then released after the introduction of the Dangerous Wild Animals Act be responsible for the populations of today? Partly, but not fully. This is no modern mystery, but the fact that you could buy a large, exotic cat from a London store such as Harrods, not many decades ago, does lay the blame to some extent on exotic purchases during a period when your average novelty pet usually came in the form of a slinking, shiny black leopard via the local pet shop or trader newspaper. To some, these animals would have made great fashion accessories, whilst to others these animals would have been great 'guard dogs', and maybe even sweet pets. But there would have been those who could not have handled such cats, and certainly when the 1976 Act was passed, the license fees would also have proven too hard to swallow, and so quite a few cats must have been released into the wild. There's no way that every cat purchased would have been found a home in a local zoo, and I'm pretty convinced that a number of zoos would have turned quite a few owners away - maybe hundreds - as they flocked to the gates to bid farewell to their beloved pets. There is also the possibility, and as shown by the capture of the Barnet lynx, that wild cats are still easily obtainable today. Whilst those which are kept legally are monitored by local councils, there are still those people out there intent on keeping exotic animals in makeshift pens, which are not always adequate enough to house an animal for that long. I'm aware that very recently two female pumas and a lynx were released locally into an area that I will not mention here.

In 2007 I received a bizarre email from Marie Jones of Luton, Bedfordshire in which she wrote:

> *'On Sunday (December 11th) late around after midnight while returning from Bedford via the A6, I saw what I think was a tall, slim woman all in black, duffle coat and black boots with big fur hood crossing the road very quickly, and with her was what I am certain was a panther. This was where the turning of Sundon Park junction and church is, on the bend. Just after the Sundon turning is. The woman was in the rain going to the quarry area. She had something big in a carrier bag with her. I see her squeeze through the railings hurriedly, and the cat followed squeezing under the gate!*
>
> *The cat seemed very tame like a domestic cat would be. It walked very close to her all the time, almost to her thigh all the time. It was not possible to see her face as she had her hood up. It definitely was NOT a dog and NO I had not been drinking either.*
>
> *It was definitely a big cat around four feet long, nose to tail about the size of a big dog like maybe a Labrador in size, with a very long tail and short legs, stocky body, the ani-*

mal had pricked up ears, and moved in a feline slinky manner rather than like a dog does. Both moved very quickly across the road from the field opposite. I was so amazed I drove up to the quarry gates to see a bit more, but the woman and the cat had vanished as if into thin air! It was all very odd.

There is a track going off to the right beyond the gates and it was very dark so I was not able to see if they went there. I looked on the ground and there were huge pug marks in the wet earth, the prints were unlike a dog in that they had no nail mark in the print. A real life enigma...who was this? And what on Earth was that cat?'

A fascinating story, if true. The witness certainly seemed adamant that the woman had a cat with her, although no mention was made of it being on a lead. Was the mystery woman simply taking her pet 'panther' on a midnight stroll, or freeing the animal in the local woods? We'll probably never get to the bottom of the story, but if Marie honestly saw a woman with a black leopard, then it's merely proof that such an animal can still be obtained.

The negative side to the theory that the animals which roam today are offspring of animals released in the '60s, is that there'd surely be more sightings? Well, in reality there *are* hundreds of sightings which each year make their way to the press, the police, local researchers and zoo parks, and there must be almost as many sightings which go unreported. However, sightings of normal leopards hardly exist, so this factor could point to the swinging 1960s fashion trend of having the customary black leopard on one's arm, as well as the occasional puma and other smaller cats. There may also have been a few people who owned cats that weren't quite as knowledgeable, and were unsure as to what they were looking after. A cat such as the golden cat can also have a dark coat, but someone may well have purchased one thinking it was in fact a black leopard. We can see by many modern reports that many people *still* aren't sure of the difference between a puma and a 'panther', so who knows what kind of cats were being obtained? The '60s and the influx of exotic cats as pets certainly goes a long way to explaining the modern sightings, but it's not the full answer.

For me though, the strongest theories to explain as to why these animals exist today concerns the Romans and also travelling menageries, for how else can we explain these brief reports of a Surrey mystery animal and others, as reported in Charles Fort's important 1931 book *Lo!* in which he writes, '*In the Daily Mail, March 19, is an account of an extraordinary killing of sheep, 'by dogs' near Guildford (Surrey)...fifty-one sheep were killed in one night. A woman in a field – something grabbed her. At first the story was of a marauding panther that must have escaped from a menagerie.*'

There is also rumour of a large, black beast from the year 940, which was said to have haunted Flixton in Yorkshire. Some claimed the creature was conjured during a dark ritual, and its gory rampage included humans as well as livestock and dogs. Later, in 1455, Percival Cresacre was killed by a mysterious felid at St Peter's Church in Bamburgh, South Yorkshire. The unfortunate victim was riding horseback through the woods when a ferocious cat leapt on him from a tree and clawed him to death. The horse took off leaving the man to fend for himself but the cat clung to his back, injuring him severely. The man was found next day, weak and bloody, by the church porch and died later. The Cresacre family, it is said, have a tiger-like cat on the family arms and also on the tomb. Some have suggested the felid is a wildcat, or 'wood-cat' as the animal was called at the time, but it seems unlikely that the wildcat, resident of Scotland now, would have weakened a man to the extent of death, despite its vicious nature. It seems more likely that Mr. Cresacre was attacked by a leopard or lynx, which was lying up in a tree. Gamekeepers and hunters killed the English wildcat prior to World War I, but in Scotland the animal remains. In his superb book *Mystery Cats Of The World (Hale 1989)*, Karl Shuker describes the felid as follows, '*The background colour of a pure-bred British specimen's pelage is buff-grey marked with several verti-*

cal stripes running down from the dark dorsal stripe to the belly. The limbs are also traversely striped, and the black-tipped tail is encircled by a number of rings (of which at least the last two or three are complete). Its forehead bears four or five longitudinal stripes running down to the neck's nap, where they converge to form the dorsal line. The wildcat can be distinguished from most (but not all) domestic tabbies by its absence of blotched markings. Generally, the wildcat is about a third larger in overall size than a domestic, its head broader, its teeth larger, its body stouter, its limbs longer and its tail shorter.' The wildcat has never been indigenous to Ireland but sightings occur, as well as in England still, many years after it was allegedly wiped out.

On January 14th 2008 the *TimesOnline* reported:

> *'Wildcats may terrorise woods again with breed-to-release project',* commenting – *'Wildcats may rule the woods once more from Land's End to John o'Groats as part of a scheme to secure the future of the endangered animals.*

> *Only a few hundred are thought to survive in the wild in Scotland, but there are hopes that captive animals will be released within five years. The project, led by the Aspinall Foundation, is designed to boost numbers by restocking thinly populated areas and returning wildcats to areas from which they have disappeared.*

> *Reintroductions are likely to begin in Scotland but conservationists hope to bring them back eventually to parts of England and Wales where they could be found until the 18th century. Scottish wildcats are Britain's only remaining native felids since the lynx vanished about 1,500 years ago. Some experts believe that loss of habitat, persecution and crossbreeding with the domestic cat,* Felis catus, *will cause the animal to die out within a decade. A survey into Scottish wildcat numbers has been launched this month by Scottish Natural Heritage. The public are urged to report all sightings of the cats, their tracks and any other indications of their whereabouts. Scottish wildcats,* Felis sylvestris grampia, *are a subspecies of the European wildcat,* Felis sylvestris, *but their fate is in doubt. Interbreeding with domestic cats has made it difficult to know whether conservation would protect the wildcat or a crossbreed.*

> *Research into cat genetics last year identified a DNA marker that, combined with analysis of coat markings, lets scientists distinguish between 'pure' and 'tainted' wildcats. SNH plans to use it to establish how badly wildcats have been contaminated by crossbreeding and how many are left. The Aspinall Foundation, which runs Howletts and Port Lympne zoos in Kent, has a male and female Scottish wildcat proved to be free of domestic cat DNA. This pair, with others bred by private collectors, will play a key role in breeding kittens suitable for reintroduction to the wild.*

> *Amos Courage, zoo director, said: "What we are trying to do is help fund a programme to run genetic tests on the wild population. There are about 400 in Scotland but there are still questions whether they are purebred."*

The legend of Black Annis may also play an important part regarding sightings of early mystery cats. This particular fiendish felid was considered supernatural at the time, during the eighteenth century, but the habits it displayed seem now to point to a black leopard. Black Annis was said to have prowled the Dane Hills of Leicestershire, and was born from an obscure poem which also concerned an old hag character that inhabited a dank cave. Annis was said to have leapt on to victims whilst hiding in trees and sink teeth and claws into the flesh of prey. Indeed, from such poems and legends we can see how such animals have faded into myth and the realm of ghosts. (See chapter, *The Others.*)

In most cases, a large cat such as a leopard would only take one sheep to eat over the course of a couple of days, administering a throat bite to bring the animal down, and at times dislocating the neck. No other animal in the British Isles kills like a leopard or a puma, but there are enough rabbits and other small prey, so an animal such as a leopard will not often expel energy on a large ewe unless very necessary. These animals are stealthy hunters which devour the innards of large animals such as sheep. Prey will often be stripped and stashed high up in trees. Numerous reports from Bodmin during 1982 involving eaten sheep, described how the flanks and shoulders of the victim had been torn away, and the flesh rasped clean. However, even if a cat had young with it, it seems unlikely that even to train its offspring, that the 'family' would injure let alone kill so many of a flock.

Dogs are certainly the most likely candidate for such attacks as they nip and tear aggressively and randomly, and not to eat, but out of sheer spite. However, some time during the 1920s, a mystery killer was attacking sheep and goats in Inverness-shire in Scotland. During the flap of attacks, where many prints were found in the heavy bogs, farmers described the predator as large, fierce, and yellow in colour. One strange attacker was shot at, and described as a large cat. Another, also a large cat was caught in a trap. These animals were identified by London Zoo as lynx.

Over one-hundred years previously a creature that become known as the 'Girt Dog of Ennerdale', in Cumberland was terrorising sheep on the England/Scotland border. The critter was killing all prey with a throat bite and draining the carcass of blood. A dog that was shot in the area convinced few that the killings would stop, for they believed that something far larger and more efficient was at large, like a lion. No-one at the time ever reported a barking creature, but something more akin to a felid but at times, striped. Similar sheep kills were also occurring in parts of Ireland around the 1870s, at Gravesend in Kent in 1905 and in Gloucestershire during the same year. The press identified this particular animal as a jackal.

In the following year the *Daily Mail* reported that some vicious animal sighted near Windsor Castle, in Berkshire, had bitten almost a dozen of the King's sheep, all of which had to be destroyed. On October 14th 1925 the *Daily Express* reported on a big, black creature stalking the night in the district of Edale, Derbyshire. This silent hunter left a trail of corpses in its bloody wake, much of these having heads and legs ripped off. Despite several hunts for the killer, nothing was ever flushed out of the undergrowth. The same could also be said for an unidentified back-breaking phantom which haunted Llanelli, in Wales during 1919. This particular prowler killed many rabbits but never ate them. It simply left piles of poor, broken bunnies. Meanwhile, in 1939 two ghost hunters visited the eerie Borley Rectory on the Essex/Suffolk border which at the time was a ruin, due to a bad fire. When they entered a room upstairs they were confronted by a big, black creature squatting in the corner that gave off an evil menace. One of the witnesses, author James Wentworth Day drew a weapon to shoot the beast, but was prevented by his colleague. Then, when the pair strolled through the orchard, a large, dark cat-like animal sped passed them into the black of night.

So, where did these mystery maulers come from? The scimitar cat became extinct more than five-hundred thousand years ago, the cave lion died out in the United Kingdom some fifty-thousand years ago, and the last leopards to inhabit Britain died out some twelve-thousand years ago during the last Ice Age, so such beasts most certainly are not survivors from then. The puma meanwhile has never been a species indigenous to Britain, although *Puma pardoides* a long-extinct relative of the puma *did* live here during the Pliocene and Pleistocene.

Whilst Great Britain once sustained a variety of species of felid, only the wildcat, allegedly confined to

Scotland now, survives.

A basic timeline of events shows that Julius Caesar headed the first invasion in 55 BC, but withdrew his advances. A century later the Romans invaded again in AD 43 under the reign of Claudius, when they landed at Richborough, in Kent, where the remains of an amphitheatre exist. Before their invasion towns such as London did not exist. It was they who founded it, in AD 50, calling it Londinium. An amphitheatre was discovered in the city in 1988 and is now open to the public. Other amphitheatre remains can be found at Chester, Colchester and Gloucestershire, namely Cirencester, formerly the Roman town of Corinium, which is Roman Britain's largest amphitheatre. The Romans conquered Wales (there is an amphitheatre at Caerleon, Gwent), the north in AD 70, and Scotland in AD 140, where an amphitheatre is situated at Inveresk, Edinburgh. They did not withdraw from Britain until AD 401. During this time however, they had the amphitheatre, their centre of entertainment - a bit like television is for much of today's general public on a Saturday evening!

In these amphitheatres, Roman citizens would flock to watch gladiators fight wild animals such as bears, lions, and leopards. Often, the fighters who took on the beasts were slaves or criminals being punished for their crimes. In many cases, these gladiators would die at the paws of an animal such as a big cat. Such a spectacle may well have influenced the more modern travelling menageries, where strange and exotic species were brought from remote regions in order to attract the curious public.

The sheer gore of a Roman gladiator battling it out with a starving leopard would have provided entertainment to thousands of roaring citizens. The volume of animals used in such battles is quite incredible and many would have been slaughtered in the most barbaric of fashion. The *Endangered Species Handbook* writes:

> 'The tradition of killing animals for pleasure has a long history in Asia and Europe. So popular was hunting in ancient Rome that mosaics and paintings often depicted this pastime as a heroic activity. Slaughtering animals was considered a form of entertainment, and people scoured the countryside for bears, lions, stags and boars to pursue with spears and dogs (Attenborough 1987). As the Roman Empire grew to encompass the entire Mediterranean basin, its citizens travelled throughout the region to hunt and bring back animals to be killed in primitive contests in the coliseums of Rome and other cities. The coliseum games continued for more than 400 years in more than 70 amphitheatres, the largest seating up to 50,000 people on stone benches arranged around a central arena (Attenborough 1987).*

> *Roman emperors carried favour with the public by upstaging their predecessors in killing more animals and producing more spectacular displays of slaughter (Morris 1990). Emperor Titus inaugurated the Roman Coliseum by declaring 100 days of celebration, during which enormous numbers of animals were speared by gladiators. On the opening day, 5,000 animals were slaughtered, and over the next two days, 3,000 more were killed (Morris 1990). The caged animals were kept underground in dungeons where they were not fed, and on the day of the festival, they were hauled in their cages onto lifts that brought them into the centre of the arena. As the crowd roared with excitement, drums were beaten, trumpets blown, and the terrified animals were set loose (Attenborough 1987). Sometimes the animals were goaded to attack one another, and at other times, men armed with spears and tridents pursued them around barriers made from shrubs in imitation of hunts in the wild (Attenborough 1987). One arena hunt resulted in the killing of 300 Ostriches and 200 Alpine Chamois (Morris 1990).*

Lions, tigers, bears, bulls, leopards, giraffes and deer died after being tormented, stabbed and gored (Morris 1990). *Big cats that had been starved were released into the ring where a human slave or prisoner of war was lashed to a post; the animals clawed at the person before they themselves were speared and stabbed by gladiators* (Attenborough 1987). *In some of the larger slaughters, 500 lions, more than 400 leopards, or 100 bears would be killed in a single day* (Morris 1990). *Hippos, even rhinoceroses and crocodiles, were brought into these arenas, and sometimes gladiators employed bizarre methods of killing such as decapitating fleeing ostriches with crescent-shaped arrows* (Morris 1990).

The Roman audiences cheered these brutal slaughters enthusiastically as a rule, but when 20 elephants were pitted against heavily armed warriors, the screaming of these gentle animals as they were wounded caused the crowd to boo the emperor for his cruelty (Morris 1990). *This did not stop their use in the games however. These slaughters virtually eliminated large mammals from the Mediterranean area.'*

Many animals were imported to Britain for the pleasure of the grisly arena battles. This shipping industry was a huge operation, with some animals being obtained from the west of India. Such wild animals were considered to be special gifts which many a barbarian monarch would offer to his overlord. In Sicily, close to the village of Armerina there exists a fresco – mural painting – showing trapping devices used to capture and crate wild animals for export. Animals such as leopards would also be caught in nets dropped from trees, and third century poet Oppian even spoke of leopards being drugged by strong wine leaked into waterholes to enable capture.

By the fourth century the attraction of the amphitheatre died out, after the adoption of Christianity which became the official religion of the Roman empire. The long production line of imported animals also dried up, and the public gradually became repulsed by the bloody battles.

If, as the facts state, the Romans imported large cats in such abundance, what are the possibilities of escapees? Very likely, I would say. And who would know, or even care at the time? No-one. So then there we have our first piece of the jigsaw. Leopards and maybe a variety of smaller cats would have been imported to Britain, some, maybe more than a few, would have escaped, and if a majority of these were leopards, as the history tells us, then already a population would have been present, a seeding vital enough to produce a breeding population of large cats.

There have also been rumours of airmen, especially during World War II, bringing large cats such as puma, to these shores as mascots. Researchers claim that some of these animals may have been let go over here, but even so, would these kind of cases cause an abundant population of felids? Well, although the answer to that is no, the animals which may have been released would simply have added to an already growing, and healthy number of wild cats already prowling the countryside of Britain. The same could also be said for the smaller cats sometimes used on boats to catch rats and mice. The ocelot and jungle cat are typical of the smaller species of felid used for such a cleaning operation which would have taken place on many boats and ships. Such animals may have been let go, or escaped once the boat had docked at its destination.

It is the travelling menagerie which provides another important clue with regards to how many of the cats of today got here. The origins of the travelling menagerie lies with the Romans and also Royalty in Europe around the seventeenth century, who would accumulate a number of beasts for their own personal enjoyment, although the first ever recorded zoos dated back to 2500 BC. The first royal menagerie was held at Woodstock Manor, now known as Blenheim Palace, during the reign of King Henry I, 1106-1135. Three leopards were given to King Henry III at Woodstock by Roman Emperor Frederick II,

47

which were moved to the Tower Of London in 1235. The Zoological Society of London was formed from this collection and what is now known as the Regent's Park site was formed in 1830. On the 24th October 2005 the *BBC News* website reported:

> *'Two lion skulls unearthed at the Tower of London have been dated to Medieval times, shedding light on the lost institution of the Royal Menagerie.*
>
> *It also shows the relationship between England's early monarchs and the 'king of beasts' was not just a symbolic one. The lions may have been among the first to turn up in Northern Europe since the big cats went extinct in the region at the end of the last Ice Age.*
>
> *The menagerie was a popular tourist attraction, hosting exotic animals.*
>
> *In addition to the lion skulls, researchers also analysed a leopard skull and the skulls of nineteen dogs. The best preserved lion skull was radiocarbon dated to between AD 1280 and 1385, making it the earliest Medieval big cat known in Britain. The leopard skull, which was badly damaged, dated to between 1440 and 1625, which covers the Plantagenet reign, the Tudors and the Stuarts.*
>
> *Despite their royal status, the cats were not treated with ceremony when they died, instead being dumped – unskinned – in the Tower's moat.'*

In the *Domesday Book*, Woodstock was described as, 'forest of the king', ground that Henry I used to house lions and leopards for hunting. The Anglo-Saxons were rather loose with their hunting laws as it was considered more of a sport, but the Norman kings were bound more strict laws, their royal hunts encased with stone walls which encased the heavily forested region.

Wealthy families would also obtain exotic species, a trend which continued up until the 1970s when it was extremely extravagant to have an animal such as a black leopard in the basement. On record there are several cases of large cats escaping from their holding and being shot, the most famous incident taking place in 1530 at a spot marked as Gifford's Cross, at Chillington Hall, West Midlands, where a 'panther' escaped from its cage and was about to attack a woman and her baby before Sir John Gifford, who owned the cat, destroyed it with a bolt to the skull.

The travelling menagerie, also known as the 'Beast Show' was the next best attraction to the waxworks and theatres. Many would flock to see dancing bears, and performing lions, and in turn organisers would attempt to bring far rarer and more exotic species into the fray, such as foreign birds and extraordinary reptiles in order to compete with one another and attract a bigger audience. These exhibitions would travel the country, stopping off for a few days and then rolling, by wagon in which the animals were housed, to the next destination. These shows were very much a zoo in motion, and animals were stocked overnight in dealers' yards. When the time came for the show, the wagons would be situated as to form an arena and a huge, attractive façade would catch the eye of the public. By the early nineteenth century many menageries were buzzing around Britain, the most well known example being run by George Wombwell, although there must have been many obscure shows on the road also. The more popular exhibitions would not merely boast exotic animals but also magicians, lion-tamers, dancers and actors, some of which would become cult figures of their time.

George Wombwell, born in 1777, was the most famous menagerie man. It all began one day when he purchased two snakes from a man at London Docks, and began exhibiting them around the local pubs Wombwell made a decent enough amount to realise that this kind of attraction could go down well with a bigger audience, and so began to form his own collection of wild animals, creatures which he often purchased from boats coming into London and which had been on world voyages. By 1830 'Wombwell's Royal Menagerie' was in full flow, and some fifteen wagons made up the show displayed in 1839. Within these wagons were paraded a variety of animals from elephants to llamas and zebras, but the most intriguing were the leopards, ocelots and 'panthers', which could have been melanistic leopards or the puma.

When Wombwell died in 1850, part of his menagerie was left to his niece Emma Bostock, who, with her husband James, ran it from 1866 to 1884, before they moved it on to their son James, who in turn sold it on to his brother Edward. It was very much a family tradition. From the 1880s the travelling show became known as 'Bostock and Wombwell's Menagerie'. By this time the rolling zoo had become a worldwide phenomenon and by the 1920s, more than seventy species of animal were put on show. The last Bostock exhibition took place in 1931 after James Bostock declared, under ill health, that no further shows would take place if there was no longer a Bostock at the helm.

A *Who's Who* of eighteenth and nineteenth menagerists lists over fifty names pertaining to exhibitions involving wild animals on the road. Sir Garrard Tyrwhitt-Drake, who owned the Cobtree Estate, near Maidstone in Kent, which had its own small zoo, was Mayor of Maidstone twelve times, and had his own travelling zoo which appeared at Southend, Margate, Crystal Palace, and Wembley. It consisted of some ten wagons. Large cats such as leopards and puma were also exhibited at shows run by Albert Haslam, who travelled around Yorkshire and Lancashire, as well as the famous Thomas Atkins who was a rival to Wombell's menagerie. Italian Stephanus Polito succeeded Gilbert Pidcock in 1810 to run the Exeter Exchange menagerie, at The Strand, London, renaming it the Royal Menagerie. It is said that the animals on display were housed in cages little better than travelling trucks. Mr Pidcock is rumoured to have been the first menagerist on record, his show dating back to 1708. His collection of animals was permanently stored at London's Strand.

Thomas Stevens was a menagerie owner from 1865, in the Liverpool area. His exhibition had several leopards, 'panthers', lions and tigers. While the imposing figure of menagerist and animal dealer John D. Hamlyn was enough to scare anyone away, his poky shop, said to have faced the walls of the London Docks, housed many small animals, but in the yard there were many big cats stored. Characters of this ilk are too numerous to mention, but we can see by this procession of menagerists the vast possibilities pertaining to populations of cats roaming the United Kingdom. Thousands of large cats must have been imported to Britain from the coming of the Romans to the travelling menageries, and escapees must have occurred on a regular basis, many of these unreported at the time.

Ballard was a menagerist known in 1751 for his troupe of monkeys and dogs, which occupied Haymarket in London. One incident related to Ballard and big cats escaping, took place on the evening of Sunday 20th October 1816, and involved *The Quicksilver*, a mail-coach running between Exeter and London. In 1987, the *Wylye Valley Life* magazine of Wiltshire, covered the story in detail, and here is author Danny Howell's take on what is now known as the 'Winterslow Lioness':

> '...the coach left for Salisbury for London. On nearing the inn known as the Hut (now the Pheasant Inn) at Winterslow, about seven miles north-east of Wiltshire cathedral city, what was thought to be a large calf was seen trotting beside the horses. The steeds became nervous, and had due reason to be, for the 'calf' was in fact a lioness which had escaped from a travelling menagerie parked at the roadside. This menagerie was shortly due to appear at Salisbury Fair (the animal also appeared at the Bartholomew Fair in 1825).

The team of horses began to kick and lash out, causing the coach to sway and panicking the passengers. The lioness began leaping at the off-leader, a fine horse called Pomegranate, badly mauling him. He was, of course, fixed in the traces and could do nothing to escape the fangs and claws of his assailant. He was a former racehorse, dubbed a thief on the course but had developed such a bad temper in the stable that he had been sold to a coach proprietor, hence his second career as part of a team pulling the Exeter Mail. The guard, Joseph Pike, reached for his blunderbuss and was about to fire when the menagerie owner and his assistants, accompanied by a Newfoundland dog, came upon the scene. The owner shouted not to shoot and the dog seized the lioness by the leg, which diverted her attention and prevented further injury to the horses. In the ensuing struggle the lioness killed the dog before running under a nearby granary; a building propped up off the ground by a set of straddle stones as a precaution against rats and vermin.

The coach-driver and the guard remained transfixed on top of the coach, fearing for their lives; while the passengers, screaming at the tops of their voices, fled for safety to the inn, bolting the door behind them. An ostler employed at the inn, settled the horses, while the menagerie keepers searched in the darkness under the granary with the aid of lighted candles. The lioness, believed to be five years of age, was normally quite tame and hearing familiar voices, allowed her keepers to catch her in a sack and carry her back to one of the cages.

The owner of the menagerie was particularly enterprising because following the incident at Winterslow, he promptly purchased the wounded horse and exhibited him alongside the lioness at Salisbury Fair. This was a successful move on his part and hundreds of fair-goers paid to gaze on in horror at the horse's injuries.

The story soon attracted national attention. Not only was it reported in newspapers; the attack was illustrated by two artists, James Pollard and A. Sauerweid. The illustration by Sauerweid, although awe-inspiring, is purely theatrical. Much rarer than Pollard's, it shows the lioness attacking the leading horse with a great deal of ferocity. The passengers fly from the coach with streaming cloaks, while men with torches come to the rescue. The Newfoundland dog is, for some reason, portrayed as a mastiff. Pollard's print, is the more accurate of the two...it shows the coach drawing up in front of the inn, with the lioness plunging at the throat of the leading horse.

The story of the lioness at Winterslow has been depicted again, more recently, when it appeared on one of the five 16p stamps issued by the Post Office on 31st July 1984, commemorating the bi centenary of the introduction to the mail coach.'

So, as you can see by the examples listed in this chapter, there is enough evidence to support the current population of large cats roaming the British countryside. Add together the many menageries, private collections, inadequate facilities at shoddy zoos, animals brought to these shores at mascots during both World Wars, cats imported on boats, the Roman amphitheatre and also a few cats purchased simply to be released into the wilds on purpose, and we have a pretty healthy starting base. It also proves that the British 'big cat' situation is far from a modern mystery, *despite* the constant reports in the press - and from many researchers - that the reason these animals are here today is simply because of the last thirty years of escapees and releases into the wilds. I simply do not go for this theory, or even the suggestion that these animals have escaped from zoos consistently enough to produce today's population. Sightings from a handful of centuries ago may not be in abundance, but then again, there were no newspapers to record such encounters, but they certainly occurred. One of the most impressive coming from the Pilgrim's Way pathway in Kent, which runs to London, where, during the 1500s, 1600s and 1700s there were reports of strange, elusive large animals prowling the route. Legend was once born of the 'great dogg' roaming the area, as well as a monster hound of Trottiscliffe, although the details of the brief sightings seem to suggest we were dealing with a large cat such as a puma or lynx. For more details, see chapters *Big Cats In The Garden Of England* and *The Others*.

I'm sure that over the last few decades cats have escaped from zoo parks. On December 7th 2001 a press release spoke of a four-year old Indian tiger being shot after it escaped from its cage at Howlett's Wild Animal Park, in Canterbury. Fortunately, at the time of the escape the zoo was not open, but the tiger was seen to be moving to an open area, and so was shot dead. However, although Howlett's has lynx, caracal, and at one time a black leopard, any animals that escape would easily be accounted for, and I'm sure the same goes for many other reputable zoo parks in Britain. However, maybe in the past such escapees were not monitored as strictly as they are now. On 18th October 1984 five tigers were deliberately freed from Howlett's Zoo Park. Two adult Indian tigers, Gelam and Putra, and three of their young were spotted one morning by the local postman. Although four of the tigers were caught, including the two adults, one three-year old was shot after being loose for forty-five minutes. The female was observed by Mrs Taylor as it stalked her goat. It then sauntered off towards Littlebourne. Marcus Matthews, once again from *Big Cats: Loose In Britain*, writes:

> '*What actually happened was that once the tiger was loose, it headed down Bekesbourne Lane. The zoo staff had discovered the escapees at 7:40 am, but they did not report that any were missing until the tiger was shot at 9:40 am, two hours later. It would appear that the Canterbury police were only informed by one of their own policemen, Rural Police Constable Nigel Chandler, who came upon the cat in Bekesbourne Lane. He was several hundred yards from where the tiger was eventually shot. He warned house-holders to stay inside, while endangering his own life. Mrs Taylor was walking up the road and she was pulled into the safety of his police car by PC Chandler. She was not angry with the zoo but was sad that the tiger was shot dead in her garden*'.

In the October of 1987 as severe, unexpected storms ripped through Kent, two clouded leopards escaped from their cage also at Howletts. The *Daily Telegraph* of 17th October wrote:

> '*Leopard at large: Two leopards* [sic] *escaped from Howletts Zoo Park at Bekesbourne near Canterbury when a tree crashed through their cage. One was recaptured but the second leopard was still at large last night.*'

There were two possible sightings of the clouded leopard before it was captured soon after. Meanwhile, after speaking at the Ashford Rotary Club in February 2008 I was approached by a gentleman who claimed that, also in 1987, a Eurasian lynx walked up the drive of his home near Port Lympne, the sister zoo of Howlett's. He told me that staff from the zoo tracked the animal in a white van with nets and had told him that the animal had escaped its cage after damage had been caused during the freak weather.

In the same year, the *Sunday Express* spoke of; '*Big cats in Life or Death peril*', dated October 1987:

> '*The future of eleven lions and tigers and two bears hangs in the balance after a council used court action to seize them from a run-down former circus. The animals used to be kept in a field near Maidstone, Kent, but after a court decided they were not part of any*

circus they were taken to Longleat Wildlife Park. Now Maidstone council has written to forty possible homes for the cats and bears, but an environment officer has warned that if nowhere is found soon they may well have to be destroyed. The animals used to be part of Cross Brothers Circus. The owner, Michael Cross, handed everything over to his friend Peter Hill, but stayed on as a trainer. Hill was then taken to court by the council after locals voiced fears about the cats escaping. Magistrates decided the menagerie was not a draw, and fined Hill £300 for keeping wild animals without a license. He dropped plans for an appeal and the council seized the animals. It is appealing for anyone who can give the animals a home to come forward.'

At Redhill, Surrey, two strange animals were sighted at a nature reserve, and were later captured and identified as coatimundi, badger-sized animals relatives of the racoon. No local zoo had lost such animals, and no owner came forward to claim them.

Whilst credibility is often added to a sighting when a well-respected member of the community is involved, we mustn't always be so sure to express sincerity to authority over a general member of the public. A letter from a police officer popped up on the internet, reading as follows with regards to a local big cat:

'I'm a policeman from the Enfield area of London. A few years back I was standing on a murder scene in Southgate for a good thirteen hours, lots of people kept asking me what was going on but I wasn't allowed to tell them. As a keen Fortean Times *(magazine devoted to the paranormal and the strange) reader I began that we had shot the Southgate 'panther', an alien big cat which had been walking down the High Street. Unfortunately several people took me seriously, including at least one journalist from the local paper. Over the years since I've heard lots of stories regarding the Southgate 'panther' roaming the Enfield/Southgate area and it occasionally makes the local papers.*

I assure you, I've worked night duty here for seven years and seen a lot of weird stuff in that time but the 'panther' is entirely my fictional creation.'

Other theories as to why these cats roam Britain is that they are ghosts of felids from Prehistoric times or demonic entities. This is something that I cannot consider, despite what many peoples opinions are of the supernatural. Black dog folklore is indeed also very potent in the world of the unexplained (see chapter *The Others*). Look back through the archives and you'll find many eyewitness reports of phantom hounds roaming Britain, also known as 'hellhounds'. Reports are very much scarce nowadays but were once in abundance. Such manifestations were often described as being Labrador-size, jet-black in colour with shining eyes. These apparitions were often considered as omens of death and misfortune, and were often sighted in dark lanes or on stormy nights. Travellers would often encounter something slinking in the fog that they would call a hellhound. Other popular names for these regional spectres are Black Shuck, Padfoot and Striker, although I have every reason to believe that early reports of these misty canids could well have been black leopards. The behaviour of such forms is more characteristic of a large cat than a roaming dog, unless of course we are dealing with some kind of unknown presence beyond our field of knowledge. However, a majority of 'black dog' encounters describe muscular beasts leaving claw marks on doors, leaping over high fences, panting heavily, prowling near streams, and even leaping from trees to attack. This is not the behaviour of your average stray dog so why should a ghostly dog, if you believe such a thing, act as such?

One theory is that the felids sighted across Britain are of survivors from the Pleistocene era. This possibility seems very remote also, and most zoologists tend to agree. Many researchers feel that the explana tion as to why so many cats roam the United Kingdom is rather simple, and those solutions have been discussed in this chapter. Although the lynx may have survived, most people tend to agree that the main influx of cats started to penetrate these shores with the Roman invasion, and the numerous other options across the centuries described above.

The only extremely strange fact to emerge out of all this, is as to why no plain spotted leopards are sighted today as mentioned earlier, or even seem to exist in older reports. Of course, reports dating back several centuries pertaining to large, exotic species in the wilds of Britain, are pretty scarce, but if we look at eyewitness reports from the last century, you'll notice a catalogue pretty much bereft of 'normal' spotted leopard sightings. As already mentioned, reports of larger cats such as the cheetah, tiger, and lion may exist in handfuls, but mainly in reference to cats that escaped from a menagerie and then were quickly recaptured or killed. Yet, when we consider how many leopards were imported by the Romans, and also for Royal menageries, it's quite baffling to note the lack of normal leopards sighted among the thousands of eyewitness reports that have been filed over several centuries, even though normal leopards were quite often housed by exhibitions and private collectors. I'm quite sure that black leopards would have been imported, despite no exact mention of 'black leopards' or 'melanistic cats' in the records, although those vague 'panther' descriptions may well have included, at the time, both the puma and the black leopard. Rather strangely, the absence of sightings concerning normal leopards almost suggests that the whole situation has come about due to black leopards only being released during the 1970s and '80s, and breeding, as they were - at one time - very much a fashion accessory and ego-extension novelty pet. But this in turn does not explain all the reports pre-1970.

The African golden cat (*Profelis aurata*) is one other cat that could at times be mistaken for the puma and also the black leopard as melanism is recorded in the species. This cat is twice the size of the domestic cat, and could explain a minority of reports of small puma and black leopard in Britain, although those maintained in captivity in Britain would have been few and far between. The natural coat colouration can vary from darkish grey to fawn, to reddish-brown, hence its name, as this is a beautiful felid. The backs of the ears are black and the tail has a black dorsal thin stripe, as well as dark bands, which has been mentioned in a few 'puma' reports. Above the eyes of the animal there are pale patches, and the throat, chin and lower area of the cheeks are white. These are powerful animals with longish legs, and feed off small prey in West and Central Africa. They'll often hunt at dawn and dusk alone, like most cats, but in the United Kingdom reports of such animals would pretty much be non-existent, unless such an animal was seen by someone knowledgeable of their cat species.

The Asiatic golden cat (*Pardofelis temmincki*) are said to hunt in pairs in their native habitat which spans from Nepal to Southern China and Sumatra. These animals also have a coat that can vary in colour from golden to reddish-brown, and melanism is not uncommon. On the face, white lines bordered with black run across the cheeks and from the corners of the eyes up to the crown. This cat is larger than the African species. Again, I'm not sure that such a cat would have been imported and maintained here.

Other cats which may well roam the United Kingdom, but in smaller numbers, are the serval (*Leptailurus serval*), which are spotted cats with large ears, and inhabit Africa. These animals have excellent hearing ability and eat small prey such as frogs, rats, fish and birds. The ocelot (*Leopardus pardalis*) roams parts of south and central America, and has a coat of chain-like rosettes. It can reach up to three feet in length, is nocturnal, solitary, and extremely elusive. During the '60s and '70s these cats were extensively hunted for their coat, and fortunately this species is now protected, although it is still under threat due to loss of habitat. Such an animal would thrive in Britain if numbers were in abundance, and many zoo parks *do* hold these cats.

Finally, the bobcat (*Lynx rufus*) is often confused with the lynx, and inhabits parts of the U.S. and Canada. It is a medium-sized cat with a ruff-like facial border. The coat appearance varies. Spots can be prominent but this density varies, and the general coat colouration is tawny.

All of the cats listed here have been sighted, not as commonly as the leopard and puma however, across the British Isles. Sightings of other cats such as clouded leopards, snow leopards, the jaguar, cheetah, and a few of the more rarer species such as the fishing cat, do exist, but there remains an inconsistency to support their existence in our wilds. Sightings of such cats would suggest that a zoo or private collection is missing a cat, rather than the slim chance that a small number exist in the countryside undetected. And, whilst the newspapers continue to dramatise reports of exotic cats in our midst, and constantly speak of 'Fen Tigers' and 'Nottingham Lions', I believe we should concentrate on the reality, which is far less stranger than the fiction reveals. Although the past remains a little cloudy as to when these cats really began to establish themselves, one thing is sure, that when the license fees were introduced in the 1970s and '80s, a lot of people let an enormous amount of cats go into the wilds of Britain.

On 20th October 2006 *IC South London* reported *'Panther prowled into my lounge'*, a bizarre alleged close encounter involving 64-year old Astro physicist Brian Shear from Nunhead Lane, Nunhead, who claimed that during the early hours of the Thursday a big, black cat strolled into his living room and settled on his sofa.

The startled witness told the press, *'It had green eyes and was between four to five feet long, nose to tail. This was no pussycat. It didn't miaow, it growled. I'd been sitting in the armchair when it walked in. I didn't try to get too close to it because I was concerned it might bite me. I just sat there and talked to it like you would a normal pussycat. I said 'Hello puss, where've you been then?' and it just growled. It seemed quite content and I didn't feel threatened. I don't think it would have harmed me. It seemed familiar with humans.'*

The witness, a diabetic, had woken during the early hours after feeling unwell and had opened his front door to let some air into the room. After being in the company of the animal for more than an hour, the creature eventually strolled out the door and headed towards Dulwich.

Could this have been the same animal which had attacked Anthony Holder in Sydenham? Was the animal almost tame, or least very used to human contact and a recent escapee from a private collection? Was the creature which allegedly attacked Mr Holder merely an escaped pet seeking human company? In such cases it's difficult to determine what really happened, if such events took place at all. Eye witness reports are vital to cat research, but can be just as frail. Whilst the witnesses remained adamant as to their experiences, such encounters are certainly few and far between, although in Surrey during 1848 an extremely obscure report emerged concerning a man who was found dead by an unnamed roadside. The body of the victim was covered in claw marks, mainly across his face and chest. Rumours at the time circulated that a wild animal had escaped from a Croydon circus although nothing was proven.

On 23rd October 2006 Peter Dunphy was driving on the M25 on the Kent/Surrey border, between the Godstone and Clackett Lane services, when he and his passenger observed a black animal running along the hard shoulder. The creature was cat-like, and described by Mr Dunphy as being three feet in length and six feet high but this measurement is altogether too odd. Maybe if the cat was six feet in length and three feet in height we could then picture a large black leopard. The animal disappeared into a nearby wood.

By 2007, the so-called Bexley 'beast' was very much active. On January 5th a woman named Kerry saw a big, black cat in local fields, and within the first four days of 2007 I'd received more than twenty reports of varying exotic species across Kent and the outskirts of the capital after several appeals in the press over the festive season.

During April '07 *News Shopper* stated *'Beast of Bexley could be out there'*, and conducted its own public poll. According to the research, 31.7 % of readers believed that some kind of 'beast' was on the loose whilst the same percentage were not sure if the animal existed, whilst 36.6 % dismissed the sightings. However, this investigation came just three days after Joanne Parfitt, 30, and Tina Rutherford, 27, spotted a black cat in Erith which was reported online on the 3rd April.

The neighbours saw the animal in undergrowth near a quarry and went to investigate. They claimed it had a thick tail and appeared to be eating something.

A similar creature was also on the prowl in the Biggin Hill area a few weeks after. An anonymous woman saw scratch marks some twenty feet up a tree and also heard the deep growl of an animal.

The deputy head warden of Longleat Safari Park commented, *"From what she has described it is possible it is a black panther."*

At 10:20 pm on April 21st, Betty Morris saw a strange black cat stalking the streets of Northumberland Heath, particularly Becton Place. Mrs Morris, 60, was about to close her bedroom window when she saw the animal sauntering along the road. She described it saying, *"...I don't think it was a panther, it was smaller, more like a black leopard and had a huge long tail"*. Despite her confusion she noted that the creature hid from three men who were strolling on the other side of the road, and then sprayed some bushes with its urine before heading in the direction of some disused garages. The woman then called the local police who probably filed the report.

News Shopper in the same month wrote:

> *'A woman has described how her, "blood ran cold", after she heard and saw evidence of what she believes is an escaped black panther.*
>
> *The woman, who does not want to be named, heard the noise of an animal growling in the back garden of her home in The Grove, Biggin Hill, around two weeks ago. She was in her garden this morning when she noticed deep scratch marks reaching almost twenty feet up the trees.*
>
> *She said: "I heard something growling a few weeks ago and it was blood curdling, but it wasn't until today I made the connection. The trees have been scored with huge claw marks going up around fifteen to twenty feet where it looks like it has leapt up to find a branch to lie on. I am really worried because a small child would obviously make a nice snack for something capable of causing such damage. Whatever it was it was obviously looking for somewhere to cool down as the weather is getting so hot. We have put chicken wire over the base of the trees to stop any more damage and I do not fancy the thought of it coming back."*
>
> *The woman contacted police and says they told her that similar reports had been made, and has also spoken to a member of staff at the Longleat Safari Park in Wiltshire.*
>
> *She said: "I spoke to a man there and described the marks and he told me it did sound like they had been made by a big cat. I also described the growl. When I first heard it I knew the sound was coming from a very large animal, and thought, that must be one*

enormous dog. My blood just ran cold, it was a low, rumbling, bubbly type of sound. Then when I first saw the claw marks I thought the badgers have been sharpening their claws again. It wasn't until I saw the marks going right up the trees that I knew something was wrong."

Ian Turner who is deputy head warden at Longleat Safari Park said; *"From what she has described it is possible that it is a black panther. It is very doubtful it would attack a human unless it was starving."*

Further north at Chiselhurst, on 1st May 2007 a black cat was seen in nearby woods by a couple. They described it, however, as being the size of a small Labrador. Then, during June, Nicole Short had an amazing sighting of a big, black cat while on a train slowly approaching Crayford Station. It was 9:30 pm when the animal, the size of a medium dog, descended a tree and bounded off into the undergrowth.

A Blackheath resident also saw a large cat, the size of a male boxer dog during August. It was slowly walking from garage roof to roof not far from the local school and sports ground. He observed the cat from his flat window and noticed how powerful it looked.

The Surrey puma was sighted 3rd September in Carshalton, near Sutton, by Darren Mason. It was 8:30 pm when the man, who was looking for hedgehogs with his family, was startled by the cat which sped across the garden. The witness told the local newspaper, *"All of a sudden this large dark animal with long legs and a long tail and the size of a Labrador darted across the back of the garden. I turned to my partner and said, 'What the hell was that?', thankfully she saw it too. It was like a puma, so fast crossing the garden in seconds."*

On 9th October a black cat was observed by a female witness at 8:00 am slinking through long grass near Croydon Airport. The animal was only fifty yards from the witness who said it slipped away behind some trees.

In November of 2007 the *Camden New Journal* of London, asked, *'Has urban Fox Turned Cat Killer?'*, after a spate of mysterious attacks on domestic cats throughout London as well as several reports of missing pets. The article continued:

> *'Cats of Hampstead Heath beware – there is something lurking in the shadows and it is not after your Whiskas.*
>
> *A series of attacks on cats in a Gospel Oak street has raised fears that a killer fox is on the loose. Cat lovers in Savernake Road believe the rogue fox stalking their gardens may have a taste for feline flesh. Brenda Morlet is, "One-hundred percent sure", that her cat, called Tony Harrison, lost his back leg in a fox attack in September.*
>
> *She said: "I have never thought a fox would do it, but six vets looked at the cat and told me the same thing – they thought it was the work of a fox. The fox chomps down very quickly. It shredded all the skin. His leg was crushed bone and sinew with a bit of foot hanging off it. His claws were broken."*
>
> *Mrs Morlet believes the culprit was a large predatory fox which was seen just two feet from her back door on the morning of the attack.*
>
> *"This one didn't have the same look as the other foxes I've seen", she said. "It was very big and it looked evil...predatory. This fox is going to give other foxes a bad name."*

She said that ten cats have gone missing from the street in the past two years – at one point they were disappearing at a rate of one a month.

Neighbour Jan Stevens believes her ten-year old tortoiseshell cat Albie was killed by a fox a year ago. His half-eaten remains were found in a next-door neighbour's garden the day after the cat went missing. She said, "People tell you foxes don't attack but occasionally there is a fox that does. There are no dogs in the houses on either side of us so what else could it have been?"

Wildlife consultant John Bryant said fox attacks could not be ruled out. "Nobody loves foxes more than I do, but it does happen," he said. "It's no good denying it, but it is rare. You can never say never with wild animals. They've all got different personalities, like people. In any species you're going to get a rogue."

It is believed the fox may come from a den of up to thirty at Hampstead Heath allotments. There are an estimated ten-thousand foxes in London. Each will cover up to one-hundred-and-sixty gardens in a night looking for food.

Elise Robertson, at Zasman Vets in South End Green, Hampstead, treated Mrs Morlet's cat without charge. She said: "As the years go on, we're seeing more atypical wounds that are being caused by dogs and foxes. The puncture wounds are completely different – they shred tissue. There are more foxes in the area, and they're hungry."

Dr. Robertson, whose cat was attacked by what she thinks was a fox, added that, "... faced with a mouldy curry from a dumpster or a nice fresh cat", the scavengers might think twice.

Mr Bryant suggests imposing a cat curfew to prevent further attacks. "Killing the fox is not the answer", he said. "They'll be replaced within a few days by other foxes."

But Mrs Morlet believes the killer fox should be shot and the council should foot the bill. She said: "I can't let my cats out because they're in his food path. Animals adapt according to their environment. Maybe we're seeing the start of the real urban fox."

In March 2008 a man and his son were watching television in their living room at Abbey Wood, between Belvedere and Plumstead, when a terrific thud vibrated the conservatory roof. The man, a Mr Roe, ran to the back door and told his son to put the light on, an energy-saving bulb that took several seconds to fully illuminate. However, upon reaching the back door Mr Roe saw the hindquarters of a big, black animal that had leapt from the extension roof on to the plastic conservatory roof, breaking a slate in the process.

Whilst sceptics still argue the existence of lynx, puma and leopard in our dark woodlands, and handfuls of researchers fume at their own frustrations at not being able to observe their elusive quarry and often do more harm than good, it is time to take a step back and realise that the only mysterious ingredient of the British 'big cat' situation is the fact that it's become a mystery at all. The lack of a serious government and authoritive investigation, continued sensationalism from the media, the hardened sceptical attitude, and the camouflaged anorak brigade spewing out mythical statistics at cuddly toy conventions, could unfortunately demote the situation into a territory now occupied by the mundane 'Loch Ness Monster' enigma and UFOs. Let's just hope the large felids roaming the UK outlive them all.

Beastly Biology

"The sheep farmers say there's a killer dog on the loose. The schoolchildren think it must
be a monster."

The Nature Of The Beast – Janni Howker

I t was Carolus Linnaeus, a Swedish naturalist (1707 – 1778) who proposed that animals of the same kind should be placed in the same species and the same genus as other similar species. *Genera* were put into orders and each order was put into classes and so on. All cats were originally put under the genus *Felis* but in more recent times the taxonomic subdivisions divided the cat family further, although the generic and subgenera status' have caused much confusion and disagreement.

Linnaeus believed that because cats were so similar (although they have also been proven to be very dis-similar) they could be grouped together as *Felis* but no longer are animals merely classified on the basis of similarity of structure, they must also be related and have the same ancestors to become part of a specified group. Cats form the Felidae family within the Carnivora order. Zoologists have sorted out many of the felids into other groups. The 'big' cats form the *Panthera* which is a species distinguished by the structure of the larynges, instead of mere size, with the smaller cats still contained within the *Felis* group although rather confusingly to some, the puma (*Puma concolor*) can grow to the size of the leop-ard which is in the *Panthera* category, however, the puma cannot roar and is the largest of the lesser cats. The cheetah however, which was once believed to only partially retract its claws, was put alone in the genus Acinonyx, a Greek word meaning 'non-movement' and 'claw' although it is understood that the claws of the felid are only slightly hooked with a less prominent sheath, whilst the clouded leopard, per-ceived as a large descendant of the small cats and considered a link between the larger and smaller cats, belongs to the *Neofelis* with the snow leopard of the genus *Uncia*.

Panthera leo, tigris, pardus, and *onca* describe the big cat family of leopard, tiger, lion and jaguar, with the fossil species of the extinct European jaguar included. All these cats are able to roar although the snow leopard has never been known to, whilst the smaller cats are only able to purr and sometimes chirp, and even scream. Large cats which purr pause for breath before continuing.

There are between 36 and 38 species of felid depending on the way some are classified as species or sub-species. During the Tertiary period, the 'age of the mammals', five periods were divided and given the names Palaeocene, Eocene, Oligocene, Miocene and Pliocene. The first of these periods began over sixty million years ago. Animals the size of small civets existed when the Eocene merged into the Oligocene, such long-limbed creatures appeared as feline-like animals and remains show large upper canines which many of the sabre-toothed cats had. All the present day 'big cats' derive from the fossils of Neofelids which date back to over thirty million years ago, during the Oligocene period. Evolution progressed from the Aeluroidea carnivores which included the Nimravidae paleofelids, which evolved on a parallel with the neofelids. Cougar-sized Pseudaelurus are believed to be the ancient ancestors to the modern cats as well as the sabre-toothed felids which first appeared around fifteen-million years ago in the form of lion-sized cats, and up until the Pleistocene era with the Smilodons. Fossil remains have never been found outside the New World and date back no further than two-and a half million years ago, and it seems that these cats with eleven-inch long teeth existed as scavengers, and also preyed on slow moving herbivores. Treacherous water-holes trapped many of these monster cats, where remains are found, yet one misconception of these cats is the belief that sabre-toothed tigers were direct ancestors of the modern tiger, however, the pre-historic forms probably became extinct long before hand. The Smilodon existed until some eleven thousand years ago in the Americas.

Large cats emerged in India, China and all over Europe as ancestral forms, and the lynx has ancestors also from the Pliocene, large cats which existed across Europe and China. By the Ice Age, cave lions and leopard-like cats inhabited Europe, with other huge felids inhabiting the rest of the world, where in time the cat family then spread all over areas of Africa, America and Eurasia although some areas which have cats have neighbouring islands which do not support any species.

Lions and cheetahs (which existed in the Pliocene) roamed freely around five million years ago with the leopards, tigers, jaguars and the now extinct Martelli's wild cat (*Felis lunensis*). This particular cat was the size of the modern wild felid and may well have evolved into the wildcat although little else is known about it. The Pallas cat is the oldest cat within the genus *felis*. The European wildcat emerged between the two great Ice Ages, with a variety of subspecies forming, although not all surviving. Cats such as the black footed cat, the forest cat and the Chinese desert cat spanned various continents with our own domestic cats developing from the African wild cats.

Many large and small cat species have become extinct over the millions of years, whilst other species have flourished. Prey for some had dwindled, whilst in other areas during periods around seven million years ago land bridges were formed, meaning that cat species crossed into different habitats, to places that were abundant with wildlife and prey. North and South America became inhabited by large cats in the forest areas, whilst other cats roamed vast desert lands created by extreme winters during the Miocene. Many cat species died out around five million years ago but restoration of species occurred around two million years later when large-toothed cats emerged in the form of Megantereon. However, extreme changes in land fauna meant that predatory cats rose and fell in population and the sabre-toothed cats were unable to catch fleet-footed prey such as antelopes, which felids such as the cheetah, lion and jaguar were able to hunt.

Around five-thousand years ago most of the ancient large cats were extinct, and up until fifteen-thousand years ago the lions and cheetahs of North America had vanished with the sabre-tooths, whilst the leopard no longer lurked in the shadows of Europe. Leopards last roamed Britain around twelve thousand years ago, whilst we have already discussed.

In 2007 there was fantastic news regarding the discovery of a new species of big cat, a Borneon clouded leopard (*Neofelis diardi*). The island species has small cloud markings and a double stripe down its back.

With the amount of large cats roaming areas of Britain, as well as Australia, and the U.S. and seemingly in abundance, is there a possibility that new species could, or already has, evolved?

Large cats such as lions and leopards have been cross-bred whilst in captivity, but to suggest that such new species roam Britain is, based on evidence, unlikely. This is despite the many reports from witnesses of cats that they simply cannot identify. Although eyewitness reports are valuable to research, whether they are supposedly credible witnesses such as doctors and policemen, or just general folk walking their dogs, it is surprising to note just how many people cannot recognise or identify an exotic cat in the British countryside.

Across Exmoor in the 1980s many descriptions of roaming cats were vague, unsure, and certainly did not seem to point to any known species of wild cat. Of course, some of the reports may well have been of domestic cats, dogs, and other animals distorted in uncertain shade and light, and more so of animals that indeed were large and exotic, but were in fact the normal species such as prowling puma and 'panther'. However, many people are insistent that they had seen black puma, which are non-existent. The black leopard is actually one of the most commonly sighted felids in Britain, although many people do not realise what a black leopard is, or even know that it exists at all.

Some witnesses describe animals too small to be of leopard size, although these animals produce between two to four cubs which could well explain many sightings of smaller, darker coloured cats. There is also suggestion that we are dealing with a completely new species of cat, or prehistoric survivor, or something akin to a monster feral cat, but in Kent there is no evidence to suggest this. The thought of bizarre mutant cats stalking the rural settings of Kent is exciting, but complete rubbish. The Asian jungle cat (*Felis chaus*) is easily able to interbreed with feral cats, as the DNA of the jungle cat and domestic cat are practically the same. Felids such as the jungle cat can roam Britain without detection, living in marshland in a similar way to the native wildcat, and also producing cross-species that the general public will not be able to identify. However, many of the sightings across Kent describe large black animals, reaching some four feet in length with, to many witnesses, '..puma-like characteristics', but the reality is they are seeing black leopards. Black leopard parents will only give birth to black young, it is a recessive gene which causes this and it continues through the species. Although spotted leopards can produce black offspring causing a mixed litter, but a black leopard cannot produce a spotted youngster. This melanism also occurs in other felids such as the jaguar.

The occasional one-off report of a cross-bred cat may occur, but the hybridisation between different species will most probably result in infertile young. In Britain there are a number of different exotic cats roaming the rural lanes and rolling woodlands. Some behave differently to one another, whilst others would not usually share the same area, let alone country. And a pairing of two different cats would produce a cat that could not produce consistent offspring, and certainly not provide Britain with its own mutant lynx-leopard! Again, something forced within a captive environment is possible as a one-off, but in the wild the chromosomes of different mother and father would not match. These chromosomes are naturally exchanged by the mother and father to go into the egg and sperm, but if the two parents are differing species, then there will be a problem with the alignment of chromosomes. In some cases where the genes within the chromosomes may not add up or may be missing, the offspring will be unable to produce young. In Scotland, the Kellas cats were the offspring of domestic cats on farms and Scottish wildcats but whether such a cat can be mistaken for the much larger black leopard seems doubtful. But then again, and as stated before, some people really do not know what they are seeing.

Whilst there is always the possibility that hybrid cats have been created in captivity and released into the wilds, it seems very unlikely that these few animals would have produced many kittens. Certainly to the extent of a new population of hybrids roaming the country. Some eyewitnesses have reported black cheetahs and cats, dark coloured but with white chests, but until more sightings occur these possible cats will have to be taken with a pinch of salt and considered one-offs - unable to produce young - or simply black leopards with their coats stained by chalk or paint.

It was once believed that only a few large cats inhabited Britain, and that somehow these certain individuals were scouring the whole country, looking for the opposite sex in order to produce offspring. Of course, despite these animals having vast territories, especially in their countries of origin, but not so much in Britain, such claims nowadays are absurd, although it is quite possible cats from Kent are slinking into neighbouring counties. Extensive research seems to prove that the cats in question patrol territories of anything up to eighty-square miles, but some of these hunting grounds will be scarred by obstacles, such as extremely strong and wide rivers, although during darkness motorways are not a problem for these highly intelligent creatures.

Each cat out there establishes its own territory, but it is very likely that in Britain territories will overlap. The ground of a puma has been proven to fade into the hunting ground of a black leopard, and that's simply down to the nature of the land and the obstacles these animals face. In some instances some of these dissecting intrusions are even too much for a cat to conquer, but a number of different species of cat are sharing habitat. This however does not mean they will breed, but they will certainly be aware of each other, but does not mean cat fights will be in abundance.

Many people believe that all cats have slit eyes, which is incorrect. A leopard has binocular vision during the nocturnal hours, and can see in black and white, as well as rely on its hearing - which is far better than a human. During daylight hours, cats can view colours; but not as well as a human. However, during the day, the pupils will become small, only to appear as small circles whilst during the night an animal like the leopard will absorb extra light. A reflective layer behind the retina called the *tapetum lucidum* allows this, and when the cat's eyes are caught in headlights they appear to glow. The lens focuses light rays to produce a sharp image on the retina. Impulses from the retina are carried to the brain by the optic nerve. Cats also have a membrane which can cover the eye to prevent dust.

All cats need to drink. Many sightings in Kent have taken place along the line of rivers, streams, and ponds. Although they use such waterways to navigate their routes and feed, they also need an area to quench their thirst. The leopard will take several laps at a puddle or waterhole before gulping it down. The cat's main sense, though, is its ability to smell, and they have a unique area on the roof of their mouth to actually taste smells, especially if they are coming from another felid. This special area is known as the Jacobson's organ and can be seen in action when a cat lifts its head to smell the air, in turn curling its lips and wrinkling its nose to allow the scent to hit the area.

The colour of a cat's coat is meant to depend on where it lives, e.g. the coat of the snow leopard is thick, off-white and with darker marking to blend in with the rocky terrain, however, a black leopard in Britain is hardly camouflaged by day to the terrain although hunting at night makes it practically invisible. However, the domestic cat has a wider range of markings and colour than the various species of wild cat. Felids are warm-blooded animals, which basically means that their body temperature stays consistent whatever the climate may be like. This is certainly an advantage when cats such as leopard and puma exist in countries they shouldn't! And when they are too hot they are able to sweat through their paw pads and noses. If enough cats exist in the wilds of Kent then they need to find each other. Bizarrely enough, a cat can communicate with another in order to tell a mate how old it is, where it lives, what sex it is and what mood they are in! Scratches, smells and sounds enable cats to find one another. By rubbing against a tree or rock a cat can leave a scent. Felids have scent glands on their chins, heads, base of their tails and between their toes. Not much is known about the cat language but like a dog their ears and tails can react to certain things and give off signals to other felids.

The territory of a male leopard could well cover the smaller territories of a handful of females, and scent marking will attract attention for mating although aggression can also be displayed in some encounters. Male cats can determine whether or not a compatible partner is a potential female. Sexual hormones are present in female urine and other secretions, and the female cats will often call to attract the attention of a male, or more than one, and even then the female may not be ready and will tend to lash out and become aggressive toward the male, and this can take days, but then finally they will mate, with the females ova only becoming released from the ovary after being stimulated by the actual mating procedure. The mating game is certainly a well constructed practice which attempts to be devoid of any kind of aggression, with the male often making tentative advances in which eventually the female cat will raise her hindquarters, whilst crouching on her stomach, lifting her tail to one side in order for the male to penetrate easily whilst he 'treads' her. The male may grip the nape of the female, something which mother cats do to 'still' their cubs, although he will be very aware of the power of the females bite in such instances.

Mating is usually over in seconds. There is no pelvic thrust as such; the excitement amounts quickly, and the male is often out of the way before he gets a frightful nip from his 'lover'. However, the male and female may copulate many times a day, up to 100 times in fact, although felids such as the ocelot will not mate so frequently..

The male penis contains a bone called the bacula which is used to caress and stimulate the females vaginal walls, and mating may continue for up to four days while the female is on heat. Cats such as the leopard are happy to mate in trees, as well as in shallow water, but such cats mate often simply because one session may not be sufficient to produce young. However, cats such as the lynx rely on the availability of prey in order to ovulate, and only become induced ovulators when prey is scarce.

Female cats will seek other males, but in smaller counties of England this is not always possible, but it certainly seems that mating does occur hence the thriving population of cats and reports of large cats with apparent young.

Thankfully, in Britain, there is not much threat to young cats, and they should be able to adapt to terrain quite easily, although in some areas the roaming female may struggle to provide food for them, despite the abundance of rabbits, birds, rodents in the British countryside. The female cat will bring prey to young in order for them to play with, and practice their hunting techniques which they will also develop by playing amongst themselves. A female cat will often return to a certain den to raise young, and the young will leave the den permanently after around six weeks although the 'family' remains intact for a couple of years. Larger cats do remain dependant on their mother more so than the smaller cats, possibly because in their countries of origin larger cats such as the leopard are able to develop hunting skills and gain strength which enables them to bring down heavy, yet often dangerous prey, whereas smaller felids take to hunting more easily simply because they hunt prey smaller than themselves.

So, if many leopards roam Britain, cats which, in their native countries bring down large prey, then why aren't they attacking humans? Well, just like any animal, it becomes used to its environment, and recognises prey from a young age. Cases in Britain that appear to show humans that have been attacked by exotic cats are dubious to say the least. Cats have an acute sense of hearing, so it would not be that easy to disturb a cat at close quarters or step upon it, or approach it easily and this has been proven with our own encounters with lynx and black leopard. Domestic cats are *not* going to be frequent prey, simply because they are not too different from their relatives. They have acute senses, and so are unlikely to sit around and wait for a large cat to come and consume them, but as in the cases which spread across London, there *were* suggestions that a large cat was responsible. Even so, if such an encounter occurred, any exotic cat isn't going to want to risk getting clawed when there is much easier prey around. The same could be said for us humans. These cats are not starving felids that will come into our villages and tear us from our gardens; they have adapted perfectly to the countryside that we believe does not provide sufficient habitat or food, despite the fact that there are more animals out there than we realise, and enough livestock which provides a twenty-four hour restaurant.

It could be said that there are as many pumas in Britain as there are black leopards, yet maybe there *seem* to be more black leopards simply because, with such dark coats, they are sighted more in daylight hours. A cat's coat is a fur consisting of many individual hairs of differing thickness and length, yet on the whole each individual hair contributes to the splendour of a cat's colour. Most of the big cats have a background colouration of fawn or gold – nature enables these cats to become camouflaged in their own environment due to their colouration, as the puma with its fawn coat patrols the rocky crevices, and the jaguar sits motionless in the glades of the rainforest. It is possible that many of the original cats were spotted or striped, or at least of a pattern that merged the two. However, like many other animals, the markings of the specific species enables it to survive in its particular habitat; firstly to conceal itself from other predators, but secondly, and more importantly, to remain hidden whilst stalking prey.

Hairs grow from the base of follicles and their structure is of a complex nature, as is the body covering of many mammals. Shorter and longer hairs provide thermal insulation and each hair is replaceable due to the fact that it has limited life. Moulting may occur during particular times of the year which may explain strange coat colours of certain cats.

The puma, although known as 'one colour', has a variety of colours in its coat which range from silvery-brown to reddish-grey, whilst a cat which lives at high altitude, such as the snow leopard has feet covered with hair, whilst the various types of lynx can appear almost shaggy and grey with spots, to reddish. The tail of the various cats acts as a balancing tool although a cat such as the lynx or bobcat has a far shorter tail. Cats such as the leopard will use its tail for climbing as a kind of balancing pole whilst the lion and its dark tufted tail has a signalling intention as it waves it around in long grass.

Despite their grace and silent stalking, cats are considered cursorial, meaning adapted to walking or running, although much of the time they sleep and quietly prowl. The leopard is the ultimate predator, it stalks quietly and closely to prey before ambushing it, and going for the throat. Or at first bringing it down by the nape before strangling. Smaller cats kill with a bite into the back of the neck, lynx go for the head, and others have disembowelled with their hind legs, but none of the cats pursue prey for a lengthy time, whilst the cheetah usually catches its prey rapidly due to its speed.

In Kent, as well as most of Britain, smaller animals which are preyed upon by these large cats are eaten to the extent where not a lot remains as to identify which animal actually killed it in the first place. Also, there are times when animals such as rabbits are left, and scavengers do increasing damage to the body as birds peck at the eyes and open wounds and foxes eat the rest. Thankfully in Kent, wild dogs do not roam the fields in abundance. These rogue canines tear at sheep, nipping and ripping, making a bloody mess, but large cats kill entirely differently. Statistics claim that thousands of sheep are lost every year to attacks by dogs.

There are some 230 bones in the cat body (humans have 202). The short and rounded skull joins to the spine which supports the body. Vertebrae protect the spinal cord which is the main nerve cable.

The cat's teeth are designed for chewing, although not all cat's teeth are as ferocious as one might think, but they can puncture with ease. The teeth and basic frame of the animal is designed on strength and agility, with powerful hind legs, strong front limbs to absorb impact of landing from great heights, and several short neck vertebrae. Sharp curved claws grow from all of their digits – one of these is the dew claw held off the ground to keep it sharp. Cats are digitigrade animals, meaning they step with their toes and claw marks will only usually be visible as the cat curls its toes to tread, leaving behind something akin to pin-prick impressions.

Claw marks can be found on the head and shoulders of prey, and the neck is often bereft of meat. In the case of smaller prey some are decapitated, whilst lambs may be completely devoured except for their hoofs. Sheep have been found lying on their side, some with ears missing, and the rib-cage exposed and picked clean. Sometimes innards are eaten but in other cases shoulders are ripped and the scene is usually bereft of blood spill. Rib-cages are usually 'rasped' and up to 70 lb of meat has been taken from local goat kills. In their countries of origin large cats such as the leopard drag their prey into trees or conceal it from scavengers, but in Kent such kills have remained in the vicinity, enabling the cat to drink its blood before clotting and to gorge itself on the crimson even if already full from a meal. In some cases, attacks on foxes have resulted in cracked bones, and examination of sheep carcasses have been found with punctured rib-cages where an animal has hit them with force. In most cases though, with regards to sheep kills, the victim is leapt upon unexpectedly and puncture marks are often evident around the neck. In Kent though, rabbit is the ideal prey, and a couple a day provide sufficient food source for a puma-sized cat. Smaller cats such as caracal and lynx can consume a pheasant or two, but during the winter the cats will scavenge, feeding off scraps thrown-out in built up areas, and clawing at sacks of rubbish.

The foxes which enter farmland and built-up areas to take chickens or other small prey tend to make a mess of it. A large cat is swift and silent, plucking prey from the night air without leaving a trace and targeting one animal at a time instead of causing a massacre. Wild dogs are full of bloodlust, beginning in a playful frenzy of spite which decimates the victim, whilst the leopard is an invisible assassin that kills for food.

A cat's claws are constructed of keratin which enables them to grab their prey, and it is the middle (second) phalanx feature which enables them to retract the third phalanx upwards and inwards to lie alongside the second. Ligaments, whilst the cats are resting, draw the claws into the fur in order to protect the claws, but to extend their claws cats rely on their third phalanges and the swivelling action which enables the third phalange to pivot at the joint of the second phalange to be thrust forward and in conjunction the claws are made to point downwards by a flexor muscle which tugs on the third phalange underneath. This way the 'toes' spread, and anything which has fallen prey to the felid will find it difficult to get away as the rake-like claws are embedded. These amazing claws also enable certain cats to not only climb well, but to climb trees with ease, although descent can be slightly more difficult.

The only other animal in the British countryside that leaves a paw-print roughly the same size of a large cat is the dog. Paw-prints are difficult to find, especially as pathways in our countryside are often disturbed, and anything from horses to cars can churn up mud, sand or any other layer which may have originally preserved a print so well. Many people can be confused by tracks, especially under different conditions where a print may have thawed in the snow or been distorted by dog tracks on a muddy pathway. Cats aren't stupid, they would much rather stroll along a hedgerow instead of traipse through a quagmire, and in some cases a cat will extend claws to grip at slippery surfaces, but dogs cannot retract their claws and usually leave a print that is elongated as compared to the cat's more rounded shape, and at the rear of the heel a cat track will show three lobes. Indeed, there are many other differences but tracking a cat's movements by way of searching for tracks is extremely difficult, especially as there are so many different breeds of dog being walked through the country lanes. However, do not always assume that a print you have found, which shows claw marks, is that of a dog. If you are convinced that you have discovered a cat print, either film, sketch or photograph it and always put an object such as a pen, coin or tape measure next to it for size comparison , but also attempt to take a cast or attempt to trace the outline accurately on a clear sheet of plastic. One other characteristic of the puma, is that when the cat walks slowly the rear feet have been known to slightly overlap the prints of the front feet. The domestic cat walks the same: they too are digitigrade and have five toes on the fore-foot, although one is extremely raised and will not show in prints.

Finally, it must be said that the best time to find cat prints or droppings, is next to a kill. When something like this occurs, it is just a question of finding out *which* cat, instead of wondering if it is a cat. The print of a lynx, despite its seemingly large hairy feet will only measure around seven centimetres on the hind foot and six centimetres wide. Such an animal also places its hind foot in the place of the fore print, and the stride length measures up to eighty-centimetres. Of course, when the lynx picks up pace the stride will lengthen. In their countries of origin the prints of wolves and lynx are often confused, which proves that in Britain it's not actually a crime to mix up cat and dog prints. Again though, the lynx print is asymmetrical. Badger prints are certainly one of the most recognisable set of tracks because of the five toes and the almost miniature bear-like quality. Sometimes, however, the inner toe is seen to be absent from the impression. Despite the fox having five toes on its fore feet, and four on the hind, four will only show on the fore also. They have thin, pointed claws the two central toe pads are positioned quite forward in the impression left, and although often confused with those left by a dog the main difference is the positioning of the pads with the dogs toe pads being in closer proximity to the main pad.

Believe it or not, the most unlikely impression at times confused with a big cat print, mainly in snow, is that left by the rabbit as it sits on its haunches. I have often received numerous photographs of tracks left by a hopping rabbit that witnesses believed to be of a large cat. This is achieved when the rabbit sits on its back legs leaving a rounded impression with indentations from its fore-legs leaving two digit marks, but even so, this is nothing like a 'big cat' - however, some witnesses believe the indentation left behind looks like a partially-thawed big cat print.

Those who tend to scour the countryside looking for 'big cats' tend to believe that signs are extremely easy to find, but this is not the case, especially when people do not know what to look for. Beforehand, it is best to eliminate the evidence left by local species such as deer, foxes, dogs, badgers etc, which can be scratch-marks, droppings, paw-prints etc. Some droppings are very common in woodlands, and you will be familiar with them no doubt, i.e. rabbits etc, but in areas where deer are rarely sighted, there are going to be signs of animals with which you are not familiar. So instead of simply looking for 'big cat' signs, try at first to eliminate signs of other animals. Droppings from cows (cowpat) and horses are easily identifiable, but badgers, deer, foxes, even otters, are signs you may stumble across and not recognize, although excrement will certainly be smaller than that of a leopard. Lynx droppings will certainly contain bones and feathers, and these deposits are often covered by the cat.

Deer droppings are cylindrical with a pointed end, resembling beans. When fresh they are very dark, often black in colour with a thin layer of slime coating them. Inside such droppings there will be signs of plant life. Red deer droppings will be slightly larger than those deposited by roe and fallow deer which are roughly the same size as one another, both being very dark in colour, rounded and pointed at one end. Deer droppings only measure up to around two centimetres in length. Fox droppings, like a majority of droppings from the carnivores are cylindrical, more slender than those of a dog with a twisted, tapering end and measuring up to ten centimetres long. They are usually black depending on the food consumed but such droppings can also alter to the particular colour of a berry that has been digested, and the droppings of a badger are similar but even more cylindrical than those of the fox and will consist of fur, insects and also seeds. They tend to leave them in a shallow pit uncovered as the badger will often return to the same small pile to excrete. Otter droppings are smaller, known as spraints, they smell fishy and are black in colour with a sticky texture, whereas sheep and goat droppings can look like large rabbit droppings around a centimetre in diameter, and the hedgehog also has black droppings which can be up to four centimetres long. Anything smaller than a fox is unlikely to be of a large cat, but if anything interests you then take a sample, by wearing gloves and using tweezers, and put your sample in a small bag.

Naturally, several species of animal may use the same pathway, and can be best observed in the snow. Early mammals in history had five toes, but a majority of such animals designed for running, such as the cats, have lost that 'thumb' as such. It is also worth noting that it's not only large cats and badgers that do damage to tree bark. The deer indulges in what is known as barking, which usually takes place in summer and winter. The deer will pull at strips of softer bark in the warmer months, causing the bark to shred upwards, exposing the wood underneath. A cat will sharpen claws on a tree and also mark via its pads, but deer certainly show similar markings and can reach high on their hind legs. Sheep and goats also mark trees, but such barking will be done to several trees at around the same height in close proximity. Even an animal as small as a vole can mark the base of a tree, gnawing away the bark but always leaving small marks where the incisors have chomped away, although they do prefer to chew roots. The hare and rabbit also gnaw at bark, the marks however go across small branches hanging down from trees, and squirrels also chomp, but this is usually high up within the branches.

Cats do not crush food. Their scissor-like teeth and rasping tongue are put into action when a felid turns its head from side to side allowing the flesh of the victim to be cut up and dissected by the carnassials. In each jaw the cats have six incisors with one canine on each side in both jaws, three premolars on each side of the upper jaw and two below and one molar on each side above. The sharp canines puncture prey by way of severing the spinal chord and then the smaller incisors in-between manipulate the food until the cat is able to swallow it. For the leopard the incisors are rather small yet enable the animal to gnaw bones and puncture skin, but it is the tongue which does most of the work. Its surface is layered with a rough texture , a carpet of pointed bumps which scrape meat from the bone of prey, as well as coming in useful for grooming and lapping at water.

In areas such as the western United States it is legal (at the time of writing) to hunt the mountain lion. Attacks on humans have been recorded, in fact a cougar can kill prey such as elk - six times its own size - and across the North numbers are increasing, as they are here. The puma is a polygamous felid which has been known to copulate over fifty times a day during a breeding period. The female will not have a den as such, but find shelter for kittens and for giving birth under tree branches or rocky crevices. Whilst hunting, the puma will find cover, moving with stealth until in reasonably close range before dashing at its prey and leaping onto its back. The initial impact can often be enough to kill some prey outright or at least knock it out. It is then that the puma goes for the throat. The cat may remain in the vicinity of the kill site for a number of days, sometimes burying the victim and then returning to uncover it for another meal.

There are many people who contact me who have a natural and genuine fear of cats such as leopard and puma prowling the local fields. They fear for their pets, they fear for their children and they fear for themselves. However, the facts are that right through the last century there were just over fifty recorded attacks on humans by cougar in North America, albeit with over ten deaths. However, the puma is way down the league of dangerous animals and stands in the shadow of snakes, bees and even domestic dogs. It could be said that children are in danger – they are relatively small, and when riding a bicycle they could be perceived by a cougar as something similar to a moving sheep or domestic cat, especially if vision is obscured and the child is on the other side of undergrowth. Large cats are coming into town, especially in Britain where woodlands are not vast when compared to the forests of Africa and the forests of British Columbia. However, they are secretive cats and so will not be taking to the streets in search of a butcher's shop! It is advised that you face a cat if you encounter one, and move back slowly, making yourself almost large, but many people when put in this situation cannot perform such cool heroics. Indeed, they *do* freeze, but in terror. Many people will turn and run, others are just put under a spell as they watch this beautiful creature, which on most occasions will slink away casually.

It is highly unlikely that anyone could get close enough to an exotic cat to injure it, step on it or stroke it (!), and such an action would not be advised. People have often reported seeing cats that appeared tame to some extent, but this is still a wild animal, and if slashed (although cats puncture, and use claws for holding prey) by one of these animals its claws would not leave thin scratches or exact parallel lines. The claws of say, a lynx, move independently, and are formed around the paw. In order for the first and fourth claw to scratch, the second and third would penetrate more than an inch deep.

Those who seek a so-called 'unofficial' animal in Britain's woodlands are putting themselves at a small risk. Flushing an animal from hiding is not a good idea at all, and this can happen as many people tend to stalk the woodlands, approaching areas on foot where they are better of staking one area out, but the trouble is with such enthusiasts is that they have no patience, they tend to be on the move, going from one area to another. However, it is unlikely that anyone can get that close to a large cat, but take into account the wind direction at all times, and try to approach from the downwind side. Being quiet is an obvious approach, but 'quiet' to a human is very different to the 'quiet' of a cat.

People tend to 'creep' through the woods, breaking twigs, cracking dry leaves, flashing away with their camera, and truly believe they are being quiet. In fact, ideal research can be done more adequately from a vehicle. A great number of cat sightings occur on roads, but also, in the wilds of Africa and the likes, much research is done from vehicles, where researchers can stop for a while and assess a situation, checking the surrounding areas. If you are able to see a cat, you can determine what mood it is in if you are close enough, and you always remain safe. If there is an area where there are young or a kill, this can be a hostile time, so again, being in a vehicle is far safer. Unfortunately, the average avid researcher is not about 'research', it's more of a case of getting together with a few friends and trudging through the woods once a sighting has been made. Nice! (And as usual, they see nothing).

Tracking an animal such as a leopard is extremely dangerous. However, as already stated, attacks on humans in the U.K. are pretty much non-existent. However, the picture changes once a person goes looking for an animal that may have young or could be protecting a kill. These animals use camouflage perfectly, but will give no warning before a charge. People that get close to such an animal will hear a deep cough or hiss as a warning. In some cases the cat may run off and then crouch, facing you, be alert to this. Signs to look for are as follows:

> ➢ Staring fixedly.
> ➢ The baring of teeth and snarling.
> ➢ Crouched head and the flattening of the ears.
> ➢ Ears held forwards and the head held up.
> ➢ Head lowered as the animal stands side-on.
> ➢ A leopard may approach several times as a warning to you to back off.

Worryingly, cougar attacks in the United States are often fatal. Even those lucky enough to escape the jaws of a hungry cat are left with terrible wounds ranging from blindness to brain damage. Those concerned about such attacks may, or may not, wish to visit the *Cougar Info* website which documents almost every known cougar attack from the U.S. to Canada, and it makes for some pretty shocking reading, especially where attacks on small children are concerned. Let's hope such terrifying and tragic ordeals do not occur in Britain.

There are some who theorise that the cats which people have seen for many decades in Britain are a species that have always lived here, and that only now are people more aware of these animals hence the more reported sightings. There is far too huge a gap between now and the period when animals such as the leopard roamed Britain, but a cat such as the lynx may well have hung on in some form as it would not have needed to venture into the territory of man to snatch sheep, and strangely enough, the earliest reports of large cats on the loose concerned lynx. People of credibility have put forward beliefs of unknown species of felid, mainly based on eyewitness reports that do not fit in with any known species of cat. In Kent, the possibility that ancient cats exist is basically nil, due to the fact that most witnesses are describing known species of large cat, such as the lynx, the black leopard and the puma. I believe that many of the questionable details are simply down to the fact that most witnesses do not know what many of the exotic cats of the world look like. I have mentioned this before, but it is true. There is a possibility that certain cats have adapted to Britain and their coat and size variation simply reflects the evolutionary adaptation to our climate, which can be said for the jaguar and the leopard. The leopard is known to be considerably larger in mountainous regions whilst in the jungles and remote savannahs it is smaller. Females are two thirds the size of the male, so once again we have a size difference and with the British leopard it seems as though we are only playing host to the melanistic version. This variation in colour is considered rare with regards to the African species but the forest dwelling leopards that have the darker coats are quite common.

The jaguar is a larger animal than the leopard, which is slimmer and longer in the leg. In Britain there are reports of black cats with very large heads like that of the jaguar – however, if more details were observed in daylight encounters, we could determine as to what people are seeing because the rosette markings of the jaguar have a central dot. Melanism does occur in the jaguar but it is rarer than in the leopard, and with this felid being the third largest of the big cats, at least some eyewitness reports would support its existence here but reports are not consistent.

During the 1980s in the west-country it was believed that many people were seeing felids not recognised by science. However, there has been no further evidence to suggest we are dealing with large, undiscovered species of cats, or at least in abundance—although as mentioned before, limited hybridisation is possible and there have been a few unique specimens discovered. There is also the possibility that we are also dealing with larger feral cats. More slender leopards have been observed in Malaysia, proof that such animals are certainly not impossible. The regions they inhabit also suggest that melanistic versions are in the majority. In an article written by Darren Naish for his blog *Tetrapod Zoology* he comments:

> '*While the conventional explanation for felid melanism is that it aids concealment in dark, forested habitats, researchers are now wondering whether the melanism prevalent in some areas has evolved to combat fungal and bacterial infections, as has been proposed for melanism in humans (Mackintosh 2001). I suppose these Malaysian leopards are of the subspecies P. p. delacouri, the Indochinese leopard. Some of the enigmatic melanistic cats that have been reported from the UK have been described as unusually gracile compared to 'normal' leopards. So... some of them might be Indochinese leopards.*'

Indeed, it must also be said that a lot of leopards which we are used to seeing on televison or in zoo parks, are often overweight where they've been cooped up and lacking exercise. Naish adds:

> '*Leopards are incredibly variable, not only in body size (adults range from 91-191 cm in head + body length, with the weight of adult males ranging from 37 to 90 kg), fur length and coloration, but also, clearly, in how robust they look.*'

In the case of the Malaysian black leopards, we are seeing an animal similar in description to the British black cats. Slender bodies, slimmer tail, with shallower bellies and slender hindlimbs. The Malaysian cats are still reasonably large, especially in the muscular stature of the forelimbs, yet when a photo of such an animal was posted on the internet, no-one who analysed the picture could identify the species - simply because they weren't used to seeing such a slim leopard. Whilst I'm sceptical as to whether Indochinese leopards are roaming the UK, the Malaysian cats are still whole proof as to how such cats differ in varying environments.

Killer cats are created by the lumbering lunatics who hunt them. Those that hang out in rural hideaways with their air-rifles at the ready. Those who set up snares in the hope of finding a manacled prize. And those who rampage across the fields with shotguns, after a local pet dog is eaten by an animal that is only doing what it does naturally. Sheep losses in Kent are not a worry when there are so many rabbits around: prey is in abundance and variety and can be obtained with ease. Kent is not a vast area, nowhere near as vast and remote as the Cornish moorlands, let alone the African plains, yet there is sufficient cover for a handful of large predators, each having its own territory whilst smaller, undetected cats mooch behind the hedgerows. They are harmless, but like most animals they can be aggressive, especially when they are protecting young or confronted by maniacal, gun-toting psychotics.

The biggest concern is the lack of so-called government interest, or examination from any recognised professional body. After the Exmoor and Bodmin 'beast' flaps, sightings of large exotic cats across Britain have become almost everyday life.

Once, the Marines were concealed in the ditches, and now with no further results, the petty politics and minor squabbles are clouding an intriguing occurrence: that large and very exotic cats inhabit this island. For some it is an alarming thought – for others one of excitement. It is already too late to even attempt to track one or two of these cats down; it is a situation not quite out of control, but it could end up that way if many of us stick our fingers in the pie without the knowledge or understanding of these animals and their way of life.

The authorities are ignorant to the situation, and for the felids in question, ignorance is bliss. Yet when it comes down to it, what are the authorities going to do anyway? Wipe them out? Accidentally injure one for it to become an irritable man-eater? Spend thousands of pounds stalking the countryside, only once again to be eluded by a creature that would always remain one step ahead? And if these animals are left to their own devices, what happens when the local woodlands and even towns are inhabited even more so by these cats? Can we afford to go with the flow, with so many people fearing that large cats will spring from the trees and eat them alive? Well, for now, yes. There is no evidence to suggest that these cats are preying on children, and any incidents that *do* take place are in an extreme minority! There are certainly more attacks by domestic dogs on youngsters.

These cats won't just go away though – evidence suggests they are breeding healthily all over Britain and there are more people who respect them as an out of place and very beautiful animal rather than despise them for being here. Unfortunately there are the selected few who continue to rampage through possible habitats, hide in the undergrowth ready to fire at any sign of movement and who blame these cats for every livestock loss. It is these people who will turn at least a handful of cats into dangerous irritable animals. But for the moment the only wild and truly dangerous animal out there is the one in the mirror.

The cats which roam Kent and Britain should be accepted as having become naturalised. Many have been, despite being ignored, let alone classed as unofficial residents. Corpses of dead felids will be extremely difficult to find, especially when we consider the lack of badger and fox bodies found in the woods. When an animal dies it immediately begins to decompose, the body's own chemicals break down the tissues.

This is known as autolysis, and putrefaction occurs when tissues are broken down by bacteria. Gases which swell the body are also released, hence the rotten smell of a carcass. Flesh-flies and blow-flies will then become part of the process, and this is where maggots come into play, as larvae which live for between five and ten days before adulthood. Maggots form after the fly has laid its eggs in an open wound. When animals die, the remains are gradually ground away by other, smaller, scavengers - bones as well

Some animals die underground too, such as the badger, but a cat such as a leopard, would - if injured - crawl into foliage to die.

Unless these felids are killed by cars, then it is unlikely that bodies will be found. A rabbit carcass even after a few weeks will be unrecognisable as the skeletal frame begins to appear. Over a year, a decomposing rabbit will succumb not only to bacteria, but also mould, fungi, worms, beetles, birds, because in nature nothing goes to waste, not even the bones which over a longer amount of time will also decompose. Although the population of cats in Britain is large, and certainly rising, searching for a body of one would be like looking for a needle in a haystack.

Finally, it has been estimated that one female leopard, in fifteen to twenty years can produce an alarming number of young. Zoologist, friend and professional animal trapper, the late Quentin Rose, once claimed that several hundred, if not a thousand large cats could roam the country in a matter of a few decades. Certainly over the course of these years, many more will be produced by those offspring. So, the future is bright for the British big (and smaller) cats. They must be protected and respected.

> *'The climax? What plain tale of science can boast of such a rhetorical effect? I have merely set down certain things appealing to me as facts, allowing you to construe them as you will.'*
>
> *Beyond The Wall Of Sleep* – H.P. Lovecraft

Kent KM Today

A Kent Messenger Group Newspaper incorporating The Kent Evening Post

Monday February 5, 1996

GILLS ACE ADE SINKS LEADERS

IS THIS THE BEAST OF BLUE BELL HILL?

Caught on film, Kent's mystery creature revealed

"It is certainly two or three times bigger than a normal cat and unlike anything else I have ever seen."

INSIDE: News...Page 2 Information...Page 15 Jobs...Page 16 Sport...starts Page 25

Soldier loses court battle

On the sick list

House sell-off?

Contract offer

Award makeover

PART TWO

Big Cats in the Garden of England

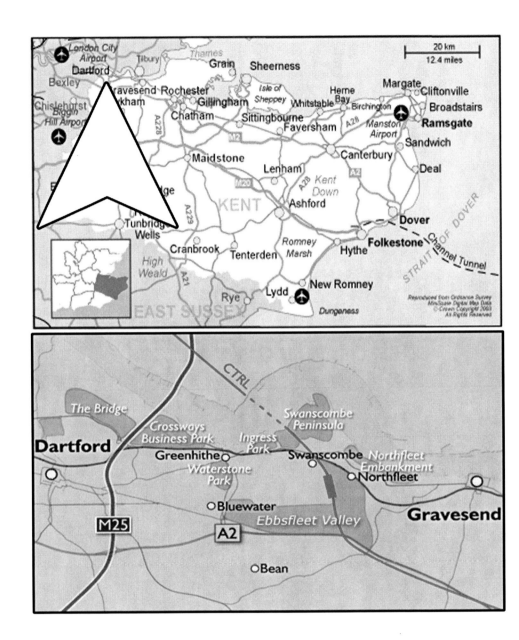

Bluewater Black Cat

'And I'm the only one who really knows about the Beast. But they'll never listen. Maybe you'll not listen either...

The Nature Of The Beast – Janni Howker

Bluewater, at Greenhithe in Kent, is a huge shopping centre, which has been described as 'an oasis in a quarry'; a vast retail complex that stretches over fifty acres and squats impressively within a cliff-face some fifty-metres deep. Europe's largest retail and leisure destination was opened on March 16th 1999, and attracts millions of customers each year, with each of these visitors estimated to spend at least three hours within the innovative framework of this gargantuan shopper magnet. People come here to purchase a variety of goods, taking their pick from a wide variety of clothes stores, right through to the latest technology and fluffy toys. They also come to dine, to watch films in the large cinema area and even to spot the occasional celebrities, who are drawn to the diverse fashion labels on offer. Yet Bluewater isn't just about hustle and bustle, for this sprawling arena is surrounded by waterways, grassy verges and towering trees, many of which originate from Florida.

It's a haven for wildlife too, with a variety of waterfowl residing there, creatures that would have been residents long before the mall was erected, back in a day when the area was nothing more than chalk pits and fields. Hopefully, after the bulldozers came in and disturbed the tranquil habitat, things would have settled to some extent and some of the natural wildlife may have come back, albeit to a rather noisy welcome as thousands of cars on a daily basis stream in and out of the car parks.

Whilst shoppers, diners, drinkers, and cinema goers come and go each busy day and evening, there has been, for who knows how long, one particular set of visitors to the area who've prowled the outskirts long before Bluewater was even a dream in the architect's mind. These particular visitors are, unfortunately not welcomed to the undergrowth, or the car parks surrounding the place despite the fact they were here many years previously. And although these frequent 'intruders' - as they are called - are hardly seen, when they are they cause quite a stir, especially among those who wish to keep such 'tall tales' quiet, in case the precious shoppers of the area are driven away, by their own obstinate fears of killer cats hoping for a feast of Bluewater shopper flesh.

These mysterious, slinking forms are not interested in the latest films on the cinema, or bothered about the current clothing range, they are simply curious creatures, wondering what in the world is going on with their territory. For they are cats. Large cats. Mainly black. Leopards in fact, and the occasional puma, like those seen in the built-up areas of London when they surely shouldn't have been. Yet they persist in travelling the nocturnal pathways into their territory, a habitat that has been obstructed by Blue-water. The animals themselves don't seem that bothered, they'll still continue their routes, and there will be times when their hunt for food, or next destination, will have to include a mooch around the car-parks or rural landscapes which flank the shopping centre.

The management seem a little bothered. They've phoned me, and asked me not to mention these sight-ings too much. Why? I don't really know. All I do know is that these cats are curious beasts. They may smell the odd bit of unwanted food thrown from a vehicle leaving the place, or they may be in pursuit of a fox which is raiding a bin near MacDonald's. They may also be stalking a swan which they've spotted as they drink from a nearby pond, but all these cats are doing is getting on with their routine, which, unfortunately for us humans, seems occasionally to come a little too close for comfort to be unaccept-able. No longer are the mystery beasts of Britain merely confined to the dark woods.

And then the hysteria starts. Not because these large, elusive cats are a threat, but because the stories suddenly become local, overblown urban legends, yarns which begin as harmless whispers that transform overnight into something akin to a frothing werewolf tale. And then the press gets involved, the head-lines get bigger, the more the Bluewater management team attempt to keep them smaller, and then the shoppers become concerned although they don't really believe. Then suddenly we have a monster on our hands - a Hallowe'en ghost story come to life. Yet there is the scepticism too, which can only be a good thing surely, meaning that these animals can continue to prowl, in silence, the darkest corners of the place. Until of course, they come out of the shadows.

> *"The thing had razor-sharp claws....", "It's eyes shined in the light of our headlights",*
> *"It was a black thing, like nothing I've ever seen before".*

The reports were becoming fantastic and exaggerated by the time the millennium had dawned. But when they started they were obscure, but - for me - nothing new considering that Bluewater sits slap-bang in the middle of several towns where sightings of large felids have been common. Gravesend (allegedly receiving its name after the Bubonic Plague hit in the 1600s, and bodies were no longer buried on land but at sea), and Dartford (situated close to the River Thames and the capital, which has seen the Romans Normans and Saxons pass through), are constantly 'hot' areas for sightings. Each of these wooded towns are peppered with creaky villages where stories of big, slinking, cats have been rife for many, many years. However, the press loved the ring to the names, whether it was the 'Bluewater Leopard' or the 'Beast of Bean', they didn't care that it was probably the same cat seen thirty miles away a week ago in some remote village, because as soon as they were able to tie a particular monster story to a very well known place, Bingo!...the whole world was interested.

Thankfully, any sightings that reached the press came from my files. Reports that I felt were too sensi tive, or of importance, remained - and still do - in my files, locked away. But occasionally a few would slip through to the local newspapers, making the whole affair a rather touchy subject for two reasons:

One, there was the concern for me that hunters, general enthusiasts, newspaper reporters, television crews and any person would start to congregate at Bluewater, in turn giving a negative vibe to the vicin ity, which - in turn - wouldn't please the management, who on one occasion sent out their 'wildlife' offi cers to scour the bushes for signs of a large predator. Now *that's* paranoia!

And two, I was concerned that there'd be an abundance of hoaxers 'phoning me all hours of the morning claiming fabricated sightings just to waste my time, and also get into the headlines. However, I knew that these particular animals - although not a threat to the area - had to be recognised, and the public made aware as much as possible. Unfortunately, the press were literally one hundred years too late in letting them know!

The Pre-Bluewater Years.

Sightings of strange, cat-like forms across the United Kingdom date back several centuries. However, some, over time, have become vague as they have been passed down, or the original references obscured, as booklets and other publications that may briefly mention such sightings, become out of print and deleted.

In his classic book *Lo!*, first published in 1931 (Gollancz), author Charles Fort documented hundreds of cases pertaining to many strange events and weird phenomena, which would later inspire *Fortean Times* magazine to form, and document bizarre happenings across the globe.

Fort wrote that in 1905, '...*near Gravesend, an unknown animal had, up to Dec. 16th, killed about 30 sheep"*, quoting the London *Daily Mail*, who spoke of '*small armies*' of men who allegedly pursued the marauder, but never sought out their quarry, which, seemed to disappear as quickly as it had appeared. Was this the first documented account of a mystery cat on the loose, stalking the marshes not far from what would, many decades later, become known as Bluewater?

One of the first mysterious predators to be shot and reported in the Kentish woodlands turned out to be a jackal, a case also mentioned in Fort's *Lo!* work. He wrote:

'*Farm and Home* – March 16th (during the same year as the previously mentioned sheep killings) – when farmers in the south of England, especially in the districts between Tonbridge and Sevenoaks, began to tell of mysterious attacks upon their flocks.

'*Sometimes three of four sheep would be found dying in one flock, having in nearly every case been bitten in the shoulder and disembowelled. Many persons had caught sight of the animal, and one man shot at it. The inhabitants were living in a state of terror, and so, on the first of March, a search party of sixty guns beat the woods, in an endeavour to put an end to the depredations.*'

This resulted in it being found and dispatched by one of a Mr R. K. Hodgson's game-keepers, the animal being pronounced, on examination, to be a jackal.'

The Times of March 2nd spoke of the predator but could offer no explanation as to how such a beast ended up roaming the local woods. According to Fort, '*Blythe News*, March 14th – *The Indian jackal, which was killed recently, near Sevenoaks, Kent, after destroying sheep and game to the value of £100, is attracting attention in the shop windows of a Derby taxidermist.*'

The *Derby Mercury* of 15th March reported that the carcass was on display in the studio of a Mr. A. S. Hutchinson who lived at London Road, Derby.

This case, which, thankfully was well documented at the time, proved that a variety of species were prowling the local woodlands. However not every mysterious sheep kill across Britain around that time, and previously, could be explained so simply, or resolved by a hunt. Thankfully - although not for the poor jackal - evidence was obtained by way of the beast being killed. Such results, however, are few and far between, even by today's standards, where hunting of varying kinds is abundant in the countryside.

Whilst a handful of cases *do* occur which involve the destroying, or injuring, of an out of place beast - whether boar, escaped hyena, and jackal - cat kills are extremely scarce, with only a few every few decades turning up dead on the roads. Often the bodies of such animals are taken away, and never seen or heard of again. Large cats that have perished after being pursued seem either non-existent, or well covered up by local folk who are more interested in the welfare of their flocks, rather than causing a fuss by way of exhibiting their surprise big game.

During the early 1930s, Mr Cuckow, who I visited during the late 1990s at his home in Cliffe Woods, described how, as a youngster of around thirteen, he had seen a 'big cat' shot in a local quarry, in the Burham area of Kent. As territories go for a large cat, Burham, near Blue Bell Hill lies across the river from Halling, Snodland, Cuxton, and Gravesend. Although there were the occasional rumours of large cats in the wilds back then, to see one shot and killed was a huge shock for Mr Cuckow, who was enjoying a game of shove ha'penny with friends. The Downs were viewable from the pub that Leonard's father owned, and as kids they would often gaze across the fields and steep hills at the inspiring rural landscape.

Whilst staring across the fields, on this particular day, as a steam engine pulled a plough across the ground, one friend of Leonard's noticed a black object that seemed to be moving slowly across the green in the distance, before it disappeared into the undergrowth like a dark apparition. Over the next few days several people spoke about the mysterious animal they'd seen up there - a mooching, powerful creature that many thought belonged in a zoo, and that should not be strolling around the tranquil fields, especially when there were kids around.

According to Leonard, whose story I never once doubted, drastic action was taken after one particular sighting, and the Royal Engineers or similar group were called in to flush the strange animal out from what they believed to be its overgrown lair. Some sixty men trawled the landscape, banging pieces of metal in the hope of driving the creature from the dark foliage. After a short time, the black animal emerged. It was a leopard, and was shot on sight.

Could such an animal have been the catalyst which spawned the generation of felids now roaming Gravesend and other parts of Kent? If the animal hadn't escaped from a zoo, had someone let the animal go? Or had it in fact been early evidence of more generations gone by? Well, there is a possibility that just as many cats were roaming the Kent woodlands then as there are now, only back then such cases were rarely documented. Sceptics argue this point, and state that if there was such an abundance of animals roaming the woods over seventy years ago, then surely the county would be running wild with exotic cats. Well, to some extent it is. However, sightings only persist in being reported when the press are willing to feature them frequently, otherwise the so called 'flaps' simply die down, and there are - of course - the many sightings that just go unreported. However, there is also a possibility that such a cat may have been an escapee - whether from a small zoo or a private collector - and that it had not been roaming the undergrowth for long until it met its maker in rather dramatic fashion. This would have been terribly unfortunate for it, when you consider that it could have lived its life eluding man. All those years ago, such appearances of large cats may well have stunned the general public far more than they would have now, although it's certainly fair to say that such reports are not really treated any differently today than they were back then as human naivety remains. Sightings of large cats aren't always taken seriously by the local press, whilst others filter through to the major tabloids, and have - on many occasions - caused mild hysteria in certain villages across the nation. Usually, when the sightings fade, or local hunts amount to nothing, the panic dissipates until the next headline foams. The previous chapter gave us prime examples of what appeared to be clusters, local intrigue, and beastly headline, it's no different wherever you go in the world, and not just regarding big cat stories.

Top: Bluewater Car Park Below: Bluewater Underground Car Park

Hoax photo of Meopham puma allegedly shot 1999

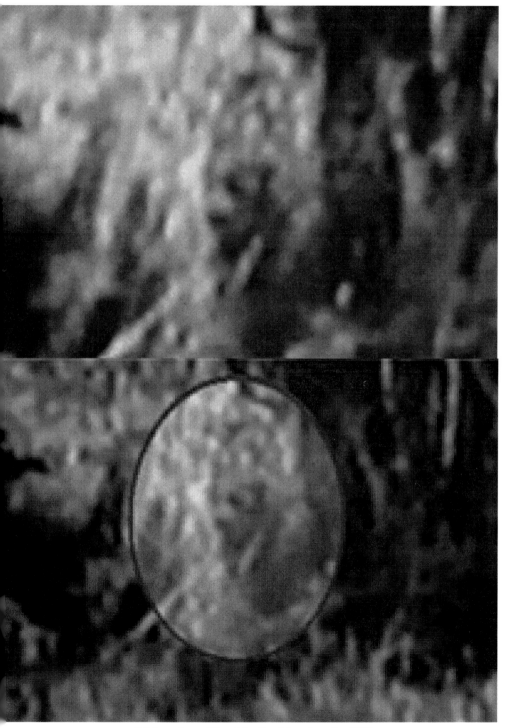

Higham lynx filmed by Ian Marsden (p. 107)

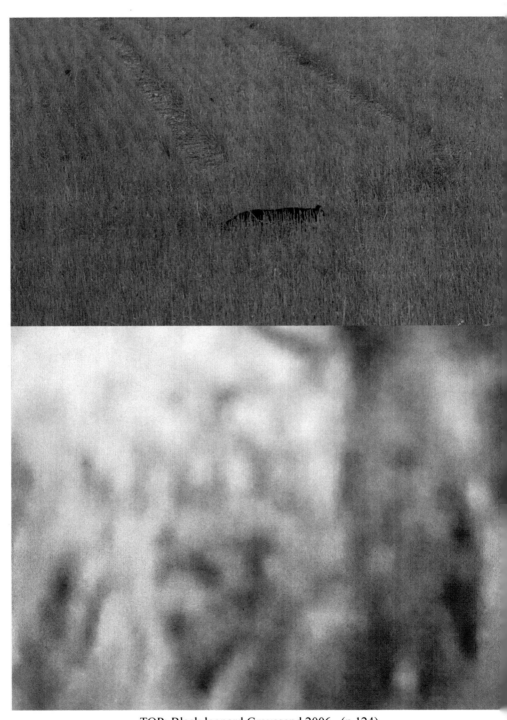

TOP: Black leopard Gravesend 2006. (p.124)
BELOW: Higham lynx filmed by Ian Marsden (p. 107)

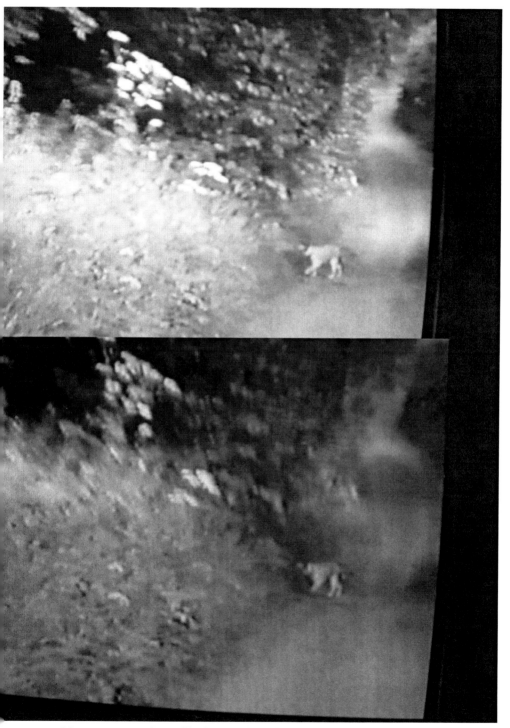

Mystery cat caught on film by member of Gravesend Historical Society.
(p. 111)

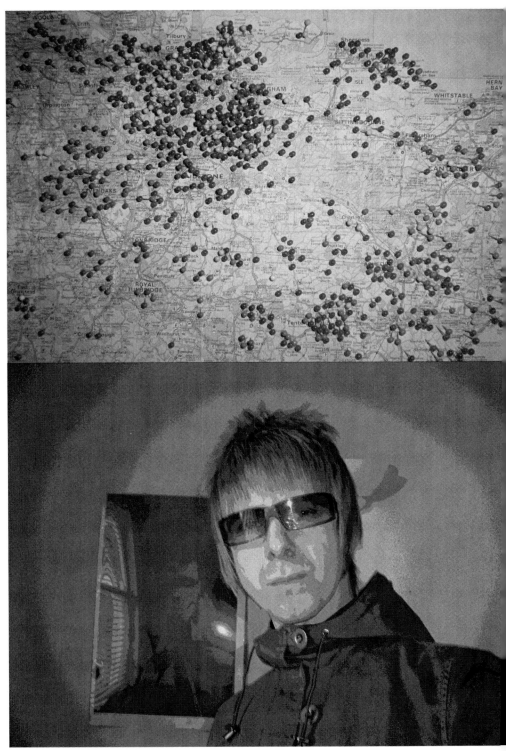

TOP: The author plots county-wide cat sightings on a map using coloured pins
BELOW: The author proving Mod ain't dead

Entrance to Borstal Fort (p. 94)
BELOW: View across Borstal.

A garden next to Rochester Castle (above) where a black leopard was seen in 1999 (p. 93)

Considering the swinging 1960s were the novelty era for keeping a big cat on a lead, sightings in Kent certainly weren't as hot as those in the surrounding counties. Large paw-prints were found in hard mud in the February of 1964 in Gravesend, but from Leonard Cuckow's sighting and a handful of others, Kent appeared to be rather devoid for some thirty of so years prior to the 1960s. Did these lack of sightings simply prove that the introduction of the 1976 Dangerous Wild Animals Act was to blame for the activity after the '60s? Or was it just a case of, like so many other counties, that people weren't coming forward to report their sightings? The Surrey puma had begun to really take off, which could have drowned reports from elsewhere, when in reality it should have brought witnesses forward from across the country. And, as we saw in Part One, parts of Sussex in the 1960s were also home to several large cats, although at the time the press would most certainly have been naïve enough to believe that only a handful of cats, or maybe even one, was responsible for so many sightings in and around the home counties. Put simply, cat sightings in Kent weren't being reported.

During late 1968 a motorist vaguely remembered seeing an unusually large black cat in the Gravesend area, which crossed the road ahead one night and slinked into the bushes. There was also talk of a family in the Thong Lane area owning a black leopard, but whether this escaped or was released remains unknown. In fact many people who owned, or allegedly kept, wild cats often mysteriously vanished along with their animals. The 1970s offered several strange events across the south-east pertaining to mysterious animal sightings and escapees. The most intriguing, which echoed the jackal incident of 1905, occurred in Sussex in 1970 when a weird creature was shot at. The British Museum at the time analysed hair samples left by the creature, and identified that the animal on the loose was in fact a spotted hyena. The animal was never captured.

Fortean Times magazine wrote of the incident, quoting from *The Times*, 23rd July 1971.

> '...*police were hunting a wild animal in the Ashdown Forest area of Sussex, which attacked a dog belonging to a farmer on the forest's edge. People who have seen the animal in the forest, including two policemen, describe it as 'like a puma', black and tan coloured with streaks of yellow, and pointed ears!*'

> *Fortean Times wrote to the farmer, Mr. Alistair Whitley, of Outback Farm, Mutley, on the south side of the forest, whose eye opening reply came six months later. The farmer claimed the animal prowled the farm from Spring to Autumn of 1971. His letter stated:*

> '*Our first signs were over-large 'dog' paw-prints on the woodland paths, and portions of half-eaten wild rabbits in the cattle drinking troughs in the fields. Our first clear sighting was when it seized our little pet dog (a Tibetan spaniel, about 10lbs in weight) at a distance of about twelve feet. I managed o throw a shovel and hit it causing it to drop the dog and make off. Subsequent and many sightings could be condensed thus; very heavy strong dog with fierce eyes and round pricked ears, yellowish in colour and splotched with darker marks. It spent much time lying in whatever field our sheep flock was in, which frightened us, but in fact it never attacked them. (Mind you, it was not with us at lambing – March – or it might have been a different story. It didn't arrive until early May). It appeared to 'camouflage' itself with the sheep to catch rabbits. It urinated in all the water troughs, and was excited by our little dogs – (we kept them shut in the garden after it came into the farmyard to catch one).*

> *We were very lucky in being helped by Dr. John Lisgoe, a marine biologist who lived locally, and a Professor at Sussex University who helped us collect paw-prints both in plaster casts and digging up the actual earth, which he took to the Curator of the Brit-*

ish Natural History Museum who positively identified the 'beast' as an African Spotted hyena, from hairs and prints. We were warned that it was very formidable as an animal which couldn't be doubted if you'd met it as closely as we had. I had a good shot at it in late October as it stood by the wood-side, but whether I killed it or just terrified it away I cannot say. It crawled into the dense undergrowth and we didn't dare follow it in case it was wounded.

Neither our family nor neighbours have seen or heard it since.'

This fascinating story is well known in cryptozoological circles, but what became of the beast we'll never know. And where its journey took it remains a mystery. However, Sussex, at the time, was also active regarding sightings of large cats, but the first close encounter in Gravesend took place in 1979 when Mr Perry was driving through Hextable, at 6:00 am, when what he described as a puma, walked across the road just twenty feet away. The witness couldn't believe his eyes, especially as he'd also seen an antelope in the Canterbury area a few years previously! To him it literally seemed like a zoo out there!

Cobham and the neighbouring Shorne, boast eerie wooded areas. Cobham has its own mausoleum (the Darnley mausoleum) which has received a lot of bad press over the years as tales of 'black magic', dark spirits, and vandalism have centred upon its gloomy confines. But such negative press simply made the area far more mystical, and today, these thickets, which are managed as country parks and have been through restoration, still offer creepy legends which sit nicely alongside the reports of large cats in the area. Shorne Wood Country Park, situated on what used to be known as the Cobham Hall Estate is one-hundred-and seventy acres of ancient woodland, which since the 1980s has been open to the public and sheltered a variety of rare and protected wildlife.

Mr Parker remembers the dark night during the early 1980s, in the Scallers Hill region, when his Alsatian dog was scratched by a big, black animal. It happened after midnight whilst he was patrolling the area with his dog, which suddenly took off after something in the darkness. He ran to where his dog had scrambled and noticed that his Alsatian was biting the tail of something, and that 'something' appeared to be an enormous cat, which, in one swipe, clawed the dog and fled into the night.

Mr Parker claimed that after the incident, and for several years, there were many reports from local residents who'd seen a black leopard with a bent tail, which he strongly believed was the same individual that had scrapped with his dog. Then, twenty-four years later in 2004, Mr Parker saw another melanistic leopard, this time at Luddesdown.

Police Officer Greg Fright was serving at Swanley Police Station, not far from Dartford, during the late '80s, when he was inundated with sightings of large cats nearby. He told me in 2004 that a very trustworthy witness had seen a big animal in Hextable around 1987, and in the same year a couple watched from their window as a puma stalked rabbits in a field in Swanley at 5:00 am.

Around the same time also Mr Clayton spoke of seeing a cat with pointed ears and thick fur on the marshes at Gravesend, ideal habitat for a cat he believed was a lynx.

Motorists seem to make up a large percentage of people most likely to see a large felid. Those who drive during very late or early hours, often to and from work are the most likely to report seeing a big cat, and most of the sightings that involve motorists concern animals which cross the road, as if these animals - as is the same with foxes - are somehow triggered by the oncoming headlights. A large cat such as a puma or leopard will lay up by the roadside at night, often in the undergrowth or roadside ditch. Such an animal may have made a fresh kill, or just eaten and is ready to move on or lay up when it is disturbed b the drone of an approaching vehicle. During the winter of 1984, at 11:30 pm near Cobham, a male witness, travelling home, was amazed to see a large, black cat run into the road after descending a mound, lope across the road and bound up the other side out of sight. The witness got a good look at the animal, which was only forty feet away, and he claimed its eyes were very bright as they reflected in the headlights. He estimated also that the animal was around four feet in length.

Around the same time there were also several rumours circulating that a Wrotham man was keeping a lion in conditions deemed unsuitable for such a large animal. However, what became of the cat - or the man - remains a mystery, but certainly any reports of lions never came my way at the time and haven't done so since. I believe that reports of lions at large in the country have to be taken with a pinch of salt, because such predators would seek large prey and are not elusive killers, hence making their survival in our wilds very remote. Four years later, in Cobham woods, Mrs Hewitt was terrified by the growl of a black leopard which was sitting in the undergrowth as she walked through the trees with her mother. It was a pleasant afternoon in 1988, but Mrs Hewitt was hindered by a cast on her leg, as she'd broken it not long before.

The mother and daughter took their time walking under the shade of the trees, when suddenly they both were startled by the sudden guttural sound. Sharon was so scared that she tried to run. Her mother glanced to the side and could see the animal, a large, jet-black felid, coiled in a ditch. It may have been disturbed by the chatting women. It is possible the animal let out the growl as a warning.

This sudden, terrifying eruption of discontent from the woods was merely the beginning.

Mr Crawford saw a black cat, long in the body, in Dartford in 1990, and also at Horton Kirby. A year later, on the 10th May, PC Ian Harvey was patrolling along the Pilgrim's Way at Trottiscliffe when a large cat, described at the time as a puma, casually crossed the road up ahead.

Just over two weeks later at Snodland, an anonymous witness called one of the local newspapers to say that a 'big cat' had made a hole in his hedge and in July, staff at an elderly home in Southfleet, saw a large black cat on several occasions in the grounds. Police were alerted, but the cat didn't show up when they arrived.

Hot summers bring the ramblers, dog walkers, youngsters, tourists *et al*, to the woods and lanes of Kent, but there has never been any evidence to suggest an increase in sightings within any of the four seasons, and this can be said throughout my years of research. Much of what has been, and still is, reported often depends on press coverage, which - in turn - may trigger someone's memory to report an older sighting, or bring forward many witnesses to fresh sightings. Vegetation is far more dense in the spring and summer months, and although prey such as rabbit is in abundance, sightings remain consistent, but do not suddenly rocket. In the colder season when foliage is thinner and prey harder to find, you would think that large cats on the hunt would be seen more often, maybe coming in to towns to search for food, but this isn't always the case, as they too become even more elusive than the prey they seek, retreating deeper into the woods.

The newspapers and other media groups adore a great mystery, but they aren't always too keen on constant coverage, and prefer writing reports on 'spooky' matters and the like around Hallowe'en, or may occasionally run a big article which usually brings out many more witnesses to strange events, and this certainly has been the case with sightings of large cats. Many researchers and writers discussing the 'big cat' situation call these periods of high activity 'cat flaps', apt considering the alternate 'flaps' domestic cats use to enter and exit homes. However, these flaps are few and far between and although the press do allow a trickle of eyewitness sightings to leak on to their pages, the clusters of sightings are the most important to any researcher, especially one who is keen on getting a glimpse of the elusive predator he is monitoring or, at times, so obsessed with.

Due to lack of press interest, the very early '90s were pretty much devoid of sightings of large cats in North Kent, but this certainly didn't mean they weren't out there or any more elusive than normal. In 1994 pensioner Edith Bryant saw a 'big cat' near her home in Snodland. During the same year a woman named Sharon was sitting in a car with her boyfriend Ian, at 2:00 am near Meopham when they observed a big, black cat as it slowly walked down the pathway by the side of the vehicle. Sharon told me that the cat was low to the ground and had a very long, curved tail. Her boyfriend was going to get out of the car, but Sharon was more concerned about her own domestic cat. A year later a friend of Sharon saw a black cat in broad daylight in Shorne Country Park only a few miles from Meopham. There were also reports from a Dartford school that a big black animal had been seen prowling the grounds. Mr Roberts was out pigeon shooting around Halling in 1995, when something caught his eye moving through long grass some sixty yards away. A large animal was creeping low through the undergrowth as if it was hunting. Mr Roberts was very curious and walked up the field towards the animal which saw him and stood up, revealing itself as a jet-black cat which simply turned around and went into the woods.

In 1996 a large black cat was seen pouncing on rabbits at Harvel in Meopham and several horses nearby often appeared spooked by something. A couple of farmers in the area also claimed that they'd lost a few sheep in mysterious circumstances in that they were cleanly eaten. A male witness named Tony was riding his bicycle near the marshes at Cliffe at midnight when a 'panther' emerged from the foliage, and crossed the lane. The man claimed he'd seen a similar cat in Northfleet a decade previously. Rumours also circulated at the time that a mini-zoo was being kept in the area of the marshes by a man who paraded his animals somewhere on the Kent coast. Apparently he had several cats which were caged behind his pub in the area, whilst a male witness out on the marshes shooting in 1997, claimed he saw a serval, although it's likely that the animal was in fact a lynx (judging by his description of a mottled, but not spotted, coat). At Stanstead in the same year, a female witness named Penny Goring spoke of several sightings of a large, dark-coloured cat, but believed it had rings on its tail. It is possible, however, that when the cat was caught in the headlights of various residents' cars, that the rosettes were evident through the dark coat.

Chickens often went missing in the area, and - on one occasion - after sheep and horses were spooked one night, foxes that were shot in the area and hung up were found next morning either beheaded or eaten.

Any cat roaming Gravesend would have a sizeable territory as heavy woodlands that merge into country parks although built up at its heart flank the town. A territory of something like a black leopard would certainly stretch as far as Dartford where sightings to the present day are frequent, as well as stretching towards the more desolate, remote marshes of Higham, Cooling and also Grain.

1998 was a significant year for my research, and for the exposure of exotic cats throughout Kent. Although the local press had had a previously fleeting interest prior to 1998, this, as you will read, was the year when things really took off and a majority of newspapers of the county followed the lead of the then *Kent Today* by writing features on sightings.

A black leopard was seen at Snodland during early '98 by a motorist driving on a back road at 11:00 pm. The cat bounded across the road ahead and went to jump a fence but somehow, according to the witness, mistimed its leap and fell to the floor. The cat then slipped under the fence out of sight as the witness drove by. Also in the January, Valerie Wynn saw a large cat which appeared in front of her headlights as she drove towards the clubhouse at Cobham's Golf Course. It was her second sighting of possibly the same animal.

One month later, Leonard Cuckow, who has already been mentioned as having sighted a black leopard in the 1930s, had another encounter with a strange cat whilst walking with his wife Marjorie near rough ground at their home in Strood. As they took a morning stroll down the disused lane, which was flanked by undergrowth, a sandy-coloured cat leapt from bank to bank just a few metres away. Leonard marked the area with a stick, and contacted me, and I visited the couple at their home. We visited the area after a long conversation about Leonard's other sightings - another had occurred a few decades ago near a local lake, of a black cat - but what he and his wife saw on their walk was altogether different. It was a lot smaller than a leopard, and could possibly have been a jungle cat.

It was on February 9th that the *Kent Today* printed one of the most intriguing 'big cat' stories of Kent's strange history. The front-page headline read *'Is This The Beast Of Blue Bell Hill?'* showing a full colour photograph of a mystery cat prowling through long grass. The article at the time was typical of so many other inaccuracies that have peppered 'big cat' folklore throughout the country. Yes, the photograph showed a wild cat of sorts, but for one, it wasn't a black leopard, or even a puma, and two, it wasn't snapped anywhere near Blue Bell Hill. The article read as follows:

> *'Caught On Film, Kent's Mystery Creature Revealed – Kent Today has reported your numerous sightings of a big cat in recent months in an area stretching from Cobham in the west to Blue Bell Hill in the east and south towards Maidstone.*
>
> *Callers have been adamant that what they saw was a puma or panther rather than a large household moggie or dog. Since our investigation began six months ago we have been looking for photographic evidence of the animal, nicknamed the Beast of Blue Bell Hill after the area where it was first sighted.*

Amateur photographer Harry Matthews snapped a large cat-like creature from thirty feet away in fields at Cooling, Rochester. The picture shows the creature, which is several times the size of a domestic cat with much longer ears and tail, lurking at the foot of a tree before it dashed off into the undergrowth.

Mr Matthews, of Herne Bay, works in the RSPB wetland area near the Thames estuary. He said, "I go everywhere with my camera and this particular time I saw it walking along a track towards the cabin where I work. I got my camera out and took a picture of it beneath the tree but then it saw me and ran away.

> *It is certainly two or three times bigger than a normal cat and unlike anything else I have ever seen. It looks much blacker than it does in the picture."*

When the photo of the mystery animal first surfaced it certainly caused a stir, and remains one of the clearest photo's ever of a strange felid roaming Britain. However, over time and after much analysis several things became clear.

- The animal was not a black leopard or even puma-size resembling other large cats reported in Kent at the time.
- The animal was not the Blue Bell Hill cat, which was making a name for itself as Cooling lies across the river, closer to the marshy areas of Higham and Cliffe.
- The photo on the front of the newspaper was misleading. At first glance it seemed to show a brown cat, long in the body with muscular shoulders and pointed ears. The animal appeared slender but had a longish, hooked tail. However, shortly after the report, another photo appeared in

the *Kent Today*. *'Well, do you think it's just a pet cat?'* asked the paper on 13th February 1998, showing a large black and white picture of the same animal, yet bounding away, with a smaller picture in black and white of the animal which appeared on the front of the paper, and next to it a photo of Harry Matthews. This time the mystery became a bigger puzzle, because although we were clearly not dealing with a photo of a black leopard, puma or even a lynx, we were certainly dealing with an unusual wild cat. The new released photo proved just how misleading the original photo was. The reality was, the cat was certainly slightly longer in the body than a domestic cat but not vastly bigger, possibly only fox-sized.

The cat in the new photo did not have a muscular frame or unusually large ears, and certainly didn't have a long, curved tail. However, none of these inaccurate details were due to attempted hoax or tampering, but simply down to the fact that the original photo of the beast standing under a tree showed a lot more undergrowth which in turn created several illusions. The muscular shoulder was in fact foliage and the hook of the tail may have also been undergrowth because the new image of the cat racing away showed its truest form. The animal was chocolate brown in colour, with lighter brown around the tops of the rear legs, and some kind of mottled marking was evident. The paws appeared only domestic cat size, there was nothing striking about the animal except its rabbit-shaped head, which has been noted in other sightings of unusual smaller cats across the British Isles, particularly in Scotland where similar cats have been recorded.

Mr Matthews at the time claimed that the animal might have been an Italian wild cat of sorts after referring to a computer encyclopaedia. Researchers who mulled over the photographs concluded that the animal was a jungle cat, or possibly a hybrid of jungle cat and domestic. Adrian Harland, big cat keeper at Port Lympne Zoo Park couldn't identify the cat, except to say it may have been a large Abyssinian-style domestic cat. Meanwhile Operation Big Cat, run by Bob Engledow from Norfolk, claimed, *'The area of countryside stretching from Maidstone to Medway does seem to be a prime area for sightings'*, although how such a group could monitor the situation from so far away had me baffled. At the time the research group was one of the countries only national registers where people could report their sightings. That trend would change for the worse soon after, when scores of 'big cat groups' formed as 'official' registers to represent Britain in order to release statistics on sightings throughout the counties.

What the photo did do was prove just how inaccurate press reports could be, but also, and rather thankfully, urged more and more people to come forward to report similar sightings. And indeed they did from all over. In the same year it was claimed that a puma-like cat was caught in a trap in Meopham woods, but the photo, which appeared on an angling forum was a hoax, showing a domestic cat seemingly hanging from a tree, although the truth was simply attributed to computer fakery.

There were several reports from the area now known as Bluewater and surrounding towns and villages. Jim Roberts came forward to report seeing what the *Kent Today* described as a 'black puma', several years ago as it stalked pheasants in the Halling area. At Hoo, past Cooling, there were several reports of a fawn-coloured cat roaming the ploughed fields, but also a handful of sightings of a big, black cat. Later in the year Mrs Barham was driving through Cuxton when she observed a black cat in a nearby field used by cows.

During the February of 1999 a black panther was spotted in the vicinity of Cobham Golf Course, and then, in March, as Bluewater opened its doors to millions of buzzing visitors, a big black animal sauntered into Rochester city centre. The *Kent Today* of Thursday March 4th reported, *'Beast Is Spotted In City Centre'* as part of their latest Beastwatch feature.

'Police are on the trail of the Beast of Blue Bell Hill after reports of a black panther prowling in

the shadow of Rochester's historic castle.

The five-foot long black feline (sic) *with piercing yellow eyes was seen in the garden of Boley Hill by cleaners in daylight yesterday. Police received a call from the distraught owner of the house at 1 pm and sent out PC Graham O' Keefe to look for paw prints and droppings.*

Police spokesman Stuart Donaldson said, "We have had calls about sightings of big cats in the past but I can't recall any of it appearing in such a built-up area. The fact that we have recorded it and sent a patrol car shows that we are taking the matter seriously."

No traces of the elusive cat were found at the scene. But Wendy Wells, mother-of-two who owns the house where the panther was spotted, said she was too scared to let her three-year old child out to play.

Mrs Wells who also has a nine-month old baby returned home to find her cleaners in a state of shock having seen the prowling beast.

She said: "It's terrifying to think that there is this huge cat out there prowling around people's gardens. How long is it safe to let your kids out, as I'm sure a small child would be quite appetising to a cat of that size. I'm scared to go out myself and now I'm definitely considering getting a guard dog."

I visited the area immediately after the sighting and assured Mrs Wells that the cat was of no threat and that sightings in the past had been very rare in such an area. Although Rochester is a beautiful and historic town in Kent - lying across the river from Strood - known for its ruinous castle, cobbled streets and Dickensian associations, it is not at all wooded. However, after a spate of further sightings along the line of the River Medway shortly after the Boley Hill encounter, it appeared to be that such an animal could well have been related to, or indeed was the same animal as the Blue Bell Hill cat, following the line of the river during the shadows of night and possibly resting up in the shrouded garden where it was seen. However, where it went straight after the cleaners had seen it remains a mystery as no further daylight sightings came – despite rumour that a domestic cat or two had gone missing in the vicinity.

Maybe the cat had slinked across the bridge that spans the river, joining Rochester with Strood, giving the cat connections to the Bluewater area, having travelled from the Halling, Cuxton and Gravesend area. We'll never fully know where the castle cat came from, but it seems unlikely that it crossed the busy bridge.

Reports of puma and black leopard were being reported from Sevenoaks, further south from Gravesend but sightings of what was to become known as the Beast of Bluewater didn't filter though until the summer.

The Bluewater Years

On the 13th August 1999 a black cat was twice seen stalking chickens at a smallholding near Meopham. The witness, Mr Davis, told local press that, *"It's definitely a cat but it's four times the size of a domestic cat. It is totally black with a two-foot-long straight tail."*

Strangely, reports of such cats with straight tales are scarce, as witnesses often note that the most eye-catching feature of cats such as the black leopard is the long, yet curved tail.

On 20th August a landscape gardener caught sight of a black panther in Dartford, a few miles from Blue-water and around the same time Norman Barnden sighted a similar creature near Meopham. The *Dart-ford Messenger* reported on another black cat sighting near Orpington during the same month.

As summer faded into the rustic haze of autumn, and the air became tinged with the scent of bonfire smoke and fizzling fireworks, and as young children took to the streets adorned in ghoulish costumes to represent All Hallows Eve, things got seriously weird for my research.

A man named Jim, who lived in Medway, often paid visits to local areas of interest, whether reputedly haunted or simply old. On the night of November 10th 1999 he visited Cliffe Fort, a derelict and remote building constructed in the mid-nineteenth century on the wastes of the Hoo peninsula. Whilst roaming the dilapidated ruins in pitch darkness, with only the aid of a male friend and torch beam, Jim picked out a set of bright eyes in the centre of the grounds, around sixty yards away. The two witnesses were so spooked by the presence, that they hastily left the fort and hurried to their vehicle. After speaking about the eerie eyes, the friends decided to leave the fort and drive home. As the car headlights came on, some-thing the size of a large dog bounded across the beam and out of sight.

Jim was only able to visit the area again a week later, this time in daylight. Luckily, he managed to pho-tograph a paw-print and saw another near one of the conveyor belts used to transport sand across the marsh.

After the experience Jim phoned me, and offered to help me with my research as he knew various places where he believed such cats could roam. He mentioned briefly something about the carcass of a goat being found at another fort over the Hallowe'en period, which intrigued me a great deal.

I investigated the area of Fort Borstal soon after the rumours began to circulate that a goat had been found dead in the grounds. I knew little about the area at the time and certainly didn't expect the series o events, which followed my visit.

From website *Underground Kent*:

> 'Fort Borstal forms part of the Chatham Outer Ring of defences, along with forts Hor-sted, Luton and Darland and the Twydall Redoubts. It was constructed by prisoners from the nearby prison at Borstal, but progress was slow. Although the land was pur-chased in 1870 construction did not begin until 1875 and fort Borstal itself was not completed until the mid 1890s.
>
> Fort Borstal is polygonal in shape and made mostly of concrete. It was surrounded by a dry ditch that was defended by firing galleries and a caponier to the rear of the ditch. At the back of the fort itself a loop-holed wall provides further protection. This wall is still clearly visible today. At the time of construction, access to the fort would have been via a roller bridge, the remains of which are still visible.
>
> Inside the fort is a row of casemates to the rear. Immediately to the left of the entrance are rooms that would have been used for officers and administrative use. To the right of the entrance are magazines and reservoirs. On the terreplein are three ammunition serving rooms with their associated expense magazines directly below them.
>
> During the two world wars the fort Borstal was used for training, and during the Sec-ond World War it was used as a heavy AA [anti-aircraft] site. AA gunners remained at

the fort until 1957. After that the Home Office took over the use of the fort and used it alongside the Borstal Institute. It was sold in 1990 with plans to restore the fort and open it as a tourist attraction. Unfortunately planning problems have prevented this project from coming to fruition.'

I never realised how a place, let alone a place local to me, could omit such an evil sense of foreboding. Sure, Hallowe'en had come and gone, but the air that surrounded the grey façade of the fort was stale and uncomfortable, despite the fact I'd visited around 10:30 am. It was a clear day, not cold, typically autumnul in its crackling aroma. However, walking to the main door of the grim building, and its outer wall, was surreal and uninviting. Daubed crudely on the iron door, which looked like the entrance to Hell itself, were symbols that many would swear were related to all manner of dark witchery and black magic. Of course, years of study of folklore allowed me to scoff at such child-like graffiti which consisted of a '666' painted on one section, and possibly 'Devil' plastered on another. Even so, whilst vandals may have been to blame, the atmosphere was altogether unsettling, even more so as I entered the door, which I realised, was not only the only way in, but also only the way out.

I stepped on to a concrete platform, and felt as if I'd stepped back in time. A mixture of Lovecraftian weirdness suffocated me, as before me stretched and loomed the pallid, crumbling remains of a fort that now presented itself as some kind of abandoned shell that could hide any number of urban horrors within its colourless frame. Suddenly, feeling incredibly alone and secluded from the rest of the world, I froze as there, on the grassy courtyard, some twenty feet from me, lay a goat on its side. Its white fur, or what was left of it, peeled back from a hideously exposed ribcage revealing a dry bed of dark blood, yellowing bone but not a sign of any glistening innards. The head of the unfortunate animal was jolted back, as if its neck had been broken, and on its neck, close to the head, was another gaping wound. The eyes were gone, probably pecked from their sockets by birds, and I'm sure that a few foxes and smaller predators had been to scavenge the remains, but what lay before me was quite shocking, in all its miserable glory. This poor goat was most certainly the victim of a big cat, very likely the same animal that had been seen at Shorts Way and further into Rochester. A prowling black leopard.

I didn't know what to take in first, the stripped carcass on the ground, or the ominous building that leered at me like some stone golem, its empty eyes the windowless frames splintered by decay and abuse. Even though I was only a few feet inside the main door, I was concerned that the entrance would suddenly blow shut and all my inner fears of childhood would swarm me, and devour my quaking soul just like that goat which lay so stiff and empty before me.

The fort was such a gloomy attraction. Small and then larger doorways pitted across its harsh face, only the greenery rear of the foreground and hilly perimeter offering any kind of summery gleam as the fresh blades of grass attempted to puncture the morose and soulless ruins. The whole place an oppressive shrine to a time long gone, but if local rumour was to be believed, I'd also heard that various tramps, drug addicts, vandals, and even black magicians had infiltrated the cavernous structure, and on varying nights either slept, lit fires, abused themselves - or even others - in the confines of this unwelcoming citadel.

My mind was awash with all manner of dark images, let alone the thoughts that a large, hungry cat might be cooped up somewhere in one of the tunnels which were rumoured to run for several miles under the river. I stood over the goat. Someone, possibly teenagers, had been here because a piece of wood was propped near the animal. There were no footprints around the corpse, and no specks of blood suggesting that whatever had killed the goat had attacked it, ending its life somewhere else, before taking it to the spot, or had disembowelled it there and then, but somehow not caressed the surrounding soil with a trace of crimson. Weird.

I took several photographs of the goat, pretty sure that a large cat such as a leopard had claimed a victim. I believed that the blow to the neck was either a ferocious throat bite that had been picked at over a few days by scavengers, or may well have been caused by a swipe from a claw. The exposed ribcage certainly pointed to a big cat kill. The gut was completely gone, the animals stomach an empty hole as if something had stripped it, and lapped at it, draining and rasping the carcass of any fresh meat. The attack had possibly only taken place around Hallowe'en and according to my source Jim, the animal hadn't been there before that time. Had a black leopard killed the goat somewhere else and then dragged it by its throat to the courtyard and had its fill? Or were there other questions that needed answering?

I scoured the fort.

The pathways were littered with debris, as if not so long ago a bomb had dropped on the building, peppering the lonely avenues with pieces of wood, concrete and other rubbish which had been left by anyone who had hung around the fort, wasting time as some kind of peculiar pastime. Why anyone would want to frequent such a formidable place I never knew, and I wasn't sure if the whispers were true or mere exaggeration spewed from residents who were convinced that one or two fires in the vaults were the work of wicked sorcerers sacrificing the animals within the vicinity under a Hallowe'en moon.

Various tunnels leading from the walls could only really be explored if I'd been accompanied by a few friends. There was no way that I was going to take a perilous journey into some unknown chasm, knowing how unfamiliar I was with the terrain and the local inhabitants. In fact, after just a few minutes of roaming the grounds I suddenly began to fear local lunatics more than a melanistic leopard or ghosts.

There were other symbols and figures painted on the walls, and stairways that spiralled into darkness. Other doorways seemed to have been derelict for centuries, which - of course - wasn't the case, but the amount of rubbish piled into the nooks and crannies simply added to the eeriness. Every step into this alien environment tightened my chest, and so, after a short spell at the place, I decided to leave, vowing to return with someone else.

When I did return a few days after, the place still had that sepulchral air about it. I showed my cousin, Jez, the place and we both found that the remains of the goat had been slung down a stairwell, which had crumbled, to a mysterious door that looked inaccessible. We tried a few of the funereal alleyways and checked on the higher ground, which proved to be fruitful. The grassy banks rose reasonably high over the courtyard and as we awkwardly stumbled to the peak, we came across three goats, thankfully alive, that were feeding on the green pasture. Surely the fort wasn't the healthiest environment for these animals, but one thing we did notice was our inability to get anywhere near them. The ground they frequented sloped dangerously towards a moat, which we couldn't even see the bottom of. Spindly trees rose from the depths, and we wondered what secrets the ditch hid. The goats were nimble, but not too wary of us unless we approached, but even then they were fleet of foot enough to easily conquer the perilous ground of dips, divots and bumps which we had to stagger across with painful concentration. Any moment one of us could be sent tumbling into a world from which we could never escape; a quiet grave from whence we'd never be rescued, and although we believed that one or two goats may have also perished in such a way, we realised that something quick and powerful must have killed the goat, the carcass of which was now crumpled in that stairwell.

Shortly after our visit, which was to be our last, as the powers that be would soon deny public access to the fort which was to be converted into living accommodation, we heard many tales from locals, possibly from the realm of folklore, although interesting all the same. Some claimed that the fort had indeed been used for satanic rituals, and that set deep within the bowels of the fort was a chamber of sorts used for animal sacrifice. It was claimed that more than thirty goats once roamed the grounds, but over time had gradually disappeared. Legend had it that such animals were caught and stabbed between the eyes, and then burned.

The truth seems less gothic, in that such an area *did* attract many a character, but many of these were probably nothing more than youths with a penchant for heavy rock music and Devil worship which - as often is the case - meant a few beers around a roaring fire, but to local residents meant extreme acts of diabolical practice. I knew of the confusion because in the mid-'80s I was one of those loiterers.

In January of 2000 more weirdness would come to light, which I will speak of shortly.

A motorist caught a glimpse of a black leopard on Shorts Way, Rochester, eight months after the Rochester castle report. The witness claimed that he was driving along during the evening in question when he spotted the big cat mooching around rubbish bags left on the pavement by residents. The animal then slinked away.

Although the area in question leads to what is known as the Esplanade, of a night the area is reasonably quiet despite the fact that only half a mile away sits the city centre. The area of Shorts Way, leading to the Esplanade is extremely built-up, but fields and marsh pepper the location, and dip into the cold waters of the river, which at night remains a silent abyss.

I received a call from a male witness who claimed that on the night of November 10th at 11:45 pm he'd driven through Shorts Way where at the time new apartments were being built, when he saw the panther on the pavement. The cat was once again sniffing at bins, and the witness got to within a few metres and noted its long tail before the cat moved off.

After conducting research of several years into sightings and other evidence of exotic cats inhabiting the wilds of Kent, I had developed several patterns pertaining to certain individual cats. Although this particular section concentrates on the Gravesham area and further north, I would just like to add that by the end of the '90s I was receiving hundreds of reports of large cats from as far a field as Dover, Deal and Folkestone, to Maidstone, Tonbridge and Sevenoaks, covered later in this chapter.

2000 was a huge year for my research, mainly regarding one of the animals roaming Blue Bell Hill, but whilst still concentrating on the Bluewater area, a lady walking with her son and three dogs, at lunch time, in the January, was amazed to see a black leopard padding along a pathway at Northfleet.

'Big Cat – Neil's On Your Tail' read the *KM Extra* free newspaper of the 6th January, stating:

> *'Neil Arnold believes he is close to catching a glimpse of a big cat roaming the Medway countryside.*
>
> *The twenty-four year old man has been tagged beast-hunter because of the way he has catalogued hundreds of people's sightings of big cats across Kent since the 1970s.*
>
> *He said: "I have pinpointed one main area where I believe at least one cat roams and I think I am very close to something."*
>
> *He is so sure he has found the habitat where a beast or beasts are dwelling that he will not reveal the location to anyone. The newspaper has agreed to his request so that we do not encourage a witch-hunt.'*

A black leopard was seen by workmen at the Southfleet Tunnel rail link construction on 19th January. Several more workmen at the time came forward to report that they'd seen a big, black cat at Cliffe one year previous. In the same month the *Medway Today* (formerly *Kent Today)* and *KM Extra* made a huge mistake. After discussing with a reporter the finding of the goat carcass at fort Borstal, I was shocked to see the story plastered all over the local newspapers, and connecting my name to something I'd discussed in confidence.

'Was fort used for satanic rituals?' asked the *Extra,* with the *Medway Today* stating that *'Symbols of the black art found at fort',* and *'Derelict fort could be haunt of the beast'.* It was unwise commentary and depicted various grim scenes that one of their photographers had discovered at the fort, and in naivety had hurried back to the offices with tales of evil which read as follows:

'Evidence of sinister satanic rituals has been discovered at derelict fort Borstal – once a proud army garrison vital to the defence of the Medway Towns.

The entrance doors to the deserted Rochester fort have been daubed with two satanic symbols and there are further signs of devil-worship inside. The carcass of a goat has been thrown into a stairwell packed with rubbish and there are animal remains in a dilapidated former storeroom at the fort. In that area the words Devil 666 are crudely daubed on the wall and there is evidence that a fire has been lit on a shoddily constructed altar.

The scene has been witnessed by Neil Arnold, from Walderslade who has visited the area for a different reason – to try and find the lair of a black panther tagged the Blue Bell Hill Beast.

Neil said, "There are certainly animal bones up there and satanic symbols. There seems to be some strange things going on there at night."

In 1991 sadistic raiders tried to kill one of the goats which roam the fort by burning it alive. Strangely, only a small number of the original twenty-strong herd of goats that have roamed the fort grounds for years seem to remain.

People living in St. Johns Way, which backs on to the fort have confirmed the late night goings-on there.

One said, "We do hear noises at night but I think it is kids mucking about."

Another said: "You see the fires lit at night and there is noise from the fort. If there are satanic goings-on in there it shows anything can happen in your own back yard."

Fort Borstal was owned by the government until it was sold at auction in 1990 for around £60,000 to the pharmacist Ulfat Hussain and his brother-in-law Tajamal Khan. They had plans to convert it into a museum, craft workshop or goat farm but their ideas fell foul of opposition from locals. Eventually they decided to pull out.

Shortly after the various reports in the press, I began to receive all manner of strange and threatening late night phone calls. Naturally, I was rather concerned - not only by the calls - but the fact that the newspaper had connected me to the activity. Yes, I'd found some very strange things at the fort, but was misquoted on several occasions. I'd grown up studying local folklore and dark tales of rituals etc, which often turned out to be nothing more than vandals, as such cults would certainly operate on a more clandestine and professional basis. Yes, there were rumours and it seems that goats had been killed over time, maybe a few of these were tortured by mindless hooligans, whilst others may well have been killed and eaten by a big cat. However, although I always appreciated that the press loved a good story, their take on the matter was disastrous.

I never believed that the fort was a lair for the local big cat, but it was certainly likely that in the still of night a hungry cat would certainly have stalked and eaten one of the goats, but for the papers to say I'd discovered some evil sect was terrible.

I refused to contribute further articles for a while, keeping my research even more under wraps than previous.

On February 2nd 2000 the *Gravesend Messenger* reported that, *'Big cat is prowling the tunnel'*, after two security men working at the Southfleet Tunnel in Downs Road, at 9:30 pm on January 19th , as mentioned earlier. Even *The Sun* newspaper mentioned the sighting. The witnesses reported the sighting to North Kent Police. Other sightings came from Fawkham when a fire fighter saw a big, black cat and a teenage electrician also saw the animal.

On the 16th February, and 19th March I finally glimpsed the so-called Blue Bell Hill Beast, which I knew I had the ability to track down. These events are mentioned in the next section.

Darenth, near Dartford became a hive of big cat activity in the summer with several sightings. On 20th June 2000 a married couple awoke at 2:00 am and looked out of their bedroom window and were startled to see a black cat, just thirty feet away, walking along the road. The animal was much bigger than a fox with a long tail and as it crossed the street it stopped and looked back at the amazed couple that were peering from their window. The next day two chickens were found decapitated in the next street.

A Wolverhampton man saw a big cat in Halling woods. He claimed he was only four feet away. On the 27th October several campers were terrified by a prowling black leopard also in Halling. They saw the cat on three occasions whilst setting up camp in the heavily wooded area not far from Cuxton. At the same time large cats were observed in Ashford, Maidstone and Deal proving to the press finally that one cat was not responsible for all the sightings!

In the more remote area of Culverstone, one of four villages which make up the civil parish of Meopham, a huge black cat was seen on one of the unmade roads.

At the beginning of 2001 I filmed a short feature with Chris Packham for the ITV series *Wildwatch*. The wildlife programme, on its second episode of thirteen, featured my research across Kent in which I presented Chris with evidence of large cats roaming the local woods. On the 20th January at Thriftwood, Dartford, a witness walking his dog claimed to see a black cat that had a striped tail. The animal made a strange sound, "*...like two magpies squabbling.*"

Five days later at Bean, near Bluewater, a male motorist driving on the B225, at 2:00 pm, saw a big, black cat cross into a nearby field.

'Black puma seen close to Bluewater' exclaimed the *Dartford Messenger*, speaking of Christine Pearson and her husband who'd sighted a big cat a week previous near the roundabout for Bluewater, at 2:00 pm.

'In the first instant we thought it was a fox, but this walked like a cat – it was definitely feline," she said.

Some confusion arose from the report. The witnesses claimed the cat was dark in colour, whereas the newspaper stated 'black puma', which of course do not exist. Did the couple see a very dark puma, or a black leopard, which often in broad daylight would look very dark brown? Other reports from varying sources claimed that the couple had seen a puma, which was reasonably rare among the countless black cat reports from the Gravesend and Dartford areas, although I knew that such an animal was out there but simply not sighted as much.

'*The beast of Bean may be a panther*', commented the *Dartford Messenger* on February 8th. Mr Tawn claimed to have seen a dark-coloured cat in Swanscombe two months previously, but said that it was too small to be a puma. Then, Mr Avery saw the cat and its piercing eyes at 5:30 pm in early February. He was driving with his wife towards Bluewater when the animal, a big, black cat, crossed the road casually in front of the car. Another report from January 30th at 1:30 am involved Mrs Merry who saw a Border collie-sized black cat whilst driving towards her home at New Barn. She reported it to the council.

On 15th February a female witness observed a black panther in a wooded area near Higham as she was collecting firewood. The cat was around three-hundred yards away and bolted into the undergrowth. The woman couldn't take her own sighting seriously, but told a friend who reported it to the *Medway Today*.

A few days later I contacted local MP Jonathan Shaw with regards to my research. He kindly approached various police Superintendents but to no avail, as any replies simply stated that such reports were not logged!

A woman from Singlewell, Gravesend was the next person privileged to see a jet-black cat. At the beginning of March she was watching television when something caught her eye at the end of her garden some one hundred feet away. The animal, which was low to the ground, was circling the pond and then it headed off towards the garden of a neighbour. Amazingly, this had been the woman's third sighting of possibly the same cat. She saw it at 10:00 am in the Spring of 2000 as she was driving through Singlewell. The animal ran out in front of her vehicle just a few yards away and leapt a fence. In 1998 she saw the animal one lunchtime whilst she was a dinner lady at Singlewell School. Many of the children observed the big cat on the field just one hundred yards away. The witness calmed the frightened children by telling them it was just a dog.

On March 8th Mr Batchelor saw a large cat-like animal in Strood, towards Higham. He was the passenger in a car travelling from Strood to Higham on the A229. As they approached Dillywood Lane something crossed the road from Chapter Farm, which the witness at first took to be a fox. As the vehicle neared the witness remarked that the animal was mottled and blackish in colour and the tail very long and curved.

However, despite being very sure he'd seen a panther, the witness then claimed it may well have been a fox with mange!

Three goats were attacked in March 2001 in Fawkham. Two of the goats were killed and the other put down. A local engineer working in the area had a close encounter with a black leopard around the same time and in the exact same area.

On 24th March a local man travelling towards Higham with his wife, at 9:00 pm observed a black leopard also. The animal emerged from the undergrowth and strolled across the road just twenty yards away. As the vehicle approached the cat it turned to look at the startled witnesses who claimed that the beast was stocky and had a patchy but very dark coat. Four days later a woman feeding birds at 2:00 pm, at her home near Wrotham Road, saw a massive black cat mooching around a series of fox holes at the end of her garden. She said, "*The animal was blackish-grey and around three-to-four foot long with a low tail.*"

Back towards Higham, Mr Clarke living in his home near the disused railway line flanked by marshes, claimed that something had been taking his ducks and leaving no sign. Whilst the area is very remote, with one dark road leading towards a small business area, details of what was actually seen seem vague. Mr Clarke on one occasion claimed to have seen a silvery animal that resembled a fox, which simply, to me anyway, sounded just like a fox. Despite the area and several details showing promise, no definite evidence came to light.

Bexley News Shopper, on April 20th commented that, '*Cats find a purr-fect county*', and that '*More than thirty people in the county claim to have seen a wild cat*', this in accordance to *Fortean Times* magazine whose annual round-up featured several reports from the Kent area. The magazine claimed that, '*…Kent is now the seventh likeliest spot in the United Kingdom for anyone to come face to face with a big cat.*'

Of course, such figures were complete rubbish but as per usual based on inaccurate statistics put forward by another nationwide big cat register.

Thankfully, with all the April Fools shenanigans over, sightings resumed as normal. On 20th April near Longfield, at Hartley, two women watched an Alsatian sized cat one afternoon from their window as it crossed the garden. They watched the animal for more than thirty seconds and were both unnerved by its presence. One of the women told me that her Irish wolfhound had returned from the woods one day with several deep scratch marks on its flanks.

Kent Messenger, April 27th, '*Proving Kent's got pussy galore*', was the tacky headline, once again echoing the *Fortean Times* coverage.

> '*Kent is a hotspot for sightings of mysterious big cats, according to a new survey.*
>
> *The research by Fortean Times, a magazine about strange phenomena, puts Kent equal seventh place with thirty-six sightings reported in the last three years.*
>
> *Kent has the same figure as Norfolk. Only four English counties had more sightings with Wales in forty-one. Scotland was way ahead at the top of the league with seventy-eight recorded cases.*
>
> *But the figures were disputed by Kent big cat researcher Neil Arnold who claims that the true number of sightings in the county is nearer to two-hundred-and-fifty. He said that the last two months alone he has had more than sixty sightings of big cats.*'

Unfortunately, such statistics have plagued big cat research since the late '90s, with the national press and commercial magazines jumping on the 'facts' and being all too hasty to report such incorrect findings. At this point I'd also like to add that several researchers nationwide quite simply couldn't understand how Kent alone could receive more than two hundred sightings, but it is easy to respond to such scepticism…or should that be jealousy?

Much of what is printed in the press is false, especially regarding big cat sightings because many of the researchers are naïve, or simply armchair enthusiasts. Whilst I respect such individuals and groups for recording and storing data, such information can never be taken seriously when simply relying on newspaper clippings. Avid researchers should know full well that if the hours are put in, not just in the field, but also bombarding the press with appeals, then it will be rewarded. A majority of the counties in England are inhabited by several large cats, so, if this is the case and the researcher is going about his work in the correct fashion, then he should be constantly inundated with information, evidence and sightings to be able to pin-point territories of such animals. Unfortunately, a majority of researchers haven't seen a thing because they tend to get impatient and give up, or constantly buzz around the countryside instead of staking out an area for months at a time, or as some claim, have seen hundreds of big cats.

With regards to Kent, by 2001 I was confident that the populations of cats were far higher than anyone else had estimated and that after receiving several sightings over a month, it was easy to determine that there were more black leopards out there than I'd originally accounted for, as well as lynx, puma and smaller cats which were more difficult to track.

A female witness named Vickie saw the Higham panther in 2001 at 10:30 pm. She was a passenger in her friend's car when the cat appeared near the Chalk Church turning. The animal ran in front of the car and into a hedge. Mrs Adams saw a cat, but not the same one during early summer. She was in bed with her husband and woke up in the night, at about 11:40 pm, to open her bedroom window which overlooks the back garden. As she pulled back the curtains she noticed a large animal walking across the lawn. She called her husband and they both watched intently as the animal, around three feet long with yellow eyes and fawn in colour and pointed ears headed towards the direction of the A226. They both agreed that the cat was almost two feet high and had a long tail.

A small black panther was seen at Downs Road, near Southfleet on 5th July at 9:20 pm by a woman driving through the area. It crossed in front of the car and was smaller than a Border collie.

Interestingly, a majority of UK-based 'big cat' researchers are baffled by sightings of smaller black cats and are adamant that such sightings must surely involve a new species of large cat roaming the rural landscape. In response to this I simply present to you the Downs Road sighting as proof that a number of smaller cat sightings are either of young leopards, female leopards, or simply the now-British black leopard, which can be compared to the Indochinese slender cats.

On 24th July a large cat destroyed a shed harbouring a rabbit in the Culverstone area. At 1:00 am a couple were awoken by a clattering noise in the garden. The woman, alarmed by the sound and thinking that someone was intruding upon their premises, awoke her husband. The sound subsided but at 2:45 am the woman went downstairs, still worried about the noises and decided to turn the security light on for a view of the garden. The sight that greeted her shocked her. The shed, which backed up as a hutch had been ripped to pieces, and scratch marks were apparent over the wood panels, but thankfully she could see that her rabbit was okay but thumping nervously.

The woman was terrified, and then heard a rustling noise coming from the direction of the conifer trees, and many of the local dogs, including her own, began to bark suddenly at the unseen presence. The next day the couple checked the shed. Something had chewed and scratched the wood, leaving puncture marks and small specks of blood from its own mouth as it had frantically gnawed.

I visited the area, a remote village built in the woods and surrounded by thickets. The roads are unmade, hazardous for a majority of vehicles, and the front gardens often open to the darkness, which surrounds.

The shed had been largely dismantled, particularly around the base. Something had pulled and gnawed free several panels leaving razor-sharp claw marks and two puncture marks a couple of inches apart. Whatever had attacked the hutch had stood on its hind legs, or at least reared up, and leaned against the shed and peered into the hutch window around four feet high and padded at the Perspex glass, but could not get at the terrified rabbit. A neighbour mentioned that a few weeks previously seven rabbits had been taken without trace. My investigations drew a blank, the surrounding undergrowth could easily hide a large cat, even during daylight. Only the local dogs would give any sign that something untoward was about.

On July 29th forty people at a barbeque in Meopham, at 9:30 pm observed a fox-sized cat that leapt into one of the parked, open topped cars. Two witnesses, a husband and wife approached the car expecting to see a fox rummaging around but instead were shocked to be greeted by a slim, sandy-coloured cat with a longish tail and a puma-like face that bounded from the front seat and off into the distance.

What was the mystery cat? The male witness mentioned that although the cat had long legs it did not have the large ears of ,say, a caracal - so had they seen a small puma?

An amazing sighting took place on August 9th when a family driving through the countryside near Gravesend at 9:00 pm spotted two black leopards in a field. At first, one witness, observed a big black cat three-hundred feet away in the middle of a light coloured field, but when the car was stopped the whole family saw another cat, smaller, 100 feet away from the other cat.

The bigger cat was estimated to measure around five feet in length and appeared to be pouncing on something, possibly a mouse. Then, the larger of the two stared at the on-lookers and moved towards the smaller felid. Another car then approached from the opposite direction so the witnesses drove off, not wanting to attract any attention to the animals.

After chatting to the wife, she told me that she believed the two cats were a mother and cub.

Six days later four youths on their bikes riding through Cobham's dense woods saw the hindquarters of a muscular, black cat protruding from the undergrowth. They reported their sighting to the *Gravesend Reporter* who put the story on the front page alongside a huge, dramatic sketch of what was meant to look like a black leopard, but looked more like a tattoo that children dab on.

During early September a couple finishing a barbeque at their Gravesend home at around 10 pm had thrown several bones into the garden for foxes to scavenge. The couple had a rest, sitting in the dimly lit garden, which was only illuminated by the glow from the windows of the house. Suddenly, an animal emerged from the dark corner of the garden and motioned towards a bone. It had a smallish head, a long tail and was around three feet long in the body. The animal unnerved the wife as it neared them, causing her husband to jump to his feet and clap his hands at the animal, which nonchalantly gazed at him, turned and slowly walked away.

After interviewing the witnesses the only thing they remain undecided upon was the colour of the cat. The husband believed the cat to be beige, but his wife said it was darker.

A few days later at 8:30 pm a girl was returning from tending to her horses with a friend in the Shorne area when they noticed a large, black animal slinking through the cornfield, which they took to be a friend's dog. When the animal suddenly grunted and began chasing something they realised in horror that it was a huge cat. One of the girls was told by a local mechanic a few days later that he'd seen a big cat, black in colour, cross a nearby road in front of his vehicle at 8:30 am and that his Jack Russell dog, a handful of chickens and a duck had gone missing.

A courier from Gravesend saw a chocolate-coloured animal near the Bean turn off during September. It was 10:30 am as he drove along a road flanked by a cornfield, which the cat ran towards. He described it as muscular with a very long tail. More than fifteen people who were out on a shoot in Meopham then observed a lynx.

A further Gravesend sighting took place on October 17th when a Chatham man driving home from work at 5:10 pm, near Thong Lane, saw an animal around fifty yards away which caught his eye. The animal, a panther, was heading towards the Gravesend Road.

A day later a black panther was seen in a Sidcup garden.

On November 1st the *Gravesend Messenger* asked, '*Beast stalks Bean... can you help?*', after my plea for more witnesses to come forward to report sightings in the area. On the same day I received a call from a Culverstone man who was awoken at 3:00 am by a disturbance in his garden. The man's Doberman was growling at something and so he got out of bed to look and was astounded to see a big black animal wrecking the rabbit hutch just fifteen feet away. The cat stared at the man as he peered at it from the back window, and so the witness fetched his dog and ventured bravely into the garden but there was no sign of the beast. Claw marks were all over the hutch, but thankfully the rabbit was unharmed, and brought inside.

Then, at the end of the month in the same area, a male witness travelling home from work during the early hours saw a large cat cross the road in front of his car. The man described the animal as silvery grey, and the size of a fox.

Over the festive season, as millions of people flocked to Bluewater, a big, black panther was seen stalking through a field near Istead Rise. Mr Lewis was taking some rubbish to the local dump when the animal caught his eye in a field around one hundred yards away. It was moving left to right towards a field of horses. Towards the end of the year a couple walking through the village of Luddesdown, at 1:05 pm saw a large, dog-sized creature moving along the hillside. The cat had a very long tail, was brownish in colour with a small head and a white belly, like that of a puma. The couple claimed to have photographed the animal but I was never able to track them down.

In the January of 2002 a countryside warden patrolling the woods of Shorne stumbled upon a huge pawprint totally unlike that of his own St. Bernard dog. Then, I got in touch with a local farmer who claimed that for a year a large, black cat had been visiting his land. He commented that he and a friend out shooting one night had the animal in their sights, its yellow eyes glowing in the torch beam, but neither wanted to shoot the creature. Then, in the summer of 2001 the farmer claimed that his Jack Russell dog had been taken by the cat and two young local girls observed the cat in the nearby woods. The farmer believed that scraps of food constantly thrown out to the foxes were attracting larger predators, which in turn were taking the foxes also.

At the beginning of January 2002 the farmer's daughter spotted the cat one evening at the back of the house. It had been feasting on some chicken bones close to the back door.

In February a dog-walker saw a big, beige-coloured cat with stripy markings under the coat close to Cobham Hall. Although the sighting was brief, the cat was only five feet away as it sprang into the undergrowth.

On the 22nd Mr Nash had an impressive sighting of an animal near Bluewater. He was driving at 1:30 am on the London Road, Greenhithe, when a van in front suddenly braked hard. The witness couldn't believe his eyes as a large black animal crossed from the direction of MacDonald's and headed up the path alongside the vehicles that had stopped, wondering what was going on. Mr Nash stated that the cat had green eyes, was around two feet high and five feet in length. In the March Mr Johnson contacted me claiming that three lynx were shot and killed on the marshes in Gravesend, but what happened to the bodies no-one seems to know.

With the vim of spring in the air, Mr Judge believed that a big cat of some sort had been urinating on his lawn at Southfleet. The witness claimed that nine patches of grass had been yellowed by something that wasn't a fox spray. Then, at Parsonage Lane, Darenth Hill, a female witness, at 5:00 am on 28th April, was driving with her friend when they both spotted a large black animal sitting on the grass verge by the roadside. Suddenly, another large cat came from the opposite side to join the other cat. On 2nd May at Vigo a local man was watching television at 1:15 am when he was disturbed by the sound of the dog flap clattering. The man was fully aware that the flap was locked from the inside at night but went to check anyway in case a fox was mooching around. As he stared out the flap he was stunned to see a large black cat scamper across the lawn and leap a six-foot fence.

The witness claimed that whilst walking his dog in the local country park he'd noticed one tree heavily scratched, but was unsure as to whether a badger had made the marks. Upon investigation I was able to confirm that a badger had not made the marks, they were too high. The bark of the tree had been scored and splintered up to around six feet in height, and the tree was located near a water hole. There were no deer in the area either.

Several more sightings would emerge from the area, a perfect habitat for a large cat to hide, with the abundance of rabbits and birds for prey, steep and winding pathways twisting through the ivy-strewn corridors and deep thickets of bracken.

Two days later, near Istead Rise, a local man whilst travelling to work at 5:30 am saw a black lump on the grass verge not far from his home. At first the witness thought it was a rabbit, until he neared, and was startled to see that the lump was in fact the head of a big, dark-coloured animal, which was pouncing, in the long grass. The cat was described as silky and slender as the man slowed the car and watched it for around two minutes before it casually slinked off towards a field.

The witness doubted himself for a while after the incident, admitting he'd been a sceptic to such beliefs and that he couldn't even tell his own wife, until he heard that his daughter, who lived only a few miles away had also seen a similar, if not the same, black leopard. Her sighting took place on the 6th near Culverstone at 6 pm. As they pulled into their road, they were amazed to see a big animal glide across the road, and head towards the woods flanking the houses.

A few days after at Vigo, at the Trottiscliffe Country Park where I'd examined the tree shredding, a witness claimed that as a coach driver pulled into the entrance of the park, a melanistic leopard strolled off into the woods, and then, at Bean, near Bluewater, on the 20th May, a woman driving at 1:15 am along the A2 and taking the New Barn/Longfield turn-off was shaken when the white van in front of her suddenly braked. Then, a black cat, much bigger than a fox, ran fast across the road, leapt a hedge and headed towards the railway line. Five days later at Southfleet Mr Mitchell was in his garden when he noticed several of the local feral cats scampering away from the old yard nearby. A bulky, black cat in hot pursuit of its meal then followed the animals. The cat slowed and as it raised its paw to take its next stealthy step, it noticed Mr Mitchell, glared at him, but was then out of sight when the witness went to fetch his girlfriend. The girlfriend then told me that her father had seen the same cat ten minutes earlier, just up the road.

On 1st June a woman walking in the country park at Vigo with her sister and dog saw a black panther emerge from the woods 25 yards away and slip into the undergrowth. Her Yorkshire terrier made a move towards the area where the animal disappeared into but the woman called the brave dog back. Seven days later six witnesses saw a black animal in fields at Meopham.

By the summer it was clear that Gravesend was a hive of activity for a black leopard or two, but at this point I was being inundated by eyewitness accounts. This is why in this chapter I have sectioned the areas of sightings, rather than supply you with an endless stream of countywide sightings, but I was receiving on average around ten or more reports a month just from Gravesend, and in July it was no different, the *Kent Online* website mentioned how, *'Big cat was sauntering along'*, and witnessed by Mrs Ellis who was driving through the under-pass of Istead Rise near Downs Road when she saw the black leopard strolling away. She described it as the size of an Alsatian but slim.

On Thursday 11th July a wave of activity occurred near the marshes of Gravesend that would spiral into a fluent bout of high strangeness that to this day remains as one of the weirdest experiences of my life.

It all began with Ian Marsden. At 7:30 pm he'd been walking his dog in local fields when he sensed a presence up ahead because the long grass in the field was moving, just thirty metres away. Suddenly, Ian saw a big black cat sit up on its haunches and gaze at Ian and his dog, which he held firmly on its lead.

Ian was rather unnerved by the animal up ahead, and so reached for a large stick in case it approached. He continued his stroll, slowly heading away from the black animal. But once again, the grass moved and again the cat emerged, sitting on its backside glaring over the top of the swaying grass at the unsettled man (and his dog which hadn't noticed the cat). Ian moved towards a stile, and peered back towards the animal, but noticed that now it was closer, and had slinked under a fence and then begun to take a direction that would eventually cause a very close encounter. Ian quickened his pace, but suddenly the animal was out of sight, and then, as if by magic, it appeared some forty metres up ahead, terrifying the witness. It was then that Ian noticed the size of the majestic creature. He said that it stood around two feet high and over five feet in length, with a long tail, wide head, and shiny coat.

It looked in pristine condition, but he was more concerned that it was a very hungry predator. Ian moved with haste, knowing that the busy road, a world away from the golden rolling fields and treacherous undergrowth, was near. Suddenly, Ian panicked and ran at the cat, screaming and waving his stick. The cat bolted, but as soon as Ian stopped, so did the cat, casually looking at him, waiting for another chance to approach. Finally, Ian reached the road and headed home where he reported the encounter, which he believed lasted around ten minutes. Thankfully, via the press he was put in touch with me, and so began a series of weird events in the local fields and woods that I would not forget in a hurry.

A day after Ian's scary episode, a neighbour also reported seeing a black panther in the same location. The woman, named Barbara, was walking her two black Labrador dogs at 4:30 pm and heading toward the stile that Ian had crossed when one of her dogs startled something large in the undergrowth. A black cat almost leapt with fright from the brambles, just fifty yards away and slinked away. The surprised witness said the animal had a mottled coat.

On the 19th July the *Medway Messenger* (the new weekly version of the defunct *Kent Today* and *Medway Today*) reported, *'How I Was Stalked By Two Black Panthers'*, and featured Mr Marsden's sighting. Ian believed that maybe two cats had been in the vicinity, the only way surely to explain how the animal that followed him suddenly appeared up ahead, although he never claimed to see two cats at once. Was this merely the press getting excitable or the unnerving thought that two predators were roaming the fields adjacent to a built-up area?

Although Ian was shaken by the incident he continued to walk the area, sticking to the more open pathways but always having a camera with him. A few times during the initial stages of the investigation he staked the area out, but then it got seriously strange.

Meanwhile, on 31st July, Mr Heart from Wrotham saw a black leopard on his drive at 9:15 pm, which a first he took to be a black sack. The object was stretched out on the drive illuminated by the security light, but when the man and his wife looked through binoculars they couldn't believe that they were watching a cat, much bigger than a domestic cat staring back at them. Then, the animal stood up, and walked off towards the fields, its long tail hanging low behind it.

On 6th August Ian Marsden took to the local fields with his camera. The sun was beaming through the sparse trees flanking the hilly field, and the view around him was clear; a large green field leading to another stretch of trees. To his right another border of trees backed with another field, and a small pocket of woods, and to his left more corn fields, a few hundred yards away from the more overgrown field where he'd encountered the leopard.

At 8:45 pm Ian sat on the bank, relaxed but observant, eyeing the dense areas at the base of the spindly tree line, hoping, or maybe not so much, that a large black animal would come into view. Suddenly, there was a movement in the tree line down the slope, around seventy yards away and something stood up, startled possibly by Ian's presence, but this thing wasn't black. Ian reached for his camera and took one picture of a form that reversed back into the shrubbery and disappeared from view.

Ian contacted me immediately, and with my father, I went to his house. He'd emailed me the photograph, and I was bemused by it. It showed an animal, standing on all fours, as if suddenly being alerted from a lying position, but as Ian snapped, the cat raised its head, and, as luck would have it, remains absent from the picture. The photo is a strange one and it was difficult to get excited for two reasons. Firstly, the photograph was disappointing; it was reasonably clear, but looked all the world like an illusion of the yellow fields of the background filtering through the section of trees, thus creating the effect of a shape, and secondly, if Ian had photographed something alive, it wasn't a black leopard and resembled, if anything, a lynx, lightish in colour, with possibly spots around the legs, although it could easily have been mistaken for a normal leopard, which although would have been something pretty amazing, would have also made sense as to why there was a black cat in the area too.

I took the photo with a pinch of salt. It was all a little too much to take in. The guy had been stalked by a leopard, or maybe two, then gone out in the hope of photographing it but somehow captured a completely different cat in the frame!

Now, Ian seemed a very genuine and enthusiastic guy. Maybe a little too over-enthusiastic, I first thought. Maybe his mind was playing tricks on him, because every time he seemed to stroll through the local fields, he'd see something strange and cat-like, and this continued for a couple of weeks. My father and I would often meet Ian in the area, knowing full well that if two leopards were out there, or even a lynx *and* a leopard, we might have a chance of tracking one of them, or at least catching a glimpse. Admittedly, the area, even in summer, was reasonably sparse, and dog walkers often frequented the stony pathways, and the few farms dotted around the outskirts didn't seem to stock enough livestock to provide a restaurant for any local felid. But there was an abundance of rabbits and pigeons, but cover was not overly sufficient, as previously mentioned. Fields stretched wide, and their idyllic scenery was only disrupted by one, albeit very busy road. And there was a reservoir very close, situated next to an orchard which dipped into a wood, and in the other direction more fields; some overgrown, spliced by tree lines and punctured by a small lake. It was all very quiet, but easily manageable, as regards determining a route for an animal to take.

After several visits to the area, which involved spraying the area with various oils and scents which should have attracted any cat walking on by, along with many hours spent with my father through the dusk and into the night, holed up on a hillside with a vantage point so we could scan the tree lines and fields, and more updates on Ian in which he claimed he'd seen two black leopards together, it was all becoming rather strange. Was Ian really seeing all this activity? Why was it that even if he went out for a ten-minute stroll he somehow came across something else? And yet, despite our hours of monitoring, there was nothing. Of course, this is often the case, such sightings are always down to chance, but a few days later we *did* have the privilege of observing something, but first, Ian was to have a memorable encounter.

The August evening was beautiful, the sun bathing the fields in golden light, and once again Ian settled with his dog on the hillside. But this time he brought with him his camcorder. At around 8:45 pm (again) a few birds in the trees ahead, the same tree line where he'd photographed the alleged cat, became disturbed and fluttered, and then flew off. Ian started the camera, scanning the line for around thirty seconds, and then, there it was. Sitting between two trees, shrouded by the bracken, leaves and dry branches, was a cat, clear as day, sitting on its haunches. It never moved, it almost seemed unaware of Ian as he glared to its right, where Ian would later tell me that a man on a cycle was travelling. Ian zoomed in. The animal was light grey, around two feet high with two large tufted ears. Its face appeared lighter, maybe white but under its lips there was a chocolate coloured beard of sorts. It was a lynx.

Ian sat, calmly, unsure what to do, and so decided to slowly crawl down the slope towards the animal. But when he raised the camera again, the cat had turned away; its rear end only visible. And then, as Ian steadied himself, the animal had gone, lost in the foliage. I viewed the film, extremely impressed, marvelling at how the animal remained so still; proof that unless one sat there as Ian had, there was not a hope in hell of knowing such an animal was even there, it was a like a ghost in the vegetation. Strangely, the cat wasn't as light or anywhere near as mottled as the cat in the photograph, but I put that down to the sunshine. But, as stated earlier, the alleged photograph I'd only taken with a pinch of salt anyway.

Sunday August 11th. It had been a few hours sat patiently observing the fields and hedges with binoculars, when I looked across towards one tree line to the right and could have sworn that something, although hazed by the evening dusk, was sitting at the base of one of the trees. Ian, my dad and I all looked through the binoculars, but weren't getting excited. We could pick out no distinguishable features except for a rough outline of what looked all the world like a lynx-shaped cat sitting on its haunches, but the reality was, we wanted much more than that, not simply the evening playing tricks with our minds and turning leaves into cat-like shapes.

At 8:45 pm (the same time Ian allegedly photographed the strange cat, and also filmed possibly the same cat) my dad moved towards the left side of the hill to observe the area where Ian had filmed the lynx, whilst me and Ian moved to our right, and scanned another tree line on the right in the hope that if something *was* around, it would come from that direction.

I had my camcorder, Ian his own camera, and we waited. Suddenly, from the right, and from the direction where we'd watched the odd shape in the tree line, a grey cat, around three feet long, leggy and with no distinguishable tail, scampered right across the field at amazing speed. It was so fast that by the time it had reached a furrow of weeds and grass, at the back of the tree line where Ian had previously seen it, I never had time to raise the camera and film, or even get my dad's attention. The animal had slipped into the dusky haze of the overgrown trench a few hundred yards away, and despite an hour of searching we didn't want to flush the cat out, but simply work out where it had gone, but to no avail, and my dad was extremely gutted that he'd missed out on this unbelievable encounter with an animal I really didn't think I'd see.

Despite more hours spent scouring the local fields of that specific location, and getting a feel for such a tranquil setting, there were times when it felt as if nothing could roam that remote place. But then, on another night, things felt strange, as if there was a non-specific presence darting through the bushes or indeed watching us. On several occasions my father and I found piles of dead pigeons on the edge of a small thicket. They had not been ravaged by a fox. Indeed, something had effortlessly stalked the low lying branches of the trees and plucked the pigeons from their resting place, and stacked them in a feathery pile.

In September, a lady walking her small dog at 4 pm near Istead Rise came face to face with a beige-coloured cat which sat on a driveway motionless. She approached the animal and told me that she got to within four feet of the cat, only its eyes moving as it watched her. The woman slowly walked away with her dog, and chirped at the animal, but it didn't react.

After her amazing encounter she told me that the animal was a lynx. It seemed leggy, it's coat biscuit coloured and mottled and had large, tufted ears. Was this the same lynx seen a few miles away or even the same cat that scratched a man's hand, as mentioned in the previous chapter?

The aptly-named Mr Catlett observed a black leopard laying a field near Cooling on the 9th September 2002. He thought it was an Alsatian at first, but when he stopped his vehicle he got a clearer view. The witness drove home to get his camera but when he returned the cat had gone.

In October, Mr White from Gravesend was cycling through Halling at 11 am when he saw a large black cat on the pathway fifty yards ahead. Although the man never saw the head or tail of the animal he claimed its coat was beautiful and seemed healthy, whilst on Sunday November 3rd at 6 pm a man named Steve, driving from work on the Cuxton Road from Snodland, saw possibly the same animal which crossed the road around thirty yards away. He said the cat was around three feet in length and had a very long tail.

Ian Marsden continued to investigate the area of his black leopard and our lynx sighting. On 16th November he staked out an area not too far away from the lynx encounter and claimed to have seen two panthers which emerged from the direction of a lane, and strolled straight passed him as he remained holed up, but unnerved slightly by their presence, although they didn't seem to notice him. Admittedly, it was this kind of luck that I was hesitant to believe in. Ian seemed a genuine guy and we had seen the lynx together, but he either had an active imagination or was very lucky. I opted for latter. I had to.

A Northfleet couple claimed to have seen a panther as they were taking at morning stroll through Shorne Wood Country Park. As they entered a clearing within the wooded location, the man stopped dead in his tracks as a black animal prowled through the undergrowth. The couple were so frightened by the sighting that they made for their car and went home.

The New Year suggested that one of the black leopards Ian had seen was still around when a man out walking his dog on New Year's Day caught a glimpse. He told the *Medway Messenger* of January 10th 2003:

> "*I reckon it was about 3:45 pm when I heard something rustling in the bushes. At first I thought it was the rain hitting the trees, but then it got louder and I heard a menacing, crunching sound. I started to feel quite nervous, I felt like someone, or something was watching me.*"

> *His dog began to growl, and the witness decided to make for home, but as he turned saw a big black animal dart across the road.*

> *He continued, "It looked like a huge black fox, or cat. But as it reached the other side*

this thing stopped and stared at me for at least a minute. I felt paralysed."

The sighting took place just a few hundred yards from where Ian had experienced his own encounters in 2002.

As the snow began to fall on the night of 7th January a man from Thong Lane woke at around 4:00 am to use the toilet. He peered out of the window and noticed a car coming up the road and then, a big black cat sprang from nowhere into the beam of the headlights and bolted out of sight. He said the cat was around three feet long and disappeared into the entrance of Cascades, a local swimming bath.

The following night the wife of the man heard a deep, guttural growl outside and believed it came from the same animal.

Things got weird again. On the same night (8th) Ian and his friend Michael walked through the local fields, as the fresh snow lay thick across the landscape like a blanket. They were hoping that if anything had been around it might have left prints.

They came across nothing but went back the following night. At around 8:00 pm they scoured the area, taking in the bottom half of the field and ascended the slope from where I'd observed the lynx. As they reached the top and looked back, scanning the white fields they were alarmed to see a big, black animal standing in the centre of the field staring at them. The cat slowly approached, Ian and Michael turned, and walked briskly uphill so the cat was soon out of sight.

Ian made it home and called me straight away and with my dad I ventured to the area. As we parked up, the snow began to fall heavily, the whole atmosphere changed, and the weather became mild, but there was an ominous feel around. Maybe it was because we knew that Ian had allegedly seen something around thirty minutes previous. At 8:45 pm (yes, again!) we met with Ian to retrace his steps through the snow. We found his tracks embedded in the quilt of whiteness, as well as fox prints and the occasional rabbit, but also a distinct set of prints that had tracked Ian's own for some distance. Ian put his hand on my shoulder, clearly shaken as he realised the cat had followed. In the darkness, but which was clearly lightened by the overpowering veil of snow, we followed the mysterious tracks. At first, whatever made them had been walking, but suddenly the impressions showed it had began to lope. At first the prints were four fist-sized impressions, no distinct claw marks, but as the stride lengthened, to over four feet, it was clear that Ian hadn't been sniffed out by a fox or domestic cat, and the slight mark at the rear suggested that a long tail had caressed the glistening snow, leaving a tubular graze.

We followed the tracks for around three-hundred yards. Ian's remained to our right some twenty yards away, those made by the cat veered slightly left, at one point they went onto a crisp bed of untouched snow, the animal circled then came back on itself and then found Ian's scent again. We reached a road covered by powdery flakes, and the prints stopped. We guessed that the prints continued straight ahead into the gloom of the neighbouring field but we were aware that Ian's journey had taken him right, across the fields and back home.

In the next field the snow had laid heavily but dark clumps of high soil were still showing, making it difficult to track the prints. We found a set of fox prints and believed the cat had picked them up, but it was getting late, the snow was thick, the air growing cooler and we made for home, Ian shaking not because of the frosty air, but with the knowledge that he'd been stalked again.

Was it the same animal seen in a Gravesend cemetery on the Thursday 9th January? Probably not. Mrs Pearson from Hartshill was looking out of her bedroom window across the graves behind her home at approximately 2 pm, when she spotted a black animal with a very long tail mooching around. She stated that although it was long in the body it was not much bigger than a fox.

The woman then saw the animal the following Sunday, on the 12th at 6:20 am.

Around the same time another woman named Sally saw a black creature the size of an Alsatian as she drove through Cliffe at 4:00 am. The car headlights picked out the animal. Another man came forward to say that whilst out shooting on the marshes with friends, they too spotted a black animal the size of a Labrador.

On the 3rd February 2003 a Gravesend man driving near Thong Lane at 10 pm saw a black leopard which once again bounded across the road and headed towards the swimming pool on the left. The witness said the animal was around six feet in length.

One month later at Cobham, a female witness driving near Henhurst Road at 11:15 pm saw an unusual animal in the road as she came around the bend. It was definitely cat-like, but sandy-beige in colour. The woman got so close that she had to beep her horn. The cat then leapt into the field. Such an animal echoed an earlier incident, when a member of the Gravesend Historical Society managed to accidentally film a cat, sandy-coloured, one afternoon whilst a passenger in a fellow members vehicle. As they came around a tight bend, the cameraman asked, *"What's that? It looks like a dog."* The animal that crossed the road and slinked into the woods resembled a lynx but its tail appeared too long. The ears were large and there were no distinct markings.

On the 30th March I was called out to look into a sighting of a cat near Yalding, near Maidstone. My dad was driving and we decided to take a look on the way home at the area where Ian had seen the black cat and the lynx. Strangely, it was 8:45 pm and pretty dark as we trudged carefully up the eerie pathway next to the shadow of the trees. We approached the area where Ian had filmed the lynx, the summer seemed so far away now as the air crisp swirled around us. Suddenly, up on the horizon I picked out a dark shape, which only became apparent as it flitted over the lights of a distant town. Something was heading down the track towards us, blotting out the orange lights in the valley. We stopped on our path and realised that whatever it was, possibly a fox, had seen us and it had veered to our left into the tree line. We had to second-guess it. Would the animal continue and walk across the field hidden behind the tree line it had entered or wait for us to slip into the field and then re-emerge and continue its journey down the path? We guessed the former and so, with torch ready we headed through the trees just in time to see the animal cross slowly on the horizon about 130 yards away. We approached, shining the beam towards it expecting to see a fox, or hoping deep down it was a big black cat, or a grey lynx. It was none of them, but instead we were greeted by a cat, fawn-dark tan coloured with a longish tail that loped across the hill. The animal stopped and looked at us, and we bounded towards it, but it moved swiftly across the slope, quickly out of the beam and into the darkness.

We shone the beam around the field and picked up a set of eyes in the distance but again the animal eluded us. Although it was a very dark night, with no moon to illuminate the fields, we estimated that the cat was around three-and-a-half feet long, with a smallish head. Possibly a puma. My dad never saw the tail but I did.

Just *what* was going on out there whilst no one was around?

It seemed that the area was simply a network of pathways that such animals, as well as foxes, could use to cross various fields, but the fact that three different species of felid had been observed within such a small area was baffling and intriguing.

On the 19th May Ian emailed me:

> '*Lynx has kittens, saw lynx and two kittens on 10th April, twice, once in morning about 7:15 and then in the evening at 7:00. Since then we have seen her quite a few times without kittens she is very active all around the area, last spotted last Saturday about 6:00 pm.*
>
> *On Sunday we saw a medium size black cat run into thicket, fifty yards in front of us. This was around 6:00 pm.*'

Activity in the area gradually died down, mainly due to the fact that I was investigating so many other sightings around Kent and Ian had other family commitments so our own particular research at the location meant less personal activity.

During the summer a thick-set sandy-coloured cat was seen in Gravesend by Marie driving at 4:30 am. The animal glared menacingly as she drove by. The witness got a good look at the animal and said it was heavily furred with a darker stretch on its back and had a long tail, although she swore that it was not a puma.

At the beginning of August a lynx was seen near the vicinity of Ian's sighting and mine although the report was vague. However, the black leopard roaming Shorne and Cobham was certainly still active and sighted between 6:00 and 7:00 pm on a back road by a motorist. And a similar cat, possibly one of the leopards which Ian saw, was seen by a woman walking her dog at 6:15 pm in the area of Chalk.

At this point even the Bluewater 'big cat' sightings had died down simply because the press had begun to realise that such animals didn't simply reside within a one-mile radius, but during late summer of 2003 a woman packing her shopping into her car at the old *Safeway's*, on Cold Harbour Lane, at Gravesend, was stunned to see a black animal sitting in the bushes a few yards away observing her. The woman walked closer and noticed it was a big cat and so immediately retreated. The cat turned, showing its long, thick tail but what astounded her more than anything was the fact that a smaller cat was sitting by the side of the bigger animal.

A black leopard was seen on 1st November at Shorne by a woman walking her Collie dog. She described the cat as, "*...the size of a large fox...running across the field up into the woods.*"

An elderly couple saw a larger black cat as they took a morning stroll with their dog a few days later at Shorne Country Park. From a distance of one hundred yards they watched a big black animal prowling through the undergrowth. The man said, "*It terrified us, it was thick-set with a long tail, we actually ran from the area!*"

Another couple walking their dog saw a dark shape in the middle of a field in Meopham on 25th November at 1:30 pm. The man approached the form and realised it was a massive cat sitting on its haunches. The following day the man returned to the area and saw the cat again.

With winter in full swing, sightings of such animals, especially lynx had fizzled completely. However two orange-yellow eyes that peered at her from the hedgerow as she came around a bend towards Vigo spooked a New Ash Green woman driving a carload of drunken friends home at 2:00 am on December 12th. The woman slowed the car and saw the rear end of a huge black animal.

A similar sighting of possibly the same animal happened seven days later near the country park when

Mrs McGill was driving towards Vigo and a large, black cat crossed the road and headed towards the park.

'I Saw A Puma' – Gravesend Reporter, of 11th January 2004.

Reporter Michael Adkins wrote that:

> *'A motorist was stopped in her tracks when a black cat the size of a puma leapt in front of her car.*
>
> *Elizabeth Smith, 52, came face to face with the cat on Thong Lane as she returned home from church on Sunday night. Whilst sceptics debate whether cats like the lynx, puma and black leopard roam the wilds of Britain, Neil Arnold said the sighting was the ninth in Gravesend in a fortnight.*
>
> *His Kent Big Cat Research organisation studies evidence and eyewitness reports of exotic animals.*
>
> *Mrs Smith said, "It leapt from the side of the road by the fields and landed in the middle of the road. It was massive, like a puma or a leopard, and took another jump on to the pavement by the houses. I just sat there with my eyes and mouth wide open. When I looked again it had gone. It is an encounter I will never forget."*
>
> *It is the first time Mrs Smith had witnessed a big cat sighting but claims her friend saw the beast on the same road 18 months earlier."*

During the snowfall of the same month, another Gravesend resident claimed she'd come across a set of large paw-prints that were on the conservatory roof! The witness discovered the strange impressions when she looked out of her bedroom window. She said the prints were far larger than any dog.

Meanwhile Mrs Eve reported seeing a black leopard from her Gravesend home on 10th January at 4:00 pm. The cat was running at pace across the green outside and headed down hill towards the A2.

Three days later a man named Richard was walking his dog in the same area at 10:15 pm when suddenly his dog became unnerved. Richard looked across the road and was shocked to see a big black cat padding along. The witness stated that it was over four feet in length, whilst on the 18th Mrs Hall observed a black leopard on the marshes at Chalk. The cat was loping casually across the ground and had an extremely long tail.

The same cat had obviously been hanging around for a while, because during early February it was seen at 11:30 am near Thong Lane again. A female motorist, a Mrs Hodges, looked across the fields and saw an animal she first took to be a black Labrador, even though it was only fifteen feet away. Being a dog trainer by profession, the woman thought about going after the animal, believing it to be a stray. But as the animal turned, and headed along the hedgerow, she got the shock of her life. The animal seemed to shine in the sun, had a very long tail and was feline in form. In the same area on Monday 2nd February Mr Chapman was putting some rubbish sacks into his garden at 3:30 am, as he was due to go on holiday and was waiting for a taxi to arrive. As he stepped into the garden, and the security light came on, he heard a thud and a scratching noise near his shed. When he looked up, fifteen feet away, a black leopard was staring down at him from the shed roof. Mr Chapman's only reaction was to suddenly clap his hands twice at the animal, which leapt down in the garden of his neighbour.

Mr Chapman called me shortly after and upon investigation a set of scratch marks were found and photographed on the back fence. I also called in on the neighbour's who also had similar marks on their fence.

Seven days later at Istead Rise a woman walking her dog came face to face with a melanistic leopard in the local woods near Downs Road. The woman actually phoned her partner to say that she was thirty yards away from the animal and that it was in a crouched position. Petrified, and taking the advice from her boyfriend, she slowly walked in the opposite direction.

Later that day at 5:00 pm, a man named 'Phil' was walking with his wife and dog in the same area, when they thought a dog was on the roam over one hundred yards away. Thinking it could possibly attack their own dog, they slowed down, and the animal coming their way stopped. It was only then they realised it was a massive black cat which was sniffing the ground. The animal then turned away, and walked into the woods.

On the 23rd of the month a woman from South America was travelling through Harvel, near Meopham at lunchtime, when suddenly a fox ran across the road thirty feet away. Two seconds later a big black cat followed in hot pursuit. The woman was amazed that such a cat existed in the wilds of Kent. She reported to me that the animal was the size of a big dog and had a distinctly long tail.

On the 29th February on the Rochester Road, near Thong Lane, a local man tended to his Alsatian dog tied up in the garden at 4:00 pm after it had spent several minutes growling and barking. As the man walked in to the garden he noticed a black shape, some twenty metres away at the end of the garden, which - in one leap - sprang over a six-foot fence and out of sight into the next garden.

After the initial cluster of sightings spring proved to be a quiet time although I remained inundated with eyewitness sightings from across Kent. Then, on 4th June Emma Turner sighted a black leopard with a rabbit in its mouth on the Fawkham Road as she drove home from work at 5:00 am. The animal was only fifteen yards ahead as it slinked into the hedgerow. Emma also told me that she saw a similar cat a year previously outside her home.

A lorry driver saw a black cat, smaller than a Labrador on 29th June at 5:00 am as he was travelling from Dartford to Swanley. The animal crossed a field towards an area used for motor cross.

"Found your website and thought that I'd run something past you that happened to me in Shorne about three years ago", wrote Mr Game in 2007.

The man, who had since moved to Germany told me, *"Early one Saturday morning, around 5:50 I looked out of my bedroom window and saw what seemed to be an enormous dark-coloured cat slowly crossing the field. I put it down to being a very big fox or too much beer the previous night. It always bothered me, and then I saw your site and realised that I might not be crazy after all.*

About two weeks after I saw this animal, a horse that was in the field had its face badly scratched..."

Shortly after Mrs Moore contacted me to say that one bright afternoon in the summer of '04 she'd been walking through Cliffe, near St. Helen's Church when she suddenly had an eerie feeling that she was being watched. She looked towards the church and noticed a cat, Labrador-sized and sandy in colour sitting by the gate. The animal appeared to have a baggy stomach.

Although startled, Mrs Moore continued walking and the cat stood up and walked off into the churchyard. Another church sighting occurred but this time at St. Michael's in Cuxton during the July when a man named Barry was walking near Holly Hill and met a large cat that was loping around the corner towards him. The cat was jet black, slender with a long tail.

'*Big Cat Population Is At Mammoth Levels*' reported *Kent On Sunday* September 5th but for the rest of the year Gravesend became eerily quiet with regards to reports. Were the press suddenly bored by the sightings? Were the general public no longer seeing the animals or simply no longer reporting them? Or had the animal moved on, retreating further into the shadows as the colder months loomed?

During the November a man jogging near Hartley was terrified by a deep growl that emanated from the undergrowth near a pool. A few days later at Cuxton, once again near St. Michael's Church, a man cycling heard a deep growl also which came from the trees flanking the pathway. Suddenly something large rushed at him through the foliage but then veered away.

Five days before Christmas a young woman riding her horse through Ashen Bank Wood, Cobham, saw a big black cat on the path up ahead some thirty-metres away. The horse the woman was on began to become agitated, but the cat slinked away, looking back one last time before creeping into the trees.

In the same year my father and myself had a bizarre experience. Although as stated the end of the year had been quiet we, one evening, randomly visited the area where I, as well as Ian Marsden, had experienced things. It ended up like something from a film. As usual we parked in the local neighbourhood and crossed the busy but dark road and headed towards the open fields. It must've been somewhere between 8:00 and 9:00 pm.

In the darkness there was a movement, something several hundred yards away - a shadowy presence on the edge of the blazing torch beam. It seemed to move so slowly by the wire fence, overshadowed by the gloom of the small pocket of trees.

We had sat watching the fields for more than two hours. Nothing had stirred in the brisk breeze under the stars. This movement however was unusual, possibly human form, ghost-like almost, but in an area where there had been sightings of a lynx, a black leopard and also the beige-coloured felid. Was the glint in the torchlight a reflective eye? Maybe. Maybe not.

We were unsure of how to act. We'd been standing near bushes staring across an open field but the object of our attention was prowling the fringe of the thicket two-hundred yards away, an inhospitable stretch of wood protected by a patch of dense brush, thorn and thicket that hides a winding, five-foot wide shallow stream steeped by slippery mud banks.

We made our move, intrigued by the presence so we steadily marched across the open field unaware of the danger head, simply assuming that the night would simply offer a quirk or mere misinterpretation, or, if we were fortunate, an elusive glimpse of local fauna, whether fox or, hopefully, a large cat of some sort.

So, we came to the area of three-foot-high bracken and bramble and decided to worm our way around the side, taking us slightly away from our concern, which may have now disappeared into the night, but it was the safest best. Within two minutes we were staring up at the imposing wood, an ominous shadow of reaching trees grasping at the black sky. There was a deadly silence.

In my right pocket was my digital camera, in my left hand a blazing torch. There was no way we could've made it this far in pitch darkness even under the glare of the moon occasionally caressed by sweeping grey clouds.

We were faced with a tricky assault course of wilderness typical of north Kent's marshes. Ahead of us ran the quiet stream; it separated us from the wood. We knew it would take a further five minutes of lumbering to reach the stream. Quietly we set off, our feet hesitantly stepping down on to unseen ground. And then the snap of my right ankle. The sick feeling in my stomach, the flash of worry for my expensive camera, damaged by my fall down the divot, and the weird rush of falling in the darkness.

I was straight back on my feet. It was a sprain, thankfully, but I could hardly put any weight on to the foot. My dad was already up ahead, several metres away, keen not to lose our quarry in the darkness. The pain was excruciating, but we were neither here nor there, in some kind of rural limbo. We knew that at least if we continued and found nothing we could go on home, but if we did find something, like a large cat, it would have been worth the pain of the fall.

We reached the stream like two characters from *Lord Of The Rings*, one a limping wreck, the other a frosted man of determination. We knew we'd have to jump it, cameras and all, with the risk of sliding into the water, dropping expensive equipment or damaging my ankle further yet we had no choice. My dad leapt with ease, however, it made me feel none the more confident. I took a breath, the excitement of spying something fuelled me and drove me on and the final leap wasn't as bad as the surprise we were about to encounter.

Once on the other side of the stream we were confronted by the wood and the orchard. Our torches were off. It was black. This was the same wood where a year or so before we'd found pigeon carcasses eerily stacked up, and had heard a terrifying scream emerge from the trees. It was the sound of no fox. It was the same area of wood where we had been watched by some 'thing' that padded a few feet in the darkness, and then moved no more. It was strange. We had to take the strangeness with a pinch of salt, however.

A small wire fence was the only barrier keeping us from entering the wood. We slunk through the fence, and softly tiptoed into the wood, hoping to determine a route that the visitor could have taken. Around us in the darkness there were the weird shadows of fallen trees, the creepy hanging vines reaching for our heads, and the soft ground underfoot. We strode on, myself less convincingly, at least fifty or sixty feet into the blackness, finding an assuring path of grass that circled the dense inner core of the thicket. And then BANG! The shot went off, the lights came on and we were in some kind of surreal game. The bullet crashed into the ground a few feet from my right foot, still throbbing with pain. Pigeons in a state of nocturnal slumber had fluttered maniacally into the sky, the rage of feathers through the leafy canopy, the hectic flap of their wings. A growling rev of an engine around thirty feet away, a spotlight centred upon us two weary travellers, and the fear of being the hunted.

My dad turned and ran, but not the way from whence we'd come but in a straight line. In a split second I realised in horror that the only possible escape was literally into thick bramble, because suddenly *there* were hunters. Fleeting shadows, some may have been in the area we'd come from, there were most definitely some up ahead, one driving a jeep up and down an unseen pathway, a person on the back shining a huge spotlight at us. We were like frightened rabbits. And my father had reacted quickly, simply shouting, "*Run!*". I followed, without ever really seeing him as more of a black blob driving through the entangled ground.

We crashed through the wire fence, reached a wide part of the stream and jumped, for what we believed in our paranoid states, was for the safety of our lives. My dad was a shadow twenty feet ahead. He'd cleared the stream, and the grasping claws of the thorn field now met his jeans. I was in full, disfigured leap. Crashing into the side of the bank face down. My ankle screaming, my heart thumping, and my mind so aware of the engine roar, the faint murmur of voices, and sheer horror of being chased by unknown persons. They knew the dark. We didn't.

I got to my feet, conscious of my camera in my pocket, the weight of my large torch, and the tingling of my hands possibly caused by nettles. I ran full pelt at the brambles, the thorns tearing at my skin even through tough trousers. Thistles biting at my ankles, treading water and quicksand at the same time. I couldn't put the torch on because surely they would see the field become illuminated.

"*Come on!*" my dad yelled. It was just another rising noise in a cauldron of confusion.

Somehow, after what seemed like an eternity, we reached a hedgerow of some familiarity. We scrambled to the darkness, deciding to glare back at where we'd been. There was a bizarre silence now. The wood was probably bereft of its rabbits, foxes and bird life now, and the pursuers had sunk back into the shadows like ghosts. We prayed they were not still following behind, but, like us, they'd have to be creeping in the darkness. Or, they'd taken to their trucks and hit the road, either hoping to encounter a limping human on the dark roads, or they'd gone.

We never saw them again. However, contacts of ours had. Pursued by the spotlight through the night. Hunted by the roar of the engine, and the shots of the gun. But these were not warning shots fired at the stars from people lamping. We were in their sights.

It was an experience to say the least, one which caused me to ponder research like this. I was left with stung hands, a bloody face, a bruised ankle, but more importantly, a question mark as to whether all this was worth it, because most researchers feel that sitting behind a computer all day is 'research', but it isn't. Some wouldn't even have the patience to spend a night in a cold field, hence their lack of evidence. But on this occasion, I felt that curiosity might well have killed more than the cat, after experiencing a scenario something akin to the movie *Deliverance*!

After the scare, we looked back on the incident and chuckled, but sincerely hoped that no large cat got in the beam of that mysterious light or within the range of the shotgun which had spent a shell towards me. It was a relief to be away from the woods that night, but the experience left us scratching our heads at an area that had offered us so much intrigue and high strangeness.

Closer to the Medway Towns, which holds Chatham, Gillingham and Strood, Mrs Smith spotted an unusual cat at 3:00 am on 11th January 2005. She was asleep in her home off Chelmsford Road when a loud screech startled her from her slumber. She rushed to the window and peered out. Twenty feet away she saw a big animal, beige in colour, speeding towards the nearby alleyway. She said the animal was much bigger than a fox.

On the snowy night of 21st February my girlfriend Jemma was laying in bed at her then Cuxton home, off Bush Road. It was midnight and her mum, Jacqui, was staring out the bedroom window watching the snow when a large, Alsatian-sized black cat padded up the hill. Jacqui called Jemma just in time to see the back end of the animal slip behind a tree. Both said that the animal was as high as the wheel arch of the car parked there that night. Immediately afterwards they went outside and took a handful of photographs of paw-prints which the animal left behind.

A resident of Singlewell, Gravesend, was walking at 8:50 pm on 14th March, towards a dimly lit area of garages to put his crook-lock on his car. As he strolled around the bend he saw an animal around forty feet away standing near his vehicle and looking in his direction.

Realising the animal was no dog or fox he became curious and walked closer. The cat crouched and then slowly slinked away, the witness quickened his pace hoping for a better glimpse. Although the cat sped up the witness got a better look as it scurried beneath a street lamp.

The man said that, "*It was quite stocky, like a lynx or a bobcat, brown in colour with a lighter underside and it appeared to have no discernible tail.*"

By the end of March big cats were getting rather a bad press across the country after an alleged black leopard attack on a man from Sydenham (see previous chapter). The drama created over the sighting, and a five-thousand pound reward offered in Oxfordshire to capture a cat after several attacks on livestock, was typical sensational commentary for a misunderstood situation. It seemed at the time, whilst scores of sightings were being reported monthly across the country but being classed as myth, it had become pretty well acceptable that large animals prowling the towns were nothing more than headlines - until of course an alleged cat attack made a real headline and everyone, including the authorities caused even more unnecessary panic by their lack of knowledge and barbaric mentality.

The authorities, whether it's the government or the police, are extremely hypocritical when it comes to the British big cat situation. It's clear that so-called wildlife experts constantly take the hundreds, if not thousands, of felids reported each year with a pinch of salt, and then 'investigated' when something occurs that is considered a threat to the public. Maybe if such authorities dealt with the situation in the first place and opened up to the public regarding knowledge and accessibility, we wouldn't continue to have such local hysteria, which - in most cases - is caused by inadequate investigation rather than the animal themselves.

After the alleged Sydenham attack, police mounted extra patrols in the area, swarming the railway lines and darkest corners, but to no avail.

During the middle of April, back in the vicinity of St. Helen's Church, Cliffe, a male motorist travelling home from work at 7:30 pm caught a fox-sized cat in the headlights as it crossed from fields and headed towards a quarry. On the 5th May a young man observed a four-foot long sandy-coloured cat at Long field, and Mrs Luck spotted a similar cat at Northfleet one morning at 3:00 am when she looked out of her bedroom window. The animal was sitting in the road and ran off towards a thicket. Had both witnesses seen a puma? The same puma?

By this time also, the beast of Bexley had been sighted on several occasions, but clearly wasn't the same animal as many sightings had fallen at the same hour. Although such animals have vast territories a cat such as a puma wouldn't walk twenty miles one night and then walk twenty miles straight back. Such animals tend to stick to an area where there is food and then move on. They can indeed cover a large amount of ground of a night, often zig-zagging through their territory, but reports certainly suggested that the Bexley cat was one of a handful within a fifty-mile radius.

On the 18th May at Istead Rise a man named Brian was mowing his lawn at 3:15 pm when he saw a huge, fawn-coloured felid run across the neighbouring cornfield. Brian told me that, "*The field was roughly eighteen-inches high in undergrowth so I walked over to the area and estimated that the animal was over two feet high and almost five feet in length. It had a long curved tail and was muscular.*"

This was just after a fourteen-year old boy on May 17th at 4:30 pm saw a big black cat near Delamere Road in Snodland. The cat appeared to be grooming itself and then leapt onto a grass verge.

The black leopard of the Thong Lane area had returned on 18th June. Hannah Warren was driving up Rochester Road at 9:30 pm when around thirty yards ahead a black cat the size of an Alsatian, crossed the road from the right, glanced quickly at the vehicle and then vanished into fields on the left. Two days later a big cat was seen at Thamesmead but at the end of June, into July, the so-called beast of Bluewater was very much in the vicinity of the shopping precinct.

Residents at the modern houses carved into one of the chalk quarry faces surrounding Bluewater reported on 28th June at 9:30 pm that a few local dogs were going ballistic for no apparent reason. Mrs Blair spotted the back end of an animal moving through her garden, heading towards Bean and the following night, on the Wednesday, the woman and her husband were disturbed by a series of guttural growls coming from the garden. Something large was out there in the darkness and was seen again on July 3rd at 8:00 pm when once again her dogs became unsettled. A cat, the size of a small Labrador slinked across the road, following the fox run, from London Road to Bean direction, just thirty feet away. The animal appeared to be silvery-grey with a long tail. The animal stopped and stared at the witness.

Two hours later the woman saw the cat again coming back.

Before this sighting on June 30th a man named Marc was sleeping in his car at 2:30 am near Downs Road. He awoke, the woods and fields illuminated by the glowing moon. Then, something around forty feet away strolled along the line of the hedgerow. It was a large black animal he'd seen previously yet on this occasion he had to pinch himself to make sure that what he was seeing was not part of a dream.

Sightings of large cats often emerge from areas where lakes are situated. Often such fishing clubs only allow members so these kinds of places are ideal habitat for an animal that requires drink, food and sufficient cover.

The Snodland Kingfisher complex has had several anglers report unusual cats over the years. During the summer of 2005 an angler and friend sitting in their swim watched a big, dark coloured animal swimming in the water on the opposite side of the lake. Thinking it was a dog they expected the owner to turn up any minute although access for the general public is prohibited at the lakes. The animal then proceeded to spring from the water, up onto the bank and run off into the woods. The following day the angler chatted to another fisherman who claimed that he'd seen it too, but closer, and that it definitely was a black panther.

On the 7th July the *Gravesend Messenger* reported:

> *'Big Cat Scare: Girls get the fright of their lives'*, commenting, *'A pair of schoolgirls were left shaken and scared after coming face-to-face with a large black cat. Megan O' Connor, 13, and her friend Georgina Broom were enjoying a day off school when they spotted the animal last Friday.*
>
> *The two, from St. George's School, were walking back home from town towards Megan's home in Packham Road at around 2:45 pm. They took a familiar route through a farmer's field behind Lane's Avenue when suddenly the cat walked out only feet in front of them. Transfixed and petrified Megan and Georgina stood watching the animal before it turned and ran away.*
>
> *The girls then sprinted home and called Megan's dad, Paul O' Connor, who returned home from work in Chatham to comfort them.*
>
> *Mr O' Connor said: "Megan said they were about three-foot from the cat, which had a long, loopy tail. She really is quite shook up about this."*

Neil Arnold from Kent Big Cat Research said the animal was a black leopard.'

Then, on the 18th July at Northfleet, at the turn off towards supermarket *Sainsbury's*, at 9:17 pm, a man named Mark was driving, and saw an animal, black in colour and bigger than a fox turn away from the road and slip into the undergrowth. He claimed that the animal had a white tip to the tail but such a detail may have been anything from trick of the light to a chalk mark.

The witness had previously seen a similar cat not too far away but commented that on this occasion the animal was smaller.

Five days later in Luddesdown, Mr Marshall was driving at 11:00 am west of the village school when a large, black cat around three feet in length ambled across the lane ahead from right to left and disappeared into the foliage. The man said that seven years previous whilst out driving with his wife he'd seen a similar animal.

Through the warmer months sightings seemed to take a sudden lull in the Gravesham area, but in September, on Wednesday 21st a Cuxton woman was alarmed by a growling sound behind her home. On the Friday the neighbour of the lady found two pigeons in the garden that had been eaten. The birds had been devoured in a very clean way.

I put a notice in the *Cuxton Parish* newsletter of October asking for anyone to come forward to report his or her sightings. A flurry of activity in the Ashford area disrupted my Gravesend-related investigations until a Mr Carter called me to say that he'd seen a large animal on two occasions. The first was in 2003 near the main Rochester to Victoria railway line one morning when he pulled into the turning to spin his car around and saw a black cat crossing the area the other side of the railway line.

On 10th October 2005 Mr Carter was walking his dog along Charles Drive in Cuxton when he saw a similar animal. He told me:

> *"There is an area of unused and unlit ground which slopes down from the road to the backs of the houses in Bush Road. I crossed the road towards this area and suddenly the dog froze in the middle of the road. He then started barking and I could not make him either move forwards or stop barking. When I shone my torch towards the area that seemed to be scaring him I saw two large yellow eyes reflected in the torch light. Once again I got the impression of a well muscled black cat around the same size as my dog, he's almost two-foot at the shoulder. The animal then moved off deeper into the trees that are in the area and I lost sight of it."*

On the 22nd October at 7:00 pm a New Barn resident was collecting garden tools from the yard when he felt as if he was being watched. The man turned and noticed a black animal, with a white chest, was sitting on its haunches and glaring at him. The witness said the animal was the size of an Alsatian and yet approached the cat but it ran off.

The witness emailed me some photos of interesting claw marks that had appeared around his shed. The marks were certainly similar to those I'd looked at in Culverstone when the shed was demolished.

After a handful of sightings it was becoming clear that at least three black leopards were roaming an area stretching from the marshes at Higham right up to Greenhithe, although deep down I knew that more black leopards were out there, spreading further towards Dartford, and yet sightings of the puma had been scarce, although I expected the lynx reports to die down.

I kept an eye on the Bluewater 'beast' story but Christmas wasn't productive and so my research at the time extended towards the Isle of Sheppey and once again towards Ashford and the vast marshes at Romney.

Chattenden is a small village in the parish of Hoo, not far from Higham. Its name means 'forest settlement', and its large wood has often been considered ideal hunting ground for a large cat or two. Witness statements seem to add credibility to the rumours. The Royal School of Engineering once used the area itself, but the now-demolished barracks were vacated during the '80s. Much of the land is now a brownfield area owned by the Ministry of Defence.

In the January of 2006 a Chatham man named Sean contacted me via email.

> *'Me and my workmate saw what looked like a large black cat twice running up the path through some woods at the rear of the MOD training area, but did not report it because we thought that people would think us a bit cranky!*
>
> *It ran up the hill faster than anything I have ever seen.*
>
> *On another occasion we were sat in a lorry up in the army ammunition dump looking sort of down on the track which leads up a hill opposite to the one we were on, we were about one-hundred metres away and I couldn't say how big it was but it looked around four feet long, but again, its speed amazed me. It was gone in about six seconds. These woods are not used that much and they are surrounded by farmer's fields.'*

In the February much of the media attention turned towards the Bexley area when the local big cat was photographed. However, on 17th February a man named James saw a big black cat at New Ash Green at 8:30 am and then the press jumped on the Bluewater bandwagon as sightings of a large black cat had come a little too close to home for some members of the public.

On the 14th March I received the following report:

> *'Me and my family were driving out of the Bluewater car park after leaving the cinema. I saw a huge black creature walking through the car park. It made me realise how easy it could have been for the cat to enter the shopping area of Bluewater. It was shocking.'*

Although the actual car park wasn't mentioned, and there are several surrounding the complex, this sighting kicked off a reasonable flap.

I received a further five emails from people claiming to have seen the animal in the same area, some reports were vague and taken with a pinch of salt, as one witness even described seeing the "...*very sharp claws*" of the animal which would have been nigh on impossible unless it was a few feet away and clawing at the person.

On March 16th the *Daily Mail* reported that there'd been, '*2,123 sightings of big cats in Britain*', according to evidence the newspaper had collected from the British Big Cats Society. Unfortunately, the statistics were once again wildly off mark, with claims that only ninety-two large, exotic cats had been reported in the Kent area during the previous year. Of course, the press fell for the inaccuracies that have peppered such investigations for more than a decade.

On 22nd March, a young woman reported that

"About half a year ago I saw something walking across Bean shopping centre. I looked at it carefully and it was like a black-brown with a bit of grey in it. My little girl was walking towards it because she thought it was a dog, as we have two. This man quickly grabbed her, and I put her in the car and drove away. I didn't really think about it but I've been thinking that if that man wasn't there I might never have seen my daughter again. I think it was a black leopard."

Again, the vagueness of what sounded like an impressive close encounter was frustrating. The description of the animal was extremely poor with no further details forthcoming, but on the Sunday night of 15th April at 10:05 pm, a Cuxton woman, standing outside her flat, was startled to see a golden coloured cat, with a "hairy face", and a long tufted tail. She added, *"It was the size of a Labrador, with a dead black and white domestic cat in its jaws. It must have been a big cat of some kind."*

Indeed, but what kind of large cat? It certainly didn't fit in with the usual panther reports, or even that of a puma.

On the Sunday morning of June 4th 2006 three witnesses reported an impressive sighting of a large cat in the vicinity of Bluewater.

"It was about 9:30 am, we were sitting in MacDonald's, Greenhithe, when we saw out of the window a cat large enough to be a panther with piercing yellow eyes. The cat was sitting just over the road in a walkway which leads to the station. A domestic cat ran past the animal which in comparison was the size of a mouse. This large cat had an extremely long tail."

Whatever wild and elusive animals were roaming the outskirts of Bean, they were certainly feeling more curious to the local smells and activity supplied by the shopping mall. This fact alarmed the Bluewater management team, who I originally contacted to ask if anything unusual had been caught on their security cameras. Although they claimed that nothing out of the ordinary had been seen, they were still very concerned about the idea that a large animal was prowling so close to busy shoppers.

Worryingly, a bounty of £1000 was put up by a shooting magazine around the same time, for anyone in the country who could shoot and kill a large cat, but the magazine was quickly condemned for what they later claimed was a publicity stunt.

On 8th July Mr Howard reported seeing a puma whilst driving home from Bluewater towards Darenth Valley. The man also claimed it had a brown mark on its face. This of course could have been anything from dirt to dried blood from a kill.

Two days later, a Maidstone woman - who at the time was working at the cinema in Strood's Medway Valley - came out of work at 12:45 am after the last showing and drove over the Medway bridge, A2/M2, to get home. As the woman was heading down the slip lane from the bridge, she saw an animal she at first took to be a fox walking alongside the road. As she neared the creature she could tell by the body shape that it was a cat. The legs were long, the tail like a cat's and when it turned to face her before scampering away, she realised it *was* a big cat. She stated the animal was brown.
On 2nd August a man driving at 8:45 am saw a big cat.

"I exited the A2 London-bound at the M25 junction. As I came to the top of the slip road to join the M25 clockwise, I looked out to the left and there in the middle of a big open yellow field was a large black cat. I got a good look at it for about ten seconds or so. It

was definitely a large cat and it was walking casually across the field. Its body was about the size of a large German Shepherd dog and its tail was an extra two to three feet long. It was the shape of something like a puma or a jaguar, i.e. slim, athletic build and you could see its shoulder blades sticking up as it walked along. The thing that struck me as unusual is that it was not smooth and short-haired like you would expect such a cat to be, but it had longer, almost shaggy hair in places, particularly towards the end of its tail and around its head and ears."

The animal sighted was certainly a black leopard. The jaguar is certainly a more stocky animal, and I've never seen any evidence to suggest that a melanistic jaguar is on the loose locally. With regards to the fur condition, I conferred with Mark L. Edgerley, who works at the Wildlife Heritage Fund at Smarden. The Big Cat Sanctuary houses several endangered species of big cat, with the hope of breeding and also re-introducing such animals to their natural environment.

He stated that:

"... if cats are depressed perhaps because of illness, injury, or lack of food they can get mange. In the case of domestics and captive zoo animals the vector / carrier is the red fox. Normally, zoos should control foxes and feral cats on site - we tolerate foxes here but only because the local population seems healthy and numbers are controlled by local farmers. If a cat were to feed on road kill fox, and it's a big 'if' as captive cats will kill but not eat fox in my experience, I guess they could pick up the mite responsible for mange.

Cats could also pick up TB from badgers and other infected road kill. They would soon show a loss of condition if they picked up this condition. Thirdly, it could just be a very old or injured cat not able to groom correctly. I have seen captive cats get very scruffy as they grow old.

Lastly, I have seen stressed cats with very, very scruffy coats. We have a tiger here who was in terrible state when he arrived but, as soon as he went through the next spring, his coat was fine again. He was moved here because he was so stressed by other tigers in the collection he came from. A big cat roaming the UK could be stressed, I guess. Strange environment, lots of humans, noise traffic would all cause stress."

Around the same time, a Higham man named Rob was walking to work at 5:30 am towards the station when he saw a big black cat sitting in a field around 400 feet away. Another man also saw the animal, and stopped and pointed towards it. The cat must have seen the men, as it suddenly sped off across the field.

Rob told me also that two months previously he'd seen three cats together. One was particularly big with two smaller animals, all black in colour.

I then received a flurry of more reports pertaining to Bluewater and the surrounding areas. A young girl was riding her bike at an unnamed rural area of Gravesend with her friends when a big black cat jumped onto the flanking fence, which shook violently and terrified the girls who peddled for home.

A family also observed a similar sized cat at Longfield, whilst good friend of mine and fellow researcher Sean Tudor sighted a much smaller cat in late August on the slip road onto the A289 Wainscott bypass, eastbound from Strood, which runs parallel with Dillywood Lane on the other side of the A289.

He told me, "*It was around 5:30 pm. The slip road is about one-hundred km long and is bordered on the right by a triangular bank of shrubs and small trees; on the left by a grass and shrubby bank leading up to the back of a housing complex. As I started to accelerate down the ramp, I saw at the end of the lane, just before the merger with the A289, a small animal emerge from the apex of the triangle of shrub – i.e. from my right, and cross the road. It was sandy-tan coloured, and had largish, pointy ears. I was immediately thinking 'fox' being a little larger than a domestic cat. But as it moved it was with definite feline motion. It was this incongruity that struck me as unusual. Of course, in the few seconds it took me to close the distance, it had disappeared into the undergrowth of the bank.*

It looked like an Abyssinian."

Strangely, several sightings had come from that area of a cat similar in size to a fox that witnesses found difficult to identify.

Wikipedia, the free encyclopaedia, states:

> The Abyssinian is one of the world's oldest known breeds, although there continues to be speculation and controversy concerning its history. Also fondly called the "Aby", in appearance, Abyssinians resemble the paintings and sculptures of ancient Egyptian cats which portray an elegant feline (sic) with a muscular body, beautiful arched neck, large ears and almond shaped eyes. Abyssinians today still retain the jungle look of Felis lybica, the African wildcat ancestor of all domestic cats.'

A man who frequently travels through Higham believed that people were simply seeing foxes, despite his own sighting of a cat-like animal he could not identify.

On the 1st September a Cliffe woman saw a long-bodied, long-tailed cat in the field behind her house. She said the animal was black and that the same animal had been observed by her husband in the July as it ran into the same field, whilst the previous year she told me that:

> "Myself and my husband were looking out of our velux window in our bedroom onto the field that is opposite our house. It was about 9:30 pm but still fairly light. We both saw what we can only decsribe as a large black cat about the same size as my German Shepherd cross Rotwieller dog, so bigger than a domestic cat. It just walked straight through the middle of the field. We just couldn't believe it and didn't think we would ever see it again."

On the 14th September the *Gravesend Reporter* wrote, 'Panther population on the increase', after an impressive sighting at Longfield in which a photograph was taken of what seemed to be a black leopard slinking through a cornfield.

A family had photographed the cat two weeks previously, in broad daylight from their home, and showed an animal, jet-black, although low to the ground, and mostly obscured by the corn, prowling from left to right.

On Dartford Heath on Friday 29th a woman walking her dog saw the back end of a black animal that she at first took took to be another dog. The animal then turned sideways and she noticed it was an extremely large cat. It was sniffing the ground and then faced her for several seconds.

The woman decided to go back the way she'd come. She described the cat as, "...*slinky, with long legs and a very long tail.*" A lorry driver named Mr King claimed to have seen a big black felid around the outskirts of Bluewater during October and then at 2:15 am during the middle of the month a husband and wife driving near Dartford Heath watched a Labrador-size animal cross the road.

The woman was previously a sceptic to such sightings but remained convinced that what she and her husband saw was no ordinary cat.

It was probably the same cat seen on October 25th by a man named Steve who emailed me the following report:

> '*I work for a well known courier and much of my time is spent driving in the early hours. It was around 4:33 am, I was travelling home towards Dartford along the A2018 when I noticed what I initially presumed to be a dog on the grass verge just beyond the Rochester Way turn off. As I approached and began to brake it then shot off across the road and into Dartford Heath. As it crossed the road it was clearly not a dog but a very large cat about the size of a Labrador.*'

Two teenage anglers saw a black leopard whilst fishing near Higham Marshes during the November and over the festive period the cat roaming Dartford Heath was seen again, this time by a group of youths camping. They fled the area but claimed that when they returned the next morning their tent had been shredded.

Was this simply an exaggerated spook tale or real encounter? On 4th December a Dartford woman, who did not wish to be named, was travelling along Heath Lane at 4:00 am and was indicating to turn right into Heath Close Road, when a large black cat emerged further down Heath Lane and was caught in the headlights. The woman stopped her vehicle in an to attempt to judge how big the animal had been, and estimated that it had measured around four feet in length.

A black leopard was then seen on the 9th at Longfield at 11:45 pm by a couple. The animal was on a bank looking to squeeze through a hole and then slinked into the hole it had found.

On the 12th December Mr Chapman who had previously seen a black leopard on his shed at his home near Thong Lane, had an even more impressive sighting of possibly the same animal. It was 10:20 am and the witness was sitting with his wife in their kitchen drinking coffee when they saw a massive black cat climbing a one-hundred-foot high birch tree in the neighbouring garden. The animal had its eye on some pigeons but it gave up the chase when it reached around fifty feet.

Heavy fog enshrouded the Bluewater vicinity around mid-December but it wasn't thick enough to prevent a road worker from seeing a big cat. He was waiting for his mates at 6:00 am on the A2 slip road from the M25, from the tunnel towards Bluewater, at the chalky area near Bean Country Park when he looked across the quarry and saw the animal slowly padding along. Whether his work mates ever believed him we'll never know, but on the 15th a man walking his dog in the same area at 9:00 am became worried when his dog froze and began staring into the undergrowth. Thinking another dog was around, he expected his friendly dog to be more curious and attempt to go and play with the other dog, but as the witness approached the wood, he was shocked to see a large black cat slinking through the woods around fifty yards away.

At the end of the month a Northfleet woman was the passenger in a car with her husband, driving near to Sainsbury's at 1:15 am when a cat, fawn-coloured but bigger than fox crossed the road ahead. It had a white chest and a very long, curved tail and glanced back at the approaching vehicle before slipping into the woods.

The witness said that the animal looked like a puma.

By the end of 2006 I was consistently receiving more than 230 exotic cat reports annually. I was finding it easier to monitor the routes of certain individuals and able to determine just how many cats were roaming the county.

2007 was an exciting year. I'd been so involved in the cat research but moving home, and writing such a variety of articles, stories and books meant a busy schedule for myself. I knew that I wouldn't be able to get out into the field as much but also knew deep down that if I'd never received another sighting via the press it wouldn't matter because my past investigations had already mapped out several territories.

The research, like the elusive felids I'd been pursuing would have to slink into the background for a while as I finished writing my first book to be published, *Monster! The A-Z Of Zooform Phenomena*, which would be far removed from my research into flesh and blood animals, and instead concentrate on mysterious yet obscure beasts from cultural beliefs and fears from around the world.

On 3rd January 2007, a Meopham man awoke at 6:15 am, looked out of his window and saw a Labrador-sized black cat walking at the end of the garden. The witness rushed downstairs excitedly but the animal was gone. That evening a local man patrolling the land behind his house with his dog was spooked by two sets of bright amber eyes which he picked up in his torch beam. His own dog had been acting strange for a couple of days, but he simply thought that a few dogs may have been in the area, but as he approached the eerie eyes he heard a confrontational hissing sound which petrified him. Suddenly, the sets of eyes moved as if they were circling him so hurriedly he rushed back indoors.

A few days later in the same region several witnesses reported seeing a big black animal in the fields behind the village hall.

Then, around the 5th January a man carrying out land survey work at Craylands Lane Chalk Pit at Swanscombe reported seeing a big animal.

"The pit is just down the road from Bluetwater it is a very secure and quiet area, enclosed by high vertical chalk walls with odd caves dotted around. We entered this secluded enclosure through two sets of locked gates. Apart from last years' activity of building up the chalk berm, levelling off the main pit and hydroseeding the area it is otherwise devoid of human activity.

We left our vehicle at the south end of the pit in an open area and worked our way north along the berm for about 400 metres. On our return about thirty minutes later, when we were approximately one-hundred and fifty metres from the vehicle we what looked like a domestic cat walking around the vehicle. We stopped and studied the cat and very quickly realised that this was not a small domestic cat. Our vehicle was facing us and when the cat passed in front we realised that, from nose to tail it was close or the same dimension as the width of the Toyota 4x4. It was walking in a slouched, stealthy manner and was approximately 0.5 m tall. We stood still, didn't alarm it in any way and after about a minute or so it slouched away into the nearby bushes.

There is a tunnel under the London Road at the north end of the pit. There we saw fresh paw marks which looked more than twice the size of my cat at home."

On January 13th, Adam Rowe reported that he'd seen a big black felid whilst driving during the early hours along Hawlry Road towards Dartford. And on the 17th a woman walking her Labrador in Cobham Woods at 4:30 pm saw a black cat stalking in the long grass. Although quite a distance away, her dog froze. The following day a black leopard was seen at Sandy Lane, Bean, and on the 22nd at 3:45 pm a woman driving up Arnold's Lane, Darenth, saw a big cat in the field behind a nearby house. She first took it to be a black Labrador, it was sitting still and looking towards the woman but when she saw it side on she realised it was feline in form.

A few days after a man walking with his girlfriend along the river near Swanscombe saw a melanistic leopard walk into the woods just off the marsh. The man claimed it was definitely a panther because he'd seen one twelve years previously, whilst fishing.

Another cat, or possibly the same individual, was seen by a girl named Emma near Dartford Heath days later as she drove along the heath. The cat was beside the road and the woman was so shocked that she almost crashed her car whilst staring at the animal.

After the initial flurry of sightings from the Gravesend and Dartford areas, the next batch of reports didn't emerge until March when a young boy claimed to have seen the panther near the cinema at Strood, and Amelia Harris reported seeing, with her mum, a black animal near Bluewater, but details were vague.

On the 23rd May the Kent Police filed a report from Dartford, at 10:00 pm of a 'black jaguar', but further information was not forthcoming. Around this time also I'd finished constructing my official Kent Big Cats website, where people could log their sightings and find out other information regarding such animals.

Sightings from the Bexley area were consistent throughout late spring whilst in the May an interesting little feature appeared in a free magazine that I have never been able to find the name of or trace the author. However, it read as follows:

Chance To Capture Big Cat On Camera

I have always enjoyed going to Bluewater because it offers a great variety of shops. It also really comes into its own when the weather is bad as shoppers are protected from the elements.

Now the shopping centre is offering something I would not expect to find there, which is even more thrilling than finding a bargain or bagging the latest fashion.

This is the chance to see a big cat on the prowl.

I understand this legendary animal has been named the Beast of Bexley. However, if it is now looking for food around the shopping centre, maybe it should now be called the Beast of Bluewater.

You would think that with all the technology we have these days, a big cat living in the south east would have clearly been caught on camera by now, and possibly even captured. Yet all we seem to get are glimpses of an animal seen from a distance, but you cannot blame the person taking the photograph for not wanting to get too close.

If the beast is prowling around Bluewater, which is full of security cameras, the chances of it being filmed properly will increase.

For once we might have something to thank shoplifters and car thieves for, as the security cameras were installed to help deal with them.

During May, something very peculiar was sighted just outside of Bluewater, but this will be discussed in the section *More Mystery Animals*.

At 7:30 pm on 26th May 2007 a man and his wife walking through fields near Cuxton took a route though a field of rape seed when they heard strange noises. At first a rustling, and then a crunching sound, as if bones were being broken. This naturally spooked the couple who strongly believed that a large animal was eating just a few metres away from them so they turned round and walked away.

On the 3rd June a man named Phil was strolling around his field near Meopham with a friend at 4:40 pm because they'd heard rumours that poachers were around. The men decided to split up. After a few minutes Phil climbed over a gate on a walkway and stepped down and two feet away came face to face with the big, black head of an animal peering from the undergrowth.

I interviewed the witness on the phone, he said:

"I was terrified. The animal was in a ready-to-pounce position, I froze despite having my air rifle and a phone with a camera in my pocket. Neither of us moved for a full minute so I decided I had to back away slowly and then I just sprinted, totally scared."

Phil said the animal was around five foot in length and very muscular. He mentioned that a few times previous whilst out with his friend he'd heard strange noises in the woods as if something was walking slowly through the undergrowth.

Via one of my websites, a man called Barry reported on 24th June that a week previously, at 3:30 am, he'd seen a massive black cat walk across the road from Dartford Park and slink into a wooded area near Brooklands Lake. On the 19th July at 6:00 pm a man, his brother, and brother-in-law were heading towards Enfield coming from Kent. They had just crossed the Dartford Tunnel near Armor Road when the witness looked out of the window and saw a big black cat in the middle of the road some twenty metres away. He said it was four times the size of a domestic cat.

A male witness driving saw a black leopard at Southfleet on 8th August at 10:15 pm, and a man named Len emailed me to say he'd seen a cat in the same month between Meopham and Sole Street. It was black in colour, three feet in length from head to back legs, with a very long tail and short legs. The man said he saw a similar animal around five years previous in the same area at 6:00 am one Sunday as he was driving.

Two sightings from the New Ash Green area reached me in September, both concerning a black leopard and on the 25th at 3:45 am a motorist had to slam on the brakes to avoid a cat, the size of a Border collie, black in colour, which raced across Heath Lane in Dartford where there'd been a handful of sightings previous.

On 7th October an angler freshwater fishing at Snodland, around 4:20 pm had a strange encounter which he called me about.

"I was walking back to the car park and waiting for my friend to catch up when I noticed

something move behind me to the left about thrity-five yards away. I turned and saw a large cat on the pathway which stood and watched me.

It was around two to three feet in length but with a long hairy tail. The animal was muscular, black in colour but with a reddish tinge but the head of the animal was a dark mushroom colour. The cat then casually walked off down the path towards where my mate was but he never saw it."

After the sighting the man looked on the internet and believed he'd seen a jaguarundi. A month previous my father was fishing at one of the lakes and was driving up a track when he saw a dark-coloured cat, bigger than a domestic cat slink into the trees. On Friday 15th February 2008 my dad saw a similar animal again, this time whilst perched on one of the swims fishing. It was around 2:00 pm when he noticed something on the opposite bank mooching about. He said it was as big as a fox but definitely a cat with a long bushy tail, smallish head and appeared to be greyish in colour.

On February 1st 2008 a woman driving home at 9:15 pm saw a big black cat along the Rochester Road near Shorne. She said that although the sighting was brief, the cat was very slender and slipped into the woods. Later on in the month an elderly woman from north Dartford, sitting up in bed at 3:30 am reading, was distracted by her growling dog. She gazed out of the bathroom window and watched in amazement as a sleek black cat with a long tail prowled along the back fence. And, on Sunday March 16th at 6:05 am a woman and her daughter-in-law travelling to a boot fair - along Thames Way, towards Ebbsfleet Station - had to be quick to catch a fleeting glimpse of a Labrador-sized black animal that bolted from right to left across the road.

The town of Gravesend is listed in the *Domesday Book* of 1086 as Gravesham, as belonging to Odo, Bishop of Bayeux, its name deriving from 'graaf-ham': the home of the Reeve or Bailiff of the Lord of the Manor, although some have suggested that the name Gravesham is from a corruption of the words 'grafs-ham' meaning a place, 'at the end of the grove'.

If so, this town, which is briefly mentioned in Mary Shelley's classic monster tale, *Frankenstein*, certainly has connections to more than one mystery, and remains a grove within which many a large cat prowl.

'There is something more than we know of in that tree, my lord. I am for an instant search.'
The Ash Tree - M.R. James

Tracking the elusive beast

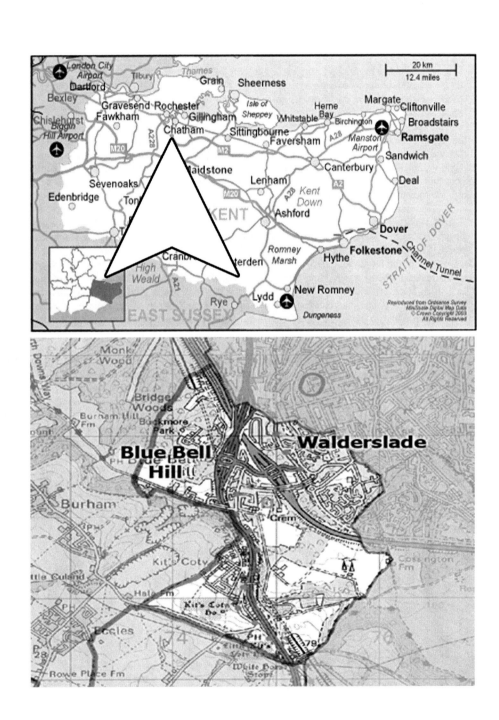

The Beast of Bluebell Hill and Others

"...something had killed a couple of pregnant ewes, and another flock of sheep had been that scared by something and chased about that one or two of them had dropped their lambs."

The Nature Of The Beast – Janni Howker

I've always been intrigued by dark tales of mystery and imagination, but since my exhaustive research into sightings and evidence of large cats roaming the county I've never dared to confuse or mingle the two. In the case of the animals which roam Blue Bell Hill, however, there must be at least some mention of the area and its high levels of, and history of, weirdness.

It was the place I grew up with on my doorstep but was always too afraid to meander through. The tales which spiralled from the blanket of woods like wisps of October smoke were at once exciting yet bordering on the evil. For Blue Bell Hill, part of the North Downs, and being an old chalk hill situated between Maidstone and Rochester, is the stuff ghost stories are made of.

The prehistoric Pilgrim's Way is a serpentine pathway that worms its way through the avenues of over hanging trees, the hills are steep, dipping into chalk quarries that remain treacherous havens for humans, but not for birds and other wildlife. The panoramic view from the picnic area on Common Road is a hive for tourists who flock to gawp across the valley, to see the sun glint off Burham's reservoir, the pillars of smoke steam from Aylesford's industrial estate—as far as the eyes can see, a green quilt of woods, small villages and odes to ancient history.

It has always been a strange area. Its most famous landmark being the Medway megaliths, Kit's Coty House and the Countless Stones. Kit's Coty House is the remains of a Neolithic chambered long barrow. The impressive and haunting stone structure is said to be older than Stonehenge, and consists of three sarsen orthostats supporting a horizontal capstone, looking almost like a stone set of goalposts sticking out from the landscape.

Website *Vortigern Studies* describes the house as such:

> Kit's Coty House stands in a field to the west (you can't see it from the road) of the
> A229 from Maidstone to Rochester. A footpath, app. 0.25 miles (0.5 km) long, leads
> towards it. The tallest stone of which is 8 feet (2.4 metres) high and the capstone 4 by

2.7 metres, which was once covered by an earthen mound of 180 feet (55 metres) long, as aerial photographs have shown. Side ditches were once up to 3.8 metres deep. This site was already famous in the seventeenth century. The diarist Samuel Pepys described it as:

'Three great stones standing upright and a great round one lying on them, of great bigness, although not so big as those on Salisbury Plain. But certainly it is a thing of great antiquity, and I am mightily glad to see it.'

Unfortunately not all people felt this way. A large stone shown on a sketch by Stukely in 1722 and known as 'the General's Tomb', was blown up in 1867. The large mound, also visible on that sketch, has also all but vanished.

Some call it simply Kit's Coty, because 'coty' means the same as 'house'. The story explaining the name tells us that Kit is Catigern who, together with his brother Vortimer fought Hengist and his brother Horsa here around 455, which is recorded both in the *Historia Brittonum* as well as in the *Anglo-Saxon Chronicle.'*

Further towards Aylesford are scattered the Countless Stones, or Little Kit's Coty House. The site is further remains of a Neolithic chambered long barrow although compared to Kit's Coty House, these stones look like nothing more than a selection of half-buried sarsen stones, which, legend has it, are impossible to count!

William Stukeley attempted to reconstruct the stones by sketch in the eighteenth century.

Both chambers have an almost forlorn look to them, set against a backdrop of green hills, fields and trees. However, according to Blue Bell Hill folklore expert Sean Tudor, the area is simply a 'special place'. Of the stones he writes:

'Like many similar sites of Neolithic age across Britain and Europe, the real purpose of these formations cannot be established with any certainty. Likely is that they had a number of functions: some for ceremonial purposes, others as track way markers and sighting points, or astronomical markers. The dominant idea, though, is that they served as burial places, which would appear to be true in part for the site known as Coldrum, at Trosley, some 8 miles to the west of BBH (Blue Bell Hill). While no human remains have been found at BBH, this is undoubtedly the favoured interpretation for Kit's Coty and many of the other structures there, prompting one commentator to refer to the complex as a prehistoric Necropolis.

Much of the air of mystery associated with BBH can undoubtedly be attributed to these legacies of our Neolithic ancestors. So little is known about them and their builders, they are a natural subject of myth and folklore. And, therefore, considering their proximity to the haunted stretch of road, it was inevitable, perhaps, that some connection would be made between them and the modern ghost story. As subjects of mystery attached to the same area, the two are naturally identified as expressions of the same mystical aura that marks BBH as a special place, instinctively identified as somewhere where strange experiences are apt to take place.

An article for the Evening Post *of 15 July 1974, for instance, noted that BBH - referring to the road, the A229 - runs across the sites of innumerable prehistoric graves, several of*

132

which, it noted, are 'known to be connected with occult practices'. Individuals too, I would discover, felt the stones 'had something to do with it (i.e. the ghost). As a taboo of many cultures, the desecration of the resting places of the dead is to virtually invite retribution; many prehistoric sites support such a tradition, with misfortune or death said to befall the guilty - which seems to be a kind of supernatural insurance policy against disturbance, reminiscent of the infamous Curse of the Pharaohs.

Some traditions state that the heavy stones were designed to imprison the spirits of the dead within their graves - an idea that dovetails to some degree with the commentary in the Evening Post, which implies that occult influences may have been unleashed by the destruction of the graves, or at least have tainted the atmosphere of the place so as to be conducive to hauntings - an idea which may not be as silly as it sounds. One outcome of my research into BBH, and noted just the same in other cases, is the correlation between outbreaks of ghostly activity and large-scale disturbance of the physical environment. Two major episodes figure in BBH's recent history - the construction of the new A229 dual carriageway over the Hill in 1970-1972, and the major refurbishment of Junction 6 of the M20 with the A229 at the foot of the Hill in 1992, the latter of which correlated very well with the spate of renewed sightings of the ghost in November 1992 - which could lead to the consideration that some of these locations may possess special energetic properties.'

Indeed, as well as the strange stone structures that puncture the skyline there have been many reports of a ghostly figure or two, said to haunt the lanes around the hill. Such sightings have been investigated by Sean, with some exhaustive details into such cases outlined on his *Roadghosts* website. Such apparitions have given the area an extra special ingredient which over the course of fifty or so years has made Blue Bell Hill one of the country's, if not the world's, weirdest locations. Although sightings of big cats date back several centuries in and around the area, the press never jumped on the bandwagon until the late '90s and so the hill has always maintained its eerie reputation via the spectral sightings rather than any of the big cat kind, but since the sightings of what was to become known as the Beast of Blue Bell Hill, the mysterious animals and ghostly forms have kind of co-existed side by side as phantasmal attractions for tourists and ghost-hunters alike.

Sean adds:

While the name Blue Bell Hill evokes images of a colourful and serene woodland landscape (of which it must undoubtedly have been deserving in its past), it seems oddly incongruous against the backdrop of the busy and noisy motorway-grade highway (A229) that defines the Hill today. Just as incongruous is the idea that the modern dual carriageway and its immediate environs could be the setting for a haunting.

The most prominent feature of the Hill today is the deep cutting and bench accommodating the A229 which grazes the face of the escarpment at the point it begins a mile-long deflection to the north. The exposed chalk cliff here, exploiting former quarry workings alongside the former Maidstone-Chatham road, combines with similarly exposed and abandoned workings just to the west to make Blue Bell Hill distinctive and easily recognizable.

Blue Bell Hill and its immediate environs have been a focus for human occupation and activity since before recorded history, long before the time of the Roman occupation when the first road was established here as a characteristically direct route to Roches-

ter, where it joined the great Roman road of Watling Street.

It is therefore not surprising to discover that over the course of its long history, the Hill has attracted to it a number of tales, many of a supernatural flavour. As author Michael Goss has pointed out, the stories regarding a road ghost are a quite recent addition to Blue Bell Hill's stock of legend and folklore, which are generally derived from or related to documented historic events or artefacts.

Sean Tudor first heard about the ghost of Blue Bell Hill on 28th February 1981 as he and his family moved from London to Kent. Like many people, the tales he heard were often vague, sinister local urban legends speaking of a phantom hitchhiker said to wonder the lonely lanes, particularly the A229, which back then was a very different setting to which it is today. He states:

'The construction of the new road - the modern dual carriageway, which now holds the title of 'A229', which was completed in 1972, was built to improve both traffic flow and safety. Construction of the new road necessitated a massive rock/earth-moving programme, reducing the dangerous mile-long 1-in-11 gradient to 1-in-18, which has left little of the original road intact between Maidstone and Blue Bell Hill Village at the top of the Hill, altering the character and appearance of the entire location.'

Much of Blue Bell Hill's ghostly legend revolves around a tragic road accident that happened on the night of 19th November 1965 when two cars crashed. Three of four women in one vehicle, a Mark 1 Ford Cortina, died. One of these women was a bride-to-be, whilst the driver in the other car - a Jaguar - was not hurt, and his partner although taken to hospital, was discharged soon after. Many researchers theorise that one of the spirits wandering the darkness is the bride-to-be, although descriptions have varied regarding the spectre, although it is generally considered female.

Legend claims that many motorists have picked up a girl on the hill who has disappeared, usually from the backseat, often before the destination she has requested being dropped off at, has been reached. Other drivers have reported hitting a girl within the vicinity, the woman often staring at the driver as she slips under the bonnet. In most cases, drivers have stopped, got out and checked for a body. They have found nothing.

There are many locations across the world which have similar cases, but the Blue Bell Hill ghost remains one of the most potent ghostly legends in the fact that it does not merely exist on whisper or local rumour, but several strong cases which date back several decades, even to before the tragic accident which took place. The area and its busy dual carriageway has also been the scene over the years for several fatal accidents, as well as other ghostly activity, some of which will be mentioned in the chapter, *The Others*.

The ghost of Blue Bell Hill hit the headlines in a big way in 1992 with researcher Sean Tudor at the core of the activity. The press, although having featured occasional sightings before, featured several stories of the ghost girl, which would run a parallel course to the big cat sightings that made the headlines in 1998. Rather bizarrely, some paranormal researchers attempted to tie the two mysteries together, believing that the large black cat seen around the haunted hill was in fact a ghost or demon of some kind, in some way similar to the phantom black dogs or hellhounds which exist in folklore. I've never believed such suggestions, but it does make for interesting reading. Mysticism has, of course, always shrouded the area.

In 1998 the Kent press created their own 'big cat' flap, albeit one some thirty years after the Surrey puma sightings, a couple of decades after the 'beast' of Exmoor panic, and a few years after the Bodmin hysteria

The Blue Bell Hill cat was described as a 'panther', or black leopard, and to newspapers such as the *Kent Today* it was a new mystery, especially after a flurry of sightings in '98 around the wooded areas and grassy slopes, although after a few months even cat sightings across the river at Strood, and from the furthest corners of Kent, were being connected to the Blue Bell Hill 'beast'! However, the press were several centuries too late!

The Pilgrim's Way, an ancient pathway which runs from Canterbury to London, was said to, in the region of Boxley, have once been haunted by a giant hound which has remained a rather obscure apparition embedded in the annals of local folklore, although such a creature may well have been a flesh and blood exotic cat, if we go on what anecdotal evidence we have.

The year was 1654 when the 'great dogg' was said to have savaged and killed a man, on what author Charles Igglesden described as, '*...the upper road*'. Although the mention is brief and allegedly from Igglesden's *A Saunter Through Kent With Pen And Pencil (Kentish Express)* work (a series of county-based chronicles covering more than thirty volumes), there is no evidence to suggest it does appear in the volumes and may simply have been information he received in a letter. Of course, such yarns sound like something akin to supernatural fiction, classic campfire tales. But consider also another sighting, this time in 1745, on the Pilgrim's Way when a peddler was killed by a, '*...lean, grey hound with prick't ears*', which at first appeared behind the man and his friend and then up ahead. Where the man was mauled he was said to have been buried. Rumours suggested that the animal was something akin to a puma for what dog has the ability to remain elusive in its behaviour in order to hunt and kill? Or maybe the mauler was a wolf.

Sometime during the 1800s two men, including Reverend Edward, or Reverend Edward H____, depending on sources, who recorded the encounter, were walking near to Maidstone towards Boxley church when, ...

> '*...at a point where the road ascends...in its course, we paused to take breath, and look't back and were surprised to see some distance behind us, and standing on the way we had come, a lean grey dog with upstanding ears...I was struck by its size...it appeared as big as a calf.*'

Was the animal merely a dog? Would such witnesses, even as credible as a Reverend would have been, recognised a slinking felid during a time when reports of such animals were rarely spoken of? In fact a similar hound was said to prowl Trottiscliffe, near Gravesend, on another pathway that has also produced several large cat sightings. Coincidence?

Fast-forward a century, and once again we come to Leonard Cuckow, who claimed to have seen a panther shot on the Downs near Burham. He told me in the late 1990s that the cat may well have escaped from Sir Garrard Tyrwhitt Drake's zoo in the grounds of the Cobtree Manor Estate, near Maidstone. Leonard said that the police approached the eccentric, twelve times Mayor of Maidstone, who allegedly owned up that it had belonged to his menagerie. Leonard also stated that despite being the Mayor and member of various zoological societies, and also a distinguished gent and pillar of the community, tales were rife of weird inter-breeding between some of the parks animal species and that such animals were also inadequately housed. Hugh William Tyrwhitt Drake bought Cobtree Manor House, its surrounding land and several farms from the Brassey family of Preston Hill, Aylesford in 1904. Eventually, the estate was inherited by his son Garrard.

The grounds were enlarged to maintain his collection of wild animals. Leonard claimed that he often went to the zoo and was allowed in certain sections that eluded the public. Sir Garrard lived in Cobtree Manor with his wife and died in 1964 aged eighty-three. The flamboyant figure left the estate in a charitable trust in 1951 for 'the benefit of the people of Maidstone', but stipulated that his widow Edna should be allowed to live there, although Maidstone Borough Council would maintain it.

In 1983 Maidstone Borough Council and Kent County Council developed the twenty-eight acres into what it is today, a museum, golf course and park, which opened to the public in 1985. According to Leonard, the thousands of yearly visitors to the zoo never heard about the frequent escapees. In 1959 it ceased as a zoo due to rising costs, labour shortages and Drake's age. A majority of the animals were sent to other zoo parks such as in the Bronx, New York.

Drake began to build his collection in 1900 and had one of the largest collections in the country. His possessions began to attract local townsfolk and around 1912 his shows aided local charities. By 1913 he owned bears, kangaroos and many birds, which he transported to Tovil, although this was to only last for a year due to the war. Soon after though, his collection was rebuilt, and after mini-tours and exhibitions a permanent zoo was set up at the estate, opened in 1934 and in two seasons attracted more than one-hundred-and-fifty thousand people.

My grand-dad Ron told me that people in show business were often invited to the zoo as were Royalty and often experienced the miniature train which took visitors from the entrance to the animal enclosures.

During the Second World War the zoo struggled again and locals feared the bombing raids would release the lions. In April 2008 a woman told me that as a child visiting the zoo she always remained terrified at how the agitated lions shook the bars of the cage to the extent that they seemed to come loose.

There is a possibility that Tyrwhitt Drake knew nothing of the animals that escaped captivity, or if he did he preferred to turn a blind eye. For the record, Sir Garrard collected the following animals over twenty years of his zoo time: Bear, baboon, bison, camel, cheetah, chimpanzee, deer, dingo, elephant, gnu, hyena, jackal, kangaroo, leopard, plus lion, llama, monkey, porcupine, racoon, rat, sheep, wild swine, wolf, yak, zebra, many birds, reptiles, horse and fish.

Did some of these creatures escape or become responsible for today's populations of exotic animals roaming the wilds? Well, as far as big cat sightings go, possibly.

The question is, if so many cats, or enough cats, escaped from the place then why weren't such animals often reported in the '50s, '60s and '70s like they are today? I think such animals were certainly observed in the Kent wilds but not reported, only a handful were ever documented, as in Igglesden's work a century or so previous.

So, has the Beast of Blue Bell Hill been with us for centuries, decades, or just a few years? Well, just like the so-called Bluewater big cats, the press has had a major part to play, and that's where we'll start.

As I mentioned in the previous section, 1998 was a huge year for Kent regarding big cat sightings. The *Kent Today* and *Medway Today* were eager to feature stories of such animals even if the reporters didn't have a clue about species or locations. They were eager to create a Blue Bell Hill beast wherever a cat was sighted. However, a trickle of reports from the early '90s suggested a variety of large cats had been roaming the surrounding areas.

Trevor Sturgess and Brian Paine mentioned a few sightings in their noteworthy *Unexplained Kent*

(Breedon Books 1997) which proved valuable to my research.
In the chapter *Big Cats On The Prowl* they list the following sightings in relation to Blue Bell Hill:

- *May 9th 1991 – A nurse at Leybourne Grange Hospital, near West Malling saw an animal she claimed was a leopard.*
- *May 22nd 1991 – Police were called to investigate a sighting of a puma made by a man in Marden.*
- *June 1991 – In Addington a big cat was blamed for eating a rodent and a resident reported seeing a large cat-like animal strolling across his garden. This sighting came a week after a motorist reported seeing a big cat on the A20 at Addington near West Malling Golf Club.*
- *August 1991 – Winifred Moss saw a large cat in her garden at Allington.*
- *May 1992 – Computer analyst Maureen Tulloch saw a puma roaming woodland near Paddock Wood which she reported to the police.*
- *September 1992 – Puma was blamed for mauling a ginger tom cat in Paddock Wood.*
- *January 1993 – Joyce Ridden reported seeing a lynx-like creature at the bottom of her garden in Wigmore, Rainham.*
- *May 1994 – Staff at kitchen and bathroom suppliers H.M. Potts, at East Malling, laid sand on their showroom car park after sightings of a big cat. Several weeks later mysterious footprints appeared in the sand.*
- *June 1995 – Retired BBC worker Eddie Dedman filmed a big, black cat on his camcorder while walking at Aylesford Priory.*
- *August 1995 – Former police dog handler Damon Hadlow claimed to have seen a black panther at Bearsted.*

The book, which focuses on various local strange phenomena, is rather vague in its descriptions of 'big cats' in that only on occasion is a black leopard mentioned, merely a 'big cat' or 'puma' is the general description, so we have to take such reports with a pinch of salt, but still note them because around the same time large cats were also reported at Canterbury, Dover and Ashford, proof that large exotic felids were not new.

Although it was clear to me that a majority of the large cats roaming Dartford and the Gravesend area were not the same animals as those in the Medway Towns due to a clash of reports, there was certainly a possibility, some of the time anyway, that black leopards and puma sighted at West Malling,

Allington and other Maidstone-related areas could have been the same animal. Again, rivers were an obstacle, but certain stretches of the River Medway were not as wide or as strong in current as that near the Rochester-Strood bridge. Further north at Halling, the river winds with tranquillity, and is only around fifty yards wide, and at certain villages such Aylesford, small bridges join the towns as well as railway lines, perfect inlets and outlets for wandering cats.

Of course, an animal crossing at Aylesford could be at Ditton in a few minutes, and a week or so later towards Gravesend, but sightings were suggesting that if anything, cats that may have been crossing were ending up in the deeply wooded areas such as Mereworth and further across into Sevenoaks.

In 1990 a man named Barry was driving near Blue Bell Hill when he saw a big black animal cross one of the walkway bridges over the main road. The witness said that he could see the white teeth of the animal. Although such a detail seems unlikely considering the witness was driving and around fifty yards away, but I perceived Barry as a credible witness after a long chat, and he also told me of several other sightings he'd experienced as well as people he knew.

In 1993 a head groundkeeper at Aylesford Priory, just a mile or so from Blue Bell Hill, reported seeing an animal that resembled a lynx as he tended to a log-pile at 4:00 pm. He claimed also that it had been seen next to the pond.

In the same year at Capstone Country Park in Chatham, a puma was observed at 1:30 pm one afternoon and the local warden was told of a strange set of large prints found in the mud. Around the same time a teacher claimed to have sighted a black panther behind the Wagon At Hale Public House, which sits a few hundred yards away from Capstone Park.

The Medway Towns are certainly built up, but there are areas that could hide a large cat or two, especially if it was a nocturnal hunter as most are. Chatham, Rochester, Strood, Gillingham, and further towards Rainham are busy areas, but if large animals are roaming the surrounding woods of Walderslade, Maidstone, Bredhurst, and Sittingbourne, then there's no reason as to why such cats should occasionally roam into these towns, whether as part of their territory whilst searching for prey.

In 1992 at Lordswood, a woman saw a light-coloured big cat, possibly a puma, by the side of the road near Gleaming Wood Drive. Again, here we have an area peppered with strips of woodland and fields, which in turn melt into other wooded areas, providing a blanket of cover for any elusive predator.

Doubt was certainly cast in the direction of such animals during the early '90s although the press towards Dover and Deal were covering big cat stories on a regular basis. In the Medway Towns, sightings of such animals were not worthy of any kind of coverage, hence the lack of reports, but as they say, absence of evidence does not always mean evidence of absence.

One morning at 3:00 am during the December of 1994, near Burham, not far from Blue Bell Hill once again, a farmer found a couple of badgers that had been eaten. The same man also told me that he saw a heavily pregnant cat and another dark animal, which had a rear white leg.

At Bearsted, near Maidstone, Mr Murdoch reported that some ferocious animal tried to kill his dog which he'd left in his car as he quickly popped indoors to fetch something. Although there was no sighting of a big cat, his dog was halfway down the road and the roof of the car looked like it had been slashed by something with razor claws. Or possibly by a dog-stealing human with a sharp instrument!

The animal mentioned earlier filmed by Eddie Dedman in 1994 at Aylesford Priory was a turning point in the local press.

'*Mystery Of Priory Beast*' screamed the front-page headline of the local *Kent Today* showing a photo of the witness and a reasonably clear image of a muscular black cat prowling through the undergrowth.

> *A camcorder enthusiast claims that he has captured dramatic footage of a big cat strolling the grounds of a religious retreat in mid Kent.*
>
> *Retired BBC television worker Eddie Dedman is convinced that the black beast he filmed at Aylesford Priory is either a puma or a panther.*
>
> *The film could prove to be the first real evidence of a big cat roaming the area, after years of reported sightings. Mr Dedman, 66, claims that several members of his family also spotted the animal merging from a row of trees in the gardens of the Priory at*

about 4 pm on Monday.

He said: "We saw it once and then it disappeared into the undergrowth. Moments later it came into view again and I managed to film it for a few seconds on my camcorder. It was about three foot long and twenty inches high and had a very long, droopy tail. It appeared to be black all over, like a puma or a panther." He added: "Everybody else who saw the animal was convinced that it was some sort of big cat and certainly not a normal one."

Mr Dedman of Sherbourne, Dorset, is visiting Kent for several weeks for a family reunion and has been staying with his nephew Andrew Deeker-Harris in Caring Lane, Maidstone.

He added: "I know that I didn't imagine the whole thing – a lot of other people saw it and I have watched the footage several times. It wasn't a case of having too many whiskies." The film was taken to Maidstone police who recorded the incident to see if it matched other recent sightings in the area.

A spokesman said: " We have had many reported sightings of big cats, but we have never seen a photograph or any proper evidence."

A spokesman for Aylesford Priory claimed that Mr Dedman had probably recorded one of several cats living in the grounds.

She said: "Our groundsman is confident that it is a black cat we have here, which is quite large and nothing to get alarmed about."

The Friars at Aylesford is a home to an order of Carmelite Friars.'

Mr Dedman's footage was certainly the first recorded evidence of a Blue Bell Hill big cat and impressive it was too, showing a large, muscular animal possibly even longer than three feet in length, high in the shoulder with a long tail. However, shortly after the feature in the local press, a Natalie Dearnaley came forward to suggest that the animal on the film was in fact her own pet cat, Sylvie!

'Is Sylvie the mystery priory puma?' asked the *Kent Today* reporter Sean Browne.

'Natalie Dearnaley says she can clear up the mystery of the large cat seen prowling in a Kent village.

She says the so-called Aylesford puma or panther, which is supposed to roam around The Friars, is no more than her grey cat Sylvie. But when I went to track down Sylvie with photographer Barry Hollis, she was determined to keep the mystery alive and was nowhere to be found.

Natalie, of High street, Aylesford, said: "I can understand why people might think that she is a puma because she is a little larger than a pet cat and she is quite muscular and walks a bit like a big cat."

Natalie moved to England from Boston, America, when she married her husband Steve and brought Sylvie and other pet cat Frank with her.

She said: "We have had Sylvie for about three years and she sort of adopted us when we were in Boston. She was about a year-old then."

The couple spent thousands of pounds in quarantine fees when they brought the cats to Kent. Natalie says Sylvie spends most of her time at The Friars hunting rabbits and be-friending the Carmelite monks who live there.

She also claims that it is Sylvie who was captured on film by retired BBC television worker Eddie Dedman, of Sherbourne, Dorset, when he spent his summer holiday there.

Natalie said: "I am convinced that the cat on the film is Sylvie and not a puma."

Despite Natalie making such claims, the photo of her silvery moggie resembles nothing at all like a black panther, and at the time of writing, I'm sure Sylvie has passed on, and yet sightings continue around The Friars.

The Carmelite Order was, according to author Malcolm John,

'...originally brought here from Mount Carmel in Palestine by Baron Richard de Gray of Codnor – legend has it that occupation began on Christmas Day in 1240. The Baron gave his Aylesford manor to these monks on his return from the Crusades. They were given every encouragement by the Bishop of Rochester and the church was dedicated in 1245 with the splendid title, 'Assumption of the Glorious Virgin'. The first pilgrimage or world visitation to Aylesford was in 1247 when the first chapter was held and St Simon Stock elected Prior General.

The order then adopted the title 'Mendicant Friars', their importance grew and centres were established in Oxford, Cambridge and London. By the time of the dissolution of the monasteries in 1583, there were over forty such centres. The subsequent history of The Friars was somewhat chequered, passing from Sir Thomas Wyatt in the sixteenth century through various owners until it eventually came into the possession of the Earl of Aylesford. The Carmelite Order purchased the building after it had been partially damaged by fire in 1930.'

Previously to Eddie Dedman's footage, a Sittingbourne man, travelling at Boxley, not far from Blue Bell Hill, in the May of 1994, at 7:45 pm saw a cat he believed was a puma. He'd been travelling from Lords-wood to Maidstone and was coming down Boxley Hill when a buff-coloured cat bounded across the winding lane. A vehicle coming up the hill had to stop to avoid the animal. The witness described the animal as the size of a large dog and having a long tail.

In 1995 a Lordswood young man and a friend out looking for a lost pet domestic cat at 1:00 am and were shining a torch through the woods when they picked up a set of bright green eyes. They claimed that the eyes belonged to a large cat, around six feet long with muscular shoulders that padded to the witnesses left before they ran from the area, terrified. The sighting was reported to the police who told the witness that the incident would be passed on to the countryside police.

In 1998 when sightings of the Blue Bell Hill creature began to be reported with some frequency a report appeared in the newspaper of a very strange sighting that actually occurred in 1997 and involved a lady named 'Marilyn', who I spoke to at length about her bizarre encounter. The woman had gone to a 1960s entertainment night at the Central Theatre in Chatham High Street which is certainly not an area you'd expect to see a big cat, in fact, no animal of any such kind has been seen there since Marilyn's odd sighting.

She had heard that a domestic cat had been stranded on a ledge on a nearby roof and after the show she came to the then Alders car park and saw the poor animal up on the height, crying in distress. However, on a separate ledge, she was amazed to see another cat, and watched it with a handful of other witnesses. They all agreed that it looked like a lynx, had pointed ears and also seemed to make a crying noise. The witnesses were so intrigued that they stayed for more than an hour watching the two cats.

Marilyn then left the scene, drove home and told her husband about the animals and decided that at 3:30 am she was going to return.

When she arrived she was surprised to see both cats still there and then at 4:00 am she was shocked even further when a larger cat, the size of a puma, appeared even higher and was pacing back and forth. She said that the animal was sandy in colour with a long tail. Marilyn finally left the area but reported what she'd seen to Maidstone Fire Brigade who allegedly investigated the area the next day and found the domestic cat, which bolted along with another cat.

No other sightings have ever emerged from the area. Of course, most places at night are quiet and any large cat can make its way across town from adjacent railway lines or woods, but this peculiar happening bugged me for a long time.

Marilyn was a witness adamant as to what she'd seen, but it just didn't add up. Had the stunned witness simply got over-excited and seen three domestic cats? What other theory could explain the incident? Okay, let's just say that a cat such as a lynx had found its way into the shadows of the town because it was hungry and had come upon a meal, being the domestic cat. Maybe the moggie, in an attempt to escape its pursuer, ended up stranded on one of the rooftops with the lynx on its tail. Even so, this doesn't explain the even larger cat. We'll never know if the largest cat was really a puma, or whether the cat with the pointed ears was in fact a lynx, maybe they were all from the same species, possibly mother, father, kitten, but such an incident remains unexplained and if it hadn't been for Marilyn's sincerity I would have laughed it off as a hoax. –And what about the Fire Brigade? What did they actually see as they came to the rescue of the alleged stranded cat? Nobody will ever know.

On the 12th December 1997, *Kent Today* reporter Geoff Maynard, who would become a vital contact in regards to my research, reported *'New sighting of the beast'*, stating:

> *'The beast of Blue Bell Hill has reared its feline head once again. There has been yet another sighting, the third, of a mysterious dark animal lurking in fields on the outskirts of Chatham.*
>
> *The latest was last summer and follows two recently reported accounts of a large cat wandering in the rural area.*
>
> *Julie and Chris Bartel, and their children Joshua, ten, Elysia, six and Susannah, four, were enjoying a family walk in the Blue Bell Hill area when they spotted the mysterious animal.*
>
> *From around five-hundred yards away they watched it stalk across a field of crops and disappear into the sanctuary of thick bushes.*

Mrs Bartel, of Hempstead, said: "We were walking along a hilltop and just saw this thing in a field below – it was like a big black creature. It wasn't a horse, it wasn't a donkey – we just couldn't make out what it was." But her ten-year old son Joshua is adamant what he saw was a cat, and a big one at that.

He said: "It had to be a big cat because of the way it was walking along and the way its tail was hanging – it appeared to be a big black panther."

Last month a motorist spotted a large, dark cat-like creature crawling through grassland off the A229 at Blue Bell Hill.

And a second witness said he saw a creature which looked like a gorilla in the same area several years ago. (Author's note: see chapter, The Others, for more on this bizarre sighting).

Mrs Bartel said: "There must be something out there if several people have reported seeing it."

Despite the rumours Kent Wildlife Trust inspectors have never seen the beast and have had no significant reports of wild animals attacking livestock in the area.'

So, had a black leopard recently been released into the wilds or were witnesses more alert after the story of Mr Dedman's footage appeared in the paper? It seemed that no hoaxes had filtered through to the press, but the name 'the Beast of Blue Bell Hill' had certainly been born around this time, immediately surrounding the area in more clouds of eeriness.

It's possible that the animal had recently been let go, or was offspring of animals that escaped the Maidstone Zoo several decades previously. We'll never know for sure, but by the end of '97 the beast was on everyone's lips, chatted about in the local pubs, feared by ramblers on the dark lanes and giving the Exmoor and Bodmin animals a run for their money.

An elderly gent named Mr Parker who was a bailiff at the reservoir at Burham said he saw a black leopard drinking from the depths in 1997. It had already startled a fisherman not long before but remained in the bushes away from Mr Parker.

In 1999 I received an intriguing letter from a Mr Lindsay Smith who spoke of two interesting sightings from 1996 and late '97, possibly early '98. He wrote:

'December 1996 – Leybourne, West Malling, on Oxley Shaw Lane between Lillieburn and Barleycorn – I was out late evening, walking my dog and just turned left out of our street, to see my dog, who always walks someway ahead, stand stock-still in the snow.

The large cat (I would have said puma/cougar, dark but not black body) ran very fast across the road from left to right, onto the large green and disappeared into a group of trees/bushes. I went after it and looked around but did not see any more. At roughly the same time an article had appeared in the KM of a local paperboy who had seen a big cat on his delivery round one morning. I believed it, no problems.

December 1997 – January 1998 (can't remember exactly) – On Oxley Shaw Lane, at junction with Castle Way/Leybourne Church – A Saturday morning, 8:15 – 8:30 am I drove right out of Willowmead onto Oxley Shaw Lane, going towards Castle Way. Just after passing the junction with Bridgewater Place, the cat ran across the road at the end of Oxley Shaw Lane, from left to right, and went into the trees/bushes which edge onto rough ground now covered by the new Autolodge and Brewer's Fayre restaurant.'

Certainly a different animal to the black beast roaming Blue Bell Hill, but West Malling would soon get a reputation for having a puma in its midst.

Between the vast Ashford woods and rolling fields of Bearsted sits Headcorn, at the centre of the northern part of the Kentish Weald. In 1998 a woman riding her horse saw a large dark-coloured cat which went into a wood, leapt a fence into a field of cows, which all huddled together.

Although the description of the animal was vague, it proved that such an animal could either roam towards Maidstone, or down towards Ashford. Was there really a Blue Bell Hill beast or simply a handful of mystery Kent cats roaming the whole county, never really restricted to one area, except by the press?

During the beginning of the year I received reports in abundance from Ashford, plus Whitstable, Gravesend and Margate all around the same time, more proof that several big animals were prowling the county. I knew that several had been seen towards Dover and Deal because these were the animals, which had made the press most frequently, for these sightings see section pertaining to east Kent.

On the 12th January 1998 the Blue Bell Hill beast came to the fore. The *Kent Today* reported that a Medway couple had seen the animal.

Blue Bell Hill's picnic area provides a spectacular view of the Downs. It was here that Steve and Amanda Arnold (no relation) from Lordswood had their close encounter. They were both walking with their toddler's when a black animal emerged from the undergrowth, ran along the bank and slinked into the bushes.

Steve said: *"It was pure black. It didn't look at us, we just heard a rustling and as I looked to my right I saw this thing pouncing downward, going very fast. It was over in seconds."*

He said the animal was as big as an Alsatian. His wife added, *"It was long-legged and skinny, that's what I'd say. Its ears were sort of floppy...short and floppy. I've never seen anything like it before, I screamed my head off."*

The late Quentin Rose, a professional animal trapper at the time was doing a lot of important research into such sightings and evidence.

He told local news:

> *"I've spoken to hundreds and hundreds of people and done hundreds of post-mortems on sheep and deer carcasses and I've identified twenty-seven parts of the country where there are regular, reliable sightings for leopards, thirty-two for puma, ten for lynx, six for jungle cat, leopard cat and ocelot and four for wolverine."* (Author's note: The wolverine is the second biggest mustelid after the giant otter, measuring over three feet long and standing up to ten inches high, they inhabit Canada, parts of the USA, Europe and Asia. They are bear-like, strong, stocky and vicious with powerful jaws.)

When asked about how the south-east figured in the picture, he replied, *"Quite heavily. I've got leopard and puma sightings in Kent, East Sussex, West Sussex and Surrey."*

A sighting backed these claims from Battle, near Hastings, where a puma had been seen on several occasions near Battle Abbey. At the time when interviewed, custodian Daryl Burchmore said, *"The witness was adamant he'd seen the beast only one-hundred yards away."*

'Is There A Beast Of Blue Bell Hill?' asked Geoff Maynard in the *Kent Today* of Wednesday January 28th 1998.

> *'What do you think there is more chance of happening – winning the Lottery or spotting a black panther on a country stroll? For an unlucky person like myself there will not be a hope in hell of either event occurring.*
>
> *But going by the stack of sightings Kent Today has received in recent months, the big cat phenomenon seems to be much more common than a lotto win.*
>
> *We have catalogued several reports from people who claim to have spotted a large black cat – either a puma or a panther – in or around the Blue Bell Hill area on the fringes of Medway.*
>
> *In the company of my trusty sniffer dogs Sherlock and Watson I set off for a stroll along the North Downs Way of Common Road on Blue Bell Hill.*
>
> *For two hours we clambered downhill and uphill in thick mud on the lookout for signs of a cat-like beastie. Our search focused on fields and an abandoned quarry area just off the A229 Chatham to Maidstone Road. The area around it is a popular spot for picnics and with walkers and we have received three recent reports of sightings of the so-called beast in this vicinity. The quarry area provides the perfect habitat for a lair cut off from the outside world in deep undergrowth. But despite the obvious potential of the area it was also obvious that we were searching for a cat in a haystack – the beastie was nowhere to be seen.*
>
> *Sherlock went darting through a hedge at one point after a black object but it was a feathery crow rather than a snarling panther. We returned from our adventure tired, muddy, cold and certain that if there is a large black cat out there it was not stupid enough to bump into us.'*

This interesting article made the full page three with various sightings mentioned.

It was a puma I saw' according to a Gillingham man Des Watson who said he'd seen a big cat or Higham Station the previous year, although such an animal was almost certainly not the Blue Bell Hil cat.

Wildlife warden Dave Hutton said: *"Nobody has actually phoned us to say they have seen a big cat and I have seen no traces myself but I am open minded about it. It is certainly possible for a big cat to be living out there."*

In another short article the newspaper mentioned:

> *'If a large cat is living in the countryside on the outskirts of Medway then where is it*

finding food?

There have been reports of farm animals being killed in the area. Kent Wildlife Trust is investigating an incident which happened over Christmas when a flock of sheep was savaged in the Holborough Marshes nature reserve near Snodland.

Trust staff are putting the attack down to a dog, but no-one saw the animal which was responsible for the butchery.

The dead sheep's injuries suggest the attacker was the size and build of an Alsatian dog – or perhaps a large cat?'

It must be said at this point that anyone at the time, or since, who trudges through the woods of Blue Bell Hill was, and still is relying on pure chance to encounter such an animal. Those familiar with the many ancient pathways that wind through the brambles will know that such dense foliage could hide several large predators that may be glimpsed only every now and then by game keepers, poachers, dog-walkers and people who ride horses through the woods.

Blue Bell Hill may always attract thousands of people each year, but its overgrown and steep-sided quarries are impenetrable and treacherous should anyone risk descending the chalky slopes into the abyss of woven trees. Even the picnic area of a night is a pitch black and hazardous slope that slips into the murky woods and gloomy valleys which spray into the neighbouring towns and villages, meaning an elusive cat could easily pad into Burham, Wouldham and the likes without being seen.

The following month the beast made the front pages, as discussed in the previous section when it was allegedly caught on camera at Cooling. Then, on the 11th February the *Kent Today* asked, *'Was mystery beast behind savaged fox?'* Geoff Maynard once again reported that:

'Further evidence has come to light to show that a panther-like beast could be roaming the countryside around the Medway Towns.

Minutes after our front page story hit the streets on Monday showing the first picture of what has been tagged the Beast of Blue Bell Hill we got a call from a John Turner.

John was out walking his dog in fields at the bottom of Blue Bell Hill on Monday afternoon when he made a gruesome discovery. He stumbled across the carcass of a fox which had been torn apart by what was obviously a ferocious animal.

The head of the fox and the front half of the body had been ripped off by a powerful killer.

John said: "It looked as if it had been killed very recently because blood was still coming out of the carcass. I didn't like to look at it for very long because all the insides had been pulled out. I just could not think of what sort of animal could do this and then I remembered the stories about the panther."

The find could be used as further evidence to prove that there is a big cat, if not more than one, in the rural area stretching from Maidstone in the south up past Blue Bell Hill to the Isle of Grain and Cobham in the north.'

A black leopard was seen stalking a cattery in Cooling for around three months, according to witness and cattery owner Vanessa Fisher. The animal had been caught momentarily in the spotlight in the garden, the most recent sighting was a few days before 13th February when her report appeared in the paper. She told the newspaper, "*I have looked out of the window and seen what is definitely a panther because it is several times the size of a normal cat.*"

A few days later the *Kent Today* asked, '*Sheep victim of the beast?*' after a sheep was found dead in a farmer's field near West Malling. A woman who found the carcass said, "*The injuries were too savage to have been done by a dog – it must have been a big cat.*"

Was mass hysteria clouding eyewitness judgement suddenly or were there really several large cats prowling the Maidstone area? If so, were the sightings of recent escapees or simply an old, much ignored mystery coming to light?

A confusing report emerged in the March of '98 as beast-fever swept the county. Mr Brownstone mentioned seeing a cream-coloured cat in the Capstone Country Park area while out walking his dog. I got in touch with the man, but he told me that he'd seen the animal in 1993 which was frustrating for me as I was keen to venture into the woods of the park. He told me that he was near one of the riding schools at the time when he saw an animal sniffing the ground that suddenly stared at him. He said it was bigger than a Great Dane and he identified it as a puma.

Shortly after I visited the area with my friend Marc Ruddy.

Capstone Park covers one-hundred and fourteen hectares of former farmland. It has an artificial ski-slope, a visitors' centre, a lake, a café, a nearby youth hostel, children's play areas and various woodland trails. The woodlands itself are old, peppered by ancient stones and other ruins. A 'capstone' is one of the finishing or protective stones that form the top of an archaeological tomb, similar to which sits at Blue Bell Hill and was mentioned earlier.

Dene holes are also littered around the fields of the park. Such holes, measuring around three feet in diameter and up to sixty feet in depth, are underground structures consisting of a number of small chalk caves entered by a vertical shaft. Dene holes may have been originally excavated for the use of chalk, for hiding/dwelling purposes, or for storing goods.

We enjoyed the day more as a stroll really, taking in the scenery, and then having some lunch: I indulged myself with two doughnuts whilst Marc scoffed a full English breakfast, and probably won't forgive me for mentioning it here! We'd spent many an hour trudging through local woods, and even Marc would never admit to being one of the most agile pursuers of large cats, and this was proven one day at Boxley when he proceeded to roll past me like a bowling ball, and bounce down a flight of some thirty wooden steps! Although he was unharmed, I almost ruptured my stomach with intense laughter as he dusted his Tottenham Hotspur sweater down and lit a cigarette at the bottom of the hill.

Marc is without doubt one of the best and certainly funniest blokes I've ever known, and I hope he recalls those days with fondness.

We circled the lake, where the odd devoted angler perched on the embankment, but there were no other visitors at the time as the wind was rather cold. We stepped into the maze of the woods that reach up on to a hill and overlook Princes Park and also stretch to Lordswood. Various signs dotted the pathways, pointers as to which birds and reptiles were common in the area, and there was also the Reptile Site, a pile of many rocks strewn at the base of slope, which allegedly hid many an adder and lizard. The local farm housed sheep, ducks and goats, plenty of prey for a large cat and the woods were full of birds and rabbits. At 3:00 pm we decided to head for home but to a path close to the lake as it appeared over-shadowed by the looming trees. The air was damp, the foliage green, moist and thick. It was a quiet area, situated beyond a hidden glade where a lonely bench sat. The pathway was hard mud, our own feet couldn't make an impression upon the surface, but it was then that we saw it, the paw-print.

It was huge: the size of my hand.

There was a set, but one print stood out, showing four toes, the other prints which didn't lead anywhere were more smudged, but the main print which we examined and photographed was around five-inches long and almost as wide. There were no claw marks evident despite the fact that the toes had made quite an impression on the soil. The heel was not evident unfortunately, but this track was nothing like that made by a dog, it was impressive considering we'd expected to find nothing on this day.

The *Kent Today* mentioned our find on the 25th March and on the 19th claimed that I was, '...*going to find the Beast of Blue Bell Hill'*, stating that I was going to camp overnight in the Burham Downs Nature Reserve, despite the fact that at night it was one of the most ominous places I'd ever visited, a tangled web of undergrowth and creepy pathways that led to the silent lake which only anglers in the past had been permitted to use, but which had attracted vandals over the years, making the place a no-go area for anyone with any sense, as the burnt out cars and eerie atmosphere stated. Of course, no-one should let local ghost stories put them off but this was one place that I felt I didn't belong, despite several late night visits, and even in the day the place had that foreboding atmosphere where the air is stifling.

Although myself and friend Marc had found the paw-print at Capstone we were rather dismayed at the fact that the so-called recent sighting was several years ago. Then, a fresh sighting was reported.

On the 3rd April two men out shooting near Blue Bell Hill claimed to have found a set of big cat prints on a pathway.

The *Medway News,* on Friday April 10th reported that, '*Mountain cat is spotted by a farmer'*, running a photo and story concerning local man Gordon Richman who, whilst tending his lambs in a pen in fields not far from Hempstead Valley Shopping Centre saw a strange cat. It was 11:30 am a week previous when Gordon walked down the slope of his small-holding towards the pen when he saw the animal. He told the newspaper, "*It was a mountain cat or cougar...it seemed very relaxed and just laid there watching the lambs. I have never seen anything like it before.*"

He described the cat as being around three to four feet in length with a sandy coat and darker face and paws.

Gordon, whose lambs remained unharmed continued that, "*Lambs were killed at Boxley and Bredhurst. Half-eaten – it was not the way a fox or dog would have done it.*" Gordon told the *Kent Today,* "*I have worked on the land all my life as a farmer and I have never seen anything like this.*"

tracked Gordon down at his farm on the 4th April with a friend, Terry Cameron. It was a blustery Saturday. The farm, not much more than field of sheep, a few horses, geese and ducks sat opposite Elm Court Garden Nursery, now called Wyevale, on the Capstone Road.

Gordon was building a stronger pen for his lambs after sighting the large cat. He told me more about the sighting: "*I was with my mate, who has sheep in the field across the road. I was already building the pen. was carrying a sheet of iron and as we approached the pen I dropped it and suddenly saw something jump. We thought it was one of the lambs. As we got nearer we saw this cougar, just sitting in the tree."*

I asked him if the lambs seemed frightened.

"No, they jumped when I dropped the metal but weren't bothered by the cat. It was silvery-brown."
He told me that he'd seen the cat on 23rd March and we chatted for hours about the local sightings when he mentioned that the police had got a cat on camera from the Boxley area. Naturally I was excited about this and probed him for all he knew.

"They had a camera at a bridge, surveying traffic, and it was caught on film but I doubt they have it any longer," he said with a sigh.

After the initial wave of excitement in reference to the local beast, it wasn't until the summer that reports began to filter through again, well, certainly with regards to the Blue Bell Hill and other Medway-related cats.

A man fishing at Burham Reservoir saw a black panther drinking from the lake and Mrs Baldwin, travelling from Borstal to Burham one evening, saw a black leopard which crossed the road one-hundred yards ahead. Around the same time a cat, described as smaller than a Labrador and tan in colour, was seen at 4:00 pm by a female witness walking her dog near the Aylesford industrial area. The animal strolled across the pathway and headed towards a nearby wood and the woman's own dog bolted after it but turned round and came straight back. The witness reported the sighting to the Kent Wildlife Trust stating that the cat had tufted ears and a tail around a foot long that had ringed markings on it.

During July the Boxley correspondent for the *Kent Messenger* said he'd seen a large cat, colour not stated, in the Harbourland area. He was walking his dogs when the felid bounded away.

He told the paper, who printed the story on the 31st July that, *"It moved like a cat and had a tail like a cat, Its head was rounded like a cats but it was too big to be one."*

Again in Burham, shortly after the Boxley sighting, a female witness walking her red-setter dog disturbed an animal that leapt into crops. She said the animal was brown in colour and had what looked like a mane, although its possible the cat may have had a disease. Then, the *Kent Today* of September 24 reported, *'Beast spooked our horses, says rider',* after two young women on horseback and riding through Hucking, near Maidstone spotted a big animal. One of the women told the paper, *"At first thought it was a fox because it had a light, sandy colour, but then I realised it was too big. It had a long tail and a cats face – it was definitely a lynx."*

Despite her statement it's clear that the witness and her friend saw a puma, but it wasn't the same large felid sighted at Sittingbourne and reported on the 29th.

'Beast was the size of a fully grown panther' claimed witness Alan Lawrie in another *Kent Today* article

> *'Two more sightings of the Beast of Blue Bell Hill have been reported. Alan Lawrie had been returning home in the early hours one morning in January when he spotted the elusive creature.*
>
> *He said: "It was about 2:00 am and I was driving down from the M2 towards Rainham when I caught this black cat in my headlights. It was the size of a fully grown panther and had bright yellow eyes. It was just rambling up the grass verge very casually."*

148

Nigel Long also contacted the paper with his story.

> 'Nigel rang in to say that, only four weeks ago while he was walking his German Shepherd dog, Max, with his nephew, he watched the animal for twenty minutes in a field behind Kemsley Power Station.
>
> He said: "I'm convinced this was a panther. It was the same size as a golden retriever but jet black and very muscular and the length of it was totally wrong. Max was terrified. We watched it and at one point it dashed towards my side of the field – it went like a rocket. It cleared a very large ditch in one single leap."

For the newspaper, Sittingbourne was a fresh area for sightings and this time they knew it could be the same animal that had been seen stalking Blue Bell Hill. I personally had a feeling it wasn't, again due a clash of sightings around the time.

In that November a man out lamping at 2:30 am near Boxley with his dogs saw an animal that had eyes the, "...colour of jade", it was a black animal moving very low to the ground which had a very long tail.

The man asked the local farmer about the sighting, but he was sceptical and claimed the 'beast' must have been a loose calf. After I spoke to the witness, he mentioned to me that a few years previous someone had a mini-circus at Stockbury near Sittingbourne, and rumour had it that the owner had lost his license and released his collection.

Another man shooting near Boxley claimed that he'd seen many pigeons eaten in the area. He believed that this was the work of a large cat and not a fox, and there were also rumours that another farmer in the Maidstone area had chickens taken on a regular basis by an animal, which during one midnight raid destroyed the entire coop.

I hoped that the local press would maintain their interest in the local legend, so as to enable my research to reach more people and thankfully, that's exactly what happened. I was able to work out several patterns to the sightings, enabling me to determine possible routes for what appeared to be at least three large cats roaming the outskirts of Medway, with more into more rural Maidstone, and across the river in more dense areas such as Mereworth. As stated previously, although I was fully aware that such animals could be appearing all over Kent, it seemed as though they were sticking to territories of around thirty to fifty-square miles. It was clear that the melanistic leopard seen during the January of '99 near Burham by a dog-walker was *not* the black animal seen at East Malling around the same time. The sightings were far too close together, even though one was at 2:00 am and the Burham report from 2:00 pm. And further proof came to light to convince the press that a variety of species were roaming, when in the same month a man investigating the remains of a dead pigeon near Boxley returned later that afternoon, and saw a puma slinking through the trees.

It was now time for the press to start getting their facts right, identifying the species, and featuring the reports more frequently, because suddenly they realised that such a situation was not some Hallowe'en story, but - in fact - a growing mystery.

On the 11th January, a woman from Sittingbourne wrote to me mentioning a sighting she'd had of a big cat on the 8th near Keycole Hospital. She caught sight of the animal at approximately 8:15 pm, approximately on the field near the back entrance to the building as she was driving. The cat stood still for several minutes in the headlight beam, allowing the witness to take in as many details as possible. The cat then headed towards the back gardens of the houses which front on to the main A2 road leading to Keycole roundabout.

She told the local paper, and me, that what she'd seen was a black panther.

On January 25th 1999 I was able to get a front page appeal out via the *Kent Today* and received scores of eyewitness reports. One was from a cousin of my father, his name is Tony, and he saw a big black panther on 3rd February during the early hours whilst on a milk round. The cat was lying on a grass verge towards Maidstone Town Centre.

East Kent Gazette, covering the Swale area, got in on the act on the 17th February, reporting, *'Sightings of areas mystery beast are on the increase',* after Mrs Godmon who was looking out of her attic window spotted a huge cat on the neighbour's drive. She told the paper, "*It was four times the size of a domestic cat. The animal had a huge thick tail that really captivated me.*"

Further details emerged suggesting she'd seen a puma.

On the 25th Feb', the *Gazette* once again ran an update on sightings.

> *'The latest sighting of Swale's mystery big cat has come in the Syndale Valley – between Sittingbourne and Faversham.*
>
> *Ten-year old Felicity De Pulford was driving with her grandad Terry Holden to his home in Newnham when the big beast leapt across a track near the car at 3:55 pm last Tuesday.*

Mr David Moor, 53, said he fully believed the latest sightings of a big cat as he himself saw the beast two years ago by Tonge Mill when driving to his daughter's house.

> "*It was a clear day and I saw what looked like a black panther at just after 9:00 am*", said Mr Moor. "*It crossed the road in front of me and went into a copse. I stopped the car to get a better look but it had gone.*"

Mr Chisman from Milton Regis saw the big cat twice from the cab of the Sittingbourne and Kemsley Light Railway engine while he was helping to ferry customers at Easter two years ago.

He said:

> "*The first time was on Easter Sunday when we had a full train of about one-hundred people. The big black cat was gracefully walking across the marsh and was about one hundred yards away from me. It had a large tail that was curled round like a hook. I wasn't frightened though because I didn't think it would come near the train.*"

The following Sunday he spotted it crouching just twenty yards away from the line waiting to pounce or nearby scavenging seagulls.

Archaeologist Mr Brian Slade, of Minster, was involved with a dig at Gilbert Farm, Minster, back in 1989 when the party of ten saw a puma stalking through the fields.

He wrote to me and said:

"We watched in amazement for five to six minutes as the big cat crept low across the marsh. Then suddenly it was startled by a gunshot from hunters and took flight. We were on the dig of the medieval stable site for several more weeks but didn't see it again."

Patches of woodland and marsh stretch from Gillingham in Medway into Rainham, to Newington, Sittingbourne, further to Faversham, Whitstable and Herne Bay meaning the possibilities have always been endless regarding populations and varying species of exotic felid. Reports from the Isle of Sheppey were also filtering through suggesting either that animals from Sittingbourne were taking to the bridge - the only way on or off the island - or that separate cats had been released/escaped on the island.

The island is only thirty-six square miles, situated off the northern coast and separated from the mainland by a stretch of river known as The Swale, but much of the land is remote marsh and farmland, and the place is pretty much bereft of woodland, remaining as a flat, open space with more development towards Minster. Despite its freakishly cold winters, forcing blustery winds across the fens and casting a vicious frost to the fields, a large cat has prowled the area for as long as anyone can remember, but during the '90s clusters of reports either suggested that local interest was building or something more than rumour was haunting the icy horizon.

Back towards Blue Bell Hill, and during the end of February I visited a man and his wife at their home at Senacre, Maidstone after he'd got the fright of his life at 5:45 one morning whilst coming downstairs for a drink of water.

The man walked into the kitchen, poured himself a drink and stepped back into the hallway to go back to bed. On his left, something through the frosted pane of the lower half of the front door caught his eye, a big head of an animal peering back into the hallway. The witness said the head was more than five inches wide and appeared grey in colour. Suddenly, the cat moved off, and the witness saw the length of its tail as it brushed the glass, leaving him shell-shocked.

The man was clearly petrified when I met him but his wife didn't seem too convinced and questioned his sanity until I mentioned other sightings. The shaken man also claimed that he'd seen a large cat shortly before one night as it slinked along the back fence and a day or two before the sighting by his door, he'd heard that a few local chickens had been disturbed.

It's possible that the man had seen a black leopard, hazed by the frosted texture of the glass, or he may have seen a silvery puma.

The Swale big cat was back in the spotlight when on the 3rd March the *East Kent Gazette* listed a few more sightings of the Sittingbourne felid. Mr Leonard Amos spotted a black panther at the top of Detling Hill. Mr Goatham claimed to have seen a large cat near Borden Lane around 10:00 one morning as he was walking his dog. The cat appeared to be standing in a patch of nettles, was black and three feet in length.

Another sighting was reported to the paper by Mrs Stephens as she was driving near Westlands School on 26th February at 3:15 pm when a huge cat strolled across wasteland just fifteen feet away and padded into some bushes.

As mentioned in the previous section regarding Gravesend's elusive cats, Rochester Castle was the scene during early March, but only two weeks later it had prowled further into town, but further away in Walderslade, where, at the time, I was living.

Even more bizarre was the fact that an aunt of my mum had seen the cat, but never knew I researched the sightings until I contacted her hastily.

On 5th March at 9:00 pm Kaye Chester, from the Weedswood Estate, was coming home from a local church meeting. She went indoors, but her husband Ron was sound asleep on the sofa so she decided to go and see a friend across the street. When she came out of the front door and looked across the road, a big, black cat came around the corner. It stopped in the middle of the road and stared at her. The animal terrified Kaye who claimed that the beast had pinky-red eyes which is not typical of the reflection of a leopards eyes, as you've already read so far. The cat had a long tail, and Kaye suddenly asked herself, "*Will it go for me?*"

She suddenly turned and ran back indoors to wake her husband. They both returned and couldn't believe that the cat was just lying down in the road. The cat looked at the couple, got up and slowly padded out of sight down a dark alleyway.

The next morning Kaye and Ron ventured out again but there was no sign of the animal, but in their back garden they discovered a half-eaten chicken - made all the more peculiar by the fact that no-one in the area, to the best of their knowledge, owned any chickens.

Again, whilst Walderslade is a very built up area, there are several woodlands which surround and also join to other areas of note. In Chatham, the Asda supermarket near Rochester Airport is backed by a small wood, but a vast wood stretches towards Blue Bell Hill, and areas such as Lordswood, and the park at Capstone are only a few minutes away by car.

An animal combing the vicinity of Walderslade has a number of dark alleyways, overgrown gardens, open, unlit fields and industrial areas to mooch around in search of prey. It was certainly likely that the animal encountered by Kaye was the Blue Bell Hill leopard, or one of a handful classed as such.

'*Is beast stalking Easter bunnies?*' asked *Gazette & Times*, after another sighting in the Swale area of a black panther. The cat was seen at 5:45 am by a woman from Bobbing Hill as it walked across the neighbour's drive. The woman had previously been sceptical about the sightings, but after her encounter believed that the animal she'd seen had driven all the rabbits in the area away, and eaten a neighbour's cat.

The creature clearly wasn't the Blue Bell Hill leopard, but the animal seen during April near Capstone Country Park most certainly was. Two teenage sisters were about to tend to their horses at the farm one evening when they saw the dark-coloured cat walking near a swampy area, a few metres from where I'd discovered the massive paw-prints previously.

The cat came into town again when it was sighted by a pensioner in Rochester, a few minutes walk from the historic castle. The woman was travelling on a bus along Old Pattens Lane one afternoon when she saw a black panther sitting on a nearby garage roof. Again, such a sighting may sound dubious but the location, an ideal walkway for a large cat at night, is only minutes from where I discovered the goat carcass at Borstal and even for a cat, just twenty-minutes from Walderslade.

At West Farleigh on the other side of the river from Teston, and near Loose, where the local valley has been rumoured to hide several large cats, a farmer vowed to shoot the mysterious animals that were killing his sheep. Although the *KM* headline was, '*Farmer to shoot killer dogs*', the reported suggested anything but dogs were to blame. It read:

'A farmer had vowed to kill any dog he sees worrying his sheep after five ewes, each with twin lambs, were savagely attacked and killed on separate nights in his fields.

John Day, of Tuttsham Farm, found the first dead ewe at the beginning of March.

He said: "We found the ewe savaged in a corner of the field. She'd been attacked in the throat and her wool and skin had been stripped and her shoulder torn off. It was a ghastly mess."

A further four ewes were found mauled to death within days of each other.

Mr Day added: "It was the same picture, the same pattern in each case. They were separated from the rest of the flock in a corner of the field and brutally savaged. It could be a fox, but we think it's more likely to be a dog, possibly more than one."

Although one of the ten orphaned lambs subsequently died, the other nine have been adopted by other ewes and are flourishing.

Mr Day, who farms a breeding flock of seven-hundred and fifty sheep has been out on early morning patrol armed with a shotgun since the attacks. And although he checks his animals daily. He admitted it was impossible to provide round-the-clock supervision.

He said: "But I will shoot any dog I see worrying my sheep. It is an horrific death for these animals and I cannot think they are being killed in this way by a wild animal."

Mr Day, whose ewes are valued at about £50 each, has appealed to dog owners to keep their pets under control.'

Strangely such concerns are still shadowing farmers today, as sheep continue to be attacked, killed and eaten by an animal they are now certainly more aware of, but still unsure of how to react against.

As the summer months thickened the vegetation, the reports failed to subside as I'd expected. It was difficult keeping an eye on reports elsewhere in the county, which were also flooding in, let alone to track the Blue Bell Hill animal which seemed to have never been out of the newspapers.

A man named Mark saw a black leopard at Leybourne Grange which again proved to be not the Blue Bell Hill animal due to a clash of sightings. A Boxley farmer had an impressive sighting whilst driving his Land Rover at 11:00 one night across his field. He'd recently erected a large fence, and was checking the area, when he was surprised to see a large black animal attempting to jump over it. The cat spotted the oncoming vehicle and ran uphill.

Teston was the next place for a black panther sighting. A man driving home at 5:00 pm saw a muscular animal which crossed the road. The man said, *"The road in question runs from the A26 at Teston to the North Pole pub on the East Malling/Wateringbury road. It runs in a general north-easterly direction and the cat was crossing right to left, so was heading south-west direction."*

A group of friends watched a large black cat near Wouldham in the summer, at 7:00 am but by the end of Autumn, the Blue Bell Hill cat was back in town. The sighting occurred in the Darland Banks area of Gillingham, which is not far from Capstone Park.

A couple were walking in the area, which is a nature reserve of green slopes and trees, and a haven for birds, when a large cat ran across their path. They described the animal as big as a Labrador with a longer tail. Although the area hadn't featured in reports before, by this time I was expecting the unexpected, and realised these animals would turn up where ever they wanted to.

A few reports, as mentioned in the previous section pertaining to Gravesend, came from Rochester, in the built up area of Shorts Way, just along from the castle, and a woman named Mrs Glover claimed she'd seen a panther in the woods of Oaklands School, on Weedswood Road, again, slap-bang in the middle of a housing estate, only minutes from where Kay Chester had seen the panther in the road.

By this point I was working with local television and radio, discussing the sightings, which enabled my appeal to reach a bigger audience. Dave Andrews saw the Blue Bell Hill beast in November as he was driving up Boxley Hill. This large village belongs to the Maidstone District, and is just four miles from the town. It is surrounded by woods and fields. Mr Andrews had to slam on his brakes to avoid the cat which ran off into a field near the Pilgrims Way and glared back at him.

He told *Kent Today:*

> *'The sun was just coming up and I could see it was a large animal and really black. I just turned the corner in the car and saw it. I slammed on the brakes and backed up the car. I was only glad that I had not been out walking the dog at the time as I often do in that area – who knows what it could have done to us?'*

The frequency of sightings around Boxley certainly tempted the local press to change their local beast 'headline' name, but by this time they were starting to realise that the areas were connected by the thick strips of woodlands.

A *KM Group* reporter, Alan Watkins, who at the time of writing still works for the now *Medway Messenger,* had his own sighting on the 9th December as he was driving along the road near the Riverside Country Park in Rainham.

It was early morning as he travelled along the Lower Rainham Road after a late night meeting when the panther walked across the road.

He told the paper:

> *"I was looking out for foxes, because there are usually lots around here at that time of night. Just at the edge of my headlight beam I saw this beautiful animal loping slowly across the road. I could clearly see its long tail on the offside of the car as I approached it. I knew immediately what it was. It was black from head to tip."*

By the end of the year, I had a feeling that I was very close to getting a glimpse of an animal. I'd been out in the field most days each week, daily taking calls, looking into evidence, and not just merely writing down a list of sightings. It got to the stage where I almost felt arrogant to the point that it would be easy to catch myself a glimpse of the Blue Bell Hill animal, however elusive it was. I also hoped - of course - that chance would play its hand too, as it always does with sightings of big cats. A majority of researchers have never seen a large cat in the wilds, whilst others claim they've seen hundreds, which is completely ridiculous. I knew, however, by pinpointing a handful of areas, that one particular night I just *had* to be in the right place at the right time. Waiting, patiently in the shadows.

Mr Ellis saw the Boxley leopard as he cycled through a winding lane at 7:20 am on his way to work, one crisp December day. He saw the cat twice, the first time it was in a clearing eating a pigeon but the second encounter was far closer as the animal rushed past him, growled and brushed his leg as it slinked away. It was the last thing he expected to see so close to Christmas.

Then, there was another encounter at Boxley, this time at night when a local man out shooting saw an animal bigger than a fox run across the horizon. He said the creature had a blunt snout and a long tail.

The millennium brought with it a series of major highs, and bizarre lows, as mentioned with the Borstal stripped goat weirdness.

Mr Botting spotted a black animal in the Darland Banks area again, the second sighting of such a creature. He'd been walking at 2:00 pm with his two dogs when the cat emerged around one-hundred feet away. He told the newly named *Medway Today*, *"It was about 18 inches high with a huge head, drooped back and a tail as long as its body."*

Two women returning from an evening out saw a large black cat at 11:45 pm on January 6th outside one of the witnesses houses near Boxley. Meanwhile a postal worker claimed to see a puma-like animal as he travelled up the Gillingham Northern Link Road at 4:00 am.

I followed the sighting up with my cousin Jez, and found that despite the rush of traffic throughout the day from Gillingham, the main road at night was dead and calm. We just weren't sure which kind of cat was roaming the area due to vagueness of sightings, but the road was only a few minutes from Darland Banks and at midnight on a freezing cold, and frosty, evening we never came across the animal.

Of course, much of my research, as it is today, went under wraps as some of the stories in the papers misquoted me once too often, attracting all manner of unwanted attention. On the 1st February 2000 the *Medway Today* reported that Dave Holmes, out walking his dog at Tonge, Sittingbourne, near the golf course, saw a large black animal that he thought at first was a Labrador until he saw its long tail and recognised the feline gait.

Strangely, much of the so-called 'Beastwatch' coverage that the local paper had featured was now being confined to small strips and snippets in the press, probably due to my lack of involvement with inconsiderate reporters. Maybe the newspaper still felt the need to feature the sightings, but because a body of the Blue Bell Hill beast hadn't turned up, they'd become bored by the reports, but it didn't stop Alan Reed reporting his end of 1999 sighting which featured in a column in the *Medway Today* on the 3rd February.

The newspaper reported that, *'Alan Reed was driving to work early one morning at the end of last year when one-hundred metres in front of his car he spotted some sort of wild cat crossing the road.*

Mr Reed had turned off the A2 in Sittingbourne and was heading up the A249 towards Sheppey when he spotted the creature in the half-light at 5:30 am.

It was moving away from the railway line towards the Milton Regis side of Senora Fields housing estate.

"It was bigger than a domestic cat, light tan with a cat-like head and small ears", he said.

"It was darker tan across its back and the tail was not full, more like a short-haired dog's, but longer than you would expect."

The story also appeared in the *KM Extra* of the 17th.

A double page appeal on the 9th February in the *Gravesend Messenger* turned my attention towards north Kent but on the 25th February the *KM Extra* ran an intriguing story of, *'Pensioner stalked by scrap-loving lynx'*, commenting that:

> *A pensioner is too frightened to leave her farmland home on Medway's rural fringe as she is being terrorised by a big cat.*
>
> *The elderly woman has talked about her experience with what she believes to be a lynx to friends and neighbours in the remote area. The animal has been on her farmland property on several occasions in recent weeks and she has watched it from her kitchen window.*
>
> *She believes the animal attacked her cat, giving it nasty cuts and leaving her with a vet's bill of £150. She says it is attracted to her house because she leaves scraps of food outside for birds and wild animals.*
> *The woman who lives on her own, will not be identified and her neighbours have asked for the location of the sightings not to be revealed.*
>
> *One of the woman's friends said: "She has seen it several times running up her garden and six feet from her back door. She is really scared of it and frightened to go out. It's quite a large cat – it's two or three times larger than a regular cat. Other people have seen it too, but she has seen it at close range. She saw it through her kitchen window and identified it as a big lynx with small tufted ears."*
>
> *The friend is so concerned that he called the RSPCA to ask if they could lay a trap for the animal but the charity said that it was not the sort of thing it would become involved in.*

Although I eventually found out the location from the reporter at the time, I couldn't quite comprehend the story. Here was a woman, allegedly scared by the presence of this animal and yet she wouldn't give out any details to anyone despite advice being offered by myself and others. Also, the article suggested that the lynx was far from terrorising her, but I also found it unusual that the RSPCA turned down the request to become involved.

Whether the animal continued to prowl around her farmland we'll never know, but I thought it was blatantly obvious that there was an easy way to not attract the animal and that was to cease throwing the scraps of food out to tempt it closer.

At this point I would just like to rewind a few days to the Wednesday 16th February to what remains one of my most amazing experiences ever involving my research.

A month or so previous I was convinced that I was closing in on filming, or at least catching sight of the melanistic leopard prowling Blue Bell Hill. My vision was realised.

At 6:55 pm my uncle Dean Wright, and his son Mark, were travelling towards Elm Court (now Wyevale Nursery) on the Capstone Road. They were due to pick up Mark's sister Louise from work. Dean occasionally put his headlights on full beam because the country lane, flanked by fields and trees, was unlit.

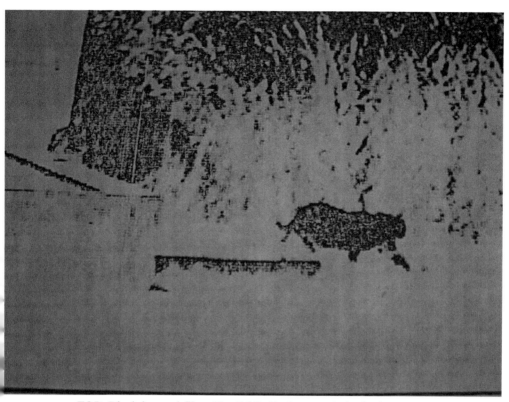

TOP: Black leopard filmed by Eddie Dedman at Aylesford (p. 138)
BELOW: Bluebell Hill beast image created by Sean Tudor

Goat victim of Blue Bell Hill beast photo (p. 94)

BELOW: Boxley Hill (p.135)

CAUGHT ON CAMERA: Is this picture taken by reader Harry Matthews the mystery beast that has been stalking Blue Bell Hill?

Well, do you think it's just a pet cat?

Harry Matthews's pictures of the `beast` of Bluebell Hill
(also overleaf) (p.91)

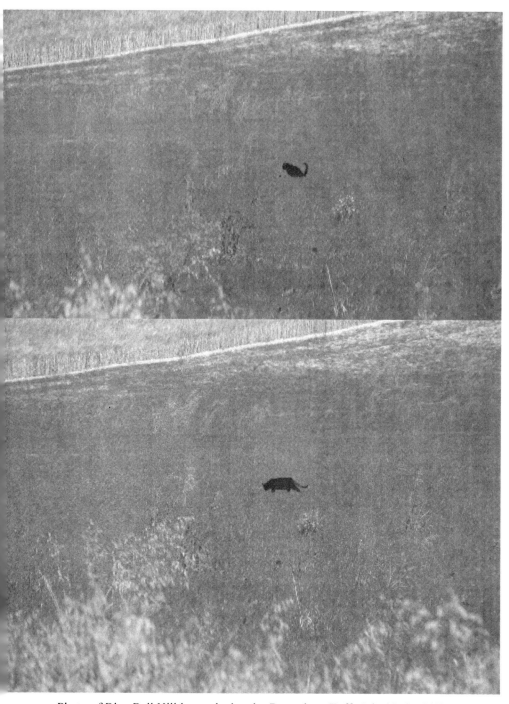

Photo of Blue Bell Hill leopard taken by Bernadette Tuffs July 05. (p. 185)

Neil Arnold at Bredhurst in 2002 next to mystery tree markings.

TOP: East Malling puma caught on film by Scott Arnold (p. 178)
BELOW: Bredhurst church where a black leopard was sighted (p. 176)

Walderslade Woods a haunt of the Blue Bell Hill beast. BELOW: St Margaret's Cemetery at Rochester where a panther was seen in 2008 (p. 191)

As they approached the garden centre which is on the right, a large, dark-brown cat appeared on the left from the tree line flanking the tight lane. The eyes reflected greenish, and the animal casually stared at the vehicle as they slowed. They described it as lean in stature with sleek fur. The cat then disappeared into the trees and although Dean stopped the car at the exact spot, there was no sign

I received word of the sighting at 9:15 pm. At the time I was out and so was my father, but he arranged to pick me up and head straight to the area of the sighting. I hoped the animal would still be about because it may have been the same animal that farmer Gordon Richman had seen stalking his lambs a few yards from Dean and Mark's sighting. Or, it may have been the black leopard seen at Darland Banks, but either way, we rushed to the area, arriving at around 10 pm. We drove up the Capstone Road taking the same route Dean had travelled but we found it difficult just stopping in the middle of the road due to other cars passing every now and then. At approximately 10:45 pm we reversed into the garden centre entrance driveway and sat in the vehicle facing Gordon Richman's small-holding. The headlights, despite the dip, were able to pick out the eyes of the sheep on the ascending field around fifty yards away. The night was slightly gloomy. To our left was a field full of grazing sheep, to our right a road leading back towards the local tip, surrounded by empty fields.

After what only seemed a few minutes, but was probably around half-an-hour, we noticed a set of eyes, yellow, although fading in and out of brightness as they caught then evaded the headlight beam, coming down the track in the farm. The outline of the form was not discernible but the head was swaying side to side, as if whatever owned those eyes was sniffing the ground. It came down a slope, towards the pen Gordon had made for his sheep, and where he saw the puma. Then we lost sight of it.

We didn't get too excited although its behaviour was strange and unlike any of the resident farm animals, and it didn't have the red tinge in the eye colour as a fox does and the eyes seemed to belong to a large head.

Despite a few minutes looking from the vehicle nothing showed so we decided to roll the car out of the entrance, and turn left back down Capstone Road. At a snail's pace we moved down the road, on the right was the tree line and back gardens where Dean and Mark had glimpsed the cat, on our left a field of sheep…and then we saw it, just sitting there, even blacker than the haze of night, on its haunches, every now and then the most reflective of eyes would turn to face us, like two lamps blazing back into the headlights. It seemed arrogant, sitting pitch against the almost greyness of the fields, and then it gazed upwards at the sheep some one-hundred feet away that had become huddled into a tight flock, fully aware that they were being watched.

My dad moved the car even slower; we hoped that another car would not come the other way. We drew level with the animal – it was twenty feet from us – and only separated from our vehicle by a thin wire fence. We sat there in silence, and the cat did also - it didn't have a care in the world. On its rear end it must've sat over two feet high. We were in some kind of surreal disbelief knowing that we were face to face with one of the beasts of Blue Bell Hill, a black leopard, yet a different cat than which the farmer had sighted.

wound the window down and then for some reason gently opened the car door. I couldn't tell by this point if the cat was looking at me because its eyes were now away from the beam of the car, but I decided to slowly walk towards it - and, as I did, it sprinted up the field, scattering the sheep; and the last we saw of it as it reached the horizon at such great speed was it fleeing into the shadows.

Immediately we reversed and took the road around the back of the garden centre hoping to catch sight of the animal, yet despite another hour or so scouring the hedgerows, fields and roads in the dead of night, there was no further sign. When we made for home we were buzzing, we knew we'd get our chance to see the animal, but not so close and we considered ourselves so privileged to have had this part-chance encounter.

It was more than likely that after we left the area the cat returned to its vigil, eyeing the sheep, but we didn't hear of any losses in the field the next day.

I'll never forget that night, it remains embedded in my memory, and yet always has that edge of unreality when I look back on it.

Apart from close family, my father and I told no-one else about the sighting for a while, as we didn't want to start a 'witch-hunt'.

On March 16th a Hempstead man named Chris saw what was likely to have been the same animal. He was walking his dogs near Capstone ski slope at 6:00 pm when he saw the animal side-on at a distance of roughly fifty feet. Although the sighting was brief - just a few seconds - Chris noticed how slender the cat was, and commented that it was smaller than a labrador, with a very long tail.

On the Sunday of 19th March at 10:15 pm Sue Pay, of Lordswood, watched a big cat walk down her road. It moved alongside the parked cars and disappeared at the end of the road.

Sue told the newspaper, "*At first I thought it was a fox but then I realised it was bigger than that. It was bigger than a domestic cat and walked with a distinctive spring in its step. I wasn't afraid but I thought 'I'm not going outside'.*"

After her sighting she saw a picture of a panther which confirmed to her what she'd seen.

On the 20th March I tracked the beast again. I heard of Mrs Pay's sighting on the morning of the 19th. At around 9:45 pm my father and I took a drive around the nearby countryside. It was a crisp night, a starry sky, with a hint of mist.

Again, after taking a look around Lordswood, we decided to park up near to where we'd seen the cat previously, that night very much in our minds. This time however, Mr Richman had given us permission to stake out his land, so we silently climbed the gate - geese cackled in a nearby pen - and walked the gravelled slope, the same path that the eerie eyes had descended just before we lost sight of them.

To our left, a large field, at the front of it, near to the road, and opposite where we'd sat before, several sheep, hilariously coughing like humans and standing agog as we positioned ourselves in the shadows. To our right, more sheep, and part of a yard that the farmer had created.

We stood, statuesque for goodness knows how long, becoming part of the scenery: the sheep used to our presence by now, a solitary horse staring at us through the descending mist.

Everything was dead quiet give or take the already mentioned guttural murmurs from the sheep, and the cold had begun to creep through the concrete, up through our feet. My gloved hands clenched my torch and binoculars tight, but the crispness was smoking the breath and tingling the cheeks.

It was between 11:00 pm and midnight (isn't it always!?) and the frosty mist had really begun to envelope the field. We were stood facing down the slope towards the entrance of the garden centre when whispered to my dad, "*Guess we better go soon,*" as we were losing visibility and with that, he looked over his left shoulder.

"*There!*" He pointed, to his left. Out of the mist, approximately seventy-five feet away emerged a long, low, slinking black form that we both watched through the binoculars. Despite the haze of the night, I could see this animal was no domestic cat or fox, it measured roughly four feet if not longer, its body stretched and back arched as it seemed to drift effortlessly over the ground. It was certainly *en route* to somewhere and not at all interested in the sheep - or us, even if it knew we were present. Maybe it had been watching us standing there and we disrupted its route, but the way it moved suggested that it had intentions elsewhere.

The sighting lasted what seemed like an eternity, but in reality it was a glimpse of around ten seconds as it descended the slope like a black phantom, and seemed to dissolve in the mist. The fog had settled in the hollow and the animal could have slipped off anywhere, but it was last seen heading towards the garden centre entrance where we'd sat a month previously.

None of the farm animals stirred, but our hearts were pounding. To twice see this amazing animal was so special, and to see it firstly stalking, and then secondly on the move just displayed to us its sheer power, grace and elusive nature. It had been a rewarding month or so.

Unfortunately, the Foot and Mouth disease epidemic eventually put paid to any more sheep being kept in the area, and sightings died down within the immediate vicinity, but I was always confident that the animal still used the route occasionally; only now there was no reason for it to linger. Prey such as rabbits were in abundance at the Capstone Park, but as far as the small-holding went, it gradually was turned into a yard where vehicles and building equipment were stored, leaving behind just a few horses and some geese - and, as far as I'm aware, these have never been attacked.

At the end of April another sighting emerged from Lordswood, although the witness claimed it was of a golden-coloured cat.

A local man got up out of bed at 4:30 am in an area not far from where Mrs Pay saw the black cat, and as he looked out of his window, he couldn't believe his eyes when a large cat stared back from the road. The witness told the *Medway Today*, "*The animal was a golden colour with a huge head and a long tail.*"

Had the man seen a puma or simply a panther under a yellow street-light?

It wasn't until the May of 2000 that local press heard whispers that I'd seen a big cat.

'*The day I finally saw mystery beast*', declared the *Gravesend Messenger* of the 3rd, and on the 9th September the *Medway Today* had the terrible headline, '*Beast is tracked down by hunter*', but it was to be another three months before another positive sighting came of a similar animal, and that was in Maidstone on the 10th August when Mr Litchfield was awoken by a terrible crying noise coming from the street outside. Although used to hearing plenty of foxes in the area the man thought this particular noise sounded like something was being killed.

The witness could hear a commotion in the bushes near a caravan parked some sixty feet away and then heard the awful sound of breaking, splintering bones. It was then that to his horror he saw a big, black cat slip out from under the caravan.

The man clapped at the animal which looked at him and walked off.

Further inspection revealed no sign of remains: it seems that this particular panther was very hungry that night.

In the same month a black leopard was seen as it bounded across a road at Wouldham, near Burham by a female motorist at 2:30 pm. However, a man named Bill, travelling from Aylesford to Greenwich, around the same time, saw a puma cross a lane at 5:10 am at West Malling. He estimated that the animal was two feet high, four feet long, with a small head and long tail. It headed towards the golf course.

On August 9th a male witness observed a black leopard near Maidstone Hospital. The man was building an extension to the hospital and driving towards the area at 7:40 am when he saw the black cat running along a tree line. Another motorist named Barry saw a panther on the Pilgrim's Way near Boxley in August, he believed the animal had a cub with it, and Mr Hutchings from Chatham said that at the end of August around 8:00 pm he was off-roading with a friend in the woods at Blue Bell Hill, near the Robin Hood public house situated on Common Road, when they observed a cat, one-hundred yards away and coming up a track. This was the same area where previously a fox had been found ripped open.

On the 2nd of September at Eccles, near Burham, at 11:50 pm Mrs Davis saw a black leopard and there was another sighting near the Lower Bell pub at Blue Bell Hill made by three witnesses who saw a green-eyed panther walking into the undergrowth.

Seventeen days later, the *Medway Today* mentioned a courting couple taking an evening stroll near the Robin Hood pub, saw a five-foot long black leopard lying in a derelict farm building. At first the witnesses thought the creature was a big dog.

I knew the witness, and certainly believed his story.

However, was it the same cat seen towards Hollingbourne railway station? A man coming out of the remote, dimly lit station was scared by the large animal which walked across the path in front of him and headed towards the trees.

An impressive sighting took place on Tuesday 3rd October very close to home when Mr Dorrington reported seeing a black leopard just a few minutes from where Kaye Chester had seen a leopard previously in Walderslade.

It was 5:30 am and the man peered out of his window into the front garden and saw an animal sniffing at the lamb bones he'd thrown out for the foxes. Mr Dorrington watched the animal for around five minutes and said it was around three feet long, eighteen inches at the shoulder, with a long tail and a smooth coat. After mooching around on the gravelled garden the cat moved away.

I investigated the area and saw the disturbed pebbles on the front garden but there were no other signs. The man was adamant as to what he'd seen because he'd been only three feet from the cat.

Another black leopard was then seen at Hollingbourne station and left a trail through long grass, and in the same month a Martin driving home from work at 3:00 through Aylesford towards Blue Bell Hill watched a panther bound across the road and into the woods.

The following month possibly the same cat, which had also been seen in Walderslade, was seen by two women as they drove by the Alexandra Hospital, Walderslade Woods Road near Tunbury Woods. Although the press were quick to publish the sighting, it was just a few easily-missed lines.

The cat was loitering around underneath a pedestrian walkway which runs over the main road. This road links to Lordswood, Hempstead and in the opposite direction towards Borstal and Rochester.

On the 16th December a former landlord of the *Lower Bell* public house gave me the following statement:

> 'At 7:00 am whilst at the front of the pub I heard a strange, deep growl and the fleeting sound of an animal passing into nearby undergrowth. It was too dark to see anything but it wasn't a dog, and it went towards the Lower Warren Road.'

Despite the local flap of sightings, and the usual reports from elsewhere in Kent such as Ashford and Sevenoaks, things had quietened down regarding the puma of West Malling, or indeed any large cats roaming other areas of Maidstone. Again, lack of press interest meant that a lot of sightings were going unreported.

By this time I turned my investigations towards Sussex, and 2000 fizzled out. For me the explosions had taken place when I saw the cat on two occasions, as mentioned. I hoped 2001 would be as interesting.

It began with a piece filmed for *Meridian Television* called *Wildwatch*, where I worked with Chris Packham, yet only a few days in I was struggling to keep up with the amount of reports I was receiving. Closer to home, my cousin Jez had a strange experience at his home near the Maidstone Road of Chatham.

He told me the following tale:

> It was Tuesday January 9th 2001, as usual my alarm sounded at 5:30 am. After trying to get a few more minutes dozing I finally gave up and crawled out of bed at 6:12 am. I made my way downstairs, my half asleep body passed my sprawled out dog Daisy, she looked up and followed me out into the kitchen and waited at the back door patiently.

> 'I take it you want to go out then?'

> I opened the back door and the dog raced out into the cold early morning air into the garden. As I was about to shut the door, a tremendous deep snarling, double-barrelled growl came from the patio, directly opposite the back door. This was a vicious growl, very low and dark as if it had come from the stomach of this unwelcome intruder. Fearing for the safety of the dog, as she is rather sensitive to someone even shouting at her, I raced out into the blackness. As I stepped onto the cold damp path, there was a shuffling sound, as if something had been startled and scrambled away.

> My initial thoughts were, that a dog, a big dog, had found its way into the garden and was startled by my dog and wasn't too amused. I scanned what I could see of the garden as it was still very early and the sun still waiting to rise, there was nothing that I could see. I could only think that if it had been a dog, it could only have come from the alley, which runs to the side of the house, to the side of the garden.

> The noise did not come from my dog. A fox could not make this sound.

Had the beast of Blue Bell Hill bizarrely made its way into my cousin's back yard during the early hours, whiffed a scent of his dog and waited for it outside? Was the animal stalking the foxes that occasionally loitered around the compost heap? At the time of writing the mysterious creature hasn't returned, but the likelihood that it was a dog is very minimal due to the fact that such an animal would have to jump a fence into the garden and the alley is limited for access.

The year started with a flurry of sightings from the Isle of Sheppey which I investigated, but a sighting of the Blue Bell Hill beast was reported in the *Medway Today* of the 12th, despite clearly describing a different felid entirely. A married couple from the Princes Park area observed a cat, around eighteen-inches high, three-and-a-half foot long, with silvery tufted ears, no visible tail and a mottled coat. They saw the cat on the morning of New Year's Day and didn't want to report the sighting due to fear of ridicule, but it seemed that the witnesses had clearly seen a lynx.

Several sightings from the Bluewater area, as previously mentioned, captured my attention and Ashford had become even hotter than the previous year with more than twenty reports reaching me by the time February was upon us.

The press did well to keep the Blue Bell Hill animal in their pages, despite a lack of sightings, and I approached local MP Jonathan Shaw to discuss the sightings, who in turn contacted several local police constabularies regarding an appeal for reports.

As more reports emerged from the Sevenoaks area, no ground-breaking information came via the local police, who seemed almost confused by my requests for information.

On Saturday April 4th 2001 my dad, Ron, was returning from Rainham in his car at around 7:50 pm, and decided to take in a rural route on the way back home to his house in Walderslade. He came along Shawstead Road, a few minutes from the Capstone Country Park and local rubbish tip. On several occasions previous he'd seen a large barn owl so hoped that he might see it again.

As my dad came down the tight lane, flanked on both sides my fields, he spotted an animal in the large field on the left which had been in the nearby, roadside hedgerow, but then proceeded to speed uphill away from my dad who'd stopped his vehicle.

He watched the animal reach the top of the slope, where the safety of trees provided cover, and the animal turned to face him, and sat on its haunches yards from the edge of the strip of woodland backing on to Lordswood. My dad turned the car around, wound his window down and sat and watched the creature for a short while. The animal got up and walked off into the wood.

He told me that the animal was a cat, the size of a fox, fawn in colour and no tail was visible. When the animal first sped away from the foliage of the roadside my dad thought it may have been a large hare, but the ears were nothing of the sort. He felt he'd seen something akin to a lynx, and strangely this animal had appeared only a few minutes away from where the couple had observed a similar animal on New Year's Day.

A man named Haniff was driving to work at Maidstone on April 17th at 5:20 am when, on Provinder Way, near Maidstone Studios, he saw a black animal emerge from the bushes some eighty yards away, pad across the road and head into St. John's School.

He told me, "*It seemed like a young black panther, around three feet in length, a very long tail.*"

The previous year a lorry driver reported seeing a black panther in the same area and came into the studios to speak of his sighting which had occurred near the entrance gates at 4:00 am.

Thankfully, the *Medway Today* wrote a big article on the sightings and I received a call from a Gillingham woman who claimed that she'd observed unusual activity at her home in Sturdee Avenue, a built-up area from where I'd never previously received any cat reports.

During early spring the frightened woman said that strange, large excrement had appeared on her lawn and then her guinea pig was taken from its pen in the April. The woman purchased two more guinea pigs, but on April 15th she was awoken at 5:00 am by the squeals of her pets. When she investigated one had gone missing and the other was frantically trying to get out of the hutch.

On the 18th April more faeces were found in the garden, and the woman's husband claimed that one morning around 5:00 am he'd seen a dog-sized black cat on the patio.

Although Gillingham is a busy area a railway line, golf course and the Darland Banks area remain not too far away, but oddly no other sightings emerged from other witnesses.

I'd been spending hours in the field, traipsing across grim marshland, holed up in damp, eerie woods, and overlooking spacious fields and had by this point become astounded at the amount of sightings I was receiving. The false statistics being put out by national big cat registers were not even close to the amount of reports I was receiving but there was no way I was going to advertise Kent as one of the most likely places to see a puma or panther. For every ten reports I was receiving I was only putting one in the paper, just so that witnesses knew that they could report their details in strictest confidence, if they didn't want their names splashed across the newspapers.

At the end of April a woman in a wheelchair in the Tunbury area of Walderslade, spotted a massive pawprint on a muddy path. She wasn't surprised. In 1999, during the summer, she'd taken her dog out for a stroll in the woods when she saw the long tail of an animal sticking out of the undergrowth.

Again, this area, not far from where a cluster of sightings would begin to emerge from, joins several other woodlands from Hemsptead, to Boxley and back to Lordswood. At night Walderslade Woods acts as a perfect forested tunnel way for any animal seeking to get from A to B.

In 1974, Mr Hamper was fourteen-years old when in the small wood behind his friend's house, near the top of Chestnut Avenue, Walderslade he saw a panther. It was between 4:30 and 6:00 pm, and only twenty yards away. In an email he told me, '*It was around five feet long from nose to tail and slowly walked across the path in front of me.*'

Also during the '70s a mysterious beast was accused of slaughtering several pets in the Constitution Road area of Chatham. A dog was eventually blamed for the attacks although the predator was never seen or caught.

In 1979 Rod Stevens was sitting in a field at 6:00 am at the bottom of the Pilgrim's Way when he saw a light-coloured cat, possibly a puma, stalking along the top of the hill. He said the animal was the size of a Labrador.

During the same decade, my grandad's brother Bill, saw a fawn-coloured cat near the tip at Shawstead. He was a passenger in a van at the time and stated that although the cat was quite a distance away, it was too big to be a domestic cat.

Such sightings certainly bridged the gap between the '70s and now, proof also that sightings were emerging before the introduction of the 1976 Dangerous Wild Animals Act.

In fact, during the 1950s, relative Joe Chester claimed that he'd seen a big, brownish cat in the Victoria Gardens area of Chatham.

A letter appeared in *Fortean Times* Issue 45 from A. Grizzell with regards to a sighting during the '80s of a big cat in Faversham. The witness wrote:

> On Saturday August 30th 1985 at about 9:30 in the evening I decided to put our corgi pup outside. I put on the kitchen lights and outside lights and looked out the kitchen door. Standing and staring at me about six feet from the door was a sandy-coloured cat-like animal about two-foot six-inches high, lithe with long legs and a long thin tail held vertical. The eyes were huge, round and bulging. It turned and disappeared it definitely wasn't a panther and was nothing like I've ever seen before.'

11:30 pm one night in darkest Stockbury, a taxi driver who'd just dropped off a fare saw a large black leopard strolling by the side of the road.

The man told me, "*It shot off into the undergrowth when it saw me but it unnerved me a great deal.*"

The following year at Shepway, at 3:00 pm during the summer a married couple both looking out of their kitchen window observed a large black cat sitting in the lower branches of a lilac tree.

A few years previously, in 1982, Mr Sharman reported that as a teenager he and a friend saw a large black cat in one of the chalk quarries which the picnic area at Blue Bell Hill overlooks. Around the same time, a man named Barry, who'll be mentioned a few times throughout this chapter, was shooting behind the Robin Hood pub when he came across an impressive set of large prints which he followed into the wood, but never caught sight of the animal which made them.

Also during the '80s the same man said that one night whilst walking his dog at Common Road he saw the yellow eyes of a dark-coloured animal and then his wife, walking in the same area shortly afterward saw a panther on the edge of the nearby field.

Around 2004 I had a wonderful conversation with a woman from a gypsy family who claimed to have, in 1987, released four female pumas and three lynx in an area of Maidstone which I will not mention.

She told me that cats were easily obtainable on the black market, and a lot of families used to have them as part of a mini-circus.

Were these kind of released animals partly responsible for the cats roaming Medway in the present?

In the June of 2001 a Chatham woman driving up the Maidstone Road, near Rochester Industrial Park saw a black panther on a track which runs into the wood.

Also in the summer, police dog handler Nigel Marshall was driving late one night at Bell Lane, when he came across a bunch of youths in a car. The man asked what the boys were up to and they claimed that they'd seen a panther the previous night and wanted to shoot it with the air rifles they had in the boot of the vehicle.

Mr Marshall said also that in the October he found an eaten fox next to the Yew Tree pub, in Maidstone. It was discovered near one of the drainage tunnels and its head was stuck in a chain-link fence but the rest of the animal had been neatly stripped.

By mid-summer, 2001 had been my busiest year with regards to cataloguing eyewitness reports.

The black leopard of Blue Bell Hill was certainly keeping a low profile but at Wateringbury, on the other side of Maidstone, a man named Shawn was driving his grandmother home one afternoon when they spotted a black panther creeping low through undergrowth in the field next to the road.

On an internet message board I found an obscure report of a tawny-coloured cat with a bobbed tail being sighted in the Darland Banks area. Was this the same animal my father had seen near the local rubbish tip?

In July a Maidstone man in the village of Loose, Maidstone, was out running at 7:00 pm when he saw a big black cat with an 'S' shaped tail on the hill leading up from the valley which runs from Tovil. He watched the animal for more than two minutes before it disappeared into the trees.

The trail of the Blue Bell Hill had certainly gone cold throughout much of the summer though but this was mainly because my research had been focusing on several other Kent towns, but the *KM Extra* of August 10th asked, *'Is this the end of the beast...?'*, an unusual statement simply because they weren't getting what they wanted from me, but at Gravesend, Mereworth, Plaxtol, West Peckham and Sussex I was bombarding the press with reports and in return receiving a wealth of local information.

It was difficult to say as to where the Blue Bell Hill cat had moved to, but in the October a Walderslade man saw the animal at 3:30 one afternoon as he was walking with his wife at Blue Bell Hill. It was only thirty yards away on the pathway, had a long tail and appeared muscular. It slinked off into the bushes, but his partner refused to continue walking in that direction.

A flap of reports from the Sevenoaks area and Ashford meant my research was required elsewhere but a Mr Fielding out walking with his eight-year old son at Boxley during mid-October, at 3:30 pm had an excellent sighting of what he believed to be a panther. *"We took a walk around the Pilgrim's Way area"*, he told me.

> *"We followed the dual carriageway near Tyland Barn which runs adjacent to the M20 towards the village of Sandling. We then followed a concrete pathway and came to an area of fields near a cottage on Grange Road.*
>
> *We heard someone shooting at the bottom of the field but as we looked across the field we saw a large animal sitting on its haunches just forty yards away. We first thought it was a dog until it was on all fours.*
>
> *It was cat-like, dark brown with a small face. Its head seemed small in comparison to the rest of its body, and it had a long tail, looked strong and had an arched back and what appeared to be a full belly. It was slightly smaller than an Alsatian. We watched it for a while as it sat back down again and then made off towards the a fence which is jumped over. We told the police about the incident."*

Had they seen a puma, judging by the head-size, or a black panther in daylight, showing its true, chocolate-brown coat?

It was a difficult one to fathom, because the witness certainly said the animal was dark enough to appear black at night, but there had been several puma reports from the area too.

On Friday 26th October fate was either smiling upon me, or messing with my mind!

It was around 8:15 am and I was on my way to work in Gillingham, travelling in a car owned by my then girlfriend Nicki. We had come from the direction of Princes Park and headed towards the roundabout outside the Wagon at Hale pub, just before the Capstone Road. There is often a busy amount of traffic congested here each morning as other motorists attempt to get to work, or get their children to school on time. On this occasion, a slightly overcast day, we approached the roundabout where we'd swing left and head up Pear Tree Lane. As we reached the pub I looked up at the sloping field on my right, as I always have done due to the fact that in the past a few cats had been seen in the area. Sitting on its haunches and almost camouflaged by the soil of the field was an animal, rusted in colour.

"*What's that?*" I yelled, but we couldn't stop, traffic was behind us, and although Nicki glanced at the animal, we couldn't look for more than a few seconds otherwise she would probably have ploughed into a postal van coming the other way.

The animal was too big to be a domestic cat yet it was cat-like. I'd seen foxes in the area before, it was nothing of the sort. It had the shape of a lynx or possibly a caracal. Had it been the cat my father had seen not so long ago?

Nicki managed to go round the roundabout again, so this time the animal was on my left as I looked into the field. It seemed to be observing the traffic and was only around one-hundred yards away.

The cat never moved, and the next minute I was on my way to the dull routine of work, leaving behind that mysterious felid I knew I'd be very lucky to see again.

My attention turned to Ashford once again, after the killing of a sheep in the Bilsington area, and then a bizarre incident occurred on the Isle of Sheppey where it was alleged that a black leopard had been shot and killed. More on this in the relevant section, however, after the strange incident, local press began to believe that it was in fact the Blue Bell Hill animal that had perished, and sent out a series of almost sympathetic articles towards my research. It was a very weird time once again, but by the beginning of November a dark brown cat was seen at Common Road, Blue Bell Hill by a Mrs Jackson who, at 10:20 pm looked out of her window, and saw the animal rummaging through the undergrowth on the other side of the road.

She watched the animal for around four-minutes, and then it ran off down the lane.

A few days later her husband saw the animal too.

I then followed up numerous Gravesend sightings throughout November, but the *Medway Messenger* were quick to promote the alleged demise of the local big cat with the headline, '*Paws and reflect - end of a legend*', which I certainly thought was dramatically presumptuous considering the amount of large cats that were roaming the county, and that Sheppey was quite a distance from Blue Bell Hill.

Of course, despite the inaccurate story the press covered, it was good publicity for the local felids once again, and by the end of the year my catalogue of annual sightings had soared to over two-hundred once again, but the headlines were certainly getting cheesier, with the *Sheerness Times Guardian* commenting '*Now it's son of Island's big cat*' after another Sheppey sighting allayed fears of the previous shooting.

Two days before Christmas a Walderslade woman walking her dog at 5:30 am near Vale Drive, Davis Estate, saw a black panther near woods. This was to be the last sighting for a couple of months and then on 4th February 2002 at 1:00 pm, two men in a vehicle travelling on the M20 at Detling Hill, saw a big, black leopard walking across a ploughed field.

Although the animal was six-hundred yards away and the rain was driving heavily against the window, the witnesses identified the animal as larger than an Alsatian dog and said also that it stopped suddenly, as if nosing the air and had one of its front paws raised as if suspended in mid-step.

A Hempstead man called me to say that he believed it was his missing Abyssinian cat responsible for most of the local sightings, despite the fact his absent pet was reddish in colour with a black stripe running down its spine, and smaller than a fox.

Also in Gillingham, a man from Cuxton, during early March at 9:45 pm saw an animal bound across the road twenty-five yards away. The animal sat on the other side of the road and remained in view for quite some time and the witness was able to get a good look at it.

He said: *"The cat was dirty-brown in colour, the size of a medium-sized dog and had a long tail."*

Such local reports on the edge of Medway were few and far between concerning this mysterious possible puma. Of course, sightings around the Link Road had happened not long before at 4:00 am but I needed to know what the animal was.

On the 22nd March a different cat was seen at Blue Bell Hill by a Walderslade man walking his bull terrier dog. It was 1:40 pm and the witness was walking down the rutted pathway at the end of Common Road which dips into the wood when a cat, the colour of a rabbit rushed across the pathway.

The man believed what he'd seen was a lynx but the animal seen at Hartlip, on 1st April was certainly no lynx, or April Fool's Day prank.

A manager at a Gillingham-based business who I worked for, for nine years, was riding his mountain bike with four friends at 11:00 pm through the country lanes when they caught an animal and its green eyes in their lights. The cat was black and shot off into the woods, leaving the five men paralysed with fear.

Six days later the animal was back in Walderslade when a woman named Shelley, driving at 10:30 pm, heading towards the main road from Tunbury Avenue, saw a large black animal by the side of the road which was about to head into a copse. The woman stopped the car quickly and the cat stared back at her before slinking away. She told me that, *"It had a long hooked tail, and overall the cat was long and slender."*

Two days later it was spotted at Impton Lane a few minutes from Tunbury Avenue and then on the 13th it was seen again nearby, this time during the afternoon by a female who was walking, with four other people in a field near the Alexandra Hospital.

Her report was as follows:

> *"Upon entering the woodland clearing we saw a large, black animal sitting upright. It was about twenty feet away. It seemed to be chewing something, and then it stood on all fours and we could see its long tail. We watched the cat for about an hour; it had no fear of us and on several occasions it went into the undergrowth and then came back out, and*

then finally headed off towards the direction of the Bridgewood Hotel."

According to the witness, the animal was seen again the following morning by one of her friends.

Then, on the 22nd of April the man who'd spotted the cat with four friends whilst cycling near Bredhurst, had an unnerving encounter again, this time at 10:30 pm near Bredhurst Church.

Again, the group had been out cycling and were travelling on foot, bikes at their side, towards the Bredhurst Bell public house. As they walked up the dark pathway they suddenly heard twigs snapping in the woods very close to them. All of the men stopped dead in their tracks and listened carefully and then a deep, guttural growl came from the blackness.

The witnesses were petrified and although one swung his bike light in the direction of the woods, they could see no sign of the animal which made the noises. They listened to the eerie noises for around five-minutes, too scared to run from the area, and then they all jumped on their bikes and headed towards the street lights of the main road.

One month later to the day, a woman and her fiancé were travelling down Boxley Hill towards *The Bull* public house, at Penenden Heath at 3:30 pm she saw a large cat in the undergrowth. The woman told me:

> *"I was looking out of the car window, to my left were lots of trees with a field beyond and at the edge of the field sat on its haunches under the trees was what looked like a lioness or a puma. I couldn't believe it, just sitting there watching the world go by through the trees. I assume the cat was sheltering from a short rain shower. Unfortunately my fiancé didn't see the cat but I know what I saw. Although it was shady under the trees it was sunny but showery at the same time, but the cat was sandy colour – not black."*

Again, I had to wait another month before a similar-sized cat was seen in the same area. A Lyn Weston who resided near Sandling, Maidstone, backing onto the Cobtree Manor Golf Club had a close encounter on the 13th June at 3:00 am.

She'd been asleep, but was awoken by what she thought was a cat fight in the garden. She owned three cats so she got out of bed and went downstairs in the hope of sorting the commotion out. Her garden, surrounded by a seven-foot high perimeter fence backed onto undergrowth flanking the carriageway.

Lyn approached the patio doors and saw all of her three cats cowering under a shelf in the garden and cornered by an Alsatian-sized animal which she could see side-on.

The animal glanced quickly at the scared woman and then she bravely opened the garden doors and attempted to shoo the beast away. Luckily for her, and her pet cats, it worked, and the animal disappeared at the end of the garden.

She'd originally been thirty feet from the big cat and said it was illuminated well by the road lamps and she stated that it was dark and mottled but not black, and it was muscular in the shoulder.

At the end of June a woman living in Loose, Maidstone, found large paw-prints in her garden which measured four-inches across. A few days after the woman found the head of a domestic cat in the garden. It had been cleanly severed and her next door neighbour had discovered a few spots of blood on his patio.

Loose Valley is around eight miles from Blue Bell Hill. It's a rural area of conservation peppered by orchards, grasslands, woods, and ponds, and harbours a variety of wildlife.

A large black cat was seen at Leybourne Grange around the same time an old work friend of mine named Andy mentioned that whilst travelling with his dad along West Sole Field Road, near Lordswood, during one evening, a black cat bounded from the woods as his father gave way to a stream of other cars.

It may have been the animal I had seen near Hempstead just a few minutes away, but a fox-sized cat seen at Lenham shortly after remained unidentified.

On July 28th the lady from Loose Valley who'd discovered the head of a domestic cat in her garden was alarmed by a deep growling in her garden as she sat on her patio with her fiancé at 12:15 am. They said the loud purring and guttural growling lasted for around three minutes from the direction of the cricket pitch which was enveloped in darkness. Suddenly, several birds resting the trees were unsettled and flew off as a strange, scream emanated from the darkness from an animal that was possibly being killed.

The *Downs Mail* of August featured a snippet on a local sighting.

'*Rhian's dogs find beast of Boxley*' it was commented after a Maidstone woman, whilst walking on the fringe of Vinters Valley Park Wood disturbed an animal which snarled at her. The animal ran off into the woods.

After the summer flurry, once again the sightings of Maidstone-related cats pretty much mysteriously ceased. The next report from around Medway came from the Lordswood area when Rod Stevens, who'd seen a large, light coloured cat in the '70s, was driving up North Dane Way, towards the top of Lordswood Lane at 3:30 pm on 14th October, with his wife. It was an overcast day pouring with rain, and as they neared a turning on the right, around one-hundred yards away a black cat emerged from a patch of trees. The animal suddenly loped across the wide road and vanished into the woods on the left.

They both agreed that the animal was the size of a labrador, very sleek and long in the body.

Such an animal may well have been the same animal I'd seen near Hempstead and which had been prowling Capstone for the last few years.

was beginning to think that this particular leopard was a female and that it had been a big male roaming the Maidstone area. Whether they had produced offspring was another question that needed answering as there hadn't been any significant reports of animals with cubs around Medway.

On November 3rd *Kent On Sunday* ran a huge appeal for me, which brought forward a stack of Ashford sightings, but the Blue Bell Hill animal remained quiet until 4th December when the *Medway Messenger* reported, '*Shining fur, glowing eyes*', in relation to a sighting of a black leopard in Rochester

> Just when you thought it was safe to go out, the Beast of Blue Bell Hill is back, bigger than before.
>
> Mary Wright, of Maidstone Road, Rochester, was out walking her dog Bonnie late on Friday when she came face to face with the panther-like beast.
>
> She said: "I normally take Bonnie and walk her near Rochester Math School and up to Sir Evelyn Road. But by the time I got in from work it was quite late so I thought we'd go

for a quick walk and then go back home."

At about 10:45 pm, Mary wandered up towards the prison in Sir Evelyn Road when she heard something rustling in the bushes.

"It's quite dark around there because there are a few trees and bushes around," she said.

"I heard noises, like someone stumbling in the bushes but we kept walking around because I knew Bonnie needed her exercise."

Just as she turned to walk back towards the main road she heard a loud crunching noise behind her.

"It sounded like a branch breaking. I looked around and I saw this thing crossing the road. Although it was dark I could see the black fur shining in the dark and a long tail waving around. It paused and looked at me and I could see yellowish eyes glowing. I honestly thought it was going to attack Bonnie", she recalled.

Mary screamed and the creature ran off towards the prison.

"I don't think I'll be walking Bonnie around there ever again", she said.

"It was really scary. Its eyes stood out like car headlights. It certainly wasn't a fox and it was much bigger than a cat. I have heard of the beast of Blue Bell Hill and we weren't too far away from that particular area."

Although it was the last Medway-related cat sighting of the year it was a huge relief to receive it. Bizarrely, the more heavily wooded areas of Kent such as Sevenoaks, Ashford and Canterbury were producing plenty of eyewitness reports, and yet the more built-up areas of Medway were somehow concealing a handful of exotic felids which weren't allegedly seen again until mid-January 2003, when it was reported in the *Medway Today* that a big cat had been prowling Hempstead once again, and had allegedly scratched a domestic cat. A couple who lived in the area claimed that what they'd seen was three feet long, jet-black and looked like a small panther. Rather oddly the couple believed that an attack on guinea pig a few weeks earlier may have been attributable to the cat, although they said that something had ripped its throat out. Considering a guinea pig is such a small animal, I wouldn't have thought that much would've been left of the victim, and a throat bite would have been pretty unnecessary.

Further away the *Whitstable Gazette* of the 16th reported, '*Big cat spotted on the prowl*' on their front page after a woman at Saddleton Road, whilst looking out of her kitchen window spotted a black leopard in the garden which was lying next to a wheelbarrow. Several sightings emerged from Faversham in the February but on the Friday night of the 28th came the most impressive piece of evidence yet that a large cat was roaming the Malling area.

Scott Arnold (no relation) of East Malling, was at home at 2:00 am and had just finished putting his son's computer games console away when something caught his eye out of the window. Scott looked across the green where he was used to seeing domestic cats and foxes frolicking around, but on the New Road, roughly one hundred yards away he found himself looking at an enormous cat that resembled cougar. It was making its way up the road from left to right, a road which in the day is rather busy but at this time was dead quiet.

Scott, a keen animal lover who'd spent a number of years in Africa and collected paintings and pictures of such wild cats, realised what he was seeing and reached for his camcorder. He claimed that he first saw the animal lying in the road and that it was rolling around, but by the time he'd steadied his camera the cat was slowly walking up the middle of the road. Under the street lights the animal's size was shocking. The central road markings were around ten feet long and this cat was more than half that length. The animal was beige-fawn in colour, massive in the shoulders, appeared lighter on the underside and had a baggy belly.

In the short film the cat is only in view for less than twenty seconds and then appears to turn right before changing its mind and continuing. As Scott attempted to zoom in he loses focus as he gets too close to a tree branch, and although the cat occasionally comes back into focus, albeit shakily, Scott told me it did indeed turn right eventually and moved out of sight.

I've watched the footage many times and believe it is the most impressive evidence of a puma in Kent. This could well be the same creature that has been heard screaming in the woods at Mereworth, yet had hardly been reported. Although the coat of the puma can certainly melt into the undergrowth, I'd been amazed at the lack of puma reports I'd received, and those which had come my way were of a smaller cat, but on this occasion we were truly dealing with a monstrous puma which has hardly been since.

A jogger running on a bridle path up through Blue Bell Hill on Sunday 23rd March 2003 saw a much smaller cat. It was 11:30 am and as he was coming down a wooded pathway, fifty yards away a cat, the size of a fox, came out of nowhere, and was sniffing the ground, completely unaware that the man was fast heading its way.

The witness clapped his hands and the animal raised its head then shrunk away into the greenery. The man told me that it was more reddish in colour than a fox, skinny, with a long tail.

Three days later a woman walking her dog at the picnic area saw a large, greyish coloured cat although further investigations were to no avail and the sighting remained all too vague to be considered as a black leopard.

Around this time much of my research veered towards north Kent again after my sighting of a beige-coloured cat on the marshes as mentioned in the previous section. However, a woman claimed to have seen a melanistic leopard near Tunbury Woods, Walderslade, in the April, and Mr Skinner contacted me on 7th June with an interesting sighting also. He told me:

> *"I saw an animal as I drove up Pear Tree Lane (near Capstone Road) a few weeks ago, about 9:00 am as I was driving up the hill towards Hempstead.*
>
> *About two-hundred yards away up from the bottom of the hill a cat-like animal ran out in front of the car from the right hand side from the trees and almost immediately turned and ran back in. The things I can distinctly remember about it as it ran were its long tail which was upright and curling or kinking over to one side at the top, the darkish tan type of colour and also its face which seemed to be a lot darker than the rest of it."*

It seemed as though the witness had seen a puma, or it had been a day time sighting of a panther, but it was difficult to say. I had a feeling that a panther appearing two hundred yards away would certainly have appeared black.

I hadn't had many local reports of puma but knew that somewhere out there locally there was one which was only turning up as regularly as a majority of the others seen around Kent. Another cat of similar colour was seen around mid-May by a woman living at Ewart Road, Chatham, not far from where my cousin Jez had heard the deep growls in the garden and also where the pensioner had observed the black cat on a garage roof whilst she was travelling on the bus.

On this occasion, the woman, who was sitting in her kitchen drinking a cup of tea, saw an animal around seventy-five yards away which she at first took to be a fox which walked along the wall along the back of the garden. As she looked closer she realised it was a large cat around four feet long, as she measured a pipe in the area soon afterwards. The cat was dark in colour and had a long, curved tail.

It may have been the same animal which a couple saw on 20th May at 10:10 am as they travelled through Walderslade Woods on the Hallsfield Road. As they approached the junction a large animal ran from left to right across the road. They said that, "*It was just a few yards in front of the car. We thought it was a fox at first and it was certainly fox-sized at the shoulder but longer in the body. It had a long tail with a rounded end and was brown in colour but its coat was covered in irregular darker blotches.*"

Had the elderly couple seen the local black leopard, with the rosettes evident under the dark coat? Possibly, and yet they didn't describe an animal anywhere near as large as what had been seen previously in the area. Strange indeed.

Nine days later at Blue Bell Hill's picnic area, a man named Colin, walking with his girlfriend from their parked car on Common Road - in the direction of the Robin Hood pub for a drink - observed a big dark-coloured cat slowly crossing the overgrown field on the left. They stood and watched it for around five minutes and said it appeared to have a darker patch on its back. Then, on June 8th possibly the same animal was seen at Wouldham by Sue Saunders at 7:00 am as she was driving up The Knole. She glanced ahead and saw the back end of a black animal disappear into the hedgerow, on the right near the local quarry. Sue told me that the year previous she'd seen a similar animal in exactly the same place, and that in 1999 something large had spooked her horses on Common Road, at Blue Bell Hill.

A month or so later eerie calls were heard from Boxley woods, a black cat was seen at Wateringbury and Mr Howard, shooting at Boxley, reported seeing a black leopard as he sat in his vehicle near the remains of an old abbey. The cat stood dead still for a moment and then slipped back from whence it came.

Another strange sighting took place on City Way at Rochester on Thursday 3rd July at 2:00 pm as an elderly woman, at her kitchen sink, saw an animal in the garden which she first took to be a fox. The creature was grooming itself but as it turned she noticed its extraordinary long tail. The woman said that, "*It was the size of a fox but greyish-beige and bigger built.*"

Just what unusual cats were prowling close to the Medway Towns? What were these smaller brown cats?

In the same month Mr Knowler saw a big cat whilst walking his dogs at 6:30 am in the East Malling area. Rumours were circulating from the area that a mystery cat had eaten a small dog, leaving only one of its back legs.

A flurry of sightings in Sussex and on the Isle of Sheppey took up a great deal of my time in the summer months, but the autumn was back to business for Maidstone connected sightings, when at 11:30 am on September 29th a mother and her son walking at fields in Headcorn saw a large black cat basking in the sunshine. They approached the animal with caution, which then got up and slinked into a hollow. The woman's son overlooked the hollow which was overgrown and although he couldn't see the cat he could hear it eating something, so they quickly left the area. In the same month the carcass of a sheep was found up a tree near Bredhurst and a Shepway woman claimed to have caught a big black cat on her

CCTV, but I never received the evidence.

A black leopard was seen on 15th October at 10:00 am by a woman as it ran across a ploughed field between the railway line and Hermitage Lane cottages at Barming. On Halloween the *Kent Messenger* reported, *'Family gets jumpy over black beast'* stating: *'Brendan Reidy and his five-year old son Daniel had the fright of their lives when they saw what appeared to be a large, black panther-like creature jump over their garden fence.*

Mr Reidy, of Barming, was gardening one Sunday afternoon earlier this month when something very big, and very black caught his eye.

"I turned my head and saw a large, dark shape leap over the fence. I thought it could have been a house cat but it was too big, then I thought it might have been a fox but they aren't black. Also, I heard the thump of its paws. Whatever it was it was travelling very fast and it was very heavy."

Mr Reidy's son Daniel was standing nearby when the creature made its appearance and was able to tell his father exactly what it looked like.

"My son was standing there, and asked me what it was. I said I didn't know and asked him what it looked like" he said. "He said it was big, and when I asked him how big he just spread his arms as far as they would go. He also said it had green eyes. We call it the Beast of Barming, it has turned into a bit of a joke in our house, we say don't go out to the wood because the beast's in there."

Meanwhile, on the 5th November a Mr Roberts saw a black panther prowling in scrub land behind Preston Hall Hospital at Aylesford. The witness told the *Kent Messenger:*

"There are a number of French doors around the pool which overlook woodland at the back of Preston Hall. I saw the big black animal walk past the doors one-hundred yards away, it was very low to the ground and five to six feet long."

Two days later the *KM* asked, *'Is black beast on the move?'* after a sighting at Bredgar, Sittingbourne, which proved that the Aylesford cat was certainly not the same animal.

Laura Lawrence, of School Lane, Lower Halstow told the *Messenger:*

"I left my sister's home to return by car to Lower Halstow. While driving along Primrose Lane, a large black cat-like animal bounded across my path and was lit up by my headlights."

The newspaper mentioned that Barming is only ten miles as the crow flies from Bredgar, and also spoke of rumour that an Alsatian had been savaged by a cat in Hucking.

Later in the month a handful of reports came from Staplehurst and Headcorn, but the most intriguing of stories came from a Gillingham couple on December 10th who claimed that they'd seen a very large puma on their land in Lower Gillingham, not far from the marshes running alongside the river. The woman, named Jan, said:

"It started in July when there were five separate sightings by four different people and then there was nothing but it appears to have come back. Yesterday it had a kill in my stable yard and it was spotted again today only fifty yards away, and we always know when it's around because our horses go mad. It is a very large brown and mottled cat with a very long heavy looking tail."

Although I looked into the reports and the woman felt very protective of the animal, the animal was far too elusive to track. Although possibly a puma, the witnesses eventually lost contact with me, but I'm pretty sure that if a large cat was going to roam the Medway Towns then the riverside at Lower Gillingham would be an ideal spot for shelter and prey.

On the last day of 2003 a girl named Natalie, a relative of my mother's, came across two dead cows in a farmer's field in Bredhurst. Both cows, one a calf, were laying on their sides with wounds evident, but the witness was wary of entering the field in case the farmer came out and thought she was trespassing. Although Natalie knew there'd been a few sightings of a big, black cat, it sounded to me like the wounds inflicted on the cows were not from a big cat. She stated that the animals seemed stiff as a board and their wounds, although clean, were not extensive but more like holes. Such strange finds have been observed throughout the world, particularly in the United States and Mexico where such 'cattle mutilations' have become commonplace. Cattle, and other livestock, have been found by ranchers completely stiff in the fields, showing signs that they've been dropped from a great height. Many of the victims show wounds to the genital areas and around the mouth as if some laser precision tool has been applied to burn away the flesh. Local people have blamed a variety of suspects; from the government, as part of some covert nuclear programme to monitor cattle eating from ground that has been previously used for nuclear testing, to extraterrestrials. But so-called experts claim that the cattle are simply being killed by predators, although cougars and coyotes do not seem to be the likely candidates judging by the weird wounds inflicted.

I knew that a large cat or two had been seen in and around Bredhurst, but attacks on cows had been nonexistent and this particular case had a touch of the very strange about it. Who knows what happened to the unfortunate victims or what type of predator caused their deaths, although in the April of the following year a farmer would find a dead calf in Newchapel as reported on the *This Is Kent* website, although this was towards Sussex.

In 2004 a man driving up City Way in Rochester, where I'd previously mentioned sightings of a fox-sized cat, was heading southbound, nearing the top junction with Maidstone Road. It was late evening and dark, and one hundred yards ahead a large cat crossed the road. It was black in colour. Then, the animal remained out of the headlines, despite a handful of Headcorn sightings in April, and a vague report of a big black cat in Walderslade on 1st May when a woman walking her dog claimed to have seen the beast on a woodland pathway before it jumped into the undergrowth.

A handful of sightings from Cranbrook, towards Tenterden were likely to have concerned one of many black leopards roaming Ashford but on Wednesday 18th May at 12:35 pm a Mr Major saw a large, stocky black cat whilst dirt biking through the woods on a track. A majority of sightings from the area concerned a very large animal.

Then, on the Sunday of the 29th a man named Mark, who I used to work with in Gillingham, who was travelling to work at 5:15 am on his scooter, was on the main road from the *Savacentre* shopping centre, near Hempstead, when one hundred yards away a cat crossed the road from left to right. He told me that it was bigger than a fox, fawn in colour, had long ears, large feet, and a bobbed tail like that of a bobcat or lynx.

On the 11th June I received an interesting email from a man regarding an impressive local sighting.

'I am contacting you to tell you that I was out with my son in Lordswood, Chatham, to-day and I saw a large black cat about eighty-metres in front of us.

We saw the cat around 2:00 pm at the top end of North Dane Way. We were walking along a pathway which is quite secluded and next to woodland, the cat walked onto the path from the left, stopped and looked at us for no more than five seconds. When I first saw it I thought it was a black dog and expected to see its owner, very quickly however I realised it was definitely a cat, arched back, tail and shape were feline. Strange as it sounds I did not feel threatened in any way and it walked off into the woods.'

Two men pulled over at Blue Bell Hill around the same time after their vehicle began to make a peculiar noise. One of the men was tending to the engine whilst the other one took a few steps down a dark pathway and saw a big, black animal which suddenly leapt into the foliage. The man told me, *"I thought it was a black Labrador at first but when it jumped I realised it was a cat with a long tail."*

Dave Parker had a fascinating sighting at 11:00 am whilst travelling to Rochester on a bus. He swore blind that the animal he saw pounce on a mouse in a nearby field was a wildcat, similar to those which roam Scotland. However, no further sightings have emerged of such an animal.

In the summer another sighting took place near Hermitage Lane, at Barming when a male witness travelling towards the hospital at 5:30 pm, looked across into a neighbouring field and saw a massive black cat slinking along the tree line. The witness was so shocked that he turned the car around and came back for a second look, but the cat was nowhere to be seen.

Two more sightings emerged from the Headcorn area of a black leopard and then on August 1st a man walking towards his plot of land attached to an orchard in the West Malling area, came across the body of a dead fox. The victim had bite marks to the throat, and the stomach had been ripped out. The witness' daughter reported to me that, *"It looked like a shark-bite to the stomach."*

On the 23rd August Mr Parker, who lives in Eccles, was walking his dog on a pathway near to the Walnut Tree pub at 7:00 am. As he came to a cornfield he saw a large, black animal slinking along the tree line some two hundred yards away. The animal appeared stocky and stood over two feet in height. Two days later at the same time, Mr Parker was in the area again walking and saw the animal which walked into a thicket.

I visited the area with my dad on the 27th and we found that the woods in the area were sufficient to harbour any number of large animals. Whilst traipsing across a field we found a dead, eaten goose. Although it could have struck a power line above and died, something had certainly eaten the carcass in a clean fashion, leaving the corpse as a stinking, writhing mass of maggot-infested pulp.

This area however is only a mile or so from Blue Bell Hill and near other relevant areas such as Burham and Aylesford. Geese were constantly observed landing in a nearby field so it was very likely that the panther had been stalking them, although rabbits were in abundance also.

At 9:30 pm on the same day Mr Entwistle was sitting in a clearing with friends at Royden Church, on Seven Mile Lane between East Peckham and Mereworth. Mr Entwistle returned to his car to get something and beeped the door with the key to open it and was startled by a big black cat which crept from the front of the car, which then walked in front of him just six feet away. The witness stood in complete shock until the cat walked out of view. Unfortunately, his friends never believed his story, but he remained adamant that he'd seen a four-foot-long panther.

A Wateringbury resident was awoken by his German Shepherd dog barking at 3:00 am during the second week of September '04. The witness, Mr Young, opened his back door expecting his dog to rush out and go to the toilet but instead, when the security light came on, he was astounded to see his dog chasing a big black cat around the garden. Apparently, the animals did two circuits before the cat leapt a six-foot fence and was gone.

On 23rd September closer to home at Lordswood, a woman named Debbie contacted me to say that her husband had been out walking that evening when he heard something walking beside him and his dog in the woods. However, the dog was quite distressed by the presence which worried the man, but as he stopped a large black animal trotted across their path. Debbie's husband said, "*It was taller than an Alsatian, but very long and slender with a long tail.*"

The extremely elusive West Malling puma reared its head on the 29th October 2004 at 11:30 am when a local man saw the cat, just off the bypass near a new mansion that was being built. The animal, which he described as fox-coloured but taller, jumped a fence next to the railway line.

A black leopard showed up at East Farleigh in mid-November and was witnessed by a male walking home across the fields at 5:45 pm. And a month later a male motorist claimed to have seen a black leopard whilst driving towards Wouldham. The cat was the size of a labrador and loped into the woods.

A girl named Liane Stones contacted me via my BBC website with an interesting report from 2004.

> 'Me and my friends were out in a rather large garden which backs onto a butchers in the Fant area of Maidstone. We heard a loud rustle in the bushes and went to see what it was. We took torches and all three of us at the same time saw two large amber eyes staring back at us. We of course screamed and ran back down the garden at which point we heard a scratching sound and a loud rustle. When we went back to the wall behind the bush there were scratches on the wall.'

Although by the end of the year it sounded as though the cats around Maidstone were very active, compared to elsewhere in the county such as Gravesend and Ashford, sightings were certainly a trickle. At West Farleigh in 2005 on 3rd January at 10:15 am Mr Robertson, travelling in his car, saw a black cat the size of an Irish wolfhound cross the road from right to left.

Later in the month during one afternoon a boy, his girlfriend and two friends walking in the woods of Common Road, near the *Robin Hood* pub, spooked themselves by wondering if they'd see the local beast, when at 3:00 pm they did exactly that. One of the witnesses claimed that through binoculars they saw the animal lying under a fallen tree just sixty-foot away. They all stood and watched the cat for around fifteen minutes and it just stared back. The group then left the area. When they returned later the animal had gone.

A Gillingham woman believed that a large cat had been visiting her garden regularly, after her first sighting in 2002. Although she was unsure of the colouration of its coat she said it was bigger than an Alsatian, and that in early 2005 it had urinated on her lawn and agitated her pet cat.

Two sightings were then reported from the Coxheath area of Maidstone, the second sighting from Stocketts Lane at 6:30 pm during a March evening. A woman named Yvonne watched a large black cat from her downstairs window as it mooched around the nearby orchard. The woman called her daughter and they watched the cat for around fifteen minutes and said that it leapt up at a small tree at one point. The cat was described as five to six feet long with a long, thick tail. At the end of the month Mr Price claimed to have been awoken at 2:00 am at his home in Barming by a horrible scream.

The man got out of bed and went to the bedroom window where, thirty feet away, he saw a fox sitting on a small wall. The fox was yelping and crying as three feet away a large, dark-coloured animal crouched low and circled the distressed fox. The animal had a long tail that was swishing behind it, very large paws and a sleek body around five feet in length.

Mr Price tapped on the window and the cat sprang away towards the main road and yet the fox just remained in its position. Although the witness remained at the window for more than thirty minutes the cat never returned, but the fox did not move.

A security guard on patrol at 1:00 am at Oakwood Park, Maidstone came out of his hut with a torch and saw a black animal with a small head crossing a path. The cat squatted then leapt up a bank towards the car park. A similar animal was seen at West Malling in the May and then on 3rd June in the Cranbrook area when a large cat was blamed for walking across the roof of a conservatory and spooking a local woman, who called the police twice.

On the 9th June at East Barming at 4:30 am a female motorist travelling towards Maidstone Hospital to visit a relative giving birth saw a labrador-sized cat, jet-black, run across the road one-hundred yards away. It moved in the direction of the river.

Three days later at Stockbury a married couple in their car travelling at 5:10 pm saw a big cat cross the road at Pett Lane. The animal was dark brown, had a long curving tail and had come from a field full of sheep.

On the 24th June Mr Smith travelling to work at 6:00 am saw a black leopard casually cross the road fifty yards ahead. It glanced at his car and then was lost in the darkness.

A puma was observed by a man named Mark walking his dog at the foot of the West Malling bypass. The cat was four feet in length.

On Sunday 10th July Bernadette Tuffs managed to photograph the Blue Bell Hill beast. I never submitted the report to the newspapers, although she did contact them with the photographs.

Her report was as follows:

It was 5:00 pm. We (my husband and daughter) missed the turning for Aylesford Priory and ended up on the Rochester Road. We turned around and drove back I believe towards Burham. Suddenly, in the field of the left something caught my eye. It was a large black cat, in the middle of the field of cut crop or grass.

It stood out clearly as it was all black. I couldn't quite believe what I was seeing. We stopped the car and I was able to get two photo's with my new camera on a 10 x zoom setting. The animal was definitely larger than any domestic cat, and was not a dog or a fox. I immediately assumed it was a panther because of the colour. We then had to drive on as the road was narrow and cars were beginning to stack up around us. We turned right into a little loop road, and came round again. My husband got out of the car to have a look and agreed it was a big cat of some description. It was a hot, sunny day, clear. The animal was in no hurry and was not at all scared or nervous. It sauntered along, then sat then wandered off again towards the corn field ahead. It is hard for me to estimate size from such a distance.

We have reported the matter to the police who have asked for my pictures, but we have heard no more about it.

What Bernadette photographed was indeed a panther. The two photos show a muscular animal, jet black, strolling upwards through the field towards the wood, and the second picture shows it sitting down, its long tail sticking out behind it.

Bizarrely the local press believed that the witnesses had only seen a domestic cat and yet on the 19th July it was seen again, this time by Mrs Peters at 4:45 pm as she was sitting in the *Fleur De Lys* pub on the Rochester Road, looking out across the field where Bernadette had photographed the cat.

This time, the cat was around two hundred metres away, again mooching along in the field. Despite telling a few people, only one man showed any interest and began to run up the field towards the cat, but the animal sensed him and it ran off towards the bushes. Then, on the 22nd four people working/drinking in the pub at lunch time also observed the cat in the same field. It went up the field again and disappeared.

Not since 1998 had I received such a cluster of reports pertaining to the Blue Bell Hill melanistic leopard, and to see it photographed in all its glory was pretty mind blowing. On the 24th August a black leopard was seen near to Barming by a man who watched the cat, at 7:10 pm as it walked along a track made by a tractor and slipped into the woods.

At the beginning of September a married couple from Whitstable were looking out their back door at 6:00 pm in the Swalecliffe area, when they noticed their pet cat cowering in the corner. A shadowy large cat had come over the eight-foot high fence and was standing, just a few feet away from the cat. Both witnesses panicked and ran out into the garden. The woman ran towards her pet cat, more concerned about its safety than her own. Her husband grabbed their cat, both of them bravely avoiding looking at the massive cat that had invaded their premises.

After the incident, when they had time to reflect on their bravery, they both told me that the animal was very dark in colour, had a long tail, and was bigger than an Alsatian.

During late summer of 2005 a woman from the Medway Towns filmed a cat she couldn't identify. The animal was seen squatting by a stile one afternoon by the woman and her daughter, not far from the Darland Banks area of Gillingham. I observed the film, and concluded it may have been a lynx although the cat is strange to say the least. The film is shaky but despite being only a minute long at the most, it's still very clear and shows an animal around the size of a fox, but with very large ears, sitting on its haunches. As the lady approaches, it shifts awkwardly, and its face comes into view, and yet resembles that of a hyena.

The lady claimed that she'd also seen the animal with a domestic cat, so maybe the animal was a peculiar hybrid, but there have been no other sightings since. However, there is a remote possibility that it was the same cat my father and I saw on separate occasions not far from Capstone Park.

A large cat was also observed near Detling cricket ground on several occasions by a man who'd gone to the area to watch his son play. He told me, "*It was a large sandy-coloured cat, the first thing that popped into my head was 'cougar'."*

An even darker coloured animal, possibly a black leopard, was seen on the 17th December at 12:00 pm by a lady driving near the Wagon at Hale pub in Chatham, near Capstone Park.

> *"At first I thought it was a large dog but the tail was far too thick and long. It was around three feet long and then the tail. It was jet-black and moved in between the derelict house (no longer there) and a gravel path."*

On the Christmas Eve in Lower Gillingham, at 1:30 pm a lady named Margaret, was sitting in her kitchen with her son and a friend looking out the window, when they spotted a light-coloured cat moving across the field a few hundred yards away.

Margaret went to fetch her binoculars, and said it was the size of a Labrador, fawn-grey in colour with a long tail. Margaret and her husband walked across the field once the animal had gone, but had another sighting as the cat raised its head from behind some black plastic sheeting, and then went away in the opposite direction.

The first three months were completely dead regarding sightings of the local big cat, but on 22nd March a man driving home from work near Hartlip at 7:00 pm, looked across the field to the left and was amazed to see a large black cat just sitting there. He was convinced he'd seen the leopard because this was the same guy who - on two occasions - whilst out with friends on their mountain bikes, saw and heard a black leopard in the Bredhurst area. On the 24th April on a very foggy night near Tunbury Woods, a teenager, who'd seen the cat previously near Lordswood whilst in a car with his dad, mentioned that once again his dad had seen the beast. It was approximately 7:30 pm, and his father saw the animal on the pathway that runs up to the crossover bridge close to the Alexandra Hospital. He was walking up a set of steps from Tunbury, and saw it ahead in the thick fog.

Fifteen minutes later the man's other son had been out jogging on the other side of the main road and claimed to also see the cat.

I visited the area immediately after, but the woods were just a grey haze of fog and it would have been too hazardous to venture down the leafy slopes into the depths of the wood when one had a job to see their own hand in front of their face. With darkness closing in, the enveloping fog was just a little unsettling and conditions were too poor to have been able to observe anything.

Possibly the same animal was seen on the Friday evening of June 16th at 9:00 pm by a man who works at Asda on the Maidstone Road, Chatham. He submitted me his report:

> *I proceeded to walk down the Chatham, Maidstone Road towards the Mid Kent College after finishing work. It was a hot evening, still sunny and just before I got to the college I noticed a large animal in a field on the same side of the college. The grass in the field was very high, but this animal really stood out as it was on a high ride approximately one-hundred-and-fifty yards away. I have no doubt that this large animal was a black panther.*
>
> *It had a very lean and muscular torso and was poised with raised rear legs and head to the ground in the act of feeding, on what, I could not see. The size of the animal seemed larger than any dog I've seen, its ears were large and pointed, and pointing backwards, the most striking thing to me at the time was its long and strong thick tail which was*

pointing upward and had a peculiar waggle. I watched this for around ten minutes before moving on as it carried on feasting.

A black panther was seen at Hollingbourne in the October by Mrs Waters between the *Dirty Habit* and *Black Horse* public houses. It was 4:15 pm, and she was driving with her son, when a cat - the size of a fox - crossed the road from the direction of the fields, and headed into the valley. The animal was sandy-coloured with a thick tail.

Shortly afterwards, a couple from North America were travelling near Bearsted, not far from Hollingbourne, at 5:30 pm when they saw a dark, chocolate-coloured cat walking along the hedgerow of a field occupied by sheep. One month later, there was another sighting in the Loose Valley of a big black, muscular cat, and during early December at 12:30 pm, Mr Cross saw a cat in Stockbury as he was gardening. He was wheeling a barrow to a rubbish pile at the end of the garden where he was working, when he saw a puma emerge from the hedgerow. It was around four feet long with a long tail.

Mr Pankhurst found the remains of a swan at Nagden Marhes, Faversham Creek which he photographed for me to have a look at. Similar attacks on swans had been reasonably common in the past at Lydd, Romney Marsh. And a man named Jim saw a beige/silvery-grey animal on Saturday 30th December as he was driving in the rain through Doddington. The cat's tail had a black tip, suggesting he'd seen a large puma.

By the end of the year figures were down slightly in reference to sightings around the Medway Towns, but remained consistent in other areas such as Ashford, and down into Sussex as well as Gravesend. By 2007 reports in the local press were pretty much non-existent or appeared as snippets from which I rarely received follow ups. It wasn't a problem, considering the file I'd created in the past, but the *Medway Messenger* had to take notice after I received a flood of sightings in the New Year.

'More than twenty big cats seen on prowl this year', wrote Sam Lennon:

> *The first four days of 2007 produced a rush of big cat sightings, with more than 20 spotted during the period. Big cat expert Neil Arnold said the reports had been throughout north and mid Kent, including Medway.*
>
> *Mr Arnold said: "This year has started manically regarding eye witness sightings."*
>
> *He added that the sightings from 1st January to the 4th were enough to match all of last December's reports. Details of pumas and black leopards being seen came from Medway, Sheerness, Sittingbourne, Faversham, Gravesend, Maidstone and the outskirts of London.*
>
> *Mr Arnold said figures show that more than 250 people have come forward in the past 12 months to tell of sightings in and around Kent alone. He said: "The winter is generally a time when vegetation thins out and these cats will search wider areas for food. They will come into back gardens and towns. Sixty-five percent of sightings this year have been in broad daylight. A majority of those involved are motorists or people out walking their dogs. The public must be informed that these animals are out there, and no longer can such animals be dismissed as folklore. Instead they must be a protected species."*

For two months I was inundated with reports from everywhere except Blue Bell Hill, despite appeals in the Maidstone press. In mid-March 2007 I received a sighting from West Malling of a large, long-tailed animal. In April a woman from the Bearsted area reported seeing a lynx that was yellowy-brown in colour with spots and another witness commented:

> I stopped once to watch the sunset at the edge of the park next to Gillingham Business Park and looked down the path at what I originally thought was a black Retriever dog. I wondered where its owners were and as no-one appeared I moved closer and scared the animal, and then it jumped over nearby brambles to hide in the scrub. I realised it definitely wasn't a dog and had a very long tail, it was a big black cat of some kind more scared of me than I was of it.

A Lee Davies contacted me also:

> In early May my girlfriend was driving past Leybourne lakes, on Leybourne Way heading towards Castle Way, when on the left hand side of the road she saw a large black cat come out from the hedge. She said it was about the size of a Labrador but slimmer, jet black with a long curved tail and pointed ears. She said the ears were the first thing she noticed, then she realised its size and curved tail.
>
> This was about 7:15 am as she works the odd day locally.

On the 23rd May a cyclist spotted the Blue Bell Hill beast at Wouldham as he rode at approximately 10:00 am near the local waterworks. Suddenly, in the field ahead all the rabbits he could see suddenly scattered and a big black cat appeared in the road, standing almost arrogantly, before slipping away. The following day at 9:00 am the wife of a Mr Stevens who'd previously seen a cat in Lordswood and also in the '70s on the Downs, was driving towards Lordswood when a labrador-sized black cat ran across the road sixty feet away.

The next sighting occurred on Friday 20th July when a taxi driver on Harp Farm Road, Boxley, saw a three-foot-long black cat cross the road and head into fields.

Another void of sightings appeared, mainly due to the fact that again, the immediate local press were not featuring the sightings and I'd been promoting my book *Monster! The A-Z Of Zooform Phenomena*, but on 9th September a black leopard was seen sunning itself in the East Farleigh area by Mr Bassett who was walking in the area close to the railway line. As he came around a bend, he came upon the animal twenty feet away. Three nights later a fisherman angling at Hunton was spooked when he found the skull of a sheep and two dead pigeons in a remote area not far from where Mr Bassett had seen the leopard. About an hour after his grisly find, the fisherman spotted a big black panther which he watched for around thirty minutes. He mentioned to me that he'd seen a big cat in Tovil a few years previous.

On September 21st Chris Hunter from the *Kent Messenger* reported on the, *'Midnight meeting with panther made me jump'*, after a Medway woman, driving between Boxley and Lordswood, on the Lidsing Road spotted a large cat.

It looked like a puma. It wasn't a lion', she told the paper.

It was long and had a tail. It was a huge cat. It looked at me like it owned the road...I jumped on the brake. If I had hit it, it would have been big enough to make a nasty dent. I jumped so much I accidentally turned my headlights off.'

The next sighting happened on Tuesday October 9th when a man called Peter was driving along Lacey Lane, Linton, and a black cat the size of a large dog crossed the road. Although visibility was poor, he described the animal as athletic looking.

Meanwhile, Bernadette Tuffs, who photographed the black leopard at Burham encountered another black cat on 20th October at 10:30 am. She was setting off on a family holiday from her home in Margate, heading for Cornwall. When they reached the area of the Detling County Show Ground she spotted a black cat in a light-coloured field. Three days later between Coxheath and East Farleigh at 7:48 am another black cat was seen on the road by a motorist and around the same time at Doddington a woman walking through woods with her son thought she was being stalked by a large animal that remained close but unseen in the woods.

On the 15th November another cat was seen around Sittingbourne this time by a Gillingham man out shooting with a friend. It was 3:00 pm and they stumbled upon two dead rabbits which they thought a bit suspicious and then discovered a dead fox with a serious head wound. Minutes later a JCB in an adjacent field had spooked a large black cat which sped across the field.

One of the men, a complete sceptic who'd criticised the big cat situation for several years said he could n't believe his eyes when he saw the cat. Of course, I'd hate to say I told him so but it's always nice when sceptics have their own sightings.

Three days later a man from Newington, near Sittingbourne at 7:35 am was looking out of the window of his spare bedroom in search of one of his cats when he:

> "...noticed a pale flash run into a large bush which is next to a garden fence which stands on the corner of the road and which is immediately in front of a large and very overgrown field. I thought it might be a new white domestic cat in the area and that it might be interacting with my own pet. I keep a pair of binoculars in the spare room and I decided to observe.

> Whilst focusing on the bush the animal ambled out. I was about eighty yards away, the weather was overcast and drizzly but the light was good.

> I was stunned to see a large cat. I would say it was about three times the size of a domestic cat with a pale, sandy body, a couple of short black stripes leading from the shoulders and a few black spots along the side of its body. It had very pointy ears and a 'beardy' type appearance around the whiskers. This was different in size and appearance to anything I have ever seen.

> It walked along next to the garden fence and then sat down. It jumped up on to the garden fence and then dropped into the garden itself. It then reappeared at the top of the back garden fence, and then dropped into the large overgrown field behind. I looked at a number of big cat pictures on the internet to try and identify what I saw 'identity parade' style. The nearest I could match was a lynx or perhaps a bobcat although the colour in the photos were not alike. The main colour was a pale sandy-yellow type shade."

On the 20th December a Mr Fuller saw a panther at 5:20 pm whilst travelling home from Sittingbourne to Maidstone. The cat raced across the road in front of the car of the witness.

To receive a flurry of sightings relating to the Blue Bell Hill animal brought back all those memories from the early days of my research when the situation was very much about mysticism and intrigue. There were no petty politics involved, or bizarre theories suggesting demonic phantom cats, or researchers displaying cuddly toy panthers at pointless 'anorak style' conferences, it was always about logging and research, the expectancy and the patience, the magic and the buzz of receiving fresh data. Maybe the area of Blue Bell Hill had something to do with it, the crackling atmosphere around the anniversary of the 1965 road accident, or the shadows cast by the looming ancient stones. Something weird was always in the air.

On New Year's Day 2008 at 10:35 pm between Teynham and Faversham a couple driving home from a friend's house caught a set of bright eyes at the edge of the headlight beam. The car was slowed and as they approached they watched in astonishment as a black animal around six feet long leapt into the hedge.

On the 2nd January a twelve-year old boy was awoken at his home at Iwade when the security light came on in the garden. He peered out of the window and saw a huge black figure perched on the six-foot tall guinea pig hutch. The creature gazed up at him, terrifying him so much that he ran to wake his mum up and tell her. When they went back to look the animal was gone.

I hoped that these sightings were of the, or one of the animals that had roamed the Blue Bell Hill area. The cat that was seen on the 22nd February 2008 most certainly was.

It was 9:40 am when a man named Richard was walking down Maidstone Road in Rochester and looked left towards the graveyard that sits bleakly on the horizon. Amongst the jutting stones, he saw a large black cat walk out. The cat had a distinctive long, curled tail and moved off slowly out of sight. Shortly after an appeal in the *Medway Messenger*, I received another call, this time from a woman named Angela who told me that on Saturday February 9th at 8:15 pm, she was in the car with her husband who was driving. They were coming from the Blue Bell Hill area, which during the colder months is always extremely dark and eerie. They were travelling along the 'lower' road, one of two adjacent and tight lanes that run from and to Blue Bell Hill, when fifty yards away a creature scuttled across the road from left to right into the undergrowth. The couple both saw the animal, but never discussed it until they got home. Angela told me that she'd asked her husband if he'd seen the animal, "*Yes*", he replied, and whether it was a fox. "*No*", he answered, "*It was a large cat.*"

She agreed.

Around the same time a puma was observed by Mrs Stockbridge in the Twydall area. She was waiting for a lift from her husband at 1:15 am, after a long evening's work. The cat strolled around the corner and slipped under a fence in the Eastcourt Lane area. She mentioned also that her husband had seen a black leopard at Otterham Key Lane whilst driving and that she had seen a black leopard at Eastcourt Lane in December '07. In the March of '08 a black leopard was also sighted near Kings Hill, at Leybourne, as well as Wouldham, but on April 9th I was to have another fortuitous encounter.

At 8:45 am I was standing on land at the rear of a house at Cobblestones, a quiet close in Hempstead. The area was once a large farm shop that stocked over ten-thousand chickens, but the area, at the time of writing, is merely a bed of chalk and dirt awaiting housing development. I was with my dad. The day was fresh, warm and very clear, the view from the land allowing the vision to stretch beyond Capstone Road and the gradually hilly rise of the field, which for around half-a-mile ascended upwards towards a scrawny fence-line, eventually fading into a thin line of trees that in the distance signalled the start of Hook Wood, a small yet dense stretch into Lordswood. The day previous I'd observed a fox nosing the ground near some horses. The fox was around five-hundred yards away yet quite difficult to pin-point as its rusty coat melted into the dry, yet short grass which faded green into beige.

On the 9th something caught my eye almost on the horizon. Beyond the field where I'd seen the fox was a section of fencing, but a further two-hundred or so yards away, there was another fence, and it was along this, that, from right to left, a black animal was slowly skulking. It moved slowly, weaving along the fence-line, and I motioned to my dad and we stood and watched it for around a minute. Although quite a distance away the creature stood out. It was long in the body, low in the back, and it moved completely unlike a dog, and if it had been a domestic cat it would have been a mere dot on the landscape. As we stood and watched it, the animal suddenly stopped, and sat on its haunches. Seconds later, it got up and continued. It reached what seemed to be a gateway or opening into the farthest field, and continued on by, but then turned back and eventually slipped off through the exit out of sight.

I am totally convinced that this animal was a black leopard, possibly the same animal I had seen with my father on two previous occasions just a mile up the road, in 2000. Around twenty-minutes after an elderly chap and a lady were walking also from right to left, with two dogs, but in the field behind the fence-line where the cat had walked. In the distance, their two dogs, one a terrier-sized white dog, the other a slightly bigger black dog, simply looked like shuffling specks in the distance, and yet they were only a few yards from where the mystery cat had walked, so their size was certainly smaller. We continued to scan the area for another five hours and saw a handful of dog-walkers in the distant field, but none of these walked the path the cat had taken and none of their dogs moved at all like the black animal.

Despite more eyewitness reports of Maidstone and Medway-related cats, I thought it rather apt to end this chapter on my chance encounter.

In relation to the oddness and mystery which centres upon Blue Bell Hill and its surrounding areas, researcher Sean Tudor pretty much sums it all up when he states:

> '*Ultimately, all we can say for Blue Bell Hill is that the evidence - the strength of witness testimony, the subtleties of detail that emerged from the case as a whole, and the remarkable similarities to events elsewhere - suggests that something of an anomalous nature appears to periodically manifest there. What that something is we may never know for certain.*'

Although he was speaking strictly of the various ghostly encounters in the area, I think it's fair to state also that the mystery of Blue Bell Hill and its enigmatic history has proven over time to be a sum of many unusual parts. I'm pretty sure that other cases within this book will prove that to you, dear reader and yet whilst I'm one hundred percent sure that the large cats which roam the black lanes and foggy fields are very real, flesh and blood creatures, putting them in the cauldron of weirdness alongside several far stranger mysteries makes for wondrous entertainment for the press and the public, because there is such a wanton requirement for such esoteric ingredients whether we understand them or not. So, there will *always* be a beast of Blue Bell Hill.

> '*Lend us a pencil,*' *I said.* '*I want to mark on the map all the places where people have seen the Beast – all the reports. Then we'll have some idea where to look.*'

> *The Nature Of The Beast* – Janni Howker

Isle of Sheppey Timeline

AD161
AD 161 is the first known date for which authentic records of the island can be found. The island is mentioned in a work entitled *Geographike Huphegesis* compiled by the celebrated Grecian geographer Ptolemy (Claudius Ptolemaeus). Ptolemy was known as Geographer, Astronomer and Historian, he named the island as "Toliapis".

664-675
Minster Abbey Completed - Queen Sexburga is the first abbess.

798
First Danish invasion. They came back in 832.

It is listed in the Anglo-Saxon Chronicles of that time, that the Vikings constantly raided the Island. The Island offered no defences to its monasteries, with ready access from the shore it was a very easy target for the Viking raiders. It is also recorded that in the AD 850's the Vikings "wintered" on the Island. They refused the local hospitality of salted meat, and by doing so forced the local residents to slaughter its breeding herds which in turn destroyed much of the farm economy.

855
Sheppey ruled by the Danes.

893
Prince Hoestan of Denmark built forts at Scipe (Shurland) and Queenborough.

1071
Canute stayed at Shurland (Scipe).

1052
Earl Godwin attacked Sheppey destroying Minster Abbey.

1066
William the Conqueror installed Barons in Sheppey.

1130
Minster Abbey rebuilt and a Parish Church added.

1248
Leysdown Church built.

1272
Harty Church built.

1279
First Eastchurch church built, it had to be rebuilt again in 1431.

1363
Queenborough Church built.

1366
Queenborough Castle built by King Edward III.

1377-99
King Richard II ordered coastal defences to be built on the Island.

1406
King Henry IV ordered better roads and levied tolls on the local ferry.

1448
Isle of Elmley granted to All Saints College Oxford.

1450
Jack Cade's rebellion attempted to seize Queenborough Castle.

1539
Dissolution of Minster Abbey, the abbey was sold to Sir Thomas Cheyne.

1558
Sir Thomas Cheyne dies. Lord Henry Cheyne (his son) disposes all of his estates in Sheppey.

1582
Queen Elizabeth fortifies Shurland and becomes the Lady of the Manor.

1579
First chemical works started at Queenborough.

1594
Queen Elizabeth re-builds Scocles Farm and indentured it to Sir Thomas Hoby.

1649
Sir Michael Livesey of Parsonage Farm, Eastchurch, signs the death warrant of King Charles I with Augustine Garland, M.P. for Queenborough.

1660
Restoration of Charles II. Livesey murdered in Holland, Garland was sold into slavery.

1665
King Charles II and Samuel Pepys mark out the site for Sheerness dockyard and garrison.

1667
The Dutch invade Sheppey.

1669
Royal Dockyard built and fortified.

1688
King James II tries to escape to France from Elmley.

1732
William Hogarth and friends made a "perambulation to Shepey" (Sheppey) and stayed in Queenborough.

1786
First Wesleyan chapel built at Blue Town followed by the Bethel church in 1787 and followed by the Roman Catholic Church in 1790.

1797
Richard Parker organised the Mutiny at the Nore.

1803
Napoleonic scare, two moats dug for defence.

1820
Admiralty House was built for William Duke of Clarence (The Sailor King) and was the last Royal connection.

1825
Sir Edward Banks planned and laid out the Crescent, Bank Terraces and built the Royal Hotel. Then in 1831 carried out further improvements to the Dockyard.

1832
Queenborough disenfranchised marking the end of it's status as a "rotten borough". A Jewish Synagogue built in Blue Town.

1834
Great cholera epidemic in Sheppey. Parish Unions established.

1836
Holy Trinity Church built. 1837 Queen Victoria ordered all the Churches to be retored.

1860
First bridge and railway built.

1888
Local and District councils formed, Sheppey Rural, Sheerness Urban and Queenborough.

1902-04
Sheppey Light Railway to Leysdown opened and electric trams in Sheerness.

1911
Eastchurch became the cradle of aviation.

1914
First World War breaks out - passports are now required to get on to the island.

1914
H.M.S Bulwark blows up at her mooring near the Naval Dockyard. 1915, *H.M.S Irene* blows up at her mooring near the Naval Dockyard.

1920
Great development in camping facilities at Leysdown.

1929
The Nore Lightship ceased to be used by Trinity House and is removed.

1931
Ferry tolls abolished after 525 years.

1939
Second World War starts. The Isle of Sheppey becomes a closed area and once again passports are required to get on and off.

1940
Eastchurch aerodrome bombed, great number of new recruits killed. Defence forts floated out in the Estuary and anti-submarine boom placed from Shoeburyness to Minster.

1948
Sheppey Light Railway closed.

1953
Flooding did great damage to Sheppey, seawall has to be rebuilt at Cheyne Rock and heightened along its 2 mile length.

1960
A new bridge for Sheppey opened by Duchess of Kent.

1962
The Dockyard closed after 290 years of service to the Royal Navy.

1974
The Island Council taken over and incorporated into Swale District Council.

1978
Island cut off from mainland by snow and floods. And again in 1979 with floods.

1983
An open prison with its own pig farm is created on the site of the former Eastchurch Aerodrome, with two more prisons built at a later date.

1987
In February the island was cut off from the mainland by snow. The military used helicopters to deliver produce to the island.

1987
Hurricane force winds devastated the Island, the historic Holm Oak Tree known as the Crusaders Tree crashes down.

Marshland - Isle of Sheppey

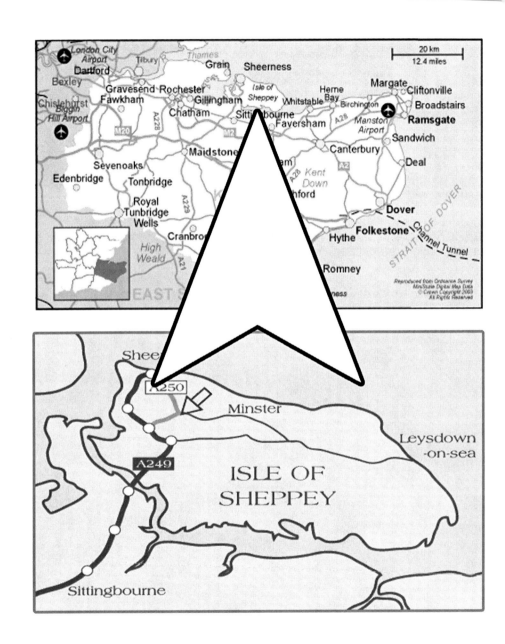

Mystery Cats on the Isle of Sheppey

"The wind was howling and growling...a wind that came off the moors, prowling the streets. You could hear it, but if you kept on listening you fancied you could hear something else. Prowling and growling. It was only the wind."

The Nature Of The Beast – Janni Howker

During the winter months, the Isle of Sheppey is one of the most inhospitable places I've ever looked in for a big cat. The bitter marshes coated in hard frost, the flat, barren landscape littered with pale green, ice-laden pools, forlorn and twisted fences attempting to maintain the desolate horizon as dead birds hang upside down in small, naked and thorny trees like morbid Christmas decorations. Across the marsh, as far as the eye can see are cold walls of mist drifting from the sea and the freezing air bites the face like no other.

According to the website of the BBC:

> *Sheppey is also blessed with some stunning scenery and wildlife. Shellness Beach, for example, is a freak of nature - It's covered in millions and millions of shells. It's also a naturist beach.*

Adding further that:

> *The Isle of Sheppey lies off the North Kent coast.*
> *The island is approximately nine miles long and five miles wide. Sheppey's main seaside towns are Leysdown and Sheerness. It has a population of 35,000.*

The Kingsferry Bridge was once the only way on and off the island but in July of 2006 a new £100m bridge was built.

The Swale Government website commented that:

> *It is expected to enhance life for the thousands of people living on and visiting the Isle of Sheppey. The new Sheppey Crossing dwarfs the existing Kingsferry road and rail bridge, which has earned the island a reputation as a traffic blackspot. Road and rail traffic used to grind to a halt each time the old bridge opened to allow river traffic to pass through; cutting Sheppey off from mainland Kent, albeit momentarily.*

With the opening, motorists can enjoy free-flowing dual carriageways carrying traffic in both directions without interruption.

Legend has always been rife that a large cat of sorts has roamed the island, sticking to the hedgerows which join each field, slinking through the thickets and plucking the abundant bird life, rabbits, and live-stock from the marsh.

Much of the legend of a big cat lurking in the shadows concerns a house on the island which was once said to have housed several exotic animals.

'Approximately twenty years ago, an awful man kept lions, tigers and pumas in his back garden on Sheppey. He was eventually caught out and fined, but not before he had let his animals free to roam the island. Luckily, all of the big cats were caught... except one puma. Over the years there have been various sightings of a big black cat in different areas of Sheppey, but it is all just hearsay. No one has ever managed to take a photo of the animal. So, is it fact or legend? No one knows.'

These comments were made on a local woman's website called *Aspirations From The Darkside*, who also mentioned that:

Sheppey is the home to three prisons. Standford Hill, a Category D prison, stands on the site of an old Royal Air Force station. It holds about 464 inmates. Elmley Prison is a Category C prison with 240 inmates. Swaleside is a high security Category B prison, and holds up to 775 prisoners, most of which are serving life sentences. Many well-known infamous prisoners have and still do serve time in Swaleside. Many a time we've been woken at night by helicopters searchlights; hunting for escaped prisoners!

So, is much of Sheppey's darker history simply exaggerated or indeed truth?

Well, with regards to sightings of large cats, I can vouch that one particular house on the island *did* keep a cat, a puma named Kitten, but such an animal has scarcely been sighted locally, with every report I've investigated instead appearing to concern a black leopard. There was one legend also that a garage possibly at, or near a pub, used to harbour a lion - but again, such facts may have become clouded over time, making the tale an urban legend.

There has been much scepticism thrown towards the possibility that a large cat roams the island, but when one considers the vast amount of prey and marsh, such habitat could certainly hide one cat.

There is also the possibility that such a cat could have come from the mainland, although personal opinion is that such an animal may have been released a few years ago because that's when the sightings really began to hit the headlines. When in 1998 the beast of Blue Bell Hill made the front page, I was able to prove that such a legend had its origins centuries previous, but in the case of the Sheppey 'big cat' finding any kind of history to the enigma has been fruitless.

The first report I have on record from the island comes from 1989 as mentioned in the previous section, when an archaeologist - on a dig with ten other people - allegedly saw a puma at Minster. Mr Oxland from Strood was driving through a marshy area at 7:00 am in November 1998 when a cat, described as sandy-coloured and four feet in length appeared. Rumours circulated previously from areas such as Warden Bay that a large cat was prowling around. The 1998 report, possibly of a puma, remains the sole report from that year although local press on the island weren't, as far as I was aware, covering any such reports. Sightings, as mentioned already, of large cats in the Sittingbourne area were beginning to trickle in but to have received only a couple within a decade suggested either that the original cats seen were misidentifications of other animals such as foxes, despite the witnesses remaining adamant they'd seen large cats, or such an animal was incredibly elusive.

However, in 1999 a report made the national press and certainly proved that something large was roaming the island. On 3rd November *Kent Today* reported:

> *Prowling big cat in attack on dog*
>
> *The dark evenings have arrived and the beast is on the prowl again – this time biting a dog.*
>
> *Police searched the Minster area of Sheppey on Monday after reports that a black panther had attacked and bitten a dog. Police received two calls from members of the public after the animal was seen at Cliff Gardens and Merrydown Hill. The cat was said to be four feet long and two feet high and one person told officers he was certain it was a large black panther.*
>
> *Another person who called police – but officers were unable to trace later – said the cat bit his dog while he was taking it for a midnight walk at Merrydown Hill.*
>
> *Swale police spokesman PC Dave Wisdom said, "It just walked up to his dog, bit it and then ran off."*

The next day the *East Kent Gazette* claimed that, *'pumas crossed to the island'* after the attack, and this report was certainly the first to speak of a large black animal. The *Daily Mirror* briefly covered the report in the same month and during the same month a Sheerness man reported seeing a black cat sitting on a garage roof, but reports certainly weren't flooding in despite appeals on my behalf.

In fact, a man contacting me in 2005 was the only other person able to give any other report from around 99, and that was vague, merely stating it involved a large cat with a smallish tail.

I found it very odd at the lack of sightings I or the press were receiving from the island, despite the fact that more heavily wooded areas from elsewhere in Kent were throwing out heaps of sightings. Amazingly another year slipped by before I received my first ever flap of sightings. Had an animal recently been released or had a large cat mysteriously resurfaced from some unknown place?

On November 6th 2000 the *Times Guardian* of Sheerness briefly reported on a 'leopard' sighting at Leysdown. Leysdown is a haven for tourists who take to the town and stay in caravans. Three days later a Swale Highway Engineer was working at dusk at Eastchurch when a black panther casually crossed the road in front of him. The man called the police who were at the scene in ten minutes but their search was to no avail. However, later in the month geese were taken from a Leysdown farm and the local farmer told me that he'd suspected a large cat - rather than a fox - had been the culprit.

At the beginning of December an angler was digging bait on the shoreline near the looming Kingsferry Bridge when he saw what he could only describe as an, "...*extremely large wild cat*", whilst on December 19th an elderly woman from Queenborough reported something even more strange, "...*a small tiger*" on a garage roof.

Here we had a small island seemingly populated by a small tiger, a black leopard, a possible lynx, and a puma. It was going to be difficult to sort out the fact from the fiction, because the island could certainly harbour smaller animals such as lynx or jungle cat and no-one would ever see them. Whilst I was keen to dismiss the tiger report, despite rumours that such animals may have once been kept in private collections locally, I knew that I had to be looking closely at sightings pertaining to black leopard and puma over anything else. But why the black leopard reports had suddenly began had me scratching my head.

If someone had let go a panther on the island, why were the sightings so few and far between? How often was it coming off the island, if at all? Was it a young cat released as a cub, or an adult?

Mrs Parish attempted to provide me with answers when on December 20th she lost her pet duck of five years, named Daisy, from her home in Minster. The duck had lived in a wood pen in the back garden. One morning Mrs Parish had found a few specks of blood and a couple of feathers in the garden and what looked to be a set of large prints. More feathers were found outside on route towards fields.

When I visited there were expectedly no signs of a large cat, but the woman who was terribly saddened by her loss told me that her five cats had all been reluctant to go outside. I then asked her if she knew anyone who'd kept large cats on the island.

> "A local man kept a black panther and a lion which used to patrol a balcony and someone else also kept two panthers."

It was intriguing stuff, more and more people were mentioning the area once being littered with a handful of cat keepers, or maybe everyone I'd spoken to had become confused. Had they all distorted the case of one man who had kept a puma in a cage? Or had there been several cats kept in cages dotted around the island?

I was sent several newspaper cuttings investigating the local beast sightings. In one it was claimed that a Minster man had lost fourteen ducks to the cat. The birds were kept in an enclosure at the man's home in Southsea Avenue.

The cuttings also cleared up quite a few confusing aspects that were peppering my investigation. The Queenborough woman who stated she'd seen a small tiger actually told the *Times Guardian*:

> "It was black and the size of a dog. I was in bed which is close to a window overlooking Queenborough railway station, when I saw it on the garage roof about ten to twelve feet from me".

The highway engineer told the press that, "It was not a dog, it was about four foot long and two feet high."

Mrs Vicky May said she'd seen a dark coloured cat with a rabbit in its mouth run across the road near the Leysdown light railway.

In the January of the following year a Marilyn Hornigold from Queenborough found her pet hen, Ginger Rogers, decapitated. She told me that although the chicken roosted in a cage up a tree, the body was found in the garden. The body hadn't been touched but the head was missing.

Marilyn, who actually lived in the house which had the huge cage in the garden, added more to the legend when she told me that it was around thirteen years ago that the puma, named Kitten had been kept b a man who had a lot of financial difficulties. She told me that he'd had the puma put down.

She also told me that in 1992 a very close friend of hers had seen a puma sitting on the roof of the then Sheerness Old Dairy on New Road.

It was clear that whether a puma had been released or not, at the time it would have been around seventeen-years old and certainly not responsible for the sightings of a black cat.

On January 8th between the hours of 12:30 and 2:00 am a local female doctor was on call. Accompanied by a fellow doctor she drove to Leysdown taking in the Lower Road. When approaching the Eastchurch turn-off they spotted the rear-end of a large cat in the undergrowth.

The witness said that it was a bright night, the moon was full and despite driving reasonably fast as she was on an emergency call, she got a good look at the hind quarters. The animal would have been around eighteen-inches high, it was a golden brown colour and the tail was long. At first she got the impression that the cat was, "...a mucky tiger", due to the varying shades and also what seemed to be patches on the coat. Despite the strange shades she simply believed that what she'd seen was a puma.

On the 10th a man, who worked at Elmley Prison as a warden, was in a van with two in-mates heading towards a field of sheep they tend, when one of the prisoners spotted a large animal sitting in a coppice just thirty feet away. The warden reversed the van and they all sat and watched a black panther which then casually got up and walked off.

The warden, when I visited him, told me, "It seemed to be a young animal, smaller than a Labrador with a long tail."

Interestingly, during the September of 2000 the warden, whilst driving with an in-mate up Jenkins Hill, observed a large, dark-coloured cat that crossed the road one-hundred yards away. The witness also told me that he knew of a man who kept lynx on the island.

This was simply another intriguing ingredient but I strongly believed that several of the rumours were confused and had all possibly been describing the captive puma called Kitten.

For me the island cat had become just as intriguing as the Bluewater and Blue Bell Hill animals, and yet here was an animal that despite having an abundance of prey to feed on, was pretty much bereft of woodland cover and instead had to stalk the reed beds along the coastal areas, as well as thickets, ditches and dykes dotted around the flat terrain.

It wasn't until the May however that a similar cat would be seen in roughly the same area. A young couple heading towards Leysdown were driving in the vicinity of the prison when suddenly, fifty yards ahead a black animal ran across the road, went up the bank and leapt over a fence out of sight.

The animal was bigger than a fox and low to the ground.

The really odd thing was, I was receiving a handful of reports from the island in clusters, and then nothing for a long stretch. In August 2001 Mrs Parish, who'd lost her duck, told me of two local men from Minster who were up on a roof working one morning when they saw the black leopard. It headed off towards an area known as The Glen. In the same month another witness came forward, Mr Richards who told me he'd seen a cat the previous January. It was 1:30 am and he saw the animal peering through his French doors, but he was to see the cat again on September 4th around 8:30 pm at The Leas, Minster. He and his partner were taking a stroll to get some fresh air when a huge black cat loped across the path in front of them. Both witnesses fled the area in panic.

The trail suddenly went cold again, but in the October the cat hit the headlines in a way I never expected, making it the most unusual account thus far of a large cat in the whole of Kent...

At first I was contacted by Hayley Robinson, the local reporter for the *Times Guardian*, who was quick to rush me startling details regarding a cat that had allegedly been shot and killed on the marsh. The story read as follows:

> '*A builder claims to have seen the big black cat of Sheppey be blasted by pheasant shooters.*
>
> *Steve Morton, 30, was working at the edge of a field in Leysdown when he saw a large cat like animal attack one of the shooter's dogs. He says it was then shot dead and picked up by the shooter who walked off with the animal's body.*
>
> *Mr Morton said: "It was about 11:30 am to 12:00 pm on Saturday October 20th. I was putting up a wall when I noticed twelve to fourteen of these shooters walking down the side of the field. I explained to one of the blokes I was working with, that the youngsters with them were beaters beating down the corn to spook the pheasants so they would fly into the air for the men to shoot. One of the dogs, a black Labrador was picking up a pheasant that had been shot when I saw a large black cat, about three-foot in length coming out of the rough ground. It headed towards the dog and then there was a tussle between them. The next thing I knew one of the men had shot the cat dead. This was no ordinary domestic cat though because when he picked it up half way down the cat's tail, its body was the length of the man's leg and its head was dragging on the ground."*
>
> *Before picking up the body Mr Morton says the other shooters gathered around to see what had been shot.*
>
> *He continued: "It caused quite a bit of commotion because these shooters are not meant to fire at ground level in case they hit a dog or a young beater. I know all this because I used to be a beater when I was younger. I'm an ex-serviceman who has served in the Gulf and Bosnia wars, I've seem some sights in my time but nothing like this. It left me speechless."*
>
> *Angela Walder, chairman of the RSPCA Sheppey Branch said: "If there are no more sightings of the black cat in Leysdown then we can say that this story may well be true."*

For me, such a story was pretty traumatic. I tracked the witness who seemed very sincere as to what he'd witnessed on the marsh. Within a week several of the local papers were quick to cover the story, although I was hesitant for it to make the headlines but knew that such an incident could not be hushed.

'*Big cat shot dead*', '*Is the beast of Blue Bell Hill dead?*', '*Big paws for thought*', wrote the *Medway Today* as various internet sites also jumped all over the story. Of course, I knew that the incident, if true had nothing to do with any of the animals in Medway and that it had been an isolated incident concerning a pretty much isolated cat, out there on the dew-damp marshes. Unfortunately the local press were keen to relate the shooting to every other exotic felid that had ever roamed the Kent countryside, so pretty much believed that all cat sightings would stop.

I was more concerned about what had actually happened on the field, knowing full well that a shooter hunting pigeons wouldn't just randomly blast at a cat that was tussling with a dog. The consequences could've been fatal, but of course, the gunman had to make sure also that one bullet was enough to kill an animal that would have certainly become even more dangerous had it only been injured.

After I wrote about and commented on the story, several people, a few of them shooters, contacted me to say that it was unlikely such an animal had been killed. Although I'd always believed that if any cat was going to get shot it would have been the Sheppey animal, considering the amount of shooting that takes place on the island, but I was still unconvinced. How were a group of shooters traipsing across the marsh able to get so close to a cat such as a black leopard? Had they merely killed a large feral cat? The questions were coming thick and fast, and because there was no body, the answers were not to be found, only theories.

One shooter was quick to dismiss the incident telling me:

> "*Most pheasant shooters would use 1 to 1+ ⅛ of an ounce of 6, 7 or even 8 sized shot. 1 ounce trap shells in 7+ ½ is common. The idea is to bring a bird down for the dogs to collect, not necessarily to kill it instantly. Even at just twenty yards one would not expect a shot that small to penetrate far into a fit, muscular animal. Each pellet would have around 2 foot-pounds of energy – very little* (a quick search on the net found a picture of a guy shot at 10 yards with 6 shot, and barely penetrated the skin!). *While it is not impossible that vital areas were hit multiple times and the animal in question succumbed, my gut feeling is that it would not have died instantly if at all. I would reach for the salt shaker as far as this story goes.*
>
> *The alternative is that this particular guy carried a gun loaded with something far more lethal – but why? And how unlucky for the cat that the one time it went anywhere near a man with a shotgun, he was using something massively in excess of what was needed for his quarry. Could he have been waiting for the cat and been suitably prepared?*"

The comments were intriguing. Had the whole incident been a hoax?

The report didn't make the *Times Guardian* until the 2nd November, by this time the *Medway Messenger* has asked readers to, *'Paws and reflect end of a legend',* despite the fact I was still receiving countless reports from elsewhere in the county.

The headlines simmered down and I wasn't sure if to cease in my research on the island, or hope that someone else would come forward with extra news of the dead animal, but on December 2nd all fears were quenched.

'Latest cat sighting may be cub' commented *Medway Today* of the 5th of December.

> *'A big black cat seen at Eastchurch on the Isle of Sheppey could be the cub of the animal shot dead by pheasant shooters in October.*
>
> *Pat Jackson, deputy manager of Elmley Prison's visiting centre, made the sighting on Sunday December 2nd at 2:40 pm. Her colleagues Sylvia Burden, Sheila Hawksford and June Bowry also saw the large animal which was walking through a field about ninety yards away from the centre.*

Mrs Jackson said: "I was looking out of the window when I saw it. It was black, very large and walking like a lion or a tiger would. I called the three volunteers over and they all agreed it was too big to be a normal cat."

Had the women merely become over-excited after hearing of the recent shooting and wrongly identified a domestic or feral cat? Or was this animal an actual cub of the panther killed in the autumn, if it had been killed at all?

No further sightings continued of the animal which I considered strange after all the fuss, so I was beginning to think that a black leopard had in fact been killed, but the whole mystery just didn't add up despite the seemingly genuine report of the witness. Why hadn't the shooter come forward to say he had or hadn't killed the cat? Surely he had nothing to hide? If the cat had attacked his dog, he could have claimed the right to shoot it - but what had he done with the carcass? Had he buried it? Set fire to it?

Of all farmers, lampers, gamekeepers and poachers I've spoken to over the years, several have come forward to say they could have shot the large cat they were seeing. A few had commented that they'd had such an animal in their sights, but just couldn't, for no reason, shoot it. Of course, I'm sure there are people out there who would gladly hunt and kill such a cat for the challenge, which I found rather disturbing, and I'd been surprised that no hunts had been gathered to comb the island, but surely there was no reason at all to harm such a cat that was doing remarkably well to stay out of the way, give or take a few sightings each year.

At times I was strongly of the opinion that there was no black leopard roaming the island, and that witnesses had maybe seen a feral cat, although there is not much to compare between the two, but witnesses do have a tendency to, at times, see things which are not what they seem. However, when sightings emerge in abundance, it's a different story.

I received footage once from a couple near Borough Green who'd claimed that - on several occasions - they'd seen and filmed a black leopard prowling in the fields behind their home. When I visited the couple they were completely genuine and adamant that what they'd filmed was a big cat, but the footage was nothing of the sort, merely showing a very wild and aggressive feral beast that certainly walked with an arrogant stride, but was nothing at all like a four-foot long panther.

Maybe the sightings of the island's cat were all from a distance, and attacks on livestock and pets had been foxes, despite the fact that farmers were completely positive that it wasn't a fox kill, as they continued to find stripped and headless animals such as ducks and geese, although attacks on sheep seemed scarce.

I took into consideration the prison warden who'd spotted, with inmates, the black cat. They never said the animal was massive, but that it was definitely a panther; so maybe I was dealing with a young cat that had been released maybe only a year or so ago.

During late February of 2002 a woman who lives near Elmley Prison was walking her German Shepherd at around 9:15 am when twenty-five metres away she saw a black cat leap a ditch and slide into the undergrowth. She said the cat was bigger than a fox with a long tail and jet-black, but it certainly wasn't the size of a fully grown leopard.

Spring slipped into summer but there were no more sightings of the animal despite press interest. However, on June 11th at 1:00 pm Mr Cross, driving with his brother along Warden Road towards the local caravan park, came around the bend and saw a pigeon in the road, and then a few feet behind, a large cat

Although flat, the Isle of Sheppey can still provide cover for a large cat. BELOW: Chequers
Road Alley in Sheppey from where a black leopard emerged in 2008 (p. 216)

The old Kingsferry bridge at Sheppey dwarfed by the new construction.

St George's School, Chequers Road, in Sheppey where a black leopard has been seen. (p. 216)
BELOW: Large dog print mistaken for big cat print on Sheppey

The house at Sheppey with the mystery cage (p.217)

side-on. Mr Cross stopped the vehicle and they watched the cat for a few seconds. He said, "*It was knee-high, black with a long tail and a square head. It was slender but well built.*"

This description seemed to match all the others from the island which made a change from the inconsistent reports that had plagued me from elsewhere in Kent describing big, small, slender, muscular, black, brown, greyish, slinky and stocky cats. However, I needed more, because this time I couldn't just accept one report and let it go for another few months. Thankfully, on the 20th June, a woman from the Warden Bay area had a strange experience. She'd found a headless rabbit in her garden and mentioned to me also that five weeks previously a dark-coloured cat the size of a sheep dog had been seen near Eastchurch at 11:15 pm.

Despite the two reports, it was becoming increasingly difficult to get witnesses from the island to come forward. Maybe this was because people just weren't seeing the animal, or didn't know where to report it, but it was a frustrating time for me. Every glimpse brought with it hope, but other reports were vague. A man photographed a set of prints near Eastchurch which were certainly from a cat, but they measured not much bigger than the foot of a domestic cat.

As summer flittered by, my research was aimed at Gravesend after the strange sightings reported by Mr Marsden as mentioned earlier in this chapter. I knew in the back of my mind that unless I went to the island and stayed there for some time, I wasn't going to receive that many reports because publicity certainly wasn't drumming up any more activity as it stood.

I waited another two months before another sighting came along, this time involving a man and his two dogs who flushed a black cat from a reed bed at Sheerness on Monday 30th September at around 2:00 pm. The cat emerged from the vegetation, jumped a ditch and disappeared into another reed bed. On the 2nd October they saw the animal again at roughly the same place and time, but I was extremely dubious of both sightings just due to the fact that some of the details I received from the witness led me to believe that they'd either made it all up, or were simply trying to track the beast themselves. Again I was deeply frustrated, but on the 3rd October a woman named Maria, driving along Brielle Way, Queenborough, with her boyfriend, at 2:30 pm saw a large black cat in a nearby field. The animal appeared to be stalking possibly a bird or a mouse. The couple were so excited that they came back for another look but the cat had mysteriously vanished.

Did the sighting add validity to the Sheerness sighting a day before? It didn't matter, I was just relieved to continue to hear of reports but knew full well that this cat had a whole island to itself, from rolling, pitted marshes to strips of undergrowth, as well as the dark alleyways that separated houses, and the cliff line.

Seven days later a Mrs Tuckwell was walking her dog with a friend at 6:30 pm near fields at Leysdown. They stood watching a field of sheep and suddenly picked out a black felid with a long tail that appeared to be stalking the flock. The animal got to within a few yards of the sheep and dropped in a posture as if ready to pounce. The animal did this three times, but not once whilst the women watched did it strike at the sheep. After around five minutes the cat decided to walk away.

Two hours previously a man driving towards the Kingsferry Bridge with his nephew observed a big black cat, around three feet long strolling across the marsh. Was this animal proof that the Sheppey cat was moving on and off the island?

Many of the questions were frustratingly unanswerable, but I began to think that the sightings were to become more than a trickle, but just as quickly as the cat had filled the imagination of the public, so it disappeared, leaving 2002 bereft of any more Sheppey sightings. I knew also that 2003 would probably run in a similar vein with only a handful of sightings. I was right. In fact it would be another eight months before the elusive animal reared its head, this time on 10th August '03 when Peter Hill was sitting with his wife and a friend at 1:00 am, over-looking the beach at Sheerness. It had been a warm day and still cool into the early hours as they relaxed and chatted. From the darkness they all watched a black cat, the size of a collie dog with a long tail stroll along the beach. The friend reported the sighting to the local paper, and then, a day later a woman walking her dog at White Way Road, Queenborough, saw a big cat in a nearby field. After such a long period of inactivity, was a minor flap beginning to take place? Surely not, I thought. Yet, during early September Mr Blackmore described seeing the same animal on the beach at Sheerness and also at 1:00am. He'd been sitting on the nearby steps and watched the cat emerge from the darkness, head towards a bus shelter, jump up on the seat, and then head off into the night.

Admittedly, I was hardly being swamped by eyewitness reports of the local beast, but a handful in a short space of time meant I could attempt to work out the route this cat was taking. During the November it showed up at Minster, at 1:00 pm near Barton Hill Farm and was witnessed by Mrs Kay who was digging soil in a car-park garden when something caught her eye around thirty feet away in a nearby field. She watched as a cat, around four feet long with a long tail strolled across the open space and went towards Barton Point. Then, the year was out with a whimper and the Sheppey leopard faded once again into the annals of the island's folklore.

During the February of the next year the cat was back, and in the same location, this time sighted by a woman named Deborah who was tending to her chickens, but found seven dead. Two of these had been completely stripped of flesh. She'd had chickens killed by foxes in the past, but there was no mess and she was sure that the local cat was to blame. Around the same time Mr Lynch was driving at 6:00 pm from Sheerness to Minster, near a local restaurant when a large black cat ran across the road some forty feet ahead towards Irwin Park. Mr Lynch claimed that the cat was over six feet in length and had bright yellow eyes.

I was pretty convinced by this point that only one large black cat was roaming the island, so expected sightings to be few and far between. Mr Lynch reported seeing something bigger simply because the way the cat moved low to the ground across the road. I didn't believe for one minute he'd seen a different cat to what everyone else had reported. On the 4th March at 11:00 am a local post woman delivering mail near Brights Wood got the shock of her life when she saw a big black cat sitting just fifty feet away. The animal, which she described as around four feet long, headed off towards the small pocket of woods, and on the 26th at Minster, a woman standing in her kitchen on Bell Farm Lane with her mother, at 1:45 pm, saw an animal at the end of the garden, forty-metres away. They described the animal as bigger than a fox with a long tail, and it headed towards the direction of the caravan park.

The next sighting wasn't reported to me until Wednesday 23rd June, at Plough Lane near Shurland Farm when two witnesses in a car, at 7:15 am, saw a cat emerge from the hedge fifteen-metres away and crossed the road, heading away from the approaching vehicle. Although the witnesses claimed the animal was black, they recalled that it had a white mark near its neck, was bigger than a Labrador but with no apparent tail. The witnesses admitted to being confused by the animal but until a similar sighting was reported, confusion was something I couldn't afford to let in. However, despite the strange details observed in this incident, not long after a couple walking along Rowetts Lane, Eastchurch, at 3:00 pm saw a large cat which bounded across the road. It leapt a four-foot-high fence.

Whilst I was ready to once again report the sighting to the press I was stunned when the witness, a Mrs Lawson told me, *"The animal was tan-coloured, bigger than a labrador, with massive, muscular back legs, a smallish head but standing more than two feet at the shoulder."*

It sounded like the perfect description of a puma, and this had certainly been my first ever reported on the island and I quite simply couldn't get my head around it. Naturally, such a cat is a very elusive animal, but why had no one else ever reported such an animal from the island? Had it recently crossed from Sittingbourne? I was completely bewildered because now people were suddenly suggesting more than one cat on the island, but this cat had been the subject of urban legends for years since the construction of the cage in the back garden of one of the houses on the island, but this cat clearly wasn't that same animal allegedly put down around 1992. And on July 1st at 9:45 pm a taxi-driver travelling along Bell Farm Lane saw a labrador-sized cat cross the road twenty-five yards away. The witness said the animal was black and sleek.

So, suddenly two sightings of two different species of cat. And then…nothing, not until December when a girl named Donna claimed to have seen a cat which she blamed for killing a rabbit in her garden. The witness also stated that the cat had often been seen near the Kingsferry Bridge and that her dog had rolled around in its scent. Then, two days before Christmas a man from Minster reported the following, *"I was walking with my dogs at 4:15 pm and I turned around and saw a big brown-black animal running about eight yards away in front of me. It saw me, changed direction and run into long grass. I called the dogs and went to look but all I could see was the grass moving a distance away."*

Thankfully I only had to wait a fortnight for the next sighting to come about. On 12th January 2005 at 11:00 am two male friends were sitting in the conservatory belonging to one of them, at Warden Bay, when they both saw a black animal moving across the field at the end of the garden a few hundred yards away. The owner of the house reached for his binoculars and watched the cat for around fifteen minutes. They both said it was around three feet in length.

They also mentioned previous activity from the last November when on the 19th something had crashed on to the conservatory roof, and neighbour's had had a similar experience around the same time. Then during early January a similar incident occurred, but no sign of the animal, and no further sign for the next few months, until Sunday 29th May when Mr Cooke walking to a friends house near Cliffe Gardens, at 11:00 am saw a massive jet-black cat as he walked up an alleyway. Mr Cooke was so unsettled by the sighting that he called the RSPCA.

Around the time quite a lot of focus was being put on the local sightings, and yet the year rolled by uneventfully regards to the Sheppey big cats. On the 27th December (yes, it really had been that long!) I received my last Sheppey sighting of the year, I guess good things always came to those who waited but this was ridiculous!

Mr Luckett wrote:

> *"1:00 pm – Brights Wood, Eastchurch. My wife and I were taking a walk with our daughter to the wood at the top of Kent View Drive. It was early afternoon and following the snow fall the sky was clear with bright sunshine. As we approached the gate to the field I saw a large black cat walking from right to left along the path directly in front of us about fifty to sixty yards away. It stopped briefly and I pointed it out to my wife. We both then watched it walk on a little further and vanish into the bushes. We investigated the area and found paw prints in the snow leading up the field into the tree line. The cat was around four feet long and two-foot tall."*

It was an impressive sighting, and one that was long overdue. As always, another followed soon after on the 3rd January at Oak Lane, Minster when a married couple sitting in their lounge at 9:30 pm were distracted by the security light coming on in the garden. Around one-hundred feet away a Labrador-sized cat, low to the ground and with a long tail, slinked by. A week previous it was seen around the same time by the couple. Even more amazingly, on the same night a woman named Pauline, who lives at Plough Lane, was looking out of her window during the evening when she saw a large cat, black, watching sheep, but they - in turn - seemed unaware of the animal stalking them. I had a long chat with Pauline who told me also that on Christmas Eve just gone something snarled in her back yard and aggravated her dog, and in the autumn she saw the cat on several occasions as it walked through the yard, but the most interesting details she told me was the rumour that some fifty-years previously a selection of wild animals were kept at the port of Sheerness. What kind of animals remains unclear.

It was certainly uplifting to talk to someone who clearly had a lot of knowledge of the local area and had had several personal sightings. On February 17th an interesting story appeared in the *Medway Messenger* in the 'County Briefing' section and read as follows:

> *'Owner and pet attacked by savage dog'* – *'An evening stroll turned into a nightmare for Michael Ball and his puppy when they were savaged by a dog running loose in a field. The attack near Mr Ball's home in Leysdown Road, Bay View, Sheppey, left him needing treatment at a plastic surgery hospital and his eighteen-month old boxer, Ruby, with devastating injuries.*
>
> *Mr Ball's wife Valerie said: "It was an horrendous attack and people need to be aware there is a dangerous dog on the loose. My husband knows the dog was big, black and heavy-set but because it was dark it is difficult to say if it was a pit bull or a Rottweiler, but it was much bigger than Ruby. The dog ran over with no colour or lead and then went for Ruby. She was lying on her back and screaming with pain as it ripped into her and my husband had his hand torn as he tried to separate them."*
>
> *Mr Ball returned home, but his injuries were so severe he was taken to Medway Maritime Hospital, Gillingham. Ruby was taken to a veterinary hospital in Maidstone. Mrs Ball said: "Her treatment has already cost £800 and it was thought she might have suffered permanent nerve damage. Mr Ball now has to go to the hospital in East Grinstead for treatment. Some of his fingers were almost torn off as he tried to separate the dogs. Swale Borough Council's dog warden is investigating the incident which happened earlier this month.'*

Personally, I didn't want to jump to any conclusions, but judging by the severity of the injuries, and the fact that Mr Ball couldn't clearly see the attacker, was there a possibility the black leopard had attempted to kill his dog? Remember a similar incident when a dog was bitten a few years previously?

Nothing came of the incident and as far as I'm aware no dog was ever found or blamed for the attack.

On the 11th May a black cat was seen near Barton point, Minster at 11:30 am. The cat was described a around four feet in length. Also during the summer a Minster man walking with his two dogs near Cliff Gardens at 1:00 am saw a big black animal cross the road near the school. The cat had short legs and long, thick tail. The cat was seen in the same area once again by a woman in the November at 10:00 am She was standing at her bedroom window with her mother-in-law looking out towards Seacliffe Caravan Park when a big black cat with a long tail casually strolled through the park and out of sight. The witness told me that the guy who owned the park had known of several sightings in the area. Then, on the 29 December, again at Cliffe Gardens, at 9:16 am, a woman named Heather spotted the cat whilst she was waiting for a bus on the Chequers Road. She couldn't believe her eyes when the labrador-sized black cat came from the direction of St Georges School, crossed the road just forty feet away and headed off into an alleyway. Seconds later, an elderly woman approached from the direction of the alley to say that a big, black cat had just brushed by her.

On New Year's Day of 2007 a woman in exactly the same area as the previous sighting was walking home from a friends when she saw the cat. It was around 4:15 pm, and the cat emerged from the alleyway it had gone into previously and crossed the road towards the school. As it reached the middle of the road a motorist had to brake suddenly in his 4x4 vehicle, but the cat remained unperturbed and disappeared out of sight.

Of all the places on the island it was quite bizarre that the cat was appearing in broad daylight and in such a built up area. Of course, the alleyways were proving crucial to its territory but it was still unusual for such an animal to be seen so frequently in such an area. Again though, the sightings suddenly ceased, until the end of June when a bizarre sighting took place. A family in a caravan at Minster cliffs saw a large cat around 2:00 am and identified the animal as a lynx. They heard the cat making "funny noises" and picked it up in the torch light before it turned away. A lynx was certainly a new one for the database, but I was always of the opinion that a lynx could easily exist on the mashes and elude witnesses. Again though, the Minster area was proving to be a haven for sightings, although several months later, on 22nd September at West Cliffe Drive I received the following report:

> A large black, cat-like animal, the size of a dog, observed lying in the sun licking its paws, for up to an hour. When moving, held its tail close to the ground – but the tail was bushy. Our first thought was that it may be a black fox, although there doesn't seem to be such a thing. It had cat-like ears.

During the same month at 10:30 pm also at Minster cliffs, a man out lamping caught a big black animal in his torch beam which jumped a fence with ease. The next day a friend of the man claimed to have seen the cat at 11:00 am when it was sunning itself in the same area. Meanwhile, brief, blurry footage of a large cat was taken on a mobile phone and posted on the *YouTube* website for a short time. Although the clip was only a few seconds long it clearly showed a black leopard, muscular in the shoulder with a long tail slinking off into the undergrowth somewhere on the island. At the time of writing it remains the best evidence as yet to suggest a black leopard is roaming the island.

On the 1st February 2008 a Mr Dixon taking a morning stroll at 7:00 am to get the newspaper from the local shop, in the vicinity of Warden Bay, saw, twenty-five yards ahead a large, dark-coloured animal he at first took to be a dog. Awaiting an owner, the witness approached, as another man walked passed, and realised the animal was in fact a cat, over two feet in length with a long tail. The observer told me he was sure it was a young looking panther. The cat was heading away and went in the direction of Leysdown, following the coastal line. It certainly wasn't the same animal seen on the 24th of February at 1:15 am. A man named Clive, from the Minster area was alerted to his garden when the security light came on, and shocked to see an Alsatian-sized black cat lope across the lawn.

Around the same time a very informative lady rang me from the island and stated she'd seen the cat, which she said was bigger than an Alsatian, near Minster, on three separate occasions in one specific place at approximately 5:45 am. The details she gave me were interesting to say the least and certainly pin-pointed one specific area where this elusive leopard crosses, an area that I certainly have under close surveillance. She also remarked that she recalled someone owning a lion, and also a chimpanzee around fifty years before in the area.

In April 2008, a black leopard terrified a woman in the Eastchurch area. Her partner had been awoken at 4:45 am by loud banging coming from downstairs. It sounded as if someone or some 'thing' was banging against the glass of the kitchen door. The man investigated but found nothing. He then got dressed and went to work. At 6:10 am his girlfriend was also awoken by the same loud banging and then the sound as if someone was running up and down the patio. She phoned her parents who, fortunately for her, lived next door, and once she knew they were awake she decided to look out the bedroom window, where she was shocked to see an enormous black cat in the vicinity of a narrow lane at the end of the long drive-way. The back end of the animal disappeared in front of some stables and then it reappeared on the lane, turned left, then quickly right and then went out of sight.

Hopefully no bodies will turn up of cats allegedly shot, but as big cat mysteries go, the Sheppey animal, or animals, remain one of the most intriguing in that we are scarcely hearing of a cat that is inhabiting a region pretty much bereft of woods. Among other bouts of weirdness, the black leopard, and possibly other mysterious felids, remains the island's most well kept secret.

The Sheppey big cat mystery deepened again. A man named Vic called me to say he'd seen the black leopard from just twenty feet in April '08 at 5:00 pm after something had disturbed his geese at his home in Eastchurch. He walked to the bottom of the garden overlooking the sea wall, and saw the animal perched, with its rear paws on the post of the chain-link fence and its front feet precariously on a freshly cut shrub stem. Startled by the appearance of the man, the cat stumbled and fell into brambles on the other side and was lost from sight. Vic told me that the animal was around two-foot-six inches long with a tail around fifteen inches long and two inches thick. Vic told me that he'd lived on the island since 1989 and we began to discuss the alleged large cat kept in a cage somewhere. Vic commented, *"Yes, I used to see it all the time and drive by, the cage was on the Queenborough Road, and it's still there I believe."*

I replied, *"That's right, but it's not connected to the sightings now because it was a puma."*

"No", he responded quickly. *"The animal was black."*

In the August of 2008, the BBC approached me to make a documentary on the 'big cat' said to roam Sheppey, with the aim of setting up a trigger-camera for one week in the hope of catching the elusive animal on film. I agreed to do the shoot, as long as witnesses were treated with respect, and all those involved were genuine. Thankfully, the three days of filming turned out to be a positive experience, and many thanks must go to Sarah Brinicombe, the show's researcher and Vince Rogers, the editor, for showing such an interest.

Although no cat was caught on the camera, which was set up opposite an alleyway, where numerous sightings of what appeared to be a black leopard had taken place previously, coincidentally, a sighting *did* emerge whilst we were filming on the first day. On Monday 11th August, after we had done a shoot on the island, I received a call from a man named John who claimed that whilst driving at 9:45 am towards Queenborough, he saw a large, fawn/sandy-coloured cat, smaller than a Labrador, prowling across a field which was occupied by some horses. The cat purposefully made its way across the pasture, and headed towards a nearby road. John stated that, *"The cat was muscular and seemed to have a dark tip to its tail."*

Bizarrely, John mentioned that two years previous, his friend, a Mr Elliot, had also seen a similar cat which they both believe is a puma - in the same area. Things certainly became weirder with regards to the legends of large cats on the island. Then, after a day filming with the BBC at Herne Bay's Wildwood Park (who, coincidentally, at the time had received a report of a dead raccoon on the outskirts of their grounds!) where I was lucky to spend some time in a cage with a lynx, we then did some more Sheppey filming at the end of August to complete the shoot.

It was here that I finally met the couple who owned the house on the island which harbours a very large, mysterious yet now dilapidated cage. Despite all the confusion and legends of the past pertaining to the cage, the couple were finally able to tell me exactly what animal inhabited the enclosure and when. Although the cage was now occupied by a very angry, hissing goose, standing inside it was quite awe-inspiring, knowing that once, not so long ago, a large cat, possibly black leopard or puma had sat there.

After a cosy chat with the house owners they filled me in on the mystery, and stated categorically that during the 1980s the house was owned by a man who kept several strange animals and one of these was a puma called `Kitten`. Despite a handful of people telling me that as they went by on the local bus, they'd seen a black animal in the cage, it seems their memories have become clouded. The puma, at around the age of four, was allegedly put down, mainly due to the fact it was too expensive to maintain, and due to its size was becoming simply too difficult to keep.

The man who lives in the house now was quick to tell me of his past playful encounters with the cat which sat in its pen, which measured around twenty-five feet in length by fifteen-feet in width. He spoke of how buses used to come by and slow down so passengers could observe the local wild cat. However, he also commented that in the '70s there were several sightings of a puma on the island, and so the owners of Kitten, to avoid people knocking on their door and accusing them of letting their cat go, put a sign up on the roadside of the cage which read something along the lines of, "Don't worry I'm still here."

So, the mystery of the caged animal is now solved, but those in the Sheppey wilds continue to baffle.

'In the centre of this room, lying in the middle of a golden patch of sunlight, there was stretched a huge creature, as large as a tiger, but as black and sleek as ebony. It was simply an enormous and very well-kept black cat...'

The Brazilian Cat – Sir Arthur Conan Doyle

Chequers Road Alley in Sheppey where a
black leopard has been seen (p. 216)

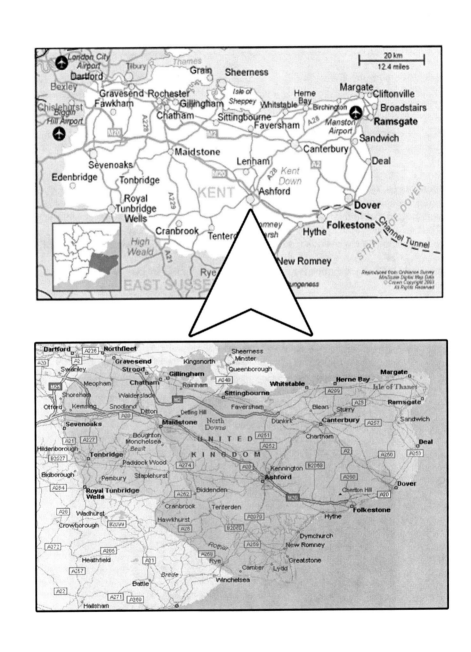

Ashford and other East Kent Mystery Cats

"Then we saw the Beast. It was one of those blurred pictures. You had to look hard but there it was. The shape of it, crouched over something, and two flashes of its eyes."

The Nature Of The Beast – Janni Howker

There are so many mysterious felids roaming Kent that in fact I could write a book on each large town and its feline inhabitants. Of course, space does not allow that here, otherwise this book would simply be devoted to the county's exotic cat populations, and other volumes would surely follow. Such turgid ramblings are quite unnecessary, hence these sections in which I can offer you a glimpse into the bewitching woods where these beasts are said to roam.

Ashford alone is probably Kent's most populated town when it comes to large, prowling cats of seeming unnature. The town sits on the River Stour, and is strong in its agricultural roots, described as:

> '…an old market town and all the vibrancy of a modern international gateway. A rich mix of historic buildings, some dating from Medieval, and Georgian times, beautiful floral displays and plenty of street entertainment create a welcoming feel, while Ashford's International Eurostar Station and street cafés lend a truly continental ambience.'

Ashford is mentioned in the *Domesday Book* under its original name, Essetesford, (or Eshetisford, Esseesford, Asshatisforde, and Essheford), the name meaning something along the lines of, 'ash trees growing near a ford', or 'a ford over the river Eshe or Eshet'. It is believed as a town to have originated from round 893 AD.

Sightings of large cats of hazy vagueness once again date back several centuries, particularly in the extensive wooded area known as Challock Forest. However, despite the thick vegetation and sprawling greenery, reports from Ashford have been consistent all through my years of research, and as mentioned above, to list even fifty percent of reports would require a whole book alone. And so, let me use this section to introduce you to the various other elusive felids roaming elsewhere in the county.

One of the first recorded 'modern' accounts emerged during the 1950s. In 2001 a retired teacher contacted the local *Kentish Express* to report a sighting she'd experienced in Broomfields, Willesborough, near the old hospital. She was only a young girl, but clearly recalled seeing a big black cat in the local fields. However, one has to only look at Ashford on a map to realise the potential habitat to hide a decent number of cats. The town and its vast woodlands, sliced by the M20, stretch into Canterbury, and slip onto Romney Marsh, an area of boggy trenches, nefarious winds and bleak, sheep-littered landscapes.

Ten years before the Ashford sighting, possibly around 1948 or '49, a man and his wife living near Nackington, south of Canterbury, spotted what they thought was a large dog on their land. The 'dog' visited the surrounding fields on several occasions, remaining along the misty hedgerows, and never once getting a reaction from their own gun dogs. Then, on one afternoon the animal leapt up a tree with ease, and left one of their dogs cowering, it was then they realised that the visitor was a large cat-like beast. It remained in the immediate vicinity for around two months, where on one trip involving the man and his brother, and sister-in-law, came face to face with it. They claimed it was a puma, and as it shrunk into the undergrowth, little did they realise this would be the last time they'd ever see the shy animal.

Canterbury, with its two castles and six museums, is still considered the ecclesiastical capital of the country, and is visited each year by thousands of tourists who revel in its historical splendour and priestly decor. Like Rochester, much of its history still remains embedded in the town, interwoven with today's more commercial structures. The view of the looming cathedral is awe-inspiring as it rises above the high street with its winding pathways which slip into medieval kingdoms almost forgotten. The rural aspect of the town is simply a wistful and calming voyage into ancient history, where villages such as the charming Chilham still promote the past with banquets and feasts and entertaining jousts.

In 1957 John Aspinall opened Howletts Zoo in Canterbury, and in 1973 started Port Lympne, at Lympne near Ashford. Both zoo parks combined house over one-thousand animals. Many witnesses who've seen large, exotic cats roaming the wilds of Kent have pointed the finger at such places, believing that cats and other animals have all too easily escaped into the wild, and never been traced. Whilst there have been reports in the past of animals such as tigers and leopards escaping from these parks, I do not believe that such escapees were responsible for much of today's populations, despite the stories I continue to hear.

In the 1960s there was rumour that an Ashford lady, possibly at Charing, kept big cats. Again, such local tales seem common, and are always uttered when new sightings turn up. There's always someone out there who recalls someone knowing someone who kept a cat, but again, whether these small collections could have been responsible for the sightings of today seems unlikely, but would certainly have added to the situation.

In 1967 a Mrs Hills from Willesborough recalled seeing a big cat whilst with her husband, daughters and dogs in Westwell Woods. Her bright and bouncing pets began to cower and whimper when they approached a clearing. Suddenly a black panther emerged from the woods, and just stood there staring at the frightened witnesses.

On the 21st December 1970 the *Evening Standard* reported that there'd been seven reports of a puma over a three-week period at Buckland Housing Estate, Dover. Four sheep had been killed in the area also.

Dover is reputedly one of Kent's most haunted places, especially its castle. The town is known as the 'Lock and Key of England', the area and its shoreline once considered a prime target for many enemies including Julius Caesar and Hitler. Today, Dover still relies on the harbour for its prosperity. It is the busiest passenger ferry terminal in the world, the busiest cruise liner terminal in Britain and a major port for freight, particularly for fruit and other perishables imported via the massive reefer cargo ships.

Neighbouring Deal was only created to serve ships who anchored there. Originally, the town didn't have a lot going for it!

Many reasons for the establishment of a small town are absent in the case of Deal: adequate fresh water, a ford across a river, or an important cross roads for example. The nearest good water was two miles away and considerable efforts had to be made to obtain a supply. No important roads passed through Deal, even today one must make a detour to get to the town.

Facts against the area as a site for a community would include the liability to flood, both from the sea and the flood plain of the River Stour, the land lying behind the shingle bank was marshy, the Sea Valley (High Street) was not dry until the 17th Century and the fact that the area could not be easily defended against attack.

writes *The Deal Maritime And History Museum* website. Today the town still prides itself in the parade of its buildings dating back to the 1800s where tales of smuggler's were once rife.

Next to Dover, along the coast, lies Folkestone, situated at the lower edge of the North Downs. It remains a popular coastal resort, and Margate even more so, which attracts thousands each year who flock to its beach and parade of seafront shops and arcades. Margate is one of three main seaside resorts belonging to Thanet, the other two being Broadstairs and Ramsgate. Despite the harsh winds and foamy tides which batter the harbours of all these seaside towns, large cats have been seen prowling the streets, not on a regular basis (with the exception of Dover and Deal), but enough to suggest that such sightings were not mere illusions or misidentifications.

During the early 1970s at Dymchurch, which is situated on the edge of Romney Marsh, a Mrs Howes, travelling at night in her car on Eastbridge Road, saw a large dark-coloured cat which crossed the road. Rumour had it that a similar cat had been seen around St Mary's Bay for many years previous.

In 2002 a Mr Bishop phoned me to speak of several incidents that took place during the '70s at Mersham, Ashford.

- 1975 – A sheep which died of natural causes was next day found completely stripped.
- 1978 – Mr Bishop was walking his dogs near to his home when a large black cat with bright eyes jumped a hedge and sped across the road.
- In the same year a female witness saw two large cats together in the High Halden area, and a neighbour of Mr Bishop said his son had seen a cat, with a rabbit in its mouth in a nearby field. The witness tried to follow the cat in his car but it jumped a four-foot high fence and disappeared out of sight.

Sightings in general from the '70s were pretty inconsistent though, especially from the towns of Ramsgate, Folkestone and Margate where any reports which made the headlines simply spoke of 'big cats' or vague details pertaining to grey or striped felids. Despite the introduction of the Dangerous Wild Animals Act in '76 there was no evidence to suggest that a great number of cats had been released in east Kent, and the '80s didn't do much to disprove this.

In 1985 a woman from Woodchurch, a few miles from Tenterden, was riding her horse with her daughter when a large slinking feline form slipped into the woods. A month or so later the woman found her foal with a huge slash in its lower jaw. Six months later the animal was found dead, but no marks were apparent although the vet claimed the poor creature had been dropped from a great height! A mysterious, non-cat related death indeed.

Mr Hirons contacted me in 2006 via email.

> *I thought I would let you know that I saw a big cat in a place called Whitfield near Dover around November 1989. I was staying on a Caravan and Camping Club Certified location while working on the Channel Tunnel Radio Communications Systems for Transmanche Link.*
>
> *One night around 2:00 – 3:00 am I was awoken up by the wheelie bin being pulled over on the left hand side of my caravan. I got up, got my torch and came out my caravan door on the right hand side, walked round, shone the torch towards the bin and was confronted by a very large cat. The cat had pulled the bin over and was looking head down in to the bin. When I came round the caravan it turned to face me. The features of the cat were distinctive yellow eyes, ears that seemed to have a point and black tuft on them and the most striking feature was black rings on its tail which was upright and the end was twitching. The cat walked slowly towards me and I backed away from it. It was less than ten feet from me. I backed away from the cat and I was really shocked to see the size of it. The cats head seemed level with my waist and I fled back into my caravan.*

Just what was this monster cat that approached Mr Hirons without any fear? Had he seen a puma, the same cat that had allegedly haunted the strip of the River Stour in the '80s and had been heard to scream on numerous occasions by local farmers and men out shooting? Possibly not. Mr Hirons claimed that whilst on a visit to Twycross Zoo, in Leicestershire, he saw an animal that resembled the huge cat, but what he pointed out was a Scottish wildcat which in no way would reach waist height. I believe that Mr Hirons saw a lynx and that its tail wasn't that long, but upstanding.

Strangely, despite the beast of Exmoor hitting the headlines in the '80s, Kent was certainly low in the league of cat sightings by county. Was this because such animals just didn't roam areas of east Kent or there was no-one interested in the reports? I opt for the latter, because the trickle of sightings still suggested that handfuls of reports were reaching the press and the police each month but being shoved to the wayside. The fact that the '90s literally exploded into life suggested that an explosion in the population had occurred, or a lot of cats had been released at one time, which seems unlikely. With regards to Kent, was the county on the backlash after fourteen years of cats inhabiting the wilds, or had the thick woodlands and expansive Downs simply refused over the last fifty years to expose their mysterious inhabitants?

During the early '90s as more and more cats began to be sighted, as covered in the previous sections, Dover, Ashford and the surrounding towns began to hit the local headlines.

On 6th March 2001 a man named Sean contacted me with an interesting tale.

> '*I am writing to inform you of a black panther I encountered in Orelstone Forest, Hamstreet on the evening of 17/4/93. As an entomologist with an interest in moths, I was running light traps within the forest with friends, and the panther was seen just prior to dusk.*'

Kindly, the man sent me a copy of the July 1998 *Atropos* magazine in which his letter regarding his sighting had been printed. It read as follows:

'…it was then that the three of us saw a large black cat leap out of the woods, over the water-filled ditch to the side of the ride, across the main ride in a single bound…(w)hile we were still taking in what we had seen the same animal came back across the ride, again in three huge leaps before disappearing back into the woodland, not to be seen again. The ride at the point where the animal had crossed was about seven feet wide while the ditches to either side were just over four feet in width. The animal appeared all black with a long, thick tail and we estimated its total length from nose to tail-tip to be five feet, including a tail-length of two feet.'

The forest, stretching from the edge of the marsh into Ashford, would become extremely active with regards to big cat sightings.

In 1994, Dover was to be caught up in a spate of sightings.

'Grey men hunt black cats' read the *Kent Today* of September 20th 1994, showing a map of cat sightings throughout east Kent, plus a photo of PC Ian Woodland holding plaster casts of alleged big cat prints.

'The Grey Men from the Ministry are investigating reports of a big cat claimed to be stalking the Kent countryside.

Officers from the Ministry of Agriculture, Fisheries and Food have contacted animal lover Dave Riches for his account of the black panther reportedly living in east Kent. The Government department has been involved in the hunt for the so-called beast of Bodmin Moor and last month officials met farmers, landowners and police in the west country to discuss their big cat.

Dave, who runs a wildlife refuge at Studdal, near Deal, is now hoping for the Ministry's support in his quest to track down and catch the animal. Sightings of the cat are still coming in. On September 5th a large black tail was seen disappearing into a hedge at the edge of a field used by horses, cows and sheep at St. Margaret's.

And last Thursday night Dave's seventeen-year old daughter Michelle and her fiancé Mark Finnis reported that they had seen two of the big cats young near Dave's home.

Dave and fellow leopard spotter PC Ian Woodland now have solid evidence of the panther – plaster casts of the animal's footprints found in a field near Ripple. And the pair say they have seen several scratch marks.'

'Eaten sheep another sign of a panther' said the *Kent Today* of Thursday 20th October 1994.

'The savaging of four sheep in a field near Canterbury this week has provided more evidence of a possible big cat in Kent.

A vet is examining the remains after two more sightings of the black puma-type cat believed to be prowling the east Kent countryside. Only the heads and skins of the animals were left on a farm at Bridge, the rest apparently devoured.

Police were called to the farm in Bourne Park on Sunday following a series of attacks on the livestock. The vet, Patricia Cornwell, was unable to say for sure what sort of animal had caused the injuries but said it could have been a feral dog or a large, cat-like animal. But she said the sheep she examined had been killed to be eaten. It was grabbed around the neck by the animal and she had found two puncture marks there.

"Large chunks near the neck and shoulder had been eaten, as well as muscle from one leg," she said.

"The flesh had been gnawed away and whoever did it certainly had a good feed. But no bones were broken or crushed."

The owner of the sheep, Claire Smith, said if she lost any more in the same circumstances she would organise a watch of the area to try to catch the killer.

A cat expert said the sheep slaughters were more evidence of a panther-like animal living in the Kent countryside.

Doug Richardson, assistant curator of mammals at London Zoo said: "The kill would be very clean, as described, and much of the carcass devoured. If it had been a dog, the kill would be messy and the animal not eaten."

But he stressed that that if a panther was at large it was unlikely to attack humans.

"It is a very timid animal and will generally look for an escape route rather than have confrontation", said Mr Richardson, who previously worked with big cats at Howletts Zoo.

Nick Marx, head carnivores keeper at Howletts, said the police had contacted him to enquire about any possible escapees following the discovery of the sheep carcasses.

He said yesterday that the park had two black leopards and added, "They were still here when I saw them this morning."

Two further sightings of a large, predatory cat in the nearby Wingham area in the last fortnight have also been reported.

The first was by Tom Sellars of Mill Road, Wingham well, who spotted the beast while walking his border collie one night.

He said: "I was in a field not fifty yards from my home when Sam pricked up his ears. I was carrying a powerful torch and when I shone it ahead of me, I suddenly saw a big, black cat. It was much bigger than my dog and I followed it with the torch beam as it bounded across the road into dense woodland. Sam shot off after it but came back a few minutes later."

He added: "I told my wife and a couple of chaps at work."

A farmer working in the area also spotted the beast while on his tractor.

He did not want to be named but said: "I have no doubt at all about what I saw. It was 9:30 am and I had a really good view of it. It was nearly four-foot long and jet black with a long tail. It gave me quite a fright."

A Canterbury woman fears her pet dog has been snatched by the mystery predator.

Julie Mousaid, says her mongrel bitch Bubbles, went missing after she let it out into her garden late one night about a fortnight ago.

She said: "Late that night something had set all the dogs off barking in the area. We often get foxes from the Old Park behind our garden but Bubbles wasn't frightened of them."

She became alarmed when she did not return and a neighbour reported hearing growling and snarling sounds.'

In the same month police in Hampshire had attempted to track down a beast on the loose and blamed for several livestock attacks in the county.

The *Kent Today* put a one-hundred pound reward out for anyone who could photograph a big cat in Kent.

On Thursday November 24th the same paper asked, *'Is this our black panther?'* after a man in the Deal area had allegedly snapped a cat sitting in a field.

'Animal lover Dave Riches who has been tracking the panther since the summer says it is a black panther.

He took a series of pictures of the big cat and a smaller grey cat, thought to be one of its young, in a ploughed field in the Ashley area, near Deal. He says the pictures have now been verified by one of the country's leading big cat experts.

"These pictures prove once and for all that these animals exist", he said.

He claims to have traced the cat and her young to the outskirts of Woodnesborough. As well as photographs of two cats he also had video footage of their footprints.

"It is exciting to be able to show these pictures to the public for the first time", said Dave, who admits he has become obsessed by the big cat.

Mr Riches who runs an owl rescue centre at Studdal, near Deal, has been lent a video camera with a powerful zoom lens by the BBC and is now hoping to capture the animals on video. He says his pictures have been verified by television wildlife expert John Hancock.

"Mr Hancock said the black cat is a panther and her young are panther crossed with another big cat, possibly a puma", said Mr Riches.

He would like to trap the animals both for their own safety and to protect domestic pets and livestock in the area. He would hand them over to a zoo or fly them to a game reserve in Zimbabwe or Asia.'

The paper also mentioned that a 'panther-type' cat had also been seen at Bysing Wood, Faversham by an angler. The actual photo shown in the paper was hardly convincing, showing a cat-like animal indeed but nothing too dissimilar from a domestic cat. I also found it strange that a so-called wildlife expert had so easily identified a panther-puma cross when there's never been any evidence as of writing that such animals exist out there. The cat photographed by Mr Riches rather suspiciously appeared a month after the reward was offered, I wonder if he snapped up the prize money? It's a shame that such pictures continue to make the headlines when they remain so indistinguished.

On Thursday December 8th the newspaper continued its big cat coverage.

> 'Zoo theory to cat mystery' – 'The big cats of east Kent could be descendants of animals kept in a private zoo more than fifty-years ago according to a wildlife expert.
>
> Dave Riches of Studdal, near Deal, believes a large cat may have escaped or been released from a private collection near Ashford. He was speaking this week after a motorist at Bilsington reported seeing a large black cat, possibly a panther.
>
> It follows a string of sightings between Canterbury and Deal, some supported by photographs, others by huge paw prints found in the areas.
>
> Mr Riches who has spent months interviewing people and collecting evidence, says there is no way they can all be the same cat. The Bilsington cat was seen by Ray Phillips, 47, from Kenardington, as he was driving along Priory Road, Bilsington with his son Dean and pub landlord Jim Andrews.
>
> Mr Phillips explained: "It was around lunch time and I saw the black animal which was far too big to be an ordinary cat."
>
> Mr Andrews, landlord of Aldington's Good Intent pub, was with him. He said: "I only caught a glimpse of the hind quarters and tail of the animal. If someone said it was a panther I wouldn't argue."

Mr Riches also advised people how to react if they are confronted by one of the big cats roaming Kent countryside.

> "Raise your arms in the air making yourself as large as possible, stare the animal straight in the eyes and shout, don't scream", he said. "The worst thing you can do is run away – the animal will almost certainly strike."

In the same year a big cat was blamed for killing sheep near Mersham, Ashford.

Unfortunately, some of the information given out by the so-called experts at the time was bizarre. Mr Riches told reporter Gary Wright, "This is almost definitely the panther that roams up to fifty miles, as far as Folkestone and Dover".

Fair comment. However…

"There is also a female lynx in east Kent. I believe she has one offspring which we have called a luma." he added.

A luma? I don't think so.

A black leopard was seen near Folkestone in 1995 by Mr Self travelling home to Hawkinge from Ga wick at around 2:00 am. He told me;

> *"I travelled up hill from Denton, to the top then along the straight bit of road where there is a big dip...as I approached the big dip I saw the cat stationary in front of me. As I neared it, it ran off into the fields in an easterly direction.*
>
> *It was at least the size of a Labrador but significantly longer.".*

On August 11th 1995 the *Kent Today* reported, *'Leopard of lily valley lives'*, commenting that, *'The beast of Bodmin is dead...but the leopard if Lily Vale is very much alive.*

> *Henry Moorhead, 39, a solicitor, told how he came face to face with it while walking his dogs near his home in Bog Wood, Smeeth.*
>
> *Mr Moorhead of Lily Vale Farm said:*
>
> *"I heard a tremendous growling, like no other I have ever heard. I thought I would soon be a statistic and froze. This big brown cat was watching me from behind some bushes. It looked like a leopard."*
>
> *Mr Moorhead's sighting has resumed the speculation about Kent's big cats. There are scores of recorded sightings since 1990 and those who have seen the animals have no doubt the county is home to panther-like creatures.*
>
> *Last year one expert suggested they were animals released from private collections af-ter a licensing shake-up in the 1970s. Another theory suggests a private zoo in Ashford released its animals just after the war. There have been four similar sightings of the animal in the past seven weeks east of Ashford.*
>
> *Mr Moorhead's mother saw a fast-moving animal cross her path in New Wood, near Smeeth, two weeks ago and a woman driving home at night saw a leopard-like animal on the road.*
>
> *Her husband Robert said: "I have no doubt there is a leopard in the area. The Ministry of Agriculture said otherwise I wouldn't believe them. I always take a stick with me walking just in case although the animal won't hurt humans. I worry about my dogs."*
>
> *Dave Riches, of Studdal, near Deal, has been tracking the Kent cats for two years.*
>
> *He said: "I had two calls yesterday about this leopard. It doesn't surprise me. It is a two-year old cub and one of eight in the county. We hope to catch one soon. When we do I will ask the public what they want me to do – put it in a zoo or let it go. I would like to let it go."*

This report appeared to be one of the first actually mentioning a leopard rather than panther or the bizarre cross-breed's they were originally coming up with. Although the press seemed reasonably unbiased to-wards such animals and their existence, it was rather worrying to know that an ordinary member of the public was attempting to trap such a wild animal.

One of the most impressive pieces of evidence came from the Barham area, situated between Canterbury and Dover in 1997. An elderly woman named Heather had found the fresh head of a sheep at the local golf course and also mentioned a black leopard sighting at Dengemarsh near Lydd, on the marshes. Heather had several sightings of large cats from 1995 onwards and often found remains of animals such as rabbits, as well as strange excrement. In 1997 also, around July, Mr Free was driving through Burmarsh, on the marshes, at 3:30 am when his van broke down. After fixing the problem he continued his journey and saw a large cat-like animal in the beam of the headlights. Around the same time Mr Webb was standing in his garden one summer's afternoon at Hamstreet, facing west across his lawn looking for his pet cat. Suddenly, he saw a large black animal running into some bushes.

Mr Moffat saw a similar animal at 5:00 am whilst walking his dog in Canterbury's Elham Valley. He would see another black leopard in 2003 whilst driving.

In 1998 a black leopard was observed near the railway line at Ramsgate, and a panther was also seen by David Matthews in Dover. He'd been leaving scraps of food out for foxes of a night, but one evening got the shock of his life when he happened upon a massive black animal just forty-foot away devouring the food. David also mentioned to me that a local vet named Mr Stattersfield, who'd also seen a big cat locally, had a theory that suggested that during World War II at Manston Airfield, Isle of Thanet, RAF pilots from overseas had brought with them large cats such as black panthers as mascots. Rumour has it that once the trips were over the pilots were ordered to let them go into the wilds instead of returning with them. Whether enough cats would have been imported this way remains a mystery, but it's certainly one theory that keeps on rearing its head.

In the June of the following year a man named Kevin was in the vicinity of Howletts Zoo at 3:00 am, rabbiting with a friend when his dog began to chase a fox that sped by. Suddenly a large cat zipped out of the darkness and had obviously been chasing the fox. Kevin's dog hastily returned, and both men shone a torch in the direction of where the animal went and picked up a pair of green eyes.

Kevin was full of information and claimed that he worked at Margate's Dreamland Safari Park some twenty-five years previously. He told me that a black leopard and two cougars had escaped from the zoo. One of the cougars was found dead by the railway line, possibly hit by a train.

In September of 1999 Mr Giltrap from Folkestone observed a beige-coloured cat in the countryside between Brenzett and Appledore on the marshes. He reported the sighting to the local police.

In the same year several large cats were reported in Dover and Folkestone, most of the animals observed were very dark brown, looking almost black in the distance. At Newington, between Ashford and Folkestone on the old A20, a witness driving saw a large black cat around three feet in length jump out of a hedge and spring across the road.

Strangely, despite the fuss being caused by the Blue Bell Hill cat, Ashford, Dover and the rest of east Kent were reasonably quiet. I personally thought that more cats were being sighted in the area, but clearly not being reported to the press on a regular enough basis. Over time this would thankfully change dramatically as I contacted more and more of the newspapers etc, in the area.

In March 2000 I received a strange call from a Mr Wilkinson who claimed that he'd been tracking east Kent cats for more than two years, and was also a part-time photographer.

He claimed that one morning at 8:00 he was walking in the dense Challock Forest area of Ashford when he heard a weird 'clunking' sound and suddenly saw an animal bounding through the wilderness. The animal was definitely a large cat, some five feet in length with a long, hooked tail. Although the animal was jet-black, Mr Wilkinson remained convinced that he'd seen some bizarre cheetah because he believed it was too skinny to be a melanistic leopard. I found this ludicrous and was also put off by the fact that his only intentions were to photograph a cat and sell the pictures.

I took the sighting with a pinch of salt, and there's been no evidence since to suggest that giant mutant cats are roaming the woodlands of Kent.

On April 28th 2000 the *Ashford Advertiser* ran the story of, *'The Big Cat Is More Than A Myth'* after Mr Myskiewiez, a tarmac worker, was driving to work in Westwell when a large cat walked in front of his vehicle.

In the autumn, Mr Pooley saw a big cat. He wrote to me in 2001 telling me of his sighting:

> *'Following your article in this weeks Kentish Express I can report a sighting of what appeared to be a large black cat moving across the top of the 17th green at Tenterden Golf Club. I was about 450 yards away and saw an animal about the size of a Labrador dog, but lower and longer and moving more cat-like.'*

On the 24th September Mr Wibley, from Ashford, was setting up his new CCTV security system overlooking the front of the house and into the next road. At 12:12 am, after the system had been running for around twenty-minutes - and had picked up a fox and domestic cat - a large animal came into view at the top right of the screen. The animal walked casually along the pavement in front of a corner house and stopped at a bush in a garden. The animal stopped for a few seconds, possibly to sniff or urinate and then turned round and went back in the direction it had come from.

I visited Mr Wibley and viewed the tape and was impressed by it. He'd slowed it down considerably so we could work out the measurements of the animal and also see its shape. The cat on the film is black, low and long in the body with an arched back, muscular shoulders and a very long tail which reaches the ground and curves upward. Although the cat is only on screen for around fifteen seconds, it is clearly a black leopard around three-and-a-half to four feet long.

The witness knew that what he'd seen was strange because not long before he'd seen a similar cat at Pluckley, Ashford.

A black leopard was also spotted in Dover at the end of the year, but in 2001 there was a flurry of sightings from Cranbrook, not far from Tenterden. The most impressive sighting concerned a milkman on January 14th at 7:45 am. He was walking his dog up a pathway between two fields when he saw something around fifty-metres away, *"...playing in the grass."* As the witness approached he got a better view of the animal, a four-foot-long black cat with a very long tail.

The man told me of at least another ten sightings over the previous few months he'd heard of, all concerning a black cat. On one occasion in 1998 it was rumoured that a leopard had attacked a Greyhound and a policeman had seen a similar animal in '96.

Also on the 14th of Jan', a photographer and author travelling with his wife at 8:45 pm from Ashford to Folkestone saw a large black panther which crossed the motorway and seemed dangerously close to an approaching vehicle. I received an interesting letter from Penny Boorman who told me of several sightings between Appledore and Woodchurch. In 2001, her husband saw a puma-like cat although nine years previously they both saw a seven-foot long black animal whilst driving one night. In March 2000 at 9:40 pm Penny was in the car at the same place of the 1992 sighting, when a big black cat suddenly stepped into the road from the foliage. The cat had its paw raised and as the vehicle approached it snarled. She told me, "*I was completely terrified of the animal. It was flat-headed, the size of an Alsatian dog and very long in the body.*"

Later that year Penny's husband saw possibly the same animal again in exactly the same area, and she also mentioned that eighteen years previous a man had seen a big black cat at Biddenden.

In the February of 2001, at 4:00 pm, a Bilsington diver braked suddenly when he spotted a large cat in a nearby field. During the same month I received a letter from a woman named Hilary who told me that during the early winter of 2000 there'd been a lot of cat activity on her ninety-acre farm in Ashford. The holding housed ducks, chickens and pygmy goats.

One afternoon Hilary checked on her goats which were kept in a forty-foot square compound surrounded by a four feet high fence. The next morning at 9:00 am Hilary noticed that two goats had gone missing without trace, so - worried that they may have been stolen - she appealed through the local press. However, a few weeks later a dog belonging to a neighbour sniffed out the remains of a pygmy goat in nearby fields. All that remained was a leg.

I also received a letter late February from a woman who told me, '*I was driving at 8:00 pm to collect a take-away from Hythe. Just on the edge of the village a black panther leapt down from the verge in front of me and up the verge into fields beyond. By chance, half-an-hour later when returning it came back down in front of me again.*'

An elderly woman wrote to me also in the spring and told me of a sighting of a lynx from the Lydd area. In the April a couple, who'd had several cat experiences in the Blue Bell Hill area, had moved to the edge of Challock Forest where they had a poultry farm. On one occasion the man of the house, named Barry (mentioned elsewhere), came across an impressive set of paw-prints on a muddy path near his home. He took casts of the prints and sent one along to me. It was certainly made by a cat, measuring four inches across by five inches.

Barry mentioned several unusual incidents pertaining to big cat activity dating back to 2000. On one occasion whilst walking his dog they were growled at by an animal up an oak tree. Then, nine of his chickens were taken in one night, with no trace, and on another occasion he observed a rabbit emerge from the undergrowth and then heard a snapping noise as if a branch had broken. Suddenly a dark-coloured big cat bounded from the woods and pursued the rabbit.

In May 2001 the *Kentish Express* reported:

> *Fresh reports of a black puma-like animal have revived speculation that a big cat is prowling the countryside. Villagers in Stelling Minnis claim to have spotted a cat, as large as a Labrador, stalking through nearby woodland.*
>
> *Eunice Holliday, from Bobbin Farm, was walking her dog through Elham Park Wood when she saw the animal.*
>
> *"It was jet black and had an erect tail," she said. "It definitely wasn't a dog – you could tell that by the way it walked."*
>
> *Her description is strikingly similar to that of another villager, Christine St-Ledger who*

also described seeing a puma-like creature the size of a Labrador.'

On May 31st a Hawkinge man found huge prints in soil in his vegetable patch and during the same time at Dymchurch, on the sea front, a male witness gardening was astonished to see a large black felid cross his lawn just ten yards away. In the June I received a call from a distressed Jan Terry from Canterbury who told me that she'd lost over forty sheep in nine years in the Elham area. She believed that a black leopard and puma were in the area because although the kills were cat-like, they were always slightly different from one another. Some lambs were left without legs, decapitated, and disembowelled, whilst others were missing their ears and lower jaw which may have suggested dog attacks.

Jane told me that two so-called researchers had looked into the killings and also that certain authorities had visited the area to monitor the predation.

Two cricket teams having a tea break at Etching Hill, Canterbury, couldn't believe their eyes, when they watched a black cat, eighty yards away skirt the cricket field and then disappear into undergrowth. The cat re-appeared several times yet seemed oblivious to its audience of more than twenty.

A woman named Rachel saw a beige-coloured cat in the July. It had long black ears and a small face and bolted through the nearby fence just twenty yards away as she and her boyfriend were just about to go out for the evening. Rachel told me that she'd been to Kenya for five months and she said what she'd seen was probably a caracal after learning about such felids.

Shortly after a man named Tim was driving at 9:15 am one Sunday to the local shop at Charing Heath, Ashford. As he approached the railway bridge a large cat, dark grey in colour came across the road from right to left, and jumped into the woods on the quarry side. In the autumn at Bethersden a Mr and Mrs Ford driving near Birch Road, saw a black leopard at 8:00 pm. Mr Ford mentioned that several people had lost their dogs in the local woods, and remains had been found to suggest that some large predator had eaten them. In October at Kennington, at 4:45 am a man walking to work saw a black panther from thirty yards. On the 3rd of the month a woman named Olive was travelling in a vehicle with three other people near Brook, Ashford, not far from Kennington. They were travelling for quite some time and became lost on a country lane. As they came around the bend they all observed a big, black cat in the road. In one movement it leapt into a hedge out of sight.

The following day Mrs McGregor was walking in woodland at Charing Heath around 7:00 pm. She was checking her land for damage after some severe winds and was parked up. With her mobile phone in hand, she strolled towards the area where her pond is situated. Whilst in the thick wood, she began to text her friend when suddenly she heard a splash. Mrs McGregor stared at the haziness of the water and was terrified to see a large, black object swimming towards her. It came out of the pond and stood before her just a few feet away, a shining panther that stopped and stared at her fixatedly. Suddenly, her mobile phone rang and the cat jumped and swiftly moved away, Mrs McGregor retreated also, but looking back she could see that the cat had gone back into the pond and headed towards the small island in the centre. She recalled to me the eeriness of the incident, "...*the animal looked so healthy and had beautiful blue eyes*" - this was a detail I couldn't fathom, although maybe its watery gaze had simply reflected the moonlight.

A local wild boar expert was walking with his Jack Russell dog at Hamstreet in early October and during their journey were joined by a stray Alsatian-retriever cross. As the three of them merrily strolled down the lane both dogs suddenly froze in terror when up ahead a chocolate-brown coloured cat emerged from the hedge and then slinked away.

The man, Mr Derek Harman, told me that in 1998 whilst at Rye on the Kent and Sussex border, he was observing wild boar when suddenly the hairs on the back of his neck stood up. He gazed around nervously and saw that he was being watched by a large lynx which suddenly spun on one paw and ran away. He mentioned also that two weeks after his lynx sighting two men hunting foxes at night in the same area caught a pair of bright eyes in the beam of their lamp. They had the animal in their sights, but could not identify it and so refused to shoot, thankfully.

On the 13th October I received an anonymous call from a young gentleman who claimed that at around 2:30 pm Ashford police were searching the south Willesborough area after a report of an exotic cat no far from the local *Asda* supermarket. The caller claimed that the cat had a den underneath the railway line.

I phoned the police, and the Patrol Room Officer confirmed that although police were in the area searching for a cat, it turned out to be a domestic. Bizarrely, twenty minutes later I received a call from a couple, Julie and Paul, who said they'd been walking their retriever dog in the same area and saw a large cat around one-hundred yards away which was bigger than their dog. They couldn't give me the colour because the sun was shining and bathed the animal which made it difficult to view as it sauntered along the horizon. They were still positive that what they'd seen was a big cat and they also stated they'd seen prints in the area which the police had seen. This suggested that whatever was out there was no domestic cat. I never found out who the mystery caller was, but had a feeling that maybe the person who rang knew more than they was letting on. In fact, I wondered if they'd let the animal go.

On 24th October the *Kentish Express* reported:

> *'Big black cat is seen after lamb killing', - 'Another big black cat sighting has been reported just days after a possible paw print was discovered close to Ashford town centre.*

> *Ruth Hoare was confronted by a large black cat as she skinned rabbits in a field near her Bilsington home.*

> *She said: "I was kneeling down when I heard a grunting and a rustle in the grass, but thought it was my neighbour's dog. When I looked up I saw the cat and as I moved towards it, it ran off really quickly."*

> *She described the animal as black, with a long tail and about two-and-a-half feet tall.*

> *Miss Hoare said her friends had spotted prints in the area and a lamb had been viciously attacked and killed just days before. She added: "When we saw the lamb we thought nothing of it. The neck had been broken and it was much worse than anything a fox could do."*

A Willesborough man named Colin Beale on the 24th also saw a black cat at 6:30 pm whilst out walking with his family. The animal was in a nearby field, around four feet long with a large, round head, short ears, and stood two feet high.

Pluckley, covering some three-thousand acres, is reputedly England's most haunted village. Locally published pamphlets speak often of the fourteen classic ghost stories of the area, but a local historian once told me that some eighty-five apparitions inhabit the dark woods and old buildings of this quaint village which is mentioned in the *Domesday Book*, where it was named Pluchelei, although the name has had various spellings, from Pluccan leah (from the old English 'plucca's clearing) to Plukele. During the eleventh century Pluckley was a bigger town than Ashford, with the main livelihood in the area stem ming from weaving.

Despite its deeply rural façade, Pluckley has been pretty much bereft of cat sightings although on November 15th 2001 at 3:28 pm, an 'elderly gent' driving in his car with wife and grandson from Pluckley Village School came out of The Street and turned left, when around five-hundred yards away the man saw an Alsatian-sized animal by the side of the road adjacent to a field. As they approached and got to within thirty yards they watched it 'drop' like a cat. It had a long tail and was completely black and moved off towards the field.

Three weeks previous the wife of the man was walking in the grounds of St Nicholas Church when she saw a gingery-brown Labrador-sized cat appear near one of the crypts and slink away.

Two days before Christmas Katrina Walker was tending to her horses in Woodchurch at around 7:30 pm. One of the horses she noticed was missing and the other was standing in the centre of the field and would not come over to her. Katrina then received a call from a neighbour who said that the missing horse was in a nearby field. It had jumped two fences!

When Katrina returned to the field with her torch, and she shone the beam towards the area where large ferns enshroud, and picked up two bright yellow eyes. She was unnerved by the presence of something she couldn't understand.

On Christmas Day a local man had an interesting encounter, which he typed up and sent to the local paper:

> 'At 8:30 am I left my home in Newton, Ashford, planning to walk through the fields to Kingsnorth and Great Chart, and return home for lunch. Just before 9:00 as I was walking along a grassy track and approaching the Bad Munstereifel Road I came across a sheep lying on its side in the track and moving feebly, clearly helpless. I was surprised to find it on the track, since the meadow on the right was separated by quite high barbed-wire fencing. Helpless myself, I decided to report it as soon as I could, passed on through a gate and turned right...I noticed that the meadow on the right seemed to be empty, although there were plenty of sheep in the meadow I had just passed. I then noticed, in the meadow, about two hundred yards away, a solitary animal which was walking about with its nose to the ground. I wondered whether it was a fox, but as I watched it I saw that it was very dark in colour, though not jet black as far as I could see.
>
> The animal looked up, saw me and ran away to the far corner of the field. Here I could hardly make it out against the dark background, but I kept staring in its direction, and after a bit it moved to my left, keeping close to the far fence and heading towards the same corner that I was making for, where the Bad Munstereifel Road crosses a dyke and the Hastings railway line. To get a better look at the animal, I started walking towards this corner, but as soon as the animal saw me move it started to race ahead. It got to the corner long before me, slipped through a gap in the fence and escaped under the Bad Munstereifel Road.'

Despite making numerous phone calls, the witness to the injured sheep couldn't get hold of anyone, due to it being Christmas, and so, later that afternoon he went back out to visit the area where the sheep was.

He continued:

'At 3:00 pm I went out again. The sheep was still alive at 3:30 and I returned home and rang the RSPCA. An inspector soon rang me and I gave her the grid reference but I said I doubted she would be able to find the sheep on her own. The next morning, having heard nothing, and feeling worried I set off at 7:40. It had been a frosty night, and though I knew the sheep were tough I was not sure whether the sheep would still be alive. I got to it just after 8:00 and found it still alive. As soon as I got back, soon after 8:30 I rang the RSPCA again and told my story again and the woman said she would deal with the matter. At 9:20 am having heard nothing I rang the RSPCA again. I explained that I should be going out again at midday and asked for the inspector to get in touch with me to show him the way. I was told that the woman inspector the day before had seen a field with sheep in it, all apparently unhurt and had left.

Soon after 10:00 am Chief Inspector Bailey of the RSPCA rang. He agreed to meet me at a convenient point. He rang again after 11:00 and we met about 11:20, walked to the sheep and found it still alive. It had a damaged hind leg, probably in jumping over the fence to escape from the animal. Mr Bailey said he would get a vet, and I asked him, if he found who owned the land and the sheep, to advise him to stop the gap in the fence through which the animal entered the meadow.'

Five days later at Hawkinge near the aerodrome, Mr Johnson, at 11:00 am was looking out from his bedroom window, and saw a large cat which was nosing around an area that was being developed. The cat was mooching between some unused piping. Mr Johnson said the animal was a puma, and had a long tail, and that a few hours later a few men showed up and began looking around the area.

Around the same time in Challock, at 5:40 am, Mr Castle was driving to Ashford and saw an animal which he first took to be a deer in a clearing on the left. As he neared the animal he realised it was a powerfully built cat, grey in colour which stared back at him through the mist. On the 2nd of January 2002 a man, driving in a transit van on the icy roads through Woodchurch spotted a puma-like cat also as it crossed the road two-hundred yards away. The next day a fourteen-year old boy was in the Bilsington area with his eleven-year old brother at 3:00 pm when they noticed the flock of sheep were huddled together and being watched by a ginger-coloured cat. The cat looked at the two boys then moved towards the sheep that scattered suddenly.

Both boys said the cat had a white chest, and was four-times the size of a domestic cat. Two days later both boys returned to the area at roughly the same time, and stumbled across a sheep carcass which had been dragged across the field. All the flesh had been removed and wool was scattered around suggesting scavengers had been at it over night. The boys took photographs of the supposed kill which were sent of to me. It was difficult to tell how long the sheep had been there. It may have been killed a week or so earlier by the cat which the boys saw, or it may have died of natural causes. It was difficult to make any judgement as the carcass was pretty much bereft of anything, wool, flesh, eyes etc, so looking at scratches on the flank, puncture marks to the throat or at how the wool had been peeled back was pretty nigh on impossible due to decomposition which had left only a skeletal frame.

In the same month at Woodchurch, a woman named Harriet contacted me to say that one morning at 9:0 her sheep were huddled together in the field. As she looked across the open pasture she watched a black cat slowly walking away from the flock. She also told me of several previous experiences. In four year she had lost around thirty sheep. In the summer of 2001, Harriet and her partner had found a freshly killed ewe shortly after she'd sighted a big black cat. And the year before, Harriet claimed that she saw her first deer, it suddenly appeared in the road up ahead, was limping and breathing heavily, whilst in 1999 during the July, one evening, around 8:40 she'd seen the hind quarters of a large, light-brown cat

That night she also found a lamb stranded near a dyke. As she approached, a large black animal leapt up from the undergrowth and sprang away. It had a very long tail. The following day a lamb was found eaten.

Lambs were also found eaten in 2002 at Petham in Canterbury. In the March at 6:00 pm at Etching Hill, four witnesses observed a jet black cat sitting in the road as they pulled out of a local park. The cat was bigger than a labrador and ambled out of sight. In May a Christina who lives east of Canterbury at Stourmoth, was washing-up when her two pet cats bolted indoors. Christina looked outside, and saw an Alsatian-sized cat stalking through the orchard. She watched it for around five minutes and said, "*...it was slightly darker than a fox and had a very long tail.*"

Shortly before the sighting a local man had his domestic cat savaged by what the vet called, "*...a wild-cat.*"

On the 16th March in fields between Ashford and Wye, at 6:10 pm, a big black leopard was observed patrolling a field adjacent to the train track. The following month George Hatch of Bethersden heard a strange noise around midnight, as if there was a commotion between animals and the frantic snapping of twigs. Deciding to take a look, Mr Hatch and his wife saw something run fast across the shingle drive and run up into a tree. At 8:30 pm later in the month at Great Stone a man named Barry Hymers was in his car with his wife travelling towards home from Great Stone, near the marshes when a large, dark-coloured cat crossed the road casually. A woman named Sally heard extremely eerie screams in the same month in the High Halden area of Ashford. On one occasion she spotted, "*....a shadowy, beige cat that moved like a ghost along the hedgerow.*"

Another sighting occurred near the William Harvey Hospital in Ashford when Mr McGoldrick was walking his dogs at 10:00 am and was stunned to see a panther sitting in the middle of a nearby field. Mrs Ranford, tending graves at a cemetery in Canterbury, saw a large, dog-sized black cat resting on a gravestone. The cat got up and wandered off. The following weekend the lady told the security guard about the sighting, and then she saw the cat again in pretty much the same area and was concerned about a couple who were strolling nearby with their child.

On 1st July a man walking on a footpath at 8:45 pm from Singelton to Great Chart, observed a melanistic leopard from fifty yards away which stared at him and loped away. A day or so later a Joyce Stone was riding her horse at Kingswood, Challock, when she startled a black cat the size of an Alsatian with a smooth coat and a small head. Two weeks later on the 15th, a lady named Lyn was travelling near the William Harvey Hospital at 11:00 am on a road through Hinxhill. Suddenly, several deer ran across the road ahead, and as she neared she saw a large black animal standing on the edge of the wood watching the fleeting and terrified animals. In the same month a cyclist emailed to report his sighting,

> 'One evening after being dropped off by my mates I decided to go out on my own. I eventually got to Saltwood woods, near Hayne Barn in Ashford. I had stopped to grab a drink from my back pack when I noticed an extremely large dog on the hill above me. It didn't really take any notice of me, it sort of looked at me and carried on with its business. Being on my own and by the entrance to the woods, I decided to get my head down and bomb straight through. It was a bit of a strange reaction for a dog but the mere sight of it was enough for me to not take any chances. Soon after I saw an appeal in the paper and realised that what I saw was your big cat. I am South African so I know what big cats are.'

On the 17th July at Mushgrove, Ashford, Mr Brown looked out of his window at 4:00 am, and saw a big black cat walk down his pathway. The animal then leapt on to the bonnet of his car which was parked on the driveway, walked over it and then leapt down and headed off into the darkness. Three days later, a woman walking to work towards the Ashford International Station, at 5:50 am, was unnerved by a black object that appeared some sixty yards away as she strolled along a toe-path. At first the witness thought it was someone's coat thrown over a tree-stump, but as she walked closer she realised it was a large animal squatting on the ground.

By late summer Ashford, despite much activity in Gravesend and Maidstone, had become a hot-bed of big cat activity, and sightings were reaching me at an alarming rate. In 2002 it would have been easy to have compiled two volumes of cat sightings *purely* from around the town, such was the influx. The press influence was also pivotal, as more and more people came forward.

- Shadoxhurst (2nd August – panther).
- Willesborough (12th August – panther), there were also reports from Dover (panther), from the St Margaret's Bay area,
- Hawkinge (August – a man pushing his baby son in his buggy towards Canterbury Lane, a large cat with tabby-like markings and also a puma),
- Chartham Hatch (August – panther in orchards),
- Lyminge Forest (remains found of dog and bird, plus deep breathing which spooked witness),
- Lydd (28th August – 10:30 am, couple driving through New Romney took an unsuitable track in a very remote area, saw a black panther spring from undergrowth. The husband had previously been a hardened sceptic)
- St Mary's Bay (15th September – black panther),
- Canterbury (mid-Sept – panther),
- Biddenden (mid-Sept – 9:45 pm – panther),
- Hawkinge (25th Sept – panther),
- Bethersden (late Sept' – panther),
- St Mary's Bay (sightings of 'marsh cats' – possibly aggressive feral cats),
- Hamstreet (27th Sept – black panther leapt from a tree), and in October one of the cats prowled very close to town, and made an appearance at the Eureka Entertainment Park. A male motorist was travelling to work there at 6:00 am, approaching the roundabout near the town centre, when he saw a black object lurking in the sidings of the motorway.
- Hawkinge (October – panther, attacks on sheep),
- Old Romney (2nd October, 10:00 pm – several teenagers saw a black panther in fields),
- Shadoxhurst (4th Oct – 10:30 pm, a man named Paul driving home from work picked up a large cat and its bright eyes in the fog),
- Alkham Valley (6th October – large cat spotted in hedgerow),
- Romney Marsh (October – three friends – two on motorbikes – approached by a big cat which ran at them. One boy sped off and the cat chased him – possible lynx sighting),
- Chartham Hatch (9th October, thirteen lambs killed over a short period, and a bullock attacked showing claw marks on the head, fox also killed in area),
- Deal, Walmer area (several sightings from September into October of several cats in the area),
- Pluckley (11th Oct – three ewes killed on Egerton border),
- Romney Marsh (12th Oct – three lambs killed, throats ripped out echoing previous attacks),
- Alkham Valley (mid-Oct – panther sighting on road),
- Hythe (9th November – panther crossed road),

- Chilham, nr Canterbury (28th Nov – four people in a car saw panther cross road),
- Pluckley (29th Nov – motorist spotted black leopard),
- Harbledown, nr Canterbury (2nd December – 11:20 pm – an ambulance crew responding to an emergency call at Faversham saw a black panther leap a nearby crash barrier. The incident was also seen by another motorist who had to brake to avoid the cat),
- Ashford cinema complex (4th Dec – a man and his son at 11:15 pm were in the car ready to go home when something walked across the car-park fifty yards away. The man started car and slowly drove towards the animal which slinked up a hill),
- Brooke Country Park – Sandgate (16th December 1:00 pm – a man named Barry sitting in his car eating saw a black panther emerge from the undergrowth),
- Kingsnorth, Ashford (December – light-coloured cat crossed road).

As you can tell by the close proximity of dates, it was increasingly difficult to keep up with the vast amount of sightings. It's strange that I often hear of scepticism towards such spates of sightings, but as I've always said, if the researcher in question works hard enough to send out appeals etc, then the witnesses will come flooding in, as proven with the cats roaming east Kent.

2003 wasn't to be any different, but judging by the sheer volume of reports I'd already received, it didn't matter if I'd never got another report again. I had the routes mapped out, and certainly realised there were more cats than I realised roaming Ashford, Deal, Dover, Canterbury etc. It was just a question of getting down there and digging myself out of the piles of sightings I was receiving daily from across the county.

In the national news *The Guardian* covered the countrywide situation, in it John Vidal wrote, '*Six weeks ago Neil Arnold got 45 reports in three days of big cats in the county, but last week his figures dropped to 20. He may be the closest Britain has to a full-time watcher, spending most nights following up reports...*', it was a nice piece of coverage because I'd been putting the hours in, but it wasn't always good being called a 'watcher' or an 'enthusiast' or even worse a 'hunter'. A couple of years later I would help Camden-based reporter Danny Robbins on his *Channel 4 Radio* show, *Danny Robbins Investigates* and I think upon meeting him he was quite surprised that I didn't come to the door with a beard, waistcoat, anorak, tweed trousers, cuddly toy panther and binoculars. He remarked, "*Neil, don't take this the wrong way but you're not at all what I expected. When I come to meet a big cat 'enthusiast' I expected someone with a beard, maybe a David Bellamy type...!*"

"*Yeah*", I replied. "*Most of them are like that..*"

"*But you're hip and quite trendy*", he added.

"*Yeah, I'm actually quite cool,*" I smirked.

"*And these people who put these cats alongside ghosts and the likes...*", he asked.

"*Yeah, they are quite funny*", I replied through a giggle.
"*There are some people who think these animals are demons from another world...*", I continued through another arrogant expression.

"*Mmm...as if they have been teleported from Africa,*" Danny responded, "*What do you think of people who say that?*".

"I think they are funny but they need a bit of a slap", I mocked.

Together we explored the subject of the so-called beast of Sydenham, but ended up waffling on about old school hip-hop, psychedelic '60s music, and generally mocking people who clamber through groves, glens, marshes and quagmires with camouflage gear on, and collect fluffy panther toys and claim to see phantom big cats on a weekly basis.

A motorist saw a puma-like animal in Sandwich during the third week of January '03. The *Kentish Express* of January 30th ran an excellent double-page spread on my research and by spring I'd received hordes more sightings, St Mary's Bay, Westwell, Folkestone, Alkham, Hythe, and the heart of Ashford where on 17th March at 5:00 pm a woman walking her dog at Great Chart saw a panther emerge from the woods up ahead. The woman was so alarmed by the presence of the animal that she ran home. Eight days later at 8:15 pm, a woman named Dawn was travelling towards High Halden with her daughter to check up on her horses, when she saw a dark-coloured cat sitting in a roadside ditch. They got to within ten feet of the animal, and noticed its eyes reflected orange-yellow. They carried on past the cat, and decided to come back for another look, and so Dawn turned the car around. Upon returning, they got a better look. They said it was longer than a fox, pure black and sleek with a long tail, and it crossed the road. Again they decided to turn around and come back for another look and the cat was still there, sitting on the opposite side of the road. The fourth time the cat finally slinked away out of sight. Around the same time a cat, black in colour, was seen between Woodchurch and Appledore, and at the beginning of April a female walking with her husband and dog at Folkestone, saw a fawn-coloured cat which she believed had attacked her dog a few weeks previous.

Also in April there were reports from Wingham, of a panther, and at High Halden. Dawn, who'd seen a cat from her car with her daughter previous, saw a slightly bigger black animal in the same remote spot.

In the May a couple travelling on the A20 to Dover approached the round-a-bout for Hawkinge and saw a large, fawn-coloured cat sneaking across a field. The animal was also seen by a bus driver. On the 4th panther was seen at Great Chart, and on the 15th a black leopard was seen near Ashford town centre by a woman walking to work during the early hours. Charing, Pluckley, Rolvenden, Dymchurch, Canterbury, Wye, and Kingsnorth, featured heavily in reports from summer through to autumn. In one particular incident a man walking his dog with his daughter in the Kingsnorth area, at the end of October, at 9:30 pm was shocked to see two black leopards running together close to a children's play area. In November Mrs Leigh had her third sighting of a black cat in Deal, whilst walking her dog at 10:30 pm at Sandwich. Two large paw prints were discovered at Chartham Hatch, and at Smeeth, three weeks before Christmas badgers, foxes and rabbit's remains had been found. The couple who found the eaten animals also had an encounter with a big, black, cat. Meanwhile, at Dover's Duke of York Barracks, just before Christmas two men travelling in a car at approximately 5:00 pm, saw a stocky, dark-coloured animal cross the road not far from the vicinity of the castle.

The end of the year culminated with a flurry of sightings. At Ash, near Dover, a man carrying a take away felt he was being followed, and watched in horror as a black shape ambled along the lane toward him. There were also sightings of black cats near Dover and central Ashford, but the biggest incident involved a certain Mr Jeffrey.

Over the course of a few weeks, Mr Jeffrey had been travelling to Canterbury Hospital on the main Dover to Canterbury road. On one occasion, on a grassy central reservation of the busy stretch, he saw a dead fox, likely to have been killed by a car. However, on several more trips he noticed that something had been eating the hind quarters of the fox, possibly another fox, but a little further along the reservation there was a larger animal, also dead, hidden partly by the grass. Its coat was sandy-coloured and covered

TOP: Ashford Big Cat paw-print 2008. (Photo courtesy Gordon Smith).
BELOW: Ashford sheep killed by large cat and scavenged. (p. 234)

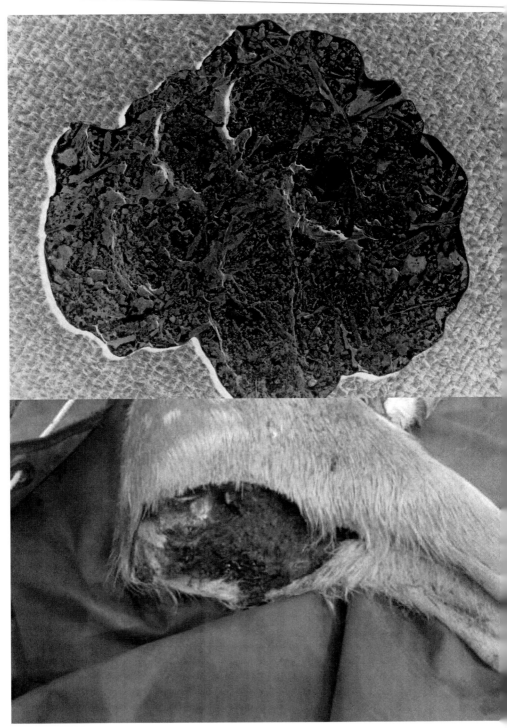

Black Leopard Paw Print taken at Ashford (p. 230)
BELOW: Deer kill Bethersden, Ashford 2005 (p. 245)

in brown rings, possibly rosettes.

Every time the witness drove by, he noticed how the coat of the animal had become more dirty, and the body clearly in a state of decomposition had become more rolled up, like a piece of carpet, as scavengers had begun to feast on what was left of the mystery animal.

Upon speaking to Mr Jeffrey I noted a sincere fellow, who believed that some kind of cat, possibly a serval, or lynx, may have escaped from one of the nearby zoo parks, possibly feasted on the fox, or crossed the busy road, and got hit by a car at some point and possibly crossed to the grassy central reservation to die. Upon visiting the road, I noticed just how dangerous it would be to pull over, but upon meeting the witness we managed to stop in a lay-by on an overcast Sunday afternoon and discuss the sighting.

The road was still pretty busy, cars roared on by at frightening pace, and I realised that even if we found the carcass we would have a few problems reaching it and hopefully bringing it back with us. We found the spot where Mr Jeffrey had thought he'd observed the body, but a search proved fruitless, and we didn't want to stand in the barrier area for too long in case we distracted several speeding motorists. Mr Jeffrey was left scratching his head; he was worried he'd appear as a fool to us, so he decided it was best to drive further up the road. Maybe he'd got the area confused, as it pretty much looked the same all the way along the road with regards to scenery. After a further few minutes, Mr Jeffrey signalled to pull over and we followed.

"*This is the spot*", he said confidently.

Again, we crossed the hazardous stretch of road, drivers hurtling by, wondering just what three people were doing bounding across the road. We hoped as well that no police car would show up.

We walked up the central reservation; a pretty bare strip consisting of some litter, pieces of tyre and long grass, and then we saw it, but our hearts sank immediately, and the look on Mr Jeffrey's face was one of disbelief. There, laid before us, was a cat alright. A toy one, smaller than a domestic cat, beige in colour with small rings on it, and a tag sticking out of it.

We laughed, but Mr Jeffrey was having none of it.

"*No!*" he repeatedly grumbled. "*This isn't it. This is the spot but this isn't what I saw, anyone can see this is a toy, something strange is going on here.*"

I took a few photographs of the forlorn toy leopard, and noted it had come from Howletts Zoo. Maybe some child had thrown it from a vehicle.

Okay, we'd travelled a long way, but there was no point dwelling on the disappointment, and we didn't want the witness to feel like he'd hoaxed us. But he remained convinced, and it was then that the mystery unfolded.

He told me that:

> "*When I first saw the carcass I rang the local newspaper about it and I think they covered the story. When I called the lady reporter back she told me she'd phoned Howletts a while after, I'm convinced they've been here, taken the real body and replaced it with the toy.*"

I wanted to laugh, not at Mr Jeffrey, but the thought of a local zoo going to such extremes to cover up the possibility that a cat had escaped from their zoo and been run over. I personally didn't think it was that big a deal, but Mr Jeffrey wanted the truth. He strongly believed that the zoo had sent someone out to get the carcass. But surely, if they wanted the incident hushed up they would have just taken the body, and not replaced it. Had the zoo 'shot themselves in the foot' by leaving an accidental clue? Had they put the toy there to make witnesses look like fools not realising that people had most certainly seen a real cat?

I was a little bemused. Mr Jeffrey remained adamant he'd seen a sandy coat with dark rings on, belonging to an animal much bigger than a fox, which over the course of several weeks had deteriorated, bombarded by fumes and the elements.

I've often scoffed at reports of covert operations being undertaken to remove bodies of alleged big cats from the highways and byways of our land, but maybe, just maybe, on *this* occasion we had been duped by forces beyond our control.

And that someone, somewhere, out there, had rolled up one night in a mysterious white van, removed the carcass of a dead, exotic animal and replaced it with a toy. Because, let's face it, we've all heard such stories, and personally I find them amusing rather than dark and sinister. I guess zoo parks have to cover their backs in some way, but in this case, even if the mystery dead animal hadn't belonged to a zoo, it possibly did now!

Around the March of 2008 a large cat was hit on a narrow stretch of road at Capel. The man who hit the animal, named Bill, contacted me:

> "I was travelling at about 50-55 mph at the time of impact; there was considerable damage to the front of my car, the fog light glass is 6mm thick and toughened – it was smashed completely. There were bloody streaks under the car with very fine hair attached; there wasn't enough to get a good sample. The body had been removed by 2:30 pm that day when I came home.
>
> The overall impression, a fleeting glimpse, was of a large cat-like animal about three feet long with pointed ears turned down on the ends, no tufts visible, overall greyish in colour with darker spots (comma shaped). Its legs were between ten and twelve-inches in length, no recollection of a tail, certainly wasn't long, and it leapt in an arched shape across the front of the car. Sorry I can't be more helpful – I kick myself that I didn't go back and look but there were several cars behind and by the time I stopped I was about one hundred yards away. A motorcyclist following me slowed down to look as the body was in the middle of the road and quite still. I have little doubt that it had been killed outright."

Whilst conducting a talk in April 2008 at Great Mongeham, I was approached by an ex-farmer who told me that during the 1980s whilst cutting corn at Deal in his combine harvester, he cut up a very unusual animal. He said,

> "We often accidentally killed foxes and domestic cats, they would dart straight into the blades, but on one occasion I went over a larger animal, it was jet-black, the size of a Labrador and it went straight into me, not much of it emerged out of the other side but I found the tail which was long."

In 2004 a panther was seen at Thanet by Mrs Johnstone in an area known as Westwood Cross. She was driving home at 11:30 pm when the big, black, long-tailed animal bounded across the road.

At the end of January an elderly lady had a fascinating tale to tell. At 10:30 am she was on a bus travelling from Willesborough to Folkestone.

Only three people were on the bus on this fresh morning. It pulled into the car-park of Port Lympne Zoo, which is part of its route, often picking up and dropping off tourists etc, who flock to the area in the warmer months.

On this occasion as the bus came out of the car-park, the woman saw a cat, sitting on a nearby bank. It was larger than a fox, it seemed pretty slender, and no-one else seemed to see the animal. Before the bus pulled away the woman got a good look at it as it crouched low near to some bushes. She described the animal as dark-coloured, but couldn't identify the species.

Had the cat escaped from the zoo? Or was it drawn to the area due to the presence of the captive animals?

A man and a friend spotted a black leopard in the woods at Shadoxhurst in the February. They were part of a 4x4 vehicle club driving through the woods. They'd parked up and spotted an impressive set of pawprints, and then glimpsed the animal which made them, a large black animal which they allegedly filmed.

Also in the February the *Dover Express* covered various local sightings, although the *'Here Kitty Kitty Kitty...'* headline left a lot to be desired. On the 8th February a couple walking at Appledore at 11:00 am spotted a black panther walking across the brow of a nearby hill. The woman believed the cat had a white tip to its tail, which is rather strange, and a detail I have always dismissed unless others report it, which at the time of writing they haven't.

Some of the year's best sightings were as follows:

February 10th – Folkestone, near Homebase, a long-tailed black cat seen diving into a hedge.

February 11th – Dymchurch, a couple were awoken by a crashing sound and thought they had intruders. The man jumped out of bed and looked out of back window and saw an animal on the roof of the neighbour's conservatory just twenty-five feet away.

February 19th – Lympne. A woman named Ruth driving from work saw a black creature in a field not far from the A20.

February 29th – 5:00 am. Aldington. A policeman walking his dog in local fields saw a dark-coloured cat, bigger than a fox in the beam of his torch.

March 19th – 7:00 pm. Aldington. A motorist saw a fawn-tan coloured cat run across the road near Bank Road.

20th April – 8:30 am. Western Heights, Dover. A dog-walker spotted a strange animal seeming to paw at a bush. The animal was on its hind legs, two-hundred yards away but was black and white in colour. No further reports of this animal.

27th April – 3:15 am. Hawkinge. A woman lying in bed was awoken by a sudden eerie growl coming from the vicinity of the aerodrome. The woman believed it was a big cat because she'd seen one locally in 1987.

6th May – 8:20 pm. The woman who reported the growling noises previous was on a coach near the Channel Tunnel when she, and several witnesses saw a big black cat run from left to right across the White Horse engraving on the hillside, and head towards Hawkinge.

- 12th May – 8:40 pm. Dover. Group of friends sitting in a flat saw a black panther cross the road near Military Road.
- Late May – Dover. A woman walking her dog saw a black panther.
- Late May – Dover. A contact of mine named Robbie discovered eaten badgers in local woods. On several occasions also he'd monitored several large cats in the area.
- Early June – 5:30 am. High Halden, Ashford. A woman named Sally was walking her three dogs in fields. She let them off the lead and lost sight of them, when suddenly a black animal zoomed by her with her dogs in hot pursuit.
- Early June – 7:15 pm. Jubilee Way, Dover. Motorist saw black leopard slinking along the line of a fence as it watched lambs in a nearby field.
- 16th June – 7:00 pm. St. Margaret's At Cliffe, Dover. Two Dexter cattle grazing the South Foreland Valley were attacked. One of the cows received scratch wounds along its flank whilst the second cow received more serious, deep scratch wounds to the hindquarters, flank and throat.
- 16th June – 5:10 am. Kingswood, Challock. Mr Beale who'd sighted a big cat before in Ashford was driving towards Challock when a large black cat with a long tail leapt into a ditch and ran into woods.
- 1st July – 9:00 am. Canterbury. Dark-coloured cat seen on road by an elderly woman and her daughter. Cat was bigger than a Labrador.
- 10th July – 1:00 pm. Between Ashford and New Romney. Mr Sear caught sight of a dark-brown cat with darker patches on its coat, sauntering along in the undergrowth.
- End of July – 3:00 am. Thanet. A Birchington woman was lying in bed awake looking out of her window when she saw a large cat, dark in colour, looking up at her from under a street light.
- 31st July – 8:15 am. Mr Parker travelling on Woodchurch to Shadoxhurst unmade road, fifty yards ahead a tan-coloured cat with a long tail crossed the road. Mr Parker saw a cat four years previous on Romney Marsh, but it was black.
- August 1st – 8:45 pm. High Halden, Ashford. Mr Fielder and his wife observed a melanistic leopard walking across a sheep field although it never bothered the flock which didn't seem too concerned about the cat.
- 3rd August – 9:30 pm. Great Chart. A fawn-coloured cat smaller than a Labrador ran across road twenty-five yards away.
- 9th August – 4:00 am. Ramsgate. A woman named Carla was waiting up for her husband who was fishing. She strode out onto the balcony of their maisonette and was frightened by a big black leopard walking down the middle of the road.
- 21st August – 7:30 pm. Wye, near Ashford. Big black cat seen lying near a fence by a man and his lurcher dog. The dog began to growl and the cat jumped out of sight over a fence.
- 29th August – 6:10 pm. Ramsgate. A woman sitting in her living room saw a big black animal in the garden.
- End of August – 2:30 pm. Wincheap, Canterbury. An elderly couple living in their ground floor flat looked out of their window towards a grassy area and saw a large cat sunning itself around forty feet away. They believed the animal was a lynx as no tail was visible, and it had large ears.
- 2nd September – 2:40 am. Westgate-On-Sea. A woman named Margaret was tending to her poorly dog in the garden when the dog began to bark. The woman shone her torch across the field and picked up a black cat with bright green eyes.
- 3rd September – 8:40 am. Appledore. A Jennifer Brown was walking her dog in fields when the dog spotted an animal up ahead emerging from the reed bed on the marsh. The dog sped toward a skinny, slinking black cat which leapt a ditch and vanished into the undergrowth.

- Sightings at Woodchurch, Kennington (3) and Aldington drew the year to a close, as Ashford made up around fifty percent of sightings received, an astonishing statistic for an area so heavily wooded.

*****

On the 4th January 2005 the same pattern emerged. At 2:00 pm Julia Campbell was looking out of her top floor office window towards woods adjacent to the Westmount Centre, Folkestone, when a large black felid, walking low to the ground, came from the wood and stuck to the shadows. A wait of eleven days seemed a lot for an area such as east Kent but on the 15th I received an email from Pauline who said,

> 'At 6:00 am, driving to where I keep my pony at High Halden, I saw what I first thought was a big fox in the middle of the road. As my lights caught it, the animal moved towards a post and rail fence, jumped onto the top and down the other side in a smooth movement. It was dark in colour.'

Six days later, a lorry driver from Brighton, driving through Romney Marsh, caught an animal in the headlights at 4:15 am as it was about to step into the road. The driver braked and the cat bounded off into the woods. He described the cat as around four feet long and black.

Large black cats were also seen at Tenterden (2), Cranbrook (4), Singleton, Charing Heath, Appledore (5), Woodchurch (4), Smeeth, Dover (6), Deal (4), Ramsgate, Hythe and Bethersden throughout the year. I think you've guessed my meaning!

The Bethersden incident was very impressive. Mr Jenkins emailed me to say that on 27th September '05 he'd found a young dead deer in a field. The poor animal had been killed near a water tank, away from the shelter of any woods. It had been dragged around ten metres. The throat has been bit in a clean and tidy fashion, and its rear end had been eaten away.

Mr Jenkins believed that a very fast predator had been responsible, and judging by the photos I received, I completely agreed. It's possible the killer had been lying up on the water tank and leapt on the roaming deer, or stalked it from the wood, pounced, and then dragged it away. Most of the carcass was fresh and intact, but the gory neck and anal wounds looked like they had been done with one bite.

On the 5th October, a big black cat was seen as it slipped through a hedge, at 8:20 am, at west Brabourne by Jennifer Wilkes. Despite my concentration being firmly aimed at Bexley and the surrounding areas, the cats of Ashford refused to rest. On the 22nd October at Kingsnorth, not far from Tesco, a man driving saw a four-foot-long black cat which ran across the road, and another sighting of a leopard took place at Brenzett a month later with further sightings from Stone Street in Canterbury, which continued into 2006.

Dover Express of January reported, *'Expert cheers year of run-in with panthers'* (who makes these headlines up?) after my recent year once again of so many sightings. On 15th January another leopard was seen at 8:30 pm by a motorist driving at Capel Le Ferne, Folkestone, and on the 28th another panther was seen between Mersham and Ashford at 11:00 pm by another motorist and his wife.

During the snowfall of February, a woman from Folkestone contacted me as she believed she'd photographed a set of paw-prints across her garden. Upon receiving the photos I concluded they were made by a rabbit as it squats, but on the 6th February at the Julie Rose Stadium, Kennington, Ashford, at 2:10 am, a man cycling home from a late shift at work was terrified when a black animal bounded across the road just twenty yards ahead. A leopard was also seen on 23rd March '06 at 11:40 pm near the station at Hamstreet. A month later, a female witness watched a small black leopard in the grounds of Appledore churchyard at 5:00 am as she stared from her bedroom window. On the 24th June, a woman and her daughter travelling between Brenzett and the local air museum, at around 10:45 pm caught an animal in the headlights about the size of a labrador with a long tail.

The first six months of 2006 had probably been the quietist ever regarding Ashford, with most sightings appearing as fleeting road encounters. But on July 5th came one of the best close encounters ever. It involved Mrs Barnes who was sitting in her car, with her daughter. They were eating a takeaway in the Eureka Entertainment Park at Ashford at around 7:30 pm. At the back of the KFC they saw an animal mooching around. It came within fifteen yards of the car.

The cat was black, had a small head, and long tail, and didn't seem put off by the people around. Possibly the same cat was seen again on the 7th by a woman named Amanda who watched the animal in a field near her home at 7:45 am. She was concerned about the amount of missing pets in the area, and also the fact that small children played in the fields.

Further brief sightings came from Warren Lane in Ashford, as well as High Halden, but on the 7th September the *East Kent Mercury* commented *'Elusive big cat is captured on film'*, stating:

'Two men have a personal crusade – to track down and capture the black panther stalking east Kent. Although they have been approached by the national press and television, birds of prey expert Dave Riches and policeman Ian Woodland decided to invite Mercury reporter Amanda McDine on one of their big game safaris.

The panther stalking the countryside around Deal has been captured on film. The big cat was filmed by a sixteen-year old boy at 5:30 am in a field behind his home. Although only a brief glimpse of the panther was recorded on film, animal experts tracking the cat say it confirms that it exists.

The big cat has been spotted many times in the last three months in the countryside between Deal and Dover. A young cub has also been seen on several occasions. On its trail from the start have been two men from Ashley, Dave Riches, of the Many Hoots Owl Rescue Centre and policeman Ian Woodland. Both admit that tracking and finding the cat has become a personal crusade. And both are confident it can be caught and kept in a secure compound at the owl rescue centre.

I joined them on a wet and windy evening in a large ploughed field near Ripple where they believe the cat has its den. We walked the boundary of the cat's territory and Dave showed me a faint cat footprint and what he believes is the cats faeces, which it uses to mark the edges of its territory. He is now planning to send a sample for analysis in a bid to gain further confirmation that the panther is there.

While walking around the cat's territory we met a couple whose garden backs onto the field. Days earlier Elizabeth had seen the panther and her son filmed it with a camcorder early the following day. The film shows a black shape slinking past a wooden fence. The animal then ran across the field but in his excitement Peter failed to get further shots.

"The film was proof that there is something out there – and I do not believe it was a big black dog." said Dave.

The two men have been contacted by national press (including The Times) and Sky Television for an exclusive story, but they decided to give the scoop to the Mercury. "The ones we will help are the papers that have helped us. The Mercury has always written great stories on us all the way through from day one..." said Dave.

We have decided to keep the exact location of the panther's territory secret for its own safety. "The one thing we do not want is for anyone to harm the cat in any way. We know it has a youngster with it," said Dave.'

I personally found this article an insult to the animal in question. Here were two guys who'd pretty much vanished since the '90s claiming that a cat with a cub needed to be captured and kept in a compound and yet they didn't want it harmed! I found it odd that such a cat, which had obviously eluded them for so long, was clearly enjoying its life in the wilds around Deal and Dover, so why on earth should it want restricting in a cage?

Ten days later, a black panther was seen at Eastry by Mrs Marsden at 1:15 pm. In October more sightings emerged from all over Ashford, as well as Whitfield, Dover at 6:50 am when a man just about to get into his vehicle noticed a three-foot long black cat walking slowly across the road.

A few days later, in early November, Mr Jarman and a neighbour both saw a black leopard near Woodchurch, whilst on the 9th December, a woman named Jan heading towards Junction 10 of the A20, just past Bockham Lane, saw a cat disappear into the banks of the M20. It was larger than a fox, with creamy-brown fur with darker circles. The woman believed it may have been a leopard – possibly the only ever sighting on record of a normal spotted leopard? However, after chatting to her and gaining more details she believed that the animal may well have been a leopard cat, a small felid from south-east Asia.

In 2007 a woman called Alison observed a black leopard crossing the Elham Valley Road on the Lyminge side of the Palm Tree Pub, as she was driving towards Canterbury. The animal came from a field on the left and walked into a field of sheep.

Among other sightings, a black panther was seen at Woodchurch on 6th Feb' 2007 at 5:50 pm by an Alison Steed, who also claimed that in the past her cat had been attacked by a big cat which left puncture wounds on top of the cat's head and also under its jaw.

On Wednesday 14th March, Doreen Barnes had an incredible encounter with a black leopard at the Eureka Entertainment Park. Again, an unlikely spot for such an incident yet, indeed, a place where regular occurrences were taking place regarding large cats.

It was 5:30 pm. Doreen was the passenger in her daughter's car. They'd been to Maidstone, and whilst coming through Ashford they decided to visit the complex, buy a take-away and eat it in the car park. A year previously they'd been eating in the same place and seen a large black cat, and this time Doreen asked her daughter: *"Wonder if we'll see the cat again?"* They both laughed as they dined.

Then, moments later, from the direction of three parked cars, a black cat emerged. No ordinary cat, but again, a big cat. Doreen and her daughter sat in amazement as the animal veered between several cars and then out of sight. Minutes later Doreen's daughter got out of the vehicle to put her litter into a bin when the animal appeared again, just a few metres away. Doreen hastily got out of the car and both of them stood, mesmerised by the animal which casually strolled around the car-park. Doreen's daughter took a photo on her mobile phone, but it had come out blurry, and the animal sat by a bush and then decided to nose through some litter before slipping away behind a fast-food restaurant.

Overall, Doreen and her daughter watched the cat for more than twenty-minutes. They agreed that it was slinkier than the animal they'd seen previously, had a smaller head and big, green eyes. A few days later, a man walking his dog in an area of Stanhope, Ashford, at 7:30 pm, noticed his dog freeze on the spot as a black leopard walked into the nearby woods. The man knew what animal it was because he'd seen it, or a similar one, a year previously at Woodchurch.

The panther of Eureka Entertainment Park was seen again around March 21st, by a Mr Coxon who was driving along the dual carriageway nearby. The cat was in a field slinking through the grass and prowled towards some trees.

Four days later a panther was seen by Mr and Mrs Harden in the Hamstreet area, and further sightings occurred through spring into summer at Aldington, Biddenden, Shadoxhurst, Dymchurch, and Kennington. On the 7th July a cat resembling a caracal was seen near Canterbury University by a male witness who was driving around 10:30 am. In the same month black leopards were also seen at Dungeness and River, Dover, whilst on the 3rd August a panther was observed at Herne Bay. A few days later a panther was seen at Ruckinge, and a lynx at Willesborough, whilst on August 23rd Matt L. reported that he was:

> "...walking to work in Folkestone, near the motorway, I saw a large black cat, that was as shocked as I was as we came within feet as we turned a corner into each other! It made a half attempt at a snarl but turned and fled quickly. It was 5:40 am and I was still shaking with adrenaline at 10:00 am!"

During early autumn, a group of friends observed a black leopard prowling near the Military Canal at Hythe. Not long afterwards I was contacted by a man named Bernie who lives in a small village between Dover and Deal. He'd heard a lot about local sightings of mysterious wild cats and told me of strange droppings he'd found and photographed in a nearby field. He mentioned several sightings of a big black cat in the area, and in 2008 he had his own sighting of a large cat.

On the 12th October, a motorist saw a black leopard whilst travelling late at night through Bilsington, and on November 6th at Great Chart around 4;10 pm, a woman and her daughter saw a black panther in a field which slinked into a hedge. Ten days later a woman walking her two dogs at New Romney saw a black felid, the size of a labrador, which excited the dogs tremendously.

On the 1st December a leopard was seen at Hamstreet, and two days before Christmas a farmer from Romney Marsh rang me to say he'd lost a sheep. He found the carcass which had a severe throat wound. A few days later a sheep five miles away was killed and eaten, and another local farmer spotted a fawn coloured cat crossing a lane in the area. On 19th April '08 a huge puma was seen near Great Chart and left a set of impressive prints, whilst another, bigger than a labrador, was sighted by an elderly couple as they sat eating at 12:00 pm in the vicinity of Sturry.

This run-down of sightings from east Kent, is only a small percentage of goodness knows *how* many I've received over the years. I'd be very surprised if there's any town in the whole of Britain that has produced, on a consistent basis, more sightings of big cats than Ashford. Of course, the heavily forested areas help their cause, and maybe several wild felids out there are constantly attracted to the local zoo parks and the cats they hold. Especially if that's where some of them came from in the first place!

'

> *"He said it was gigantic with yellow eyes. The next day he said it had green eyes."*
> *The Nature Of The Beast* - Janni Howker

Toy leopard found at Dover in place of exotic cat. (p. 238)

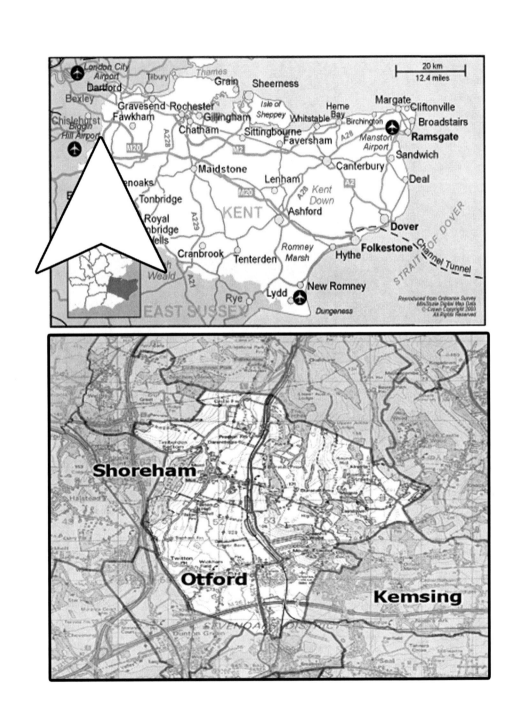

The Otford Panther and Others

'Next, the Beast got into the playground. I don't mean the actual creature itself, but the rumour of it.'
The Nature Of The Beast – Janni Howker

The so-called Otford 'panther' could well have the biggest territory of any of the Kent cats, yet as an elusive, prowling, local mystery cat it's never really made a name for itself, headline wise. Naturally, the press in the area were desperate to have their own 'beast' - but 'Otford panther,' despite its genuine existence, just never sounded quite right. And here was a creature, that one week could be roaming the fringes of Gravesend and Dartford, and becoming a Bluewater 'beast', the next it could be padding through Tonbridge and across into the ancient woods of Mereworth, just a few miles from Maidstone, or indeed taken a trip to the vast forest areas of neighbouring county Sussex. And so, the Sevenoaks 'panther', or puma, or whatever else was out there, was certainly one of the most difficult animals to track, despite an increasing number of sightings. And, like a majority of other Kent cats, the Sevenoaks-related animals certainly had their 'moment' as such in the press, but it was never to become a household name.

Deriving from the Saxon word 'seouenaca', pertaining to the growth of seven oak trees which grew around a small chapel in the Knole Park region, the town began life in 800 AD. Author Malcolm John, in 1978 wrote, *'The town was originally called Sevenoke and in the 18th century was commonly known as Sennock.'*

Situated to the east is the one-thousand acre Knole Park which could be the main reason as to why so many exotic cats lurk in the local woods. Thousands of deer inhabit the vast woodland, and at its centre lies Knole House, where the Sackville family reside. The park's biggest claim to fame, in my eyes anyway, comes from 1967 when *The Beatles* filmed two promotional videos in the grounds; *Strawberry Fields Forever* and *Penny Lane.*

There do not appear to be, on record, many accounts of large cats strictly in Sevenoaks area previous to the 1960s. And yet in neighbouring towns, and certainly in Sussex, (as you'll read later), reports emerged in abundance.

During the late '60s at Brasted, Westerham, a teenage girl walking with friends had a very close encounter with a black leopard which came from nearby undergrowth in the vicinity of Elliots Lane, and proceeded to sit down in front of them. The girls were naturally hesitant to approach but after a few seconds the cat walked away casually. The '70s were pretty much a non-event rather peculiarly, considering sightings were being reported elsewhere, and the 80s were as dead as the jackal shot in Sevenoaks in 1905, which certainly suggested that no cat owners were releasing their animals in abundance. Unless, of course, they were taking them elsewhere.

In September of 1994, Mr Bloom travelling from Eggpie Lane in the Weald, near Sevenoaks towards Leigh, saw a melanistic leopard, and possibly in the same year a cat, black in colour, was seen at dusk in an unknown location within Sevenoaks; but reports certainly weren't flooding in... and neither were they trickling in, strangely enough!

Two years later Mrs Salter saw a black panther as she was driving in the Westerham area, but for the next two years no reports whatsoever were filed regarding Sevenoaks, despite 1998 certainly being the 'year of the beast' after the exposure of the Blue Bell Hill animal which provoked many people into reporting their unusual sightings.

In 1999 *This Is Kent And East Sussex* reported, *'I saw a puma in town'*, Trish Fermor wrote, *'A teacher claimed this week he felt like, "...someone out of The X-Files", because no-one believes he saw a mountain lion – also known as a puma – in Southborough.*

Jonathan Eastal, 36, was driving to his parents home in Valley View when he saw the large cat standing on the side of the A26 near its junction with Harland Way. He spotted the creature at 3:45 am on Sunday January 17th and is adamant it was not a fox. He said, *"It was about the size of a big fox but it had a cats face. It was standing on the side of the road about eight feet away and looking at me. It was lion-coloured, sort of sandy, and looked in good condition. I drove past but decided to turn the car round and go back. By the time I got to where it was it had gone. I did see another car, perhaps the driver saw it too."*

On the 2nd February the same paper told of the, *'Big cat sightings flood in from worried locals'*, which seemed to kick off a slight snowball effect regarding local reports.

> *'A mystery puma is skulking around the Tunbridge Wells area, according to readers who have flooded the Courier with calls. Readers telephoned to back up the story of Jonathan Eastal, with claims that they too have seen the pumas in Southborough, Tonbridge, East Peckham and Lamberhurst.*
>
> *Spanning two years, many have waited until now to speak out for fear they would not be believed. Deirdre Morris, 67, of Tunbridge Wells, twice saw a black animal she thought was either a puma or a panther. She first saw it while walking her two dogs in the woods on Southborough Common in July last year, she said: "It had a small head with little pointed ears, and a long back, long tail and long legs. It was stalking through the undergrowth."*
>
> *Keen jogger Richard Jacobs, 41, of East Peckham, found company as he pounded the midnight lanes. "It was on my left in a ploughed field about two-hundred yards away. I think the pat of my feet startled it. I was slightly awed by it as though I had been in the company of a big cat."*
>
> *Ann Wood, of The Ridgeway, Tonbridge, saw the puma in a neighbour's garden last week. "I knew it was not a fox,", she said. "It had a tiger-like face." She believes the puma could have mauled a cat whose carcass she found on Tonbridge football ground.*

*Nick Weal, 31, of London Road, Tunbridge Wells, saw a beige-coloured cat crossing the
road in front of his car in December.*

*He said: "It was slimmer than a lion but it was big. The police are not concerned. It's
about people's safety. It is a wild animal. Who knows what it is capable of."*
*Angela Brewster of Berkeley Road, Tunbridge Wells, said her son Callum, who was eight
at the time, heard a lion-like roar. He was out with a friend when he heard it.*

*A cat was also seen on January 16th just past Shipbourne. A woman said: "I thought it
was a fox but it had a cat-like face, I thought I was seeing a ghost."*

*Marie Sharman, 70, of Speldhust Road, spotted the animal in the school playing field off
Broomhill Road last week. She heard her dog barking in the garden and first thought it
was a fox.*

*But others believe people may have been mistaken. Brian Burren, of Rusthall, who regu-
larly goes badger watching in the early hours of the morning, has seen a sandy-coloured
badger which he believes people may mistake for a puma. Iain Luxford, west Kent police
spokesman, confirmed the police had received one report of a sighting. He said: "At this
stage the sightings are all over the place and are infrequent so it is difficult to know what
we could do."*

*RSPCA Supt Stuart Farmer confirmed there had not been any recent reports of pumas,
which can be any colour, in the Tunbridge Wells area. He said: "It would be very unusual to see a puma. They are not found naturally in the wild. A large cat would only be
on the loose if it had got out of a private collection and we've had no reports of any going missing."*

*Supt Farmer said people could have mistaken the creature for a large domestic short-
haired cat which can be two-foot long.'*

This article pretty much summed up a lot of the press reports at the time and also confirmed my feelings
that local authorities were completely useless when it came to investigating reports. Worryingly, such
inadequacies are still reflected today, but what irritates most is how someone can come forward and so
easily dismiss so many reports of what were clearly puma and black leopard in the area. Unfortunately,
the press report claiming that '…pumas, which can be any colour' was certainly an impressive inaccu-
racy which would no doubt have caused confusion in the public. Given such a statement, and also considering the ignorance of local authorities, it was quite clear as to why there'd been no Sevenoaks sightings for twenty years – because people were indeed too afraid to report such sightings. Firstly, the press
were getting the stories wrong, although at least they were showing an interest. Secondly, the police did-
n't have a clue how to file the reports or look into the sightings. And thirdly, the RSPCA were making
bizarre statements instead of actually looking into the eyewitness sightings.

On the 8th the *Courier* reported that, *'Lynx spotted twice in Kemsing'*, stating that:

*'A lynx-like creature which witnesses say measures six feet long from head to tail has
been spotted prowling gardens of Kemsing.*

And a similar creature has been seen by no fewer than eight people south of the district.

The mysterious animal was seen at Highfield Road property on Wednesday afternoon by three Biggin Hill-based builders working on the empty house. Earlier it was spotted by a gardener in the village. One of the builders, who did not want to be named, said: "It suddenly appeared out of some bushes and sat on the grass for half a minute, just watching us. It was sandy-coloured with pointed ears and looked like a cross between a lynx and a cougar. It wasn't sleek and didn't walk like a cat. It sort of lolloped along. It definitely wasn't a fox, cat or dog. It was well built and muscular. We ran to get a camera but by the time we got back it had gone. The property has been empty for a while so maybe it's just been hiding out there."

This is not the only reported sighting. Gardener Brian Judd, 56, from Park Lane, Kemsing, claims to have seen a wild cat while working at a Pilgrim's Way property last year.

"We were working out in the garden when we spotted something behind a boulder. It jumped up a tree in one bound. The first branch is six-foot from the ground and when it went to take it at full stretch, its tail was dragging on the grass. I know what I saw and this was no domestic cat."

Despite the confusion it seems that once again a puma was in the vicinity. However, on the 18th things became more confused when the *Courier* ran the story:'

Sightings of wild cat point to lynx', 'More than one wildcat is prowling the Sevenoaks countryside, according to a dangerous animal expert.

Multiple sightings of the sandy coloured fox-like creatures have been supported by dangerous animal trapper and consultant Quentin Rose. He identified the animals as caracal – African lynx – which are, he says, breeding in the area.

After reports last week of sightings in Sevenoaks and Kemsing another four witnesses have come forward including Chronicle deputy editor Andrew Cruickshank.

Former sceptic Mr Cruickshank, 34, says he saw a small wildcat not dissimilar to a caracal lynx early Sunday morning during a round of golf.

He said: "I haven't really believed other people's stories but perhaps now I should eat my hat. I spotted the animal crossing the fairway in front of the 7th green and I knew it wasn't a fox from the way it lolloped when it ran. It had brown fur and was the size of a fox but didn't have a bushy tail – it was not the size of a domestic cat or dog. I knew it must have been the wild cat."

In a letter to the *Chronicle*, Sevenoaks paramedics Julie Hewitt and Lynda Davis also claim to have seen a lynx-like, tan-coloured, muscular animal with pointed ears walk across the Tonbridge Road a year ago while on duty in the early hours of the morning.

And Chris Peppiat, of Kemsing, believed that she had seen a similar animal in her garden on Wednesday of the previous week.

"It just sat there watching me," she said. "It was slightly bigger than a fox, was sandy brown in colour and had very distinctive ears. It was definitely bigger than a domestic cat and moved like a big cat."

Expert Mr Rose, of Gloucestershire, said: *"These animals have been roaming the area for many years. They are not indigenous and are a among a number of cats released back into the countryside after the Dangerous Wild Animals Act of 1976. They are potentially dangerous only if cornered or surprised. They tend to avoid people and are very rarely known to attack."*

For me it was good to see an expert such as Quentin Rose involved in the research, and it certainly steadied the confusion. But it was strange how one moment large pumas were being seen, then a black leopard, then no puma or panther and suddenly a handful of animals resembling the caracal. This was typical of the time, and an example of how people then begin to think they've seen the same thing despite the fact they may have seen a different wild cat entirely. However, this also produced a negative effect because people at the time who'd seen a panther, weren't coming forward because they often felt that the press were only interested in sightings of a caracal, and so in turn witnesses to other cats were keeping their stories to themselves for fear of ridicule. The lack of expert opinion from the likes of the police and the RSPCA wasn't helping the cause either.

Suddenly, the caracal reports ceased, and the puma was back. One such animal, described as, *"...the size of a German Shepherd, milk chocolate in colour with a long tail"*, was seen at Ide Hill's Emmetts Garden by a family having a picnic on the picturesque National Trust grounds. On the 21st April it was reported that a similar cat was seen at Riverhead, it was eating some dog food. The description however was vague with witness Horntvedt Phillips stating, *"It was not a domestic cat or a dog. It was bigger than a fox with a long tail and short hair."*

In September, five months after the initial cat-flap, a Crowborough motor technician observed a black leopard in the Rotherfield area. At the time another clever RSPCA spokesperson claimed, *"It is very rare for big cats to be living in the wild in Britain."*

Despite the scepticism, on 4th November '99 the *Courier* reported, *'Big cat spied at school'*, stating:

'A mysterious wildcat has been spotted roaming the grounds of Sevenoaks County Primary School.

Margaret Sharp's sighting on Wednesday afternoon last week follows several reports earlier this year of lynx-like creatures in Kemsing, the Otford Hills and Knole Park.

Walking down Bradbourne Park Road Mrs Sharp thought her eyes were deceiving her when she saw the creature sitting on a bank behind the school building.

"I could see over the wall into the grounds which are fairly wild. On a bank in the distance I could see the animal sunning itself like a cat. It was sitting upright and had very pointed ears which made me think it wasn't a big dog," she said.

"I looked at it for between five and ten minutes. It was sandy colour and stared at me with very bright eyes. Another person was walking up the road and I hoped she would reach me in time to see it as well but as she came up beside me the animal disappeared."

Headteacher Fred Sandall said he had not heard about the sighting but he would investigate the matter and alert the caretaker.

"It is quite important, because we are using the site after dark now," he said.

Indeed, a sighting near a school should have had the police appealing for calm, but the cat itself remained as quiet as the constabulary, because the next reported sighting never filtered through until the February of 2000 when a Sherry Griffin spotted a black leopard opposite Otford surgery. She told the paper it was big, very fast and heading for Eynsford Road.

In the June of the same year a woman contacted me to report her experience.

> *'Tunbridge Wells – Nellington Wood, Rusthall. My daughter and I were badger watching in a meadow just outside of the wood one evening about 8:00 pm. We heard a terrible sound that lasted about two to three minutes. It was a snarling, screaming and growling all at the same time. My daughter who was eleven then, started crying. We were terrified and ran half a mile to the road and then walked in the middle of it in case there was something lurking in the hedges. People have said it must be a fox but I've heard that plenty of times and it was nothing at all like that. We will never go into the woods at that time of day again.*
>
> *I've had to put up with a lot of stick from people, but a local farmer has heard a big animal padding up the stream.'*

The woman was clearly unnerved by the encounter. It's possible that she'd heard an animal such as a fox being killed by a large cat.

Also during the warmer months a man named Mike, who was walking his two dogs on a track from Kemsing to Otford, at 6:00 am saw a black panther on the footpath up ahead. Although the animal was some four-hundred yards away he instantly knew it was a large, wild felid.

A cat was also seen around the same time near the Chiddingstone causeway, towards Leigh. On this occasion, a female motorist saw a sandy-coloured big cat sitting in a field behind a gate. Then, a woman named Julie, walking her two German Shepherds through woods at Olbury Hill, on the A25 just outside Sevenoaks, spotted a large, tawny-coloured cat in a nearby field which she identified as a puma. During October, 'the season of the witch', Miss Palmer, driving at 11:30 pm observed a sandy-coloured cat with tufted ears which ran across the road some fifty feet ahead as she was travelling at Bidborough. A panther was seen between Hadlow and Tonbridge one night by a motorist, but monitoring the sightings at the same time I determined that such cats, could well have been the same individuals also seen at Orpington and further north into Bromley, as well as towards Gravesend, and because the lack of reports was correct to assume so, although deep down knew that Sevenoaks and the surrounding villages most certainly had their own small population of a variety of species of cat, but the reports were simply too few and far between to pin-point exact routes at the time.

One of the major tabloids had briefly spoken of a leopard sighting at Shoreham, six miles north of Sevenoaks, but the bombardment of reports from Gravesend was overwhelming at the time, so maybe I neglected doing investigations and appeals in Sevenoaks hence the lack of sightings.

The *Courier* of 8th February 2001 ran the story, *'Kent and East Sussex: Paws in hunt for panther'*, commenting:

> *'Promising big cat sightings in the Kent and east Sussex area have come too late for Canadian tracker Simon Goldfinch. He has been forced to return home to his wife Vee and baby in British Columbia without getting to the bottom of the long running mystery.*

Mr Goldfinch, 47, has been catching all kinds of ferocious animals in Canada for twelve years but was unable to get a fresh lead on the beast before jetting off last week. However, within days of his departure the Sevenoaks Chronicle and our sister paper, the Courier, received word of large paw prints in the area. After last month's snow fall Lynn and Graham Briggs from Weald were out walking their two dogs, Erik and Amy, on Big Meadow, behind Nizels Golf Club.

Mrs Briggs said: "As we were walking along my husband suddenly shouted out, "What the hell are those!", as I looked sown I saw huge paw prints, I looked for claw marks that would indicate the sign of a dog but there weren't any. The prints were about three-and-a-half inches wide, which would make it a very large cat. Although I am convinced there is a panther roaming about, what I saw was very strange indeed."

Peter and Shirley Chamberlain, from Tunbridge Wells, had a close encounter with a fawn-coloured 'bobcat' while driving through Crowborough before Christmas.'

The tracker claimed that although he was disappointed not to have glimpsed a large cat, he vowed to return to bag himself a cat which in turn he would give to a zoo. Thankfully, as far as I'm aware, Mr Goldfinch never returned.

Although situated near the town of Maidstone as a parish of Malling district, Mereworth's ancient and foreboding woods could hide any number of cats whose territory includes Sevenoaks, Tonbridge, and further north. The village has the Wateringbury Stream winding through it, such a waterway snakes for around four miles. Author William Cobbett once wrote during the 1820s, *'From Maidstone to this place Merryworth is about seven miles, and these are the finest seven miles I have ever seen in England or anywhere else.'*

Indeed, his compliments were accurate; for the village is the epitome of Kent and its rural landscape - a wild haven of deep, dense woodland that melts toward the delightfully-named villages of Plaxtol, Borough Green, Dunks Green and West Malling, with Sevenoaks not far away.

On the 22nd February 2001 I received an interesting letter from a Mereworth resident named Margaret who had farmed in the area since 1971. She told me how each morning and evening she'd tend to her flock on her land over-looked by the shadows of Mereworth's ominous tree lines. Before the Christmas of the previous year she'd heard from a neighbour that a big cat had been seen around the village and that a dog, which had died of an illness and been put down had allegedly been dug up by the mystery marauder. Margaret was interested in the story but thought no more of it until Sunday 18th February, of which she wrote:

'I went round the sheep as usual with my torch at about 9:00 to 10:00 pm. I was half-way across the field when I heard the big cat. It was a bit like a cat but much louder, deeper, throatier, richer, it was a lovely call. I am not a nervous person but I froze on the spot. I waited but only the one call. It was north of me so I would say between Mereworth and Borough Green.'

It was always a pleasure to meet and speak to people such as Margaret and that's one of the greatest thrills in doing this research. There are so many genuine people out there seeking advice, and an abundance of characters to meet, some bizarre, some very friendly, others who at first are very hesitant of speaking, but Margaret was one of those kind people, who over time would send me cuttings if ever there were sightings reported in the local press.

Jane Snook saw a black panther at 8:00 pm during the March of 2001. She was driving on the Otford to Sevenoaks road when the animal, the size of a Labrador, with a long, hooked tail ran across the road and leapt over a wall.

This Is Kent And East Sussex reported on the 12th March that a tawny-coloured beast had been seen in Hildenborough, not far from Leigh. Doug Aldred was astonished to see the animal twice in a week as it prowled through his flower bed. He described the animal as like a lynx. He believed the cat may have been stalking the ducks in the garden next door.

Shortly afterwards, Mrs Kyd, driving with her husband at 10:00 pm through the back roads from Riding to Hildenborough Lane, saw a cat in the headlights which was dark in colour with a very long tail. Certainly not a lynx. Then, on the 16th March came a bizarre sighting involving witness Barry North who was working at *The Bull* pub near the primary school in Otford. It was around 8:40 pm, and Barry had been taking crates outside, when he heard footsteps on the roof of the school. Thinking intruders were present, Barry went back into the pub and asked two colleagues to come and investigate with him. As they returned, Barry and one of the other men saw, some twenty metres away, a large, cat-like animal padding back and forth on the roof, which was situated around ten feet from the ground.

The cat was silhouetted against the night sky and the witnesses vision slightly hindered by a security light, but Barry was certain that the big cat was staring down at something on the playground. Both men watched the cat for around ninety seconds but when it flicked its tail, Barry's colleague ran in terror back to the pub.

They both described the cat as almost four feet in length and eighteen inches high; very dark in colour, possibly a puma and not a panther and it was very lean.

After the incident Barry phoned the RSPCA who didn't call back until the next morning.

Mr Rotherston saw the so-called Otford panther and reported it to the local *Chronicle*. He claimed it was a puma.

On Wednesday 4th April Sally Alston was driving, with a friend, at 7:00 pm at Ide Hill, Sevenoaks, down Hanging Bank Lane. Around fifteen feet ahead a cat-like animal crossed the dark lane. Thinking that it was a black fox, Sally stopped the car and asked her passenger about what they'd seen. They both claimed the cat was slender, the size of a labrador, with a long tail, and that the animal was very dark in colour. Two days later a tawny-coloured cat was seen on the prowl in Plaxtol by Bridge Trust secretary manager Niall Willis. He was on his way home from Tonbridge when at 8:00 pm he caught the creature in his headlights on an access road off the A227.

He told the paper:

> 'The animal was definitely not a fox and had the appearance of a very large cat with a flat face and a long tail. It had the colouring of a small puma. It jumped on the wall abounding Fairlawn Estate, crouched down for a few seconds and then jumped down.'

The small flurry of sightings enabled me to conclude that some of the individuals roaming Gravesend and Maidstone were not the same cats being seen at Sevenoaks. It was always nice to receive a couple of sightings just a few hours, or a day apart.

Several sightings from the Gravesend area drew my attention but on May 15th Mrs Branston, driving through Sevenoaks spotted a big, grey-coloured cat, possibly a puma. It was around 10:45 pm and she was travelling uphill, west towards Boar Place at around 20 mph when a cat began to bound alongside the car towards open land. She told me, *"The animal was stocky with a long tail, it was going faster than the car."*

On the 23rd May at Dunton Green, between Otford and Riverhead, at 5:45 am, Mr Williamson pulled into *Tesco* garage to fill his car up as he was due to travel to Brighton. Whilst topping up his petrol he caught sight of an animal over one hundred metres away which was walking towards the main road. It was a cat-like animal, muscular with a long tail, jet-black in colour.

On 25th May I finally managed to put a huge appeal out via *The Kent And Sussex Courier* whose stories cover much of the Weald. From Borough Green I received an interesting call from a Tony who claimed that he'd had two of his pygmy goats killed in mysterious fashion. He'd gone on holiday and left his small-holding to be monitored occasionally by a friend. The holding consisted of around 500 chickens, all protected by an electric fence, and the two goats in a six-foot-high compound.

The two goats, weighing around seventy-pounds each, were found dead. The smaller of the two victims had puncture marks on its throat, but the larger animal had been devoured to the extent that all that re-mained was the head and hooves. It was a grisly find for Tony's friend, who immediately told Tony of the grim discovery. Unfortunately, Tony burned the carcasses before I could take a look at them.

On Friday 1st June Tony found the carcass of a chicken in a nearby thicket, it was in a tree! I visited the farm shortly after; it was perfect for a large cat, with fields surrounding the farm, and then heavy wood-lands stretching for miles.Tony mentioned to me that during early May he'd glimpsed a large black cat which darted into a hedgerow.

Also on the 1st June a smallish, sandy-coloured cat was seen killing a cockerel at 7:00 am in the vicinity of Hildenborough. Eleven days later in Sevenoaks, a local man saw a panther in the garden of his bunga-low. In July a beige-coloured cat was seen at Chiddingstone, as it crossed a road at 10:30 pm.

A black panther was seen by a woman driving her burger van through East Peckham during the summer. Also during July, Dave Smart was walking home from the local pub in the vicinity of Matthews Lane, West Peckham, at 11:20 pm. It was a reasonably light evening, and although Dave usually walks in the area with his dog and torch by his side, on this occasion he had neither.

Whilst near Forge Lane Dave heard something in the undergrowth nearby. A long, black animal, very low to the ground slinked across the road. He knew it was a leopard as he'd seen the cat in 2000 at the same spot one night whilst with his dog. Again, he was walking from the public house, but on that occa-sion he caught a pair of yellow eyes in the torch beam. The cat climbed up the bank. On the 4th August a Chatham family were travelling towards Crowborough, but had to turn the car around due to a road clo-sure. At 8:00 pm they were on the A227 to Tonbridge/Ightham and drove by a small wooded area when, just twelve feet away a black leopard strolled through the brambles.

The woman, Tracy, was the only witness. Her husband was busy with his eyes on the road and the four kids in the back of the vehicle weren't paying attention, but Tracy was adamant as to what she saw, she reported to me, *"...it was like the one out of `The Jungle Book`, very dark and a small head, small rounded ears, long legs but with a long tail."*

On the 6th September the *Sevenoaks Chronicle* were all too eager to print photographs of a set of paw-prints they believed belonged to a big cat, which were found in Knockholt, but despite the fuss, the prints were clearly belonging to a dog, showing claw marks, looking extremely symmetrical in shape and nothing like a print a cat would leave.

During the October I recorded a special show for *Radio Kent* as part of a competition. A young lady named Samantha Webb was hoping to become a radio disc jockey, and was conducting her entry for the competition from her farm in Plaxtol.

Plaxtol lies south of Ightham and has a thirteenth century fortified residence called Old Soar Manor. The village is a delight to travel through, although at night the area is a little like entering the twilight zone as spooky lanes drift into the woods and road signs seem to lead bewildered drivers back to where they started.

Samantha wanted me on her hour-long show, because over two weeks four lambs had been killed in a very unusual manner. Samantha took photos and sent them to me, and I was delighted to be on her show which centred upon her family and living on the farm. The poor lambs however had certainly been victim to a large cat. The bodies were untouched around the head and front half, but the rear had been eaten away so cleanly. There had been brief sightings of a large black cat, but the gamekeeper, despite seeing a black panther in the local wood, believed that the lambs had been killed and eaten by badgers. This angered me. It was clear that the lambs, which had been eaten around two days apart, were taken by a cat and when I visited her home on my birthday on 19th October, along with my grandad; most of the community were convinced that some kind of wild cat was on the loose.

A few weeks previously a motor mechanic was travelling home from Seal at 6:30 pm, just approaching Underriver when a black cat, the size of a large Alsatian crossed the road. The witness, a Charles Priauix-Wells, of Hildenborough had previously been a sceptic regarding sightings, but was amazed by what he and his friend had seen.

He told the paper, '*Visibility was good and the animal was very low and sleek. It moved like a cat and disappeared up a driveway.*'

On November 6th Samantha Webb contacted me again, this time to say that a beige-coloured cat had been seen on the back road to Ightham. The animal was described as having a black tip to its tail and being slightly bigger than a Labrador and was seen on the 1st.

The attacks on the lambs didn't continue, but strange scratches on trees were observed in woods around Rusthall. Robert Lindley, who contacted me with photographs, had been walking through Denny Bottom when he came across a western red cedar bearing curious marks. The slivers of the bark were hanging off the tree, as if something had stretched up and clawed at the bark. Some argued that the marks were made by badgers, but the markings appeared to be too high.

In the January of 2002, a male motorist travelling home from Borough Green to Tonbridge through the back lanes near Plaxtol, was surprised to see a flock of sheep standing in the road at 10:30 pm. The man fetched his girlfriend who'd worked with sheep in the past, and when they returned, she found that several of them had large scratch-marks on their flanks. The police were called, and traced the owner, who said that somehow the sheep had jumped the fence. It seems that something hadn't only spooked them but also attempted to bring a few down. Whether any were killed and eaten after this, remains unknown.

A massive black cat was seen on the 25th February, by two relatives as they headed through Borough Green to Seal. It was around 6:30 pm but very dark, when two green eyes appeared, and headed toward their car. The animal crossed the road around twenty feet away, and the witnesses both described the cat as alsatian-sized with a big head.

Much of the spring was a non-event due to lack of press interest, although the summer had several interesting reports, the first was on Seven Mile Lane as lorry driver Simon Bates was driving through Hadlow at 11:30 am. He slowed his vehicle right down to get a better look at the black cat in the nearby field which was slowly crossing the grassy area and remained in view for over two minutes. A black leopard was also seen on 24th June at East Peckham.

A puma was also seen on the Tonbridge/London road by Jane Bennison on 20th July at 1:00 am, who called the animal thinking at first it was a fox, but as it emerged from the shadows Jane became unnerved, slammed the door, and put her shutters down.

On Thursday 1st August a man named Bill was walking his dogs with his wife in the Ightham Mote area of Sevenoaks, when they came across some black, silky hairs caught on a wire fence. Although the dogs were playing-up, Bill didn't think much of the hair but took a few of the strands. He sent them to me but they seemed to belong to a dog as they were rather long, although the previous year they had seen a black leopard at the same location.

A woman named Gene spotted the Otford big cat, firstly in mid-July at 7:50 am as she was sitting in her conservatory, when suddenly a powerful looking tawny cat came around from the side of the house and headed towards the dense woods. On August 19th, at approximately the same time, Gene was once again relaxing in her conservatory, this time with her husband and her aunt, when her aunt "came over very strange" and had a look of utmost horror upon her face. Gene wondered what she'd seen, her aunt replied that a big, black, animal had emerged from around the side of the house, and headed towards the woods. Seven days later Gene, was standing outside with relatives and their three dogs, when a screeching cry came from the woods. The dogs bolted in terror.

It's certainly this kind of experience which leads many researchers to believe that black leopards are being sighted alongside pumas. However, I've seen no evidence to support this in Kent. Just because a black leopard is seen in the vicinity of a puma does not mean these cats are happily hanging around together and mating, because as far as I'm aware, they are not. It's only natural that a variety of exotic felids are sharing their territories, but as far as hybrids of panthers, puma and lynx are concerned, I remain unconvinced.

A taxi driver travelling near Knole Park during mid-September, at around 1:30 am, saw a pure black cat, the size of an Alsatian, on the side of the road. He got the impression that the cat seemed malnourished. Later in the month, a Mereworth woman said that her fifteen-year old son had been walking her collie dog down a track, at 6:30 pm, when he was startled by a rustling noise in the bushes about ten yards away. His dog became nervous, and began to whimper, when suddenly a large, black cat emerged from the foliage, leapt across the track, and fled. The boy ran home to tell his mum of the encounter.

On the 28th October at 11:00 am Mr Harvey was travelling near Otford Manor and saw a panther crossing the road forty yards ahead, but the next sighting, in the Ide Hill area, didn't take place until 11th January 2003, when a man named Gerry was strolling through woods fifty yards from his home at 11:00 am and came across a dead doe. The animal was lying on its left side on flat ground away from the road, but Gerry didn't believe it had been hit by a car. The neck appeared to have been broken, as the head was arched back. The neck had been stripped of flesh, and the local woodsman agreed that the death was suspicious. On 14th April at 9:15 pm a couple walking through Whiteley Woods in Sevenoaks saw a black cat-like creature jump over a fence, but the Otford panther didn't raise its head again until early summer when a couple, previously sceptical about big cat sightings, were travelling at dusk from Shoreham to Otford Road, when they saw a cat quickly rushing across the road, about two-hundred yards in front of them. Throughout the rest of the year, sightings of Sevenoaks' mysterious felids were few and far between.

A puma was seen at Kemsing during early July as it casually strolled across her lawn. On the 1st August the local *Courier* reported:

> 'Strange beast spotted on the prowl at nursing home', - 'A big cat the size of a German Shepherd dog has been sighted prowling around Sevenoaks.
>
> The mystery beast was spotted outside Pinehurst House nursing home, in Seal Hollow Road, by a care assistant who works there.
>
> Helen Kelly said: "I was pulling back the curtain in a room just after 5:00 am and I saw what I thought was a fox. Then I noticed its tail which was not like a fox and also it had a mottled coat. I was really surprised – it was definitely a cat of some sort."
>
> Another resident, who reckons he spotted a similar animal to the one seen by Mrs Kelly, is Otford barber Stan Miles.
>
> Mr Miles, 61, said: "I looked down my garden and saw what looked like four small bears playing around. They were black, chunky creatures about the size of a Rottweiler and they left small, lozenge-shaped print marks in my garden. They came quite close to my back door but then disappeared – I haven't seen them since."

This was certainly an impressive - and important - sighting of a family of black leopards, but no-one else at (or about) the time observed several cats together which is rather strange. It's always a relief to hear reports of two or more cats together, suggesting offspring, but reports tend to be scarce, so a sighting of four black cats was a thrill.

On 7th August at 8:00 pm a man and his father-in-law driving through the rural area of Bewell Reservoir near Wadhurst, Tunbridge Wells, were hoping to park up and take some photographs of the local water and so they reversed up a track and took a few snaps. After taking the pictures they drove slowly back up the incline which was quite bumpy, and as they reached the brow of the hill a big black cat strolled from right to left across the road just twenty-five metres away. Both men couldn't believe their eyes but never had time to reach for the camera. One of the witnesses told me that the sighting lasted around six seconds.

A panther was seen on allotments at Quakers Hall Lane on Saturday November 1st at 7:45 am. The *Courier* claimed to have received four sightings in the last month. On December 2nd at 10:00 pm a black leopard was seen at Sundridge, roughly five miles east of Sevenoaks.

During the snowfall of January 2004 Mr Rose found large paw-prints in woods at Penshurst, Tonbridge and spoke to the local farmer who said he'd lost several sheep.

Reports were certainly decreasing in the Sevenoaks area, on 23rd April the *Courier* reported, 'Farmer shocked to find dead calf', commenting:

> 'A young farmer striving to build up the beef herd at the family business in Newchapel was shocked to find a six-week old calf dead in the field after an attack from an un-

known animal.

Daniel Wickington, 23, of Churchill Farm, found the distressed mother wandering in the field looking for the calf which had lost an eye, one ear had been bitten off and part of its nose. He believes one or two dogs were responsible, "...or I have even read in the farming magazine that a big cat can do this sort of thing", he told the East Grinstead Courier.

"I think whatever it was held the calf by the nose and it suffocated. One dog on its own wouldn't have been able to get the calf down because it weighed eighty kilos. It took me and a seventeen-year old student a lot of effort to load it onto the trailer."

A possible puma was watched through binoculars in the Westerham area at the end of August at 10:30 pm. Mrs Burwood looked out of her bedroom window and saw a large cat, greyish in colour with a long tail and pointed ears as it mooched around a disused dog kennel. The animal then ran up a tree, sat in its branches and made eerie screeching noises.

At River during mid-September a dark-coloured animal was seen crossing the road by Peter Ward as he drove near the *Golding Hop Inn.* Despite scores of sightings reported in the Sussex-based newspapers, reports of large cats were not appearing all too frequently in the papers further north, which was frustrating.

On February 7th 2005 Alan Thomas was on a train to London, at around 10:30 am as the train approached the station before Sevenoaks, Mr Thomas observed a massive brown cat walking across the golf course on the right-hand side. The cat was only thirty yards away. A man named Mark contacted me with the following report:

'I was out walking my dog around 5:30 am on March 8th in the fields near where I live, at first I thought it was another dog but there was no owner. My dog Charlie was restless and wanted to chase it, good job he was on the lead. I am convinced it was a big black cat, it was as tall as a Labrador and had a long tail. The sighting was the back of Tonbridge football club, on the outskirts of Hildenborough.'

A panther was seen on 23rd April near Tonbridge, and again in early May, and on the 16th June the local *Courier* reported:

'Beast strolls into sight', - 'A Plaxtol man has spoken of his close encounter with a big cat in broad daylight.

John Barker was driving home from the shops with his daughter last Thursday (9th June) when the beast appeared from the undergrowth and crossed the road about two car lengths in front of him on School Lane.

He said: "We were talking about how we were worried about foxes because we have chickens at home, then she said, "There's a fox daddy". I just thought, that is a big cat, it had a long tail, big eyes and ears like a lynx but without the tufts. There was a striped look about it with a sandy background. I saw the slinky movement that they have, you could see its shoulders moving up an down."

spoke to the witness after the sighting, because I was slightly confused by the details the newspaper had given. He told me that the cat was around two feet high with a long tail, yellow eyes and its fur was like an, "...*oak colouration*", it also had stripes on its shoulders and was only the size of a dog fox. After much discussion we agreed he may have seen a jungle cat, also known as swamp cat and reed cat.

I received another report from Kevin Davies, an Aldershot man who was driving along the M25 anti-clockwise on the 27th May at 5:40 pm when he saw a large black cat running across the bridge over the motorway between Curry Farm and Sepham Farm. At first he thought it was a dog.

When I spoke to him for extra details, he confirmed that the area was at the junction close to Sevenoaks, possibly between Knockholt and Otford. He believed it was a black leopard as he'd seen a normal leopard in South Africa.

On 30th July at 11:30 am a black cat of some considerable size was seen running across a field east of the A21, before Tunbridge Wells, by Sue Owen as she was driving south.

Towards the end of the year the *Courier* were quick to report, *'Is there something nasty lurking out in the woods?'* after a motorist had discovered a dead deer in woodland near Ightham. The witness told the paper that the deer had bite marks on it which could have been attributed to a big cat. He found the animal as he pulled into a lay-by on the A25 to make a phone call. He got out of his car and took a wander to stretch his legs when he found the lifeless animal. He told the paper that there was no visible damage to the body except for a wound on its side.

However, I examined a photo taken at the scene and confirmed that a big cat had not been the culprit and that the deer had most certainly been hit by a car.

Meanwhile, a handful of reports emerged from the Bedgebury, Wadhurst, Hawkhurst and Goudhurst areas, and on the 28th May 2006 at 9:30 pm near Penshurst, a woman driving saw a dark-coloured cat run across the road. The cat then stopped by the side of the road, and the woman approached and got to within ten feet before it leapt across the road to the right. She strongly believed it was a panther and that it was very dark brown with the rosettes visible. It was another six months before an animal in that area was sighted, this time at West Peckham when a motorist named Ken, at 11:15 am saw a melanistic leopard run across a tight bend he was taking.

2007 was certainly a hectic year for my research, but you can observe already that Sevenoaks was struggling to have its own mystery cat because the territory was so vague. And the sightings, when they did occur, had no real theme or consistency to them. There could never be an Otford panther, or Hildenborough beast because one moment such a cat could have been in Dartford, the next in Sussex, and there were proving to be too many gaps to fill in between the sightings.

As the snow fell during February '07 a married couple looking out of the window of their home in Riverhead were stunned to see two black animals stroll across the disused land at the end of their garden seventy feet away. Both animals were bigger than a Labrador dog, thick-furred, and after they strolled away they left large prints in the snow. Again, this was another impressive sighting and yet no other sighting emerged of two cats together.

The police logged a report on April 20th 2007 at 4:19 pm of a black leopard in Sevenoaks, but no other details were forthcoming. The following month a big black cat was seen by an Emma Holmes in Sevenoaks at 5:00 am as she attempted to deter a fox from her garden by banging her window shut. During late August / early September between the hours of 7:00 and 7:45 am Wendy Stevens had observed on three occasions, a strange cat in fields between the Otford road from Sevenoaks and the lakes. She told me:

> "*This is a large wildlife reserve that borders on to town. Between us and this field, sometimes children play football, we have watched this cat for around ten minutes each time. The first time we saw it, we thought it was a puma. I have lived in Argentina and Brazil for twenty years and have seen these cats there. In the last two weeks we have twice seen a younger, smaller more orange-coloured cat. It is significantly larger than a domestic cat.*"

After the initial fuss, it seemed that it was only a domestic cat in the end, which I found amusing yet bizarre!

On Saturday 29th September on the A21, half a mile from the Westerham turning, a man driving at 11:30 am towards Sevenoaks saw, whilst with his wife, a leopard moving between fencing heading towards an open field. A lady named Jean coming from the outskirts of Groombridge, at 11:00 am saw a black cat, smaller than a Labrador which crossed the road in front of her. She told me it "…*was an awe-inspiring sight and a shock!*". On the 13th October at 5:15 am a guy named Steve was on his way to work at the junction of Hildenborough Road and Riding Lane, near Tonbridge, when a large black felid the size of an Alsatian crossed the road in front of his vehicle. Steve said:

> "*It was caught in my headlights and the coat looked dull or matt black. I was not going very fast as a few days previously I had seen a deer and was worried I may hit it if I saw it again.*"

Another report came from the same time and in the same area of Riding Lane. A man was driving with his fifteen-year old daughter and they were just three-hundred yards from their house when a cat froze in the headlights about twenty feet away. As the man drove closer the cat ran into a hedge. The animal was described as black with a long tail. On the 25th October a couple driving through Hildenborough were amazed to see a black leopard walking down the road towards them, before it jumped into a hedge and on November 5th another strange, black animal was seen near Hildenborough, but this will be covered in the next chapter. However, it was certainly thrilling to receive a cluster of reports from the same area near Sevenoaks, and as proof that several animals were still out there inhabiting the woods. Of course, and as per usual, the sightings suddenly ceased again and the leopards, pumas, and other mystery felids said to haunt the woods and lanes of the area shrunk back into the shadows. Until the next time…

> '*With long bounds the huge black creature was leaping down the track, following hard upon the footsteps of our friend.*'

> *The Hound Of The Baskervilles* – Sir Arthur Conan Doyle

Shadows across the Border

"It had eaten a lamb right out of one ewe and broken the back of another".
The Nature Of The Beast - Janni Howker

Whilst this book is very much a Kent affair, there will certainly be occasions when my words, and most definitely my research, stray into other territories and dark corners of neighbouring places. I would like to briefly, or as briefly as possible, mention a few sightings linked to Sussex, which may well have connections regarding territory with Kent. For such is the vast stretch of woodland that spreads through much of Sussex, that legends there are rife also, and the local folklore of the county, such as Kent, is peppered with horrifying tales of strange beasts and plagued by mentions of slinking felids. Again, due to the expanse of land which Sussex covers, it is very difficult to surmise exactly as to where particular individual cats roam. From Hastings, down in the east, to Brighton on the coast, and East Grinstead on the edge of the Ashdown Forest, reports of black leopard, puma and lynx have been regularly made. We'll probably never know where one territory begins and another ends, but hopefully this section on exotic felids roaming Kent can be concluded by way of a quick tour of Sussex and its prowling inhabitants.

Like most counties across England, a majority of sightings began in the 1960s and '70s when it was certainly more popular not only to own a big cat, but also quite common to let one go!

A website on the folklore of Sussex states:

'Sussex was originally Suosexe or Suoseaxe, then Suoseaxnaland, meaning the land of the South Saxons. Many names in Sussex are Saxon names, the Saxons having invaded in 477AD, settled the lowlands of Sussex and named most of what we see today. When the Normans invaded in 1066, their manors provided a few new names, but the Saxon names were mostly kept and recorded in the Domesday Book, although probably not correctly, by the Normans. The people wandering the countryside collating all the information for the Domesday Book would have written down the names as they were told by the locals with their thick rural Sussex accents. Modern problems have been caused by the Ordnance Survey who got several names wrong and appeared to make quite a few

THE USUAL SUSPECTS:
(Facing page) FROM TOP: Black leopard, Puma,
BOTTOM ROW: Eurasian lynx (left) Jungle cat (right)

up as they created the maps we see today. Unfortunately, most people have only these maps to go by.'

In 1961 a strange incident took place on the main road into Brighton and was told to me by a man from the area called David. He said that on the A23, Mill Hill, where there were a set of pylons, he'd been hanging around with around twenty friends who all flocked to the roadside after a bad accident had just taken place. As they all approached the crash, a black panther suddenly emerged from the hedgerow and ran across the busy stretch of road. The friends stood agog and they all saw that the cat had something in its mouth and the animal headed uphill towards a coppice. As the boys recovered from the shock they spoke to one of the police officers at the scene who told them that the accident had been caused by a motorist swerving to avoid a black cat that had crossed the road. Various members of the ambulance crew had allegedly seen a black panther emerge from the roadside, and with it were two smaller cats. The animals headed towards an old farm.

I wonder just how many accidents each year on the roads are caused by drivers swerving to avoid, or hitting, large, exotic cats? Incidents such as that may be scarce but certainly have happened in the past on more than one occasion.

In the October of 1964 the *Midhurst And Petworth Observer* reported that at Robins Garth Kennels, in West Sussex, a woman walking her dog in woods had seen the back end of a puma which her dog attempted to chase. The story claimed that the cat screeched and hissed at the dog before bounding away. On the 23rd November 1965 several sheep were killed on a farm at Plaistow, West Sussex. Two policeman observed a cat resembling a puma in the Ashdown Forest but *The Times* of the 23rd July claimed that, '*...the cat was black and tan with streaks of yellow*'. This was the case that would become known as the Sussex 'hyena'. And in 1972 the *London Evening News* reported that a large cat-like animal had been seen running at 35 mph on the Polegate to Folkington Road. Three years later at Brooks Green, near Horsham, a large cat made two horses throw their riders, two teenage girls. Police allegedly found strange hair on a wire fence. Shortly afterwards, a female witness saw a possible puma near Peas Pottage and someone claimed that the beast had been captured by the police near to Brooks Green. In his book *Big Cats: Loose In Britain*, Marcus Mathews, in briefly covering Sussex big cat reports comments, '*Two weeks later it was discovered that a man kept a puma on his farm at Southwater, Sussex. The ten-month old puma was blamed for the sighting, although this was never proved.*'

On 18th July 1977 a Douglas Brownjohn observed a large, grey, lean cat with a small head and long tail in the grounds of a nursing home at Patcham, Brighton. The cat ran off into the bushes. In the summer of 1979, as mentioned in Graham J. McKewan's *Mystery Animals Of Britain And Ireland*, a Colin Carter was walking along the South Downs in the Belle Tout area, near Eastbourne, at around 9:00 pm when he saw a large black felid that crossed the path ten yards away. A Mr and Mrs Clarke saw a similar creature on 10th September 1979 as they walked through Tilgate Forest.

Locals claimed that the animals may have come from a zoo park at Berwick.

Meanwhile, Mr Hannam told me that in the '70s whilst driving at quite a speed through Horsham and Five Oaks, West Sussex, he almost hit a cat the size of a Labrador, but with a shaggy coat. In 1980 M Weaver, whilst walking with a friend in the Ashdown Forest during summer, saw a large black cat walking along a pathway. He described the cat as around eighteen-inches high. In the same year on the Kent and Sussex border, and as reported in the *Sussex Courier* of 13th December, a Lawrence Sharpen was turning his car at the Curfew Inn crossroads when his headlights picked out two yellow-orange eyes. When he clicked on the full beam he spotlighted a black cat running across a grass verge.

The Daily Telegraph of 16th August 1987 reported, *'Tiger snatched'* – *'Two tiger cubs were snatched from Gerry Cottle's circus near Eastbourne yesterday. Animal Rights protestors are suspected.'*

Tony Wareham contacted me in the June of 2002 to report a sighting he had in Sussex during the '80s.

"The incident occurred in August 1987, I was employed as a night driver at the time. I regularly used the road from Burgess Hill to Haywards Heath. The particular night in question I was driving in a southerly direction from Haywards Heath to Burgess Hill at 1:30 am. As I negotiated a bend in the road I saw a black creature over two-foot at the shoulder and about six-foot long, powerfully built with a tail that seemed relatively short compared to its body size, the tail was rounded at the end and quite thick. I noticed that the ears were round, somewhat similar to a Teddy Bear, with no tufts or straggly hairs. The animal looked directly at my vehicle where I noticed that the eyes reflected a bright green, the animal picked up from the road what I assumed to be a road-killed rabbit and bounded across the road from right to left."

During late 1987 rumours were circulating that a lynx-like cat was on the loose in Danehill, a village on the edge of Ashdown Forest.

In 1995 magazine *Fortean Times* listed the following Sussex-related big cat sightings:

- 15th February – Ashdown Forest at Forest Row. Spotted by Gail Brooker in headlights against the snow. Another sighting about a week earlier.
- 31st March – Lewes outskirts. Fox-sized cat with dark stripes and pointed ears, seen in floodlights by tennis court. Cat of similar description seen at Rodmell in mid-April.
- 16th April – North Chailey. Dark brown cat, seen by Hylda Lumsden who made a sketch of the animal.
- 4th May – Kilnwood, South Chailey. Seen by two young girls.
- 26th May – Bough Beech.
- Late July – Bognor. Lynx-like creature caught in headlights.
- Early Aug – Stedham Common, near Midhurst. Fawn-coloured. Similar creature seen half a mile away on 29th August – muddy brown with flecks, blunt nose and long tail. A few days later, this second sighting was said to be of a fifteen-year old yellow-eyed Burmese blue-cream domestic cat.
- Early November – Henfield. Orangey-brown about two-foot, six inches tall with a three-foot tail. Mention of a lynx like creature seen near Bognor in the summer.

In 1997 a lady from Forest Row saw a large, tanned cat running across a field which she described as bigger than an Alsatian. On 14th May 1998 an elderly lady in Tower House Close, Cuckfield, observed a black panther from her bedroom. It was on her lawn just five yards away. In the June a local school teacher from East Grinstead saw a large black cat with a very long tail prowling around the playground. The teacher told other staff about the cat and they all agreed to keep it quiet so as not to unnerve the children. The following year on 11th March a cat described as, *"Tawny-brown with black markings, and a curly tail"*, was seen once again at Tower House Close, whilst in the Autumn, Mr Shepherd reported to me that:

> *"At Sedlescombe, from Hastings, at 4:30 pm I was on my motorbike, turning off the A21. Approaching a sharp hill at 45 mph I slowed as I came to a bend and noticed a car parked on the side of the road. The driver was in the road and staring at something. I stopped and saw, just thirty feet away a sandy-coloured, large cat which was strolling across the road. The motorist looked at me in disbelief."*

During October 1999 a black leopard was sighted by a woman whose parents had moved to a large home, with several acres of land, near Battle. The cat was seen circling a well in the garden, terrifying the witness.

I visited the home of the family in 2000 with my dad and cousin Jez. The place the family had moved into was quite impressive. It allegedly once belonged to a rather strange family who neglected most of their animals, including cattle which were found knee-deep in excrement. Rumour had it also that the family once owned a large cat, or cats, and this was proven when I was shown a pen in the yard which clearly wasn't made for a dog. The pen was made of bricks, around ten feet in length and five feet high, with small flaps either side which would enable the owner to slot food in. In 2000 the family had several experiences with a big cat on the land. The only bizarre thing which took place on the day of the visit, was my father being chased by several cows in a field, as he was inspecting an eaten pigeon. The fenced-in herd weren't too keen on the intruder, but seeing my dad run and vault a high wire fence in one jump was at once impressive and hilarious.

This Is Brighton & Hove reported on 3rd November 1999, *'Panther spotted by dog walker'*, stating that it had been seen at Redford, near Midhurst. According to the press, two years previously, police marksmen had surrounded a copse at Bracklesham Bay, near Chichester after reports a panther had been seen in the undergrowth. To their embarrassment the animal turned out to be a domestic cat.

At the turn of the millennium my research had spanned across Kent into Sussex. Here is an abbreviated list of Sussex-related sightings since 2000:

- The family from near Battle, as recently mentioned spoke of a cat sighting in the March of 2000. The youngest daughter saw, from the house, a large black animal sitting near a hedge and it was staring back at her. It was 9:00 am.
- April 2000 – Family as mentioned above. The mother who contacted me saw the rear end of a black cat going into bushes. Her husband told me that one night he'd driven home, it was pitch darkness and he parked on the drive. Suddenly some large animal leapt up at him, and he could hear it panting in his face. He realised it wasn't a badger but that, or a stray dog was the only animal he could think of, but he strongly believed it may have been the cat that once lived there.
- October 2000 – *Daily Mirror* reported that, '*A black cheetah-like animal has been seen in church grounds at Shoreham.*'
- December 27th 2000 – Uckfield. Mrs Taylor saw a black leopard from twelve feet in her garden. The cat jumped a six-foot fence. Rumour that Lewes police had received a photo taken by a woman of a leopard on a patio in the Iford area.
- February 27th 2001 – Newick, near Uckfield. A panther was reported in a garden.
- April 2001 – East Grinstead, Holtide Common, 4:30 am. Motorist observed black panther heading towards forest.
- August 26th 2001 – A mid-Sussex resident saw a puma on the lower slopes of Wolstonbury Hill, Hurstpierpoint. The cat was fawn-coloured.
- September 2001 – Black leopard seen between Balcombe and Worth.
- October 2001 – A woman named Gill told *Mid Sussex Today* that at her home at Chelmwood Common, on several nights weird, eerie throaty coughs had been heard from the nearby woods.
- 28th October 2001 – A Mr Barton from Newick, Uckfield, saw a lynx run across road at 11:30 pm.
- October 2001 – Henfield. A woman reported to me that over a seven-week period a large animal had been coming into her garden and drinking from her small pond. The woman also heard deep growling noises which terrified her. I advised her to get rid of the pond.
- October 2001 – Lynx seen at Sydney Farm, Cuckfield.

- November 2001 – Newick. A farm worker reported he'd wrestled with a lynx after he disturbed it whilst clearing undergrowth.
- December 21st 2001 – West Sussex. Man and woman travelling through Billingshurst and Pulborough, around midnight when a large cat-like animal was caught in the headlights. The animal was described as light brown and having thick fur.
- Summer 2002 – Panther seen on country road at Hastings.
- 3rd August 2002 – A Mrs Turner driving towards Petworth, saw a muscular, brown, but fox-sized cat cross the road.
- 14th August 2002 – *This Is Brighton & Hove* reported, *'Mystery cat on the prowl'*, after several sightings in the Midhurst area.
- Summer 2002 – A man on a motorbike travelling towards East Grinstead saw a panther bound across road and leap fence.
- Approximately 2002. An elderly woman at an unnamed location in Sussex arrived home late one night and fell asleep on the couch. She was awoken by a strange noise as if something was scratching at the front door. Intrigued by the noise the woman investigated. There had been heavy snow fall that night, and outside the door she discovered a set of large prints that crossed a field.
- 2003 – date unknown. Woman named Mandy walking dogs at unnamed location in the county saw a black leopard which slinked into woods.
- March 2003 – Patcham. Mrs Masters observed a cat with a long tail that was fawn-tan in colour which was looking around some bins before moving away between two houses.
- April 2003 - Several newspapers including the *Daily Mirror* reported on a black leopard sighting from Portslade region. A milkman saw the cat on Southdown Road and the police received more sightings of the animal which was reported to have measured seven feet in length.
- 12th May 2003 – A woman named Carol, travelling at 8:30 pm towards Ditchling Common, near Burgess Hill saw a panther with green eyes standing in road.
- June 2003 – A man walking with his eight-year old daughter on the South Downes near Storrington, was startled by a five-foot long black leopard that was stalking deer.
- 26th June 2003 at 4:30 am. A Steve Ellis was on his way back from Haywards Heath at Fox Hill when a black panther crossed two-hundred yards away.
- August 2003 – A Dawn Tan took photographs of a set of large prints in Battle Woods, Hastings. The witness, who'd lived in India and tracked tigers and leopards was convinced the prints belonged to a large cat.
- 12th August 2003 – West Chiltington, West Sussex. Two men spotted a puma.
- 24th August 2003. Couple walking down Lyoth Lane, Linfield near Haywards Heath, saw a cat, black in colour, which emerged from the darkness of a driveway.
- September 2003 – Burgess Hill. Man walking dogs in Bedelands Estate saw a cat at 4:30 pm. Another cat of similar description seen between Haywards Heath and Burgess Hill.
- 26th September 2003 at 3:30 pm – Mrs Williams walking her dog in the Forest Row area, East Sussex, spotted a puma in a field.
- Late September 2003 – Black leopard encountered by a woman behind houses at St Wilfrids Road, Burgess Hill. Chickens taken at Muster Green by an animal described as large, and grey with long legs.
- 18th October 2003 – 11:30 pm, Maple Drive, Burgess Hill. Male witness watched a black panther jump onto his neighbour's shed roof.
- Late October 2003 – Black leopard seen by woman in Lewes Road, Haywards Heath. Remains of fox found in Turvey Wood, Haywards Heath. Black leopard also seen on edge of Downlands School in Hassocks.
- May 2004 – *This Is Kent* reported on 28th that a passenger on a train on the Bluebell Railway saw a puma sunning itself between Kingscote and Sheffield Park.

- 1st July 2004 – 8:50 am. Peasmarsh, Rye, East Sussex. On road which runs between Flackley and Ash Hotel, a large reddish-brown cat was observed crossing the road thirty feet in front of female witness. She described the cat as, *"Three feet long, eighteen-inches to the shoulder, short stubby tail, pointed ears and white markings on both cheeks."*
- 7th July 2004 - 9:30 am. Male motorist saw a long tailed, dark tan-coloured cat, with black markings on its rib cage, run across road in Sandhurst area.
- 8th August 2004 - 12:30 am. A man named Matt and his girlfriend were walking at East Grinstead when they were circled by a cat, described as, *"...bigger than a fully grown cat, large ears, pointy chin, the fur was a light brown covered in a mixture of darker spots and stripes, with a short tail."*
- Late August 2004 – *Lewes Today* website reported that a cat resembling a mountain lion had been seen near Piddinghoe at around 3:30 pm the previous Thursday. Laughably, Sgt Alan Leslie told the *Express* that, *'These animals can travel up to one-hundred miles in a single night.'*
- September 2004. Crowborough, East Sussex. A lady named Dawn saw a black leopard one-hundred feet away in a field whilst walking her dog and chatting on her phone. She'd seen a similar cat previously in the area.
- 23 April 2005. 10:10 pm. Two people in a vehicle observed a black panther in the East Grinstead area as it crossed road.
- July 2005. Mr Martin saw a big cat at 5:00 am in East Sussex. The man, a landlord of a pub, looked out of the window at Boreham Street and saw a black cat sitting in the middle of a nearby field. Several other sightings emerged from Cuckmere Valeey, Seaford and Glynde up to the Cuckoo Trail and Hailsham. In the same month a large trap was set up by so-called animal welfare 'experts' after reports of a large cat in the Worthing area. Several newspapers and local *Meridian News* reported that officer Billy Elliot was tracking the animal, possibly a lynx, and that a trap had been set up in the front garden of a house in Carnegie Close.
- 19th August 2005. *This Is Kent* reported that several cat sightings had occurred in the Uckfield area. A motorist driving on Horsted Lane, in Isfield saw a long, slender cat on the road, whilst other reports were made from Millennium Green at Ridgewood.
- 25th August 2005. Fifteen sightings reported of a large, cat-like animal in the Upper Hartfield area, although the fact that reports emerged from Cat Street may have suggested a hoax, however, a delivery driver claimed he'd seen an animal as big as a lion, but police who followed up the reports found nothing.
- May 2006 – Linfield, West Sussex. Couple observed puma whilst driving.
- June 2006 – Jogger in the vicinity of Findon village saw a black leopard. In the same month a leopard was spotted at Beachy Head, as reported by *Eastbourne Today*.
- 13th July 2006 – *Sussex Express* ran the story that a Windmill Hill resident, Angela Pearce, saw a big cat whilst driving in Burwash. The cat, a black leopard was lying in the road.
- August 2006 – Lorry driver saw a tan-coloured cat in a field near Crawley.
- December 2006 – Sussex police allegedly dealt with more than twenty cases of big cat sightings in 2006, including a case concerning several sheep found with their ears bitten off.
- 20th December 2006. A daughter and her friend driving back from a pub they work in at Arlington, East Sussex saw a dark-coloured creature which was about to cross the road. The cat shrunk back into the woods.
- January 2006 – A Langney man named John Hescott saw a black cat the size of a Labrador whilst walking with his dogs near his home on the Faversham Road. He reported the sighting to the police. A spokesperson commented that, *"Many big cat theories have been put forward but none, to my knowledge have been substantiated by firm evidence."*
- March 2007 – A black leopard was sighted by a Joanne Walsh who was travelling on the train from Brighton to Croydon. She told a local paper, *'It was a large black animal moving in a cat-like manner with very defined muscle tone and a long tail.'*

Big cat faeces in Sussex BELOW: Sussex lamb kill (p. 275)
(All pictures in this section courtesy Graham Bennett, taken 2008).

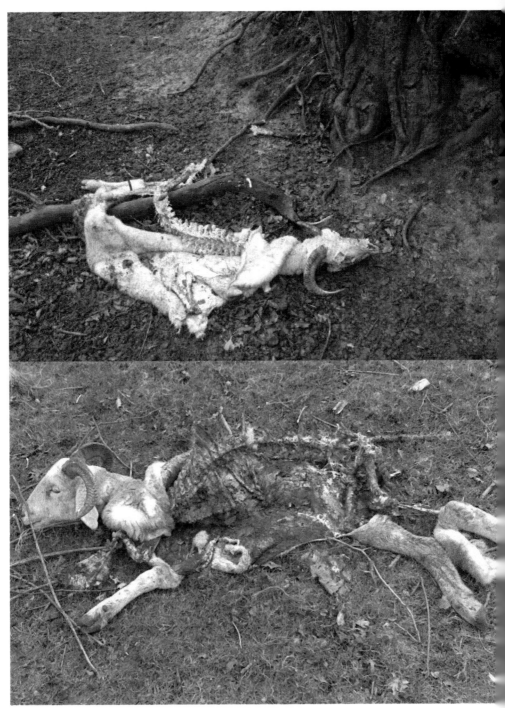

Sussex sheep kill 2008 (Courtesy: Graham Bennett)

- July 2007 – Sheep mysteriously killed in the Crawley region.
- November 2007 – *Hastings Observer* reported that a dog-walker named Doreen Newlyn, saw three big cats in St Leonards. She was taking a stroll with her spaniel Shadow, in the vicinity of Bexhill Road, near the council refuse tip, when she saw the jet-black animals which caused her own dog to freeze on the spot. She told the paper, '*When I saw the first one I was a bit shocked then when the second one walked through the bushes I was gobsmacked. The third one was lying in the under-growth and just got up and crept away. We didn't hang about, we went straight back to the car and went home.*' Bizarrely, a wildlife expert named Trevor Weeks dismissed the sighting. The man, who runs the East Sussex Wildlife Rescue and Ambulance service commented that, '*I have investigated a number of these sightings over the years and they have all turned out to be false.*' In other words, every time he'd followed a sighting up the animal was never around when he got there.
- 7th December 2007 – 12:00 am. Stocky, brown cat with short tail seen in Hastings area. Witness identified animal as a lynx.
- December 27th 2007 – The *Observer* reported, '*A South Cliff resident has seen what she reckons is a large wild cat running through her garden. Now Joyce Prichard is wondering if anyone else has spotted this mysterious creature. "About a month ago was the first time I saw it", said Joyce. "I was sitting there and a big black thing went past. Then I saw it again on the 27th – it was very fast, and it was much too big to be a fox. It had got a long tail and a long body, it was definitely not a dog. It was like a puma or a panther."*
- December 2007 – A woman from Battle in East Sussex contacted me to report several sightings of a large cat on her land. A dismembered deer had been found in local woods and the woman's husband sighted a big, black animal. A horse was lacerated a few months previous and two sheep were found dead in early December, and another turned up eaten a week later.
- December 2007/January 2008 – Farmer Graham Bennett lost a handful of sheep over the Christmas period in the Ashdown Forest area, commenting, "*I have lost five ewes since Christmas, two I have never found the carcasses. Off the three I have found all have the skins rolled back to the back bone the skeletons have been intact, basically whole with the legs still attached (by sinews, if not jointed) The lower legs interestingly have the skin/fleece loose like a sock. The whole carcass cleaned of meat even down the socks. In all cases the head and neck have not been touched. The necks were dislocated which is not unusual for cat strikes. I have paid most attention to the last ani-mal since my conclusion has been confirmed. I thoroughly examined the neck for puncture marks which can be indicative of certain cats with the resultant dislocation of the neck on the last ewe I couldn't find any wounds. The carcasses are licked clean with the very rough tongue. One ewe is the untidiest example of the three the other two were extremely clean to look at. All had not been dead any length of time in my opinion as the eyes were still intact and shiny, the crows had not been at work, after four/five hours the eyes had dried out. I lost a lot sheep last year more than the previ-ous year (my first). Fly strike took its toll but sheep went missing, without finding any carcasses, and my fences were in good shape. Who knows in hind sight some could have been taken. Which brings me to the strength of these cats. They are capable of carrying off a sheep, over fences and gates and can climb trees with a carcass. Henry O_____ told me a friend of his found a sheep up a tree. He saw a large cat three years ago and has lost sheep in the manor as I described. I am not sure he agrees with my explanations.*" I looked at photographs Graham took of the sheep and con-firmed that a large cat had indeed killed them. The animal had also left excrement near the carcass, a sample of which was sent to me. The slaughter continued…almost two a week, and a bag full of deer and fox skulls also as sign of one or possibly more large felids present.
  16th March 2008 – A group of people including a woman named Penelope pulled over at noon to watch a black leopard as it loped up a field and went into a hedge. The cat was seen near Jevington as the witnesses were heading towards the A27 in East Sussex. A smaller black leopard was also seen near Hailsham by a woman walking her dog.
  4th April 2008 – Black animal around three feet long seen at Pevensey.

The list of big cat sightings from the south-east seems endless, and so too are many of the theories, although a majority of these are quite absurd. By analysing the evidence I have presented, there is no proof that an unidentified species of cat is roaming Kent. Despite a few reports of strangely marked cats I see no reason to believe that such animals are completely new species. Until a handful of carcasses turn up in Kent, around London, and Sussex of unknown cats, then I'm under no illusion that such animals out there prowling the woods are something beyond our knowledge.

Year after year magazines, newspapers, websites etc, feature their annual 'big cat' reports but there still seems to be a lack of knowledge, and lack of direction, with frustrating 'investigations' which are simply based on the views mostly, of an armchair enthusiast.

It's my view that the British cat situation should not be a mystery, but but we often find the subject relegated to the realms of folklore, anorak UFOlogy and the likes. This is a field that should be relying on serious investigation and not paranormal associations.

Charles Fort, the original clipper collector had theories that large, out of place cats were in fact teleportations from other countries, and that many sightings of unusual animals were possibly the work of a cosmic jester. At the time this was a naive explanation for a relatively new enigma but such views are still commonly found 70 years on. Many other explanations abound too.

- **Releases**

Few people will actually admit to having released ABCs (ABC is an abbreviation of 'alien big cats', a terrible term used for out of place exotic felids). Unsurprisingly, there are not many people from thirty or so years ago who would have released cats into the wilds on purpose and then casually come forward to tell of their act. A majority of owners who did dump their cats would possibly have said, when asked what happened to their pets, that they had died or maybe escaped, but not many owners would have told the press, police or a so-called 'big cat' researcher of their thoughtless actions. In over fifteen years of research I have come in contact with no more than twenty people who claimed to have let a cat go, or knew someone who owned a cat, or more than one cat, and released them.

Rumour has it that when the 1976 Dangerous Animals Act was introduced, more than 100 people flocked to London Zoo with their pets but were turned away. Even if this figure is exaggerated, just twenty people letting felids wild into the local woods is a startling statistic and certainly a concrete base for today's reports/populations to stem from. Other owners, who possibly panicked when they realise they couldn't afford their animals, must have either been turned away by other zoo parks across the country, or simply drove their animals into remote woodlands and bade them farewell.

Researchers often seem to ignore the fact that the cats released would take no time at all in breeding. the black leopard was the popular pet in the 1960s, such animals when released would take on large territories and easily meet up with other leopards, and mate. The 1976 Act is not the sole reason as to why so many cats roam the UK today despite many researchers' claims that it is, but admittedly it is one of the main ingredients of the phenomenon.

- **Escapes**

Another common researcher suggestion refers to possible escapes of large animals from menageries and circuses and points out that few of these tales have ever been substantiated – but, if anyone, even a zoo in the past, had lost a cat, would they always be honest and own up? Of course not. The Romans, as discussed elsewhere within this book, imported thousands of animals into their amphitheatres. Did none of these animals escape into the wilds? Of course, some escapees may have been easy to catch, but in such cases cats would not have been tame, but felids captured in places such as Africa and brought over to the UK. If a leopard or puma had escaped, would there have been a mass hunt to look for such an animal? Possibly not.

During the times of the Roman settlements, there were no records as such of big cat sightings, and the same could be said for the 1800s when travelling menageries roamed the country.

It's likely that there were many obscure exhibitions travelling the countryside, as owners sought a quick buck to earn a living. Not in every case would the vans/cages etc. which housed such cats have been adequate enough, and then, when such animals escaped, that was it; the vans would have rolled on. There must have been cases also where almost entire menageries were released into the wilds. Such incidents still occur today even despite such strict laws, so one can imagine how many wild animals were released into the local woods over the last two to three hundred years.

In 'big cat' research there are countless 'legends' pertaining to sightings dating back to the 1700s, 1800s and early 1900s. However, there were no registers as such to record sightings and no armchair enthusiasts to collate them, so such reports remain murky with only handfuls making any kind of news and being included in newspapers at the time, as well as personal journals, church records and the like.

The failure of the police and other pursuers to capture such animals is often cited as a point against the presence of flesh-and-blood large cats in the UK countryside.

Whilst no black leopards have turned up having been shot, smaller cats such as jungle cats have. Lynx have been killed on the roads but the scarcity of such evidence is actually as expected.

These cats are very elusive animals. In their countries of origin they shy away from man, and in the UK, despite the countless sightings, they still hunt mainly during dusk and throughout the night. Over a century ago police hunts and other vigils would have been very few and far between, but what frustrates and seems to confuse so many cat researchers and sceptics nowadays is the fact that these cats seem to elude pursuers so easily. No credit is being given here to naturally elusive cats which in most cases can sense when they are in the presence of humans. Police, the army and researchers tend to arrive on scene too late – even ten minutes is sufficient for the cat to be long gone.

Tracking a cat such as leopard, puma or lynx is extremely difficult, and the police and other authorities cannot afford to spare the time to frequent certain areas to pursue their quarry. The cats don't have to be that secretive when they are being hunted/pursued incorrectly. Even the press fails to understand as to why these cats aren't turning up in photographs all the time, and when a cat is filmed they complain it's too fuzzy, but are they really stupid enough to believe that a black leopard will hang around long enough, and be happy enough for a photographer to get within ten feet for a quick snap? In the past, cats have escaped from menageries, from zoo parks, from imported shipments, and the figures alone, which we'll never find out, would certainly have been the reason as to why we have cats today.

- **Prehistoric Survivors**

It's sometimes suggested that UK ABC's are a relict species of pre-Ice Age big cat, still hiding out in the wild.

Although the lynx may have survived in remote areas, there is no evidence to suggest we are dealing with a new species of cat, because the facts state that a majority of sightings involve simply black leopards, puma, lynx. The answer is right there in the definition of the species, so why do people need to create bizarre theories that prehistoric cats are roaming the country? The problem is, many researchers cannot pigeon-hole some eyewitness reports, and so wonder just what is out there in those woods. Yet, whilst eyewitness reports are vital, they can also be vague or exaggerated. We mustn't forget also that we are dealing with a variety of species of cat in the UK. Indeed, the jungle cat is able to breed with the domestic cat, so I'm unsure as to why there is excitement over reports of overly large domestic cats, or even feral cats. This situation is happening in Australia where monstrous cats, yet resembling feral cats are being seen on a regular basis.

Also, we mustn't forget that the cats that inhabit Britain are now *British* big cats. They are the offspring of cats from decades, possibly centuries ago. Leopards will naturally be smaller than their relatives from Africa and Asia, as the prey is smaller and the range is smaller, yet many researchers cannot understand why many sightings of black leopards involve smaller cats. Maybe they are slinky females or young. What's the confusion all about? (See earlier analysis of this.) There is no evidence at all in Kent to suggest we are dealing with new species of cats, so why should this theory apply elsewhere in England?

- **Hybrids and mutants**

Reports of differently coloured cats - presumably of different species - being seen in the same general area has given rise to the suggestion that cross-breeding could be occurring. For example, sandy-coloured cats resembling pumas have been sighted in the vicinity of black panther-like cats.

However, there is no proof as yet that leopards and puma are breeding. There is a remote possibly in the few-and-far-between cases of 'sandy' and black animals that we are dealing with Golden Cats. These can be melanistic. As pumas cannot be black, I'm unsure as to why such theories continue. If by some miracle a black puma turns up, then we'll look at the evidence but it's unlikely to occur.

Similarly, it's been suggested that mutants will spontaneously occur which differ from their parents; for example, a black puma being born of normal pumas. However, there's no evidence to suggest we are dealing with hordes of mutant big cats out there. Researchers tend to become excited by reports of black leopards which seem to have smaller, puma-like heads, but this is annoying. In Kent, we are simply dealing with, as mentioned before, smaller leopards, *and* smaller puma that are evolving in the UK. They are not animals brought over from the USA, Africa or wherever and released here. Only the press still believe that!

- **Secret societies**

It's been suggested that big cats are imported and secretly bred by criminal gangs for cat-baiting entertainment, or to act as hounds in deer-hunting, and are released if injured or they become difficult to maintain.

However, I do not believe this goes on to the extent where an abundance of cats are being bred and released. It is possible that a cat such as a lynx could be released as part of some rich hunter's game, but until such a covert operation uncovers such a scenario, there's no telling. There may indeed be an influx of cats trickling into the UK by ways not as yet spotted by researchers.

- **Cover-ups**

We are getting into the Fortean realm here, a quirky world that attempts to wield together all aspects of the mysterious, but it is something that must not be allowed to interfere with cat research. We are some times invited to believe that the Government knows about the problem and hastily hides the evidence whenever it can. While the cat situation in the UK is not recognised as official, or a protected or at least admitted species, then there will no doubt be theories such as this. I'm pretty sure that bodies of cats, and sheep kills, have been taken away for examination, but that's natural. The government does know that 'big cats' exist in the countryside, but what can the government do? What would the government have to hide? They could waste precious time of the police and the Marines and send marksmen out into the valleys to maybe pick one or two cats off, but what will that achieve? Nothing.

The public would not resort to mass hysteria if the government admitted 'big cats' are roaming our woods, but because these cats don't officially exist, shouldn't such carcasses and evidence at times be cleared up? Of course. But for every sheep kill secretly cleared away, there's always another four or five around the corner that many get to see.

- **Non-biological origins – Black Dogs, Tulpas (thought-forms) and demons**

A recurring folklorist idea is that today's black large cats and the black dogs of British folklore are one and the same – either the black dogs of old might have been misidentified black cats all along, or today's cats are really yesteryear's black dogs.

Researchers should not be confusing roaming big cats with phantom animals. Black dogs, hellhounds etc, or whatever you may call them exist on some other level not related to black leopards. Such phantom hounds which have become known by many names such as Black Shuck, Padfoot and Striker, are part of a complex folklore, and whilst old, murkier reports of padding, agile 'black dogs' with glowing eyes may well have been old sightings of black leopards, the actual legend of the black dog certainly does exist, and should never be melted into the British cat situation. See chapter *The Others.*

The occult sometimes gets the credit for the manifestations of cats in the countryside – It's sometimes claimed that the cats are tulpas materialised through some kind of ritual, or are demons (or daimons, as the ancient Greeks called them), and should be catalogued alongside elves and pixies.

Now, I've written a book on 'tulpas', 'thought-forms' and manifestations, but in no way are these cats some kind of strange materialisation or image conjured up and I cringe at the theory. For any self-respecting researchers to come up with such drivel is embarrassing to the situation. People are seeing large exotic cats in the wild, what's the big deal? Where's the mystery? And why do certain people always link simple things they cannot understand to such ludicrous, un-related anomalies?

As for the demons, this is the most hilarious and ridiculous theory I have ever heard in my life and makes me feel ashamed and embarrassed to be part of the whole situation when a so-called researcher comes up with such vomit. Whilst we do indeed live in a peculiar world, to suggest that these cats roaming our woods date back to the dawn of time is a joke, and some serious head checking needs to take place here. It's not a mystery at all that such animals are here.

It's notions such as this that causes the 'big cat' situation in the UK to be lumped in with so many other anorak phenomena such as UFOs and the recent 'ghost' craze made even more sickening by the *'Most Haunted'* dramatics on television.

A recent article in *Fortean Times* concludes that

> '...*websites dedicated to collecting and commenting on ABC encounters have proliferated in the past five years, and ABC witnesses are increasingly likely*

to report their experiences to a website rather than a newspaper or the police. In one way this is unfortunate as few of the individuals or groups running the sites make their reports public, and so sightings reported only to them can be lost to general research.'

So, what exactly *is* this general research? Sightings plastered all over the internet, areas of sightings advertised to hunters and more plundering researchers who then write articles stating that these animals are from other worlds. Why should serious researchers share information with the police? In my experience all the police will do is file the report, or turn up, look around, and then vanish without a clue. Why should serious researchers become part of groups who spew out mythical statistics, based upon armchair enthusiasts who've collated dramatised newspaper clippings? It's a vicious circle that resembles the weird ol' days of UFOlogists with their petty politics and freakish theories.

Whilst some cat reports *do* not seem to fit into the known species bracket, the lack of consistency in such reports means that they cannot be taken seriously, or must at least be taken with a pinch of salt until further evidence presents itself. However, to place such animals into a realm of fantasy is complete madness, and it is nonsense like this that will prevent the much-needed proper research from gaining any credibility.

'I lay in bed. I couldn't believe it. I lay there and everyone thought I was lying through my teeth – or that I was delirious with the pneumonia. Of course all the flaming sheep killing stopped! The Beast was lying under half a ton of peat and water and moss. No-one would even go and look!'

The Nature Of The Beast – Janni Howker

Gordon Richman, the farmer on whose land, near Wyevale Nursery, the author sees a black leopard, and Mr Richman sees a puma (p.147)

PART THREE

More Mystery Animals

Wolves in the Weald

'Deep and terrible, the snarling, half-mad growls and barks continued;
always in mounting volume, but with hideously significant pauses.'

The Dunwich Horror – H.P. Lovecraft

I have drowned you in eyewitness reports of exotic cat sightings, and smothered you with the evidence and data which proves that large, elusive felids are in our midst. Now that you have had the chance to come up for air and crawl from the shadows, I introduce to you another strange menagerie from the rural canopy, a further delve into Kent's half-hinted creatures that roam and seek shelter within the florid avenues of summer, the ice-moulded tunnels of bitterest winter, the dew-damp mornings of a shower-drenched spring, and the smoking bonfire scent of a rustic autumn.

'Primarily medium-sized flesh eaters, canids are more omnivorous than many carnivores, taking as food invertebrates, plant matter, and carrion as well as the prey they kill themselves. They are adapted more for endurance than for speed, and they catch prey by pursuit over long distances in relatively open terrain until the prey tires. Kills are made by grabbing for the nape of neck and tackling the prey to the ground. The neck grab is followed by a violent shake, which may dislocate the neck of the prey. Large prey may be immobilized by biting into the soft parts of the underbelly, often resulting in disembowelment and death from shock. Sense of smell is acute and appears to be critical to these animals, as is hearing, but sight is less developed. Canids have deep-chested bodies and a long muzzle.'

– Animal Diversity Web

The Family Canidae is formed of thirty-six species including the following:

- Short-eared dog (Genus Atelocynus)

- Dogs, wolves, jackals, coyote (Genus Canis)

- Crab-eating fox (Genus Cerdocyon)

- Maned wolf (Genus Chrysocyon)

- Dhole (Genus Cuon)

- Falkland Island wolf (Genus Dusicyon)

- African wild dog (Genus Lycaon)

- Raccoon dog (Genus Nyctereutes)

- Bat-eared fox (Genus Otocyon)

- South American foxes (Genus Pseudalopex)

- Bush dog (Genus Speothos)

- Grey foxes (Genus Urocyon)

- Foxes (Genus Vulpes)

If we exclude dogs and foxes, with which we are familiar in the United Kingdom as our pets and urban scavengers, you may be shocked to know that at least three other members of this family have allegedly been sighted in the county of Kent and its outskirts over the last two centuries!

Within the Genus Canis sits the coyote (*Canis latrans*). Its name translates as 'barking dog', a close relative of the grey wolf (*Canis lupus*), although far more slight within its frame (weighing on average around thirty pounds) standing not an inch over two feet in height. The coyote, an omnivore, is whitish-grey in colour although the coat can have a tanned hue and reddish tint, and its ears and nose are pointed. They inhabit North America and hunt in small packs, and also alone.

In 1884, according to *Land And Water* of 19th July, and to quote the *Beastwatch* website:

> '*The superintendent of London's zoological gardens was given a coyote that had been found in Epping Forest. It was speculated that four coyote cubs had been brought to England in a ship belonging to Mr J. R. Fletcher some years previously. They were thought to be fox cubs and were released into the forest. The coyote is referred to in the report as a prairie wolf.*'

Epping Forest stretches for some six thousand acres and could hide an animal such as a coyote for some time. Large cats such as puma and black leopard have also been sighted in the woods which creep towards Essex, as mentioned in previous chapters.

One of the best-known mystery animal sightings pertaining to Kent and the canidae family concerns the Sevenoaks jackal (*Canis aureus*) as mentioned in the chapter *Big Cats In The Garden Of England*. Another similar incident involved the Sussex hyena, mentioned also in the same chapter.

In 1961, on 22nd February, is was alleged that a wolf had escaped captivity in the vicinity of Clapham Common, London. The animal was said to be tame and one of a pair kept by a woman in an enclosure constructed of wire. Despite local fuss and fear, the animal had become trapped in a gap between the walls of St. Paul's churchyard and an adjacent building. The police buzzed around the area like bees around a hive and cordoned it off so that no excitable child could aggravate or distress the poor animal. However, although a constable wriggled into the gap to reach out with a wire loop extended from his gloved hand, the terrified creature was said to have died on the spot of a heart attack.

Around 2005 a friend named Chris Eades told me that, whilst living in the Battersea area, he recalled from childhood around twenty-five years previous, several nightmarish tales that would send him cowering under the bed sheets. One of these yarns concerned rumour that wolves were inhabiting the local woods! I have always been fully aware of strange creatures roaming the thickets, but wolves – surely not?!

Then I came across the incident from 1961 that may well have sparked off such a legend, even if the reality was not quite as sensational or dramatic as the possibility that howling grey outlaws were spooking sun-bathers on the common. Locals had been whispering of an unusual beast, like a big dog, grey in colour, with pointed ears lurking on Clapham Common. The common itself is over two-hundred acres situated between Clapham, Battersea and Balham. Enough grassland to hide a wolf?

In his 1964 book, *Wolves And Werewolves (Robert Hale Ltd)* author John Pollard commented that:

> '*A thousand years ago wolves were common in the great forests of central England, and during January, called 'Wolf Month', by the Saxons, packs of hungry beasts roved the wild country north of the Thames. Indeed, the menace was so great to travellers leaving the city that a special grant of land was made by the good Abbot Leofstan of St. Albans to one Thurnoth and others in return for keeping the woods between the Chiltern Hundreds and London free from wolves. In some places where the presence of wolves constituted a special danger, hospitals were set up for the protection of travellers. One of the most notable was built in the time of Athelstan in Yorkshire, and a farm at Flixton is called Spittal to this day. According to one authority, Blaine, records still existed at Flixton, Hackston and Folkston in the middle of last century of payments made for the destruction of wolves at fixed rates per head.*'

Such wolves, were said to have prowled many known battlefields, especially in the Kent area. Pollard adds:

> '*...tradition has it that the bodies of the English who fell at Hastings were devoured by the savage denizens of the Weald*', and, '*...if we can believe Shakespeare or his sources, loud howling wolves greeted the Duke of Suffolk when he landed at night near Dover.*'

It is claimed that the last wolf to have been killed in the Scottish Highlands was in the year 1743. Of wolves further south, author Anthony Dent in his *Lost Beasts Of Britain (Harrap 1974)* writes:

> '*There can have been no more wolves in the southern Pennines by the end of the fourteenth century. This is the latest possible date from the writing of the romance of Sir Gawain And The Green Knight. The earliest is 1360. It is a story of the supernatural, and it relies, like all good ghost stories, on a realistic setting against which the supernatural element is contrasted. The setting is somewhere in the north-west Midlands, the Green Knight goes hunting in what might be the Derbyshire Peak District, or Rossendale Forest in Lancashire, or one of the many chases in between these. These hunts are described in highly realistic details, and the quarry is deer, boar...and fox. If in the second half of the fourteenth century there had been enough wolves in the South Pennine country to be worth hunting it is not likely that people like the Green Knight would have taken fox-hunting so seriously.*'

Experts believe that Cumbria was the final setting for England's last wolf. Others claim that Penzance in

Cornwall saw the last wolf. Whatever the truth, it's clear that such animals have certainly not hung into the modern day as it is suggested with animals such as the lynx. And yet, whilst large cats such as black leopards and puma roam this small island, there are, in-between these now regular reports, cases which involve wolf-like animals. Of course, such animals may well have escaped, or may indeed be one-off cases, yet they do indeed persist, suggesting that such animals do roam the woods but somehow are able to remain far more elusive than their relations which perished a few hundred years ago. Are such animal really escapees from zoo parks? Ghosts of our once glorious nature? Or, in fact, smaller animals which people in turn mistake for wolves? Let's look at the evidence.

It has long been suggested that wolves be introduced back into Britain, mainly into the Highlands o Scotland. Zoo parks such as Howletts currently hold several wolves. On November 9th 2006 *The Inde pendent* newspaper said:

> '*Call of the wild; re-establishing our lost wild animals'*, stating, '*If Peter Clarke had his way, the countryside would be a fiercer, more romantic place. There would be wolves in the hills and lynx in the forests. Rivers would be home to the long-lost British sturgeon, while beavers would build their dams in the headwaters. Maybe the odd walrus would be lying up on an offshore island.*
>
> *Clarke, a former environment policy adviser to the Thatcher government, is spokesman for a shadowy group called the Wild Beasts Trust. The trust attracted attention recently when Clarke let slip that it was holding six lynxes and two wolves which it planned to release in Scotland. Nothing more has been heard of the release, but the trust reflects a broadly-felt frustration with the lack of progress in re-establishing our lost wild animals.*
>
> *Britain and Ireland have turned their backs on the rehabilitation of our extinct big beasts. The beaver, lynx, wild boar and wolf are not prehistoric. All are now known to have lived in Britain until early modern times. Many would love to see their return. But the government, bowing to the landowning lobby, is adamantly opposed. Last year, the Scottish Executive turned down a detailed proposal to release beavers in western Scotland. Yet other EU countries have successfully re-established beavers, lynxes, wolves and even bears.*
>
> *Clarke points out the contradiction between release of big wild birds and the non-release of big wild mammals. With six million birdwatchers in support, the government has countenanced the release of red kites all over Britain, and is considering releasing giant sea eagles. But the beaver, it seems, is a beast too far.*
>
> *For some, the attraction of a land with beavers and other once indigenous large animals goes well beyond ecology. "The soul of a location is changed by the presence of these long-extinct species," says Clarke. "A wolf howling on a moonlit night transforms the poetry of a glen."*
>
> *The return of the big mammals may in fact be closer than we think. While the new chairman of Scottish Natural Heritage has ruled out any repeat effort to re-establish the beaver, there are well-founded rumours of at least one semi-wild colony in Scotland, (it seems they escaped from a private wildlife farm and built a dam on nearby land).*'

There may be a remote possibility that some lynx have already been released into the wilds of the U

These will certainly do no harm, but what of the sightings of wolves? If the hundreds, if not thousands of reports of leopards and pumas are not taken seriously, then surely the occasional story of a roaming wolf would easily slip by the wayside?

On the 27th November 2007 *The Daily Telegraph* wrote:

'Wolf and lynx could be re-introduced to the UK', - 'Bringing back animals which were hunted to extinction in Britain - including the wolf, lynx, beaver and wild boar - would not be difficult, according to a new report. The animals could be brought back to live free in the wild without posing any great threat to people, crops or the environment, it is claimed. A report from the Wildlife Conservation Research Unit at Oxford University (WCRU) said while further work needed to be done on their impact, there was no obvious reason to block their return.

The animals roaming free in remote areas would enhance the natural environment and as a bonus they could form the basis of a multi-million pound tourist industry. Wildlife tourism in the UK is thriving particularly in Scotland where the reintroduction of the osprey attracted on average 33,600 visitors between 1998 and 2001 while the Red Kite Centre, Wales attracted 33,350 visitors in 2004. The possibility of the animals' return is raised in the State of Britain's Mammals report for 2007 Mammals Trust UK, which looks at the challenges wildlife will face in the 21st century.

Professor David Macdonald and Dr Dawn Burnham, from the WCRU identified a range of factors including climate change, the spread of infectious diseases, agricultural and forestry practices, and human activity which will all combine to put increasing pressure on the UK's fragile wildlife populations.

Earlier this year the UK Biodiversity Action Plan (BAP), added 16 new habitats, 8 terrestrial mammals and the common seal to the UK's Priority List of Species and Habitats. The report says that wild boar are already living free and breeding rapidly across several south-eastern countries after escaping from farms. They were a potential threat to people and dogs and caused damage to crops and through rooting to wild flowers, particularly bluebells, and trees. But they also played an important role as ecosystem engineers increasing habitat diversity and in places they were regarded as an asset because they provided sport and meat to the hunting sector. Similarly beaver had also escaped into the wild and one was living quite happily near Oxford. Even in the worst case scenario, where beavers caused damage to trees, the cost would only be tens of thousands of pounds while at best the costs would be negligible. But their presence would contribute to wetland creation helping with consequent water purification and they were useful in flood retention.

"The end result appears to be a very healthy balance sheet in favour of reintroducing the beaver," the report says. Studies surrounding the reintroduction of the wolf to Scotland, where it was hunted to extinction in the 18th century, found that highland farmers were the most likely to be affected because they would lose livestock. But they were not absolutely opposed to the wolf's return as it was 'restoring the balance of nature and preserving Scotland's heritage'.

They recognised the value of wildlife tourism and knew they would be compensated if they lost sheep to predation. The studies had found that 1,000 square kilometres could support 25 wolves and that they would keep down deer populations and save the expensive cost of regular culls in Caledonian pine forests. The lynx had disappeared during medieval times because of deforestation, declining deer populations and persecution but all these had now been reversed. The EU Habitats Directive had also stated that the European lynx should be considered for reintroduction. Studies by Aberdeen University had identified two areas in Scotland which would provide suitable habitat for lynx. It had been estimated that current deer populations could support 400 lynx in the Highlands and 50 in the southern Uplands.

The report identifies the brown hare, mountain hare, red squirrel, hedgehog, harvest mouse, Scottish wildcat and grey seal as all being threatened British mammals whose populations were in decline. One high point has been the recovery of the otter which had suffered severe decline in the latter half of the 20th Century because of pollution. But the clean up of rivers had resulted in the otter's recovery and continued expansion.'

The *Illustrated London News* of 14th June 1879 spoke of an unusual animal that caused minor hysteria in the Southampton region.

'Captain Sir Allen Young's pet Esquimau dog was either stolen or wandered from the Arctic ship Pandora as she lay in Southampton harbour after returning from the polar regions. Quite a panic arose in part of Hampshire where this most valuable and harmless animal was wandering about, and every sort of story was circulated of the ravages and dangers the country was subject to. The people began to think their sheep, pigs and children were in danger; some said it was a gigantic black fox, others said it was a Canadian wolf. Expeditions were organised to attack it, and after being chased for some miles by people on horseback, it was ultimately shot and exhibited at sixpence a head in Winchester market place. There could be no doubt about the dog's identity for Sir Allen Young afterwards got back his skin.'

How many more strange, dog-like animals have escaped into our woods? Judging by the next batch of weird sightings of muzzled marauders, quite a few.

From the *Press And Journal* of 22nd August, 2000:

'A visitor to the North-east claimed last night that he had encountered a wolf in the wild during a recent holiday.

Conrad Sheward, 62, was on a shooting trip with friends when he saw what he was sure was a wolf roaming Clashindarroch Forest, near Huntly.

Mr Sheward, from Gloucester, was driving up a hill with friend Richard Brundle and Mr Brundle's 15-year-old son, Tom, when made their apparently startling discovery last Monday morning.

"We opened the locked forestry gate and drove through about 100 yards and then came to a bend," said the lawyer.

"About 120 yards away, there was an animal in the middle of the road sideways on to us. turned and looked straight at us. Initially I though it was a huge fox. It was grey with a whitish tail but it was too big for a fox."

Mr Sheward, who has been visiting the north-east for nine years, said he had seen wolves in the flesh at wildlife parks and was convinced his eyes had not deceived him.

"I have got no doubt in my mind that it was a wolf. I would have known if it had been a dog."

Mr Sheward had been staying with friend Jim Copland, from Aberdeen, who has been shooting tenant at the Forestry Commission-owned land for 18 years. Mr Copland, 73, said he had never seen or heard reports of a wolf on the estate - but was not overly surprised at his friend's apparent sighting. He said he had been told of reports that wolves were being released into the wild in the Highlands. The presence of the predators would be a major setback for local farmers whose livestock would come under threat, added Mr Copland.

He said he first suspected the animal might have been a giant cat such as a puma - revealing that a feline beast had been shot and buried in the forest two years ago. "Wolves are a dangerous animal which would prey on livestock," he said. Some conservationists have appealed for the reintroduction of wolves in the Scottish glens to save the countryside from an explosion of red deer.'

In Derbyshire, north east of Buxton, there is legend of a creature known as the 'speed wolf'. The animal has often been seen running at tremendous speeds through the countryside. In 1925 a similar howling black beast was much heard of in the Edale area. In Wales during the eighteenth century legends were rife of prowling wolves. One such beast was said to have lurked between Wrexham and Denbigh, and savaged men as well as livestock. The beast was never caught. Mystery wolf-like animals have also been rumoured to exist on the moors of Devon and Cornwall, the marshes of Pevensey in Sussex where before 1939 it was told that several large, grey creatures roamed. Other places said to be inhabited by wolves are the Cannock Chase area of Staffordshire, and also Scarborough where Mr Ted Beverley heard of such a creature in 1958. Beverley was the ex-Superintendent-in-chief of Skegness police and mentioned that he'd heard of several wolves being shot in the area of Messingham Common during the early part of the century. On the *Wild About Britain* website, a nature lover named Andy commented on the forum:

"…I was a teenager I was fishing on Scarborough Marine Drive late at night when an adult timber wolf walked past on the opposite side of the road.. Must admit to some nervousness at the encounter. Sadly it was shot the following morning. It had escaped from the local zoo."

During 1904 several wolves turned up in the news, one from the Cumwhinton area of Carlisle and another in Newcastle. Were these beasts really the last of the original survivors or escapees?

The *Daily Telegraph* of April 1985 wrote, *'Wolves were no risk'*, after rumours circulated that five of the animals had escaped from Colchester Zoo. The truth suggests that only two wolves actually escaped and were found soon after.

So, how does the county of Kent figure with regards to wolf sightings? Well, although legends and sightings seem sporadic, I've filed quite a number of alleged wolf sightings from the region. Some of these cases of course may actually concern smaller species such as the jackal which have been incorrectly identified, but it seems that whilst these occasional reports can be taken with a pinch of salt, eyewitness reports suggest that some kind of wolf-like, or member of the canidae family does indeed roam Kent.

Rather more worryingly is the fact that such stories are not misty anecdotes of forgotten lore, but rather recent sightings.

In 2008 I spoke to an Ashford man who claimed that during the early to mid-1990s, he'd seen a wolf cross the road not far from the Aldington area. Despite being mocked by friends and family he remained positive as to what he'd seen.

The most impressive and bizarre sighting of a wolf-like animal to come from Kent reached me in the May of 1999. It was around 6:00 am and the witness, a male, was driving home from working nights. His route home to Cliffe Woods took him within the vicinity of the Great Chattenden Wood, where I'd received a few cat sightings in the past. On the phone he told me his amazing story.

> "I know the woodlands well, I fly birds in the area all the time. I caught a creature in the headlights, it was nosing the gutter and then seemed to spring up and then run off into a field of rape seed. I stopped the car and had a look around but there was no sign. Now, I know the difference between foxes, dogs etc, and this thing was not cat-like, it was a Maned wolf. I couldn't actually see the mane but I know a lot about animals and this thing shocked me. I told my wife about the sighting and it went no further than that until I read your article in the paper. I've no idea how it got there and I don't know of anyone else who has seen it but if I'd had a gun I'd have shot it."

The witness, who I spoke with for quite some time, said that the animal wasn't muscular, but the size of an Alsatian, and very long-legged, almost stilted. The animal had a long snout, a bushy tail and was thin.

The maned wolf (*Chrysocycon brachyurus*) roams the pampas plains of South America and does look similar to the red fox. The creature is mainly nocturnal, reaches over four feet in length and stands around eighteen-inches in height and weighs up to fifty-pounds.

Had the witness seen a large fox? Judging by his details and sincerity it seems that what he did see was something other than a fox or a dog, and he was quick to mention the maned wolf instead of being vague. Unfortunately, I've received no further reports of the animal since, but then again, a majority of such sightings always seem to be one-off occurrences, which either suggests that the witnesses got it wrong, or indeed an elusive, night-prowling variety of wolf species does in fact inhabit the heavily wooded areas of Kent, but somehow eludes man.

In March of 2000, Miss Nolan, a former newspaper reporter, came out of the offices in Gravesend at around 7:30 pm and walked to her car. She was startled by a creature eating an old sandwich at the kerb. The animal was like a big dog, cream in colour with big patches of brown over its coat, and a long, curling tail. She was terribly spooked by the beast which peered at her intently, and so she scrambled to her car and drove away, leaving the mysterious beast to its meal. The lady, who was a reliable contact of mine within the media informed me that the animal looked like an African dog of sorts, such as a jackal. The first possibility is the side-striped jackal (*Canis adustus*) which reaches almost three feet in length and has white and black stripes on its flanks although these are often indistinct. These creatures, when roaming parts of Africa are known to come into towns and forage for scraps. The black-backed jackal (*Canis mesomelas*), which roams east and southern Africa is roughly the same size and has a distinctive black 'saddle' of sorts over its shoulder. Other more remote possibilities are the African wild dog (*Lycaon pictus*) which is endangered in Africa, and known as the 'painted wolf' due to its coat of varying patches. Had something like this been released or escaped from a private collection?

During the late '80s a wolf was seen by a Mrs Joy on the outskirts of Ashford. She watched the animal for several minutes as the haze of dusk fell on the woods. The animal was creeping along the fence line, and was bigger than an Alsatian with a long muzzle.

A handful of brief 'wolf' sightings occurred around Ashford after the millennium. Local press attempted to explain them. On 11th June 2002 *Kent News* wrote of the *'Hunt for the beast of Egerton'*, commenting:

> *'Sightings of panthers or other deadly beasts roaming the countryside are a fairly regular occurrence but sadly the animal in question is rarely identified.*
>
> *Not so with the latest sighting in the south east of a mysterious creature said to resemble a large fox or wolf. But the so-called beast of Egerton is actually a pet dog.*
>
> *Gvir belongs to a breed known as Canaan and originates from the desert wastelands in the middle east. Untamed by man until seventy years ago, centuries of evolution has equipped it with the ability to endure extremes in temperature and harsh climate.*
>
> *So eight weeks after he first went missing there's every chance Gvir is still alive. It's hard to overestimate Gvir's pedigree. The Crufts best of breed winner has himself sired dozens of champions. In the dog world this canine is a one off. There are only eighty Canaan's in the UK and Gvir's owner Lorna Hastings owns five of them.*
>
> *Anyone spotting him is urged not to approach. Canaans won't let strangers near. Instead eyewitnesses are being advised to call the dog warden department at Ashford Borough Council.*
>
> *Gvir has recently been sighted near Tudely and, on Wednesday 7th, between Staplehurst and Marden.'*

Several sightings from the Charing area of Ashford may well have concerned the stray dog, but eye witness accounts varied. On one occasion a wolf-like animal, but only the size of a small dog, was observed crossing a road and slipping into the woods.

On the 23rd January 2007 a man named Stevie reported:

> *"On the A20 road from Charing to Ashford, was wondering if anyone else saw the wolf that I saw? It ran out of the woods and over the main road, stood right in front of my car and then carried on to the other side. It was around 12:00 pm and I'm ninety-nine percent sure it was a wolf."*

Mr Young saw a similar animal on 3rd August 2004 in the same area whilst driving. A year later, during the summer, I received an eerie report of a strange creature via the *Your County* website who I'd contributed articles for. The report read as follows:

> *'Dear Sir, I have recently read your interesting article on strange creatures sighted in Kent. This is a subject that has always intrigued me and although somewhat vague, I have an addition in what you may be interested.*
>
> *My good friend recently stayed at a cottage in Dode, near Meopham over the weekend and during the afternoon, whilst relaxing and admiring the view from his dwellings, he and his partner witnessed an unusual sight.*

A white animal emerged from the woods at the side of a field, across about a quarter of a mile over a field and back again. Not that strange you might think, but apparently this happened in about twelve seconds! The animal looked as though it was after a group of rabbits and it ran faster than a horse. The action was more of a bounding than a run.

I enquired as to the size of this creature and was informed that it was much bigger than a dog but not as large as a horse. In fact, a fox was witnessed passing through the same field and was minute in comparison. I am afraid that's it, no other clues are offered. I do not question my friend's authenticity one iota.'

This was certainly a weird incident, and a pity that no actual description of the animal was given. Cer tainly, the Meopham area had its fair share of big cat sightings, but this creature seemed bigger and pal in colour. Naturally, I took the sighting with a pinch of salt and assumed such a creature would never b seen again.

The area of Dode is peculiar indeed. In fact it is considered a lost village which, during the Black Deat of the thirteenth century, was wiped of its residents and remained uninhabited for fifteen years. The church, all that remains from the fourteenth-century, is situated at the end of a 'no through road'. Th building has been restored and is used for weddings, but the place has several legends such as connec tions to black magic and the spirit of a seven-year old girl rumoured to be the last survivor of the plague Legend also speaks of a well, which was removed from public view, and was said to be haunted by young child. Other researchers believe the place to be haunted by other apparitions as well as curse ground, and I've also received several big cat sightings from the area.

During early September 2006 a Mrs Whitmore contacted me with an even stranger sighting than th Dode occurrence. She wrote:

'It was 1:00 am and myself and my husband were on the dark road coming from Bluewa- ter, the slip road on to the A2. The road has a diner and a car wash on it, but is always pitch black at night.

From the side of the café a few yards ahead emerged a huge, white animal which crossed the road slowly. As it reached the other side of the road it glanced back at us as we slowly drove by. It was terrifying. It was not a big cat or a dog, but something resem- bling a wolf but stockier and bigger and whitish-grey in colour. The animal had a snout like a German shepherd dog and large pointed ears, one of which was darker in colour than the other.'

I was certainly excited, but bemused by the sighting. The creature sounded ghost-like if anything but wasn't something I was willing to consider, and the witnesses were very sincere and unnerved by the encounter. I filed the report, as I had with the Dode one, and again hoped that another sighting wou take place. It did.

A lady named Zoe contacted me as she was shocked by what she'd encountered on the same stretch dark road outside of Europe's busiest shopping precinct. On 25th May 2007 at 2:30 am she reported:

'I narrowly missed a large white canine which looked like a wolf or husky dog and as large, on the road leading on to joining the M2 coast bound from Bluewater. I could see another in the distance. I think it's the old part of the A2. Lorry's park up on the left and

there's a trucker's café on the right. I saw the animals just before the café.'

Amazingly, Zoe had to swerve to avoid the animal which caused her to run her car off the road. Luckily, she was unhurt and aided by her friend who was driving behind her. Bizarrely, Zoe's friend never saw any animals on the road! Zoe added that:

'It was the size of an Alsatian and looked fluffy like a husky. Friends and I thought it may have been a guard dog escaped but the colour and the shape makes me think otherwise.'

Just what eerie creatures were people seeing around the black lanes of Bluewater? Mere dogs? I appealed for witnesses regarding stray dogs in the area but received no replies. The case remains a mystery, like so many other alleged wolf sightings, but could be explained in the next chapter, *The Others*, as could the next weird sighting.

On November 5th 2007 at 12:30 pm Mrs Margaret Phipps had a bizarre encounter with a strange creature. She phoned me after I'd sent an appeal out via the Sevenoaks press regarding big cat sightings, but what she experienced was something slightly - though significantly - different. Margaret was driving through Hildenborough where around the same time I'd received a couple of reports of a black leopard. Along the B245 she passed Nizels Lane, then Bank Lane just along from the *Iveco* transport place. It was a clear day, no other cars about. Suddenly, not far from the *Cock Horse* pub, she noticed a black creature emerge from a woodland path and head in her direction. She slowed the car right down and as she neared the animal on her right, she was intrigued as to how black it actually was. At first she thought she was seeing the panther everyone had been talking about and reporting, but as the beast came closer she got an even better look.

The animal trotted along the path and as it got to within a few yards it veered into the road in front of the vehicle as if it was going to cross the road. Mrs Phipps braked suddenly, worried she may hit the creature. She beeped the horn but the animal didn't seemed alarmed and just gazed at her. The beast then moved back on to the pathway and walked down the side of the car. Mrs Phipps then watched in amazement through her rear-view mirror as it walked down the centre of the road until out of sight.

She reported the sighting to the *Courier* but what she told me was very odd. She described the animal as bigger than an Alsatian, but extremely pitch black all over. The ears were pricked and it was long in the body with a long, curved tail, but it was not cat-like because the face was that of a strange wild dog. Mrs Phipps recognised it as very peculiar as she used to breed German shepherd's but she'd never seen anything so weird. She was fortunate enough to see the animal from different angles and she was quite baffled by the long snout, like that of a wolf. Although she wasn't frightened by the animal she told me that something wasn't right about it and that if she'd been walking in the area and seen it she would have most certainly crossed over to avoid it.

Again, no further evidence came to light of the mystery prowler.

On Saturday 1st March 2008 at 2:00 pm a man from Walderslade saw a creature in an area once again known for its big cat sightings. Tunbury and Walderslade Woods in Chatham link to Boxley, Lordswood and Hempstead, but on this occasion what was seen most certainly wasn't a large cat.

'I was laying on the front room floor with my dog, I caught a slow moving, tall, skinny animal-like object in the corner of my eye.

Too tall to be a cat, anatomically incorrect to be a dog. Although it did have the propor-

tions of a Greyhound or a cheetah (tiny waist, long spindly legs). I rushed to my garden to see what it was only to catch it slowly stalking through a slim gap in the fence. It was mainly grey in colour, but it had short, rough hair similar to that of a mangy fox, but this was certainly too tall and slender for a fox, and like I said, moved like a cat.

One of the most sinister things to me was the reaction of my dog. He is a rough collie and the most docile animal on record. Never barking or anything, never showing any sign of aggression and genuinely not showing interest in anything other than sleep. Since seeing the said creature, my dog has been frantically attacking the spot where the thing left the garden. Day or night my dog paces this spot growling and seems to be nervously listening to something from the woods behind.

After losing sight of it, I rushed to the upstairs of the house to watch it enter the woods which back my garden. From there I could only make out slow moving movement between the bushes. I am confident that this is not a fox, domestic cat or dog. I only wish I'd seen its head, as its sinewy, tall body is unrecognisable to me.'

I phoned the witness who told me that after looking on the internet the closest animal that compared to what he'd seen was a jackal. He told me also that the tail was long but the animal was not a wolf.

The golden jackal (*Canis aureus*) is native to south eastern Europe, parts of Africa and Asia, and measures over three feet long. The coat of such a creature varies from grey to light brown to pale gold but it is not a tall, sinewy animal. Had he seen a jackal? The coyote (*Canis latrans*) is native to North America, and is a slim animal measuring around three feet in length and has a buff coat. However, how would a coyote have got into the woodlands of Walderslade?

Maybe the witness had seen a young wolf, possibly a grey wolf (*Canis lupus*) which inhabits Europe, Asia, Greenland, and North America. It is the largest member of the canid family, and the sightings around Bluewater certainly described very large animals. It measures up to five feet in length, whereas the smaller red wolf (*Canis rufus*), which lives in North Carolina, USA, and was recently rediscovered in Texas by CFZ associate Chester Moore Jr., measures up to four feet long but such animals are critically endangered.

The Sevenoaks Jackal killed in 1905 (p. 77)

The Boars are back in Town

*'Then the storm of swine noise came again, beating up in a gigantic riot
of brute sound that roared through the room, piping, squealing, grunting and howling.'*

The Hog – William Hope Hodgson

The Great Storm of October 16th 1987 was a tragedy. My sister Vicki was about to be born at any time, it was three days before my birthday, and trees, fences, cars and roof tops were whizzing across the streets as if they'd been thrown by some unseen giant hand of the elements. It was a terrible time, and I wasn't sure if my mother was actually about to give birth to some kind of demonic entity, an unholy arrival accompanied by the raging storm as windows rattled. Winds left a trail of destruction in their wake, lives were lost, buildings were blown away, electricity failed across the county, and almost three-thousand calls for help were received by local authorities as the River Medway flooded its banks and huge trees crashed through houses. Several landmarks were demolished by the gales, and woodlands were flattened with ease. More than sixty-five families were made homeless, and businesses - particularly local farms - suffered loss of crops. Dangerous animals were also escaping into the wilds as pens and cages lifted off the ground and once stable enclosures were mangled by the storm. The bird park at Blean allegedly lost more than twenty-thousand pounds worth of birds and Howletts had six animals escape. How many others escaped their enclosures, unrecorded, and are responsible for today's populations of exotics?

Of the mighty boar, researcher Jonathan Downes wrote:

> *'Once upon a time the gentry sallied forth on horseback to hunt the wild boar. They were the fiercest game animals of the British countryside and were responsible for the deaths of many a foolhardy hunter. They were hunted to extinction by the end of the sixteenth century, although many authorities believe that the only animals left alive in Tudor times were actually semi-domesticated creatures kept in deer parks purely for their use as a game animal.'*

Kent author Charles Igglesden, in his *A Saunter Through Kent With Pen & Pencil*, the fourth volume of 1902, and pertaining to St Michael's, near Tenterden, wrote of the Boar's Isle, stating, '*Local tradition points to the place as the favourite haunt of the boar*', whilst in his sixth volume of 1909 in relation to Dunkirk, he comments of Blean Forest, '*...the forest in which bears and wild boars were wont to live long after they were extinct in other parts of England.*'

In order to pay their bills in the 1980s, several farmers began housing such creatures in miniature theme parks alongside other animals such as bison, in order to attract people on a frequent basis. Boar sausages were also high on the menu in several restaurants.

Many animals have been freed from captivity on purpose in the past and the Great Storm of 1987 certainly played a huge part in introducing the hairy beasts into the countryside where they remain today. However, many people believe that such animals are a severe problem. They can be very aggressive, especially when protecting young, and devour anything they come across, especially crops. In the '80s the existence of such a creature in our woodlands was treated as myth despite countless sightings in areas such as Paddock Wood, Tenterden and Romney Marshes. Now, it seems, such beasts are a problem. In 1994 the *Daily Mail* reported that four Argentinean peccaries had been released by vandals at West Blean, but recaptured quickly.

In June of 1999 various land owners decided it was time to organise an emergency mass meeting. These beasts had certainly struck fear into the hearts of men a few centuries previously and now it was happening all over again. Was the circulating dread justified?

Video footage shown on local news showed these seemingly docile creatures foraging in Kent and Sussex, particularly in the Beckley area where it was rumoured that more than sixty were thriving, and males were said to weigh up to four-hundred-and-fifty pounds. By day, such ugly forms were plodding through farms, but at night they appeared far more destructive. Hunter and conservationist Angus Irvine commented at the time that, *"They don't exist in law and the government has to decide whether they exist. Maybe then we can make decisions from that point."*

Oddly, the reaction of some campaigners at the time resembled that of primal hunters grasping their spears and taking to the woods with angered faces in order to kill as many tusked hairballs as possible. Such radical opinions and extreme acts provoked a poster campaign that was obviously intended to shock people and to turn them against the countryside's new inhabitants. The mock poster read:

> '*A mother and daughter were killed while walking through an English woodland along a public footpath. Their dog, it is believed, disturbed the boar which charged out of the undergrowth killing the young girl instantly, and so severely wounding the mother by ripping with its tusks, that she subsequently died.*
>
> *What are the authorities doing about this new menace? Not much, it appears!*'

Already the creature was being turned into a barbaric monster and yet attacks were scarce on humans Damian Green, then Conservative MP for Ashford said:

> *"If the wild boar population is growing fast and is likely to start intruding on human life then we need to find a method of control."*

Despite the anger of some landowners towards the animals, others were less concerned and stated that such creatures should be classed as endangered species and left alone.

Derek Harman, a boar expert and former gamekeeper, at the time commented:

> *"I disputed a Ministry of Agriculture estimation last year that stated the boar population was only around one-hundred. Since the government figures last year there have been fifty boar shot in the Kent and East Sussex border and that hasn't made any dent in*

the population. I think they should be classed as game animals exactly the same as deer. The deer legislation would be adequate to cope with wild boar."

A farmer named Ian Douglas claimed he was almost attacked by a boar but shot it just in time, and yet he remained sympathetic towards the animals, commenting on local news that:

After looking at the boar on the ground after I'd shot it I thought it was scary but I do have a sneaking regard for them because there are people out there shooting away just so they can say they've bagged a wild boar, all the while the poor young ones are dying and the big old ones are still there getting on with it. They are the dangerous ones and they are the ones producing more and more."

Farmers and land owners were obviously trying to control a problem long before it got out of hand. At the time the boar were healthy, but they could eventually be on their way out again, the only hope is that it breeds rapidly, even producing smaller, blacker species after breeding with escaped Vietnamese pot-bellied pigs.

However, Jonathan Downes wrote:

'More ominously, the wild boar carries with it a real threat of conveying disease be-tween herds of outdoor pigs. With Swine Fever rife on the European mainland there is a huge risk if the disease jumps across the channel. MAFF have even had reports of wild boar mating with outdoor sows, giving rise to litters of stripy pigs.'

[MAFF was the UK's Ministry of Agriculture, Food and Fisheries.]

The Kent area is certainly suitable habitat to hide such creatures. It has vast marsh-lands and rolling fields, with open spaces and deep woodlands. They were once a deli-cacy on many a local menu until many of the animals broke free from their pens. In Romney Marsh a fifty-pound peccary allegedly attacked a man and his three large dogs in the '90s. The animal had been on the run for a week but it was tempted back to its pen with a lusty sow. Other sightings at the time took place at Herne Bay, parts of Devon, Gloucestershire, Dorset and also Hampshire.

On November 13th 2005 a witness told the *British Wild Boar* website:

'I have seen a wild boar at the edge of the road, a very large animal I might add. The incident happened when the animal was startled by the head lights of my vehicle at approx: 6.30 pm. The boar was standing at the road edge on the A272 Piltdown, East Sussex. He was large and had all the features of a boar, he jumped back turning on his hind legs and made way into the under growth. My wife and daughter saw the animal also. A very exciting moment for me and I thought that you would like to know.'

Sightings in Kent and East Sussex have become reasonably common. Appledore, Tenterden, Lympne, Ruckinge, Warehorne, Wittersham, Bilsington, Aldington, Bedbegury, Coxheath, Hamstreet, Wrotham, Tonbridge and Rolvenden seem to be the most likely places to spot one.

On 14th October reporter Laura Smith-Spark for *BBC News* wrote:

'Wild boar move faster than Linford Christie, weigh up to 400 pounds but can turn on a

sixpence - and they have big tusks. All of which begs the question, what was I doing in woodland on the borders of East Sussex and Kent trying to track one down?'

Well, after reports as many as 1,000 wild boar are roaming free in the South East - an area better known for its proximity to London than its wildlife - I was keen to see the evidence for myself.

My guide was Ian Douglas, a farmer from Woodchurch in Kent who has spent more than a decade following the creatures, learning their habits and shooting the odd few as game. As we headed down a leafy path into the Forestry Commission-owned woods - bordering land belonging to pop star Paul McCartney - he issued his first instructions.

"If we do come across a boar, don't move. You won't have time to run away or climb a tree - just stand still and we'll work out what to do next."

Not the most comforting words but they inspired an unusual thrill of danger.

Mr Douglas, a veteran of countless trips into the woods at night when the wild boar are most active, has had several close encounters.

"The most I've ever seen together at one time was nine adults and their piglets," he said.
"One time I was here and I just felt the hairs rise on the back of my neck - I knew something was there.

When I turned round there was a sow and her piglets, watching me. I hadn't heard a thing."

The signs of the animals' presence are everywhere, once an old hand points them out. Furrowed turf by the path - which would barely have warranted a glance before - turns out to be a prime indication of wild boar.'

This investigation came a week after the same sources reported,

'Government experts are compiling a report into the problem after scientists said a colony of the omnivorous animals grew up in south east England following storms in 1987 and 1989 when 15 of them escaped from farms.

Keith Taylor, of the British Wild Boar Association, said drastic action is needed.

He said: "We think that ideally they should be culled, but it's easier said than done because they are nocturnal and are difficult to find. It would certainly require a team of professional stalkers to find them and professionally cull them, so we don't have members of the public or anyone else going out on a wild boar hunt."

A massive boar was hit and killed by a car in the Gloucestershire area in 2002.

Despite the opposition the boar face, in February 2007 a research student named Tasha Sims had something more positive to say on the matter, stating:

'Wild boar are extremely shy and intelligent creatures. They are scavengers, not preda-

tors. They do not attack other animals unless cornered or threatened. They don't attack people's dogs, as has sometimes been reported. This is a sizable population, but the truth is that there isn't much left of their preferred habitat of woodland anyway, and their spread is prevented by civilisation and motorways.

My study shows that there is room for man and boar to live side by side, if we are prepared to be a bit more accommodating.'

On the 27th February 2008 *Kent Online* website added, in a report by Sinead Hanna, that, *'A leading Kent conservation charity has praised plans for new legislation to help control England's wild boar population.*

The Department for Food, Rural Affairs and Environment (Defra) recently announced a policy and action plan to protect and manage feral wild boar in the UK – many of which live on the Kent and Sussex border. The plan gives landowners and local communities new powers to selectively cull boar in their area in order to control numbers, but will also establish rules - for the first time - on how to humanely kill the animals. Wildlife and conservation experts have, for years, been concerned about the lack of legislation protecting the UK's wild boar, which allows hunters to kill them inhumanely and indiscriminately.

Herne Bay-based conservation charity and wildlife park Wildwood Trust, which has its own family of wild boar in captivity, said the Government's plans would go a long way ensuring the species' presence in England for the foreseeable future. Press officer Martin Nicholls said:

> *"We are very pleased Defra has made this move, and we have been encouraged by their recent work in bio-diversity and conservation. At the moment, anyone with a shotgun licence can go out and kill a boar however they like. The new plans will mean people will probably have to obtain a licence to hunt them, with more legislation and rules on how to control them humanely."*

Descended from the domestic pig, wild boar – or *Sus scrofa* – died out in the UK around 300 years ago, but escapees and illegal releases from farms across the country led to herds of boar flourishing in several areas. Woodland across West Kent and Sussex has the largest feral breeding population in the country – the official number is 200, though experts believe it is closer to 400.

Though extremely fast and aggressive if their young are threatened, recent risk assessments by Defra found boar do not pose a national threat to the environment, farming or public safety. Announcing the action plan, Biodiversity Minister Joan Ruddock said:

> *"It is important that communities and land owners are allowed to decide the future of their wild boar population based on their local situation. The Government's support will help them make the right decisions for where they live."*

But the announcement was not welcomed by everyone.

Wild boar expert Dr Martin Goulding, from Cheshire, criticised Defra for not immediately releasing clear guidance on culling boars to stop sows or females crucial to a herd's survival from being slaughered.

He said:

"Defra has rushed out this announcement because of media hype, but nothing concrete has been decided yet about when to cull them, how to cull them, and protecting sows and piglets. There is a great need for education and awareness about this species before any action is taken so that people's first reaction to boars isn't to be scared of them.

There may be a need for a cull in the future, but whether today is the day for it is debatable."

And speaking of wild, snorting, grunting things, I'd like to leave this section by finishing with a London-related tale.

An obscure legend was said to exist in the passageways beneath the capital during the mid-1800s and remains one of London's most forgotten mysteries, yet echoes a more potent urban myth that has plagued New York's sewer system since the early 1900s, being the possibility that alligators inhabited the murky waterways and pipe systems, feeding on rats and garbage. In the case of London's inhabitants, there is a rumour that in 1851 beneath Hampstead, feral pigs, or hogs were prowling the depths of the sewers! Legend has it that a pregnant sow somehow ended up trapped in the gloomy tunnels, giving birth to a happy litter of excrement swilling, offal consuming offspring, even more ferocious than their known relatives that may have inhabited some nearby yard.

Sceptics at the time argued that such animals had never been seen or heard to grunt through the drain grates, but believers in such quirky tales claimed that the reason for this elusive behaviour was simply down to the Fleet ditch, which, once encountered from the mouth of the sewer at the riverside, would have flushed the piggies back to their lair after failed attempts to swim against the rapids.

If only pigs could fly!

Wild boar at Wildwood - a Kent animal sanctuary

Other Out-Of-Place Animals

'On a sudden the stars began to blink more fiercely, a faint wild light overspread for a minute the bleak landscape, and he saw approaching from the moor a figure at a kind of swinging trot, with now and then a zig-zag hop or two...'

The Vision Of Tom Chuff – Joseph Sheridan LeFanu

Wallabies, indigenous to Australia, hop on their long back legs using the extended middle toe as an extra limb segment. These marsupials bear live offspring, and have been sighted throughout Sussex since the 1950s, and in Kent since the '70s. Such animals are thought to have escaped private zoo parks, especially after the Great Storm which possibly increased the populations.

In 1973 sightings took place in the Ashdown Forest of Sussex. A farmer from Tunbridge Wells reported that wallabies and kangaroos were always escaping from a pen on land between Tunbridge Wells and East Grinstead. In 1976 a wallaby was reported once again at the Ashdown Forest area. More recent sightings suggest that the populations have far from depleted. A kangaroo-like animal was reported on 21st April 2005 by *Farmers Weekly* staff. A motorist from Kent was shocked to see a large kangaroo hopping along side a road before disappearing up a farm track and into woodland. The marsupial was spotted along a road between the villages of Ide Hill and Sundridge early on the Wednesday morning. The driver reported the sighting to Kent police who said they would pass the information on to the RSPCA, but said they could not look for the animal as, *"...it had left the highway".*

"To the best of my knowledge there are no kangaroo-related crimes, so the public would not thank us for sending an officer to look for it," a police spokeswoman told the paper. *"There are better uses for our resources,"* she added. This is the first sighting of a kangaroo in Kent, however, there have been a number of sightings of wallabies so it was more than likely one of them.

The *Daily Mirror* once reported in the '80s, *'It's Enough To Make A Policeman Hopping Mad'* - claiming: '

> *...a big police hunt is on for two wallabies on the run. The wallabies, smaller versions of the kangaroo, escaped from Heathfield Safari Park, Sussex. Now one of them has been spotted leaping over hedges in Kent. Mr Julian Moore, 18, who works at the safari park owned by his father, Dr. Gerald Moore, explained that they are not really dangerous but have a tendency to kick. He said: "We have a devil of a job keeping them from vaulting the enclosures. We keep on building higher fences - but once a wal-*

laby, even a small one, decides he is going, it's pretty hard to change his mind. The two missing animals are about 3 ft 6 inches high and greyish-brown."

In 1908 wallabies were introduced to the forests of Horsham by Sir Edmund Loder. On 24th October 2000 a London-based website ran the headline:

'Kangaroo Blamed for Attack on Dog: South Londoners 'distressed' by animal-on-animal violence!'

'A mystery creature - thought to be a kangaroo - has been terrifying women and attacking dogs in Beckenham, (near Bromley) South London. Yesterday the animal made two women jump with fright as they were walking their dogs through Beckenham Palace Park. Jim Horn, manager of the park, said: "They were visibly distressed. One said her dog came flying out of the bushes after being kicked by the creature." Council workers who went to investigate failed to catch sight of the assailant, but found a set of footprints which they believe could belong to an escaped kangaroo. A park worker who discovered that tall shrubs had been munched on said: "This could only be the work of a tall creature, like a kangaroo. We don't know where it could have come from." Park owners, Lewisham Council, have urged members of the public not to seek out the animal. "Kangaroos are potentially dangerous and the last thing we want is anyone getting hurt," a spokesman for the council said.

Animal welfare experts have sprung into action after reports that a 6ft kangaroo is prowling a golf course and park in south London. Members of Lewisham Council's animal welfare department have found a set of paw prints - but so far the creature is keeping one jump ahead of them. Beckenham Place Park manager, Jim Horn, said that several golfers had reported seeing the animal but the latest sighting was made by two women walking their dogs (as mentioned previous).'

Various sightings of a wallaby-type creature emerged from the area of Lenham, Maidstone. On one occasion it was sighted around a storage yard and photographed by a Nick Perry. After several reports the animal was given the nickname of Wesley but rumours circulated that the beast had been hit and killed by a car on the A20. Shortly after the incident, more wallabies appeared in the area. On the 24th May 2007 a motorist travelling from Lenham to Doddington was held up on a narrow lane as two large lorries attempted to pass one another, when suddenly a wallaby sprang across the road.

I received two more interesting wallaby reports also, which are undated but between 2000 and 2004.

"We have just returned from a holiday in the New Forest. On Tuesday evening at around ten o'clock I am almost certain the car headlights picked out a wallaby at the side of the road. This was on the Lymington to Brockenhurst road about half a mile from the station at Brockenhurst. Was I seeing things or is there a wallaby at large?!"

And:

"I just saw a wallaby in my garden. It is 10:00 pm and dark/dusk - I was doing some 'hedgehog watching' and suddenly a wallaby appeared, moved quickly up and down the garden and into the flower border and then came down to the pond to drink. The pond is near the window I was watching from - and so although is was quite dark - I managed to see it reasonably clearly. I live at Kingston, which is four miles south of Canterbury."

Rather ironically, on Monday December 6th 2004 the *Daily Mail* reported that an Australian couple on holiday in Buckinghamshire were amazed to see a wallaby hopping along a railway line at Stoke Mandeville. Although no-one knew where the animal had come from, one was reportedly killed two months previously whilst crossing the M40 near Stokenchurch. On a more ferocious note, in August 1983 at Hawkhurst, two brothers, Mark (11) and Peter (9), were playing in their garden at Slip Mill Lane at around 7:30 pm when they saw an unusual creature fall from a nearby tree. The boys were unnerved by the animal because they thought it was a bear. Police were called to the scene, but their search found nothing except a few scratch marks on the bark. However, when the youngsters were questioned they told the police:

> "...the animal was bigger than our dog (weighing 60lb) and covered in shaggy brown fur, and had long black claws. They claimed to have chased the animal away.

No further sightings of the beast emerged.

Two years previously there had been reports of a bear on London's Hackney Marshes. The story made a few brief headlines, but the creature was never seen again. On the 27th December 1981 four youngsters came face to face with a creature they described as, "...*a giant great growling hairy thing*", during the snowfall. One of the witnesses, Tommy Murray, aged thirteen, claimed that the beast raised itself up on two legs as he and his friends scrambled across the fields to flee from the animal. This sighting came shortly after Tommy and his friends had found a set of unusual prints which finally lead them to the creature. Tommy was so unsettled by the incident that he cried his eyes out to his mum and dad who in turn phoned the police. Some fifty police turned up within the hour to scour the marsh, and footprints - analysed by experts and confirmed as belonging to a bear - were found but no trace of the creature could be found despite helicopters and marksmen present. Locals claimed that the police had been hoaxed but a chief inspector at the scene commented:

> Although I didn't see the boys myself, I'm reliably informed that they were very frightened by what they saw. They were not hoaxers, although, of course, they may have been hoaxed.

Although the inspector hadn't dismissed the possibility that someone had dressed up as a bear, he added:

> The search itself was interesting; it was winter and there was about two inches of snow. I saw three sets of prints that to me were strange. One of the prints was on an island which had a perimeter fence and a locked gate. The other two lots were near marshalling yards. All three were on virgin snow and could not have been made by a hoaxer because no other prints were near them or led to or from them.

Although the mystery has filtered into obscurity over time, it is interesting to note that the previous December, two dead bears were found in the River Lea at Hackney. Even more bizarre, the animals had been decapitated and completely skinned! In 1961, golfers at Croham Hurst in Surrey saw an animal they described as a bear. It was black in colour, around three feet tall and disappeared into the woods when it was approached. Police officers suggested that it may have been a dog, but there was more chance of it being a leopard!

From the *West Sussex County Times* : 31st Oct. 2007

> 'Llama mystery - Police have sparked a search for a mystery stray llama spotted near Faygate last week. The exotic beast was seen by the side of the A264 just after midnight

on Thursday October 25. Police attended the scene and checked with local farms, but could find no trace of the animal.'

One of the oldest accounts of a mystery animal in the county comes from the *Maidstone Journal* February 2nd 1802 and is briefly mentioned in Robert H. Goodsall's book *A Fourth Kentish Patchwork (Stedehill 1974)*, and, to quote:

'*The woodmen of Boxley Hill, zealous to imitate their superiors in the chase, on Saturday last turned out, at Upper Blue Bell, a marten cat, which had 15 minutes grace before it was pursued by three couple and a half of beagles. After affording an excellent run of two hours and a half, it was taken in a tree, with great difficulty; and we hear, this animal will be turned out again next Friday morning on the same spot, when a number of sportsmen are expected to participate in this new and entertaining hunt.'*

Goodsall adds:

'*That marten-cats, no doubt of the 'Beech' variety, should have inhabited the North Downs woodlands as late as the nineteenth century is something of a surprise for writing in the 1860s'.*

J.G. Wood, in his well-known *Illustrated Natural History* commented:

"*The Martins are nearly banished from the more cultivated English counties, but still linger in some numbers among the more rocky and wooded portions of Great Britain. In Carnarvon and Merioneth they are still tolerably numerous, and are frequently hunted by hounds, as if they were foxes or other lawful game.*"

The beech marten, or marten cat (*Martes foina*) measures under two feet in length but its range is not a extensive as the pine marten (*Martes martes*) which is more cat-like in its movement. The pine marten a British resident, albeit one of the rarest mammals on the British List. The beech marten, however, is by current thinking at least - not, and never has been a UK resident. If we are looking for credible wi nesses to unexplained creatures then look no further than policeman S. Bishop who, on April 16th 195 came face to face with an unusual creature at Dumpton Park, Ramsgate. The animal he saw ambled o of the bushes and appeared to him as Alsatian-sized, but being covered with large scales, having a lor snout, short tail and very long claws. The policeman couldn't believe his eyes, and so called for back-u but the creature was nowhere to be found upon returning to the spot!

This much documented case has never been fully investigated or resolved but the most likely candida for what was observed may well have been a pangolin. These are similar in shape to the armadillo a the anteater, and although they are bereft of teeth, they use their long tongue to lap up prey such as i sects in their countries of origin, these being the southern parts of Africa and Asia. However, whilst su armoured creatures can grow to almost three feet in length, they are not the size of an Alsatian as r corded by the witness all those decades ago. The giant armadillo (*Priodontes maximus*) is bigger than t pangolin, and roams south and Central America. This creature isn't as armoured as the pangolin and appears as if covered in small plates, but still has long claws which compare to the pangolin. At the tin of the sighting some researchers put forward the suggestion that the policeman had seen a porcupine b such creatures, which inhabit Africa, have a coat of spines and long whiskers also. Whatever the case, was likely to have escaped from a private collection or a pet shop. It's a shame that such a mystery an mal sighting remained stale for so long. The fact that it remained so dormant has prevented further up date investigation, because surely at the time other people must have see the animal?

During the '70s *Fortean Times* magazine reported on the flying squirrel of Tatsfield, Kent. Such an interesting animal, native to southern Asia, is a glider rather than a flier and reddish-brown in colour. It hunts at night and glides by stretching out its limbs and spreading a membrane.

A witness reported:

> *"...I was coming round a bend of a country lane and saw this grey creature fly across in front of the car, from one tree to another. The front and rear limbs of the creature appeared to be joined by a flap of skin and it floated and clung to the bark. I'm sure sightings would have been few and far between but I actually saw a similar, if not the same creature again shortly after, but on the other side of Tatsfield."*

No further reports emerged of the animal, but in London during Autumn 2007:

> *Wimbledon Guardian* 3rd Oct. – '*Is mystery squirrel playing possum after un-Common sighting?*' – '*Walkers on Wimbledon Common could be forgiven for thinking they are nuts following reports of a mystery mammal. According to an eyewitness a strange animal similar to a squirrel is hiding out on the common leaving people wondering what kind of beast it could be. So far educated guesses on website Wild About Britain have included the Australasian sugar glider, the North American flying squirrel or another species of possum. Rather more tongue-in-cheek suggestions have included a flying womble - on account of the common being home to the fictional TV characters. Wandsworth's Kolin Barnz, who spotted the beast while on the common, said: "It was squirrel-like but its face looked more mouse-like, with long whiskers, black eyes and small ears. As it jumped between trees, flaps of skin stretched between its front and back legs and it gilded to the next tree. I couldn't believe my eyes. How the animal got to its new home is anyone's guess, but it is possible it could be someone's escaped pet.*'

Wesley the wallaby photographed by Nick Perry. (p. 301)

Two Tone (p. 309)

From the Depths

'Come not between the dragon, and his wrath'

King Lear – William Shakespeare

The tales which have rolled off the tongues of many an excited fisherman remain some of the most appealing to me. Of course, many such spun yarns of monster fish in local lakes, or from windy piers puncturing salt-water waves, are usually exaggerated, but that's the magic. I recall being very young and accompanying my dad on several jaunts across the outskirts of Medway to find overgrown swims in which to tempt all manner of fish from the inky waters by often an orange tipped float. The trudge through the reeds, with a mountain of fishing gear on our backs, was often a perilous journey through wiry quarries, swampy fens, leering woods, and prehistoric looking valleys. Of course, these places were not so remote as to suggest that they'd been unexplored - but the fact that anglers only had been permitted to use these little bays, dotted around the mirror-like calmness of the creeping depths, certainly supplied the biggest air of mystery to me.

There were always the legends of ghosts said to haunt the misty banks and shadowy tree lines, but once an angler is perched on that embankment, his peg becomes his own personal habitat to fulfil his quest, not just to tempt bream, roach, perch, tench, gudgeon, eels etc from the deep, but also the possibility that a large, lazy carp may take the bait and bend the rod into the murkiness or even more exciting, the possibility that some aggressive pike would crash into the keep net and attack the silvery shoal we'd already accumulated in the heat of day. Personally, I was more distracted by the irritating insects which used to buzz my ears, and then, as dusk fell the flitter of swooping bats. At times I spent the fleeting hours dissecting maggots on a fragile, metal chair, and then felt my heart thump my chest as my orange float bobbed on the green waters amongst the myriad of ripples, algae, bubbles and floating pads. To me, these trips were akin to a monster-hunt for a child. I was convinced, in my imaginary world anyway, that far stranger things inhabited the depths, even though a majority of the lakes fished were hardly bottomless, but even so, that humid air and strong smell of damp trees, meaty bait, dirty rain, and my dad's stewed flask of tea will remain long in the memory as he plucked fish upon fish from the steaming waters where foggy ghosts seemed to dance upon the surface like apparitions of anglers who maybe had been dragged to the pits in the past by unknown creatures resting on the silt.

Sea fishing was less adventurous for me simply because it lacked the rural surroundings, and instead the exposure to the elements would result in a guaranteed cold, an aching back and frosted fingers. Sure, there was the possibility that any kind of creature could bend the rod and snap the line as its leathery

307

head emerged from the foamy waters and a wet, dark back broke the surface, but the stretch of shingle beach ripped by gale-force winds was less appealing to me. Either way though, the water always terrified me, whether it was a roaring sea fading to grey in the distance, or a still lake just fifty feet across. My mind raced, and the water became just as unknown as the black sky of night, and after indulging myself on the twisted stories of H. P. Lovecraft, I knew my fishing days were numbered…along with the fact that I hadn't a clue how to set my fishing gear up, and instead decided to munch on my packed lunch whilst my dad affixed float, reel and line and cast at the mirror. It must have annoyed him also when every time I had a bite, I would raise up suddenly from my chair.

A majority of these tranquil lakes were set deep into the areas where large cats have since prowled. Leybourne, Burham, Maidstone and Snodland, to name but a few, harbour lakes just off busy roads that are half a world away from the roar of traffic. The Kent coast is an historic attraction, from Dover's white cliffs, to the eerie, coast-lined wrecks at Sandwich. To me though, every wreck, every sunken boat, every lost swimmer, and every vibration around the float could well have been caused by an unseen monster. As a youngster introduced to the Loch Ness 'monster', giant snakes said to slither through the Amazon jungle, and eels with heads the size of armchairs, I always made a fantasy out of the most mundane surroundings and situations. Of course, as a kid I never dreamed that one day I would stand on the shore of Loch Ness and stare into the black water as several tourists leapt up and down excitedly and pointed at another boat wake in total belief that it had been caused by 'Nessie'. And yet every emotion felt whilst searching Kent's bogs, swamps, ponds, lakes, rivers, and streams for strange creatures originates from the days of watching the float waver in the breeze on a hazy day, and that's why this particular section is dedicated to my dad Ron, the finest of anglers.

Monsters of the depths, of whatever size and elusive nature have always been recorded. Once again referring to Goodsall's *A Fourth Kentish Patchwork*, he writes, '*Kentish Gazette, June 21st, 1814:*

> *An extraordinary large trout, of the salmon species, was caught on Tuesday last in that branch of the River Stour, which passes through the Black Friars, in the centre of this city (Canterbury) by Mr. Linom. It measured in length from snout to tail, 2 feet 7 inches, in girth 1 foot 8 inches, and weighed 17 lbs. It had been observed in that part of the River for two years past, and it is supposed had been attracted there by the offal from a fellmonger's yard, in the vicinity.*'

One of the most monstrous of fish was caught in Maidstone in July 1774; a great sturgeon which once were common in the Medway. It is mentioned in J.M. Russell's *History of Maidstone* book, published in 1978. The creature measured seven-feet and four-inches and weighed 160 lbs. In June 1879, another fine specimen was caught, this time longer at seven-feet nine-inches but weighing slightly less at 132 lbs.

Author Charles Igglesden speaks of other large fish in various volumes of his *A Saunter Through Kent With Pen And Pencil* series. One such tale concerns a large fish called George which inhabited a lake in the Sturry area. The enormous trout had never been caught - only glimpsed - and such was its mystical nature that local fisherman began to oppose any visiting angler who attempted to catch it by throwing rocks, sticks and stones at the water to urge George to flee from the bait being lured. Then, on one rare day, a London angler caught the mystery fish, but as soon as rumour spread like wildfire around the lake all fishermen present came to the aid of the trout, pushing aside the once celebratory angler, and at once tossing the gasping trout back into the waters. The London man was sent on his way, and George slipped back into the depths. At Fordwich, near Sturry, a twenty-eight pound trout was caught and exhibited at Canterbury Museum.

Another tale concerns several overly large pike rarely caught from underneath the bridge at Aylesford

As mentioned in Igglesden's third volume, the pike legend also states that one particular specimen was seen to eat a fox, and in volume eight, in relation to Leeds Castle, near Maidstone, he writes:

> *'In the outer hall are cases containing three huge pike captured in the moat, where for many years they must have roamed and sunned themselves under the walls of the old fortress. The heaviest weighed thirty-six pounds, another turned the scale at twenty-nine pounds, but a third, although much larger than the rest, weighed less when found dying in the water. When in health it must have scaled over forty-pounds.'*

At the time of writing, the record weight for a pike, as accepted by the British Record Fish Committee, is 46 lbs 13 oz caught by Mr Lewis at Llandegfedd Reservoir in Wales in 1992, although the Scottish record belongs to Tommy Morgan who hooked, in 1945, a 47 lb 11 oz pike in Loch Lomond. There has been much debate among anglers as to who really holds the British record for the biggest pike caught by rod and line and a majority of fishermen lean towards Morgan's monster. The world record for a pike comes from the Lake of Grefeern, Germany. The fish caught was 55lbs 1oz, and taken by a Lothar Louis in 1986.

Every angler dreams of catching a whopper, and in the UK the quest for the biggest carp is the aim of a majority of fishermen. The record specimen, named 'Two-Tone', has been lured from Conningbrook Lake, in Ashford, on several occasions, each time with the record being broken by a small measure. 'Two-Tone', named after its recognisable shades of scales, currently weighs in at 67lb.

These fish certainly weren't the mystery creatures that got away, but many do, and not all are recognisable monsters.

Kent, Sussex and Essex. Three counties steeped in lore. Buried treasure, great battles, murder, mystery and rural beauty. A far cry from vast, cold, icy lakes, or inhospitable mountainous regions, and a million miles away from tales of rising, coiled serpents or bubbling, frothing lake demons. Or so you would think.

Various cathedrals, crypts and churches around these areas boast peculiar carvings, stone gothic sculptures and fossilized images that would seem to speak of fairytales, myth and bygone eras of exaggerated yarn. There is an apparent contradiction of discovering such bizarre tapestries inside Christian arenas, where fire-breathing forms spout flames at leather-winged gargoyles. Such houses of the holy are adorned in these 'evil' pictures, as if some sadistic graffiti artist from medieval times projected his stone masonry from the inner sanctum of his dark matter, instead of aptly decorating such a pure environment. And for many, such carvings are perceived as religious symbols, as representations of a good versus evil emotion, or vivid sermons of an undiscovered language. And yet, whilst many of us may be intrigued by such complex artwork do we ever consider the possibility that such gothic creations may well be assembled as historical accounts of real creatures, great beasts that have since been driven from the once magnificent forests into the modern world of mythology?

If ancient carvings from ancient civilizations are accurate then for some reason modern man has either mocked at such wild imaginings, or simply ignored or - more likely - misunderstood. Whilst every artist has his own unique hand, there are many minds to become confused and to misinterpret, but when understanding tales and sketches from the past we also open a world torn from us and whilst we may never be able to imagine such times, we have to consider how, in five hundred years from now, our current ideas and creations will be perceived. If we are quite adequate in our recordings then those that uncover our secrets will have a pretty good idea of how we lived and what we lived with. The same must surely be said not only for our prehistoric ancestors, but those who existed only four to five hundred years ago.

If all wildlife on this precious planet is obliterated within two hundred years, the humans that inhabit the earth in three hundred years will find tales of bears, rats, horses, elephants, fish, insects, etc quite ridiculous. Even if one or two species are wiped out, can you imagine what people of the future would make of a description of a jellyfish or an anteater? The same must be said with regards to stone-carvings left by those during the twelfth century. For however much interpretation is dredged from such bestial poses, i also becomes informative to the cryptozoologist or folklorist who gazes wildly at leering scaled serpents and giant felids. And these creatures are more strange in that they are depicted in a Kent church and not some remote African village where lore maybe rife.

Sea-serpents, dragons, monster snakes and river entities once inhabited Kent and the surrounding areas as they probably did the whole country. Whether encounters with humans were often is difficult to say but amazingly, to this day, it would seem that some leviathans still lurk around the Kent coast, and in murky lakes, occasionally offering themselves as they did so long ago when so many other animals such as wolves and wild cats were native to the gardens. There are records of such bizarre monsters, as I will reveal to you, but such obscure yet fantastic tales are hazed by the passing years and scepticism. Incidents of today which involve unexplainable and uncategorized creatures, are defined as 'paranormal' and either scoffed at or investigated to no real conclusion. Many of the winged beasts and great serpents have been replaced locally by mysterious felids, ghostly black dogs, and - across the continent - by hairy hominids and vampire-like spectres. How would we explain such mysteries to future generations?

Saint George and the Dragon is a popular story that is seldom taken out of mythological context. A medieval mural in Dartford dating back to the 1300s pays homage to this 'battle' of good versus evil, which places such as Canterbury Cathedral have often drawn from in their carvings without ever acknowledging some cryptozoological puzzle. For these are true recordings of monstrous encounters I'd always imagined.

There are some two hundred lakes, rivers, pools, and coastal areas in Britain, said to be, or to have once been, inhabited by one beast or another. Many such creatures are said to reside in areas known for their vast waterways, i.e. Scotland and Ireland and so, in comparison, the county of Kent (and its neighbours contain mere puddles. And yet gargantuan forms have been recorded around such dingy lakes, vein-like rivers, and small but thick woodlands over the centuries. St. Osyth, Henham, Saffron Walden, Hornde and the appropriately named Wormingsford are all areas within Essex that were once haunted by a phantom of serpentine proportions. Dragon-like creatures were said to inhabit the forests of Sussex, a county also known for its snakelore, but Kent seems too frail in comparison with regards to historical monster But in more recent history sightings of such abominations have been impressive.

One bizarre lake monster event occurred during the fifteenth century and a record of it exists within chronicle that is found in Canterbury Cathedral's library. On Friday, 26th September 1449, two enormous reptilian creatures fought on the banks of the River Stour, where they were watched by a number of locals. The two beasts were watched for a fair time and the locals noted that one was a reddish and spotted monstrosity, the other, black and the victor as it eventually sapped the life from the other before returning to its weedy lair. Ever since this startling incident, the area has been known as Sharpfight Meadow.

Whilst such an event would stick in the minds of many for so long, I find it disappointing that many details are left unmentioned of this particular leviathan combat. For instance, what did the animals look like? Considering the local folk watched in admiration for so long, the fact that only details of body colour seem apparent questions their judgement. How big exactly were these fearsome beasts? Did the creatures spot the witnesses to their struggle? And if such an event can become immortalised in a Canterbury chronicle, why does it seem that no other reports of such creatures exist from that period? Indeed from such an era it may be fair to say that such creatures were almost accepted by the locals but also m not have been as fearsome or as exotic as one might think. From this period leading up to the late 1800s, reports of large snakes seem quite common, especially from the Sussex area which over the centuries spawned so many tales of dragons and water-horses.

Firstly though, let us concentrate on another leviathan legend from around that period. It concerns the county of Suffolk, according to a chronicle from 1405, where at Bures, near Sudbury, a huge creature appeared. Vast in body with crested head, teeth of a saw-like nature and an enormously lengthy tail, this rampant reptile slaughtered many sheep throughout the county and in one incident attacked and allegedly ate a shepherd tending to his flock. Such a monster had often been hunted, tracked and rounded by local archers whose arrows could not penetrate such a leathery hide but it would seem that after several attempts to destroy the flesh-eating demon, the archers could only drive the beast into the local marshes where, fortunately for them, it never returned from.

Again, such a story reeks of fairytale imagination but if such a record does speak the truth then once again details of the creature's appearance are scarce, despite mentions of the teeth, tail and body-size. So, do such records speak of bloody encounters with real dragons, forgotten living dinosaurs or merely fuel modern imaginations which make too much out of minor battles with snakes and lizards or out-of-place, escaped crocodiles?

The lore of the dragon has a history that can be traced right across Europe to China and America but do such magical and wondrous stories merely distort mild encounters with pythons, or salamanders or even alligators? In Sussex the legend of the dragon seems confined to the west. Such serpents often considered omens of misfortune, unlucky signs and general mongers of doom. From the eighth century there are accounts of such creatures, records stored in Anglo-Saxon chronicles which speak of , '..wondrous adders that were to be seen in the land of the South Saxons'. Ethelward's 770AD chronicle gives mention to, '..monstrous serpents that were seen in the county of the Southern Angles that is called Sussex.' Whilst modern man becomes engrossed by such legends, in his mind they exist in the realm of myth and fantasy, but what is bizarre is the fact that bones of Iguanodon have been unearthed in Tilgate Forest, an area not far from St. Leonard's forest where famous dragon lore was born. The ancient woodland near Horsham was said to be inhabited by a dragon which was eventually slain by a local hermit during the sixth century, but there was also much mention of giant adders lurking in the undergrowth which were allegedly banished when St. Leonard killed the dragon.

A pamphlet produced in 1614 gives another version of the St. Leonard's dragon tale in more detail. It claims that the fearsome beast used to have a territory of four miles within which it would consume large amounts of cattle and travellers. The pamphlet also states that the serpent of the forest always left a path of glutinous slime in its wake and that such an ooze would have a fetid reek. Finally there is a detailed account of the creatures size:

> *'The serpent is reputed to be nine feet, or rather more, in length, and shaped almost in the form of an axeltree of a cart; a quantitie of thickness in the middest, and somewhat smaller at both ends. The former part, which he shoots forth as a neck is supposed to be an elle long; with a white ring, as it were, of scales about it. The scales along hist backe seem to be blackish, and so much as is discovered under his bellie, appeareth to be red; for I speak of no nearer description than of a reasonable ocular distance. For coming too neare it, hath already beene too dearly payd for, as you shall heare hereafter.'*

The creature is also described as having large feet, although the author seems to believe that dragons have no feet and simply glide upon their ribs and scales. The creature is also perceived as arrogant, almost standing to attention when detecting prey and upon a great neck looks and listens about. However, the most startling description from the pamphlet mentions, '...*on either side of him discovered, two great bunches so big as a large foote-ball and (as some think) will in time grow to wings.*' And so, such a record would seem to describe something akin to the jabberwocky, a great, leathery winged beast unlike any animal ever native to this county or country.

The pamphlet read like an old crypto-chronicle, detailing witnesses, the diet of the animal (rabbits), attacks on livestock and domestic pets and further sightings of other serpentine creatures. Another pamphlet, entitled *A True Relation of a Monstrous Serpent seen at Henham (Essex) on the Mount in Saffron Waldon,* spoke in detail of a reptilian animal sighted several times during the spring and summer (particularly May) of 1669. There is no telling if such serpents were ever slain by members of the local community, but such heroic tales make for good, pleasant night-time reading. Indeed, if the truth be known, such beasts would have merely moved cross country to seek more food and shelter because a four-mile territory wouldn't be sufficient for a fox let alone a mammoth dragon, so maybe once again we could be dealing with something akin to an adder, or an escaped pet such as a cobra.

If such creatures were factual forms then like so many mysterious creatures upon this globe, they would have been misunderstood, elusive, in some cases slain or died a natural death in some remote cave. And the possibilities as well as territory would have become endless if such monsters did indeed have wings.

The next set of leviathan tales of any detail emerged during the 1700s and 1800s. A change in cultural beliefs may well have turned the dragons of the past into great snakes, or indeed both of these creatures co-inhabited the South-Eastern counties.

Sussex history tells of an encounter at Hayward's Heath around 1794 when a huge snake, which had terrorised locals and livestock, was shot dead. The fact that this 'monster' only reached five feet in length disappoints the modern researcher who becomes disillusioned by such tales of gargantuan beasts. Whilst such records cannot be totally dismissed, it would seem that many of the creatures involved in the scare stories measured between five and nine feet in length and seem more snake-like than dragon. The report from the Heath also speaks of the various witnesses who encountered the 'beast' and their mention that the creature always disappeared under the earth when approached. This is hardly the behaviour of a flesh-eating monster, or indeed a dragon. Another report, this time from 1867, within the woodlands of Fittleworth, Sussex, concerns another strange creature far more snake-like once again, especially in the fact that it often hissed and spat at those who accidentally stumbled upon its lair. The creature was never said to have harmed a soul though and so once again the legend of the dragon sinks into fantasy and the reality of the snake, possibly an adder, comes to life, turning the incident into a rather mild and vague nature tale.

Strangeness around Fittleworth does not end there though. Also around the same time, and with possible relation to the same animal, various locals had horrifying experiences with an 'oudaciously large' (as described in Sussex dialect) 'dragon' which inhabited a lair near a pathway and would never let anyone pass without omitting a terrifying hiss and putrefying stench which always drove the unfortunate traveller back from whence he came. I imagine that the pathway must have become awfully overgrown and perfect hideaway for such a creature considering no-one ever managed to walk the area and to wear away such a route. Again though, I believe some kind of snake was responsible because whilst so many villagers were frightened of the creature, there are no reports of anyone being eaten or descriptions of a roaming beast of massive proportions. No dragon, however elusive, could reside next to a pathway and not be hunted to extinction, unless it was the product of hysteria. A phantom.

With so much supposedly fictional artwork protruding eerily from places such as Canterbury Cathedral and Leicestershire's St Mary and Hardulph Church, we cannot pretend that such caricatures are of ord-nary animals indigenous to the British Isles. None of our current wildlife are bestowed with long-necks, or – indeed – bipedal, as depicted in the Leicestershire carvings which clearly show animals with great hind legs and two smaller fore-limbs whilst large, long-necked quadrupeds feed in the background on plants and trees. And these unknown species sit so comfortably alongside more recognisable birds and humans as if they shared the environment not so long ago. Or were the artists in question merely creating monsters as guardians, in the same way as stone gargoyles which loom over many old structures throughout Europe. Various Kent cathedrals and churches parade many a strange stone sculpture, from fire-breathing foxes to barbaric forest wildmen, and many a winged beast.

Judging by even more recent accounts of huge serpents and other aquatic oddities, it would seem that the Loch Ness monster has many relatives which not only inhabit grim, remote lakes, but also the vast oceans. Unfortunately, such cases have well and truly been drowned by the Nessie enigma, a 'monster' made immortal despite whatever is proven or disproved in the future. Indeed, many authors quote the first Nessie sighting from the year AD 656 when St Columba supposedly cast the beast backed to the depths of the inky waters after it attacked a swimmer, but as recent as the eighteenth century people have been attacked by lake gargoyles. A man swimming at a lake called Lyn-y-Gader, in Snowdon, Wales was eaten by a leviathan in front of his friends who watched from the shore as a long object approached the man, raised its head and pulled him down to his watery grave, wrapped within its oily coils. Even more recently, and certainly more local, at Rye in Sussex, as chronicled in a 1926 work, a courting couple were walking their dog one evening across a field when a peculiar horse-like creature with great staring eyes galloped past them. The man pursued the animal in time to see it leap a fence and to splash into a large, deep pool. Whether such an apparition ever existed in reality is another thing. Water horses and kelpies are not common to the South-East, or indeed the reality of nature, but then again neither were dragons. The kelpie was often considered a spectral beast, more accustomed to the next chapter, but as you'll discover, it is very difficult to decide where to draw the line. Were kelpies - horse-like spooks - said to lure travellers to their deaths, something akin to fiery dragons? Were dragons simply misinterpreted snakes? Are all of these creatures participants of a more complex puzzle?

Those who take the stone carvings from the churches and cathedrals seriously translate them as complex human emotions and literally cloud any other interpretation which may lie within. For stone-masons to sculpt sadistic images of confronting dragons, figures being attacked and devoured by serpents, and ape-like bipedal creatures of unknown species, does not, for me anyway, represent human instincts, or in the case of woodland deity carvings, symbolise lust. When the Danes and the Norwegians spoke of such beasts they never translated great battles as conflicting emotions but recorded such encounters as one would nowadays if they stumbled across a big cat in British woodland. Basically, if records of ancient origin exist with regards to serpent and lake monster encounters then indeed such incidents must have occurred. 336 BC is the date of the first account of a reptilian leviathan encounter, involving King Morvidus of Wales who was consumed by a monster which was eventually slain by Peredur, the son of Earl Efrawg, at a place called Llyn Llion. However, it would seem that the same sort of dragon was encountered in Wales around 1693 on the River Conwy and was also killed.

It would seem that the South-East counties monster lore exists on few and far between recorded encounters. Kent seems pretty absent amongst the legends of Essex and Sussex in regards to dragon-like forms. However, a researcher from Maidstone named Tom Atkinson, who I was contacted by in February 2008, told me of a Kent 'dragon' as mentioned in Charles Igglesden's 1906, Cranbrook volume seven of his *A Saunter Through Kent With Pen And Pencil*:

> *'The magnificent wooded park of a hundred and fifty acres is richly watered by a huge lake, made in 1812, and a smaller one within the garden grounds, while further west is an old mill pond that rejoices in a curious legend. It is an old one, and the subject of it*

must be very ancient indeed, and as rare as it is horrible. Nothing less than a flying dragon is said to haunt the pond, but on certain or uncertain nights of the year it wings its flight over the park and pays a visit to the big lake yonder. But he always returns to the mill pond and it is said to pay special attention of a vicious kind to young men and women who have jilted their lovers. A legend with a moral is this. But a winged dragon! A dragon of the ordinary kind is bad enough, but a flying dragon! Augh! It is Mr Tomlins opinion that there is stronger evidence of the existence of this dragon than of most of his kind, and of his fires having gone out in the closing years of the last century. Nothing short of this monsters malign influence could account for the curious fact that, till the coming of Mr Tomlins eldest daughter, no child has been born at Angley for upwards of a hundred years.'

An intriguing tale, albeit as my source Tom Atkinson suggests, '...*tongue firmly in cheek there I think but I would certainly steer clear of Angley Park if I was a local rogue.*'

In more modern times, other strange watery beasts have been observed on several occasions around the county, albeit creatures which not entirely fit into the dragon bracket but which certainly slot nicely into the 'serpent' section. During February 1993 several on-lookers witnessed a long-necked animal swimming slowly in the northern part of the Thames Estuary at Leigh-On-Sea at Essex. More details of the sighting were not forthcoming, such as size or colouration, but seven years later I was told of an amazing serpent sighting whilst interviewing a local man from Canterbury with regards to a black leopard encounter in 2000. The witness to the 1999 sea-monster is a highly respected and known author on fishing, often works for local radio and television. His sighting is as follows:

"I was fishing off Folkestone Pier with a fellow angler when in the distance we saw a black object. I looked through my binoculars and saw a huge animal that I can only describe as a sea-serpent. The creature was roughly one-hundred feet long and seemed to be diving and then resurfacing. We both watched it for about thirty minutes and it was so ridiculously large that I laughed and did not tell anyone else about it. The animal had a long neck, moved very slowly and looked all the world like the Loch Ness monster plesiosaur that people talk about. It was massive".

A two-hour telephone conversation seemed to convince me that what the witness saw was indeed a huge sea creature of some sort. The witness had spent a full hour talking to me about his angling adventures but only when I mentioned sea- serpents did he mumble something along the lines of, "...*I've seen one of them.*" Such a comment intrigued me to ask more.

Whilst a one-hundred foot leviathan of the deep seems too immense for Kent, although historical reports suggest otherwise, let us look at two other strange sightings from the Kent coast which took place at the beginning of the twentieth century and the middle part. These reports have been aired in Graham J. McEwan's excellent 1978 book, *Sea Serpents, Sailors and Sceptics (Routledge & Kegan Paul 1978).*

The first encounter took place in 1912 from St. Margaret's Bay, near Dymchurch. The report is vague but concerned Mr. Stone and others who saw a serpent which the author categorises as a long-necked seal. During 1950 a similar creature was spotted at Cliftonville, between Margate and Broadstairs, by John Handley. Indeed, around this period many so-called serpent sightings were later considered long necked seals and such a creature may well have been responsible for an encounter in Suffolk from 193? when on the morning of October 21st two men, Ernest Watson and William Herrington, went out in their boat to lay nets, but were shocked by the appearance of a grey, long-necked, sixty-foot long beast. As they returned to land the animal thrust its neck out of the water some thirty metres away before shooting off at great speed (thirty knots allegedly) before diving below, leaving a commotion amongst the waves.

The encounter made the headlines not just locally but nationwide, with the *Daily Mail* and *Mirror* running articles on the incident. It also seemed to echo the sighting of a long-necked animal seen in June 1931 by Mrs Sybil Armstrong at Thorpeness, Suffolk.

It would seem that the Thames Estuary is the most likely place for a large animal to be seen. Whilst the 1993 sighting was brief, during the Summer of 1923 Captain Haselfoot and crew of HMS *Kellett* were surveying an area of the estuary known as Black Deep. It was around nine o'clock in the morning when they observed a long neck rise out of the water some two hundred yards away from the ship. The neck was around seven feet high and seemed to submerge and then resurface on a number of occasions. Interestingly enough, the area where the creature was sighted had been closed to shipping for over eight years. So had the Kellett disturbed the lair, or resting place of this creature? Captain Haselfoot also managed to sketch the creature's neck, and what appeared to be a head. It is difficult to get any information from the drawing which simply shows a black long neck, a small head and what appears to be a mouth either with whiskers, some sort of beard or what could merely have been dripping water. It is the classic 'Nessie' head and certainly not of a long-necked seal.

Graham J. McEwan discussed in length the possibility that the long-necked seal could well solve the mystery behind many 'sea monster' sightings. Such an animal would have, obviously, the long-neck, a small seal-like head, a bulky body lacking distinct tail, four large flippers and a vertical undulation, as well as reaching lengths of around sixty feet. The creature is likely to be a pinniped due to the fact that it has webbed feet or flippers, and - like a sea lion - can bound across land. It is also said to leave a greasy wake. However, the 1999 sighting from Folkestone sounds more like a prehistoric monster rather than large seal. Other possibilities of such ocean leviathans lie with everything from giant eels, huge turtles, zueglodons, elephant seals, and oarfish (which rarely surface). However, the more exciting species concerns those that are seen in lakes, pools and rivers. Snakes, giant catfish, lizards or indeed unknown and now extinct creatures could well explain the scattered reports from the south-east over the centuries. If such accepted creatures such as catfish and lizards had been responsible for such folktales though, then surely stone-masons would have carved accurately as they did with other sculptures. I find it bizarre that, after so many years, many ancient paintings and carvings still cannot be deciphered by our experts. It would seem that dragons and 'monsters' did haunt the seas and lakes, but such times have been hazed by the constant misinterpretations.

And so to the present and the serpents and dragons seem mere whispers on the wind. However, as recently as July 2001 a mysterious, smooth-skinned monster was spotted in a Kent river. The River Darent (Darenth), a Kentish tributary of the River Thames, had attracted many anglers and newspapers in the hope of fishing out a dark-skinned predator which was consuming the native residents on a route from Westerham through to west Kent, to Dartford and then into the Thames Estuary. The prime suspect for such obliteration was a wels catfish, estimated to be five feet in length and caught, but put back by a fifteen-year-old local boy named Oliver Parker-Grater. The forty-pound fish was released back into the river simply because Oliver never realised how dangerous it could be to other wildlife, causing alarm to the Kent Fisheries Team who believe that the fish could well cause damage to domestic pets and young children. Fishing expeditions were sent out to catch the monster fearing it would be a threat to the native brown trout. Adrian Saunders of the Fisheries Team said the fish must be caught immediately:

> *"My suspicion is that he has swum down river towards the Dartford Creek area and could even be in the River Thames. Small rivers like the Darent are not the natural habitat of catfish. It is a very ugly fish with a huge bulbous head and a wide slash of a mouth lined with hundreds of razor-sharp teeth. They are very strong and put up a huge*

fight. It is likely this has been put into the river illegally for someone's angling fun but it can be a threat to the environment, making a big impact on local fish stocks."

So, will a five-foot-long catfish go down in the folklore records alongside an elusive five-foot-long snake mistaken for a dragon? Probably not. Whether there has ever been a connection between ancient, local carvings of dragons, serpents and reptilian beasts and historical encounters with similar creatures we will never know but there is one sculpture within Canterbury Cathedral that I wish to pay special attention to also. It is that of a huge cat-like form, which has been officially recognised as a 'panther'. The sculpture shows a muscular felid strangely breathing fire but there is no doubt that it is a wild cat of some kind. The carving has been translated as follows by author J.H. Vaux who in his pamphlet *The Canterbury Monsters (Meresborough Books 1989)* comments:

> '*If we assume that we have here another example of the panther breathing out the fire of the Sweet Breath of Innocence ,then again it is Good overcoming Evil'.*

Make of such a translation what you will but if the panther does indeed represent any kind of reality and goodness as one, let us hope that the many which currently inhabit Kent and the surrounding counties are not as fearsome as the dragons and serpents as before. For such a phenomenon proves just how ironic some of those carvings are, even if they were the work of mere medieval jester. I'm just not sure who is having the last laugh.

Dragon expert and good friend Richard Freeman, author of the comprehensive book on dragons, called *Dragons – More Than A Myth?* (CFZ Press 2005), told me:

> "*Some UK dragons were undoubtedly exotic reptiles escaped from early collections such as the Wormingford dragon of Essex (probably a big crocodile). Others are less easy to explain. There are over ninety dragon legends in the UK and many seem to relate encounters with a species of huge reptile unknown to modern science. Today, a surprising amount of modern day sightings of dragons are reported especially from Asia. Forget demons, vampires and werewolves; the dragon is the most ancient and powerful monster of them all. Cave paintings of it go back 25,000 years. Dragons have always been with us and I think they always will.*"

In his excellent book, *From Flying Toads To Snakes With Wings (Llewellyn 1997)* Karl Shuker writes of such beasts as being:

> '*...probably specimens of crocodile or one of the large species of African or Asian monitor lizard, imported into Europe as curiosities for private ownership or as exhibits in travelling menageries. Some may have escaped and survived for a time in the European countryside, alarming anyone who unsuspectingly encountered them, until they were eventually killed.*'

As for snakes, the adder (*Vipera berus*), the grass snake (*Natrix natrix*) and extremely rare Smooth snake (*Coronella austriaca*) are native to Britain, but could such creatures be considered dragons? It is also assumed that Britain harbours only three lizards, the viviparous lizard, or common lizard (*Lacerta vipara*), the sand lizard (*Lacerta agilis*) and the slow worm (*Anguis fragilis*), which is an anguimorph lizard despite looking like a snake, within the diverse superfamily of the Lacertilia suborder distributed worldwide.

However, other exotics have no doubt been imported throughout the centuries, and during the '70s Pat Langridge recalls seeing an luminous green lizard near his home in Cuxton. He claimed the lizard was the size of the common variety, around four-inches in length, but spectacularly green and certainly not a native species. The wall lizard and green lizard have been introduced over time as alien species, and maybe a selection of exotic escapees could well have spawned dragon legends, but we would still have had to have dealt with the much larger lizards and snakes for such fuss to have been caused.

In 1222 there was mention of 'dragons' over London, although such a record remains vague except to say that a terrific thunderstorm ensued.

During the 1700s, and mentioned in *The Gentleman's Magazine*, to quote:

> '*In the beginning of the month of August, 1776, a phenomenon was seen in a parish a few miles west of London, which much excited the curiosity of the few persons that were so fortunate to behold it. The strange object was of the serpent kind; its size that of the largest common snake and as well as could be discovered from so transient a view of it, resembled by its grey, mottled skin. The head of this extraordinary animal appeared about the same size as a small woman's hand. It had a pair of short wings very forward on the body, near its head; and the length of the whole body was about two feet. Its flight was very gentle; it seemed too heavy to fly either fast or high, and its manner of flying was not in a horizontal attitude, but with its head considerably higher than the tail, so that it seemed continually labouring to ascend without ever being able to raise itself much higher than seven or eight feet from the ground.*'

Even more amazing was the fact that the magazine recorded, in 1797, another flying serpent account, this time between Hyde Park Corner and Hammersmith, on 15th June at 10:30 pm. The witness, a J.R., wrote a letter describing the weird encounter, stating, '*...the body was of a dark colour, and about the thickness of the lower part of a man's arm, about two feet long.*'

The beast was already beginning to resemble the first encounter.

The witness continued:

> '*...the wings were very short and placed near the head. The head was raised above the body. It was not seven or eight feet above the ground.*'

Whilst the creature seemed very flesh and blood, almost like a flying snake, the letter ended in morose fashion, concluding:

> '*...being an animal of such uncommon description, I was particular in noticing the day of the month, and likewise being the day preceding a most dreadful storm of thunder and lightning.*'

Dragons over London too? Surely not. However, the most modern account has become known as the Brentford Griffin, which I wrote of for the *Londonist* website as part of my weekly column called *The Saturday Strangeness*:

> '*During the middle of 1984, a Kevin Chippendale was strolling along Braemar Road, when he observed a strange dragon-like creature in the skies near the Green Dragon apartments, rather coincidentally! He claimed that the beast resembled a dog but with wings and a beak. Mr Chippendale saw the creature again in the February of 1985 and said that the apparition bore some resemblance to the creature painted on the sign of*

the Griffin Public House. A friend of Kevin's, an Angela Keyhoe also claimed to have seen the flying monster. She was on a bus journey when she saw it sitting on the gasometer next to the Waterman's Art Centre. She said it resembled a giant black bird. Several passengers on the bus apparently saw the creature, and so did psychologist John Olssen, one morning whilst he was jogging near to the Thames. Sightings seemed to escalate, and the legend was featured in the press and also on The Six O' Clock News.

Although many claimed that the entire 'Griffin' fiasco was a hoax, it has embedded itself into local legend. A pamphlet on the series of reports was written by Andrew Collins in 1985.

Now, whilst such a creature may well have been nothing more than fanciful rumour, I would like to share with you a letter, submitted to Fortean Times magazine, during the May of 1998, from a Mr Martin Collins who believed that such a monster may well have been more than local hoax.

He wrote: 'I first encountered the story of the Brentford Griffins while I was at St John's School in the 1950s (note: some thirty years before the first sightings!). St John's in those days sat in the shadow of Brentford's football ground, Griffin Park. Inquiring why there were so many griffin references in Brentford, I was told that it was due to the family of griffins that lived on Brentford Eyot, an island in the Thames.

The story of how they got there was that the first griffin was brought to Brentford by King Charles II as a gift for his mistress, Nell Gwynn, who had a house in the Butts at Brentford. One day the griffin was playing on the banks of the River Brent, which flows past the Butts, and fell in. The hapless creature was washed down the Brent into the Thames, finally being washed up on Brentford Eyot. As it was assumed to have been killed, it was left alone and was able to live on the Eyot for many years – griffins having a lifespan of centuries. Then Sir Joseph Banks brought back a griffin from a Pacific island where he had been with Captain Cook. This griffin was originally housed in the Pagoda in Kew Gardens, which is on the opposite bank of the Thames from Brentford Eyot where it found a mate awaiting it. There was soon a whole colony of griffins and they spread out from the Eyot all over the town of Brentford, where they can still be seen to this day, if you look closely enough.

This story has stayed with me... it is a nice bit of Brentford mythology.'

Again, in his book *From Flying Toads To Snakes With Wings*, Shuker writes:

'Relics purportedly from griffins – those fabulous monsters with the body of a lion but the head, wings, and forequarters of an eagle – have also been documented. Their long talons were once highly prized, because they were reputedly able to detect poison and many were brought back to Western Europe by crusaders during the Middle Ages. Sadly, however, they invariably proved to be antelope horns, sold to the gullible fighters by African entrepreneurs.'

He adds:

'As noted by Edward Peacock (The Antiquary, September 1884), a griffin claw preserved

in the Brtitish Museum is believed to be one of two contained in 1383 within the shrine of Saint Cuthbert, at Durham Cathedral. It resembles the horn of an ibex.'

The ibex is a wild mountain goat.

1205 remains the earliest date of a strange dragon-like beast seen in Kent, Maidstone to be precise and recorded by the Abbot Ralph of Coggeshall who wrote of a very strange beast that was discovered after a severe thunderstorm that rained down all over England. The beast itself was a messy carcass, something dark and hideous with an assortment of limbs, the belly of a human, the head of an ass and which it gave off a foul odour. No further record of this abomination exists, but we assume that an air of the unnatural must have exuded from it otherwise such a sight would not have been recorded. Whether it was a dragon we'll never know, but such a creature must either have been on the ground and fried by a lightning bolt, or descended from the zenith like a meteorite, crashing into Maidstone.

Less weird, but as equally out of place, was the whale which drifted into Kent as commented on by the *Kent Messenger* of 27th January 2006 in response to an incident which involved a whale turning up in the Thames - *'Whale's arrival caused excitement'* :

> '...56 years ago, the River Medway had a whale drama of its own. The whale involved was of a much rarer species than the northern bottlenose whale in the Thames. In October 1949, records author Bob Ogley in 'Kent - A Chronicle of the Century Vol 11', '... there was great excitement at Rectory Wharf, Wouldham, when the body of a narwhal arrived on the shore via the Medway. 'It is only the second example of the species to be washed ashore in this country in 500 years. The whale's body was taken to the Natural History Museum, in London.' So, what is a narwhal? Narwhals are usually found in Arctic seas and rivers where they feed on cuttlefish, crustaceans and fish. The most unusual feature of the narwhal is that it has only two teeth in its upper jaw.'

A whale which caused excitement in the Thames in 2007 also triggered this article from the *Times Online*:

> 'The wonder last month of a whale in London recalls an episode 350 years ago. In the summer of 1658, the appearance of a whale in the Thames at Greenwich gave rise to wide excitement. The best-known literary witness to the event is that of John Dryden. He recalls the phenomenon in his Heroique Stanzas, Consecrated to . . . Oliver Lord Protector, figuring it as an advance tribute to Cromwell, who was to die three months after: '. . . first the Ocean as a tribute sent. That Gyant Prince of all her watery Heard; And th'Isle when her Protecting Genius went, Upon his Obsequies loud sighs confer'd.'

Adding natural-historical detail, the diarist John Evelyn reports the whale's stranding at low tide. It *"was killed with a harping iron, struck in the head"*, where after with *"a horrid groan, it ran quite on shore and died"* (Diary, June 3, 1658). His description is corroborated by a newsletter from John Barber to Viscount Scudamore (June 8, 1658):

> The people of this Towne have gratified their eyes for almost a weeke together with a Succession of novelties: Green-goose-faire is the preface to the trapanning of a young whale betwixt Blackwall and Greenwich: a strange and unwonted spectacle here; it is sayd to be faeminine, & about 58 foot long, & about 12 in thicknesse; She was first discovered neare Blacke-wall, pursued by hideous cries of watermen, strucke first by a fisher man's anchor, throwne from a bold hand, & then attempted by severall engines,

V[iz.], musket-shot, resented his wounds soe highly that he made an outcry the most terrible that fancy could create; in fine they kill'd him, & drag'd him at a loyter [lighter, a boat used for lading] to Greenwich where then thousands of people in a day are to see him: men & ladies are carried on porter's backes to him as he lyes in the water . . . to the great content of the beholders: a gent that I know, with 7. or 8. more were at once in his mouth: his tongue is the whole breadth of his mouth: of the tonge of some great whales have bin made no less then 4. tun of oyle, as I am told: but as for the throat of the greatest Leviathan it is no wider than the thicknesse of mans arme, which confirmes that of Jonas to be purely a miracle: This monster hath hugely inrich'd Greewich & Deptford, but is now remov'd to Blackwall to perfume that place, for he stinks intollerably: some say the protector doth challenge it, as being a fish royall, but had it bin but a sturgion the Lord mayor might have had it.'
(British Library, Add MS, 11043, f. 107)

In the December of 1763 was also recorded that a live whale, measuring over fifty-six feet appeared on the shoreline at Seasalter.

It is these tales as such which create monster legends.

On 10th March 2008 the *Medway Messenger* reported, *'Porpoise is seen in river'*, commenting:

'Medway could have its own answer to Jaws. A creature with a shark-like fin has been spotted swimming up and down the River Medway and is thought to be chasing shoals of fish.

But the fin actually belongs to a Harbour Porpoise and not a Great White Shark. One resident described the marina mammal spinning in the water, while others said it looked like it was playing. The Harbour Porpoise is one of the smallest marine mammals and is commonly seen alone in shallow waters or estuaries. Some have even been spotted hundreds of miles from the sea.'

In the same edition of the newspaper, it was also reported that, *'Dead dolphin found after sightings'*, *'The body of a dolphin was discovered on Wednesday afternoon in Milton Creek near Sittingbourne.*

It's thought it may have been the same creature that was seen earlier in the day in the River Medway at the Medway City Estate. And Jason Carter, Kent co-ordinator for British Divers Marine Life Rescue (BDMLR) thinks it may have been the same dolphin that was seen in the Medway at Strood Bridge earlier on the same morning. It is believed the animal was an Atlantic white-sided dolphin usually found in the North Sea off the coast of Scotland.'

On 20th September 2007 *Dive Magazine* reported, *'Kent dolphin a danger, say police'* – *'A dolphin that has been swimming off Folkestone in Kent for the past year has become a danger to bathers, according to police. Nick-named Dave, the bottlenose dolphin has allowed swimmers to touch him and to ride on his back in the waters off Sandgate in Kent. However, police have warned that the dolphin has become so humanised he could pose a threat.*

"A wild dolphin can injure a human and there have been fatalities in the US." said PC Andy Small of Kent police. "There are fears that as Dave becomes used to human con-

Exhibits at Rochester Guildhall Museum
(TOP: Cabinet of curiosities BOTTOM: ammonite) P. 332

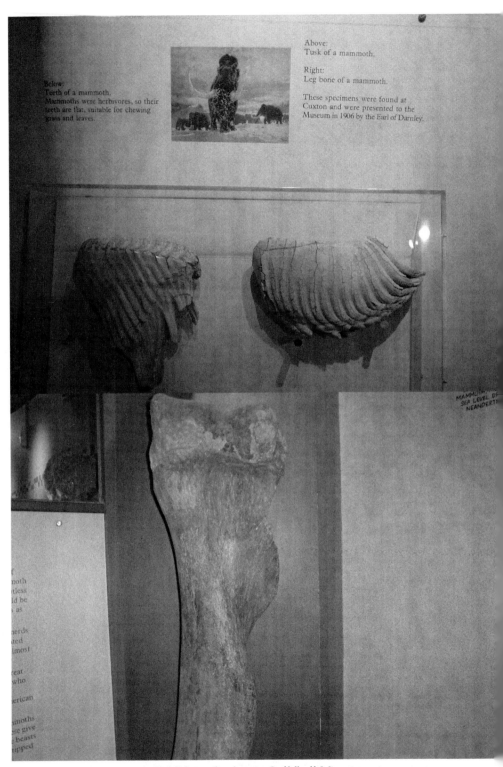

Above:
Tusk of a mammoth.

Right:
Leg bone of a mammoth.

These specimens were found at Cuxton and were presented to the Museum in 1906 by the Earl of Darnley.

Below:
Teeth of a mammoth.
Mammoths were herbivores, so their teeth are flat, suitable for chewing grass and leaves.

Exhibits at Rochester Guildhall Museum
(TOP: Mammoth teeth BOTTOM: Mammoth leg bone) P. 332

TOP: Mammoth tusk in Guildhall museum p. 332
BOTTOM: Carving of giant pike (p. 310)

TOP: Reconstruction of 2008 Medway Monster (courtesy *Medway Messenger*)
BOTTOM: The Swanscombe skull (p. 332)

*tact, he actually becomes a danger. Dolphins start to display their dominance and that
is when there is a likelihood of danger."*

*Police are also concerned about injury to the dolphin, following reports of small craft
getting too close to the dolphin.'*

The *East Kent Gazette* of 3rd March 1999 reported on others visitors to Milton Creek:
*'The wildlife of Swale is certainly getting more exciting - and I'm not just referring to
those who frequent its nightclubs!*

*Telephone calls from readers have already alerted us to sightings of some sort of wild
cat in the Sittingbourne area. Now we hear about seals cavorting in the Creek at Milton. According to information reported to the newsroom, two of the sleek swimmers
have been seen on several occasions bobbing up and down in the waters of the Creek.
As with the big cat story, we'd love photographic evidence of these unusual visitors.'*

A seal pup became separated from its mother at Broadstairs during the autumn of 2005. Bay inspector
Tom Phillips rescued the baby which was taken by the RSPCA. A month later the common seal was released off the coast of Rye. Another pup was also discovered on the shore at Cliftonville, whilst a year
later a pup was photographed basking in the summer sun at Dover. On 31st October 2006 *Kent Online*
reported, *'Seal on the Medway attracts huge attention'*, after an adult seal was seen cavorting on the
shore, but 2008 was the busiest year for such visitors. In January a three-year old grey seal appeared to
be stranded at Main Sands, Margate, and was aided by Horizon Sea Safaris, and transported to Goodwin
Sands. Then, a seal that became known locally as Simon, became famous for its ventures close to Maidstone. The animal was first recorded around Allington lock and filmed on March 16th. The animal had
been seen hunting fish and eels. Reporter Chris Hunter reported, *'Animal rescue teams will not step in to
save a lonely seal which has become 'landlocked' in a freshwater river'.*

*Last week the Kent Messenger reported on how a seal, dubbed Simon, had swum up the
River Medway and through Allington lock; where the 19km freshwater river reaches its
tidal limit. The lock had been open due to high spring tides but has now been shut, ef-
fectively trapping the coastal animal up-river. Since then the saga of Simon the seal has
continued, with the animal continuing up through Maidstone town centre and on to East
Farleigh. Representatives from the RSPCA and British Divers Marine Life Rescue say
they do not plan to remove Simon, who, they insist, remains 'happy' where he is catching fish. However, Mark Stevens, director of BDMLR admitted seals normally live in
colonies and that Simon was stuck by himself unless he worked out how to operate the
lock system.*

*He admitted there wasn't much chance of Simon meeting a female companion in East
Farleigh, "They don't all need to breed, just like not all humans need to breed."*

BDMLR chairman Alan Knight however admitted that seals had been known to upset fishermen in the
past. He said: *"In Scotland they were going to shoot a seal that was eating salmon but we said, why don't
you make it an honorary club member, and they did, and they got loads of good press."*

On April 9th Alan Smith reported that:

*'The worry is over. Simon the seal will not spend the rest of his life as a lonely bachelor
marooned in the upper reaches of the River Medway.*

The seal, which has attracted a huge amount of interest since he was first spotted at Allington lock, near Maidstone, has shown he is perfectly able to cross through to the tidal downstream section whenever he wants.

It appears he uses the underwater sluice gates which are opened at high tide to pass through from one reach of the river to the other. He was spotted Tuesday happily frisking around downstream of the lock by a Peter Russell who was taking a stroll. Several people, including Ross Duddell, secretary to the Friar at Aylesford Priory, have also spotted Simon fishing in the river near the priory.

On Friday 11th April the *Kent Messenger* featured an email sent in by a Dawn Coutts, who reported, '*Not long ago, I was walking along the bridge above the River Medway, near Maidstone town centre, when I saw a head like thing, My mum thought it was a seal. I didn't believe her until I got home and looked at the newspaper. It really was a seal's head*!'

On a rather more sombre note during the late '90s the local wildlife trust were becoming alarmed at the amount of dead otters turning up in the county, particularly Sevenoaks, with one corpse being discovered near the railway line. Otters have been pretty much of a rare species in Kent, making the sudden emergence of carcasses a mystery.

Biodiversity Sussex website commented:

'*In the middle of the 1950s otters were considered to be common and widespread across much of England (Stephens, 1957). However, by the early 1960s otter hunts in this country were reporting diminishing hunting success and it appears that otter populations crashed across England in the late 1950s and early 1960s. This was due mainly to the introduction of organochlorine pesticides (Lloyd, 1962; Anon., 1969; Anon., 1974). Organochlorine pesticides, used in sheep dips and as cereal dressing, tend to become concentrated in eel tissues. Those eels not killed directly become poison reservoirs for otters and other predators, which subsequently suffer from elevated levels of mortality and low breeding success (Chanin & Jefferies, 1978). Otters are at the top of the food chain, and because of their natural fat reservoirs, they are highly susceptible to the accumulation of fat soluble pesticides and other toxins. In high doses, toxins can reduce breeding success and immune system function.*

By the late 1970s only 6% of sites inspected in the UK showed signs of otters and they were largely absent from the midlands and southern England (Lenton et al., 1980). Voluntary and later compulsory bans on the use of organochlorine pesticides coupled with a ban on the direct persecution of otters in the 1970s has enabled otter populations in some areas of the UK to begin to recover. However, in many areas of England farming has intensified since the late 1950s and much of the riparian vegetation that otters once used for cover has been removed. This together with increased disturbance from human activity and continued building and infrastructure developments along riversides and in floodplains has restricted the otters' recovery in the Midlands and in the south and east of the country.

The otter is currently recovering nationally with most counties in the UK seeing some regular otter activity, although breeding activity is still low in many areas. Otter populations in the South are moving South eastwards from the South West counties, and

Southwards from the Thames and Kent regions.'

On November 18th 2005 in the capital, the *South London Press* covered a strange story of an alleged alligator sighting.

> *'RSPCA inspectors were called to reports of an alligator in a popular park. They rushed to Tooting Bec Common after a member of the public discovered the three-and-half foot "gator" on Sunday morning. But once on the scene, RSPCA Inspector Ian Gough identified the creature as a Bosk monitor lizard. It had died, unable to survive in cold weather. The reptile was the second monitor lizard to be found in the wild in South London in the last few days. On Thursday last week a Nile monitor was discovered alive in a Lambeth park. Monitor lizards feed on a diet of mice and chicks and can grow up to 6ft long. The RSPCA recommends the reptiles are not kept as domestic pets because of the space required and the expertise needed to keep them in good health. Inspector Gough said the Bosk monitor had probably been kept as a pet but escaped. He said: "We were called at around 9.30 am on Sunday to reports of an alligator on Tooting Bec Common. It was reported to be lying at the common next to Elmbourne Road. When I arrived there I realised it was a Bosk monitor. It was dead and had lost one of its legs. It might have escaped from someone's home or been dumped there after it became ill. It was in a poor condition. Monitor lizards come from warm climates and cannot survive in cold conditions like the current cold snap."*

Of course, it's not actually unusual for such smaller exotic pets to go walkabout. If every sighting was logged of someone's errant lizard or snake, I'm sure there'd be thousands of reports of such 'monsters'. Only the more peculiar remain of interest, such as this tale, although from further a field reputedly of a crocodile, which I wrote for my *Beasts Of London* blog.

> *'Posters warning of a small crocodile-like creature living in a pond in Shirley are a hoax. Croydon Council has denied issuing the signs, which bear a fuzzy reproduction of its logo, saying it is the work of a prankster. News of the croc broke on Monday on a local website Then another contributor posted a mock-up picture of a croc sitting on a grass verge near one of Croydon's trams. The following morning a copy of the poster arrived at the Guardian offices, with an anonymous hand-written note saying: 'Council are trying to keep this quiet. The posters - several have been posted round the park - warn of a small crocodile-like creature living in Millers Pond, which is thought to be an escaped pet which has thrived due to the recent hot weather.' It signs off with: 'Important: do not approach creature.' A council spokesman said: "The sign is obviously a spoof sign put there by a prankster and is not an official Croydon Council notice."*

This fiasco emerged in September 2003 but died down rapidly, bit it did echo a similar incident which took place in Finchley, North London in 1996. On this occasion an-off duty RSPCA Inspector was walking his Labrador dog along a stream at Dollis Brook. His dog decided to go for a wade and a splash, only to return with quite a catch, the decomposing remains of what appeared to be a crocodile measuring around five feet in length. The corpse was sent to London Zoo, but no further information emerged.

Another similar dead end was also reached in the hunt for the alleged freshwater shark said to have clamped its jaws around the foot of Jenny Pickles as she swam in a reservoir south east of Heathrow Airport in 1997. The woman kicked out at the unseen predator and swam to shore where her wounds were examined by a marine biologist who concluded that a shark had taken a nip at her. Of course, most freshwater sharks are reasonably small and mild-mannered, except the bull shark, but in my opinion there was more chance of the attack coming from a big catfish or a pike. In March of 1962, a three-foot long lizard-like creature was run over by a car in Friern Road, East Dulwich, south-east London. RSPCA officers were quick to arrive on the scene and concluded that the animal was nothing like they'd seen before! A zoological expert from London Zoo also looked at the animal and he too commented that the sandy-coloured reptile was like no other species. Yet, despite the intriguing find, it is alleged that the reptile was buried somewhere in the leafy suburbs. Shame.

In Horsham, West Sussex, a pike known as 'the alligator' has maintained its mythical status for several years in the vicinity of Roost Hole pond. The ferocious fish, known as the freshwater shark in angling circles, weighed around 35 lb when last hooked. The predator has a taste for ducks and any toes that should be bravely dipped into the cold waters. Warnham Mill Pond near Horsham is another dwelling of a monster pike. Its claim to fame was the devourment of a Jack Russell terrier which decided to take a paddle. The pike is rarely hooked, but can often be observed lazing under the bridge.

> September 21st 2007 - 'A young mother was in the bath with her baby when a 5ft python slid out from under it. Leanne Smith, 18, screamed as it hissed at her and four-month-old Millie', reported the Daily Mirror. 'She scooped Millie into her arms and leaped over the snake which experts believe was ready to pounce. Leanne, who lives with boyfriend Ben Payne, also 18, in a council flat in Dartford, Kent, said: "It was huge and it just sat there hissing and looking at me. "I just screamed and screamed, which was probably the wrong thing to do as it started to hiss at me even more. "I jumped over it and called the RSPCA. They said it had probably got in through a pipe and was ready to attack me. "So I locked the bathroom door and waited for them to take it away." An RSPCA officer caught the royal python - a non-venomous constrictor that crushes its prey - and a neighbour experienced in looking after large snakes is caring for it while the owner is sought. Ian Stephen, London Zoo senior reptile keeper, said: "It would have been more aggressive than usual because it would have been very stressed and afraid, cold, confused, hungry - and more scared of Leanne than she was of it."

In the September of 1976 it was recorded that hordes of poisonous adders were converging on a beauty spot known as The Humps, in Canterbury. In the July of the same year giant jellyfish swarmed around the south-coast, and an animal resembling an alligator was rumoured to have lurked in a pond at Warden Bay, on the Isle of Sheppey.

Of course, like so many anglers' tales of the "...one that got away", there are often stories of large, alien beasts wading through the waters off the coast or in the local lake. In fact, if I had a pound coin for every tale I've heard of a monster-haunted lake locally I'd be quite well off in the pocket at least. Terrapins pools, scorpions on the sea wall, lizards on the marshes, giant catfish in the streams, exotic snakes on the banks. Many are simply rumour....but many are also true stories of animals that have escaped into the wilds, been exaggerated over time, and become mini-monsters in our own back yards. They are not really mystery animals, just out of place.

In 1926 a mysterious creature was being seen in the Vale of Heath pond at Hampstead Heath. Dogs appeared to be spooked by the creature that would occasionally surface, whimper and then plunge back into the depths. Then, on the 25th August an angler snagged something that appeared to be too strong for resident fish. He sought help from another fisherman who came to his aid and together they reeled in a small seal. The fishermen overpowered the aggravated and frightened animal and took it to the Vale Health hotel where the proprietor, a Mr Fred Gray found a large fish tank to put, and exhibit the animal in as the local legend. A reporter from the *Daily Chronicle* followed the story up, as did the *Evening*

News, and a Mr Shelley, from London Zoo confirmed that the creature in the tank was in fact a wild seal that must have been dumped. Then, after the strange catch, it was revealed that more of the animals could well be living in the pond as sightings had apparently dated back two years, and Mr Gray claimed that the creatures must have come from the River Thames, reaching the pond via the River Fleet, but London Zoo dismissed such claims, stating that no-one had ever reported seals making their way up the Fleet.

On November 2nd with the mystery long faded, another seal turned up in the pond. An angler hooked the animal which he described, *"Fought like a lion and barked like a dog"*, but the creature unfortunately died on the shore from the wounds caused by the rip of the hook. However, the carcass was taken away by the fisherman who stuffed it and put on display at his home. The seal which resided at the hotel, lived a long and healthy life. In 1992, an eight-foot long grey seal was seen swimming in the River Thames, very close to Westminster. Proof that the experts aren't always right.

In 1994 Hampstead Heath was once again in the news, with *Big Issue* magazine reporting on the lethal crayfish that had been discovered in a bathing pool frequented by local men. The crustaceans, known as the Louisiana reds, have been known to bite, and such forms also carry a virus known to kill native crayfish. Whilst residing at his terraced house in Kentish Town, during the 1980s, Christopher Fowler began to catch glimpses of unusual whitish creatures in his back garden. After finally finding the time to fully investigate, and to dismiss such possible hallucination on his own behalf, Mr Fowler was astounded to discover several albino, lobster-like critters which plagued his yard for several months. A friend of Mr Fowler's, whilst visiting one evening, almost stood on one of the bizarre creatures whilst exiting the back door. They could not understand how such things had got there. Had they been dumped there by someone, maybe as restaurant rejects? Had seagulls plopped them down after snatching them from market stalls?

After much confusion, Mr Fowler's friend decided to have a specimen investigated by the Natural History Museum's Crustacean Section, where they concluded that such beasts were in fact Turkish crayfish (*Astacus leptodactylus salinus*), aggressive and rather large sea creatures which had also been observed in Camden's canal system. According to the further investigations, although the river was very much running underground, the waterway was in fact still linked to the drainage system between the roads and the canal. The crayfish, apparently, had used the system and emerged in Mr Fowler's garden, due to the fact his drainage outlet was uncovered.

Also in the 1990s, thousands of insects resembling cockroaches descended upon Woolwich, in south London, particularly in the vicinity of Globe Industrial Estate. The two-inch-long forms, with large antennae, were swept to London via a freakish flood but from where no-one knew. Such creatures were deemed harmless.

During 1975, shortly after the mentioned Hampstead storm, a Kensington man discovered a West African python on his window ledge after one heavy rainfall. The creature was carted off to London Zoo.

On 26th May 1984 Mr Ron Langton was enjoying some late-night television at his home in East Ham when he was unsettled by a peculiar noise outside. It sounded for all the world as if his roof was being hit every few minutes or so, and all over, by something which slapped as it made impact. The strange noise went on for quite a few minutes, but Ron was too relaxed to go outside and take a look, thinking it was heavy rain. The next morning the man was amazed to find six fish scattered on his roof and lawn. The fish measured approximately twelve centimetres long and appeared to be flounders and whiting.

A more extreme fish fall was record at Canning Town when two witnesses discovered some forty fish strewn about the gardens. Theories put forward were either a water spout from the Thames had lifted the fish or seagulls had dropped them, but the solutions seemed even more bizarre than the odd events. In February 2004 people travelling on the boat, *Thames Bubbler*, at Dagenham, were astonished when what appeared to be a piranha dropped from nowhere, and slapped onto the deck. The Environment Agency theorised that a seagull had dropped the fish, despite the piranha belonging to waters some five-thousand miles away in the murky depths of the Amazon. Those who observed the fish noticed that the beak marks of a gull were evident, but the only suggestion they could come up with as to why the fish had made its way to London, was as an import which was then discarded in the local waters, where it would have perished due to the cold.

The Wildlife Crime Unit of London's Metropolitan police commented on their website:

> *'Exotic Species in the Wild'* – *'Over the years many species which do not normally live in the wild in Britain have been deliberately released here and many of these now have established populations in the wild. This can have a serious impact on our own wildlife as these animals are often more successful than similar species already living here, and a number of previously common British wild animals are now threatened by the presence of exotic species which compete with them for the habitat and food supplies in the area. The Grey Squirrel, from North America, is probably the best known exotic species living in the London area, but there are many others including Muntjac Deer from South East Asia, Red-eared Terrapins and Bullfrogs from the USA and Ring-necked Parakeets from India. In 2000 the Metropolitan Police and London Zoo even caught a lynx which was roaming free in North London. Many of the terrapins and bullfrogs are examples of household pets which were deliberately released by their owners when they became too big or too difficult to look after. This is against the law, as in Britain it is an offence to deliberately release any species which does not normally live here.*

> *How you can help - If you are thinking of buying an exotic pet make sure that you know as much as possible about how to care for it, how large it will grow etc., before you buy. If you have an exotic pet which you are unable to keep any longer please contact a reputable animal welfare organisation like the RSPCA who may be able to help to re-home it. Remember, it is against the law to release it.'*

A Rochester man got a surprise in 1995 when he peered at his window box from his flat window and saw a four-foot long iguana!

In the same year the East Sussex Wildlife Rescue team were looking at evidence which suggested that terrapins were surviving healthily in the UK. I'd heard several local rumours of such creatures inhabiting nearby ponds after being released as pets.

Our only real evidence of once great beasts roaming the Kentish lands lies in the fossil records. When you consider the variety of remains excavated from the chalky hills of Kent and Sussex, I'm surprised that far more animal ghosts have not been seen, should you believe such! In Swalecliffe, the remains of hippopotamus were dug up in the early 1900s. In the 1800s giant tusks, as well as bones, of a great elk and the skull of a lion were unearthed at Blue Bell Hill. Why aren't there ghosts of prehistoric creatures? In a strange book from 1861 entitled *Round About Kits Coty House: An Essay In Popular Topography* there is mention of several finds beneath local chalk in the enormous quarries.

> *'From a quarry of the lower, or earliest, deposit of the chalk in the pits about there,*

Mr W.H. Bensted of Maidstone obtained the remarkable fossil Turtle, named in honour of the discoverer Emys Benstedi, and fully described in the Philosophical Transactions For 1841. The skeleton is perhaps the most perfect and beautiful ever discovered, and appears to have belonged, as did also a specimen from the same quarry, previously described by Professor Owen, to a fresh-water species inhabiting our pristine lakes and rivers.'

The author also goes on to speak of:

'Thanks to the genius of Mr B. Waterhouse Hawkins, the grounds of Crystal Palace have been peopled with life-like restorations of the Dragons of this remote period. Peering over the neck of land below his larger group of Pterodactyles, the head of this gigantic lizard (Mososauraus) armed with terrific teeth, is seen rising from the lake. Few of the thousands who see him daily at the Palace, realize the startling fact that he was once a denizen of famous Kent, wallowing unwieldy in its waters, and startling the lesser fry from their propriety. Yet, in the choice museum at Chillington House, Maidstone, now the property of the town, there is a fine specimen of the tooth of this Saurian – not brought, as you might be guessed from parts beyond sea, but actually from the chalk at Upper Halling. But you must not quit the contemplation of this monster without a scrutinizing gaze at the Pterodatyles on the cliff above, squatting on their haunches with wings dispread, and out-stretched necks, as if they had just been in the water for divers purposes, and had come out for sun-dry reasons, according to the venerable joke. For these Pterodactyles, too, were once amongst the tenantry of pristine Kent. Some bones discovered in the Burnham chalk were described, in 1841, as a humerus, and two distal terminations of tibias, resembling in form, proportion and size, those of the albatross, and apparently belonging to some long-winged water fowl.'

In November 2007 the *Hastings Observer* reported on a remarkable find:

'A new species of dinosaur has been discovered from bones dug up in Hastings.

The remains, found in Ecclesbourne Glen in the early 1890s by a fossil hunter, had sat gathering dust locked in a cabinet in the Natural History Museum. It was given a brief review by expert palaeontologist Richard Lydekker in the days after it was found but then lay untouched for the next 113 years. That was until a palaeontology student researching his PhD noticed something distinctive about the bones. A closer look at the backbone confirmed his suspicions and the new species, the Xenoposeidon, was discovered.

Part of the sauropod family, the Xenoposeidon - roughly translated as Alien from the Sea - was about 50ft in length and weighed a mammoth seven-and-a-half tons. A herbivore, it would have roamed the area around 140million years ago, thriving during the Jurassic and Cretaceous periods. Portsmouth University student Mike Taylor, who made the discovery, was understandably excited by the find. He said: "It leapt out at me as being different. I've spent the last five years doing nothing but looking at sauropod vertebrae so I immediately realised it was something strange. It didn't look like any dorsal I'd ever seen before."

Taylor and fellow palaeontologist Dr Darren Naish, used the likely position of the bone to estimate the size and shape of the animal. From this they established Xenoposeidon is *not only a new species, but probably a new family of dinosaur. Mr Taylor said: "The big advantage we had over Lydekker was 113 years of research during which time a hundred sauropods had been named, many of them from excellent remains. There were lots of animals we could compare our specimen with, and lots of useful papers describing and discussing them. It was quickly apparent my first instinct had been right: this bone had belonged to a previously unknown species. Although no precise records were ever made of where the bone was found, Mr Taylor suspects Hastings would be the best bet for any budding bone hunters. He said: "We know Rufford (the expert who found the bones) did most of his collecting in Fairlight and Ecclesbourne Glen. That is certainly where I would go looking for more of it."*

The area in and around Hastings is well-stocked in dinosaur fossils and has a long history of yielding important specimens. In fact, fossil bones now regarded as dinosaurian were reported from Hastings as early as 1829 and a predatory dinosaur, the Becklespinax, was first un-earthed in nearby Battle.'

In 1913 at Upnor, remains of an elephant were discovered by a Mr. S. Turner, of Luton, Chatham. A great leg bone was excavated after it was found in a ditch, and the remains are stored by the Natural History Museum in London. In 1906, bones of a mammoth, found in Cuxton, near Strood, were presented to the Rochester Guildhall Museum by the Earl of Darnley. The large teeth, a leg bone, and tusk can be seen on display at the present time at the museum which is situated on the High Street, a few yards from the Rochester Bridge.

Many intriguing discoveries have been unearthed in the county. One such artefact is the 'Swanscombe Skull', now housed at the Natural History Museum. Three fragments, found in 1935, 1936 and 1955, between Gravesend and Dartford, are the earliest human remains, dating to between 250,000 and 350,000 years ago. They were discovered at Barnfield Pit, and belonged to a female hunter-gatherer, a nomadic soul who would have used stone tools and weapons, and provided a link between earliest hominoids and modern humans, and may also lead to the comparatively recent but extinct Neanderthals.

Rochester's Guildhall Museum displays a true cabinet of fossil curiosities. Several teeth and a vertebrae from a species of shark found at Wouldham sit among Trilobites (marine creatures who inhabited the seas long before the dinosaurs ruled), Crinoids (marine organisms), Sea Lilies (deep water dwelling animals which resemble plants), Brachiopods (shellfish), and also bark and leaves from Carboniferous plants. Plesiosaur teeth found at Burham, sea urchins discovered at Cuxton, an Abbey Wood Sand shark and teeth belonging to a Mastodon (a mammoth-type creature) and woolly rhino also line the shelves.

One-hundred million years ago in the Cretaceous chalk (formed of a sediment of shells and algae) period, Medway was under sea level. The waters would have been inhabited by the most widely-known fossil of today, that of the ammonite, which the Rochester museum also harbours. These creatures, which first emerged around four-hundred and fifty-million years ago, died out with the dinosaurs, their spiral ribbed form evident in many fossils in museums. These predators, belonging to a group known as cephalopods (marine creatures having a head/mouth surrounded by tentacles), which includes the squid, cuttlefish, nautilus, and octopus, would have lived in Medway's depths alongside primitive fish, flatworms, jellyfish, sponges and seaweed.

I would like to end this particular section with a truly amazing monster story that came my way just as I submitted this book for publication, so such a tale, as you will read, is certainly fitting as a climax. With reports of dragons, dinosaurs and other aquatic creatures allegedly roaming the waters of Kent and the surrounding waterways, the *Medway Messenger* of July 7th reported on, *'Monster Mystery: Could there* be something fishy going on in the river?', with reporter Luke Hollands writing, *'Does the River Medway have its own Nessie?*

> *A strange creature has been spotted swimming against the tide near the Esplanade, Rochester.'*

Immediately this pricked up my ears, not just because it was a local monster report, but actually came from the stretch of water that flows behind my apartment! Hollands continued:

> *'On Thursday (3ʳᵈ July) the* Medway Messenger *newsroom received calls from Rochester residents who said they had seen the strange sight in the water. Some believed it was a pod of porpoises but one woman thought she had spied a single animal. She said: "It was about thirty-feet long, dark brown and mottled grey in colour. It was undulating like an eel and swimming towards* Amadeus *nightclub."*

To the paper I commented that it was more likely that witnesses had seen a string of porpoises, a boat wake or exaggerated an eel or even misinterpreted a log. As of writing no further reports have materialised. The stretch of water mentioned slinks under Rochester Bridge and worms its way along what is known as the Esplanade, a long stretch of road flanked by apartments and park land. The river is seventy-miles long and eventually enters the Thames Estuary.

In February 2009 I received an even more intriguing report, from a Richard Mann who told me that around twelve years ago, he saw a terrifying creature in the same stretch of the river. He'd been sitting on the flood defence wall at Strood, close to the Civic Centre, and decided to take a stroll down the steps to a muddy walkway when suddenly he spotted a circular object, black in colour, at the foot. As the tide approached, this thing uncoiled itself, and swam out into the water. Richard was so alarmed by the creature that he fled, and every time he subsequently had to cross Rochester Bridge, he would run like the wind in case he saw the beast again, and this was *indeed* a beast! Richard believed the creature to be almost thirty-feet in length, and in form resembling an eel or snake, and as it moved away waves, crashed against the steps.

On another note, Herne Bay also got monster fever with the *Medway Messenger* of July 4ᵗʰ 2008 commenting, *'Monster turtle from the deep'*, after a spate of mysterious animal deaths had plagued a pond in Strode Park, to reveal a snapping turtle. According to the report:

> *'For at least two years staff at the foundation for people with disabilities could not work out why moorhens, ducks and fish were dying in their pond. There had been sightings of a shelled creature swimming around the murky waters. But we just thought it was a terrapin", said maintenance worker Rikki Carter. "Then we decided to drain the pond and got rid of one-hundred years of muck. After that we managed to get a little terrapin out. Then another staff member said they had seen a big turtle and it had hissed at them."*

> *The hunt to capture the monster of Strode Park was on.*

> *"It just evaded us every time", said 24-year old Mr Carter. "I kept throwing nets at it but last week it nearly pulled me in." Finally on Friday it was taken captive. Mr Carter said: "I saw it by a sluice and managed to get it with a bigger net. It was a beast, a dinosaur. We called it `Jaws` at first but changed it to `Snappy`!"*

The creature was taken by the RSPCA and now resides at an animal sanctuary in Essex.

TOP: The author with TV Presenter Chris Packham in 2001 BELOW: The author today

Up in the Sky

*'Owls screech overhead, strange insects rustle in the fallen leaves, shadows from overhanging branches
flit across the path and quaint trunks of lightning-stricken trees stand out from the gloom, white and barkless,
taking the shape of gigantic mortals or untameable beasts of forest glade.'*

A Saunter Through Kent With Pen And Pencil (Vol III) – Charles Igglesden

I n 2006 the *BBC News* website reported on a giant bird on the loose locally, stating, *'Lethal 5ft Bird Escapes in Kent - A 5ft bird that could, according to the RSPCA, kill a human with one strike of its 6-inch claws is on the loose in Kent.*

Ralph, a South American rhea, fled his enclosure in Benenden on Monday after his owner introduced pigs to his pen. RSPCA spokesman Roy Jezard said the birds would also go for people's eyes with their beak, and said their strength was "unbelievable". He added: "People want to pat them, but I don't recommend it. If you see it, report it to the RSPCA or the police." Mr Jezard said rheas were not a problem in a paddock. But he added: "Running up the street, with lorries, cars and dogs barking, they get startled and tend to kick out in defence, and can do quite a bit of damage."

Three rheas had originally escaped from their enclosure at the smallholding.

The owner of the flightless birds, Sue Savage, said: "I bought some pigs and introduced them to the rheas but the birds didn't like the look of them, leapt the 4ft fence and took off."

RSPCA officers captured one, which was 6ft tall, by manoeuvring it into a cul-de-sac using a van and dustbins. Another returned home of its own accord.

Mrs Savage said three-year-old Ralph was last seen on Hemsted Forest Golf Club, near Sissinghurst, on Monday.

"They can run up to 20mph and blend into the background quite well because they are dark grey. It would startle the hell out of you if you saw it."

She has put up wanted posters around Benenden and warned local farmers to be on the lookout. The birds were naturally tame and could be kept without a licence, she added. "Generally they're placid but it's when they get spooked that they can become a different

bird and I wouldn't want to grapple with one unless I was a professional." She said the birds were kept for their eggs.

"They lay between 200 and 300 each year and these sell on Ebay (auction website) for £30 each." Mrs Savage, 44, and her husband Mike, 46, keep 10 rheas at their farm as well as pigs, chickens, horses, sheep and geese.'

On 15th November 2006 *Sky News* reported on several sightings over the UK of large birds resembling vultures.

'Huge vultures have been spotted circling the skies above the UK.

The scavengers, seen as harbingers of doom, are usually more at home in places such as South America, Africa and India. But the birds, with a wing-span of up to nine feet, have been seen in Norfolk, Snowdonia, Bodmin Moor in Cornwall - and even in Croydon. An Indian white-backed vulture has also been spotted in Richmond Park, London.

Andre Farrar, of the Royal Society for the Protection of Birds, told The Sun it is thought the bird had escaped from captivity.

He said: "Vultures are not long-distance flyers and there is no way it could have flown from India. They do seem to be the sort of bird that is capable of escaping from captivity."

Indian vultures are dying out as they often feed on dead cattle which have usually been injected with an anti-inflammatory steroid, which poisons them.'

Another report commented:

'Rare sighting of vulture in park - The vulture could be one which escaped from a zoo in Staffordshire. There has been a sighting of a vulture in a London park, according to the Royal Parks Agency (RPA). Bird watchers who have seen the bird in Richmond Park, south-west London, have identified it as the endangered Indian white-backed vulture. The Royal Society for the Protection of Birds (RSPB) said the bird could be a vulture named 'Bones' that escaped from a Staffordshire zoo in August. The RPA said it was not native, so had probably been released or escaped. A RPA spokeswoman Louise Wood said: "We don't believe it is roosting or feeding in Richmond Park, but it has been sighted in the vicinity." But, she added it had not been seen since Saturday. Cath Harris of the RSPB said: "Vultures can fly fairly large distances, and Britain is a fairly small country, so it's possible there are no more than two". She emphasised that vultures do not pose any threat to local wildlife, and that they would most likely feed on a diet of road kill. "They're scavengers - they don't kill," she said. A vulture was spotted in Snowdonia six weeks ago but RSPB conservationists said they did not think this was the same bird.'

In 2004 the *BBC* reported that:

'Escaped eagle captured in London -Zookeepers tracked an eagle to a park after the bird escaped from its tether in north London. Delilah, a six-year-old African Tawny Eagle, is thought to have freed itself from London Zoo at about 1230 GMT. Londoners

enjoying the sunshine watched as zookeepers wearing leather gloves and carrying food followed it to parkland at neighbouring Primrose Hill. Delilah was safely recaptured at about 1545 GMT - after keepers spotted frightened birds circling the eagle Robert Goodchild, from London Zoo, said Delilah - who has a 6ft wing- span - had probably got carried away by the strong wind. He and colleague Claire Horton easily found her, as seagulls and crows were making such a racket. "She's been off work all winter so she's very unfit, Primrose Hill is about as far as her range would have taken her," said Mr Goodchild. "We tried coaxing her down but because of the windy conditions she couldn't get close enough to land properly." Eventually fatigue and the circling birds overhead forced her down on Primrose Hill. He was surprised Delilah had managed to give them the slip by somehow untying her tether. "It's very unusual. There's a special knot we use which is very difficult for a bird to be able to undo," he said. Although tired, Delilah managed to eat all her food when she got back to the zoo which is a good sign, he added. Eyewitness Kate Newman said: "There were lots of seagulls in the air and birds going mad and there was a big circle of people - in the middle was an eagle sat on the ground. "[The keeper] just went straight up and got it and another guy came up in a van and fed it a couple of little chickens, then they left."

During the late '90s and a few years before the London sightings there were several reports of big, black birds over Kent. One such flapping wonder was said to have been an escaped vulture, yet sightings ceased suddenly with no resolution. In 1998, whilst investigating sightings of large cats at Blue Bell Hill, I filmed a strange bird on a hillside. The bird was bright green, and certainly not native to these shores. It turned out to be a parakeet. Little did I realise that these birds were flocking to the county, and perching above the streets of London and Surrey also. Nine hundred were recorded from Lewisham alone, and over four-thousand in Surrey. The ring-necked parakeet is native to Africa and parts of Asia. In 2007 the government were considering a cull to control the birds, with ornithologists of the belief that the para-keets were competing for food and nesting space with native birds.

The RSPB claimed that records of such birds invading the UK dated back to 1851. The *Kent Today* asked, *'Have You Seen The Green Alien?'* after several more sightings.

It seems obvious that the likelihood of alien species of bird landing on our rooftops is reasonably high. All manner of large birds have been seen soaring in the skies of London. In 2007 there were reports of a mystery bird believed to be an eagle or a buzzard flying over Wandsworth. A Kingston man from the autumn claimed the bird he saw stood over two feet high, whilst another large bird was photographed over Battersea. In 1997 an eagle-owl was observed perched on St. Paul's Cathedral and certainly affected the flow of traffic. According to reports, the bird was also seen over Camden and Hyde Park and even attacked a man's dog in Regent's Park. Unfortunately the bird turned up dead five weeks after the initial excitement. It had died of a bacterial wasting disease, and its leather anklets were proof that it had es-caped captivity.

In 2007 it was reported by the *Wildlife Extra* team that:

'A Squacco heron appears to have made itself at home at the Crossness nature reserve in Bexley, South East London. It is claimed that the last Squacco heron seen in London was at the Kingsbury Reservoir in 1866, but there have been some other more recent reports.

There have been around 50 reports of Squacco heron's in the UK over the last 50 years or so, and there are unconfirmed reports of another Squacco in another part of Kent too. There have also been sightings of a Purple Heron and a Quail (the latter hasn't been seen in this borough since 1969) The Squacco was spotted on the afternoon of 29 May and has been seen on the Southern Marshes of Crossness ever since. The Squacco heron is mainly found in southern Europe, though it winters in Africa.

The sighting follows a £500,000 project at Crossness by Thames Water, Bexley Council and the charity Groundwork. Work has involved restoring reed bed and ditch habitat for water voles and creating a new wader scrape which has attracted the heron. The site has also been opened up to the public with a wildlife viewing screen enabling ornithologists to get close to the bird without disturbing it. Crossness Nature Reserve is a small oasis within an industrialised urban environment, providing a unique opportunity to escape city life and enjoy one of the last remaining areas of grazing marsh within the Greater London area. The reserve is part of the original Thames floodplain known collectively as the Erith Marshes. With much of the marshland having been developed to provide business and residential opportunities, the creation of Crossness Nature Reserve in 1996 secured part of this important, declining habitat for nature conservation and public access. As a result of the regionally important communities of wetland birds, plants and invertebrates, the site has been awarded Local Nature Reserve.'

In the same year on 8th May the *News Shopper* reported, *'A missing bird of prey with a 10ft wing span has been found safe and well'*.

'Crews from Dartford fire station joined the search for Tiny, a condor who went missing during a display at Eagle Heights Bird of Prey Centre, on Sunday. The crew used thermal imaging equipment to try to find the bird, who landed in a rapeseed crop field, close to the centre's grounds in Eynsford. But their efforts were unsuccessful and the search, led by centre staff and RSPCA officials continued.

Luckily, Tiny was eventually found during a helicopter search last night. Condors are members of the vulture family and are the largest flying land birds in the western hemisphere. They have black plumage with a frill of white feathers around their necks.'

In June 2007 fourteen glossy ibises made several bird watchers excitable as they appeared in the skies of Kent, Gloucestershire and Surrey. It was the first time such birds had been seen since 1867.

In 1974 a West African crowned crane was gliding through the skies near to West Drayton, on the outskirts of the capital. Reports had gone on for more than two years but whether all reports concerned the same bird we'll never know, yet oddly, fifty-two years previously a more sinister flying creature was seen in the area, particularly in the grounds of the local cemetery. It was claimed that the mystery bird-like creature had a six-foot wingspan and was often heard screaming. It's difficult to say whether such a case was simply down to misidentification or merely a ghost story.

The strangest Kent-related bird tales make for interesting reading. In 1948 south Kent was besieged by an unusually large number of rooks. The black hordes allegedly invaded from France and damaged crops in the Romney Marsh area. The National Farmers Union assembled to organise several shooting parties such was the plague bestowed upon them and their productive land. However, the bizarre and over whelming flock were left to their own devices until they flapped away, never to return. In November of 1999 at Mill Hill, in Minster, fifty-six year old Mrs Jackson was riding her horse one evening when large, winged 'something' attacked her. She told the local newspaper:

"It's the most bizarre and frightening experience. I was thrown and the horse bolted

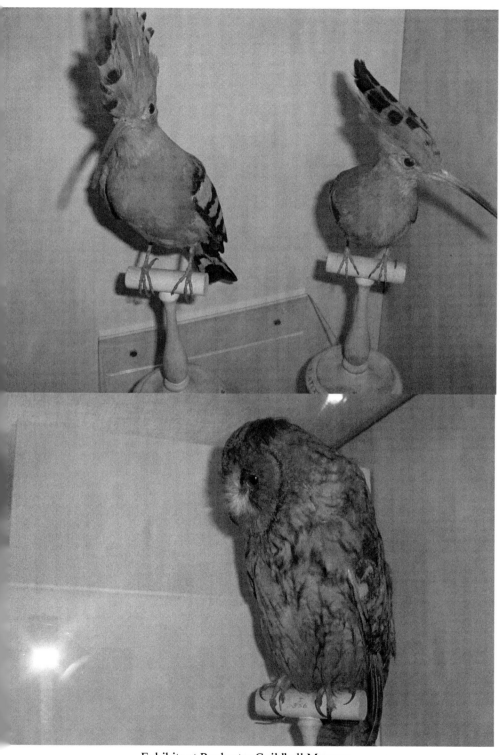

Exhibits at Rochester Guildhall Museum
(TOP: Hoopoes BOTTOM: Long-eared owl) P. 342

Exhibits at Rochester Guildhall Museum
(TOP: Golden oriole   BOTTOM: White tailed sea eagle P. 342)

but fortunately a workman on a nearby building caught him before he ran into the busy Chequers Road',

and with regards to the bird simply added, "*...had an enormous wingspan.*"

Again, to quote the important works of Charles Igglesden, in reference to Leeds Castle he writes:

'*...other old stuffed denizens of the deep waters can be seen in glass cases, as well as rare birds shot by the moat, or in King's Wood – the coverts that adjoin the Park. Here is a brace of peculiarly crossed pheasants, between a golden and an ordinary pheasant, the cock bird falling to the gun of Mrs Wykeham-Martin, who is an excellent shot. Then there is a pair of ospreys, as well as a bittern, all shot by the moat; and a whole case of white pheasants shows how varied has been the breed of birds on this estate.*'

The *Kentish Gazette* of October 14th 1814 wrote:

'*Last Tuesday a water fowl of species totally unknown in this country, was shot in a pond belonging Mr. Stephen Grantham, at Stoneham, near Lewes, where it had settled among some tame ducks.*

Its plumage is beautifully variegated and the breast exhibits a spot, coloured exactly like the breast of a partridge. It measures across the back to the extremity of each wing, four feet seven-inches, and from the bill to the tip of the tail, which is short, two feet four-inches, and weighs five-pounds, fourteen-ounces. Its wings appear especially formed for long flight, and the heads of both pinion bones are quite bare. The bird does not appear to have come under observation of any of the authors of natural history, except Berwick, who describes a bird nearly resembling the one in question, and calls it an Egyptian goose, but he at the same time confesses that he never could meet with one to enable him to give drawing of it.

Two woodcocks were last week shot in the neighbourhood of Lewes.'

We return once more to Charles Igglesden who whilst speaking of Tenterden writes of a huge bird, almost as a local folktale in relation to the place known as Heronden.

'*It is said that the place derived its name from a family of Herons. This is probably the case, but I cannot refrain from giving an old legend connected with the place, and which, if true, might have caused the place to be called Heronden.*

Once upon a time – so the story goes – the tiny child of a woodcutter in Heronden Park was wont to play from daybreak to nightfall in an opening among the trees. Here, too, came herons in great number, and in course of time would stand around the little girl, allowing her to stroke their downy feathers and place her arms around their tall thin legs. But one day a huge golden eagle swooped down upon the child, lifted her by its cruel beak and soared away into distance. At the approach of the eagle the simple herons had vanished into the trees, but when they saw their little friend carried off, and heard her piteous cries, they rose in a body and gave chase to the thief. And they reached him just as he lay his victim on the ledge of a distant rock. He fought and struggled with his pursuers, but although many fell dead and wounded, the others persevered and conquered.

When the woodcutter arrived he found his child caressing a heron, and at her feet lay the eyeless body of the dead eagle. And henceforth, adds the legend, the spot was called Heronden.'

On 11th April 2008 the *Kent Messenger* ran a story on *'Flying visit from doorstep hawker'*, commenting,

'When William Coomber opened his back door one afternoon, he didn't expect to be greeted by a rather large bird looking for a way in.

But the feathered friend wasted no time in soaring straight into the Woodville Road house, in Maidstone, and having a look around. Mr Coomber's daughter-in-law Alison said: "We thought it was a hawk of some sort but we weren't sure – it looked as thought it was chasing a smaller bird, as there were feathers all over the downstairs hall."

The bird eventually settled by a window in an upstairs bedroom and Mr Coomber, 74, took the chance to photograph his unexpected guest before releasing it – but was sure to don several layers of protective clothing and a pair of goggles for the job.

Mrs Coomber said, "He wasn't going to take any chances with the animal. He got such a great picture of the bird, we thought someone might be able to tell us exactly what kind of bird it was – and how common they are in this area."

Mr Coomber's picture was published on our website and online readers were quick to help. The overwhelming verdict was that it was a sparrowhawk, a view shared by the RSPB.

A spokesman said: "Sparrowhawks are becoming much more common now after steadily rebuilding in numbers since the 1960s. When I went bird-watching in Kent in the 1980s, seeing a sparrowhawk was a notable experience. Now I'd be surprised if I didn't see one."

In Rochester's Guildhall Museum there are several impressive stuffed birds on display, the most interesting of these being a large, albeit juvenile White-Tailed Sea Eagle *(Haliaeetus albicilla)*. The bird was shot in the Parish of High Halstow by a James Marshall on November 8th 1879. Such birds are the fourth largest eagle in the world. The BBC website states that such wonders are thought to be vulnerable to the point of extinction, although reintroductions are on the cards.

Also in the glass cases of the museum sit various other stuffed winged specimens. Hoopoes *(Upup epops)* do not breed in the UK, but as many as one-hundred can be seen during the Spring along the South coast as they migrate North to Europe from Africa, over-shooting their journey. These exotic looking birds are the size of a mistle thrush, have striking black and white wings and a crest of feathers upon the head which becomes raised when excited. Two Hoopoes, one shot in Seasalter in 1865, the other in 1886 in Tenterden, are displayed in Rochester. The Golden oriole *(Oriolus oriolus)*, known for its flute-like whistle, and in the male individuals, its striking yellow body and black wings, has also made its way to the south-coast. One male is housed at the museum, recovered from Dover in 1883. These birds, according to the *RSPB* website, are extremely secretive and difficult to see.

Another elusive bird, which sits alongside the Osprey and the Honey Buzzard as stuffed specimens, the Long-Eared Owl *(Asio otus)*. One was shot in Parkwood, at Rainham in 1865 and is on display

These buff-brown coloured birds breed thinly across the UK.

Thankfully, not all uncommon visitors to these parts are only viewable in display cases at museums. If rare bird sightings over Kent are your thing, then be sure to go online and check out the various websites who log reports.

Author Charles Fort wrote of many insect swarms around the Kent coast in *Lo!*, mentioning that in the July of 1869, and according to the London *Times*, '*...a tropical, or sub-tropical insect, a firefly (Lampyris Italia) had been caught*', in the garden of an Ashford man, but such a record was explained in the July when a man came forward to claim he'd kept twelve of these insects and released them in Dover. He also goes on to speak of huge swarms of aphides on the south-coast, ladybird invasions in Ramsgate, one of which I recall when I was a toddler in the 1970s, and literally ominous clouds of ladybirds over Ramsgate in the 1830s. Dover was also plagued by such creatures, with many researchers claiming that the insects were far larger than the normal ladybirds we'd been accustomed to seeing, and that they were yellow in colour. Wasp swarms invaded Ramsgate one summer in the 1830s and horrid 'thunder bugs' clouded an area between Wingham and Adisham, around the same time crane flies converged upon London. Fort also records that a bizarre amount of winged ants descended upon Maidstone in 1870, but in today's climate, such reported invasions now seem rather normal as our lands are besieged by foreign insects and mighty swarms.

So, out of place animals aren't exactly mystery animals, but they are made mysterious often by those newspapers etc, who report on them. There is no real mystical eeriness about a bird that has travelled too far north or a snake that has escaped a private collection. The real mystery always remains something unseen and unanswerable, whether it's the unknown creature in the local lake that snaps the lines of fishermen and devours the ducks, or the shadowy wolf-like form that appears on a country road and then never shows its face again. Real mystery animals are often fleeting, half-hinting at the sinister, occasionally melted accidentally into the realm of folklore, and always existing at the corner of the retina as some unguessed, unfathomable, untraceable form.

Casting a line into the chasm of a lake is like stepping into the woods on a pitch black night. Who knows what really lurks out there, scurrying at the edge of the torch beam, prowling by the light of the bestial moon, swirling beneath the ripples and toying with the mind like a cat with a mouse. We've always been deeply superstitious as a race and despite our often sceptical mindset, we must realise that even as we quash our fears over time and construct a wall of mundanity around such mysteries, they will always be out there, often as originally harmless animals, but which, over a short period of headlines and rumour, will become as mysterious as the monsters we've always grown up with and feared and often attempted to block out, but they'll always keep re-emerging because deep down we need them to.

'Let your imagination loose – go back to centuries gone by – think of what strange, weird, wild scenes have been enacted here'.

A Saunter Through Kent With Pen And Pencil (Volume V) – Charles Igglesden

The Others

*'She could see nothing of it, she said, but that it was a moving form: only she had an impression
that when it returned to the church, as it seemed to do in the end of the dream, it turned its head:
and then, she could not tell why, but she thought it had red eyes.'*

An Episode Of Cathedral History – M.R. James

omething very weird this way comes. And for those of you who have overdosed upon the
strange writings of authors such as H. P. Lovecraft, you'll no doubt wallow in this high level of
oddness; a true menagerie of the damned, a surreal safari into the peculiar and eerie creatures
that would no doubt have been cast from the Ark, and given their own insanely psychedelic zoo.
They are the monsters from the id. That place of unknown architecture and alien design, a plateau of
ethereal scavengers, seemingly unholy creation and disturbing illusion.

There are certain beasts, or things, seemingly of this world, or void, which quite simply do not add up.
They are something akin to a feverish nightmare, a concoction, or boiling cauldron of almost fantasy and
freakish myth, and yet they are seen. Often only once, but they exist, whether as a relation to the human
psyche, or as spiritual forms, or as story, who knows, but they are out there, waiting in the woods, in the
darkest places, our fears, our dreads, the shadows of the unknown. You may call them supernatural, or
connect them to the paranormal, but I do not. They are something far more complex than the pigeon-
holes we try to encase them within. They must be catalogued, because they remain as an important part
of our folklore, even if they are never understood, and they will certainly never be proven. They aren't
ghosts, although that's our easiest explanation, but they aren't as simple as the ghost of the next door
neighbour's dog, because what I'm about to discuss and chronicle, are in fact in a field, as such, of their
own. It is a remote location, either deep within us as a race, or somewhere through the fabric of time. I
touched upon a handful of Kent-related anomalies in my book *Monster! The A-Z Of Zooform Phenomena*
because the term 'zooform' was the only word which could loosely describe such spectres which are a
sum of many bogeymen, campfire critters, clandestine creatures and true monsters. And they will even
remain out of the reach of cryptozoology, the study created to seek out mysterious, hidden animals.

This chapter explores the unfamiliar dimension inhabited by a horde of entities, which, despite appearing
to haunt the woods, skies and waterways of the county, quite clearly are something more than your average out-of-place animal. At times it may get confusing, or even ridiculous as I offer to you a selection of
screaming, shape shifting, at times vague, often red-eyed, flying, creeping, buzzing, glowing, and unusually menacing creatures which only you can decide whether they exist in our 'reality', or as legend, or
maybe just as well constructed hoax or misidentification of natural phenomena. For centuries mankind
has spoken of many mysteries which have remained with us on a consistent level - whether it is spirits of

the dead roaming ancient grounds and old buildings, or peculiar lights whizzing across the skies and their occupants allegedly abducting members of the public. Or even tales of bipedal man-beasts striding through the forests. We've turned such mysterious forms into household names, i.e. Bigfoot, Nessie, UFOs, Bermuda Triangle, all the old, classic enigmas which we continue to debate, and are often regurgitated in book after book. However, this time, it's time to read of local equivalents that range from the somewhat fleeting and misty, to the downright horrific. We don't know what they are, and it's my guess that we never will find the solution, because we somehow need these night prowlers, in the same way we've always had a thirst for vampires and werewolves and other ghouls stalking our fairytales, turning them into gothic nightmares. Hopefully, this chapter will give you an insight into a selection of 'monsters' which have roamed, prowled and slinked through the local fields and woods, but which only surely appear if there is someone there to see them. Let us not fall into the lacklustre hands of regurgitation where, for many decades, local authors have vomited forth book after book of replayed imagining and theories, because as armchair enthusiasts they've never had the heart, mind or hunger to seek the more obscure mysteries by skinny-dipping in the darkness. In fact, there are many so-called 'monster' hunters' across the globe who have probably never left the comfy confines of their armchair or the migraine inducing snare of the computer screen, and yet for so long have theorised, debated and corrected those who have got off their backsides and looked into the darkest corners. Monsters are out there, in some form, whether as fears, hallucinations or genuine force, and there must be real people out there to find them, and this book is the first Kent-related book to investigate such matters. Forget the run of the mill ghost stories, the same old tales spewed from so-called societies and clubs who offer nothing more than false membership, petty politics and ancient beliefs. Let us find real monsters, the kind of fiends and grim omens we've always been terrified of. Look under the bed and in the closet, recite the spell of your local urban legend, and scan your torch beam across the wastes of a foggy night. Face the facts, we'll never find where these things come from or why they continue to haunt us, and much of this cul-de-sac investigating is simply down to the lack of fresh evidence and story, so come, let's meet some monsters we'll never contemplate.

Some of these weird monstrosities may be considered as omens of death, symbols of malevolence that no doubt in the past would have been connected to black magic and the appearance of the Devil. Nowadays when such terrifying manifestations appear we do not know how to identify or relate them because mankind has so many mixed beliefs and opinions, so maybe that's why such 'demons', 'goblins' or 'angels' or whatever you want to call them have no real face or purpose. They are either here to toy with us which suggests an intelligence beyond our comprehension, or they are merely things accidentally invoked by humanity, in the same way we once believed in fairies at the foot of the garden, or fire breathing dragons writhing within the clouds.

We begin with an age-old legend which is rife throughout world folklore and has often been covered in supernatural-related books, and that is the lore of the Black Dog.

> *'Never in the delirious dream of a disordered brain could anything more savage, more appalling, more hellish, be conceived than that dark form and savage face which broke upon us out of the wall of fog.'*

> *The Hound Of The Baskervilles* – Sir Arthur Conan Doyle

- **BARKING UP THE WRONG TREE**

> *'About seven years ago (the late 1990s) I was still living in Kent in a town called Tenterden. Myself and three mates used to regularly drink in Smarden, which is just a few miles from Pluckley. The route we would drive home was a single-track back road, with the odd house and a few farms. We were driving back at about 11:45 pm on an*

October evening with patchy fog.

We had reached the straight bit of road and ran into a thick bank of fog when a shape in the middle of the road forced us to slow down. A huge black dog was stood there, side on. If I had to guess I would say it was similar to a very thick-set Labrador. We had slowed to a walking pace then stopped. The car we were in was a Mini and it was level with the window on the driver's side as it walked alongside us and towards the back of the car, at which point Jane, the driver, hit the gas!'

The above report came via the *Fortean Times* message forum, from eyewitness James Sanderson who believed he'd encountered a phantom black dog, or 'hellhound' on this dark, foggy night in rural Kent. Encounters of this kind have proven to be quite frequent over the last few centuries, often nightly beasts which exude a malevolence far more than any stray, flesh and blood dog, to the extent that witnesses often realise that what they are seeing is something unnatural, something often foreboding, despite no evidence to suggest so except the eerie presence, the oft' reported blazing eyes and the ability to vanish, sometimes into a ball of flame or with a flash of blinding light.

No-one is quite sure why these hounds exist, some exist as the representation of good and evil, others are connected to waterways and ancient pathways, whilst other spectral dogs may take on the form of other phenomena, from ghostly figures to eerie light formations. Whatever their purpose, those who encounter such creatures know they are seeing something distinctly weird, often menacing - an omen of misfortune, a wandering spirit believed to lead weary travellers astray. They often are silent, except for those which carry chains around their necks. They are often large and black, except for the eerie white dogs, as well as those across the world that have been described as fiery red, or with varying tints, and their eyes are often ablaze, as they slink across moonlit roads, or disappear into balls of flame.

Great 'dog' beasts exist as monstrous legends throughout history. Those that roam the lanes of Kent could well be no different, or indeed phantasmagoric reflections of Cerberus, the three-headed dog of Hades, or Garm, the watcher at the gates of Helheim, the Norse realm of the dead, a dog said to be drenched in blood and have four eyes. Names such as Stryker, Padfoot, and Black Shuck have become similar 'monsters', but now they do not walk the banks of the River Styx, but merely the local streams and tranquil roadways, or corpse paths, where once funeral processions would march. As such cases have been documented, researchers continue to dissect the phenomenon in an attempt to give the presence of such ghost dogs a meaning, although there possibly is none. Such bizarre canine forms have become a very British phenomenon, restricted to crumbling churches and foggy graveyards, or misty waterways and overgrown pathways, yet such dogs have their place in world folklore, and although their appearance may vary depending on the differing cultures and communal beliefs, they seem to belong to the same pack. However, as discussed already, because of the dogs and their relation to the English countryside, their appearance has often been connected to sightings of black leopards and other mystery cats. Researchers continue to ask questions such as, are the black dog sightings of centuries ago, really of black leopards? Or, are black dogs and big, black cats both of ghostly nature? I'm of the firm belief that there is no connection whatsoever, but when certain mysteries share location, we have a tendency to relate them, but as far as black phantom dogs and big cats are concerned, they are worlds apart. Fact.

In phantom dog lore, the Cadejos of Costa Rica are black and white hounds which are said to represent good and evil, the black dog obviously connected to the dark side, the lighter companion seen as something akin to a guardian creature. Such creatures have never been connected to reports of big felids.

The Devastating Dog is said to devour children in parts of Hawaii. There has never been a case to suggest these hounds exist in reality but clearly they do exist as something akin to a bogey creature. A similar entity roams an apartment block in Syria but takes on the form not only of a black hound but as swirling mist. In Babylonian lore the Alu are said to be a family of evil spirits said to take the form of a pack of frothing hounds, while in Japan a fierce hound is known as 'mountain dog' or Yama Inu and is said to resemble a wolf-like creature said to prey on lost and lonely travellers. In the Philippines the local ghost dog is the Bagat, and although harmless it tends, like so many other hellhounds, to appear during severe storms. In France the phantom hound haunts the foggy moors of Brennilis, where it is believed the 'gates of Hell' are hidden.

In New South Wales, Australia, a pony-sized white dog was seen in August 2001, and on the border of Canada a creature known as the Lightning Splitter Hound once stalked a house in Montana. The United States has a veritable feast of bizarre phantom hellhounds, the Snarley Yow is one of the most famous salivating dogs, existing in the Pacific Northwest where it is seen along Alternate Route 40 in Frederick County, often observed by travellers. In the northern area of Frederick a blue phantom dog is said to haunt an old house, whilst the Graveyard Dogs are certainly the most commonly known hellhounds, large spectral dogs often found in old slave cemeteries. The beasts have been known to appear headless or carrying heavy chains around their necks. In Maine in 1996 a creature known as the Dark Dog was sighted by several researchers into the paranormal as they were driving up a remote road near Portsmouth. The beast emerged from a gloomy pit and gave off a pungent odour. In Pennsylvania, strange howls often heard throughout Colebrook are blamed on a pack of hounds, whilst the Fence Rail Dog, also known as Red Dog Fox, or Yakehtan Ami, by the Cherokees, is a road wraith said to appear along a stretch of highway which runs from Pennsylvania in the north to Georgia in the south. The hound appears to symbolise several fatal accidents that have occurred on the road.

In Scotland the Famh is a massive spectral dog, one of several to lurk in the Highlands, whilst the Earth Hounds are smaller, ferret-sized animals with dog-like heads said to lurk in graveyards, and in Wales there are many also, including the Dogs Of Hell which are more commonly known as Cwn Annwn.

In England the most potent hellhounds are the already mentioned Stryker, Padfoot and Black Shuck alongside the Devil's Dandy Dogs, Wisht Hounds, Guytrash and the Irish Pooka which takes on several forms, such as fairy, horse and local bogey spirit. It is also known as Phooka and Puck. Black Shuck roams the Essex, Norfolk and Suffolk coast line, whilst Padfoot prowls Lancashire and Yorkshire, but such hounds and their alternate names tend to melt into one another.

Smaller black dogs are considered as benevolent and often sighted by people during illness as a sign that they are going to improve in health.

In Kent, reports of black dogs are not frequent but those which have been seen have been quite significant cases, and not your run of the mill, fleeting glimpse.

- **BACK TO THE HILL**

'Weird accolade for local haunt' read the *Medway Today* of 4th May 2001, stating that, '...*a village in Medway has been named the weirdest in Kent'*, and continued that, '...*Blue Bell Hill is the only place in the county listed in* Bizarre Magazine's *'Weird Britannia League'. The village was chosen because of the ghostly hitchhiker who appears and disappears as drivers approach. It is also home to the mysterious 'panther'-like animal known as the 'beast' of Blue Bell Hill. Kent came eleventh in* Bizarre's *league.'*

And now you'll read why...

It was the Monday evening of 22nd January 2001. A motorist travelling towards the Medway Towns from

TOP: Leeds Castle (p. 358) BOTTOM: Shurland Castle (p. 359)

Are these the portraits of the dogs who still haunt Leeds Castle? (p. 358)

TOP: The Bluebell Hill hag (p. 355)
BELOW: Sean Tudor, expert on the Bluebell Hill road ghost

TOP: The Downs around Bluebell Hill BELOW: Reconstruction of phantom hitchhiker

TOP: Kit's Coty house (p. 131) BELOW: Quarries around Bluebell Hill

TOP: Reconstruction of road ghost BELOW: Snake Quarry, Bluebell Hill

Bluewater, nr Bean. Rick Flynn set off for home around 10:15 pm and reached Blue Bell Hill around 10:35 pm. It was a cold, wet and windy evening as Rick reached the foot bridge that crosses near to the Ayelsford turn-off, Maidstone bound. All of a sudden a white-coloured Alsatian-size dog ran across the road at great speed, causing Rick to brake hard in the rain. His front wheels locked due to his sudden braking and he released them just in time to avoid skidding on the slippery surface. Rick noticed that a dark-coloured Mercedes Benz was coming at quite a pace down the fast lane, it seemed as though the driver was sure to hit the animal. However, the animal moved at great speed, heading under the central reservation then straight over the Chatham bound carriageway where there were no cars in sight.

Rick reached home, palms sweating, body shaking, unsure of what he'd seen.

Whilst large cats have been seen in these dark, wooded areas, Rick was certain he'd seen an Alsatian-like dog, and not a cat. Such a phantom has at times been connected to a ghost girl seen on the hill, but with a variety of 'ghosts' associated with the location, and varying legends, it may be all too complex, and maybe unnecessary to connect the two. Throughout the UK, ghostly, often black dogs are associated with old pathways, ley-lines and churchyards. In the village of Pluckley a small white, spirit dog is said to haunt St. Nicholas' churchyard as well as a variety of other phantoms. The dog is occasionally seen running from behind the crooked tombstones, fleetingly across the path of frightened ramblers. Other spectral hounds are believed to haunt areas which experts believe they once guarded.

In March 2008 fellow researcher Tom Atkinson spoke of an intriguing legend in connection to the mysterious hill which related to both phantom hounds and the road ghosts said to linger within the vicinity. However, before I go into that I'd just like to share with you this important case to tie the tales together. To quote from road ghost researcher Sean Tudor:

'*In January 1993, reports started to come in of a wholly different kind of character encountered on Blue Bell Hill. In the early hours of 5th and 6th January, two families travelling home encountered a frightening figure that crossed their path at the same spot on a dark, remnant stretch of the Old Chatham Road - the former main route between Maidstone and Chatham before the construction of the current A229 in the early 1970s, and which now, as a feeder road, runs parallel for a short distance before joining the faster route further uphill.*

When Claire Ogley of the Kent Today *first called me to ask if I had ever heard of a ghost of an old woman being seen on Blue Bell Hill, I answered 'no'. I then asked her what she knew. The menacing witch-like apparition she described sounded too bizarre, too fairytale-like to be true - except that, at that time, one family, very much frightened by the experience, had come forward to say that it had happened to them...*

The Maiden family's experience had taken place at around 12.45 am on 6th January on their journey home to Rochester following a night out. The account given here differs in minor detail from the original Kent Today *version. It was, for instance, a clear, cold night - far from the foggy conditions described in the newspaper account. The location also differed - not the Chatham-bound carriageway of the A229 - but a section of the lonely backwater route just to the west that, in the past, had featured in at least one account involving the ghost-girl.*

There were five people in the car: Angela Maiden, her husband Malcolm (who was driving), Mrs Maiden's mother, her young daughter and a family friend. The daughter was asleep, but everyone else witnessed the event. The family had come up from Ayles-

ford, turning northward onto the Old Chatham Road at the Lower Bell crossroads (a location, again, that features as a reputed 'picking up' point for the ghostly girl hitch-hiker in the early history of the case). Some 300 yards (275m) further up, at Kit's Coty Cottage, the road makes a sweeping bend to the right. As the car started to turn into the bend, the Maidens saw a figure start across the road from right to left in front of them. Mr Maiden immediately slowed down.

"At first I thought it was [somebody in] a fancy dress costume," said Mrs Maiden. "It was wearing a long dress, very old-fashioned, that stopped mid-calf. It had a tartan shawl round the top and a bonnet with a brim." She remembered remarking to her husband: "Somebody's playing a prank."

But then the car's headlights fully illuminated the figure. "It was like when you trap a rabbit in your headlights. It stayed dazed, hunched over without looking at us. As we got alongside it we were almost at a standstill. All of a sudden it was 4ft [1.2m] away from the car. It rounded on us really quickly and I saw the face. It was totally horrific... very small, black beady eyes. It was like a wizened face. The worst thing of all was the mouth. It opened and [it] was like an empty black hole. My mother was sitting directly behind me. At the same time I remember we said, 'Oh, my God.'

With the figure's mouth agape, a hissing sound filled the car, even through the closed windows. The figure was carrying a spray of twigs, which it raised and shook threateningly. Mrs Maiden quickly engaged the car's central locking, instinctively bringing her arm up to protect herself.

With all this going on, Mr Maiden, panicking, was trying to get the car in gear to get away. As he did so, and started to pull away, Mrs Maiden's mother turned to watch the figure, which started toward the nearside kerb, where it seemed to vanish.

"My daughter woke up feeling a terrible atmosphere in the car. I couldn't talk; all you could hear was everyone breathing. I've never felt evil before and I've never been so terrified. I felt as if I had looked into the eyes of the Devil."

This horrifying account had a strange connection to the story Tom Atkinson mentioned to me although his version was more of an urban legend, but one which emerged a few years previous to the nasty encounter involving the Maiden family.

He said:

"I was particularly interested to read about the phantom dog seen near Blue Bell Hill, it reminded me of a story that went around my school in the late 1980s about a ghost dog on the hill itself. Obviously we had all heard about the phantom hitchhiker on the hill and the endless re-tellings of this story sometimes led onto discussions about a particularly unpleasant old woman's ghost who was also rumoured to haunt the hill. The story was a bit vague but the gist of it was that she would walk next to the carriageway with a dog on a leash. When a car approached she would send the dog running out in front of the vehicle, causing it to swerve. Both the dog and the old bag would then vanish. I'm afraid I don't have any further details – it was just one of those vague rumours that circulate at school."

Yet, what a fascinating rumour and one that seemed to speak of a wizened, hag-like figure which since the Maiden incident, Sean Tudor has discovered could have some truth in an old woman said to once live on the hill, who used to frequent the woods and pathways of a night collecting sticks, possibly for firewood. Was such a woman, the local reclusive oddball, responsible for some kind of curse put on the hill? Was the crone a witch? Was it her ghost guarding the hill, forcing motorists to swerve to avoid her pet dog?

There are certainly many unanswered questions which simply add to the mystical draw of the eerie hill. As Mr Tudor states in his research, there are several similar wizened road horror's throughout world folklore. Some are perceived as gypsy-type characters, others as local hermits, or are there even deeper, more complex possibilities? Sean states:

'Folklore (and world folklore, at that) - as I have suggested, is replete with such characters, many of which bear more than a passing similarity to the two aspects and habits of the Blue Bell Hill 'ghost'.[7] However, their best recognition is found in Celtic and pre-Celtic mythology, in the Cailleach of the Scottish Highlands (or in Ireland and the Isle of Man, the Caillaigh or Cailleac), the tutelary earth and mother goddess, and most especially, in the form of Hekate, the Dark Goddess of early Greek tradition. The Cailleach was an ancient figure of wisdom and supernatural power who was commonly depicted as a hooded crone or hag (caille meaning hood or veil, the title itself lending itself to interpretation as hooded hag or, interestingly in terms of the phantom hitchhiker comparisons, veiled nun, representing the transition, through Christianisation, from pagan goddess or semideity into nun).

Her common depiction as the personification of winter, and her triple form of Virgin, Mother, Crone (or the Woman Who Devours Men), representing seasonality and the nurturing and hostile faces of nature, have clear relevance to the forms and timing of appearances at Blue Bell Hill (frequently given as 'winter'). In some traditions, she is depicted as transforming into a beautiful girl.

Turning to early Greek tradition, to the pre-Olympian earth goddess Hekate, we find further eerie echoes of Blue Bell Hill's dark ghost. Like the Cailleach, Hekate (Hecate in Latin) has been featured as one aspect of the primordial triple-goddess: Maiden (Hekate), Bride (Persephone), and Mother (Demeter). In the most ancient depictions, she is portrayed as a 'bright-coiffed' girl or young woman, in keeping with her function as attendant, guide and guardian - a role demonstrated most famously by her leading of Persephone back from Hades to her mother, Demeter, after hearing her cries from her cave dwelling. (As with the Cailleach, it is difficult to overlook here the apt comparison to Blue Bell Hill's own triple set of Young Girl (Maiden), Young Woman (Bride (or Bride-to-be?)/Mother), and Hag (Crone/Mother)). Thus, her image and sanctuaries were erected at doorways and gateways, to ward off outside evils. Similarly - and significantly in terms of our interest - as 'goddess of the crossway' (crossroads), and protectress of roads, her three-headed or three-faced likeness was set up to watch over and act as a guide to travellers. But it is Hekate's transformed later guise that finds greatest recognition here. For from c.400 BC (and particularly since Roman Times), the darker aspects of Hekate's character became dominant. And along with her changed character and function, came a wholly different and frightening image. Instead of the youthful, benevolent goddess - we find instead perhaps the quintessential expression of the evil supernatural hag - a terrifying chthonic goddess of magic, of the waning (dark) moon, the night, and death.

Known variously as the Crone Goddess, Goddess of witches, the Veiled One, Goddess of Midnight, Queen of the Night, and Queen of Restless Ghosts, this Hekate was said to walk the highways of night (particularly at the dark of the moon), crowned with coils of wild snakes and wielding 'terrible black torches'. With her wandered a train of fearful ghosts: deceased humans, apparitions and dogs. Since crossroads were associated with her, these especially became the realm of these 'outcast and accursed spirits', which, in many cultures were said to include the restless spirits of suicides, those who had suf-fered a sudden or violent death, or those who had died childless. Some of these spirits merely frightened men; others were said to bring bad dreams, illness or madness.'

Sean's exhaustive research proves that all manner of mysterious, possibly separate issues can be con fined under one roof if we choose to bracket it that way. Suddenly, a seemingly explainable hitch-hiking ghost now has connections to Greek and Roman mythology, phantom hounds, an old crone, witchcraf etc, making the hill a cauldron of strangeness. Some places are weird. Some weirder than most!

A phantom black dog is rumoured to haunt Leeds Castle a few miles from Blue Bell Hill. It was claime that during the fifteenth century an aunt of Henry VI practiced several diabolical practices and wa charged with the dabbling and imprisoned for life. Legend claims that it was around this time that th hound began to manifest, and the beast since then has always been connected to the dark arts, although majority of reports simply describe a black, retriever-type dog with curly coat that would vanish into thi air, but not exactly emit any menace. One particular story suggests that the dog is a good omen. On on occasion a family member saw the dog whilst sitting on a window seat over-looking the moat. Th woman was so intrigued that she got up and walked towards the animal which suddenly disappeared. was then that the bay where she'd been relaxing cracked and crumbled into the murky depths of the mo: below. The lady was sure that the phantom dog had saved her life.

There have been reports in the grounds of a similar hound and also around nearby areas such as Holling bourne. Is the beast related in any way to the selection of dog collar's displayed in the castle museum Or is the hound really the embodiment of cursed evil?

After visiting the castle and speaking with the staff, it seems that the black hound is no real mystery, b simply the ghost of a dog owned by Lady Baillie, an Anglo-American heiress. She purchased the cast in 1926 and after her death, the building was handed over to the Leeds Castle Foundation. Staff als speak of a smaller dog haunting the place. A white, terrier-like dog has been heard scratching at a few the doors, and was also a pet of Lady Baillie.

During the mid-'90s, my mother was suffering with pleurisy, a condition of the lungs which causes i flammation and shortness of breath. One night she was sitting up in bed at home in Chatham. She hadn been asleep, she was in too much discomfort. As she sat there, wide awake, she looked towards the co ner of the room towards a chest of drawers, when she noticed a dog, jet-black in colour and the size o: spaniel, with floppy ears sitting on the furniture. The animal was staring at her, its eyes were just like a dog, and not glowing or in any way fiery. My mother felt no malevolence from the dog, and despi blinking several times to make sure she wasn't dreaming, the dog remained. Then, after a short time, simply vanished.

My mum recovered shortly after the incident and to this day believes the dog was an enlightening sign.

My sister Vicki was only a small child when she visited the Chatham home of relative Joe Chester w my mother, and observed a ghostly dog which scampered along by the sofa. She was terrified by t creature which she claimed was an awful sight, despite Joe and my mother not seeing the form. In 20 my sister also saw the apparition of a brown cat on three occasions, in the home of her boyfriend's parents at Strood.

- ## MORE BLACK DOG TALES

On the desolate Isle of Sheppey, and mentioned in Igglesden's twenty-eighth volume of *A Saunter Through Kent...* he writes of Shurland Castle:

> *'And here is another weird story. My informant is a lady who lived there, and, referring to the tradition that Shurland is haunted, says, "Strangely enough I myself never had any fear, although no one else would stay in the hall at midnight in the dark. I had no fear either of the ghostly lady in the black silk or of the big black dog sometimes seen or of the ringing of the bells from some unknown cause. Then there was the sound of the horse's hoofs outside the front door, and it was said that a hearse passed by. We would rush to the door and open it, but nothing was to be seen. All bedroom doors were locked at night and any dog would whine if you tried to get him to pass into one of these rooms and absolutely refuse to enter. Door handles would keep turning, and fingers would run over the panels of the door. Huge hairy spiders infested the place, and it was always said that they foretold death. Outside at night owls screeched and weird noises kept the inmates of the mansion awake, and it was difficult to persuade guests to stay."*

There's a ghost story for you!

Iggleseden writes of another phantom dog in his Benenden coverage within the second volume, stating:

> *'But one more ghost story and I must finish my saunter through this interesting and picturesque old Wealden village. Skull's Gate Farm lies just off the Cranbrook high road, and it is said that many years ago an old man was murdered near here under revolting circumstances, and, what is more horrible, his ghost is still to be seen traversing the roadway. Why, I am told that only last winter a bicyclist says he distinctly saw the apparition following close behind his machine as he toiled up Skull's Gate Hill. And the shape of the ghost was remarkable – it had a long body like a dog, with four legs, but its head was human. How shocking!'*

At Great Chart, Ashford there has been much confusion as to whether a phantom dog or bull-like beast appeared on one occasion. In a book entitled *Ghosthunter Walks (SB Publications 2005)* by Rupert Mathews, he comments:

> *'The phantom that came to Great Chart appeared just once, but in such spectacular form that it immediately became famous and is still recognised as a remarkable apparition. On a summer's day in 1613, just as the vicar, Hadrian Savaria, began his sermon a gigantic black bull suddenly appeared in the middle of the church. The good folk of Great Chart were understandably terrified and there was a general move to get away from the snorting, stamping beast. The bull glared around with burning red eyes that seemed alive with malevolence, then it charged. Three men fell before its horns and pounding hooves before the monstrous bull hit the North Wall and exploded into a ball of hellfire which demolished part of the wall, singed the good Rev. Savaria and left behind a curious odour.*
>
> *It has been suggested that the destructive bull of Great Chart was an example of the*

entirely natural phenomenon known today as ball lightning. This occurs usually during thundery weather when a small mass of super-charged air turns into an electric plasma, appearing as a floating globe of burning air.'

Even stranger then that the Great Chart bull appeared on a bright summer's day, bereft of storm.

However, in 1993 a motorist claimed to have seen a big, black creature like a dog, with fiery eyes as he was driving up a lane in Great Chart.

Strangely, or merely coincidentally, Igglesden in his third volume of *A Saunter Through Kent...,* from 1902 wrote of a sign board of the Black Dog dangling at the front door of a house in Great Chart. Possibly not connected to any devilish manifestation, Great Chart was subjected to a big earthquake in 1580. A phantom hound is also said to pad through a manor house in Willesborough, and the Barrow Dog was said to have been sighted in the Chilham area in the 1940s.

With regards to fiery anomalies, a weird ball of light was observed in the late 1800s by travellers, who were reputedly led to their death in the Marden area, which was once known as Marshden. Such peculiar marsh lights have become known as will-o'-the-wisps. In 1927 similar bobbing balls of fire were seen by campers in the Upstreet area. The orbs bounced along the top of some apple trees.

Several spooky encounters across the world involving black hell hounds have involved witnesses who noted that such creatures exploded into a ball of flame, transformed into hovering spheres of light or gave off a strong, burning stench or transformed into orb-like forms. Bizarrely, this characteristic also applies to encounters with a whole myriad of ethereal beasts. Even reports of bigfoot from the Pacific Northwest often describe a sulphuric odour and glowing trails.

Another legend of a similar fiery intruder reads as follows:

'*The Tudor historian John Stowe, who was born 1525 and died in 1605, recorded a strange story told to him by his father - 'My father told me that, at St Michael's church in the Cornhill ward, London, on the night of St James, certain men were ringing the bells of St Michael's, in the loft, when there arose a tempest of thunder and lightning, and a thing of an ugly shape and sight was seen to come in at the south window, and it lighted on the north. For fear whereof, all the ringers fell down and lay as dead for a time, leaving the bells to ring and cease of their own accord. When the ringers came to themselves, they found certain stones of the north window to be razed and scrat as if they had been so much butter, printed with a lion's claw; the same stones were fastened there again, when it was repaired, and remain so to this day. I have seen them oft, and have put a feather or small stick into the hole where the claw had entered, three to four inches deep.*

At the same time, certain main Timber posts at Queen Hith were scrat and cleft from top to bottom, and the Pulpit Cross in Paul's churchyard was likewise scrat, cleft and overturned. One of the ringers lived in my youth, whom I have oft heard to verifye the same to be true, and I have oft heard my Father to report it'.

Black dog legends are rife in the neighbouring counties. Again, these manifestations have been tied in the 'alien big cat' mystery. South-west of Arundel, Sussex, in the village of Yapton, locals are said to fear the ghostly dog, so much so that they once left their doors open so that such a phantom could roam freely on its path. South of the Surrey border near Haslemere there is an area known as Black Dog Cop whilst a Black Dog Lane runs from old Crawley High Street to West Green and Horsted Heynes, Sussex also has a place, marked on old maps, called Black Dog.

The village of Henfield, West Sussex, harbours a black dog legend, a phantom said to be calf-sized and eyes ablaze although many legends from Sussex often revolve around old smugglers who were said to have created such 'monsters' to prevent local folk from loitering around wooded areas where these mischievous crooks hid their goods. The 'beast' of Bouley Bay in Jersey is another of these so-called legends created by smugglers. Such a demonic, saucer-eyed dog is said to roam the shoreline as a scare tactic offered by the crooks to frighten off intruders into their clandestine activities. Were most black dog legends of Sussex mere creations of smugglers? It is said that many local villains used to conceal their stash of gold in old cemeteries and dark woods and often return to their villages with tales of haunted locations, warning the townsfolk to steer clear of the treacherous bogs and inaccessible thickets, and yet on most occasions it seems as though such sly thieves were simply protecting their loot.

The 'wish (or wisht/whisht) hounds' of Sussex are the most commonly known spectral canids, alongside the likes of Black Shuck, Padfoot etc, and also haunt Dartmoor in the westcountry. Rarely though are such dogs sighted in packs across the county, despite the legend that a wild hunt, including the sound of yapping hounds and the thunder of horses hooves, can be heard near the Ditchling Beacon hillfort. A solitary hound haunts Windover Hill above the Long Man Of Wilmington etching, and it is the South Downs area where most reports seem concentrated, which could suggest some ancient pathway or old location once guarded by these hellhounds.

At Jevington, East Sussex, a black dog is often sighted fleetingly before vanishing, whilst at Alfriston also in the east, two spectral dogs, one black and one white, are sighted around the full moon on the dark roads heading towards Town Fields. The black phantom is said to overlook the flint wall of the road and then run back from whence it came. The whitish hound is said to be the omen of death, an animal murdered, along with its master, the heir of the Chowne Estate, by a group of farm labourers. The dog is rarely sighted now, maybe because the remains which were buried at the side of the road were excavated and buried at a more appropriate spot, allowing the spirits to rest, however, in his 1884 work *Our Sussex Parish*, Thomas Geering mentions part of a song concerning what was to become the White-Way ghost:

> '*When evening closes in with shadows grey,*
> *And the ghostly vapours overhang White-Way,*
> *And the crescent moon hangs gloomy in the west,*
> *'Tis then the spirit of young Chowne can't rest,*
> *But walks abroad with melancholy stride,*
> *Adown the path that skirts the chalk hillside.*'

Another road, that which runs east-west to the south of Lewes and Mount Caburn, is haunted by a Labrador-sized black dog which disappears as soon as it is sighted. So does that mean if no-one is there to see it, it does not appear?

Most legends pertaining to these phantom hounds concern a general fear of the dark from the locals, who often speak of these hounds emerging from the shadows once the sun has gone down. Reports from the daytime are rare it would seem. Not even poachers and the like tread the valleys east of Philpots Promontory Camp, in the parish of West Hoathly after dark. The 'gurt black ghost hound' prowls the area which locals call an 'ellynge place', meaning 'eerie'. The hound is called 'Gytrack', similar in name to the 'Guytrash' hound said to haunt the north of England.

Black Dog Hill south-east of Ditchling, West Sussex, is haunted by a headless black canid, the road haunted could possibly be an old Corpse Way or 'coffin road' which points directly toward Westmeston Church. These roads were once said to be the common routes used when the dead were transported for burial. Could such hellhounds be guardians of the dead?

Why are reports of phantom black dogs less common now then say thirty or forty years ago, and previously? Has the British 'big cat' situation literally swamped such a phenomenon out of existence? It seems likely. Reports of hellhounds, spectral dogs and 'wish hounds' are now few and far between. Black animals creeping through the fog now become black leopards, fleeting, fiery-eyed creatures slinking into hedgerows are mystery cats, and whilst the age-old Black Dog legends remain fossilised in their chosen towns, like so many other mysteries before them, they have transformed, or died out even, despite once being the common fear of men. They exist as bad omens across the world, from Iraq's chained phantoms, to Holland's Doberman-like hounds. They exist in some form or other, and certainly to the extent of being taken very seriously, but whether they hang on in there as they have done, as a phenomenon only time will tell, but if we put them alongside the potent canine forces that exist throughout Egyptian lore, or Greek mythology, then these hellhounds, and harbingers of doom should remain active for as long as the Earth remains round.

From the dark, dank pea-soup fog ridden alleyways of Victorian London, to the modern, neon-corridors of human traffic and vehicle congestion, the capital has always had its quirks, its sinister corners and misty, murky annals of folklore.

Legends of bizarre crimes have littered the seedy underworld of the smog-choked streets, tales of eerie spectres being whispers of the stale air, spewed from the pallid sky as local yarns and spun tales of the community. Yet, the vibrancy and technicolor splendour of the bustling city has often blurred, obscured and quashed the ill rumours, but even though the city never sleeps, there are many a phantom and grim apparition that remains to creep.

Briefly, London has its share of 'hellhound' legends. A black hound was seen during the 1960s on the Wandsworth Road. Researchers claimed that the form was the ghost of an animal killed on the road. The hound would often be seen disappearing into 523 Wandsworth Road, and the haunting occurred for more than four months. Similar harmless ghost dogs have been seen in South East London where a phantom dog was said to prowl the Anchor Tavern, and another pub, the Spanish Galleon of Greenwich was also said to be haunted by a large mastiff hound. However, the lore of the black dog often concerns hounds which are sinister, often appearing as omens of death or ill luck as discussed. Meanwhile a dog resembling a dachshund is said to haunt an area of Baker Street also, but London's most famous phantom hound was that which resided at the old Newgate Prison, a slithering, ominous spook which gave off a nauseating odour. Legend of the beast dates back to the reign of Henry III during a period of extreme famine where the prisoners were often rumoured to have fed upon one another. One such victim of cannibalism, who was rumoured to be a sorcerer, claimed vengeance upon the inmates when a frightful, red eyed phantom hound materialised in the vicinity. According to legend, the evil beast ripped many of the felons limb from limb, its blood soaked jaws dripping to the icy floor. Other prisoners simply died of fright, terrified of the oncoming sound of padded feet in the corridors. The phantom hound was said to have haunted the prison up until its demolition in 1901 where it was thought to be no more, yet rumour has it that sightings and strange odours are still reported, suggesting that the harbinger of doom was not confined to the dank annals of folkloric horror.

In his book *Ghosts Of London (Jarrold 1982)*, J.A. Brooks writes, '*It must have been known in folklore long before anything was written down: the earliest record of its existence dates from about 1596 and was written by an inmate named Luke Hutton.*' Hutton was hanged in 1598 but his versions of events have been oft' repeated and re-read. One fascinating account of the beast, dating from a 1638, called *The*

Discovery of a London Monster, called, the Blacke Dogg of Newgate, as follows:

> *'I maintained that I had read an old Chronicle that it was a walking spirit in the likeness of a blacke Dog, gliding up and down the streets a little before the time of Execution, and in the night whilst the Sessions continued, and his beginning thus.*
>
> *In the raigne of King Henry the third there happened such a famine through England, but especially in London, that many starved for want of food, by which meanes the Prisoners in Newgate eat up one another altue, but commonly those that came newly in, and such as could make but small resistance. Amongst many others cast into this Denne of misery, there was a certaine Scholler brought tither, upon suspition of Conjuring, and that he by Charmes and devilish Whitchcrafts, had done much hurt to the kings subjects, which Scholler, mauger his Devil Furies, Spirits and Goblins, was by the famished prisoners eaten up, and deemed passing good meate. This being done, such an idle conceit possessed the mindes of the poore Prisoners, that they supposed, nightly to see the Scholler in the shape of a black Dog walking up and downe the Prison, ready with ravening Jawes to teare out their bowles: for his late human flesh they had so hungerly eaten, and withal they hourely heard (as they thought) strange groanes and cries, as if it had been some creature in great paine and torments, whereupon such a nightly feare grew amongst them, that it turned into a Frenzie, and from a Frenzie to Desperation, in which desperation they killed the Keeper, and so many of them escaped forth, but yet whither soever they came or went they imagined a Blacke Dog to follow, and by this means, as I doe thinke, the name of him began.'*

OTHER PHANTOM ANIMALS

Do phantom dogs chase phantom cats? Reports of spectral felids are certainly few and far between in Kent. Most reports concern your average spirit of a domestic cat, like that which is said to haunt Maidstone Museum and seen as recently as February 2008. The cat is said to be white and fluffy, but hardly removed from the same etherworld as phantom black dogs. At Pembury, which is circled by Tonbridge, Royal Tunbridge Wells, Paddock Wood and Goudhurst, several hauntings are said to occur at the Old Church and Old Bayhall Manor. On one occasion, several decades ago a researcher named Frederick Saunders, accompanied by a Kenneth Jeffrey, spent the night in the area. Sanders reported, whilst seeking the vault of an Anne West, who was the last mistress at the hall:

> *'As we stood silently near the old tomb a noise like a subdued rustling became audible, followed by a light thump, followed again by jerking, gritty sounds. Turning, we glimpsed a small black form bounding along the pathway. It was a black cat at full gallop and it quickly disappeared into the gloom on the further side of the graveyard...'*

At Sissinghurst a phantom black cat has been reported in a house at Branden. Those who've seen the mysterious animal say it is impossible to touch, let alone catch and every time the felid appears there is a strange sound of purring and the flapping of wings.

During the 1950s, 88 Newark Street, in Whitechapel, London, was said to have been the prowling ground of a ghastly cat-like form which was often seen by children residing at the house. At the time the family reported that six years of bad luck befell them, and there was always mention of a gloomy atmosphere within. Another phantom felid haunted Great Tower Street, in the vicinity of All Hallows, near the Tower, before the 1940s. The eerie cat lingered around the original church until it was obliterated by German bombers during WWII. On one occasion a group of witnesses claimed that a ghostly woman transformed into a big, black cat whilst the most peculiar phantom cat appeared at Regent's Park during the 1930s. A zookeeper was strolling the grounds with his granddaughter when a lion, with a glowing coat appeared. As the man approached the great cat faded away. Strangely enough, the next day when the keeper went to work, he was told that one of the lions had died the previous evening, at exactly the same time as the spooky encounter!

In 1992 in north-west London at West End Lane, a ghostly golden-coloured cat surprised several witnesses, although they may have seen an elusive local puma which they couldn't identify at the time.

A record from 1674 suggested an apparition of a big cat lurked in a haunted London house and read as follows:

> 'News from PUDDLE-DOCK IN LONDON or, A Perfect particular of the strange Apparitions and Transactions that have happened in the House of Mr Edward Pitts next Door to the Still at Puddle-dock' – '...Mr Pitts takes the Loaf off the Dresser to cut bread to lay on the Table, as he was cutting the Bread he spied upon the Dresser a great thing like a Catt, at which being a little affrighted, he started back Presently calling to his Wife, saying, here's a Catt, I never saw a Catt in this house before, upon which, this Cat-like thing seemed to slide off the Dresser, giving a thump on the Boards, and so vanished away. All Mr pitt's Family then in the Room, but none could perceive this strange Catt but only his daughter of about 15 years of Age, and himself; and they say it was as bigg as any Mastiff Dog; but they could not perceive that it had any Leggs.'

Folklore author Joan Foreman had an unnerving encounter with a very eerie presence in Kent at a Goudhurst school whilst vacationing, which she wrote of in her book, *The Haunted South (Hale 1978)*, she says, of the account, which I believe took place around 1955:

> 'My sole encounter with it – and once was enough – was at the beginning of the only summer vacation I ever spent in the place. Most of the staff had departed for far-flung and no doubt exotic holidays, and I found myself working and sleeping alone in the oldest part of the building for about three days until I, too should leave.
>
> My study bedroom was a largish room looking on to the garden; a pleasant enough place, though hot in summer and cold in winter.
>
> On the second of my three nights I awoke about 3:30 am. It was the time of a summer's night when dawn was about to break, when the cracks were appearing in effect without making any appreciable difference to the darkness.
>
> I came awake abruptly, from full sleep to full awareness at once. And the awareness announced that something was crouched on the floor of my bedroom to the left of the bed. I did not need to turn my head to know where it was. Indeed, I could not have turned had I wanted for I was paralysed by fear. Even the fear was not normal, for it was a kind of thick terror, like a blanket in which I was rolled. All I could do in that petrified state was to turn my eyes toward the creature on the floor.
>
> It was about two feet in length, I suppose, the size of a large cat or a small corgi. It resembled neither of these. It had a pair of huge nocturnal eyes like those of a lemur, and these were the clearest feature of the apparition....With all its exudation of evil it

was at the same time mocking. It stared at me for what seemed like half an hour, and I stared back, playing rabbit to its snake...After what seemed an interminable time the clarity of the thing beside the bed began to fade, its light to dim, and its malevolent emanation to lessen. With this diminution the room which had been bitterly cold, began to grow warmer. In a few minutes it had disappeared entirely leaving a very shaken and occupier of the bed.

Some two or three years after this incident, I met the person who succeeded me on the staff of this school, and was told that she had had a similar experience in another bedroom in the same wing, though in her case the 'animal' had appeared on the window curtains.'

On a less sinister note, Kent is littered with various other ghostly tales pertaining to animals. Although they are rather your average spook tale, they are quirky and worth a mention. At Faversham, two separate incidents to record, the first concerning a ghostly fox said to haunt the railway bridge, although sightings are few, and also the rumours that there was once a local woman blamed for witchery for it was once said that she owned a hideous beast, something akin to a cross between a goat and a dog. The whispers of her sorcery eventually got round and she, along with her peculiar pet, were killed, and said to forever haunt the area as lonesome spirits. Faversham was once an area said to be inhabited by witches, many whom were executed in the 1600s.

It is strange how witchcraft is often blamed on such apparitions. The often misinterpreted word 'witchcraft' often sends shivers down the spine of those who have, for centuries, misunderstood it. It conjures images of grim tales of voodoo, possession, sorcery, diabolical summoning, curses and witches entertaining monstrous apparitions. Many of the 'satanic panics' have been nothing more than media conjuration whereas the fascination of white magic has been somewhat clouded by the imaginary dark blanket of so-called devilish cults. Yet, during the famous witch trials of many centuries ago, there were indeed cases in witch so-called 'witches' and sorcerers were accused of cavorting with demons and raising familiars.

Condemnation of Edmund, Earl of Kent on political grounds; had obtained important information from a demon through the mediation of a friar. Edmund is brother of Edward II (murdered). Condemned in Winchester Parliament of 1330. Kent had heard that Edward was still alive and his consequent action in Edward's interest was the pretext for his conviction and execution on March 19th. Whole affair engineered by Roger Mortimer (lover of Queen Isabella), young Edward III not yet in charge. On March 24th Mortimer sent a letter to the pope explaining and justifying the crime; declared that Edmund had got the info from a demon conjured by a friar. When Mortimer was condemned the following November, the parliament surely had the matter of the demon in mind, saying that he managed to convey the report that Edward was still living to Kent, whereupon the Earl investigated the matter, *'...by all the good means he new of'.*

During 1534 the Holy Maid of Kent vented her unhappiness with regards to a tree upon some land. Such an outburst was taken by the then King Henry as an insult. Allegedly, the maid had also told the king that should he ever leave Queen Catherine, then he would die within a few months. Of course, such remarks led to the maid's persecution. In 1586 Joan Cason was accused, via 'witchcraft', of killing a child named Joan Crook. She was tried at Faversham and accused of having familiars. She was sentenced to death. 1671 saw a Woolwich widow tried in Kent for feeding, entertaining and employing a familiar that looked like a rat. In 1692 three women were accused of consulting and covenanting with strange creatures in the shape of mice.

Whilst the witch-craze sparked many unnecessary executions, several centuries later the public and the press still interpret 'witchcraft' as something sinister, despite the fact that it's difficult to often siphon out the yobs from the vandals, the drunken rock fans from the amateurs, with a majority of these not having a clue about either white or black magic.

During the late 1960s at Fordwich a tortured kitten was discovered and reported to a local newspaper. The poor creature bore marks to suggest it had been burned, and near the body black candles were found, and according to the media, a 'witches circle'. A few years after several animal skulls were found in the chimney of a Chatham house. One of these skulls was coloured black, and a museum owner identified it as possibly belonging to a boar or a bear which have been used for ritual purposes.

The village of Cobham has a dark history, particularly in the area of the mausoleum buried in the woods. A dating couple allegedly uncovered a red circle daubed on the ground, the sacred hexagon of Solomon in the centre. A gored rabbit and an eerie doll were also found in the area. The press had a field day. Around the same time coffins were desecrated in the Canterbury area after which the police acknowledged was indeed the work of drag-crazed vandals, although how they knew this is anyone's guess, but I guess that anyone can be blamed as a Satanist!

During the '80s a local 'witch' was driven from her home in Medway, and the haunted area of Blue Bell Hill has often been associated with dark magic, although white witches often operate in the area. Yet those who stumble upon such practices are obviously dramatic enough to run to the press and the police with tales of sorcery and ritual. White witch Kevin Carlyon has visited the area on numerous occasions, legend even has it that the Kits Coty house was formed by four witches on a dark and stormy night, although this is simply untrue, yet very eerie folklore. Just like much of what Wicca is about. And whilst the Devil may truly exist, those that practice witchcraft have a true connection with nature, and not the underworld.

In his first volume of *A Saunter Through Kent With Pen And Pencil*, Igglesden wrote of Wye and it once famous holy well near Brook Road. The waters of the well were so blessed that they reputedly cured all disease. He wrote, '*It is recorded that a dropsical woman who drank the waters vomited two black toads, which changed into dogs and then asses – then vanished.*'

Indeed, a fine fable if ever there was one. Yet he also writes of a place named Robin's Croft in Chilham, an old vicarage said to have been haunted by a flame-wielding monk and a skeletal horse. A white stallion is said to haunt Michelham Priory in East Sussex and also the Bramber area. Another ghostly horse was once rumoured to glide along the lanes of Canterbury, more specifically Littlebourne Road. On several occasions in the not too distant past police were called out to investigate several reports of the mare. The local panic began when Miss Dorothy Ramsay was driving home late one night, she said, "*The horse seemed to fly up from the road like a great shadow. It landed on top of my sports car and smashed in the roof and windshield. After that it vanished.*"

Then, several motorists reported colliding with the phantom, leaving police scratching their heads and commenting that, "*We don't want to start a ghost horse scare, but we have searched for the animal without success.*"

Whether there was any truth in the rumour I'll never know, but as a young child growing up in Walderslade, there were always local ghost tales to be spoken of, in a similar respect to Tom Atkinson and his Blue Bell Hill crone with the dog. An obscure and terrifying ghost story of sorts emerged from the woods surrounding Walderslade, Rochester Airport and Blue Bell Hill, although it may have been nothing more than a school urban legend. However, 'Thumper' or the 'Reggae Woman' may have been one and the same thing, a bizarre manifestation said to have made a 'thud' noise at it ran at tremendous speed through the black woods of a night. Some whispers mentioned that 'Thumper' was a witch, or voodoo woman, so the term 'Reggae Woman' may have been a loose description pertaining to a dark spectre with long hair, wearing odd garments, who knows? However, being a child and growing up with the theme tune to the strange Roald Dahl television series *Tales Of The Unexpected*, the last thing I needed as I strolled up to bed in my Liverpool pyjamas was that damned musical score and the image of the silhouetted woman dancing in flames, and the legends of Blue Bell Hill echoing through my skull walls. 'Thumper' also may have been a monster rabbit that was imagined after terrified teens, hanging out in the thickets, misinterpreted a haunting 'thumping' noise which they attributed to the frantic beating of its back leg on the soil, but the legend remains clouded, yet vaguely frightening. Or it may have been a roaming wallaby, or something far weirder, we'll never know. I guess that like boggarts and other fears, they can be whatever we want...or don't want them to be.

The county of Sussex has a most intriguing legend, that of the spectral bear said to haunt the grounds of Verdley Castle and appear around the festive season. A team of psychics visited the location in 2004, and their expedition was covered by the *Midhurst And Petworth Observer*. The castle dates back to the thirteenth century and it was in the forests as claimed, that the last bear was killed. Unfortunately, the psychics, although providing a wealth of other historical information could not determine as to whether a phantom bear roamed the vicinity, sightings seem scarce and much of the local townsfolk have never even heard of the legend although folklore states that white, black and brown bear have been reported there, in spectral form.

However, the phantom bear said to have prowled the Tower Of London is certainly one of the most popular animal ghost tales, as once stood the site of an ancient menagerie within the vicinity. Sighted around 1815, the apparition was said to have haunted the Jewel Room. On one occasion a guard was confronted by the spectral beast and lunged at it with his bayonet. His weapon drifted through the creature. Legend has it that the guard died soon after from shock. This is certainly an often repeated anecdote.

Another weird form also haunted the room, that being a cylindrical nightmare witnessed by Mr Edmund Lenthal Swift who was Keeper of the Crown Jewels from 1814 to 1842. It was he who received message of the phantom bear, but during the October of 1817 whilst relaxing with his family they were approached by a tubular, giant floating worm-like and misty apparition which swirled ominously around the table before vanishing near the window.

Black, brown and white spectral bears have also been sighted around Glebe Place, in Chelsea. These ursine manifestations are perhaps connected to bear baiting in the area during the 1600s. One such form is said to prowl the riverside, and another at Cheyne Walk.

A large bird-like spectre known as the Puck Bird is said to haunt Fittleworth in Sussex. Tales originate from the 1800s of a disease bestowing creature that haunts rural pathways. Legend has it that should any traveller pass the bird then cursed they must surely be. However, one of the most fascinating animal hauntings of the county emerged from 2007 when BBC Southern Counties reported, 'The Ghostly Peacock' -

'Every Halloween we get inundated with spooky stories but none quite as strange as this one.... Is there something unusual haunting the A267 south of Five Ashes? Or is there a perfectly reasonable explanation?

According to Trevor Weeks, the Rescue Co-ordinator for East Sussex Wildlife Rescue & Ambulance Service, something very peculiar is happening outside Heathfield. In the last two nights, he has been called out between midnight and 1:00 am to a peacock which had almost caused a road accident on the A267 south of Five Ashes.

The first call, on Tuesday 31st October, came just minutes after the 'witching hour' from a lone driver going south. They thought they had seen a peacock in the road and believed it might have been hit. A call to the WRAS sent Trevor out into the dark and chilly night in the rescue ambulance to find the bird, but when he arrived he could not find any sign of a peacock injured or otherwise. However, in the early hours of Wednesday morning, he received a second call, this time from a lorry driver, who was sure he had seen a peacock and thought he had actually hit the bird.

"He waited for me to arrive and I found him checking his lorry to check if the bird had been caught underneath" said Trevor. "We checked the wheel arches, looked at the road for signs of blood and feather but could not find any trace of the bird. This is really odd" said Trevor. "It was too big to be a pheasant and it's tail length was different."

He told BBC Southern Counties that there are peacocks living in the area as they escape from private collections and they can survive successfully in the wild. They can also fly short distances.

"I do believe the drivers saw a peacock but what was really strange is that usually when a bird is involved in an accident, there are a few feathers or a bit of blood at least, but there was nothing. It had completely vanished into nowhere. We don't normally deal with escaped domestic pets, but as they had tried other rescue centres and not had a response we attended. I'll be interested to see if we get another call tonight of this phantom peacock...."

An unidentified white bird is said to flutter around Arundel Castle when a death is about to occur, and a white deer is said to haunt West Grinstead in Knepp Castle. Another strange bird-like form said to haunt Sussex is that which is known from an 1868 account from Ashington. It concerns a blacksmith's wife who was found one morning deeply disturbed after an alleged visitation from a white, duck-like bird. She screamed at the animal which ran away, but afterwards she was of the firm belief that such a form was indeed a bad omen and that a stroke of ill luck was due to follow. Despite local suggestion that the troubled woman may have just seen a normal animal, she was convinced that due to its extremely whiter than white appearance, the bird was most definitely spectral and its aura otherworldly.

'Something had caught my ancestor on a dark valley road, leaving him with marks of horns on his chest and of ape-like claws on his back; and when they looked for prints in the trampled dust they found the mixed marks of split hooves and vaguely anthropoid paws.'

The Unnamable – H.P. Lovecraft

The Horror of the Humanoids

*'You could imagine the Beast roaming about in this wild wasted place, lapping the water
in the beck, washing the blood off its teeth, licking its claws, watching us, hidden in the
rocks, or among those black twisted trees.'*

The Nature Of the Beast – Janni Howker

They come from places unknown. Yet they should not surely walk through these woods, where glades afresh act as glistening pockets, sheltered by over-hanging trees which reach to the soil such as spindly fingers. The land runneth with strange imagery, but surely not with monsters that are beyond the realms of even this tranquil garden. Now this is where Kent and the surrounding areas get really weird...

Whilst the man-beasts known as the Yeti, Bigfoot, Sasquatch, Skunk Ape, Orang-Pendek and the Almas are known worldwide, and pursued greatly by cryptozoologists, and even some scientists, strange, bipedal humanoids from the United Kingdom are lesser known. Ape men have intrigued from the hills of Wales, as have bipedal were-creatures, and there is also the well known shadowy figure, the 'Grey Man' of Scotland's Ben MacDhui, a shadowy spectre of immense proportions, said to haunt the Cairngorms, which sceptics put down to mountain myth and local panic.

Several counties within England such as Sussex and Lincolnshire are rumoured to have witnessed shadows cast by fleeting man-beasts and monkey-men, although such lore is reasonably brief. The most known cases of English man-beasts are without doubt the tales of the 'Shug Monkey' (paranormal-related beast either in the form of black dog or spectral, hairy creature said to lurk in the Rendlesham Forest area of Suffolk), the Athelhampton 'ape' (a spectral primate said to have haunted Athelhampton House in Dorset), Devon's ghost ape (a primate said to haunt Dartmoor), the Bolam 'beast' (a muscular, hair-covered entity said to prowl woods around Northumberland), the Man-Monkey (a bizarre beast said to have terrorised locals within the vicinity of the Union Canal in Shropshire from the year 1879) and a handful of others, but surely such sightings are mere folklore or of escaped monkeys and surely not concerning hulking beings from a place we do not know of? The original speakings of such woodland prowlers originated in the tales of the Wild Man, or the Men of the Woods or the Wudewasa, strange, club-carrying, muscular men of some height, often hairy and bearded, at times preferring to walk on all fours, and often depicted in Medieval paintings and sculptures, and staring wildly from church carvings. Such beings were often connected to the rural landscape and considered symbolic, whilst to some such humanoids were outcasts, shunned by the local people and cast into the shade of the forests to live as wild people, who occasionally would venture into villages and steal food, or even women and children, making such predatory 'people' into bogeyman-type figures.

Such Kent hominids have never really been chronicled, until now. Only since stumbling accidentally on such brief reports have I managed to construct this section pertaining to such phenomena. In fact, the only 'humanoid' case which has been chronicled time and time again, as far as I'm aware, is that of the Hythe 'being' which scared a group of youths in the 1960s, and became a case quite well known within UFO circles, and sneaked its way into such classic works as John Keel's *Strange Creatures From Times & Space* (Sphere, 1975), but it mainly made its name in connection with the Mothman sightings of West Virginia which took place not long after the original Kent incident.

For those unaware of the Hythe 'Mothman' case, here is a brief summary of what took place on that cold, night of November 16th in 1963:

> '*Four young people*', Keel wrote, '*...were walking home from a dance along a quiet country road near Sandling Park, Hythe, Kent,...John Flaxton, 17, was the first to notice an unusually bright star moving directly overhead. They watched it with growing alarm as it descended and glided closer and closer to them. It seemed to hover and then dropped out of sight behind some nearby trees.*

> '*I felt cold all over*', Flaxton recalled. *He and his friends had seen enough. They started to run. The light bobbed into view again, and this time closer, floating about ten feet above the ground in a field some two-hundred feet from the panic-stricken quartet.*

> '*It was a bright and gold oval*', one of them reported. '*And when we moved, it moved. When we stopped, it stopped*'.

> *Once more it went out of sight behind the trees along the road. Then suddenly there was the snapping of twigs and branches and a huge black figure shuffled out of the bushes towards them.*

> '*It was the size of a human*', Mervyn Hutchinson, 18, told police later. '*But it didn't seem to have any head. There were huge wings on its back...like bat wings*'.

Apparently, five nights later Keith Croucher, 17, saw a similar mystery, floating object crossing a football pitch on the Sandling Estate. Then, two nights later John McGoldrick and a friend began investigating the reports and allegedly found an area that looked as though it had been flattened by a craft of some sort, but their most impressive discovery was a set of large footprints. The prints were two feet in length and nine inches across. On December 11th McGoldrick and a newspaper reporter saw a strange light the sky that illuminated the woods.

I've personally never been overly interested in reports that tie together bigfoot-like creatures and UFOs and although the Hythe apparition was not exactly described as a bigfoot or remotely ape-like, the case seemed to pick up some amount of credibility and certainly involved a weird humanoid figure. At the time UFO researchers jumped all over the case, and since its time it has been looked upon as the close relation to West Virginia's Mothman, a hairy red-eyed and winged humanoid said to have haunted the Silver Bridge area, of Point Pleasant, USA, in the '60s. Now, with both cases firmly buried in the past, seems to me that because the Hythe incident was pretty much a weird one-off encounter, there is no re reason to bracket it with any other anomalous phenomena. The sighting of the humanoid was brief, an almost vague. Some researchers even claimed it may have been the spectre of a man dressed in red carrying a lantern, at times said to appear in the vicinity. The creature never flew, spoke or gave off any smell so for all we know such a case, although well documented, could have been a hoax and doesn't even really fit in with the creatures I'm about to describe to you. However, it certainly put Hythe and the su

Hythe mothman

TOP: Marc Ruddy walks the Pilgrim's Way in search of mystery animals
BELOW: Sherwood Avenue Woods where Maureen saw a man beast (p. 374)

rounding areas on the map of high strangeness. If anything though, the case must be forgotten unless the creature returns. We'll never know whether the spectre was in fact alien, ghost or illusion but I've decided to speak of it, as many have, because it pertains to Kent, but as a case it is now a distant memory, and unless it appears again I hope this is the last we'll hear of the incident.

Strangely, during the 1980s a weird thing involved myself and my best friend at the time. At around the age of eight I became good friends with a neighbour named Brett who would become my best friend for several years. Strangely, Brett always used to speak of a strange 'evil eye' which used to appear in his room of a night and occasionally shift around the room, always staring at him until after a few minutes he would run screaming from his bedroom to fetch his mum or dad who would visit his chamber of slumber, but find no eerie eye.

One summer evening, myself and Brett were throwing a tennis ball to each other outside of my house. We must've been around eleven-years old at the time. It was quite late, but the warm air and dimming sky were not to put us off from playing into the night. At the time, outside my parents' house, there was a small green, only sixty yards or so long. It was square in shape and located in front of three neighbouring houses. To the extreme left of my home there was a large tree - it's still there as I write - and that's where one of my strangest ever experiences took place.

Brett was standing at the edge of the green near to the shadows of the tree. I was standing at the other end near to my front garden, and we were throwing a tennis ball to one another. After a day of football in the sizzling heat, as well as playing with numerous figurines and also various other sports, we decided to see the night out by chatting and just lazily throwing the ball to one another.

Brett will always admit he was hardly sportsman of the year, but he tried his hardest at whatever he did. After several throws, I launched one and as the ball was heading towards Brett, curving in the air, he must've lost the flight of the ball in the gloom of dusk. The ball seemed to drop straight through his hands and hit him square in the face. Brett dipped his head, and both his hands clasped his face. Between giggles I ran to his aid. He was okay, we both saw the funny side. Suddenly, something happened we could never explain. From the tree next to us, some fifteen yards away, something large, possibly the size of a human, jumped from the branches. These branches, belonging to the tree which is an oak, must have been some thirty feet in the air, and yet whatever it was, it hit the ground running. Immediately, myself and Brett, who weren't facing the tree by then, heard the thud of footsteps bolting across the blanket of grass, twigs and leaves, and heading towards us. I remember us looking at each other in terror and running for our lives, ending up at the big, wooden gate of the side entrance to my house.

To this day I've never been able to explain how something, which clearly wasn't visible, had managed to leap from the tree, and break into an instant run, and seemed as heavy as a human. There was no sound of it hitting the ground, just the leap and then the steps. It was a very odd incident. I hope Brett still recalls it, but managed to escape from the weird eye that used to appear in his bedroom. I lost touch with him during the later school years, but we shared some fun, and indeed strange times.

Twenty years previous to the Hythe incident in an area of woodland on the east coast of England, the Shirley family were one of only a handful of witnesses to an English werewolf-like creature. The following report, although brief, and obtained from an American website called *Cryptomundo*, has, allegedly, been passed down through several generations and stood the test of time as a family incident of the most unusual nature.

Pat Shirley, whilst having a picnic with her grandmother in the woods, described seeing a creature that was only described as, "*...being covered in flaming red hair*", and, "*...possessing a pair of huge and* *powerful jaws*". Apparently the beast was seen only briefly before it moved off into the trees.

Again, there is that urge to become excited by such a tale, but again, the details are all too vague to pass judgement. However, in the summer of 1975 a very strange and close encounter took place.

The woods, at the top of Chestnut Avenue, Waldersalde, literally three minutes from my house as a kid, were never inhospitable areas, but merely heavy coppices that have since been wiped away by housing estates, leaving only a strip of thicket. The small wood itself didn't even stretch for a mile, and dipped in to the local 'village' where a handful of shops sat, and still do. However, a few hundred yards from Walderslade 'village' is Sherwood Avenue, which backs on to a bigger strip of woods which large cats have used frequently, connecting their territories of Walderslade Woods, Hempstead, Lordswood and Boxley. Again though, the wood is no forest, but like any wood at night, it remains silent and uncanny, two dense blankets of wood sliced by a muddy path. What a woman named Maureen saw, and never spoke of until she confided in me in 2006, was very much a Kentish bigfoot, something quite unique. This is an account never before published that has remained in her mind for more than thirty years! This is what she told me:

> "*I was in the woods behind Sherwood Avenue, in Walderslade in the August of 1975. I was eighteen at the time and myself and my ex-husband were about to light a small fire, as it must have been around 10:00 pm, quite dark. My husband was crouched down sorting the fire out and I was standing. It was then that I saw them, two piercing, reddish eyes just around ten yards away. I froze in terror, because this thing was big. It was around seven feet in height but in the darkness I could make out the bulk of it. It's figure wasn't like that of a man, it was a mass, a hulking figure, like it was hairy. I really thought I'd seen the Devil!*".

I was intrigued and yet unnerved by the horror in her voice.

> "*I just stood there and then it seemed to lower, quite slowly and after a few seconds it disappeared behind heavy foliage, but I could sense it was still there. I immediately made excuses to leave and we did, and I kept that terrifying night with me and never spoke to anyone.*"

So many reports of this ilk, especially from Kent are all too brief, but Maureen's sighting is very impressive. However, it seems clear that what she saw on that breezy summer's night was not a flesh and blood creature, simply because I do not believe that an undiscovered ape or sasquatch relative could inhabit such land. This may, of course, sound sceptical towards other reports of this type, but all around the United Kingdom, reports of this kind straddle a fine line between manifestation and the absurd. Were wolves and bigfoot-like humanoids cannot exist in our woodlands as real creatures, the only species of primate known from Europe is the Barbary ape (*Macaca sylvanus*), from the Rock of Gibraltar, but maybe as some form that dates back several centuries to a time when yarns of Wildmen, or the Wudwus were recorded, these being alleged men of the forests. This does not mean to say that I doubt the existence of undiscovered man-beasts in the Himalayas or the Pacific Northwest, but in England, and Kent of all places, I remain very sceptical. So, what was, and is, still being sighted?

In 1997 a motorist reported to the *Kent Today* that he'd seen a creature resembling a gorilla in the thick woods surrounding Blue Bell Hill. Details, which appeared on December 5th were vague, but maybe there was a remote possibility that some ape had escaped, but there are no zoo parks within the vicinity so maybe the witness had seen a small monkey that had burst free from its cage?

In 1964 the *Kent Messenger* reported, '*Terrified villagers declare gorilla warfare*', commenting,

'*January 24th: Two gorillas, who escaped from John Aspinall's private zoo at Bekesbourne yesterday, roamed the area for five hours, defied all attempts to catch them and caused terrified villagers to demand tighter security immediately.*

The gorillas are Kula (a male weighing 16-stone) and his mate Shamba. They just walked out of their cage while it was being cleaned and played happily on the lawn in front of Howletts Cottage by the drive leading to Aspinall's mansion.

Nine policemen arrived from Canterbury, followed by the fire brigade but the animals resisted all attempts to lure them back to their cages with oranges, preferring to drink milk left on the cottage doorstep. The foremen fixed up their jets and sprayed the gorillas with ice-cold water. Kula quickly ran back to his cage but Shamba disappeared. Minutes later an attic window in the cottage was flung open and Shamba peered out. Leaning on one elbow she waved gracefully to the crowd which had gathered below. Then deftly she clambered out of the window, dropped down on to a wall and, encouraged by the jets of water, lumbered off to her cage. Inside the cottage there was chaos. Shamba had knocked over furniture, pulled books from the bookshelves and broken several bottles.

Chairman of the parish council, Mr William Wallis said today: "There is something wrong with security at the zoo and we are demanding action now. It is a terrifying thought that they can escape like this. A few weeks ago a council tenant heard a knock at his door and there was a gorilla outside."

In July 2006, a primate escaped from London Zoo. Local press quickly heard of the story:

Visitors to Regent's Park witnessed some disgraceful monkey business today as a primate from London Zoo swung into action and made her Great Escape. Betty, a 10-year-old squirrel monkey is still on the loose after she spotted her opportunity for freedom when staff left a branch of a tree next to her enclosure growing too long. Today crowds watched the monkey running through the trees as staff waited for the moment to tempt her back home. It also emerged that the cheeky monkey may have been plotting the breakout for some time.

A spokesperson said: "The monkeys have really been hurling themselves from tree to tree and can travel quite a long way." David Field, London Zoo's Zoological director said: "She's certainly made a monkey out of us! She is merely visiting the park. We train the monkeys to come back to their quarters and she will return later in the day when it becomes quieter. We will encourage her to come back with a favourite treat of mealworms. We have also separated the other squirrel monkeys who are calling to each other and that is also a way of getting her to come back. She will be feeling vulnerable because she will not feel safe outside her familiar enclosure. The monkeys are a very tight-knit group. Squirrel monkeys are very inquisitive, exploratory and active creatures who like to swing on their branches. Part of the reason she left may have been the fruiting trees, since they like to eat fruit and leaf buds, as well as foraging for juicy grubs. They are not a dangerous animal – their enclosure is a walk through exhibit – and they pose no threat to the public. However keepers are monitoring her to make sure she does not come down from the trees, since we wouldn't want her to meet a dog. Their uniforms will also make her feel more reassured as she is used to them. The keepers found her out this morning. She will have escaped by a branch that was overhanging the enclosure. There are tree surgeons in there now making sure all the escape routes are closed."

- **APES OR MONSTERS?**

Another man-beast sighting took place in Friston Park, nr Newhaven in the neighbouring county of Sussex. On November 18th, 2002, at 2:30 am, Phil Hayman had parked his lorry up to stretch his legs when he spotted a large figure in the woods. The form was illuminated by a red light which was situated on a forestry machine in the woods. Mr Hayman was unsettled by the presence and hurried back to his cab but still had time to shine his torch at the being which rushed off into the darkness. Phil claimed that the creature wasn't human because he saw no skin colour reflected in the flashlight beam, and suggested it may have been covered in hair for it was dull in colour.

In the winter of 1967 at Winterfold in Surrey, a motorist pulled over on a dark, remote road to clean his windscreen. As he looked along the road he noticed a huge figure standing there which gave off a foul odour. The strange beast seemed to have a glowing, oblong-shaped head!

On the night of February 11th 2006, and as reported on the *Unexplained Mysteries* forum, a similar man-beast was observed in south-east England. Unfortunately the exact location was not given.

The witness was taking out the dustbins when he was unsettled by a weird sound he could only describe as low pitched, very deep, like a distant rumble. The strange noise seemed to be coming from the pitch black woods at the end of his garden. As the witness walked down his garden, to the wood, only separated by a fence, he thought he could see two glinting circular objects that seemed to be a dull yellow in colour. Rather unnerved by the objects, which he likened to cat's eyes, the man switched on the security light which seemed to make the two glinting objects glow brighter and the rumbling sound deepen. As soon as the witness reached the very bottom of his garden, the sound almost became unbearable from the woods. However, he managed to get a closer look at the two glinting 'eyes' which he believed were on the sides of a head of some kind of dark form. The 'creature' appeared to be humanoid and covered in hair, and stood over six feet in height. Then, as the rumbling increased, the man finally fled, scrambling back to his house, and slamming the door shut on the cacophony. Later on that night he heard the rumbling again and once more saw the dark, muscular form, only this time it was in his back garden. The being seemed to move around in peculiar hopping fashion, and had strange humps on its back. The terrified witness wasn't brave enough to go back into the garden, but the next morning he found all his rubbish strewn across the garden, and the wire fencing, erected to prevent rabbits escaping, was flattened to the ground, and in the woods there were several broken branches as if something had crashed through there.

I discovered that during the May of 1961 at Bilington, Kent, two schoolgirls watched in horror as a hairy being emerged from woodland and stood in a nearby field. The form then scurried off towards the trees but as it turned the girls said they noticed it had a tail. A creature hilariously dubbed a 'catgarookey' was said to be lurking in the woods of Salisbury, Wiltshire, and reported in the summer of 2005. The beast was said to be a hybrid of kangaroo, cat and monkey with a striped tail. Although such a creature was dismissed as possibly an escaped racoon, it did remotely echo a tale from 1877 in the same place concerning a local 'wild man' said to inhabit the woods. The monster came into a farm and attempted kidnap the wife of the farmer. In Sherwood Forest, Nottingham, a hairy, red-eyed, bipedal man-like creature has been observed on several occasions. Any coincidence here between Sherwood Forest and Sher wood Avenue where Maureen saw the red-eyed hulk?

In November 1991 Kevin Payne had an alarming encounter close to Blue Bell Hill. He hadn't told anyone of his scare until I spoke to him in a pub one evening whilst discussing folklore. His account reads as follows:

Mr Payne and three friends, one a taxi driver, the other two, old territorial army mates, had been on a pub crawl in the village of Burham, near Blue Bell Hill. They had done this many times before, and then, like this particular night would head in the direction of the far end of the village, toward Aylesford, to a bridleway that led up through farmland and deep into the woods of Blue Bell Hill, where they had found a few years before, a small clearing to light a fire and camp.

On this night, as they ambled up the steep bridle way that ran between farm fields, there was no moon above, the only light being from the windows of an old farmhouse, four to five hundred yards away. Mr Payne's three comrades were strolling just in front of him singing some bawdy song, when he heard one of them shout, "...*what the Hell is that?*", the two others followed with expletives and as he pushed his way to the front, in the total darkness directly ahead, which led to the woods, were two very large red eyes staring at them, approximately twelve feet ahead, slightly higher than their own eyes, accounting for the slight elevation of the path, that would make this apparition six to seven feet high. In the confusion caused by this sudden appearance, one of the witnesses, who was Mr Payne's sergeant in the T.A., suggested it might be a large bull or something, whilst the others argued with him in hushed tones, all the while Mr Payne automatically reached down feeling for some kind of ammunition on the rough pathway, and luckily found two large flints.

The lads, due to fear and being obstructed by this thing, started shouting and swearing at it, but the only thing it did was occasionally blink, but very slowly.

'*Staring intently at these eyes was almost hypnotic...*", Mr Payne described many years later, except that fear made one look down from them every so often. After around what seemed like ten minutes of this eerie game, Mr Payne let fly with one flint which seemed to miss, then he threw the other, which he was certain landed on target, but he heard no thud of connection, just the noise of the flint landing on the rough of the bridle path, and then all was suddenly silent, no sign of the eyes. Had the spectre dashed away? As Mr Payne took one step ahead, the eyes appeared again, only this time, around six feet away and about three feet above him, resulting in all the witnesses screaming, "*Run!*", fleeing for their lives back down the pitch black path, tripping on the loose stones, and bumping into one another, at the same time dragging one another by any limb they could grasp so that no-one was left behind. They eventually made it to the bottom and on to the Burham road, sober and exhausted.

For some years after, the friends would often discuss what it could have been that they encountered that night but remained mystified.

Just what sinister apparition with fiery eyes was lurking in the woods at the foot of Blue Bell Hill? Does it remain there dormant?

We'll never know what the witnesses actually saw on those chosen nights in one of Kent's most mysterious places. Reports are few and far between which could of course suggest sporadic sightings of an escaped animal, but what animal had red, glowing eyes? Or, on each occasion the witnesses were prone to hallucination, despite their conviction that what they saw was actually there, in front of them.

In the summer of 1999 Kevin Payne's sister, Claire, had a terrifying encounter in the area of Luddesdown, where Dode Church is situated. She'd gone for a drive with her boyfriend to the Golden Lion public house and at around 11:45 pm decided to take a trip to the church. The couple parked outside the church gates and Claire decided to have a cigarette and a stroll, whilst her partner decided to remain in the vehicle. She was certainly brave!

Claire climbed over the locked gate, and a few minutes later found herself next to the old well. Suddenly two heavy footsteps approached from the blackness, but the noise they made suggested a cloven-hoofed pair of feet, which were coming towards her from the direction of the dark lane. The footsteps got to within a few feet, and although Claire was unnerved she did not run from the area. There was a silence for a few seconds, and then a most horrifying growl, something akin to a bear. However, whatever made the noise must have been around eight feet in height for the growl emanated from above her. Claire's boyfriend, despite being in the vehicle twenty feet away, heard the sound, leapt out of his skin and screamed, "Get in the car!". Claire leapt the gate without glancing back, she dived into the vehicle and they sped away leaving the unknown presence in the blackness.

When they got back to Medway, the pair told a male friend of their scary night at Dode, despite scepticism and a heated debate, all three, accompanied by the friend's greyhound, decided to head back to the place. Claire stayed in the car this time whilst the two men and the dog patrolled the area with flashlights. They walked around the back of the old church, and it was here that the deep growling began again, a fiery roar from the field below them, leaving both men scrambling for their lives, the dog also keen to get back to the vehicle. The dog cowered and whined in the backseat, and despite seeing nothing both male witnesses claimed that what they heard was, *"...ungodly"*.

A lady named Charlotte contacted me with the following bizarre email:

> *"In November 2008, on my drive back to the University of Kent, I spotted something which completely scared the life out of me. It was about 11:00pm and I was just turning onto the Dover and Canterbury sliproad after the Dartford Bridge, when I saw 'something' in the distance. It was on the opposite side of the motorway running fast towards the sliproad. Within seconds it had reached the sliproad where I managed to get a better look at it.*
>
> *It was just metres from my car. It was well over six-feet in height, and completely black all over with a slightly pointy shaped head. It ran on two legs, which were extremely long in comparison to its torso, the arms were the same. The thing that scared me the most though was the way it ran. With each stride it took, the leg would bend and the bent knee reached all the way to the creatures face! Its arms were really long and also bent in a weird position. The creature had a humped back and was really skinny. It scared me so much my hands came off the wheel and I almost crashed."*

London boasts a rather obscure yet fascinating haunting pertaining to a weird ape-like form. The story emerged from the 1900s and was mentioned in Elliot O' Donnell's classic *Dangerous Ghosts* (Const Books 1954). The tale revolved around Mr Ward, a man from the capital who was a keen hunter and explorer who'd taken a trip to Sumatra where he encountered a woman, akin to a local witch who cursed him after he shot dead her pig-tailed macaque. Shortly after the accident, Mr Ward, whilst on his expedition, was mauled by a tiger and then stung by an insect. Such was Mr Ward's pain and fever that he returned home to his Hampstead house, where he remained in his sick-bed for a while. Whilst sweating of his fever Mr Ward was tormented, on various nights by a spectral ape, which, the local priest and a friend suggested, may well have been nothing more than severe hallucination from the fever. However, on night, whilst the priest and Mr Ward's friend stood guard outside the room, the spectral primate paid a visit. Mr Ward screamed in terror and was then found unconscious by the two guardians. The priest crossed himself, and as Mr Ward came round, the jabbering victim asked, *"You believe me now don't you?"*, and the priest replied, *"Something terrible was in the room. I saw it very distinctly. It was simian just like you described it Mr Ward, and very diabolical. It vanished as soon as I prayed. It won't trouble you again."*

After the horrific encounter the beast never returned and Mr Ward made a full recovery. **Other peculiar and terrifying humanoid figures exist throughout the lore of the south-east region. These however differ from the seemingly hairy, red-eyed beings.**

On May 6th 1961 at Keston between Bromley and Biggin Hill, a strange entity was observed. Keston Ponds are three watery abodes, one natural, two man-made, which attract many anglers each year. On this particular day two schoolgirls were terrified by a cloaked figure wearing a tall, dark hat and a glowing belt, which glided around them. Little else has been reported on the spook. Interestingly also, there is said to be a phantom hound in the area.

Such a humanoid phantom does bear some resemblance to Spring-Heeled Jack, the versatile, leaping apparition said to have haunted Victorian London as a darkly adorned, mocking caped villain. At the time it was said that the elusive assailant was seen in Kent also, whilst a handful of reports from London stated that a creature like a bear was in fact to blame for the sightings, although during the hysteria several falsities emerged. In his book *The Legend And Bizarre Crimes Of Spring Heeled Jack (Muller 1977)*, author Peter Haining, in the chapter entitled *The Agile Murderer*, comments briefly on the Kent apparition as, '...*a Devil on springs*', said to haunt rural pathways. In Croydon in 1803 a similar spook adorned in grim mask and cape haunted the area near the *Hare & Hounds*, Purley Way and was said to have leapt more than fifty feet to avoid a large crowd of on-lookers.

During the 1970s a Cuxton man named Paul, recalled how one afternoon whilst at school in the village, a group of girls began screaming and pointing at the trees of the wood which backs onto the school field. Paul said he ran over to find out what the commotion was all about when one of the girls claimed that a creature resembling a small monkey was watching them from the trees. Paul never saw the animal but was unnerved by the girls and their screaming frenzy and certainly believed their tale was more than just a school legend. On a slightly different note, whilst at infant school I recall a legend pertaining to the gloomy corridors and ice-cold toilets, it was something rarely whispered, but I distinctly remember one girl mentioning a beast resembling a giant squirrel (how giant, I do not know!). The monster was said to scratch with its claws or possibly stab with a knife, anyone brave enough to venture into the cubicles at dark. It was a bizarre and nasty legend and I never discovered how it came about and I'm sure no-one ever experienced the critter because no-one visited the loo at night! An even eerier legend is connected to the village of Upnor, an area known for its castle which was completed in 1567, and in its construction borrowed heavily from Rochester Castle's stonework to speed up the process. In Old English the name Upnor meant 'at the bank' translated from its original name of 'æt þæm ōre' and then in Middle English 'atten ore', changing in 1292 to 'atte Nore', but the meaning altered eventually to 'upon the bank', and by 1374 'uppan ore' was translated as 'Upnore', a place of two villages, being the Lower and Upper situated on the western bank of the River Medway. An interesting fossil find took place in 1913 when a straight-tusked elephant was dug up, an extinct species related to the now living Asian elephant, said to have wandered the land during the Middle and Late Pleistocene. However, the real mystery of Upnor concerns a bogeyman-type figure known as the Bogman! I'd never heard of such an apparition until I stumbled upon its presence in a 2001 book called *Medway Towns (Ottakar's Local History Series)* and compiled by Stuart Beaney and Diarmuid O' Leary, but the tale itself was told by William Hamper who I mentioned in the second chapter.

So, the Bogman. It may sound like a cartoon character, but what we know of such a spectre is in fact quite alarming even if its façade is often vague, or confused. Hamper writes:

> '*I first heard of the ghost of the Medway Bogman in 1974 from an archaeologist who had long frequented the Marshes at Upchurch. He had, he claimed, seen the spectre himself on several occasions.*'

Despite claims from the archaeologist that the spirit may have been of a Neolithic hunter, descriptions vary, yet often, even from its obscure origins, seem to describe more of a monster rather than mere human. One legend claims that the humanoid roamed the marshes after 1930 when the mummified corpse had been unearthed in a peat layer and that the only reason the being was discovered was due to a police investigation into a missing local schoolgirl. However, this is where the story drifts into urban legend. According to the yarn, a girl's shoe was found in one of the hands of the corpse and that a pathologist, upon analysing the red sandal, needed to break the fingers off in order to retrieve the shoe. Hamper continues:

> '*Several years later the body of the missing schoolgirl was finally discovered beneath the vegetable patch of the local gamekeeper. The only item of clothing missing from the corpse was the left shoe. Folklore has it that the gamekeeper never stood trial for the murder of the schoolgirl, as shortly after the grisly discovery, he himself was the victim of toadstool poisoning apparently administered by the schoolgirl's great aunt.*'

However, Hamper also goes on to state that the archaeologist recalled that no remains were in fact ever found of a Bogman, and this is where the story becomes a monster tale. Some claim that the Bogman runs in bizarre fashion, and its head appears broken, and dangles hideously behind it as it lopes across the misty marsh. Another legend claims that the Bogman has his head on backwards, leaving some to believe that the humanoid, when existing on this Earth as a human being, was hung, but now wallows through the quagmires disfigured by his hanging. Hamper states:

> '*Some accounts had him in possession of a gallows tattoo, which eyewitnesses claimed was visible on his upper arm, other accounts omit the detail.*'

However, the most intriguing details suggest that the mystery being may well have been accompanied by two spectral hounds, and other versions state that the Bogman was a local bogeyman, a mud-caked fiend with a shock of bright red hair said to attack schoolgirls up until the 1950s, when it was alleged, the ghoul was exorcised from the marshes, but other versions of the legend claim that the monster prowled not just the Upnor area but as far as Chatham, and particularly the gloomy tunnels of Fort Amherst and Fort Pitt. Mr Hamper also writes:

> '*There is yet another, more far-fetched legend attached to the Medway Bogman. Before the Second World War his remains were on display at East Gate Museum in Rochester. The most extraordinary aspect of this part of the legend is that the exhibit somehow came alive and escaped during an air raid on the Medway Towns. It is true that at around the time of the Second World War, sightings of the Medway Bogman were verging on the hysterical.*'

After reading of such a legend I was bemused as to how such a yarn had remained so obscure. Despite trawling various sources there is no other mention of the Upnor spectre, but similar bodies have been discovered throughout Europe encased in muddy tombs, often showing signs of hanging, strangulation or having their throat cut, possibly connected to sacrifice. A specimen excavated in a Danish peat bog was over two-thousand years old, despite its face being well preserved, and the man had been murdered, the corpse having a garrotte around its neck. It is believed the sacrifice was made to a fertility goddess. In 1984 in Cheshire, peat-cutters found a similar being from the Iron Age who became known as Lindow Man. Grains of mistletoe pollen were found in his stomach and his throat had been cut.

So, was the Medway Bogman merely the produce of local fired imagination, or a sum of several parts, a ghost story doing the rounds for decades but altering via each generation? No-one will know for sure, but hopefully the mention of him here and in William Hamper's feature, will bring him back to life once again.

It could be said that a majority of creatures within this chapter are simply too inconsistently sighted and half-hinted to exist and that they are unreliable, but that is the magic of the real mystery 'animals', and exactly how they become sinister ghost stories. Of course they are unreliable, because they have no reason.

Kevin Payne points to the spot where he saw a red-eyed humanoid in 1991 (p.377)

TOP: Eastgate House which used to be the Guildhall Museum, allegedly the home of the Me
way Bogman (p.380) BELOW: Reconstruction of Gladwishwood Zombie (p.387)

The Unnamable Anomalies

'With the years the legends take on spectral character – I suppose the thing, if it was a living thing, must have died. The memory had lingered hideously – all the more hideous because it was so secret.'

The Unnamable – H.P. Lovecraft

In 2007 I was sent two interesting reports of a vague 'monster' from the Clapham area of West Sussex from Patrick Noble - a researcher on the *Ghost Connections* website. Clapham has a long history of alleged satanic worship, rumoured cults, and the like, but what I was told was something very different. One concerned a dog-walker, who was approaching the driveway to a church in Clapham, when he saw a six-foot tall, skinny, humanoid, black in colour running from a field across in front of him. The being was hunched, and its chin appeared to be joined to its chest. A woman then also claimed to have spotted the beast, again in the Clapham area. The thing looked at the woman, straightened itself up, and then sped off into the woods.

Although to be taken with a pinch of salt, this particular faceless entity simply adds further air of mystery to the Clapham Woods region. A fawn-coloured bipedal creature was also reported from the Ashdown Forest area of Sussex. The sighting took place in the October, or possibly November of 2006 during the day in the 'Five Hundred Acre Wood' area, popular with visitors due to its *Winnie The Pooh* connections. A witness was walking along a path, came around a bend and saw, on the track ahead, a five feet tall creature, like a human but covered in brown hair. The beast ran from the witness along the line of the stream.

Patrick visited the area, and believed that the witness may have seen a deer on its hind legs, reaching up at a tree.

During the March of 2007 the *Ghost Connections* team visited an undisclosed location in Kent not far from Lenham after sightings of red-eyed creatures, near the local church. Believing the sightings to involve nothing more than wallabies, the team investigated the area and found a set of bizarre and very large footprints. To quote researcher Dave Godden in his email to me:

> *'There were probably about 10 - 15 in total leading towards the road. The ground became drier as we progressed. Each print can easily fit an adult human hand... The best one has a discernable heel impression and what could be an arch (i.e. a higher area). There is a large amount of disturbance and each is about 1/4" deep. There was a discernable inter-digital pad (ball) and digital pads could be made out which may have*

been four or maybe five - difficult to tell. There were no discernable claw marks. The track was in a straight line with no other print to indicate a quadruped and the stride was easily more than I could comfortably stride with my 33" legs.

The exact location of these tracks was found coming out of the ancient woodland and towards the road from a large beech tree at the junction of footpaths. There are tyre treads along the footpath and these prints were found (along with human shoe prints and horse prints) along the raised area between the tyre treads.'

After examining the photos of the strange footprints, the team discovered that it appeared they belonged to something akin to a bear, but without the distinct claw marks, although such animals don't walk on their two legs for great distance, and certainly don't inhabit the woods of Kent.

Kent, and much else of the south-east region is a haven for sightings of weird and occasionally wonderful creatures, but a majority of the encounters appear to have sinister relations, like all great campfire tales. The encounters as mentioned above are just the tip of the iceberg when it comes to almost random, and very surreal incidents involving people who seem to unintentionally invoke these 'demons', 'spirits' or 'ghosts'. These are the spectres which rarely leave tracks, or remain so obscure that literature has overlooked them as they've hid in the shadows of human memory. Many such local tales and urban legends do admittedly become distorted over time, but that's because they are passed on as word of mouth spooks and bogeymen, each time exaggerated and made scarier by those who speak of them. And some weird forms and beasts, despite only one rare glimpse, still stand the test of time.

This section, and the book as a whole, is my attempt to log and chronicle so many bouts and glimmers of local strangeness pertaining to the startling, seemingly baleful, and peculiar, monsters that have invaded our inner space. They must be recorded, whether you dismiss them or not.

Charles Igglesden wrote of a strange set of creatures in the fourteenth volume of his *A Saunter Through Kent...*, 1920, in relation to Bearsted, in Maidstone. To quote:

'Thanks to the liberal restoration of the fabric – several times since 1863 – Bearsted church is in a state of superb condition. The exterior of the windows in the south and east has been so thoroughly repaired that very little of the original stone is left, but on the north wall the mullions are left and some of the tracery is exceptionally good.

The feature of the church is the tower, well-proportioned, conspicuous in its garb of ivy from base to turret top. A turret stairway runs up at one of its corners, having its buttresses placed at angles. Just below the parapet are several carved stone heads, some almost hidden in the ivy, but more remarkable are three large stone animals at the corners of the embattlements of the tower. Some good folk of the village will tell you that these are the figures of bears – naturally bears in Bearsted – and I have heard others say they are actually intended to be lions. All this indecision is somewhat a reflection upon the skill of the sculptor, but he has at least given the old gossips of the village a chance to make their little joke. It is that the lions, or bears, or whatever they are, come down and feed in the churchyard when the clock strikes midnight. And the great jest of it lies in the fact that there is no clock in the church.'

In his 1983 book *Kent Lore*, Kent author Alan Bignell wrote of the gargoyles:

'The tower of the church is embellished with three mysterious stone beasts, one on each

of the three corners. No one has ever been able to say with any sort of finality what the creatures are supposed to be, or why they were put there. Indeed, pretty well all that is known about them, locally at an rate, is that on one night of every year the three jump down from the top of the tower, stretch their legs a bit on the green and then always without being seen return to their perches to gaze over the surrounding roofscape with stony stoicism for another 365 days.'

Researcher Tom Atkinson also brought to my attention a similar legend pertaining to a stone carving in All Saints churchyard, in Loose, near Maidstone. Roger Thornburgh, in his 1978 book, *Exploring Loose Village (Loose Amenities Association)* says:

'On the south side of the church tower there are two table tombs, memorials to the Crispe and Penfold families who occupied Old Loose Court for many years. Just behind is a pillar memorial to the Charlton family of Pimps Court along Busbridge Road. Its top is curved with three hideous faces, intended, so it is suggested, to frighten away the Devil.

Tradition has it that if you stick a pin in the yew tree, run around it anti-clockwise twelve times (at midnight some say) and look in the small tower window above the Charlton memorial, you will see a face. Younger villagers add that what is seen is the missing fourth face from the top of the pillar. An older and much more macabre version of the story is that having stuck a pin into the tree and run around it twenty-four times, you stand on the table tomb near the porch, look through the little trefoil window and see a woman killing a baby. These fragments of folklore seem to be as near as we in Loose can come to having a resident ghost.'

The Loose legend, like so many local tales, mentions the Devil, and so does the village of Newington, which has the unusual, and creepy, boast of having been allegedly visited by the Devil, or at least a similar humanoid. A local priest allegedly started the tale that he, one day, had been visited by the Devil who had warned him to cease with the ringing of the church bells. The wardens enquired as to what the being looked like, and the priest replied that it was, "*Black as the night from head to toe, not a hair on his head, a beak of a nose, a gash of a mouth, and a great long tail with a fork on the end.*"

Naturally, the wardens believed the priest and were stunned at the thought of Satan himself visiting the church. The community was terrified by the alleged visitation, but the priest insisted that the bells ring out forever more. After several weeks, and then months, the village returned to normal, until one night when a terrific thunderstorm battered the area, and strangely, seemed centred upon the church with skies seemingly clear elsewhere. Lightning speared the building, villagers screamed and scurried through the downpour like drowned rats, and loud booms rang out across the sky, crops were destroyed, the ground a sodden state, but still, despite the evil weather, the bells rang out. Then, the storms ceased, and burning sunshine bathed the church and the surrounding area, drying out what was left of the crops, as gentle showers oddly only fed the harvest of the neighbouring villages. The cruel sun blazed down, scorching for weeks, withering the trees, the plants and the hopes of the sizzling villagers.

Then, late one night the priest who'd defied Satan's orders, saw the horned humanoid furiously cavorting on the porch of the church and holding his hands to his leathery ears as the bells chimed into the sky. A local witness claimed that he'd seen the Devil on the tower parapet, holding a large sack. In the sack, and confirmed by the eerie silence of the yard, were the bells of the church, however, as the bell thief of utmost malevolence bounded down from the tower, he slipped, dropping the sack, spilling the bells on to the floor. As Satan swooped to the ground the witness, cowering at his window, saw the Devil leave a footprint on a nearby stone before leaping away, obviously beaten by the holy order.

The next day the print, measuring some fifteen-inches long was there for all to see. Proof that some unnatural presence had visited Newington, and left its grim mark upon the village.

Such tales will surely be remembered for many years to come as they uniquely, as entities, have somehow left their unusual mark on the landscape, whether as a strange footprint, or the fact that they leer as gargoyles from their stony perch.

However, the following humanoids have hardly embedded themselves in folklore, but hopefully now they have been recorded here they'll take their rightful place in the weird realm of what we know as the south-east and its mysterious happenings. A few obscure tales from Sussex also speak of bizarre beings. Edburton, in West Sussex was said to be haunted by an incomprehensible entity, said to have been the size of a cow and have glowing eyes. The beast roamed the area, near Henfield, during the nineteenth century and terrified smugglers and villagers alike. In Eastbourne, at the Claremont School, in 1918, it was alleged that novelist Pamela Frankau, whilst around ten-years old, observed a small, albino figure which ran across the bedroom floor and went out on to the landing. Also in Sussex, a phantom known as the Gripper Ghost is said to haunt St. Leonard's Forest. The creature is thought to be headless and once attacked several riders in the area of a night, and remains something of an obscure ghost story, like so many of the entries in this section.

On 12th July 1975 near Worthing, in Sussex, four witnesses observed an unidentified craft which had landed on a footpath in the vicinity of Highdown Hill. As they approached the shimmering object they saw a humanoid with a grey body and a face like a lemon! Before the observers could get a better glimpse one of them was blasted by a beam from the ship, knocking them down. All four witnesses then scrambled away.

The witnesses recovered from their shock and returned to the scene where they discovered a strange glowing powder where the object had sat. Strange aerial lights had been seen in the area during the '60s, whilst children often avoided the area for fear of the local ghost, although legend remains clouded.

In the January 2008 issue (12) of *Beyond* magazine, zoologist Karl Shuker wrote of several mystery creatures said to haunt the British Isles. One such beast was witnessed by Jacki Hartley who contacted the magazine in October 2007 to speak of her spine-chilling encounter with a creature that was to become known as the Bat-Winged Monkey Bird!

To the magazine, Jacki wrote:

> '*Back in 1969 I was four years old and travelling back from my auntie's house in London. Dad had been driving for about half an hour and we were going through the countryside. I was in the back of the car when I suddenly heard an awful, screeching scream. Mum and dad were in the front chatting and heard nothing. It was twilight and as I looked out of the back window into the trees, I saw what I could only describe as a monster.*
>
> *It had bat wings which it unfolded and stretched out before folding back up again, red eyes and a kind of monster monkey-face with a parrot's beak and was about three feet in height.*
>
> *To my four-year old mind it was terrifying and I had nightmares for weeks. I did not have a name for this thing in my vocabulary and so called it the Bat-winged Monkey*

Bird as it seemed to be such a weird mixture of animals.

I saw it again late one night when I was eleven from the back window of the car on our way home from Hastings, I think we were travelling through Robertsbridge and I saw it for the third time last year (2006).

It was 4:30 in the morning and I was awoken by the same horrible screeching sound. Thinking someone was being murdered in the street I jumped out of bed and ran to the window, catching the tail end of it as it flew past. I knew immediately what it was…the same horrible monster thing I had seen all those years ago, the Bat-Winged Monkey Bird was back.'

Jacki then conversed with researcher Karl Shuker, who included her recent report of the beast in the magazine.

'My recent sighting was at 4:30 am on October 19th 2006 outside my bedroom window, I saw the tail end of it fly past after the awful screeching noise woke me up. My address is in Tunbridge Wells in Kent.

The time before that I was on my way back from Hastings in Sussex…as for my parents, they just laughed and said I must have fallen asleep and had a nightmare. They weren't interested and simply dismissed it, even though I had nightmares about it coming to get me. Although the creature looked solid flesh and blood and made an awful sound, I think it could be paranormal in origin, as I have never seen or read about anything that even vaguely resembles it.'

Just what did Jacki experience, screaming into the night, and heading for the woods? Her sketch, even as four-year old, showed a creature bat-like, and also resembling an owl, and it is the owl which I'm beginning to side with in relation to what she saw. However, Jacki remains convinced that the creature was something very abnormal and certainly not identifiable as an owl many years after her first dreadful experience. If such a creature belonged to some unknown realm, is seems to be connected to Jacki's state of mind, the human psyche, as many of these seemingly real yet absurd beasts are. The Owlman of Mawnan was a feathered man-bird that haunted the churchyard of Mawnan Church in Cornwall during the 1970s scaring several witnesses, often teenage girls, and younger. Such a monster was often sighted as it perched on the branches of a tree in the grounds of the thirteenth century church. The being was described, during various encounters as red-eyed, grey in colour, and vaguely resembling an owl although far more sinister with odd legs which many witnesses believed at first belonged to a man in a costume, until their hearts began to pound with fear. The feet of the creature were often described as being like black crab claws, and despite sporadic sightings to the present, and across the globe of similar winged entities, there has never been a solution to such winged horrors.

One other weird humanoid said to haunt the outskirts of Kent is the so-called zombie of Glad Wish Wood at Burwash, situated between Tunbridge Wells and East Sussex. Rudyard Kipling spoke of the place as, *'…full of a sense of ancient ferocity and evil'*, and the encounter of Arthur Warnford seems to echo Kipling's words, and also the fear of the locals in regards to the unnatural setting.

Mr Warnford spent much of his time strolling around the local fields and woods, and Glad Wish Wood always tempted him to within its grim and wiry framework, a place of dread, atmosphere and history. On the particular evening in the September of 1956 Arthur walked along the edge of the wood, dusk had yet to fall, the birds were still happily singing in the tall trees, and all was calm as he swung his ash stick merrily through the wood. Arthur had strayed slightly from his usual path, and suddenly, despite his own annoyance towards himself for day dreaming, the air became heavy, menace seemed to enshroud the thicket, and a heart-jolting screech pierced the air. It could have been an owl or a rabbit Arthur thought to himself, nothing at all to worry about, as he was quite familiar with the sounds of nature and also the unpredictable atmospheric changes in the intriguing woodland. Arthur strolled on, aware that dusk was hanging in the air, and after half a mile he stumbled into a patch of thicket that seemed eerily quiet, and then there was the presence, as if someone, or 'thing' was also in the wood. Surely nonsense, he thought to himself but why the very strange feelings? Again, Arthur walked on, slightly worried at the lack of a pathway before him and the clawing brambles and snagging vegetation. Again the shriek filled the evening air. Fox? Rabbit? Bird? And then the noises as if something larger than fox, rabbit or bird was lumbering through the woods. Arthur began to panic, aware that the path he required was possibly nearby yet out of view amongst the spillage of greenery and thorny foliage. He wasn't sure if he'd walked in a circle, or where he was actually going, and he was angry at himself for his unusually poor navigational skills. He sensed the dread within, disorientated, the sweat forming on his forehead. Was it the heavy oppression of dusk or the sudden wall of fear encasing him causing his senses to become confused? Yet there, behind him, something crashing through the scrub…a person….no, …a figure most certainly, was it a ghost? Darkly adorned, the being emerged from the shadows and bracken, stumbling, faltering, an awkward - maybe limping - and jerking and that awful wheezing, rasping gurgle from the oesophagus, dying, mournful gasp. Are they wings flapping by its side? Or maybe arms in spasm, ragged in unkempt tatty cloth? Yet the figure comes closer still. Arthur trembling as its legs catch on the brush, pulling nettles and ivy from their root. And the face. Oh no, the face of the thing. Merely a jaw-dropping skull, rotten, with deep, sunken, barely visible eyes, yawning from the chasm of the sockets. The face of decay, putrefying ogre from some indefinite place. Was this a nightmare? How could Arthur wake as the monster from the worst of ill dreams smothered the air, reached for him, its black eyes searching him, its putrid head bobbing, twitching, the yawning cavernous mouth babbling and choking on the evening air.

Then the humanoid was upon him, but with all the strength he could muster in the sapping dusk, Arthur cracked his walking stick over the cranium of the being, and then darkness…

Arthur stirred. He was on the ground amongst the greenery. The evening seemed still, calm and how should be. No sign of the nightmarish phantasm that had invaded his privacy. Had he imagined it? He looked quickly at the stick by his side. It was indeed broken, but where was the creature he'd struck so heavily with one mighty blow? Was it an apparition of the undead? Some flesh-eating marauder from the very depths of Hell? A formidable spirit? Hallucination?

Rumour has it that what Arthur encountered may well have been the spectre of a man named Dave Leany, once hanged in the area yet wrongly convicted of murder in 1825, who, before his death, warned all his accusers that he would return from the grave and forever haunt the area.

Whatever the ghoul of Glad Wish Wood was, whether a ghost, zombie or winged-entity, we'll never really know, but I'm pretty sure that such a presence remains in that wood, albeit dormant, awaiting another hour of reprisal.

The 'space ape' of Sheppey certainly won't have been remembered…until now. This peculiar oddity was encountered at approximately 10:30 on the night of March 22nd 1979. The local police received several reports from motorists that a wacky creature had been sighted near the Kingsferry Bridge. Although the figure was only the average height of a man, it looked like an ape but was dressed in a silvery costume. One witness claimed he never saw the face of the suited space-beast because it wore a visor and a back seat passenger in another passing vehicle confirmed this detail. One can only assume that the creature moved like an ape, hence the name 'space ape' but apart from that there seems to have been nothing a tually ape-like of the beast.

The police received so many calls that they investigated the area immediately, but found no trace of the humanoid. It was believed that most of the motorists were travelling around 40 mph, so may not have had much time to survey the creature before them, and despite the fact that most statements matched, all they could describe was a figure in something akin to a diver's outfit. So, maybe that's exactly what they saw!

A similar 'space' entity was seen in 1954 at Tenterden by a Maureen Garner who was walking to her kitchen when she was accosted by a seven-foot tall humanoid wearing a blue suit that seemed to glimmer. Maureen stood transfixed watching the intruder, but she did not feel frightened. She noted that under its tight-fitting helmet the cheekbones were high, the mouth a slit and eyes very blue. The complexion appeared perfect although it had no eyebrows, and after almost a minute the figure simply vanished.

Two helmeted apparitions seized a London woman during the early '60s one morning at 8:30. She'd just awoken to the brightest of days when she was alarmed to see two figures either side of her which had put thick, metal bands on her wrists. From these bands came wires, and she was shown a series of images on a television screen before they left. Apparently, the figures returned a month or so later and repeated the process.

Read through a lot of literature pertaining to UFO sightings and alien abductions and you'll come across several of these type of scenarios where people have allegedly been woken up, shackled and either taken aboard vast ships or shown a series of weird images on screens. Whether this is mass hallucination, government interference, alien intervention etc, we'll never know, and whilst such humanoids are not exactly mystery animals or monsters for that matter, there is always, in folklore, a fine line often between things such as the space ape, and UFO-related strangeness. This isn't to say however that there is always a connection, but us humans tend to construct one.

In the August of 1967 in south London a married couple and another male witness saw a shape fifty feet above the ground which had a yellow glow. The craft was around twenty feet long and descended to the point where it was just hovering off the ground. Then, a very weird humanoid creature emerged from the object. The witnesses noted it had webbed hands and feet but very quickly went back into the object which took off.

These kind of cases are extremely difficult to judge, but when we consider the amount of bizarre incidents, weird sightings and surreal events that plague the people of this planet, we must at once approach with caution but not necessarily cast aside everything as too crazy to evaluate.

Take for instance the form called a giant jellyfish by the local press, and seen in the skies over Kent. Was the flying serpent of the zenith a real creature? A spaceship? Or natural phenomena?

Kent Today – 7th April 1999 – 'A motorist has told police she was followed along the M2 for nearly 15 miles by a mysterious flying object that hovered above her car. The woman was with her husband and a friend who also saw the UFO which they reported when they arrived home at Gravesend.

The police said the woman driver, who has not been named, said the strange flying object followed them along the London-bound carriageway of the motorway from Faversham to Blue Bell Hill at Chatham where it disappeared. Police have so far been unable to find any explanation. Police spokesman PC Dave Wisdom said the driver described the object as transparent with lights underneath which followed the car about 20ft from the ground. Checks were made with other areas and Maidstone police had also received reports about lights in the sky that evening. But it appears these were probably laser beam searchlights being used to advertise a town centre pub.'

Meanwhile:

Gazette & Times of 14th April, - 'Motorists watched in wonder as they followed an unidentified flying object swirling around the night sky above the M2 motorway, from Faversham to the Medway Towns.

Two couples returning from the coast on Good Friday saw the object which they described as, "...like the bottom of a jelly-fish", circling close to their car, just past the Faversham turn-off.

Mrs Pauline Davis (51) had her attention drawn to the strange phenomena when her sister Mrs Val Springhall noticed the sky looked strange. Mrs Davis described it as being transparent, with white lights swirling around. The object disappeared, then re-appeared about 20ft from the car. It eventually disappeared when the family reached Blue Bell Hill, near Chatham.

Mrs Davis, from Gravesend, said, "I was dozing off when my sister said she saw it in the sky. When I looked I knew I had never seen anything like it before. A lorry in front of us was swerving all over the road, so I think he may have seen it too. It just kept swirling like the bottom of a jelly-fish. You couldn't see an object, just lights. We called the police when we got home and they said there was a light show at Detling, but when we went back along the motorway there was nothing. If there is a simple explanation for what we saw, I wish someone would tell me."

And on the same day *Kent Today* reported:

'You can sleep safely in your beds - Medway may not have become a hotbed for paranormal activity after all. The source of an alleged UFO sighting over the M2 could have been a giant laser image from a nightclub in Maidstone, we can reveal.

Last week we told you how a motorist claimed to have travelled 15 miles between Faversham and Blue Bell Hill with a mysterious flying object hovering above her car on Good Friday.

Valerie Springhall and her sister Pauline Davis were terrified when what they described as a 50ft long jellyfish-shaped object appeared to deliberately keep them under observation.

"I was absolutely terrified" said Mrs Springhall. "I have never seen anything like it before in my life and I don't want to repeat the experience. It was around 50ft long, fluorescent white, and changing shape from round to oval as it revolved. At one stage it tipped over slightly as we could see small fluorescent circles in its main body."

But the answer may be the laser lights emanating from Atomics nightclub in Maidstone town centre.

Sean Tudor, who writes articles on spooky happenings in the Blue Bell Hill area, believes lights from the nightclub laser show are capable of shining across large distances and is the most likely explanation for the sighting.

He said, "My girlfriend and I happened to be out in Maidstone on Friday and saw the jellyfish display again swirling on the underside of the cloud cover over the town - which confirms to me that the UFO witnesses probably saw something like this the previous Friday. The display clearly has a powerful beam and would be seen for some distance which might extend as far as the M2 at Faversham but would, under the right conditions, almost certainly overplay the M2 closer to Blue Bell Hill. The reason it disappeared at Blue Bell Hill may have more to do with a confined arc the display travels than any sinister association. This doesn't definitely explain the story but the very close descriptive and behavioural similarities suggest strongly that this might be so."

On the 28th April *Gazette & Times* reported:

'The UFO sighting over the M2 motorway on Good Friday was also seen in the hamlet of Bedmonton, near Wormshill. Mr Don Brown and his wife told the paper of their strange experience after reading the report two weeks ago, which they say described exactly what they saw. The couple were settling down for the evening on Good Friday when Mrs Brown noticed something in the sky. She called her husband who went out to look at the swirling object above.

He said, "It was a clear night and there was nothing in the sky to suggest where the lights were coming from. It rotated from left to right in a three-quarter circular movement. It was there from 9:30 pm and it was still there when we went to bed at 10:30 pm."

The following day Mrs Brown asked her friends whether they had seen the swirling object but drew a blank. It was only when a friend told her about the report in the newspaper that the couple realised they had not been alone in what they saw. One explanation for what these and similar UFO sightings in the sky above Swale might be has been put forward by a local taxi driver. Carol Perry, who first witnessed the mysterious swirling lights in the sky two weeks ago whilst parked outside a fare's house in Roseleigh Road, Sittingbourne, believes they might be reflections on the sky of laser lights from a nightclub in Maidstone. A few days after the first sighting, Mrs Perry dropped off a fare at Maidstone and saw the lights emanating from Gabrielle's nightclub.'

Unfortunately, the mystery of the monster flying jellyfish or the weird lights, if they were lights at all, dissipated and the case remains unsolved, like so many others, until the next time…

The nights here are long sometimes – very long; but they are nothing to the restless nights, and dreadful dreams I had at that time. It makes me cold to remember them. Large dusky forms with sly and jeering faces crouched in the corners of the room, and bent over my bed at night, tempting me to madness.'

A Madman's Manuscript – Charles Dickens

Despite the variety of spectres, and sheer unnerving nature of some of those experienced in this chapter, it's clear that across the world, and not just in Kent, people are continuing to encounter strange forms. Some of these could well just be the ghosts of animals once said to inhabit the land, or creatures which were once pets. However, there is a clear indication that not all is right with some of the bizarre and downright eerie manifestations that seem to seep into 'our' frame of life on occasion. Such incidents are often fleeting, at times vague enough to not be taken seriously by the sceptics, but they have occurred, and those that are caught within such oddness are convinced of what they have seen, even if much of their experience is moulded by their mindset or belief system. And the same can even be said for the countless number of people who observe mystery, and seemingly very real, animals across the world. Kent is only a diminutive county on a small island and yet it is a treasure trove of peculiar data and incident which dates back to the dawn of man, but unfortunately many of those early tales have been lost, or over time been dismissed and cast aside due to lack of evidence. I will admit that evidence appears to be lacking in so much of what I have discussed in this book, but that is the power of the mystery, or the local legend. In the end, people don't want to see such riddles solved, or bodies of mystery animals turning up, because they have such a need for these things to be out there. Of course, there are the sceptical folk, and the scientists who want hard matter, and this is understandable, but in the case of the prowling felids roaming the woods, unless the time is put in by more people, such answers will never come to light. They will always remain as hazy photographs, as fuzzy film footage, and leaving signs such as the devoured prey, but much of this is to do with us and our failings and not the elusive nature of the beast. The evidence is there, I have it, but nothing ever comes of it. It's not meant to.

This planet is not likely to give up its entire box of secrets, and new species of animals are likely to be discovered long after science has given up on the hope that new mammal species still exist. And even this small island of ours, and the Garden of England within, will always harbour a rural jigsaw where I'm pretty sure a piece will always remain missing.

'It is almost dark. All is silent. Even the flocks have ceased to bleat. The long-winged heron descends upon the tall grass by the side of the narrow ribbons of water, still glistening as the sun goes down; the curlew wails his last good-night; only an owl hoots as he blinks his eyes from the bough of the churchyard yew.

Then darkness. The marsh sleeps.'

A Saunter Through Kent With Pen And Pencil - Charles Igglesden

'They asked for my story. I have told it. Enough.'

The Woman In Black – Susan Hill

Sources and Acknowledgments

The following books were consulted during the writing of this book :-

A FOURTH KENTISH PATCHWORK – ROBERT GOODSALL (1974 STEDEHILL)

AROUND HISTORIC KENT – MALCOLM JOHN (1978 MIDAS BOOKS)

A SAUNTER THROUGH KENT WITH PEN & PENCIL – CHARLES IGGLESDEN (VARIOUS : KENTISH EXPRESS)

BEYOND THE HIGHGATE VAMPIRE - DAVID FARRANT (1991 B.P.O.S.)

BEYOND THE IMPOSSIBLE - RICHARD LAZARUS (1994 WARNER)

BIG CATS: LOOSE IN BRITAIN - MARCUS MATHEWS (2007 CFZ PRESS)

CAT COUNTRY - DI FRANCIS (1983 DAVID & CHARLES)

CHAMBER'S GUIDE TO LONDON THE SECRET CITY - MICHAEL CHAMBERS (1975 OCEAN)

DANGEROUS GHOSTS - ELLIOT O'DONNELL (1954 CONSUL)

DRAGONS: MORE THAN A MYTH - RICHARD FREEMAN (2005 CFZ PRESS)

EXPLORING LOOSE VILLAGE - ROGER THORNBURGH (1978 LAA)

FOLKTALES & LEGENDS OF KENT - GEOFFREY M. DIXON (1984 MINIMAX)

FORTEAN TIMES: YESTERDAY'S NEWS TOMORROW - Edited by PAUL SIEVEKING (1992 JOHN BROWN PUB.)

FORTEAN TIMES: GATEWAYS TO MYSTERY Edited by BOB RICKARD 1993 JOHN BROWN PUB.)

FORTEAN TIMES: DIARY OF A MAD PLANET - Edited by PAUL SIEVEKING 1991 JOHN BROWN PUB.)

FORTEAN TIMES: IF PIGS COULD FLY - Edited by PAUL SIEVEKING 1994 JOHN BROWN PUB.)

FROM FLYING TOADS TO SNAKES WITH WINGS - KARL SHUKER 1997 LLEWELYN)

GHOSTHUNTER WALKS - RUPERT MATTHEWS (2005 SB PUBLICATIONS)

GHOSTS OF LONDON - J.A. BROOKS (1995 JARROLD)

INSTRUMENTS OF DARKNESS - JAMES SHARPE (1996 HAMISH HAMILTON)

KENT LORE - ALAN BIGNELL (1983 HALE)

LO! - CHARLES FORT (1931 GOLLANCZ)

LOST BEASTS OF BRITAIN - ANTHONY DENT (1974 HARRAP)

MEDWAY TOWNS - S. BEANEY & D. O' LEARY (2001 OTTAKAR'S)

MONSTER! THE A-Z OF ZOOFORM PHENOMENA - NEIL ARNOLD (2007 CFZ PRESS)

MYSTERY ANIMALS OF BRITAIN & IRELAND - GRAHAM J. McKEWAN (1986 HALE)
ROUND ABOUT KITS COTY HOUSE - ? (1861 ?)
MYSTERY CATS OF THE WORLD - KARL SHUKER (1989 HALE)
OUR SUSSEX PARISH - THOMAS GEERING (1884 METHEUN)
SAILORS, SEA SERPENTS & SCEPTICS - GRAHAM J. McKEWAN (1978 ROUTLEDGE & KEEGAN PAUL)
STRANGE CREATURES FROM TIME & SPACE - JOHN KEEL (1975 SPHERE)
SUSSEX GHOSTS & LEGENDS - TONY WALES (1992 COUNTRYSIDE BOOKS)
THE UNXPLAINED: STRANGE ENCOUNTERS - ? (2000 PARRAGON)
THE BEAST OF EXMOOR - DI FRANCIS (1993 JONATHAN CAPE)
THE CANTERBURY MONSTERS - J.H. VAUX (1989 MERESBOROUGH)
THE HAUNTED SOUTH - JOAN FORMAN (1978 HALE)
THE LEGEND AND BIZARRE CRIMES OF SPRING HEELED JACK - PETER HAINING (197 MULLER)
THE SMALLER MYSTERY CARNIVORES OF THE WESTCOUNTRY - JONATHAN DOWNE! (1996 CFZ COMMUNICATIONS)
THE VAMPIRE TERROR & OTHER TRUE MYSTERIES - PETER HAINING (1981 ARMADA)
THEY WALK BY NIGHT - MICHAEL HARVEY (1968 ACE BOOKS)
UNEXPLAINED KENT - BRIAN PAINE & TREVOR STRUGESS (1997 BREEDON BOOKS)
WOLVES AND WEREWOLVES - JOHN POLLARD (1964 HALE)

I would like to thank the following people, websites, newspapers, radio stations, magazines and oth‍ media sources for helping me with my research over the years.

Animals & Men, Appledore Heath Parish Magazine (Jennifer Griffiths), *The Argus*, Ashford Rota‍ Club, *Aspirations From The Dark Side, Ashford Advertiser*, ASPR Radio, Tom Atkinson, *Atropo‍* Austinist, Bart Nunnelly - Mysterious Kentucky), BBC Kent, BBC South-East News, BBC Radio Ker‍ Graham Bennett, *Bexley Times*, Bexley U3A, *Beyond*, Biodiversity Web, *Bizarre, Blythe News*, Briti‍ Hominid Research, British Wild Boar, *Camden New Journal, The Cat* (Tom Briggs), CFZ, Channel Radio (Danny Robins), Chatham Rotary, Loren Coleman, Cougar Info, Craig - Texas Bigfoot, CP, Cry‍ tomundo, Cryptozoology, Gary Cunningham, Cuxton Parish Newsletter, *Daily Express, Daily Ma‍ Daily Mirror, Daily Telegraph, Dark Lore*, Dartford Messenger, *Dead Of Night*, The Deal Maritime History Museum, *Derby Mercury, Dive Magazine, Dover Express*, Downs Mail, Joe Durwin, Ch‍ Eades, *Eastbourne Today, East Kent Gazette, East Kent Mercury, Encounters, Evening Post, Farm A‍ Home, Farmer's Weekly*, David Farrant, Farshore's, *Fate, Faversham Times, The Field, Folkestone He‍ ald, Fortean Times, Gentleman's Magazine*, Ghost Connections (Paddy and Dave), Ghostfinder's Rad‍ Scotland, Ghostly Talk, *Gravesend And Meopham Rotary, Gravesend Messenger* (Michael Barna‍ Karen Jeal,), *Gravesend Reporter*, Great Mongeham Society (Diana Knight), *The Guardian*, Willia‍ Hamper, *Hampstead & Highgate Express, Hastings Observer, Hawkinge Gazette*, Howletts Zoo, Patri‍ Huyghe (*Anomalist*), Hythe Live, IC South London, Kent Angling Preservation Society, *Kent & Sus‍ Courier, Kentish Express* (Simon Alford), *Kentish Gazette, Kent Messenger* (Emily Hall), *Kentish Tim‍* (Ed Cook), Kent Online, Kent On Sunday, Kent Parishes, Kent Today (Geoff Maynard, Toby Smit‍ Kent Wildlife Trust, KM Extra, KMFM (even if the songs drove me insane!) Laist (Zach), *Land A‍ Water*, Paul Langridge, Lark FM, Lesley - Beyond The Dial, Lewes Today, Lionel Beer, Local Ra‍ *Londonist, Maidstone Journal*, Maidstone Library, Maidstone U3A, Maureen, *Medway Matters, Medw‍ Messenger* (Janine Nolan, Alan Watkins), *Medway Today, Mereworth And West Peckham Record, M‍*

ridian News, Meridian 'Three Minutes', *Midhurst And Petworth Observer*, *Mid-Sussex Times* (Susan King), Mihali Moore, MonsterUSA, *Mystery Animals Of Ireland* (Nick Sucik), *New Jersey Devil Hunters* (Laura Leuter), *News Shopper*, Rachel Nolan, One-Eye Grey, Paranormal Database, Phillyist, Port Lympne, *Press And Journal*, Pulse Talk Radio, Roadghosts, Albert Rosales, Quentin Rose (RIP), Round Tables, Saga, *Sevenoaks Chronicle*, Shades, Jonathan Shaw - MP, *Sheerness Times Guardian* (Gemma Constable, Hayley Robinson), Sky News, Snopes, South East London Folklore Society, Southern Counties Radio, *South London Press* (Zoe Walker), South London Radio, Strange USA, Strood Rotary, *The Sun, Surrey Advertiser*, *Sussex Express*, *Sutton Guardian*, Richard Syrett, TAPS Family Radio, Tetrapod Zoology (Darren Naish), The Other Side, *This Is Brighton & Hove*, *This Is Kent And Sussex*, *This Is Local London*, *The Times*, *Time Out* (Sara O'Reilly, Annabel Bates), Trashotron, *Tunbridge Wells Extra*, Tuesday After Twilight (Chad Austin), Twickenham Times, UFO Info, UFO Magazine, UFO Mystic, UFO Seek, UK Paranormal Research Society, Underground Kent, Unknown Creature Spot, Vortigern Studies, Joshua P. Warren, *Waterlog Magazine*, *Weekly News*, *West Sussex County Times*, *Whitstable Gazette*, Wildwatch (Chris Packham), Wikipedia, Wildlife Extra, Wildlife Heritage Fund (Mark Edgerley), Mike Williams, *Your County* (Steve Morris).

SPECIAL THANKS

This book didn't take long to write in comparison to the dark voyage of my first book *Monster!* However, this book has always been in the making, and I would like to say that this work would not have been made possible were it not for all the witnesses who have contacted me over the years to report their sightings and stories, all the farmer's who have confided in me and let me onto their land, the handful of policemen who've been helpful, as well as so many newspaper reporters and the like who've aided me in my research.

More importantly there are a select few people who I'd like to give extra special thanks to, some for their unconditional love and understanding, others for nurturing my ego!, and some for giving me the opportunity and outlets to express myself. They are as follows:

My dad Ron, you're my hero, and despite never following in your foot-balling footsteps as I probably should've, I hope I have made you proud with my skills of documenting the contents of my head and this weird county. Thank you for all the trips, for sharing some amazing experiences, and for being the greatest dad. X

My mum Paulene. You must have taken so many phone calls over the years for me, and given me so much support and love, and artistic flair. You are such a strong and beautiful person. You mean the world to me. X

My sister Vicki, well, what can I say. You're the most amazing person, so talented, and you've been there for me through everything and always believed in me, and I'll always believe in you. All the years we've shared have been so special and will last forever. You're the best. You rock! I love you X

My nan, Win, and grandad Ron. Magical grandparents, so caring, thoughtful and just everything to me. Always in my heart. X And Doris, the nan I never knew X

Emma, my Pinkcess! - Thank you always for being so understanding, and for all your constant love, affection, patience, support and vampish mystique and for being in my surreal world. Forever X

Jez, you're like a brother, and we've shared so many strange and hilarious trips, from rock 'n' roll to hunting vampires. You'll Never Walk Alone.

Jonathan & Corinna Downes of the Centre For Fortean Zoology, your support is immense, thank you for all you've done and for giving me an outlet for my work.

Richard Freeman, a true gothic monster-hunter, Sean Tudor, a great friend, and a real researcher, Joe Chester, for the support and many hours over many years spent discussing weirdness, Nick Redfern, thanks for all the US publicity and promotion, Karl Shuker, Mark North, Vince Rogers, Sarah Brinicombe, Graham Inglis, Linda Godfrey, Terry 'Dred' Cameron, Marc Ruddy, Jacqui Ford, Sue, Bob and family, Lesley & Ian in South Carolina, Mr Wyatt and Adam Smith for the wicked illustrations of me... anyone I forgot? Sorry!

> *'Are there here and there sequestered places which some curious creatures still frequent, whom once on a time anybody could see and speak to as they went about on their daily occasions, whereas now only at rare intervals in a series of years does one cross their paths and become aware of them; and perhaps that is just as well for the peace of mind of simple people'.*

The Vignette - M.R. James

About the Author

N eil Arnold is Kent's only monster-hunter.

He runs *Kent Big Cat Research,* the county's only research into large, exotic cats roaming the wilds, he is the author of *Monster! The A-Z Of Zooform Phenomena,* which he describes as "National Geographic meets Marc Bolan", which was named the 2007 Fortean Zoology Book Of The Year by cryptozoologist Loren Coleman.

He has an obsession with misty graveyards, vamp-a-go-go women, the films of David Lynch, glam-rock and '60s culture, a true dedicated follower of fashion whose surreal safaris have enabled him to appear on national television and international radio, give lectures on his expeditions and research, and encounter all manner of weird and wonderful beasts and characters, from Satanists, to rock stars, and from alleged vampires to big cats.

He lives opposite a haunted castle in Rochester, Kent, with his girlfriend Jemma.

Since a very young age he has collated evidence of strange, and mysterious creatures roaming Kent and the surrounding areas. He believes in monsters more than he does himself.

THE CENTRE FOR FORTEAN ZOOLOGY

So, what is the Centre for Fortean Zoology?

We are a non profit-making organisation founded in 1992 with the aim of being a clearing house for information, and coordinating research into mystery animals around the world. We also study out of place animals, rare and aberrant animal behaviour, and Zooform Phenomena; little-understood "things" that appear to be animals, but which are in fact nothing of the sort, and not even alive (at least in the way we understand the term).

Why should I join the Centre for Fortean Zoology?

Not only are we the biggest organisation of our type in the world, but - or so we like to think - we are the best. We are certainly the only truly global Cryptozoological research organisation, and we carry out our investigations using a strictly scientific set of guidelines. We are expanding all the time and looking to recruit new members to help us in our research into mysterious animals and strange creatures across the globe. Why should you join us? Because, if you are genuinely interested in trying to solve the last great mysteries of Mother Nature, there is nobody better than us with whom to do it.

What do I get if I join the Centre for Fortean Zoology?

For £12 a year, you get a four-issue subscription to our journal *Animals & Men*. Each issue contains 60 pages packed with news, articles, letters, research papers, field reports, and even a gossip column! The magazine is A5 in format with a full colour cover. You also have access to one of the world's largest collections of resource material dealing with cryptozoology and allied disciplines, and people from the CFZ membership regularly take part in fieldwork and expeditions around the world.

How is the Centre for Fortean Zoology organized?

The CFZ is managed by a three-man board of trustees, with a non-profit making trust registered with HM Government Stamp Office. The board of trustees is supported by a Permanent Directorate of full and part-time staff, and advised by a Consultancy Board of specialists - many of whom who are world-renowned experts in their particular field. We have regional representatives across the UK, the USA, and many other parts of the world, and are affiliated with other organisations whose aims and protocols mirror our own.

I'm new to the subject, and although I am interested I have little practical knowledge. I don't want to feel out of my depth. What should I do?

Don't worry. We were *all* beginners once. You'll find that the people at the CFZ are friendly and approachable. We have a thriving forum on the website which is the hub of an ever-growing electronic community. You will soon find your feet. Many members of the CFZ Permanent Directorate started off as ordinary members, and now work full-time chasing monsters around the world.

I have an idea for a project which isn't on your website. What do I do?

Write to us, e-mail us, or telephone us. The list of future projects on the website is not exhaustive. If you have a good idea for an investigation, please tell us. We may well be able to help.

How do I go on an expedition?

We are always looking for volunteers to join us. If you see a project that interests you, do not hesitate to get in touch with us. Under certain circumstances we can help provide funding for your trip. If you look on the future projects section of the website, you can see some of the projects that we have pencilled in for the next few years.

In 2003 and 2004 we sent three-man expeditions to Sumatra looking for Orang-Pendek - a sem legendary bipedal ape. The same three went to Mongolia in 2005. All three members started off merely subscribers to the CFZ magazine.

Next time it could be you!

Project Kerinci, Sumatra - 2003
In search of the bipedal ape Orang Pendek

How is the Centre for Fortean Zoology funded?

We have no magic sources of income. All our funds come from donations, membership fees, works that we do for TV, radio or magazines, and sales of our publications and merchandise We are always looking for corporate sponsorship, and other sources of revenue. If you have any ideas for fund-raising please let us know. However, unlike other cryptozoological organisations in the past, we do not live in an intellectual ivory tower. We are not afraid to ge our hands dirty, and furthermore we are not one of those organisations where the membersh have to raise money so that a privileged few can go on expensive foreign trips. Our research teams both in the UK and abroad, consist of a mixture of experienced and inexperienced per sonnel. We are truly a community, and work on the premise that the benefits of CFZ member ship are open to all.

What do you do with the data you gather from your investigations and expeditions?

Reports of our investigations are published on our website as soon as they are available. Pre liminary reports are posted within days of the project finishing.

Each year we publish a 200 page yearbook containing research papers and expedition repo too long to be printed in the journal. We freely circulate our information to anybody who ask for it.

No. Each year since 2000 we have held our annual convention - the *Weird Weekend* - in Exeter. It is three days of lectures, workshops, and excursions. But most importantly it is a chance for members of the CFZ to meet each other, and to talk with the members of the permanent directorate in a relaxed and informal setting and preferably with a pint of beer in one hand. Since 2006 - the *Weird Weekend* has been bigger and better and held in the idyllic rural location of Woolsery in North Devon. The 2008 event will be held over the weekend 15-17 August.

Since relocating to North Devon in 2005 we have become ever more closely involved with other community organisations, and we hope that this trend will continue. We also work closely with Police Forces across the UK as consultants for animal mutilation cases, and we intend to forge closer links with the coastguard and other community services. We want to work closely with those who regularly travel into the Bristol Channel, so that if the recent trend of exotic animal visitors to our coastal waters continues, we can be out there as soon as possible.

We are building a Visitor's Centre in rural North Devon. This will not be open to the general public, but will provide a museum, a library and an educational resource for our members (currently over 400) across the globe. We are also planning a youth organisation which will involve children and young people in our activities. We work closely with *Tropiquaria* - a small zoo in north Somerset, and have several exciting conservation projects planned.

Apart from having been the only Fortean Zoological organisation in the world to have consistently published material on all aspects of the subject for over a decade, we have achieved the following concrete results:

Disproved the myth relating to the headless so-called sea-serpent carcass of Durgan beach in Cornwall 1975
Disproved the story of the 1988 puma skull of Lustleigh Cleave
Carried out the only in-depth research ever into the mythos of the Cornish Owlman
Made the first records of a tropical species of lamprey
Made the first records of a luminous cave gnat larva in Thailand.
Discovered a possible new species of British mammal - the beech marten.
In 1994-6 carried out the first archival fortean zoological survey of Hong Kong.
In the year 2000, CFZ theories where confirmed when an entirely new species of lizard was found resident in Britain.
Identified the monster of Martin Mere in Lancashire as a giant wels catfish
Expanded the known range of Armitage's skink in the Gambia by 80%
Obtained photographic evidence of the remains of Europe's largest known pike
Carried out the first ever in-depth study of the *ninki-nanka*
Carried out the first attempt to breed Puerto Rican cave snails in captivity
Were the first European explorers to visit the `lost valley` in Sumatra
Published the first ever evidence for a new tribe of pygmies in Guyana
Published the first evidence for a new species of caiman in Guyana

EXPEDITIONS & INVESTIGATIONS TO DATE INCLUDE:

- 1998 Puerto Rico, Florida, Mexico *(Chupacabras)*
- 1999 Nevada *(Bigfoot)*
- 2000 Thailand *(Giant snakes called nagas)*
- 2002 Martin Mere *(Giant catfish)*
- 2002 Cleveland *(Wallaby mutilation)*
- 2003 Bolam Lake *(BHM Reports)*
- 2003 Sumatra *(Orang Pendek)*
- 2003 Texas *(Bigfoot; giant snapping turtles)*
- 2004 Sumatra *(Orang Pendek; cigau, a sabre-toothed cat)*
- 2004 Illinois *(Black panthers; cicada swarm)*
- 2004 Texas *(Mystery blue dog)*
- 2004 Puerto Rico *(Chupacabras; carnivorous cave snails)*
- 2005 Belize *(Affiliate expedition for hairy dwarfs)*
- 2005 Mongolia *(Allghoi Khorkhoi aka Mongolian death worm)*
- 2006 Gambia *(Gambo - Gambian sea monster , Ninki Nanka and Armitage s skink*
- 2006 Llangorse Lake *(Giant pike, giant eels)*
- 2006 Windermere *(Giant eels)*
- 2007 Coniston Water *(Giant eels)*
- 2007 Guyana *(Giant anaconda, didi, water tiger)*
- 2008 Russia *(Almasty)*

THE CENTRE FOR FORTEAN ZOOLOGY

www.cfz.org.uk

Other books available from
CFZ PRESS

Other books available from
CFZ PRESS

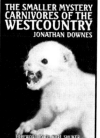

THE SMALLER MYSTERY CARNIVORES OF THE WESTCOUNTRY
Jonathan Downes - ISBN 978-1-905723-05-8

£7.99

Although much has been written in recent years about the mystery big cats which have been reported stalking Westcountry moorlands, little has been written on the subject of the smaller British mystery carnivores. This unique book redresses the balance and examines the current status in the Westcountry of three species thought to be extinct: the Wildcat, the Pine Marten and the Polecat, finding that the truth is far more exciting than the currently held scientific dogma. This book also uncovers evidence suggesting that even more exotic species of small mammal may lurk hitherto unsuspected in the countryside of Devon, Cornwall, Somerset and Dorset.

THE BLACKDOWN MYSTERY
Jonathan Downes - ISBN 978-1-905723-00-3

£7.99

Intrepid members of the CFZ are up to the challenge, and manage to entangle themselves thoroughly in the bizarre trappings of this case. This is the soft under-belly of ufology, rife with unsavoury characters, plenty of drugs and booze." That sums it up quite well, we think. A new edition of the classic 1999 book by legendary fortean author Jonathan Downes. In this remarkable book, Jon weaves a complex tale of conspiracy, anti-conspiracy, quasi-conspiracy and downright lies surrounding an air-crash and alleged UFO incident in Somerset during 1996. However the story is much stranger than that. This excellent and amusing book lifts the lid off much of contemporary forteana and explains far more than it initially promises.

GRANFER'S BIBLE STORIES
John Downes - ISBN 0-9512872-8-1

£7.99

Bible stories in the Devonshire vernacular, each story being told by an old Devon Grandfather - 'Granfer'. These stories are now collected together in a remarkable book presenting selected parts of the Bible as one more-or-less continuous tale in short 'bite sized' stories intended for dipping into or even for bed-time reading. `Granfer` treats the biblical characters as if they were simple country folk living in the next village. Many of the stories are treated with a degree of bucolic humour and kindly irreverence, which not only gives the reader an opportunity to re-evaluate familiar tales in a new light, but do so in both an entertaining and a spiritually uplifting manner.

FRAGRANT HARBOURS DISTANT RIVERS
John Downes - ISBN 0-9512872-5-7

£12.50

Many excellent books have been written about Africa during the second half of the 19th Century, but this one is unique in that it presents the stories of a dozen different people, whose interlinked lives and achievements have as many nuances as any contemporary soap opera. It explains how the events in China and Hong Kong which surrounded the Opium Wars, intimately effected the events in Africa which take up the majority of this book. The author served in the Colonial Service in Nigeria and Hong Kong, during which he found himself following in the footsteps of one of the main characters in this book; Frederick Lugard – the architect of modern Nigeria.

CFZ PRESS, MYRTLE COTTAGE, WOOLFARDISWORTHY BIDEFORD, NORTH DEVON, EX39 5QR
w w w . c f z . o r g . u k

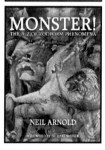

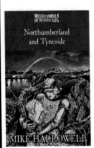
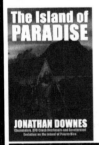